THE ROUTLEDGE HANDBOOK TO THE POLITICAL ECONOMY AND GOVERNANCE OF THE AMERICAS

This handbook explores the political economy and governance of the Americas, placing particular emphasis on collective and intertwined experiences. Forty-six chapters cover a range of Inter-American key concepts and dynamics.

The flow of peoples, goods, resources, knowledge and finances have on the one hand promoted interdependence and integration that cut across borders and link the countries of North and South America (including the Caribbean) together. On the other hand, they have contributed to profound asymmetries between different places. The nature of this transversally related and multiply interconnected hemispheric region can only be captured through a transnational, multidisciplinary and comprehensive approach. This handbook examines the direct and indirect political interventions, geopolitical imaginaries, inequalities, interlinked economic developments and the forms of appropriation of the vast natural resources in the Americas. Expert contributors give a comprehensive overview of the theories, practices and geographies that have shaped the economic dynamics of the region and their impact on both the political and natural landscape.

This multidisciplinary approach will be of interest to a broad array of academic scholars and students in history, sociology, geography, economics and political science, as well as cultural, postcolonial, environmental and globalization studies.

Olaf Kaltmeier is Professor for Ibero-American History at Bielefeld University.

Anne Tittor holds a PhD and is a research associate at the Department of Sociology at Friedrich-Schiller-University Jena.

Daniel Hawkins is the Director of Research at the National Union School of Colombia (ENS).

Eleonora Rohland is Professor for Entangled History in the Americas at Bielefeld University.

THE ROUTLEDGE HANDBOOK TO THE POLITICAL ECONOMY AND GOVERNANCE OF THE AMERICAS

Edited by Olaf Kaltmeier, Anne Tittor, Daniel Hawkins and Eleonora Rohland

Routledge
Taylor & Francis Group
LONDON AND NEW YORK

First published 2020
by Routledge
2 Park Square, Milton Park, Abingdon, Oxon OX14 4RN

and by Routledge
605 Third Avenue, New York, NY 10017

First issued in paperback 2022

Routledge is an imprint of the Taylor & Francis Group, an informa business

Publisher's Note
The publisher has gone to great lengths to ensure the quality of this reprint but points out that some imperfections in the original copies may be apparent.

SPONSORED BY THE

Federal Ministry
of Education
and Research

British Library Cataloguing-in-Publication Data
A catalogue record for this book is available from the British Library

Library of Congress Cataloging-in-Publication Data
Names: Kaltmeier, Olaf, 1970- editor.
Title: The Routledge handbook to the political economy and governance of the Americas / edited by Olaf Kaltmeier, Anne Tittor, Daniel Hawkins and Eleanora Rohland.
Other titles: Handbook to the political economy and governance of the Americas
Description: Abingdon, Oxon ; New York, NY : Routledge, 2020. | Includes bibliographical references and index.
Identifiers: LCCN 2019037595 (print) | LCCN 2019037596 (ebook) | ISBN 9780815352686 (hardback) | ISBN 9781351138444 (ebook)
Subjects: LCSH: Latin America–Economic policy. | Latin America–Economic conditions–21st century. | Latin America–Politics and government–21st century.
Classification: LCC HC125 .R679 2020 (print) | LCC HC125 (ebook) | DDC 330.97–dc23
LC record available at https://lccn.loc.gov/2019037595
LC ebook record available at https://lccn.loc.gov/2019037596

ISBN: 978-1-03-240082-2 (pbk)
ISBN: 978-0-815-35268-6 (hbk)
ISBN: 978-1-351-13844-4 (ebk)

DOI: 10.4324/9781351138444

Typeset in Bembo
by Integra Software Services Pvt. Ltd.

CONTENTS

CONTRIBUTORS

The Editors

Olaf Kaltmeier is Professor for Ibero-American History at Bielefeld University and Director of the Maria Sibylla Merian Center for Advanced Latin American Studies (CALAS). His research focuses on (Post)Colonial Studies, Multiculturalism, Indigenous Movements, and Ethnicity. He is also a main editor of this Routledge Handbook Series *Rethinking the Americas*. His most recent book is *Refeudalización. Desigualdad social, economía y cultura política en América Latina en el temprano siglo XXI* from 2018.

Anne Tittor holds a PhD and is a research associate at the Department of Sociology at Friedrich-Schiller-University Jena. Her research focuses on development theory, environmental, social, and health politics in Latin America, as well as social inequalities and social movements. She is also co-editor of *The Routledge Handbook to the Political Economy and Governance of the Americas*. Her most recent publication, that she co-edited, is *Globale Ungleichgewichte und Soziale Transformationen. Beiträge von Dieter Boris aus 50 Jahren zu Lateinamerika, Klassenanalyse und Bewegungspolitik* from 2018.

Daniel Hawkins is the Director of Research at the National Union School of Colombia (ENS). His research focuses on workers' rights, labor impacts of Free Trade Agreements, the informal economy, and socio-labor standards in global agricultural supply chains. He is also co-editor of *The Routledge Handbook to the Political Economy and Governance of the Americas*. One of his most recent publications, that he co-authored, is *Trabajo decente y saludable en la agroindustria en América Latina. Revisión sistemática resumida* from 2018.

Eleonora Rohland is Professor for Entangled History in the Americas at Bielefeld University and Director of the Center of InterAmerican Studies (CIAS). Her research focuses on climate impact and disaster history. One of her latest publications is *Changes in the Air: Hurricanes in New Orleans from 1718 to the Present* from 2018.

The Contributors

Antoine Acker is an Assistant Professor at the Department of History at the University of Zurich. His research focuses on global and environmental history. His most recent publication is *Volkswagen in the Amazon: The Tragedy of Global Development in Modern Brazil* from 2017.

Christian Ambrosius holds a PhD and works at the Institute for Latin American Studies in Berlin. His research focuses on remittances, political economy, as well as economic development. One of his most recent publications is *What Explains the Speed of Recovery from Banking Crises?* from 2017.

Mark Anner is an Associate Professor of Labor and Employment Relations and the founding director of the Center for Global Workers' Rights at Penn State University. His research focuses on how sourcing dynamics in global supply chains impact working conditions and shape patterns of labor resistance. One of his best-known books is *Solidarity Transformed: Labor Responses to Globalization and Crisis in Latin America* from 2011.

Ricardo Antunes is Professor of Sociology at the Campinas University. His research focuses on labor sociology, social theory, new labor morphology, and the working class. His most recent book is *The Privilege of Servitude* from 2018.

Maria Backhouse is Professor at the Department of Sociology at Friedrich-Schiller-University Jena. Her research focuses on environmental sociology, political ecology, development theory as well as postcolonial critics. Her most recent publication, that she co-edited, is *In Hörweite von Stuart Hall: Gesellschaftskritik ohne Gewähr* from 2017.

Joachim Becker is Professor at the Department of Economics at Vienna University of Economics and Business. His research focuses on development economics, state theory as well as regional integration and disintegration. His most recent book is *Neo-Nationalismus in der EU: sozio-ökonomische Programmatik und Praxis* from 2018.

Manuela Boatcă is Professor at the Department of Sociology at Albert-Ludwigs-University Freiburg. Her research focuses on macrosociology, theories of inequalities, postcolonial studies as well as theories of social change and research on violence. One of her most recent publications that she co-edited is *Global Inequalities in World-Systems Perspective: Theoretical Debates and Methodological Innovations* from 2017.

Tobias Boos works at the Department of Political Science at the University of Vienna. His research focuses on populism and middle class in Latin America, as well as state theory of the Global South and political economy. In 2017, he worked as a co-editor together with Gregor Seidl on the special issue of the *Journal of Development Studies* (*JEP*) on Middle Class in Latin America, Volume XXXIII.

Paul Bowles is Professor of Economics and International Studies at the University of North British Columbia. His research focuses on globalization and regionalization, critical development studies, as well as extractivism. One of his most recent publications is *Resource Communities in a Globalizing Region: Development, Agency, and Contestation in Northern British Columbia* from 2016.

Ulrich Brand is Professor at the Department of Political Science at the University of Vienna. His research focuses on resource and environmental politics in Latin America, the crisis of liberal globalization, social-ecological transformation as well as the imperial mode of living, and critical state theory. One of his most recent publications, as a co-author, is *The Limits to Capitalist Nature: Theorizing and Overcoming the Imperial Mode of Living* from 2018.

Martin Breuer is an academic assistant at the Center for InterAmerican Studies at Bielefeld University. His research focuses on the history of development assistance and Andean history. One of his most recent publications is "Exploring the International Labor Organization and its technical assistance activities in the field of indigenous peoples: The significance of Human Rights and the Andean Indian Program (1954–1968)" from 2018.

João Paulo Cândia Veiga is Assistant Professor of Political Science and International Relations at the University of São Paulo. His research focuses on global and transnational governance, international policy economy, labor and environmental standards, as well as private regulation and corporate social responsibility in transnational corporations. His most recent publication, together with Scott B. Martin and Katiuscia Galhera, was from 2019 and is titled *Labor Relations, Conflictual Cooperation and Retail in Latin America: The Case of Walmart in Brazil.*

Juan Camilo Cárdenas is Professor at the Department of Economics at the Universidad de los Andes in Colombia. His research focuses on studying how cooperation emerges through the interaction between institutions and decisions using experimental and behavioral economics. One of his most recent publications, together with César Mantilla and Santiago Gomez, was published in 2018 and is titled *Between-Group Competition Enhances Cooperation in Public Goods Appropriation Games.*

Lucía Dammert is Associate Professor at the Universidad de Santiago de Chile. Her research focuses on Latin America, public security, organized crime, and criminal justice institutional reforms. One of her best-known publications is *Fear and Crime in Latin America: Redefining State-Society Relations* from 2012.

Karin Fischer holds a PhD and is head of the Politics and Development Research Unit at the Institute of Sociology at Kepler University in Linz. Her research focuses on global political economy and north-south relations. One of her most recent publications is *Neoliberal Think Tank Networks* from 2018.

Thomas Fischer is a Professor at Catholic University of Eichstätt-Ingolstadt. His research focuses on development in Latin America, asymmetric power relations, collective memory, as well as construction of identity and history of Latin America within the process of globalization. One of his most recent publications, which he co-edited, is *Kolumbien heute. Politik, Wirtschaft, Kultur* from 2017.

Barbara Fritz is Professor at Freie Universität Berlin for Latin American Economics. Her research focuses on economic development and development theory. Together with Daniela Prates and Luiz F. de Paula she published *Global Currency Hierarchy and National Policy Space: A Framework for Peripheral Economies* in 2018.

Katiuscia Galhera is a Professor at the International Institute of Social Studies at Erasmus University Rotterdam. Her research focuses on gender and labor, social movements, transnational corporations, global supply chains, and Latin American political economy. Her most recent publication, together with Scott Martin and João Paulo Veiga, is *Labor Relations, Conflictual Cooperation and Retail in Latin America: The Case of Walmart in Brazil* from 2019.

Virginia García-Acosta is Social Anthropologist and Historian at CIESAS (Center for Research and Advanced Studies in Social Anthropology) in Mexico. Her research focuses on food history, disaster, and risk. Her next forthcoming publication is *Historical Perspectives in Risk and Disaster Anthropology: Methodological Approaches.*

Juan Grigera is an Honorary Research Associate at the Institute of Americas at the University College London. His research focuses on economic development, economic policy analysis, as well as development countries. His latest publication is *Populism in Latin America: Argentina and Brazil between Old and New Forms of Populism* from 2017.

Steven High is Professor of History at Concordia University. His research focuses on transnational approaches to working class history as well as forced migration and the history of deindustrialization. One of his most recent publications is *One Job Town: Work, Belonging and Betrayal in Northern Ontario* from 2018.

Tina Hilgers is Associate Professor of Political Science at Concordia University. Her research focuses on comparative politics, clientelism, and urban violence. One of her most recent publications, together with Laura Macdonald, is *Violence in Latin America and the Caribbean: Subnational Structures, Institutions, and Clientelistic Networks from* 2017.

Richard Huizar is Assistant Professor of Political Science and director of the Latin American and Latino Studies Program at William Paterson University. His research focuses on comparative politics, international relations, Latin American politics, and Mexican politics. His most recent publication is *Why was Yacimientos Petrolíferos Fiscales (YPF), Argentina's National Oil Company, Privatized?* from 2019.

Kjeld Jakobsen holds a PhD in International Relations. He worked as a consultant on international relations, development cooperation, and labor issues in Brazil. Currently he is an international adviser of the Worker's Party and consultant for the Trade Union Confederation of the Americas.

Alke Jenss holds a PhD in Sociology and is Senior Researcher at Arnold Bergstraesser Institute Freiburg. Her research focuses on the intersection of critical political economy, state theory, urban (in)security, and development studies with particular reference to Latin America. Her most recent publication, which she co-edited, is *Globale Ungleichgewichte und soziale Transformationen* from 2018.

Andrés López Rivera is doctoral researcher at the International Max Planck Research School on the Social and Political Constitution of the Economy. His research focuses on transnational governance, international political sociology, as well as epistemic authority. His most recent publication is *Chronicle of a Schism Foretold: The State and Transnational Activism in Ecuador's Yasuní-ITT Initiative* from 2017.

Lachlan MacKinnon is Assistant Professor of History at Cape Breton University. His research focuses on deindustrialization, labor history, ecology and the environment. One of his most recent publications, as a co-editor, is *The Deindustrialized World: Confronting Ruination in Post-Industrial Places* from 2017.

Laura Macdonald is Professor in the Department of Political Science and the Institute of Political Economy at Carleton University. Her research focuses on Latin American, Mexican, and North American politics as well as Canadian foreign policy and democracy and civil society. One of her most recent publications that she co-edited with Tina Hilgers is *Violence in Latin America and the Caribbean: Subnational Structures, Institutions, and Clientelistic Networks* from 2017.

Scott B. Martin is Professor and works at the Department of International Affairs at the School of International and Public Affairs at Columbia University and for the Graduate

Program of International Affairs at The New School. His research focuses on comparative and transnational labor politics, comparative social policy, corporate social responsibility in transnational corporations, and Latin American political economy. His most recent publication as a co-author, together with João Paulo Veiga and Katiuscia Galhera, is *Labor Relations, Conflictual Cooperation and Retail in Latin America: The Case of Walmart in Brazil* from 2019.

Franz Mauelshagen is a Senior Scientist at the Anthropocene Network, University of Vienna, and an affiliated scholar at the Institute for Advanced Sustainability Studies in Potsdam. His research focuses on the history of great transformations, sustainability and resilience in a deep historical perspective; climate history, history of climate science and climate policy; global environmental history as well as the history of (natural) disasters. One of his most recent publications, which he co-edited, is *The Palgrave Handbook of Climate History* from 2018.

Belén Olmos Giupponi is Associate Professor of Law at Kingston University London. Her research focuses on regional human rights systems and the interplay between transnational human rights law and other disciplines. One of her most recent publications is *Rethinking Free Trade, Economic Integration and Human Rights in the Americas* from 2017.

Mirko Petersen holds a PhD from Bielefeld University where he is member of the Center for InterAmerican Studies. His research focuses on Populism, Latin American politics in the 20th and 21st centuries, as well as the relationship between the Soviet Union and Latin America. His most recent publication is *Geopolitische Imaginarien. Diskursive Konstruktionen der Sowjetunion im peronistischen Argentinien (1943–1955)* from 2018.

Dieter Plehwe holds a PhD and works at the Berlin Social Science Center (WZB). His research focuses on the history and variety of neoliberalism. Together with several co-authors he published *Nine Lives of Neoliberalism* from 2019.

David Pion-Berlin is Professor of Political Science at the University of California, Riverside. His research focuses on civil military relations, defense, and security mainly in Latin America. His most recent publication, which he co-authored with Collin Grimes, is *Power Relations, Coalitions and Rent Control: Reforming the Military's Natural Resource Levies* from 2019.

Josef Raab is Professor of North American Studies at the University of Duisburg-Essen in Germany. His research interests include Inter-American Studies, ethnicity (especially U.S. Latinas and Latinos), borders, cultural hybridity, and the whole range of U.S. American literature from the 17th to the 21st century. He has also written on U.S. Catholicism, the German presence in the United States, city narratives, television, film, and transnationalism. From 2009 to 2018 he served as the founding president of the International Association of Inter-American Studies. Additionally, he is a co-editor of *The Routledge Handbook to the History and Society of the Americas.*

Fabricio Rodríguez is a post-doctoral researcher at the Department of Sociology at Friedrich-Schiller-University Jena and an ALMA (Asia, Latin America, Middle East, and Africa) Fellow at the Arnold Bergstraesser Institute in Freiburg. His research focuses on global power structures and the political economy of oil, minerals, and biomass. One of his most recent publications is his doctoral thesis *Oil, Minerals, and Power: The Political Economy of China's Quest for Resources in Brazil and Peru* from 2018.

Wagner de Melo Romão is a Professor at the Department of Political Science at the University of Campinas. His research focuses on democratic innovations, participation, public policies, as well as political parties, and political institutions in Latin America. His most recent publication that he co-authored is *Democratic Innovations in Municipalities* from 2018

María Josefina Saldaña-Portillo is a Professor of Social & Cultural Analysis at New York University. Her research focuses on Latin American and Latinx Studies; Indigenous Studies; globalization and immigrations studies; development studies as well as cultural studies. One of her most recent publication is *Indian Given: Racial Geographies across Mexico and the United States* from 2016.

Olga Sanmiguel-Valderrama is Associate Professor at the Department of Women's, Gender and Sexuality Studies at the University of Cincinnati. Her research focuses on neoliberal economic policies, military aid, as well as labor, environmental, and equality rights for women and racial minorities. Her most recent publication is a co-edited volume titled *Global Women's Work: Perspectives on Gender and Work in the Global Economy* from 2018.

Stefan Schmalz is Professor at Friedrich-Schiller-University Jena. His research focuses on work and industrial sociology, international and comparative political economy, development research as well as political sociology. His most recent publication is *Machtverschiebungen im Weltsystem. Der Aufstieg Chinas und die große Krise* from 2018.

Ursula Stiegler holds a PhD in Political Science and works currently for GIZ (German Corporation for International Cooperation). Her research focuses on governance, migration, and development and pro-poor financial sector development. One of her publications, which she co-authored, is *Remittances for Financial Access: Lessons from Latin American Microfinance* from 2014.

Aaron Tauss is Associate Professor at the Department of Political Science at the Universidad Nacional de Colombia. His main research interests include international relations, international political economy, and geopolitics. One of his best-known books is *Sozial-ökologische Transformationen – Das Ende des Kapitalismus denken* from 2016.

Paul-Matthias Tyrell is a research assistant at the Center for InterAmerican Studies at Bielefeld University. His research focuses on borderlands and North American economic and political history in the 1920s.

Jonas Wolff is executive board member and head of the research department "Intrastate Conflict" at the Peace Research Institute Frankfurt (PRIF). His research focuses on the transformation of political orders, contentious politics, international democracy promotion, and Latin American politics. One of his most recent publications is *Socioeconomic Protests in MENA and Latin America* from 2019 which he co-edited together with Irene Weipert-Fenner.

Carlos del Valle Rojas is a Professor at the University of La Frontera. His research focuses on intercultural communication, cultural studies, and different modes of cultural representation. Currently, he directs the international research network project "Converging Horizons: Production, Mediation, Reception and Effects of Representations of Marginality" and is director of the journal *Perspectivas de la Comunicación*. One of his most recent publications, which he co-edited with Francisco Sierra, is *Communicology from the South: Critical Perspectives from Latin America.* from 2019.

María Fernanda Valdés holds a PhD in economics. She is a consultant in the area of inequality and works as a coordinator of tax issues for the Friedrich-Ebert-Stiftung in Colombia and Latin America. Currently she lectures on taxation at the Universidad de los Andes in Bogotá. Furthermore, she worked as a researcher for the Colombian Ministry of Healt for the network "desiguALdades.net" at Freie Universität Berlin and the Deutsche Gesellschaft für Internationale Zusammenarbeit (GIZ). One of her most recent publications is *Reducing Inequality in Latin America: The Role of Tax Policy* from 2016.

Henry Veltmeyer is Professor of Development Studies at the Universidad Autónoma de Zacatecas. His research focuses on the political economy of development, critical development studies, and political sociology. One of his most recent publications is *The Essential Guide to Critical Development Studies* from 2017.

Lucrecia Wagner is a researcher at the National Scientific and Technical Research Council (CONICET) in Argentina. Her research focuses on environmental conflicts mostly related to mining and fracking activities, with particular emphasis on the relationships between socio-environmental movements and environmental governance. Her most recent publication is *Agricultura, cultura del oasis y megaminería en Mendoza. Debates y disputas* from 2019.

Dorothea Wehrmann is a research associate at the German Development Institute (DIE). Her research focuses on aid effectiveness, international and transnational cooperation, as well as partnerships and networks, and private sector engagement. Her most recent research is *Critical Geopolitics of the Polar Regions: An Inter-American Perspective* from 2018.

Rudy Weissenbacher holds a PhD and works at the Department of Economics at the Vienna University of Economics and Business. His research focuses on development studies, international political economy, as well as regional integration. One of his most recent publications is *A Ladder without Upper Rungs: On the Limitations of Industrial Policies in TNC Capitalism. The Case of the European Union* from 2018.

ACADEMIC ADVISORY BOARD

ACKNOWLEDGMENTS

The history of the project to organize a multi-volume handbook on critical key topics of Inter-American relevance dates back to the research group "E pluribus unum? Ethnic Identities in Transnational Integration Processes in the Americas" that Sebastian Thies, Josef Raab, and Olaf Kaltmeier organized at the Center for Interdisciplinary Research (ZiF) at Bielefeld University. So, our first thanks go to the ZiF who had enough confidence to fund this research group in 2008 and 2009.

This handbook would not have been possible without the support of the German Ministry for Education and Research (Bundesministerium für Bildung und Wissenschaft) which funded the research project "The Americas as Space of Entanglement" conducted by Wilfried Raussert and Olaf Kaltmeier from 2013 to 2019 at the Center for InterAmerican Studies (CIAS) at Bielefeld University.

In the context of this project, a special editorial office for the handbook-project could be installed. Martin Breuer and Johanna Lehmann did an extraordinary job to manage this office. Grace Dolcini made an excellent correction of all entries. Nora Willenius, Rosie Thomas, and Tamar Mota did their best to support the editorial office. For the translation we would like to thank Kate Berson, Christopher McCallum, Alice Nash, and the University of Massachusetts Amherst Translation Center.

Furthermore, we want to express our gratitude to Ashgate and Routledge who supported the handbook right from the beginning. At Ashgate we would like to thank Kirstin Howgate and at Routledge Claire Maloney and Rob Sorsby.

Last but not least, we would like to thank all authors of this dictionary for their encouraged engagement in this publication. And we would like to express our very great appreciation to more than 112 reviewers of our Academic Advisory Board who contributed greatly to the quality and Inter-American outreach of each entry.

Olaf Kaltmeier
Bielefeld
July 2019

GENERAL INTRODUCTION

Olaf Kaltmeier

The Routledge Handbook to the Political Economy and Governance in the Americas charts the field of Inter-American studies, focusing on the transnational or hemispheric dimensions of economic, political, social, and geographic dynamics that shape the different societies and communities in the Americas. It seeks to provide the framework and the tools needed to explore the hemispheric space of entanglements in the Americas as a new perspective in transregional area studies (Smith 2010; Wesley-Smith and Jon 2010; Kaltmeier 2017). Conceptually, it stresses the dimension of "inter" as a discursive zone to capture the dynamics, negotiations, and power relations of knowledge production from diverse loci of enunciation. The *Routledge Handbook* is thus based on an approach of globally entangled spaces and histories that has far-reaching methodological implications.

Beyond the critique on "methodological nationalism" and container thinking, the production of horizontal methods based on reciprocity and dialogue is required in order to construct a common basis of understanding (Corona Berkin and Kaltmeier 2012). In doing so, the Handbook is inspired by recent debates in cultural and postcolonial studies in the humanities and social sciences that have challenged traditional conceptualizations that have had the tendency to essentialize and universalize Western concepts that are grounded on particular local European experiences (Mignolo 2000). This means also taking into account the different geopolitical loci of enunciation within the Americas, due to different cultural and political regional differences. Thereby, the differences cannot only be limited to the linguistic divide between Anglo- and Latin America. Instead within these linguistic spaces, there are enormous cultural-political variances and multiple entanglements that have to be taken into account. Furthermore, postcolonial approaches have illuminated the important contributions of other epistemic communities, especially indigenous and Afro-American, as well as nonacademic actors, such as social movements and non-governmental organizations, for the emergence and constant redefining of key concepts in the Americas. Therefore, actors that are involved in multi-sited constellations must be taken into account, from governmental, non-governmental actors, to cultural producers and the media, as well as different cultural and geopolitical loci of enunciation. Thereby, it must be acknowledged that the academic field is still a privileged site of knowledge production with highly symbolic capital, but it is not the only site where knowledge is produced. Decentralizing the existing knowledge hierarchy and the search for dialogue with other sites of knowledge production is thus another challenge for dialogical area studies taken up by this Handbook. In this sense, it is not the aim of this Handbook to provide a unilateral and homogenous narration of political economy, geopolitics and, governance in the Americas from a single perspective. Instead, it explores different and entangled perspectives on the same concept.

In doing so, dialogical approaches – like the one developed in this *Routledge Handbook* – cannot aim to arrive at a consensus. A final definition of a concept would mean that there is nothing left to say, this would be the end of dialogue. Instead, we hint at the permanent process of knowledge production and underline that polyphony and the understanding of difference might be more important than the definition of "universal truths." This does not open the path for "alternative facts" or relativist partial truths. Instead, it helps to understand different positions on a broader contextual and epistemological level, and invites engagement in political-academic debates. In highlighting the contested character of key concepts that are usually defined in strict disciplinary terms or in regard to specific – often unconsidered – geopolitical standpoints, the Handbook provides the basis for a better and deeper understanding of Inter-American entanglements.

To secure the excellent quality of the texts, all entries underwent a strict double-blind peer-review process, where authors from the North were especially reviewed by experts from the South and vice versa. Furthermore, all entries have been discussed intensely in the editorial conferences by the editors of this three-volume *Routledge Handbook* project.

Beyond its particular focus on political economy, geopolitics, and governance in the Americas, this Handbook is the second volume and an integral part of a broader project on "Inter-American Perspectives" consisting of two further Handbooks, the first volume, the *Routledge Handbook to the History and Society of the Americas* and the third volume, the *Routledge Handbook to the Culture and Media in the Americas*. Each of the three volumes consists of two thematic parts which are introduced by a conceptual essay. The current volume consists of a first part on "Political Economy" and a second part on "Geopolitics and Governance." The volumes generate and systematize knowledge about the Americas by a collection of key terms discussed critically through an interdisciplinary and meta-reflexive lens. The three Handbooks are cross-indexed. The arrow (→) marks a cross-reference, the Roman number indicates the volume and the Arabic number refers to the chapter. For example (→ Pan-Americanism, II/40) means that the entry on "Pan-Americanism" is in Volume II *Routledge Handbook to the Political Economy and Governance in the Americas*, Chapter 40.

Due to its transdisciplinary approach, the *Routledge Handbook to the Political Economy and Governance in the Americas* is of interest for a broad array of academic disciplines, especially Cultural Studies, History, Sociology, Social Anthropology, Political Sciences, Political Economy, Environmental Studies, and Geography, as well as different areas studies such as U.S.-American and Latin American and Caribbean Studies. Thereby, this Handbook does not just list political institutions and economic indicators or narrate macro-regional dynamics; instead, it makes the effort and provides the tools for a terminological and methodological rethinking of (trans-)area studies in the current era of globalization.

Inter-American key topics on political economy, geopolitics, and governance

The Handbook on Political Economy and Governance in the Americas is divided into two main parts. The first part on "Political Economy" deals with concepts and dynamics related to political economy, containing twenty-two thematic entries. The second part is concerned with Inter-American concepts and dynamics on "Geopolitics and Governance," with twenty entries on key concepts. Furthermore, each of the two parts provides an introduction with a general overview of the specific theoretical debates in regard to the main topics.

In the vein of Inter-American Studies, this Handbook seeks a different take on transnational phenomena, cherishing the goal of developing a critical dialogical methodology by decolonizing key concepts, paradigms, and theories (for Inter-American Studies see: Quijano and Wallerstein 1992; Salvatore 2006; Mignolo 2008; Raab 2008; Rinke 2012; Kaltmeier 2013, 2019; Raussert 2017). In order to un- and rethink common concepts in terms of dynamics of Inter-American entanglements, the Handbook proposes a two-fold interdisciplinary dialogue, which refers first to crossing the boundaries between the established area studies and, second, to that of the academic discipline.

The Handbook's goal is to provide a critical vocabulary within a dialogical and horizontal framework between North and South as well as South and South in the context of processes of globalization. The most basic yet essential requirement of a critical handbook of Inter-American Studies is the acknowledgment of the multiplicity and simultaneity of knowledge production in different areas and various disciplines. The differences need to be recorded, contraries and similarities juxtaposed, and the existing sources of knowledge mobilized, including extra-academic ones. It is important to understand the different meanings and connotations the same concept may have in different contexts and from the perspective of different loci of enunciation in unequal power relations. In order to do so, the methodological apparatus of historical semantics can be used. German historian Reinhart Koselleck (1992, 2011) was interested in tracking the meaning of a concept in diachronical as well as synchronical terms. Today, it seems difficult to reconcile both perspectives. While Bielefeld historical semantics (Steinmetz 2008) is especially interested in the diachronical dimension, the Cambridge School (Pocock and Agard 1996) gives preference to the analysis of concepts in its specific spatiotemporal context. In this Handbook, the pretense to do historical semantics in strict methodological terms is not intended. Rather, there is an inclination toward cultural and postcolonial studies and its focus on the context, arguing that in the Americas, a whole variety of different contexts need to be dealt with. First, there are different linguistic spaces and geopolitical units, but also within these spaces, variety is given, basically in regard to coloniality and the multiple social and cultural fragmentations derived from it. This means that concepts are also contested – by different meanings and even counter-concepts. This perspective has been exemplified in regard to critical development studies by the *Development Dictionary: A Guide to Knowledge as Power* edited by Wolfgang Sachs (1992), which became a benchmark in post-development approaches.

For the studies of the Americas an interdisciplinary perspective is necessary. After all, different disciplines provide optional insights and open windows for dialogue and exchange. Thereby, this *Routledge Handbook* draws particularly on those interdisciplinary approaches shaped by Post-development Studies, Critical Geopolitics, Cultural Geography, Critical Development Studies, Postcolonial Studies, Political Economy, Environmental History, Gender Studies, as well as Global History and Globalization Studies. Beyond the "parochialism" (Sayer 2000) of disciplines, a topic-based approach is proposed that does not create a unified definition of an issue, but that sheds light on the cultural construction process of a concept and the different notions by which a single concept is framed. In order to grasp the notion of entanglements, the concept of dialogue has been put in the center of the methodological reflections. The goal is to capture the multiplicity, simultaneity, mobility, dialogical, and often conflictive (ex)change of knowledge. This is also revealed in the definition of the structure and topics of this volume.

In order to identify the relevant topics in each volume of the Routledge Handbooks, we worked in interdisciplinary and interregional editorial committees including scholars from North and South America as well as from Europe. Finally, the work of these committees was discussed in several conferences of the editorial board consisting of the editorial teams of all three Routledge Handbook volumes. As the Handbooks are not concerned with the universal definition of concepts, independent of place and time, we have chosen topics and concepts of Inter-American importance that are under debate and on the move. In this sense, we want to reveal how the same term or topic can be conceptualized in different ways depending on the locus of enunciation and the particular moment in time.

This special way to unthink concepts in an Inter-American perspective is revealed in the topic`s general structure. Each entry starts with a short general description of the topic. This introductory part could include a short history of the concept or etymological considerations, especially in regard to the Americas. Second, the main part consists of discussion of the topic in its Inter-American dimensions. Here, we propose to take into account three heuristic approaches: (a) Comparison: This refers to the description and analysis of the same topic in different, separated contexts; (b) Transfer: This refers to the flow of meaning and knowledge from one context into another. Here, we are interested in the itineraries of the flows as well as in the adaption of a new meaning in a new context; (c) Entanglement: This refers to the *mestizaje* and hybridization of different meanings through interchanges. Thereby, new meaning can be produced. The entry concludes with a final discussion of the topic, where the authors can reveal their own opinions.

Beyond this dialogue distilled in each entry, and beyond the lively discussions on the structure of each volume, there is also a dialogue between the volumes. We would like to invite the readers to an entangled reading. This means that we do not prefer a linear reading of one page after the other, but a flâneur-like cruising from one entry to the other. Cross-references between the entries of all volumes support this way of reading within each volume and within the three Routledge Handbooks. In this sense, each volume is also an invitation to you, as a reader, to engage in dialogue with the text you read. We hope that you will enjoy this dialogical knowledge production as much as we, as authors and editors, have.

Historical thresholds in Inter-American entanglements

The following pages aim to provide the reader a toolkit to connect the different thematic entries on key concepts in Inter-American studies and to put them into a broader historical context. Inspired by the history of ideas suggested by Reinhart Koselleck (1992, 2011) this Handbook identifies decisive historical thresholds or turning points that mark the end and the beginning of new historical conjunctures with far-reaching consequences for the construction, transformation, and application of the analyzed key concepts (Kaltmeier 2019). Historical thresholds, historical moments or condensed time spans, catalyze the resemantization of existing notions and the emergence of new key concepts. What were these decisive moments where the meaning and cultural significance of important political, economic and geopolitical concepts in the Americas changed profoundly?

From an Inter-American perspective applied in this Handbook, the emergence of the U.S. Empire in the aftermath of the Spanish-U.S.-American-Cuban-Filipino War in 1898 has been chosen as a fundamental threshold on the eve of the 20th century. This war has also transformed the self-understanding of the United States in regard to its Southern neighbors as expressed in its growing political interventionism (→ II/36), economic imperialism, as well as self-declared claim in regard to not only hemispheric but also global geopolitics (→ II/34). With the beginning of the 20th century, a profound geopolitical shift in global power relations toward the Western Hemisphere, and in particular the U.S., could be observed that led journalist Henry R. Luce (1941) to baptize this century as the "American Century." The quest for U.S.-American hegemony after 1898, after the end of Spanish dominance and in competition with the British Empire and the emerging German Empire, is linked to a plea for freedom on the one hand, and to a realpolitik on the other hand that considers Latin America as its neo-imperial backyard. In this sense, the Pax Americana is also based on military force, from the gunboat policy over counter-insurgency to the nuclear superpower (→ Military, II/37). At the same time, the U.S.-American way of life fostered by the cultural industry and mass consumption became a leading set of values, was often experienced in Latin America in terms of cultural imperialism. The emergence of the U.S.-American 20th century is contested in an Inter-American entangled way by anti-imperialism – a concept that emerged in the United States after the Spanish-American War – and whose main protagonist were Latin American intellectuals, like Cuban José Martí and Uruguayan José Enrique Rodó as well as the U.S.-American based Anti-Imperialist League.

The next Inter-American threshold, already in the 20th century, is marked by the success of the Mexican Revolution, probably best expressed in the progressive Mexican constitution, and the U.S.-American entry into World War I, both in the year 1917. The conceptual history of socialism has been written basically from a fairly Eurocentric point of view; yet from an Inter-American perspective, the experience of the Mexican Revolution has to be highlighted as the first social revolution of the 20th century that possessed open socialist and anarchist aspects, and that coined the concept of socialism in different ways. In 1910, a broad uprising began in Mexico against the technocratic and authoritarian regime of Porfirio Díaz that culminated in the first revolution (→ II/44) of the 20th century. The revolution found a prominent institutionalization in the constitution, where important social rights have been granted, e.g. in regard to the redistribution of land (→ II/15) or labor representation (→ II/14). This constitution was not only inspired by the U.S.-American one, but also by the socialist constitution of the recently founded Soviet Union, as it also contains crucial demands of the anarchist movement. In the U.S. main social reforms took place after the Wall Street Crash of 1929 (→ Crisis, II/4). The onset of the Great Depression suddenly made possible many of the reforms for which socialists and anarchists had been fighting for decades: the right of unions to organize, state pensions for the elderly, welfare programs for the poor, etc. According to historian Alan Brinkley (1995), this era marked "the end of reform," with the administration of Franklin D. Roosevelt introducing with his New Deal policy just enough reform to undercut calls for revolution, to preserve capitalism (→ Class Struggle, II/3). In this context Italian Marxist Antonio Gramsci coined the new concept of Fordism (→ II/10), derived from automobile-magnate Henry Ford, to describe a new formation of industrial capitalism (→ II/2). Simultaneously, in many Latin American countries populist governments were established (→ Populism, II/43) that pursued economic policies of endogenous industrialization based on import-substitution and that replaced often traditional dependencies of the *hacienda* regimes by new forms of clientelism (→ II/29), often related to corporatist forms of labor representation.

While the European powers were in crisis due to the tumults of war, U.S. foreign policy was basically focused on the Western Hemisphere – oscillating between the Big Stick policy and the Good Neighbor approach (→ Pan-Americanism, II/40). Especially during World War I, the U.S. expanded its geopolitical power in the Western Hemisphere through the occupation of Nicaragua (1912–1933), Haiti (1915–1934), the Dominican Republic (1916–1924), and Cuba (1917–1922) followed by several interventions in Central America (Panama, Guatemala, Costa Rica, Honduras) at the beginning of the 1920s. This interventionist policy was accompanied by a dramatic expansion of U.S.-American economic activities in Latin America (→ Interventionism, II/36).

The end of World War II is considered to be the next historical threshold as it marked the beginning of a global geopolitical transformation that can be described best as the Pax Americana: the reordering of the world under U.S.-American hegemony. This period is also frequently described by historians as the Cold War, which began in 1947 when U.S. President Harry S. Truman's announced "the Truman Doctrine." This first public articulation of a U.S. foreign policy dedicated to the "containment" of communism ushered in a nearly fifty-year-long epoch in which the United States consistently justified all actions against the "red threat." In 1946, the U.S. Army School of the Americas, located in the U.S.-controlled Panama Canal Zone, was founded in order to instruct the armed forces of Latin America using training programs that were compatible with United States customs and geopolitical trajectories (→ Military II/37).

The climate of anti-communism extended beyond the United States throughout the Western Hemisphere (Iber 2015). Instead of a Panamerican integration based on a dialogue among equal neighbors, a Pax American international institution building took place. Notably, the USA and nearly all Latin American countries committed to hemispheric anti-communism by signing the Inter-American Treaty of Reciprocal Assistance in Rio de Janeiro, commonly known as the Rio Treaty (1947). Having arranged a military–political alliance among nearly all countries of the Western Hemisphere under U.S. hegemony, the Inter-American system took another important step on April 30th of 1948 to its formalization through the foundation of the Organization of American States (OAS). On a global scale, the Pax Americana also led to a considerable building of international institutions that followed the bipolar logic of the Cold War. In 1949, the North Atlantic Treaty was signed in Washington to create NATO as a defense alliance against the communist block. In this context, the concept of development (→ II/6) received a completely new meaning and was introduced as a policy concept on a global scale by President Truman in his 1949 inaugural address after the end of World War II. This concept of development is related to the emergence of institutions such as the International Monetary Fund (1947) and the World Bank (1945).

Nevertheless, the conceptualization of development through capitalist modernization theory did not remain uncontested in the Americas. Of particular importance for the introduction of new concepts and the re-semantization of existing ones in political economy was the theory-production of the 1948-established UN Economic Commission for Latin America and the Caribbean (in Spanish: Cepal) in Santiago de Chile. In the 1960s and 1970s, Dependency Theory became the main critical approach for Latin American societal realities that also openly addressed Inter-American relations of dependence (Kay 1989). With its origins in Latin America, Dependency Theory soon became an Inter-American approach related to U.S.-American Neo-Marxists, such as Paul B. Baran and Paul Sweezy as well as German intellectual Andre Gunder Frank. This school of thought had an enormous impact on the reconceptualization of a whole slew of political–economical concepts discussed in this *Routledge Handbook* such as modernization, nation-state (II/38), and development (→ II/6).

In this sense it is possible to argue that 1947/8 was a threshold for the establishment of the bipolar Cold War order, and at this same time, it opened a horizon of contestation and creative searches for a third path. In Argentina, Juan Domingo Perón promoted the idea of an Argentinean third way between "greedy capitalism" and "totalitarian communism" (Petersen 2018). On a smaller scale, Costa Rica decided – in a context of worldwide growing militarization – to be the first country to abolish its army after the short, bloody Costa Rican Civil War in 1948 (→ Military, II/37). However, the space for maneuver was limited. The Cuban Revolution of 1959 (→ Revolution, II/44), which was first an anti-imperialist uprising against the dictatorial regime of Batista, had to reinforce its alliance with the Soviet Union after the missile crisis and the failed U.S.-organized invasion in the Bay of Pigs.

In the United States, Inter-American relations also increasingly became a matter of domestic policy for the U.S. Mexican anthropologist and indigenist Manuel Gamio who had already written *Mexican Immigration to the United States* (1930) and *The Mexican Immigrant: His Life Story* in the early 1930s. He was obviously influenced by the emerging Chicano and Latino movements that had founded the Confederación de Uniones Obreras Mexicanos (1927) and the League of United Latin American Citizens (1928), as well as the La Asociación de Jornaleros (1933). However, it was the Bracero-program and its effects that profoundly accelerated the question of Latinidad in the U.S. The Bracero-program was intended to fill the labor shortage in agriculture during World War II (Chavez 2008). While the Latino-movement had some success in the politics of recognition, in 1950, mass deportations of Mexican migrants started establishing a continuing important field of conflictive Inter-American relations. Nevertheless, from 1951 to 1964, a yearly average of about 200,000 men and women continued to come to work in the U.S., contributing to a growing Latinization of the Anglo-American North. For the sending countries, the income became of growing economic importance, even still at the beginning of the 21st century (→ Remittances, II/19).

In the Americas, the years between 1968 and 1973 mark the next crucial threshold. The year 1968 is the paradigmatic year for social revolutionary activities and revolts (→ Revolution, II/44). And 1973 represents the year of political reaction with the coup d'état against the socialist government of Salvador Allende and subsequent military dictatorship (→ Authoritarianism, II/25), as well as the establishment of a neoliberal model in Chile (→ Neoliberalism, II/16). A similar emblematic condensation of this turning point took place in Mexico where the utopian horizon of the Mexican 1968 movement vanished with the Tlatelolco massacre where police forces and the military killed around 400 peaceful demonstrators. The Bolivian military ended, with the support of U.S. secret service, the guerrilla of Ñancahuazú with the symbolic execution of Ernesto "Che" Guevara in 1967. One year later, the powerful mobilization cycle of the civil rights movement in the U.S. that began in 1955 came to a violent end with the assassination of Martin Luther King in 1968. In several Latin American countries as well as in the U.S., the libertarian and emancipative cycle closed, or was stopped by violence, burying the ideas of social and cultural revolutions, and initiating a new conjuncture of neoconservative backlash. The United States were not only involved in several regime changes. They also proliferated a counter-insurgency policy in the region. From the 1960s onward, the aforementioned School of the Americas taught specific anti-communist counter-insurgency strategies, including torture (→ Human Rights, II/55). Several future Latin American dictators passed through this institution, as part of a general pattern of U.S. support for right-wing dictatorships (Schmitz 1999; Gill 2004).

The oil crisis (→ Energy, II/7) and the collapse of the Bretton Woods system in 1973 indicated the beginning hegemony of neoliberalism (→ II/16). The rise of this new concept dominated the political debate until the midst of the 1990s. In the Americas especially, the examples of the Pinochet dictatorship (1973–1990) and the Chicago Boys in Chile and of president Ronald Reagan in the U.S. (1981–1989) marked the neoliberal experience of structural adjustment programs (→ State Transformation; II/21) and shock therapies that favored privatization (→ II/17) of state enterprises, low taxation (→ II/22) for the rich and transnational corporations (→ II/23), deindustrialization (→ II/5), leading to higher levels of informality (→ II/13) and new relations in regard to gender and work (→ II11), which provoked dramatic gaps in social inequality (→ II/20). The reign of neoliberalism went hand in hand with the external debt crisis in Latin America (→ Crisis II/4) and the rise of global financial markets.

Globalization and a new wave of democratization (→ Democracy, II/23) characterize the profound transformations at the threshold of the years 1989/1990 that is shaped by the implosion of the Soviet system, which led to the formal end of the Cold War in 1989. This collapse of the socialist block marked the end of an existing alternative to the capitalist system (→ Capitalism, II/2). In the midst of the crisis of socialism, Latin American revolutionary movements and governments had their own problems. In Cuba, the economy nearly collapsed in the "special period." In Nicaragua, the leftist Sandinistas Government, with Daniel Ortega at the forefront, was defeated in the 1990 elections by conservative Violeta Chamorro.

From a Latin American perspective, this threshold was often interpreted as marking a turning point toward a new wave of democratization, ending the Cold War dictatorships and authoritarian regimes (→ Authoritarianism, II/25) following the anti-communist doctrine of national security. The most striking example for the transition toward democracy (→ II/32) was the end of the Pinochet dictatorship and the assumption of office of the first democratically elected president in Chile since the violent end of Allende, Patricio Aylwin on March 12, 1990. Three days later, Fernando Collar de Mello took office as the first democratically elected president in Brazil after twenty-nine years of dictatorship. And in 1993, Juan Carlos Wasmosy became the first elected president in Paraguay, after nearly forty years of the Alfredo Stroessner dictatorship. In El Salvador, guerilla leaders and government representatives ended twelve years of Civil War. In Haiti, liberation theologian Jean-Bertrand Aristide waked the aspirations for liberation and social equality and was elected in 1990. In all these cases, a reconfigured civil society (→ II/28) was identified as one of the main drivers for democratization.

With the end of the bipolar world, the United States of America established itself as the unique world power. In geopolitical terms, this situation required from the perspective of the U.S., a New World Order. Free trade became a core principle for the post-Cold War era. In Latin America, the common market of the South, the Mercosur, was established and the United States envisioned the whole Western Hemisphere from Alaska to the Antarctic as a free-trade area (→ Global Commodity Chains, II/12). The first step to realize this vision was the establishment of the North American Free Trade Area (NAFTA) between the U.S., Canada, and Mexico in 1994 (→ Regional Integration, II/18).

A new element of the post-Fordist regime (→ State Transformation, II/21) was the rapidly growing importance of the financial markets in the 1990s and a similar rapid de-industrialization (→ II/5). The breakdown of the Bretton Woods system provided the conceptual room to understand money as a commodity, and the informational–technological innovations in the stock markets accelerated the worldwide circulation of huge amounts of money, including financial speculations, in real time. The unregulated financial speculation and the new global financial regime created new economic crises (→ II/4). After the NAFTA agreement and the subsequent de facto dollarization of Mexico, the Tequila crisis and its effects rippled across the South American content, where among other effects, Ecuador was forced to replace its national currency completely with the U.S. dollar in 1996.

A further important aspect of the 1989/90 threshold was the rising information age (Castells 1996). The informational–technological innovations like the World Wide Web in 1989 and the establishment of the first Internet connections as well as the programming of the first known internet webpage made a big difference in all social fields. Furthermore, new biotechnological innovations, especially in the field of gen-manipulation for agro-industrial purposes, led to a new green revolution in agriculture (→ Land, II/15). In this context, new concepts like the neologisms "internet," "webpage," and "email" emerged and created a different sense of the world related to new temporal experiences of instant time communication or the vanishing of space as structuring element in social life.

However, globalization was not only an economic and technological issue. The wave of democratization also opened a window of opportunity for other societal concerns, such as the ecological question (→ Nature, II/39). In 1992, the United Nations Conference on Environment and Development (UNCED) held the Earth Summit, or Rio Conference, in Rio de Janeiro, putting the concepts of sustainable development, climate change (→ II/30), and man-made natural disasters (→ II/33) on a global agenda. In the context of an accelerated process of globalization, the early dynamics – namely the conquest and colonization of the Americas – also came to the forefront. Facing the preparations for the commemoration of the 500th anniversary of the beginning of the conquest marked by the arrival of Cristobál Colón in the Americas, massive indigenous protests broke out to demand social inclusion, cultural recognition and new regimes of citizenship (→ II/27)

In this sense, 1990 not only marked the consolidation of a neoliberal worldwide free-trade regime, it also marked the beginning of new contestatory and social movements – such as the indigenous, the environmental, and the alter-globalization movements – that envisioned new utopian horizons of expectations of environmental justice (→ II/8), participation (→ II/41), defense of the commons (→ II/31), social equality (→ Social Inequality, II/20), democratization (→ Democracy, II/32), and multicultural recognition.

The 21st century began in the Western Hemisphere with an unexpected loss of political control of the United States over their southern neighbors, which can be interpreted as the first threshold in the second millennium. After the emergence of U.S.-democratic imperialism in 1898 and the following establishment of the U.S. as the only remaining superpower, in the 2000s, Latin American countries took self-determined development paths in a way they had not done in historical periods before. The efforts to transform the Americas into a free-trade area – the Free Trade Area of the Americas (FTAA) – under U.S.-American hegemony failed in 2005, because of the rejection of most Latin American countries (→ Regional Integration II/18).

In addition to this rejection, in a seemingly paradoxical historical *détournement*, Venezuelan President Hugo Chávez proclaimed in January 2005 at the fifth World Social Forum, the Latin American project of the "Socialism for the 21st Century." Hugo Chávez came into power in 1998 followed by Luiz Inacio "Lula" da Silva in Brazil and Néstor Kirchner in Argentina in 2003 as well as Tabaré Vázquez in Uruguay and Evo Morales in Bolivia in 2005. Socialism was not the only concept that reemerged within this so-called "Pink Tide." Given the ongoing Latin American economic dependence on natural resources, the traditional concept of extractivism (→ II/9), actualized with the prefix "neo-," also became an important concept of the political economic debates, especially in regard to environmental justice (→ II/8). It is also related to the ongoing problem to satisfy the rising demand of energy (→ II/7) – nowadays by new "green economy" means such as biofuels or hydro- and aeolian-power.

The South American progressive turn also found its echo in the North. In the United States, Barack Obama became the first elected president of African-American heritage in 2009. And yet, during the Obama presidency, police violence against unarmed black civilians became so widespread (and well-documented on social media) (→ Security, II/45) that a new movement, Black Lives Matter, formed to combat it.

The years of 2016 and 2017 marked the threshold of the end of the progressive conjuncture most notably with the impeachment – or cold coup d'état – against president Dilma Rousseff from the Brazilian Worker's Party and the election of Donald Trump as the president of the United States. Both cases went hand in hand with a significant shift in political communication (→ II/42). Offenses, defamations, and fake news were used to dismantle political correctness, multiculturalism, as well as feminism and LGBT+ rights. Supported by conservative religious beliefs, and especially by fundamentalist protestant churches, ultraconservative attitudes were promoted. The promotion of whiteness – against the multicultural politics of recognition – is a particularly important feature of the 2016/17 threshold in identity politics. This turn is accompanied by a growing social inequality (→ II/20) which on a global scale has reached yet unexperienced levels. The presidency of billionaires such as Mauricio Macri (2015–2019) in Argentina and Sebastián Piñeira (2010–2014 and since 2018) in Chile implied the end of a cycle of progressive governments and the recovery of a conservative economy of "austerity," the abandonment of social policy, and a refeudalization of political culture (Kaltmeier 2018).

The year between 2016/17 also marks a significant turning point in regard to multilayered conjunctures of international and regional institution building. The United States – under the lemma of "America first" – withdrew from several international agreements, such as the Paris climate agreement (→ Climate Change, II/30). Furthermore, institutions of Inter-American integration, such as the NAFTA, are under reconsideration, while the U.S. pursues a more protectionist policy abandoning the paradigm of global free trade that goes hand in hand with a strict border control policy (→ Borderlands, II/26). In a similar vein, ultraconservative Latin American governments in Brazil and Argentina have dismantled the institutions of Latin American integration founded in the 2000s, withdrawing themselves from Unasur, Banco del Sur, and TeleSur.

National protectionism also reveals itself in regard to transnational migration. The amplification of the fortified border between the United States and Mexico is the highest expression of a broader phenomenon of xenophobic anti-migrant attitudes, not only in the Western Hemisphere, but worldwide. In this sense, it seems that 2016/17 will turn out to be a significant turning point that stops the international institution building of the post-World War II period, as well as the globalization peak of the 1990s. As we are in midst of this threshold, it is too early to analyze the cultural and political impacts on key concepts in the Americas. Nevertheless, it seems that especially in the field of identity politics, massive transformations are taking place, while the horizon of expectation is mostly not directed toward a utopian better future, but in a nostalgic way toward the recuperation of a supposed lost idealized past. With regard to the urgent ecological question our (post-) modern understanding of time and historicity will also probably change profoundly. The neologism Anthropocene, introduced by geologist to term a new geological age based on human-made transformations of the Earth (→ Nature, II/39), highlights this tendency.

Works Cited

Brinkley, Alan. 1995. *The End of Reform: New Deal Liberalism in Recession and War.* New York, NY: Knopf.

Castells, Manuel. 1996. *The Rise of the Network Society.* Oxford, UK: Blackwell.

Chavez, Leo R. 2008. *The Latino Threat: Constructing Immigrants, Citizens, and the Nation.* Stanford, CA: Stanford University Press.

Corona Berkin, Sarah and Olaf Kaltmeier. eds. 2012. *En diálogo. Metodologías horizontales en Ciencias. Sociales y Culturales.* Barcelona: gedisa.

Gill, Lesley. 2004. *The School of the Americas: Military Training and Political Violence in the Americas.* Durham, NC: Duke University Press.

Iber, Patrick. 2015. *Neither Peace nor Freedom: The Cultural Cold War in Latin America.* Cambridge, MA: Harvard University Press.

Kay, Cristóbal. 1989. *Latin American Theories of Development and Underdevelopment.* London: Routledge.

Kaltmeier, Olaf. 2013. *Transnational Americas: Envisioning Inter-American Area Studies in Globalization Processes.* Trier and Tempe, AZ: WVT/Bilingual Press.

———. 2017. "Doing Area Studies in the Americas and Beyond. Towards Reciprocal Methodologies and the Decolonization of Knowledge." In *Area Studies at the Crossroads: Knowledge Production after the Mobility Turn*, eds. Katja Mielke and Anna-Katharina Hornidge, 47–67. New York, NY: Palgrave.

———. 2018. *Refeudalización: Desigualdad social, economía y cultura política en América Latina en el temrano siglo XXI.* Guadalajara: Universidad de Guadalajara.

———. 2019. "General Introduction to the Routledge Handbook to the History and Society of the Americas." In *The Routledge Handbook to the History and Society of the Americas*, eds. Olaf Kaltmeier, Josef Raab, Michael Stewart Foley, Alice Nash, Stefan Rinke and Mario Rufer, 1–13. New York, NY: Routledge.

Koselleck, Reinhart. 1992. "Introduction." In *Geschichtliche Grundbegriffe*, Vol. 7, eds. Otto Brunner and Werner Conze, 5–8. Stuttgart: Klett-Cotta.

———. 2011. "Introduction and Prefaces to the 'Geschichtliche Grundbegriffe'." *Contributions to the History of Concepts* 6, no. 1: 1–37.

Luce, Henry. 1999. "The American Century." *Diplomatic History* 23, no. 2: 159–171. www-personal.umich.edu/~mlassite/discussions261/luce.pdf. Orig. pub. 1941.

Mignolo, Walter. 2000. *Local Histories – Global Designs: Coloniality, Subaltern Knowledges, and Border Thinking.* Princeton, NJ: Princeton University Press.

———. 2008. *The Idea of Latin America.* Malden, MA: Blackwell.

Petersen, Mirko. 2018. *Geopolitische Imaginarien: Diskursive Konstruktionen der Sowjetunion im peronistischen Argentinien (1943–1955).* Bielefeld: Transcript.

Pocock, John Grevile Agard. 1996. "Concepts and Discourses: A Difference in Culture?" In *The Meaning of Historical Terms*, eds. Hartmut Lehmann and Melvin Richter, 47–58. Washington, DC: German Historical Institute.

Quijano, Aníbal, and Immanuel Wallerstein. 1992. "Americanicity as a Concept, or the Americas in the Modern World-System." *Social Science Journal* 44, no. 4: 549–557.

Raab, Josef. ed. 2008. *Hybrid Americas: Contacts, Contrasts, and Confluences in New World Literatures and Cultures.* Münster: LIT.

Raussert, Wilfried. ed. 2017. *The Routledge Companion to Inter-American Studies.* London and New York: Routledge.

Rinke, Stefan. 2012. *Lateinamerika und die USA: Eine Geschichte zwischen Räumen – von der Kolonialzeit bis heute.* Darmstadt: WBG.

Sachs, Wolfgang. ed. 1992. *The Development Dictionary: A Guide to Knowledge as Power.* London: Zed Book.

Salvatore, Ricardo D. 2006. *Imágenes de un Imperio: Estados Unidos y las formas de representación de América Latina.* Buenos Aires: Editorial Sudamericana.

Sayer, Andrew. 2000. "For Postdisciplinary Studies: Sociology and the Curse of Disciplinary Parochialism/Imperialism." In *For Sociology: Legacies and Prospects*, eds. John E. T. Eldridge, John MacInnes, Sue Scott, Chris Warhurst, and Anne Witz, 83–91. Durham, NC: Sociology Press.

Schmitz, David F. 1999. *Thank God They're On Our Side: The United States and Right-Wing Dictatorships, 1921–1965.* Chapel Hill, NC: University of North Carolina Press.

Smith, Neil. 2010. "Remapping Area Knowledge." In *Remaking Area Studies: Teaching and Learning Across Asia and the Pacific*, eds. Terence Wesley-Smith and Jon Goss, 24–40. Honolulu, HI: University of Hawai'i Press.

Steinmetz, Willibald. 2008. "40 Jahre Begriffsgeschichte – The State of the Art." In *Sprache – Kognition – Kultur*, eds. Heidrun Kämper and Ludwig M. Eichinger, 174–197. Berlin: Walter de Gruyter.

Wesley-Smith, Terence, and Jon Goss. eds. 2010. *Remaking Area Studies: Teaching and Learning across Asia and the Pacific*. Honolulu, HI: University of Hawai'i Press.

PART I

Political Economy in the Americas

Edited by

Anne Tittor

FRIEDRICH-SCHILLER-UNIVERSITY JENA

Daniel Hawkins

NATIONAL UNION SCHOOL OF COLOMBIA

In collaboration with

Bernhard Leubolt

KATHOLISCHE SOZIALAKADEMIE ÖSTERREICHS

1
INTRODUCTION
Political Economy in the Americas

Anne Tittor and Daniel Hawkins

Economic and social structures in different societies and communities across the Americas and the Caribbean are very much connected and, in many ways, entangled. An Inter-American approach offers a novel way of more adequately identifying and examining these structures, drawing on recent debates in cultural and postcolonial studies in the humanities and social sciences. It challenges traditional conceptualizations and their tendency to essentialize and universalize concepts that are grounded in local experiences. Furthermore, Inter-American approaches welcome the important contributions of non-academic actors, especially from social movements and the field of cultural production, in harnessing new meanings and concepts which are key to understanding the diverse interconnections of all types of human interaction across the Americas and the Caribbean.

Inter-American approaches as a new lens within political economy

The Inter-American focus is increasingly discussed in media studies (see *The Routledge Handbook to Culture and Media of the Americas*), migration research, as well as transborder studies and has gained ground in history with perspectives such as Entangled Histories and Global History (see *The Routledge Handbook to History and Society of the Americas*). In the field of political economy and governance, the Inter-American approach is still a relatively new perspective. Nonetheless, the key ontological starting point of Inter-American perspectives on political economy and governance is to highlight the multidirectional flows and entanglements of politics and economic production and exchange, across and within the diverse regions of the Americas and the Caribbean. Herein, attention is paid to the heterogeneity of these interactions, which throughout history have been much more complex and multifaceted than is often depicted by perspectives which only highlight the North-South structural power inequalities. Without negating these power asymmetries, it is important to stress their perpetually evolving dynamics. The historically unequal market relations between Canada, the USA, Latin America, and the Caribbean influenced the institutional architecture of the nation-states of the region. As the discourses of development and underdevelopment set hold and were gradually molded within policy, visions of governance and notions of political and economic opportunities as well as constraints were affected, as is discussed in detail in the entry on Development (→ II/6). Nonetheless, neither these discourses or the economic exchange (industrial goods in North America and mineral and agricultural commodities from Mexico to the South) that undergirded Inter-American relations, during colonialism and after independence, were completely binary and path dependent. For example, even after the formulation of the Pax Americana development paradigm based on the Three Worlds – officially projected in Harry Truman's inaugural presidential address in 1949 (Escobar 1998) and institutionalized via development missions, such as the one led by Lauchlin Currie to Colombia in the same year (Sandilands 2015) – many countries of the Americas continued orienting state policy in line with more heterogenous proposals made by leading Latin American scholars, such as Raúl Prebisch and his team at the Santiago-Based ECLAC (Economic Commission for Latin America and the Caribbean) offices (Prebisch 2016).

Nonetheless, efforts to disentangle Latin American and Caribbean societies from the nexus of economic and political power further north need to be understood within the two-pronged structures of the "coloniality of power" (Quijano 2007) and the boom-bust cycles of capitalism and their distinct manifestations and impacts depending on, to a great extent, the asymmetrical but systemically linked production and export structures found across the region. The changing historical forms and theories of the state express the changes in social relations and how the local, regional, and global were articulated and crystalized in the concrete forms of state apparatuses and discourses, as is discussed in the entries on State Transformation (→ II/21), Capitalism (→ II/2), and Crises (→ II/4) in this volume. The North American version of Fordism-Keynesianism both influenced and was shaped by the evolving regimes of accumulation that emerged across the Americas in the Post-World War II period. Their transregional interactions display the complexity of shaping and conceptualizing models of production and their modes of governance, socialization and the multiple terrains of contestation they face, as discussed in the entries on Fordism (→ II/10) and Transnational Corporations (→ II/23). Furthermore, the practices and discourses of imperialism not only engendered processes of socio-cultural, economic, and political emancipation, but were also often emblazoned in the images of the multiple and diverse guerrilla groups (both urban and rural) that rose across Latin America and the Caribbean from the 1950s onwards. The battle of ideas went beyond the policies of distinct U.S. governments, from Kennedy's Alliance for Progress to Nixon and Reagan's War on Drugs, or of Castro's project to vanquish U.S. dominance in the region and unify Latin America along the lines of Simón Bolívar's vision at the beginning of the 19th century. The 20th century was rife with social processes of transnational collaboration and support in the fields of labor, human rights, indigenous, and environmental struggles, to name only a few (Anner 2011).

The transregional nature of these interactions forged common fronts of political and economic contestation, many of which were institutionalized in diverse ways across the Americas, becoming key factors of influence in how trade union movements, for example, organized themselves, both in terms of their representation, nationally and regionally, as well as how their alliances shifted across space and time, points that are well covered in the entry on Labor Representation (→ II/14). Furthermore, even the coffee economy, of primary importance to the economic development of Brazil and Colombia as well as many Central America countries, especially throughout the 19th and 20th centuries, evolved along disparate institutional and regional lines in each country due in much part to the intricate social and market relations producers and their respective national coffee federations maintained with U.S. toasters, traders, and the U.S. Government (Topik and Samper 2006).

Economic structures and capitalist dynamics beyond borders

The inter-American perspectives, developed within the study field of political economy, are especially useful in crossing boundaries (spatial, historical and conceptual) as a means of examining the diverse interactions between political and economic structures and the agency of territorially based but regionally and globally bound social actors. The emergence of the neoliberal project, geographically located in the Chile of Pinochet's initial period, but ideologically and institutionally tied to the political and academic platforms projecting change in the USA and their consolidation through U.S.-backed military interventions and the dominance of *Reagonomics* across the region during the 1980s, is well illustrated by the entry on Neoliberalism (→ II/16). The entry on Privatization (→ II/17) moves on from here, reflecting on how concrete policies to privatize state assets across the Americas were justified by the emerging elite consensus against what was perceived as excessive state intervention in economic affairs. But the implementation of such doctrines, although more emphatic in Latin America than elsewhere, also encountered more acute opposition and social conflict, a reflection of its enormous social impact, while also molding many of the tensions in state-market-society relations in the intervening decades across the region, with distinct manifestations dependent on the specific institutional configurations and sectoral foci of actual privatization projects. In a similar manner, the entry on Deindustrialization (→ II/5) discusses a common pattern in different nation-states across the Americas, heavily influenced by the changing hegemonic ideas concerning the principle objectives of economic policy. As the entry shows, across the entire continent, millions of industrial jobs were lost, while at the same time there was a trend toward financialization and the installation of export-processing zones, commonly known as maquiladoras; both resulting in the demise of industrial hubs and the simultaneous growth of peripheral neighborhoods across the geographies of the mega-cities and other urban centers of the Americas.

Examining the inter-American entanglements from within the field of political economy permits a more fluid conceptualization of the ongoing changes within structure-agency in concrete socio-spatial contexts. For instance, looking at the ever-more complex modes, forms, and varieties of economic activity across the Americas, from within this lens, highlights the multiple entanglements between the spheres of economics and politics, allowing one to delve into how agency molds evolving structures to create patterns of integration along global commodity chains, which are transformed through the processes of cooperation and competition by lead firms and other downstream and upstream agents. The diverse reconfigurations of distinct chains of sectoral economic interaction (for example, the automotive, textile, and agro-industrial and mining sectors) and their socio-spatial manifestations across the Americas and the Caribbean are well encapsulated and summarized in the entry on Global Commodity Chains (→ II/12).

Land, without doubt is positioned at the crux of issues concerning how wealth and power are distributed within and across societies. In the Americas, with its complex practices of colonialism and imperialism, conflicts over access to, use of, and ownership of land have always been central themes that influence development models, state forms, and broader social conflict. While the social sciences tend to examine land conflicts from within the lens of conflicts between nation-states over their territorial boundaries, inter-American perspectives, grounded in the field of political economy and combining other fields such as agrarian studies and ecology, as discussed in the entry on Land (→ II/15), examine the social implications of different types of land appropriation and land use over time and across geographies, as well as give voice to the processes of social resistance to such projects and processes.

Overcoming methodological nationalism and Eurocentrism

Inter-American perspectives on key concepts from the field of political economy allow for fruitful discussions and reflections on how socio-economic power structures in the Americas were historically constructed and how they operate today, either spreading or becoming fractured due to the heterogeneity of the interactions between social groups within and across the Americas. They allow for more fluid discussions of the multiple political, economic, and social relations that connect people throughout the Americas and shape the societies of the continent. Most of the contributing authors to this volume faced the challenge of having to grapple with the fact that the literature they refer to rarely discusses the advantages and disadvantages, or at least the complexities involved in pursuing an Inter-American approach. Nevertheless, the editors asked for the discussion of a certain term and its relevance for societies in North-, Central-, and South America, as well as the Caribbean, and that they offer reflections regarding the multifarious interactions and relations between them. Most authors refer to literature that can be located in the field of *Global Political Economy*, and as such, even though these texts may adopt different theoretical frameworks (often Liberal, Marxist, or Realist), implicitly, they often reproduce universalizing hypotheses that perceive the market, the state or the capitalist mode of production as being omnipresent, always shaping the object of analysis despite the concrete place at which a certain development is evolving. Other literature sources are framed within the *Latin American Studies* field (an academic arena constructed in Europe and the U.S. during the Cold War period, which is strongly susceptible to tendencies of othering). Finally, also highly influential is the literature from within the field of *Development Studies*, which stresses the importance of inequalities between certain world regions, but often has an underlying idea of progress modeled in a Eurocentric and unilinear way.

This is not the only challenge. The disciplines of Sociology, Political Science, Economics and Anthropology have emerged and evolved over the past two hundred years very much rooted in the nation-state project and a system of academia that has encouraged the compartmentalization of knowledge production. Economy, society, and social problems are – in most cases implicitly – confronted in reference to a specific nationally defined society and often underestimate transnational and transborder dynamics. The disciplines emerged within bourgeois-capitalist industrial social spaces and – with a few exceptions – referred to specific nationally defined societies, the French, the German, or the English. Additionally, these societies systematically ignored the dynamics of colonialism and imperialism, which make transparent their position of power within the world (Boatca 2016, 1). They conveniently overlook the crucial influence that colonialism and enslavement played in their recent history. As argued by Wimmer and Glick Schiller (2003, 107), it is important to understand how concepts, such as the modern nation-state and national populations, developed not in insular territorially constrained spaces, but rather in transborder ones, across which colonial and imperial domination and ideologies evolved alongside counter discourses of popular sovereignty and movements of independence. In recent decades, a growing number of authors have stressed the need of thinking beyond the nation and of transcending methodological nationalism (Levitt and Khagram 2008; Vertovec 2009). However, while this critique pervades the field of study of international relations, political economy, embedded in its epistemological starting point of examining the interactions between states and markets from within the framework of capitalism and its intrinsic drive to expand globally through time-space compression, is helpful in moving analyzes beyond the confines of nation-states and the international system. Despite this caveat, in practice, much of the related literature is still often drawn toward the supposed centrality of the nation-state.

Related to the conceptual pull of the nation-state as being the key realm of explanatory pertinence, an additional, but related, problem is that many of the concepts are not only developed within the nation-state paradigm, but also with a universalist gesture. European and Euro-American colonial expansion and domination constructed a division of universal/superior versus particular/inferior knowledge. This was done by viewing others in the 16th century as "people without writing" and in the 18th and 19th century as "people without history." Such colonial perspectives were transformed, particularly after the Second World War, into the academic mantra of "people without development" (Escobar 1998) and more recently, in the early 21st century, of "people without democracy" (Grosfoguel 2011, 7). Current discussions, for example about the state and its transformation (→ II/21), are still shaped by ideas of a Western, democratic, well-organized state which is constituted against the construction of a "failed state," which threatens both itself as well as global stability and security (Rotberg 2002, 5). In this kind of thinking, the West is blessed with certain positive attributes such as an inherent drive toward democratic institutions, while any of its authoritarian experiments are conveniently ignored (for example, the Inquisition, and the governments of Mussolini, Hitler, Franco, Salazar, among others) and antidemocratic practices such as colonialism, the slave trade, and imperialism, which all have their roots in Western rule (Stam and Shohat 2012, 65). Additionally, they tend to obscure the multiple contributions of Western democracies in subverting democracy in the Global South (in alliance with local kleptocrats and/or dictators) and negating democratic tendencies in the non-European world. Non-Western social systems are seen in these readings as Oriental despotisms, or as societies without (functioning) states.

Overcoming such limitations, while offering short summaries of the main historical developments and theoretical debates that have entangled some of the most important concepts of political economy and governance, is a significant challenge. Numerous scholars from the study areas already mentioned have examined imperialism-colonialism (Petras and Veltmeyer 2016; Robinson 2003) as well as class and identity-based social categories/movements/groups (Duany 2002; Schütze 2013). However, they rarely do so from epistemological standpoints that highlight the intertwining of social-political-economic processes and projects that have a special resonance in the Americas, based on geographical, cultural, institutional and economic similarities and the distinct impact made by European and U.S. colonialism and imperialism across the continent.

This part of the Handbook, offering a political economy overview of inter-American perspectives is a way of transcending L.A. Studies, U.S. Studies, Indigenous and Black Studies, with their differing binary views on interactions, and opening up new dialogues between and within all these institutional, historically constructed, schools/perspectives on specific areas or subjects in the Americas.

A political economy perspective – from a Marxist approach to a diverse field of study

The different entries of this book all apply a perspective of political economy. Broadly speaking, political economy is interested in the interaction between politics and their material bases – or how economic issues shape political interests, processes, and outcomes and vice-versa. Although Marx was certainly not the first political economist, today, many political economist perspectives depart from the Marxist understanding that consciousness is determined by the social being and that political and economic interests and activities are intrinsically intertwined. Engels once wrote that political economy is the science of the conditions and forms under which various human societies have produced and exchanged and, on this basis, distributed their products (Engels 1877).

The political economy of *Tierra del Fuego*, for example, is different from that of England and therefore it makes sense to study the concrete situation of a specific place in the world and how its present systems and societal and institutional configurations are embedded in its historical social processes. Nevertheless, some changes have effects on very distant places; it is indeed one of the characteristics of capitalism that certain processes, such as the commodification of land and labor, occur globally, even though the process of commodification takes place with the help of non-market factors, what Jessop (1990) terms the extra-economic realm. In contrast to classical economics as a discipline, political economy perceives the market as being socially constructed and embedded and politically regulated. Instead of creating abstract models based on rational choice theories or individualist assumptions, political economy examines the interactions of market exchange and political governance from within the lens of concrete social relations and their configurations. Of central concern is how market exchange and politics are perpetually fraught by conflicts over wealth distribution and power relations. Political economy also places importance on structures and the effects they have on influencing diverse trajectories of path dependence.

Political economy perspectives place importance on examining one of the intrinsic tensions within global capitalism, taking into account its multifarious institutional forms and organizational models across different nations and regions as highlighted by scholars of the Varieties of Capitalism perspectives (Coates 2005; Hall and Soskice 2001), as well as the political need for territorial boundaries and fixed governance time frames and the market's contrasting craving for geographical expansion and time-space compression (Gilpin 1987; Harvey 1982, 2006). Indeed, temporalities and geographic dimensions are increasingly important in understanding the uneven processes of capital development and how crises and conjunctures manifest themselves differently across the global economy and how they create dynamic forms of resistance and complex transformations within social institutions and governance mechanisms. The two elements of crises and conflicts, the first, rooted in the inherent contradictory relation in the capitalist mode of production – between use-value and exchange-value – and the second, as expressions of how different social groups, positioned antagonistically in relations of (re-)production-distribution, come into conflict over surplus value (the rate of labor exploitation in the production process) and the related mechanisms and processes, through which people are both swept into and also expelled from wage relations in their temporal and socio-spatial dimensions. The two entries on these key terms, Crises (→ II/4) and Class Struggle (→ II/3), outline the evolving theoretical debates on how these concepts are defined by political economy perspectives, while also examining the changing contours of their development across the Americas, with special emphasis given to reflections on how recent crises related to the financialization of capital have influenced new struggles against it, while also generating new forms of understanding class politics and worker identities.

While political economy is often associated with the Historical Materialism of Marx, it is not limited to it. Indeed, traditionally, the field of political economy has been traversed by scholars with diverse theoretical perspectives as to how markets and states interact: classical liberal economists who highlight the importance of market efficiencies and the benefits of the international division of labor via comparative advantage, which sow the seeds for international peace and cooperation; realists who highlight concerns of economic nationalism and conflict over the distribution of wealth and power within the international system, in which monetary relations, trade and foreign investment are the key variables of analysis; and of course, Marxists who prioritize how the international capitalist system is grounded in relations of imperialism and colonialism, whereby unequal economic and political relations are the very basis to the system's reproduction (Cox 1987; Gilpin 1987, 2001). Such viewpoints are far from exhaustive and, especially in recent decades, a plethora of heterodox political economy perspectives have attained resonance across the Americas and beyond.

As already discussed, the key topics, included in this volume, while drawing on a variety of debates and theoretical reference points, all share the common dominator of adopting critical perspectives from within their specific analytical field. Not content with describing the structures, conjunctures, and dynamics of market-political entanglements, they seek to question how they came into being, how they have been reproduced, to the benefit and harm of which social groups and agents, and how, indeed, may such inequalities of power and wealth be dismantled. Any critical political economy perspective (including a critique of political economy) should examine the standpoints and normative judgments from within which these critiques are made (Sayer 2000, 81). Criticism pre-supposes the possibility of a better way of life, and many concepts, such as uneven development, offer conceptual possibilities for critiquing the socio-territorial inequalities pushed forth by capitalism, while also mapping out possibilities for resistance against them.

Decentering and engendering political economy

An easy way to define the field is to "think about political economy as the study of the social relations, particularly the power relations that mutually constitute the production, distribution, and consumption of resources" (Mosco 2010, 24). Political economy seeks to understand social change and historical transformation, what possibilities exist to overcome the inequalities and injustices of the current mode of production, and the prevalent relations of consumption and exchange. Diverse theoretical and epistemological standpoints are important for several reasons. One of them is that Marxism, as well as most traditional perspectives of political economy, often reproduce the unilinear notion of development and in so doing, ontologically, they conform to many of the binarisms associated with Eurocentrism and so-called Western exceptionalism.

The problem of such ontological groundings can be displayed via the work of Grosfoguel (2011) as he traces Europe's colonial expansion across the Americas. From a Eurocentric point of view, the origins of the so-called capitalist world system are primarily produced by the inter-imperial competition among European Empires. The most important motive was the need to find shorter trade routes to the East, which led to the accidental "discovery" and subsequent invasion (colonization) of the Americas. This development led to the inculcation of an economic system grounded on capital accumulation and the profit motive in a region of the world previously isolated from the ruminations of such a system. This analysis posits Europe as the center of capitalism and the dominant node of its reproduction, naturalizing colonialism, and European domination of the Americas, and privileging economic relations over all others. The class structure of Western capitalism becomes the key analytical tool, despite the historical processes by which, in the Americas (and beyond), commodification, proprietary relations, and wage labor were gradually forged across the region on the back of non-capitalist relations of slavery, serfdom, the annihilation of millions of indigenous and Black African lives, as well as socio-cultural practices via violence, forced religious acculturation, and the negation of citizenship or basic rights for all those with non-European descent (Orlando-Melo 2017; Shapiro 1999).

Indeed, not only have diverse labor regimes (and modes of production) coexisted, they have also collectively formed the basis to fomenting the engine of commodity extraction (→ Extractivism, II/15) across the region, which was, for so long, one of the key elements in the international system of triangular trade that propelled European expansion and industrialization (Braudel 1984). This system, grounded in the destruction and impoverishment of tribes, communities, and the world view of civilizations, simultaneously established an international division of labor between the core and periphery (industrial and primary-goods' production, respectively), together with an inter-state system of political-military organizations controlled by European males and institutionalized in colonial administrations (Wallerstein 1979). "The Americas were not incorporated into an already existing world economy. There could not have been a capitalist world economy without the Americas" (Quijano and Wallerstein 1992, 549). Colonialism actively promoted a global racial/ethnic hierarchy that privileges European people over non-European people (Quijano 2007), as well as a gender hierarchy that privileges males over females and patriarchy over other forms of gender relations (Enloe 1990; Spivak 1988). Colonialism comes along with a sexual hierarchy that privileges heterosexuals, a religious-spiritual hierarchy privileging Christianity, as well as an ecological hierarchy whereby the Western conceptions of "nature" dominate, and a spatial hierarchy where the urban dominates and destructs the rural, among others (Grosfoguel 2011, 10).

This example shows that decentering/decolonializing key concepts is no easy task and that there is no single way of undertaking it. As such, it is vital that academics address this issue and promote a plurality of approaches – feminist, decolonial, dependency or world-system approaches, or others that derive from critical development studies, etc.

A second strand of challenges comes from feminist political economy because for too long political economy was guilty of focusing more on (paid and regulated) employment to the general exclusion of efforts to systematically analyze the gender division of labor and the social category of gender structures. Such structures were often left invisible with the associated power relations overlooked to the detriment of a broader and more critical understanding of key concepts such as work, class or development. What kind of activity is perceived as work, and how different types of work are paid are very much tied to gender relations. As the entry on Gender and Work (→ II/11) discusses, there are changing patterns of discrimination of women in the area of work across the region.

The transition to capitalism involved not only the enclosure of peasant and indigenous lands, but also the redefinition of productive and reproductive tasks, defined by the gendered division of labor and fomenting a dominant culture as to how families in "modern" societies should be constituted around certain conceptions of femininity, which were deeply inscribed in (especially women's) bodies (Federici 2003). Mainstream theories in macroeconomics, trade, finance, migration and the environment are also grounded in a very traditional understanding of gender roles and fail to acknowledge explicitly or implicitly that global restructuring is taking place on a gendered terrain (Bakker 1994; Young and Scherrer 2010, 10). Political economy should, therefore, focus on the provisioning of human life rather than the study of choice under conditions of scarcity and extend the study beyond the formal economy as a means of examining more deeply the relations between markets and firms, states, and households and how all of them are structured in gendered relations (Sayer 2000, 83). In line with this thinking, various entries in this volume systematically discuss the gender dimension of certain fields, for example, the entry on Land (→ II/15), on Remittances (→ II/19), and, as already mentioned, Gender and Work (→ II/11).

The kind of concepts analyzed

In this volume, certain different middle-range concepts were prioritized despite one challenging exception, the entry on Capitalism (→ II/2). Most entries do not intend to offer the highest level of abstraction of the concepts. Instead, they combine historical and theoretical overviews with empirical observations from across the Americas. Those middle-range categories were chosen, which, from an inter-American focus, seemed especially interesting or were theoretical concepts developed in the Americas. For example, Extractivism (→ II/9), Environmental Justice (→ II/8) and Global Commodity Chains (→ II/12). These entries use specific lenses to examine the dynamics and injustices of the global division of labor and trade in terms of how profits are extracted across different socio-economic geographies, where and to whom they are distributed, and which actors from where remain relatively excluded from sharing in such wealth, while also bearing the bulk of the externalities associated with these development models. All three examples are also concepts which have traveled across the Americas and beyond, via academic reflections, institutional debates, and forums of social activism, metamorphosing in the process, from one context to another. Environmental Justice (→ II/8), for instance, was developed within a protest movement to frame injustices and problems, whereas the already mentioned concepts of Global Commodity Chains (→ II/12) and Extractivism (→ II/9) were developed within an academic arena as a means of better understanding how and where specific types of capital accumulation and profits were generated and how they are distributed or concentrated, via the interaction of states, transnational agents and market mechanisms. Despite their academic origins, these concepts are both used and hotly contested by workers' organizations and environmental and indigenous movements across the Americas and beyond in their present struggles.

It is also obvious that not all concepts are equally important across all countries and territories, and applicable to all contexts. Several entries prioritize the debates and developments of concepts across specific socio-spatial contexts of the Americas and the Caribbean, as for short entries it is impossible to discuss all concepts in every society across the continent. Nonetheless all authors highlight the regional entanglements and connections between struggles, structures, and phenomena.

A second set of entries are those concepts that examine transnational flows and interactions, such as Remittances (→ II/19), Transnational Corporations (→ II/23) and Regional Integration (→ II/18). These categories have been generated to describe the exchange or flow of commodities, trade, and money or as a means of focusing on how certain actors within these flows have gradually managed to challenge and even supersede nation-states as the chief agents both in terms of regulation and circulation dynamics. Such perspectives of political economy are relevant in that they challenge the still pervasive notion found in certain perspectives of international relations which contend or implicitly uphold the view that nation-states and the global political system still remain the key agents and structures for understanding all economic and political transformations and tendencies across the globe. As the entry on Regional Integration (→ II/18) shows, there have been different and even contradicting attempts of regional integration – some with a Pan-American, others with a Latin American and/or Caribbean, focus inspired by Bolivarianism. Numerous political networks, institutions, and cooperation projects have been started, strengthening cooperation on different issues; many of them lost significance after political and government changes.

A third set of concepts are brought together in this volume as a means of examining social stratification and the dynamics of work and, as such, they represent abstract issues of analysis within political economy. The associated concepts could be classified as "must haves" in a volume of political economy, and they include the entries on Labor Representations (→ II/14), Class Struggles (→ II/3), and Social Inequalities (→ II/20). The authors describe empirically how these topics have developed within different American countries and how struggles and developments in certain countries are entangled. In contrast, the topic of Informality (→ II/13), which is also part of this thematic group, is itself a category that stresses what many Eurocentric and mainstream economic approaches fail to see and accept: that the majority of the global workforce, almost five decades on from the initial academic attention given to the dynamic of economic and labor informality, is still not engaged in the "formal" economy or employed by formal firms with legally accepted contractual labor relations. Instead, in a direct rebuttal to Modernization Theory and a great deal of Development Theories, these workers face not only systematic exclusion from exercising their labor rights but also precarious and indecent working conditions, even while they both individually and collectively uphold the very capitalist development model that denies them the agency they so obviously exert.

A fourth set of concepts discusses historical dynamics and how economic structures and their conceptualization have changed over time: historical phases and ideational orientations. In this subgroup we include the concepts: Deindustrialization (→ II/5), Fordism (→ II/10), Neoliberalism (→ II/16), Crisis (→ II/4), State Transformation (→ II/21), and Capitalism (→ II/2). In the development of these entries, the respective authors were asked to, once again, grapple with the endemic issue of Eurocentrism in the development of the key debates and reflections that have taken place across the Americas. In a precariously poised attempt to balance the need for discussions of the universalist nature of the bulk of the academic literature on such topics with an epistemological stance that highlights the need to unearth many of the place-specific (in a socio-geographical sense) developments of these concepts, the authors often use the comparative method as a means of showing the uneven nature of theory and empirical development of these concepts historically across and within the Americas and the Caribbean.

A last set of entries can be named exemplary policy fields: Energy (→ II/7), Land (→ II/15), Taxation (→ II/15), and Privatization (→ II/17). For these topics, the authors discuss how certain historical developments (many of them dating back to colonial times) have shaped the inequalities and power structures of a certain field. A good example is energy by which many social conflicts all over the Americas are connected. Who produces energy in different territories, and, under what conditions, and how energy is distributed or exported within the respective country, and finally, who appropriates the benefits, are all contested questions. The entry on energy takes the political-economic perspective of Political Ecology to explore the issue of "energy" while discussing how the specific materialities of distinct kinds of energy are deeply articulated within societal power relations.

At the same time, the entries on different policy fields show how more recently, many social movements and progressive governments across the region have attempted to reform these respective fields, but so far, with only limited success. As the entry on Taxation (→ II/22) shows, there are areas where a North-South divide is still very clear: While most of the income and profit taxes collected in the U.S. and Canada stem from personal income tax, countries in "the south" have proven to be "allergic" to personal taxes. Countries in South America rely more on indirect consumption taxes and therefore have less room for redistribution compared to those in North America.

Taxation, in the same way as almost every topic discussed in this issue, is intrinsically linked to Social Inequalities (→ II/20). As the entry on social inequality shows, the Americas – especially South and Central America – are considered two of the most socially unjust regions in the world. These inequalities do not only persist in terms of income and opportunities, but there are also manifold intersections of race/ethnicity, gender and class. Throughout the economic and political development of the Americas in the last two centuries, inequalities have been modified, some have been weakened, while others have deepened, but immense social inequalities continue to be the motive for many social struggles as well as for migration processes and transnational networks constituted by them and therefore even contribute to strengthen the existing entanglements in and between societies and communities of the Americas and the Caribbean.

Works cited

Anner, Mark. 2011. *Solidarity Transformed: Labor Responses to Globalization and Crisis in Latin America.* Ithaca, NY: ILR Press, an imprint of Cornell University Press.

Bakker, Isabella, ed. 1994. *The Strategic Silence: Gender and Economic Policy*. London: Zed Books.

Boatca, Manuela. 2016. *Global Inequalities beyond Occidentalism*. New York, NY: Routledge.

Braudel, Fernand. 1984. *Civilization & Capitalism. 15th–18th Century. Vol. 3. The Perspective of the World. Translated by Sian Reynolds*. New York, NY: Harper & Row.

Coates, David, ed. 2005. *Varieties of Capitalism, Varieties of Approaches*. Houndmills: Palgrave Macmillan.

Cox, Robert. 1987. *Production, Power and World Order: Social Forces in the Making of History*. New York, NY: Columbia University Press.

Duany, Jorge, ed. 2002. *The Puerto Rican Nation on the Move: Identities on the Island & in the United States*. Chapell Hill, NC: University of North Carolina Press.

Engels, Friedrich. 1877. "Anti-Dühring. Part II. Political Economy. I Subject. Matter and Method." *Marx-Engels Archive*. www.marxists.org/archive/marx/works/1877/anti-duhring/ch13.htm.

Enloe, Cynthia H. 1990. *Bananas, Beaches & Bases: Making Feminist Sense of International Politics*. Berkeley, CA: University of California Press.

Escobar, Arturo. 1998. "Power and Visibility: Development and the Invention and Management of the Third World." *Cultural Anthropology* 3: 428–443.

Federici, Silvia. 2003. *Caliban and the Witch: Women, the Body and Primitive Accumulation*. New York, NY: Autonomedia.

Gilpin, Robert. 1987. *The Political Economy of International Relations*. Princeton, NJ: Princeton University Press.

Gilpin, Robert. 2001. *Global Political Economy: Understanding the International Economic Order*. Princeton, NJ and Oxford: Princeton University Press.

Grosfoguel, Ramón. 2011. "Decolonizing Post-Colonial Studies and Paradigms of Political-Economy: Transmodernity, Decolonial Thinking, and Global Coloniality." *Transmodernity, Journal of Peripheral Cultural Production of the Luso-Hispanic World* 1, no. 1: n.p. https://escholarship.org/uc/item/21k6t3fq.

Hall, Peter A. and David Soskice, eds. 2001. *Varieties of Capitalism: The Institutional Foundations of Comparative Advantage*. Oxford: Oxford University Press.

Harvey, David. 1982. *The Limits to Capital*. Oxford: Blackwell.

———. 2006. *Spaces of Global Capitalism: Towards a Theory of Uneven Geographical Development*. London and New York, NY: Verso.

Jessop, Bob. 1990. *State Theory: Putting the Capitalist State in its Place*. Cambridge and Oxford: Polity Press.

Levitt, Peggy and Sanjeev Khagram. 2008. *The Transnational Studies Reader: Intersections and Innovations*. New York, NY: Routledge.

Mosco, Vincent, ed. 2010. *The Political Economy of Communication*. Los Angeles, CA: Sage Publications.

Orlando-Melo, Jorge. 2017. *Historia mínima de Colombia*. Madrid and Mexico: Turner Publications/El Colegio de México.

Petras, James F. and Henry Veltmeyer. 2016. *Power and Resistance: U.S. Imperialism in Latin America*. Leiden and Boston, MA: Brill.

Prebisch, Raúl. 2016. "The Economic Development of Latin America." In: *ECLAC Thinking: Selected Texts (1948–1998)*, ed. Ricardo Bielschowsky, 45–84. Santiago de Chile: United Nations. Orig. pub. 1948.

Quijano, Aníbal. 2007. "Coloniality and Modernity/Rationality." *Cultural Studies* 21, no. 2: 168–178.

Quijano, Anibal and Immanuel Wallerstein. 1992. "Americanity as a Concept: Or, The Americas in the Modern World-System." *International Social Science Journal* 44, no. 4: 549–557.

Robinson, William I. 2003. *Transnational Conflicts: Central America, Social Change, and Globalization*. London and New York, NY: VERSO.

Rotberg, Robert I. 2002. "Failed States in a World of Terror." *Foreign Affairs* 81, no. 4: 127–140.

Sandilands, Roger. 2015. "La misión del Banco Mundial a Colombia de 1949, y las visiones opuestas de Lauchlin Currie y Albert Hirschman." *Revista de Economía Institucional* 17, no. 32: 213–232.

Sayer, Andrew. 2000. "Moral Economy and Political Economy." *Studies in Political Economy* 61, no. 1: 79–103.

Schütze, Stephanie. 2013. "Chicago/Michoacán. The Construction of Transnational Political Spaces." *Latino Studies* 11, no. 1: 78–102.

Shapiro, Michael J. 1999. "Triumphalist Geographies." In: *Spaces of Culture: City, Nation, World*, eds. Mike Featherstone and Scott Lash, 159–174. London, Thousand Oaks, CA and New Delhi: Sage Publications.

Spivak, Gayarti Chakravorty. 1988. "Can the Subaltern Speak?" In: *Marxism and the Interpretation of Culture*, eds. Cary Nelson and Lawrence Grossberg, 66–111. Champaign, IL: University of Illinois Press.

Stam, Robert and Ella Shohat. 2012. *Race in Translation: Culture Wars around the Postcolonial Atlantic*. New York, NY: New York University Press.

Topik, Steven and Mario Samper. 2006. "The Latin American Coffee Commodity Chain: Brazil and Costa Rica." In: *From Silver to Cocaine: Latin American Commodity Chains and the Building of the World Economy, 1500–2000*, eds. Steven Topik, Zephyr Frank and Carlos Marichal, 118–146. Durham, NC and London: Duke University Press.

Vertovec, Steven. 2009. *Transnationalism*. London: Routledge.

Wallerstein, Immanuel M. 1979. *The Capitalist World-Economy: Essays*. Cambridge: Cambridge University Press.

Wimmer, Andreas and Nina Glick Schiller. 2003. "Methodological Nationalism, the Social Sciences, and the Study of Migration: An Essay in Historical Epistemology." In: *The Transnational Studies Reader: Intersections and Innovations*, ed. Sanjeev Khagram, 104–117. New York, NY: Routledge.

Young, Brigitte and Christoph Scherrer, eds. 2010. *Gender Knowledge and Knowledge Networks in International Political Economy*. Baden-Baden: Nomos.

2
CAPITALISM

Juan Grigera

"Good heavens! For more than forty years I have been speaking prose without knowing it." Monsieur Jourdain's discovery in Molière's *The Bourgeois Gentleman* could be paralleled to a fair amount of scholar studies in the Americas. Discovering and unraveling what appears to be sometimes natural has been a daunting task and a cornerstone of critical thinking since the 19th century. Acknowledging and studying the system under the term "capitalism" is still today a signal of the attempts at denaturalizing and historicizing the system against the numerous attempts at peddling it as a part of human nature.

How has capitalism in the Americas been defined, thought, discussed, studied? How was this agenda shaped? What would be a roadmap to the study of these issues? Should the issue of capitalism in the Americas be addressed? Or rather that of (Latin) American capitalism? Should whether the Americas are capitalist be questioned? Or rather, since when have they been capitalist? The variety of responses to those questions can certainly provide us with a clue and a basic roadmap on how the issue of capitalism and the Americas should be questioned and rethought.

To what extent is capitalism a useful term to describe and analyze the social formations of the Americas? If it is, since when should this analysis begin? As much as capitalism used to be a term rarely used outside Marxist thought (something that has changed, but not significantly since Dobb pointed this out in the 1950s), its suitability for the Americas was contested even within Marxism. A pervasive dismissal of the concept stems from the erroneous idea that Marx writings referred only to England in the 18th and 19th centuries.

Instead of attempting to give a definition of capitalism and a description of the main characteristics of the system in the region, what follows moves directly to the question of when and how societies in the Americas "transitioned to capitalism." It will become apparent through the exposition of this debate that no single definition of capitalism exists. This approach allows for a pluralistic and historical presentation of the issue of capitalism in the region. Particular attention will be given to the lesser known Latin American debate and the recent rebirth of these discussions, highlighting the interest in the question of the relationship between capitalism and slavery (→ I/18).

The origins of capitalism

Characterizing contemporary societies of the Americas as capitalist would not raise any reasonable objections today, after one accounts for the special case of Cuba and leaves space for the caveats of a few localized exceptions (e.g. "uncontacted" Amazonian dwellers or several nonetheless formally subsumed indigenous communities in several places including Canada, the U.S., or Bolivia) (→ Indigeneity, I/31). This same statement, however, would have meant taking stance on a contentious issue during most of the 20th century in Latin America, and it would be meaningless (or more specifically would imply naturalizing capitalism as a system) if one is not able to identify temporarily and spatially the development (→ II/6) of capitalism in the Americas as a region.

Different variations of what could be grouped together as "discrete models" have been used to explain the origins of capitalism in the Americas. These explanations are rooted in the simple idea that whichever social formation existed before was at one specific moment in time violently disrupted (→ Conquest and Colonization, I/7), creating a historical discontinuity that led to capitalism. One such model entailed finding the real (or true) "bourgeois revolutions" in the Americas (in an ideal type that attempted to closely follow the French or the English Revolutions) (→ Revolution, II/44), either by forcing the Latin American Wars of Independence (1808–1830) into that category (e.g. W. Z. Foster, Manfred Kossok) (→ Independence Movements, I/10) or by splitting the event in two in the case of the U.S.: the American Revolution and the U.S.-American Civil War. Even beyond the historical question of the nature of these events, the existence of revolutions is introduced as a substitute for the question of capitalist development. By grounding the upheavals on the diffusion of "bourgeois ideas" (a complex and diverse spectrum ranging from the Bourbon Reforms, figures such as Bolívar or Lincoln, and "the American Jacobins" such as Toussaint Louverture in Haiti, Miguel Hidalgo and Morelos in Mexico, or Artigas in Argentina), these models presuppose the fertile material conditions for their expansion and their triumph in the hands of an existing bourgeoisie, thus substituting the question they were set to explain (why this specific class came to exist in the first place) with the narrative of how it managed to assert politically its socio-economic hegemony.

A second type of discontinuous narrative is the one that searches for the origins of capitalism in the spectacular turning point of the conquest. In the case of North America, the capitalist nature of English "settlers" is assumed, thus capitalism is seen as "disembarking" from the ships (e.g. Carl Degler or more recently Daron Acemoglu, James Robinson). In Latin America, the capitalist nature of the conquest has been more contested, but the "legacy of the conquest" (→ Postcolonialism, I/38) has been frequently used in the explanation of the "original sin" of underdevelopment (→ Development, II/6). These models deprive the Americas of agency or history, sending all pre-conquest societies to the dustbin of history. By assuming the actual outcome of the process of colonization as the only possibility (i.e. that European capitalist expansion was inevitable) and avoiding any reflection on the actual interaction of these societies, these narratives naturalize capitalism's dominance over any other social formation.

The debates on a "transition" were a departure from these discrete models. These were in term marked by a theoretical "great divergence," that was expressed by the two poles of the Dobb-Sweezy debate of the 1950s. These two perspectives (thereby enunciated polemically for the first time, but both with long-standing traditions) still broadly inform many of the later developments. Brenner said in 1978 that Dobb's thesis "continues to be a starting point for discussion of European economic development" (121). One could say that is still valid today, to map the debates in the Americas.

Dobb in his *Studies in the Development of Capitalism* (1946) gave analytical primacy to production as the key to understanding the dynamics of a social system, and thus defined the capitalist mode of production after the predominance of social relations of production based on a private profit motive. Dobb saw the crisis of the 14th century as proof of the stagnant and unproductive character of the feudal system and dated the transition to the capitalist mode of production to be after the increase in the productivity of labor within feudalism made the change from serfdom to wage labor viable and subsequently dominant. The English Revolution would then remove the super-structural remnants of the feudal system. The transition was thus not a single event in time but a long and complicated process. For Dobb, this process was not driven by the expansion of markets, the rise of the bourgeoisie, or the growth of cities, but rather it was the consequence of the internal dynamics of feudalism.

In Latin America, the interpretation that understood the social relations of production as key to defining the capitalist mode of production was dominated until the 1970s by the "feudal thesis" or "feudal diagnosis." Succinctly stated, this Marxist reformulation of an idea from 19th century political thought attested to the non-capitalist character of Latin American social formations, and was ascertained from the prevalence of backwardness, *latifundios* and peonage (or serfdom), which showed the region had not (yet) seen its transition to capitalism. This conflation of forms of exploitation, relations of production, and modes of production somehow already present in Dobb's original argument was augmented in these debates where any form of non-wage labor and feudalism were equated. The thesis was supplemented with a unilinear or stageist conception of history (i.e. that underdeveloped countries lacking the preconditions for capitalism must first pass through a stage of capitalism before moving to a socialist stage). This idea was central to the politics of the Communist Parties in the region that advocated popular fronts and the need to fight for a capitalist stage as a first and necessary step toward a socialist revolution (→ Socialism, I/42). Another necessary historical complement included an explanation of the Spanish and Portuguese conquests as the product of feudal dynamics. The conquest in this view was the product of a typical feudal expansion (such as the *reconquista* or the Crusades) in search of land (→ II/15) and tribute. The thesis has lost political relevance after the crisis of Stalinism, though it was also important in informing a shared set of views with modernization theories at the time (→ Modernization, I/35) and probably still today (i.e. underpinning some of the calls to "develop" the region). The uses of feudalism have also been key (and somehow still relevant) to the "agrarian question" (→ Land, II/15) and in explaining the different development paths in Latin America and the United States.

A first systematic refutation of the feudal thesis came from what has been later on grouped under the idea of "circulationism." In the late 1940s, Caio Prado Junior (2011) in Brazil and Sergio Bagú (1949) in Chile independently contended that the nature of the maritime expansion was that of establishing "colonial capitalism," not feudalism. For them, these societies were structured after a mercantile logic from the very origins of the colonial formation (→ Colonial Economies, I/4). In this sense, the colonial expansion produced the precise opposite of feudalism (characterized as a system of production for use, a system of subsistence). Commerce was its disintegrating force, one that was constitutive of the colonial world since the conquest. Colonial capitalism was then organically structured around profit-oriented productive structures, intended for the supply of the world market: the social system in the region was externally determined. The colonial enterprise was highlighted as a mercantile exploitation of primary commodities (→ Extractivism, II/9).

In the mid-1960s, the modernization promises of import-substitution industrialization began to falter and the Cuban Revolution reopened the debate on the possible transitions to socialism (→ I/42). These were fertile grounds for a radical critique of development discourses, modernization theories, and stageism (→ Development, I/6). They drew from these critiques of the 1940s, but also advanced a strong set of new claims. One of those was extending the validity of the mechanisms described for colonial capitalism into the explanation of contemporary underdevelopment: economic surplus was systematically transferred since the conquest from the periphery to the center (Cardoso and Faletto 1969; Frank 1967). The idea of declining terms of trade (between primary products and manufacturers) was generalized to account for every commodity produced in the periphery, in what was called unequal exchange (→ Global Commodity Chains, II/12). Underdevelopment, they contended, had been wrongly confused with feudalism. It was in fact "developed underdevelopment" that is the manifestation of advanced capitalism in the periphery. Dependency theory also criticized the dualism prevalent in CEPAL and modernization theories: "backward" regions (agrarian, traditional, stagnant, or archaic) were as much part of the capitalist system as the "modern" ones and the constitution of these two "poles," or of these two "opposing societies," was the result of a single, intertwined historical process (Oliveira 2003; Stavenhagen 1965).

The Latin American debate became at this point enormously rich and heated. A very influential response to dependency theory came from a clever articulation of Althusserianism and the feudal thesis made by Ernesto Laclau (1971). His proposal began distinguishing modes of production from socio-economic formations, thus unfolding the question of the capitalist nature of Latin America into different but interconnected areas. Stressing the heterogeneous character of the region's economic system, Laclau concluded that several modes of production existed that constituted different parts of a single system articulated by mercantile relations. Laclau reasserted the weaker elements of dualism: "backward" (or feudal) regions were inserted in the socio-economic system (and not isolated as in modernization theories) but this did not make them capitalist. This allowed for a partial rehabilitation of the feudal diagnosis and introduced the idea of articulation of modes of production (that required finding the "dominant" one in this articulation). Unlike the former, the latter feudalism-hypothesis was a powerful idea in the debates to follow within and beyond Latin America.

The attempts at characterizing Latin American societies as heterogeneous, i.e. not "fully capitalist" were not only attempted within Althusserianism. The idea of multiple coexisting systems was appealing and widely accepted, though it opened the issue of which mode of production was dominant within this heterogeneous coexistence. Garavaglia (1984), for instance, argued that the specificity of Latin American colonies' lack of any hegemonic mode of production was precisely due to colonialism. Enrique Semo (1973) understood that from the beginning New Spain was integrated with commercial capitalism but in a pluriparticular (i.e. heterogeneous) way, where tributary despotism, feudalism, and "embryonic capitalism" coexisted (and a pre-capitalist nature dominated). Many others saw capitalism as dominant within this heterogeneity: Horacio Ciafardini (1984) proposed the usage of formal subsumption to understand "backward" regions; Bolívar Echeverría proposed the concept of "barroque societies"; René Zavaleta Mercado that of "*sociedades abigarradas*" (variegated societies), all of which developed an idea of "juxtaposed elements" already present as early as Mariátegui's *Seven essays* (1928).

In many of these cases, a common thread was the idea that capitalism as a term was used in a Eurocentric fashion and that it was only partially applicable to the heterogeneous social formations found in the Americas. Though insisting on the heterogeneous character of the region's capitalism implicitly romanticized Western societies as homogeneous, this also led to a different type of criticism of dependency theory, an interpretation that searched for the peculiarities of Latin American societies: endogeneism. "Endogeneism" insisted that though the colonial economy was indeed part of the capitalist system (or a system in transition to capitalism), it followed its own evolution, one that was the product of its internal balance of forces and that was qualitatively distinct from those in the West and not merely externally determined by its insertion in the world market. Endogeneism revolved around several attempts at defining a "colonial mode of production" (sometimes in dialogue with Samir Amin's definition of the idea, sometimes defined anew) as well as recognizing the specificity of colonialism in a particular region. Sempat Assadourian (1984) sustained the idea that the historical peculiarity of Latin America laid in the compatibility between feudal and archaic forms, as well as merchant capitalism, since the former allows maximum surplus appropriation by the latter. For Assadourian, this convergence explains the subsistence and even the expansion of these pre-capitalist structures within the colonial space, including different labor forms such as slavery and other types of coerced labor (→ Unfree Labor, I/19). A somewhat different vision was that of Ciro Cardoso and Héctor Pérez Brignoli (1984), who also insisted on the diverging evolutions of societies within the region. For him it was key to note that the areas of contemporary Mexico or Peru developed (coerced) labor from indigenous peoples (→ I/11), while this option was not possible for Brazil or the southern United States that thus resorted to slavery, nor for the North American east coast where production was based on a small scale.

Spelling out the consequences of these divergent developments was key in understanding social dynamics and later advancements of capitalism in each of these areas. Yet another stream within endogeneism can be exemplified by Fragoso and Florentino (1993). They coined the idea of "archaism as a project" to account for the peculiar shape of the colonial society that placed the merchants at the top of the social hierarchy (and at the appropriation of surplus), in particular those who monopolized contact with the metropolis (→ Colonial Economies, I/4). This peculiarity was central for them in understanding contemporary underdevelopment and the survival of modern archaisms. Overall, endogeneism maintained that the specificity of the colonial mode of production was relevant in understanding not only the reinforcement of pre-capitalist conditions in the periphery, but also its very own contribution to the European transition to capitalism (see Laclau 1971).

This shift from dependency and external mechanisms toward endogenous explanations of the origins and development of capitalism somehow had a parallel in the European and North American debates. Simultaneously to Latin American endogeneism, the Dobb-Sweezy debate was revived on the transition to capitalism sparked by the works of Robert Brenner. Succinctly stated, Brenner (1978) explained that the pattern of agrarian development in Europe can be found in the specifics of local class relations and the constraints that property relations impose on local actors. Taking this model to the U.S., Charles Post (2011) has recently argued that "The American Road to Capitalism" can be explained by a "collision course" set between the North (rapidly expanding based on the subordination of petty commodity production) with the South (that was an obstacle for the former because of its dependence on a slave-form of pre-capitalist production that conspired against the development of a national market and states) (→ Nation and State Building, I/16). The American Civil War that lead the North to triumph and expand is the outcome of the development of local conditions of class struggle (→ II/3) in what is now the U.S. In other words, capitalism in America is the product of these endogenous conditions, not the legacy of "settlers" or a "bourgeois revolution."

Capitalism and slavery

The debate on the North American transition at its forefront contains the issue of how to characterize the "peculiar institution" of slavery (→ I/18) and its relationship with capitalism. In Latin America the consideration of slavery is of insurmountable importance to the understanding of the development of some countries (particularly Brazil, Cuba, and Haiti) and has varying degrees of importance for the rest of the region. Slavery is also in all cases a peculiarity when comparing the historical trajectories of the Americas with those of Western Europe and beyond. The extent of actual and potential entanglement and comparison of the debates between North and Latin America is in this topic particularly interesting.

As referenced before, C. L. R. James (1938) and his ex-student Eric Williams (1944) sought to debunk the liberal narrative of abolition as being essentially the product of British humanitarianism (→ Enlightenment, I/18). It was in this process that they challenged the assumption that capitalism was developed both independent of and against the slave system and spelled out for the first time the taboo that the modern world is the product of slavery as are many of its contemporary concrete and abstract legacies. This included pointing out the role of cotton in the industrial revolution, mostly produced under slave labor. The abolition of slavery for cotton producers was thus the product of a new historical moment, one when capitalism no longer needed slavery but rather consumers and a more efficient and less capital-intensive method of commodity production. This argument was extended to Cuba and Brazil as well in the 1960s (Cardoso 1962; Ianni 1988; Moreno Fraginals 1964).

In making an explicit link between capitalism and slavery as primitive accumulation, these early works relied on the common assumption of the backwardness of the slave system. Productivity was seen as stagnant and the slaves as a less efficient labor force in their inability to compete with wage labor, thus underpinning the declining economic fate that led to the abolition of the slave trade first and of slavery altogether later. This line of thought argued that the wage labor and slave systems (the North and the South in the U.S.) were competing against each other within the same space. This view of slavery was coherent with the dominant narrative of the system as a pre-capitalist enterprise dominated by non-innovative paternalist landlords and slave owners (e.g. Eugene Genovese for the U.S. or Gilberto Freyre for Brazil).

It was the work of cliometrics (Conrad and Meyer 1958; Fogel and Engerman 1974) that severely challenged this assumption in the U.S. and contended that the southern states' 19th-century slavery was highly profitable, with rising productivity (even at higher rates than the first postbellum years under share cropping), and competitive. The dynamism of the slave system (with staggering figures of output growth in cotton production) was empirically challenged at first by social historians on the left, but after a phase of scrutiny was reconciled with the idea that there was greater fluidity between slavery and capitalism than previously thought.

A recent second wave of studies of slavery and capitalism have understood slavery itself to be governed by the capitalist logic in many more dimensions than previously acknowledged, thus further debunking the idea of relationships of traditional patronage. Walter Johnson, Edward Baptist, Calvin Schermerhorn, Robin Blackburn, Sven Becket, or Greg Grandin for instance have detailed how the slave system was governed by the marketplace, and how it was deeply permeated by trade, productivity targets, and a complex financial system (that for instance even accepted slaves as collateral for credit). The extent of market dependence of slave owners and how deeply intertwined financial institutions were with slavery was further evidenced in complex mechanisms such as bankruptcy, secondary markets of slaves (similar to the *escravos de ganho* in Brazil), and Taylorist labor practices. This picture further details how modern nation-states, financial companies, and world-scale consumption were built "upon the backs of enslaved Africans," fueling industrialization, urbanization (→ I/45), and class formation as part of a process of primitive accumulation. But beyond this, the reading attempts to show that slavery was embedded within, rather than replaced by, modern capitalism.

The comparisons between slavery in the U.S. South and Brazil have been recurrent since the classic comparative works of Freyre or Genovese. The two abolition processes (one mediated by a massive armed conflict, the other relatively peaceful), the fate of slaves after it, the differences in the rates of manumission, and productiveness all called for different explanations and many different dimensions of comparisons. There are two, however, that are interesting to note in the context of the debate of capitalism. First, the idea that Brazilian slavery was more "benevolent" than that of the U.S. (and this, in turn, due to the differences between Catholicism and Protestantism) was the subject of the first round of myth debunking by the "Paulista school" (lead by Florestan Fernandes, Emília Viotti, and others). But it was only later on that Sydney Mintz linked the question of differing degrees of cruelty, exploitation, and racism to the modes of the integration of the colony to the world economic system. In this sense, this issue was restored in the problem of slavery and capitalism (or at least its subsumption to capitalism), making the intensity of exploitation of labor and land, and the control of the metropolis over the colony the explanation for the differences between the U.S. and Brazil. Second, the persistent association of slavery and backwardness in contrast with the U.S. has not been significantly challenged in Brazil. Barbara Weinstein attempted to explain this peculiarity of scholarship to the debates on slavery in the early 19th century, where a "weak" defense of the system by slave masters (as opposed to a "strong" defense in the U.S. South, even claiming it as harmonious and morally superior than the inhumanity of the free-market system) made the argument of slavery as a necessary, though transient and backward evil (and framed it consistently as an anachronistic phenomena since as early as 1822).

In the rebirth of the debates of capitalism and slavery, it is interesting to recapitulate the previous discussions of the transition and origins of capitalism. On one side, the necessary revision of a certainly evolutionist/progressive narrative that began asserting slavery as inefficient and thus deducing from that its inevitable falling behind to modern/efficient capitalism has led to associate growth and progress with capitalism. The fascinating descriptions of the complexities of the institutions of merchant capitalism, as well as the descriptions of the integration of the slave system into the world market seem not to have been sustained by the theoretical development of the concept of capitalism. Instead, the existence of capitalism has been quickly deducted from processes as evidence. These shortcomings fail to recognize both the historical antecedents of merchant capital institutions not related to capitalism (e.g. the elaborate financial system of ancient Rome) and only rely on a feeble association of pre-capitalism with stagnant productivity and lack of pressure on the pace of labor. When these aspects are challenged by historical events, this is often attribute to the force of an imagined capitalism.

At the same time, the critique of the "circulationist" approach to slavery as capitalism on the grounds of its insertion into the world market had several appealing conclusions when pointing out the social relations of production created by the slave system. There are many challenges relevant to this approach, since there seems to be a quick association of the legal status with a relation of production as well. Arguably, slaves working for a salary and living on their own but paying a fixed amount of money to their owners are engaged in social relations of production similar to that of a serf, despite their status as slaves. This could be another layer of conflation to the one Banaji has warned about: one that equates a form of exploitation to certain relations of production to a mode of production, creating a simple taxonomy of discrete categories of what counts as capitalism and what does not, while in fact they are not reducible, one to the other.

Final discussion

As shown, the contending definitions of capitalism have also been the product of explanations of its origins (or lack thereof) and have also been tied to divergent political strategies. This sketch of the debates has shown how capitalism's origin can be attributed to both discrete and continuous models of transition, external and endogenous change, as well as the specificities of colonialism and slavery's influence the development of capitalism in the Americas (→ Colonial Rule, I/5; Colonial Economies, I/4; Slavery, I/18).

This approach to an outline of "capitalism in the Americas" has followed an exposition of these problems guided by the question of capitalism's historicity. Before concluding, it is worth spelling out which assumptions were considered (and which were not) in the process. First, it has not been assumed as a universal truth that historical transitions have shaped and still shape the current configuration of capitalism in the Americas (no matter to what extent this has been the implicit or explicit premise of most of the historical debates). This hypothesis (under different variations, for instance that Latin American underdevelopment needs to be traced to the specificities of the transition, its lack of, incomplete character of, etc.) (→ Development, II/6) relies on assigning a greater importance to national and historical features than structural characteristics, shifts in the world market, and contemporary class struggles (→ II/3) that would not be shared across the explanations mentioned. For example, the specifics of Mexico's neoliberalism (→ II/16) needs not necessarily be traced to the origins of capitalism in Mexico. Second, it is fair to recognize that no discussions of how to offer a periodization of capitalism in the Americas have been attempted. Finally, the historical debate has also been used in trying to explain the contemporary patterns of capitalist dynamics and development in the region. This was seen as another dimension that explains how studying capitalism contributes to conceptualizing these varieties and also how peculiarities constitute a vantage point to approaching the region. Among the many ways of both defining the regions as reasonable units of study (arguing respectively that Latin American or North American countries have more traits in common within the region than with other economies of the world or that capitalism as a system has a common regional logic to be untangled), the impact of different forms of transition to capital is a prominent one. Other typologies include discussing the form of integration to the world market, or the conditions that specific commodity staples impose on development paths (→ Extractivism, II/9) and arguably these too can be better understood when looking at the historical development of capitalism.

In sum, understanding the need to develop a conceptual tool that both sets up the basic characteristics of the system and historicizes its development is key to any critical approach to the social sphere.

Works cited

Assadourian, Carlos Sempat. 1984. "Modos de producción, capitalismo y subdesarrollo en América Latina." In *Modos de producción en América Latina*, ed. Carlos Sempat Assadourian et al., 114–146. Mexico City: Siglo XXI.

Bagú, Sergio. 1949. *Economía de la sociedad colonial: ensayo de historia comparada de América Latina.* Buenos Aires: El Ateneo.

Brenner, Robert. 1978. "Dobb on the Transition from Feudalism to Capitalism." *Cambridge Journal of Economics* 2(2): 121–140.

Cardoso, Ciro Flamarión S., and Héctor Pérez Brignoli. 1984. *Historia económica de América Latina.* 2 vols. Historia 10. Barcelona: Crítica.

Cardoso, Fernando Henrique. 1962. *Capitalismo e escravidão no Brasil Meridional.* Sáo Paulo: Difusáo Européia do Livro.

Cardoso, Fernando Henrique, and Enzo Faletto. 1969. *Dependencia y Desarrollo En América Latina.* Mexico City: Siglo XXI.

Ciafardini, Horacio. 1984. "Capital, comercio y capitalismo: a propósito del llamado capitalismo comercial." In *Modos de producción en América Latina,* ed. Carlos Sempat Assadourian et al., 111–113. Mexico City: Siglo XXI.

Conrad, Alfred H., and John R. Meyer. 1958. "The Economics of Slavery in the Ante Bellum South." *Journal of Political Economy* 66 (2): 95–130.

Fogel, Robert William, and Stanley L. Engerman. 1974. *Time on the Cross: The Economics of American Negro Slavery.* Boston, MA: Little, Brown & Co.

Fragoso, João, and Manolo Florentino. 1993. *O arcaísmo como projeto: mercato atlântico, sociedade agrária e elite mercantil no Rio de Janeiro, c. 1790 – c. 1840.* Rio de Janeiro: Diadorim.

Frank, Andre Gunder. 1967. *Capitalism and Underdevelopment in Latin America.* New York: Monthly Review Press.

Garavaglia, Juan Carlos. 1984. "Un modo de producción subsidiario: la organización económica de las comunidades guaranizadas durante los siglos XVII XVIII en la formación regional altoperuana rioplatense." In *Modos de producción en América Latina.* Cuadernos de Pasado y Presente 40. México City: Siglo XXI.

Ianni, Octávio. 1988. *Escravidão e racismo.* São Paulo: Editora Hucitec.

James, Cyril Lionel Robert. 1938. *The Black Jacobins.* New York: The Dial Press.

Laclau, Ernesto. 1971. "Feudalism and Capitalism in Latin America." *New Left Review* I (67): 19–38.

Moreno Fraginals, Manuel. 1964. *El ingenio.* La Habana: Comisión Nacional Cubana de la Unesco.

Oliveira, Francisco de. 2003. *Crítica à Razão Dualista – O Ornitorrinco.* 1a ed. São Paulo: Boitempo Editorial.

Post, Charles. 2011. *The American Road to Capitalism: Studies in Class-Structure, Economic Development, and Political Conflict, 1620–1877.* Historical Materialism Book Series 28. Leiden and Boston, MA: Brill.

Prado Júnior, Caio. 2011. *Formação do Brasil contemporâneo Colônia.* São Paulo: Companhia das Letras.

Semo, Enrique. 1973. *Historia Del Capitalismo En México.* México City: Ediciones Era.

Stavenhagen, Rodolfo. 1965. "Siete Tesis Equivocadas." *El Dia,* June 25.

Williams, Eric Eustace. 1944. *Capitalism & Slavery.* Richmond, VA: University of North Carolina Press. 93 (4): 829–72. doi:10.2307/1863526.

3

CLASS STRUGGLE

Ricardo Antunes

The modern theory of class struggle has its roots in the thinking of Karl Marx, who affirmed that the proletariat, for being dispossessed of the means of production, would be the main class capable of dissolving capitalism (→ II/2). Being the responsible class in the process of value and wealth creation, it could develop political and social consciousness to be able to abolish private property and the class society. As capital is created by the exploitation of the workforce and the extraction of surplus value, Marx (1996) described a fundamental and insuperable contradiction in capitalism, between bourgeoisie and proletariat. It is exactly this contradiction that is fundamental in class struggle.

In order to overcome this contradiction, the proletariat should develop class consciousness, organizing politically and in trade unions (→ Labor Representation, II/14) to be better able to confront the capitalist's interests, to understand the complex connections guaranteeing domination in the system, and thereby working toward the construction of an effectively emancipated society.

Nevertheless, it is a difficult venture to understand class struggle in its particularities in America, a continent originating from modernizing colonization (→ Conquest and Colonization, I/7). This is especially the case because the Western Hemisphere is divided along the lines of North America led by the United States and Canada, and Latin America, with Brazil, Mexico, Argentina, Peru, Bolivia, Cuba, etc. These differing historical trajectories have determined the articulation of class struggle in the region until today.

The first popular struggles in the Americas

Throughout its history, the colonial "New World" was a scenario for numerous revolts and rebellions. The secular fight of the indigenous peoples (→ I/11) against the expropriation of their wealth and culture in the Americas is well known. This fight began a powerful resistance against the troops of the metropolis and the white European colonizers (→ Colonial Rule, I/5). Later, the struggle assumed the form of a fight for independence against colonial and neo-colonial domination (→ Independence Movements, I/10), and the expropriation and dispossession of land (→ II/15) and companies taken over by big corporations from the U.S., and other European or Asian imperialist countries (→ Transnational Corporations, II/23). The fight of black slaves (→ Slavery, I/18) for their emancipation was as intensive as the fight of the indigenous peoples. The revolution of the black slaves in Haiti, in 1791, is an important landmark, as the first of many revolts envisioning the abolishing of slavery (James 2013) (→ Revolution, II/44). The struggle of the Quilombo dos Palmares in Brazil during the 17th century is another important historical event, as it represented a considerably large black community, living free and collectively for more than fifty years. Both experiences indicate that the process of emancipation was marked by the interconnectedness and transversality between class and race/ethnicity (Prado Jr. 1969) (→ Intersectionality, II/32; Race, I/39; Ethnicity, I/25).

In the middle of the 19th century, the continent also witnessed the first surge of wage workers, when the industry began to develop, particularly in the Thirteen American Colonies, especially in New England in the north, where the process of capitalist industrial modernization (→ I, 35), began in contrast to the agricultural south, marked by slavery (Genovese 1976; Williams 2013). In Latin America however, these activities developed later and always dependent on foreign interests (→ Development, II/6).

According to Florestan Fernandes (2009), the system of colonization in Latin America had different phases (→ Conquest and Colonization, I/7). First, a form of unlimited colonial exploitation evolved, permitting the creation of a complex articulation between the colonized dominant classes and their counterparts in the colonizing countries. The fights for independence opened what Fernandes called the "second form of external domination," characterized by the disaggregation of the old colonial system, when various European nations assumed the control of exports and imports in Latin America to benefit from trade with the colonized world (Fernandes 2009, 22–27) (→ Global Commodity Chains, II/12). The economic centers retained control of the market via neo-colonialism, in which the proprietors of the native primary goods came to appropriate the portion which was exploited by the exterior in the old colonial system in the past (→ Extractivism, II/9). This was the first impulse toward the constitution of a capitalist market.

Thereby, a new era of external domination formed by the end of the 19th century, assuming its proper imperialist form, in which dependent capitalism became historical reality in Latin America. According to Fernandes, it expanded during the 20th century, via the big corporations controlling not only the agricultural sector, but also the industrial, commercial, service, and financial sectors (→ Transnational Corporations, II/23). This was the beginning of total imperialism, under U.S. hegemony, but also with European and Japanese participation.

In this context, Latin America, despite being predominantly agricultural, began to develop some industrial activities, e.g. in Brazil, Argentina, and Mexico, as a consequence of the association of the dependent bourgeoisies with their U.S. American counterparts. The U.S. had formed as a young imperialist bourgeois nation, searching for a role as a performer in the international division of labor, whereas Latin America "integrated" itself in a dependent and subordinated place. A strong movement of migration (→ I/15) from Europe and Asia has been part of this process since the 19th century, driven by growing urban-industrial activities into the American continent (→ Urbanization, II/2), especially into the USA, Brazil, and Argentina (Godio 1972).

Under these historical and structural conditions, the urban working class was constituted, organized mainly in the industrial centers, ports, railways, civil construction sites, mines, etc., leaving specific marks for the American working class: a direct transition from unfree labor (→ I/19) (African or Indigenous) to salaried labor (mostly by European descendants). Thereby, the transition from feudalism to artisanry until capitalist industrialization did not transpire, as the classical form of the bourgeois revolution, but rather a direct transition from agricultural-based colonial slavery to urban wage labor materialized.

In this process, the first workers' associations, trade unions, and parties were created (→ Labor Representation, II/14). Influenced by anarchism (or anarcho-syndicalism), socialism (→ I/42), and communism, various communist parties were founded in Brazil, Chile, Mexico, Argentina, Cuba, Peru, etc. Catholic trade unionism also developed and spread throughout Latin America. In the U.S., trade unionism also developed, with the creation of the American Federation of Labor (AFL) in 1886, in the context of strike struggles. The AFL acted in a reformist way, refusing political struggles and maintaining a corporatist position. In 1935, the AFL merged with the Congress of Industrial Organizations into the well-known AFL–CIO, the biggest trade union entity in the U.S. and Canada, searching for ways to fight communist influence (Silver 2005; Van der Linden 2013; cf. Casanova 1984).

Since the transition from the 19th to the 20th century, there are numerous examples of strike movements. In 1886, in the U.S., one of America's most important struggles took place demanding a reduction of working hours, and turned the first of May into the symbol of the worldwide struggle of the working class despite not being celebrated in every country. In Latin America, there were the General Strikes in Brazil 1917, and in 1918 in Uruguay. Other important examples include the strikes against Tropical Oil (1924 and 1927) and against United Fruit Company (1928) in Colombia, typical of the exploitation of the southern region of the continent by North American companies (Casanova 1984; Silver 2005; Antunes 2011; Van der Linden 2013). In this context several workers' organization emerged to foster class struggle: such as the Central Obrera Boliviana (COB) during the Bolivian revolution in 1952; as well as of the Central de Trabajadores de Cuba (CTC) during the revolution led by Fidel Castro, and Ernesto "Che" Guevara in 1959 (→ Revolution, II/44); the Conferderacion General del Trabajo (CGT), created in 1930 in Argentina; and the Confederacion de Trabajadores de Mexico (CTM), created in 1936. These are all important examples of trade union centrals, reflecting the political and ideological differences in the Latin American workers' and trade union movements (Rama 1967; Casanova 1984). These kinds of organizations shaped the experiences of socialist class struggle during the 20th century in Latin America.

In the middle of the 20th century, the expansion of capitalism and the generalization of Taylorist-Fordist patterns of production (→ Fordism, II/10), especially through the North American automobile industry, resulted in the formation of a more concentrated working class. This configuration enabled, *ex post*, the development of a new phase of class struggle. In 1936, according to Silver (2005), with the advances in the automobile industry, workers occupied the car body factories Fisher, in Flint, Michigan. In the next year, 1937, the largest U.S. industrial corporation, General Motors (GM), was obliged to sign a contract with the United Auto Workers (UAW), an entity with its main strength on the factory shop floor. In this context, an important wave of strikes led to rising rates of workers' organization and unionization in the factories (Silver 2005, 58–59). The strike of the occupation in Flint was initiated by a small militant core of workers who knew how to catalyze the sentiments of trade unionists and of revolt in the base. It led to a dramatic breakdown of the number of cars produced and forced GM to abandon its anti-trade-unionist position and negotiate a collective bargaining agreement with UAW. The automobile industry, the heart of capitalist production in the USA, showed its weaknesses, opening a cycle of victorious workers' struggles.

During the 1970s, after a broad policy of expansion of its factories to other regions, GM constructed various factories in the south of the U.S., with preference for rural regions and small cities. This "Southern Strategy" failed, as "[i]n 1979, UAW were able to extend all the agreements with GM to all factories in the South" (Silver 2005). In this confrontation, UAW once again capitalized on the role of the workers of the automobile sector, paralyzing the work in strategic units for the production of the main GM car models. The strike in strategically located factories enabled UAW to impede the production of two best-selling car models (ibid., 60). The automobile corporations responded even harder and outsourced their productive units to more distant areas, thereby gradually weakening the power of trade unions. Thus making the 1980s a decade for the expansion of power of the ruling capitalist class.

Whereas in the U.S., class struggle centered on industrial sectors linked to the automobile industry, in Latin America it was more diversified. Apart from industrial workers, e.g. in the Brazilian industrial region of São Paulo, or in Córdoba in Argentina, class struggle also gained space among the rural and agricultural workers. There are various examples in Mexico, Uruguay, the Bolivian miners, Columbian service workers, indigenous communities in Peru and Bolivia, the popular rebellions in Haiti and Cuba, among others. These struggles were geared against the super-exploitation of work and precarious working conditions and envisioned new social achievements, many times evolving into revolutionary struggles, such as in Mexico (1910), Bolivia (1952), Cuba (1959), Nicaragua (1979), etc.

In Argentina, the "Cordobaza" occurred in 1969, in the important industrial belt; in Brazil, the workers' strikes in ABC Paulista (an important industrial pole for the Brazilian metal industry) emerged in 1979/80, among other examples. Class struggle in these important confrontations was centered in the automobile industry. In Brazil, this was the initiation of the "New Trade Unionism" (*novo sindicalismo*), differing from the old state-controlled trade unionism, fighting against super-exploitation of work during military dictatorship (→ Authoritarianism, II/25). In Argentina, the movement fought for the seizure of power, openly confronting Peronism.

Class struggles took different forms throughout Latin America and for a myriad of reasons. The predominance of agriculture in Latin America generated a strong class of peasants, responsible for a large number of uprisings and struggles, e.g. the Mexican Revolution of 1910. However, in some cases, the struggles were against bourgeois reformist governments, such as Argentinian Peronism or Brazilian Getulism (→ Populism, II/43). Other movements were against military dictatorships, such as in Chile, Uruguay, Brazil, Argentina (Rama 1967; Lora 1969; Casanova 1984; Antunes 2013).

Nevertheless, a particular and very important characteristic for understanding class struggles in the Americas is the central significance of dependence center/periphery. In Latin America, a particular kind of dependent capitalism in relation to the North American center developed: a self-destroying capitalism, economically outward oriented and internally socially disintegrated. The native bourgeoisies guaranteed their local domination by preserving and amplifying their links of dependency toward central bourgeoisies (especially North American). Thereby, capitalism developed in the periphery in a complex dialectic between the archaic and the modern, between the new and the old. This interaction became a crucial condition for the expansion and accumulation of capital in the center. Neither the dependent dominant classes nor the capitalist class in the center showed any interest in eliminating this relation of subordination, as both benefited directly as a result of the process. Therefore, the super-exploitation of work, or the differentiated rate of exploitation (Mészáros 1995), continued, guaranteeing the further suction of excess surplus value in the periphery and its absorption by the center, forcing the bourgeoisies to realize an extraction always at the limit of absolute and relative surplus value.

According to Marini (2008), the dependent economies, exploit the native working class more and more, envisioning higher rates of surplus value, produced to guarantee their profits, but also a surplus to transfer to the central countries. This is done via three intimately articulated mechanisms: salaries below the costs for reproduction; extension of the working hours (absolute surplus value); and a constantly rising intensification of work (Marini 2008, 124–127; Biondi Guanais 2016). A good example is GM, a company with a strong presence in Latin America in which the average payrate per hour was significantly lower in Latin America when compared to Europe or the U.S. (Praun 2016). In this scenario, class struggles in America evolved throughout the 20th century. But especially from the beginning of the 1970s onwards, this situation changed profoundly with the acceleration of the process of the globalization of capital, which affected class struggle in America even more.

Class struggle in the era of globalized capital

From the 1990s onwards, with the application of the neoliberal principals based on the Washington Consensus (→ Neoliberalism, II/16), productive state sectors, such as steel, telecommunication, electric energy, banking sector, railways, bus lines, etc., were significantly privatized under the hegemony of financial capital (→ Privatization, II/17). This phase of globalization of capital penetrated production worldwide (Chesnais 1996). The erosion of regulated work, characteristic for most of the 20th century, was amplified by outsourcing and flexibilization as well as informal labor patterns were expanded to further intensify the mechanisms of the extraction of surplus value (→ Informality, II/13). This new reality reconfigured the class struggles on the American continent.

The bourgeois class suffered from major changes that not only affected its traditional sectors, such as agriculture, commerce, industry, and banking, with the latter two originating or directly linked to the financial bourgeoisie. In addition, the sector of agribusiness grew exponentially, and the service sector was increasingly privatized. The middle classes amplified and diversified: in their upper layers, they confused themselves with the managers of capital; and in their lower layers, they snarled with the new service proletariat. Additionally, with the expansion of corporations, upper management sectors – such as Chief Executive Officers (CEOs) were strengthened and directed the larger corporations controlling the global value chains (→ Global Commoditiy Chains, II/12) through their own personal networks. This also established the dominant patterns of labor exploitation with differentiated hourly rates varying in the distant regions of the capitalist world. The working class in the new international division of labor saw an significant expansion of new workers on the one hand, especially in the service and agricultural sectors in Latin America, e.g. in Brazil, Mexico, Argentina, Uruguay, and Columbia (Braverman 1974; Panitch and Albo 2014). The feminization of the workplace was another important development, with rising rates of female participation in the labor market in practically all productive sectors (→ Gender and Work, II/11). On the other hand, the industrial proletariat was also reduced in various areas, such as in the U.S., where Detroit was transformed into a ghost city (→ Deindustrialization, II/5). In a nutshell, the working class became more complex, heterogeneous, and fragmented even further (Valencia 2003; Bialakowsky and Antunes 2009; Silver 2005; Antunes 2014).

At the peak of Taylorism/Fordism (→ II/10), the power of a factory was measured by its number of workers – the *mass worker*. In the era of flexible accumulation, the successful companies were those with the smallest allotment of workforce, as they were able to raise their rates of productivity strongly, as a result of technological advances (Harvey 1989). One of the most profound consequences of these changes is the fact that informality (→ II/13) has become less and less the exception, but tendentially has developed into the norm.

Precarization has become a central element in the dynamics of flexible capitalism, intensifying even more in the absence of trade union opposition (→ Labor Representation, II/14).

The results in the U.S., Chile, Mexico, Brazil, and Argentina are alerting: deregulation of social rights, outsourcing, precarization, and flexibilization of the workforce in most diverse forms, apart from a strong attack on autonomous and class-based trade unionism, trying to transform it into a partnership- and negotiations-based unionism for the companies. The maquiladoras in Mexico are a classical example, producing semi-manufactured U.S. products with low costs, especially labor costs, resulting in a deepening of the precarization of labor (→ Social Inequality, II/20).

In this context, new challenges have arisen for the workers' and trade union movement. On the one hand, the globalization of capital has strengthened the increasingly transnational bourgeois class. On the other hand, the working class is still predominantly nationally organized and thus weak in the sphere of international class struggles. Therefore, it would be crucial for the working class to advance in the direction of international organization (Bernardo 2000; Antunes 2013).

The strike of GM employees in Flint in the U.S. in 1998 is an emblematic example. Initiated by a small strategic unit of the company, it lasted for 54 days and paralyzed 27 of 29 productive units of GM, with profound repercussions in other countries, such as Canada, Mexico, or Brazil (Moody 1998). This unit produced necessary car components for the production of cars in the other factories. With the paralyzation in Flint, step by step, other factories became paralyzed, affecting practically the whole global production process of GM. As indicated by Moody (1998), in this era of internationalization, the workers have shown resistance against the system of just-in-time production. Emblematically, the strike in Flint showed that the globalization of capital can be confronted by the workers' movement on the global scale.

Other strikes and events have proven significant in recent years in North America for their redirection of attention onto class struggles. In the U.S. the United Parcel Service (UPS), a postal company uniting 185,000 part- or full-time workers, went on strike in 1997. The unification of these different groups of the working class in a fight for equal rights guaranteed the victory of the strike. Noteworthy strikes occurred also in Canada, executed by public sector employees, especially during the 1990s. Later, in 2011, the mine workers of the transnational corporation Vale Inco, in Sudbury Ontario, also carried out a powerful strike (Van Velden 2007). A notable example of struggle was also the riots of Los Angeles, California in 1992, with the decisive dimensions of ethnicity (→ I/25), race (→ I/39) and class, as the mobilizations were triggered by strong racism, affecting the black and poor working class most strongly. Another important example is the Battle of Seattle in 1999 against the World Trade Organization (WTO), opening up a new phase of struggles against the globalization of capitalism (Silver 2005) (→ Alter-Globalization, I/21). And in 2011 the Occupy Wall Street movement denounced the hegemony of financial capital and its dreadful social consequences (→ Social Movements, I/41). This opened the floor for an important debate about interconnections between work, unemployment, crisis (→ II/4) and financialization, issues which were not at the agenda in the U.S. before.

In Latin America, there were also various cycles of strikes, initiated by diverse sectors, such us industrial workers, agricultural workers, public employees, and a diversity of middle-class sectors, such as professors, bank employees, etc. In Brazil, there were four general strikes during the 1980s, when the country had one of the highest strike rates worldwide. In this decade, there was also the resurgence of class-based trade unionism with the creation of the Central Única dos Trabalhadores (CUT). CUT was founded in 1983 originating in autonomous trade unionism independent of the state. In the same decade, the Workers' Party (Partido dos Trabalhadores – PT; 1980) and the Movement of Landless Rural Workers (Movimento dos Trabalhadores Rurais Sem-Terra – MST; 1984) were also founded.

Other intense mobilizations occurred in Mexico in the sectors of mining, metal, electricity, agriculture, public sector, and university professors in opposition to neoliberalism (→ II/16). The strike of public professors in Oaxaca in 2005 was a strong example of struggle against the destruction of public education (→ I/24) by the neoliberal governments. It turned into a popular rebellion shaking Mexico's political system. And even before the 2005 strike, the Rebellion in Chiapas in 1994 united important indigenous and popular communities of the south of Mexico symbolically creating an opposition to the North American Free Trade Agreement (NAFTA) at the same time (→ Regional Integration, II/18).

There were also important examples of social struggles in Argentina. In December 2001, the unemployed, called "piqueteros," rebelled and took down various governments. Making use of road blocks, they paralyzed the traffic in the streets, impeding the circulation of goods and persons, directly affecting the movement of capital and denouncing unemployment. There were countless popular assemblies in the neighborhoods, and hundreds of occupations of factories (called *fábricas recuperadas*). The cases of Bruckman (textile), INPA Fábrica Cultural (tube factory), Hotel Bauen in Buenos Aires, Zanon (ceramics) in Neuquén and La Toma (supermarket in Rosário) are rich examples for the working-class experiences to combat unemployment and self-manage the companies. Similar movements also took place in Uruguay, Venezuela, Columbia, Peru, Brazil, etc. and reflect the new modalities of the confrontation between capital and labor in Latin America (Armelino 2004).

Brazil has also faced many noteworthy incidents in which class struggle and its movements were highlighted. For example, another important struggle has been pushed forward by the MST against mass land privatization, agribusiness, GMO-modified food, and toxic fertilizers (→ Land, II/15; Privatization, II/17). Their actions are based on the organization of rural workers, small peasants, and unemployed in general. Via occupations, squatting, and encampments, they fight for the acquisition of land, and for the right to work and survive. There is also the Movement of Workers without a Roof (Movimento dos Trabalhadores Sem Teto – MTST), who fight for housing and against the deterioration of living conditions in the cities (→ Urbanization, I/45). Both movements, MST and MTST, define themselves as workers' movements and by their respective struggles. The Free Transport Movement (Movimento pelo Passe Livre – MPL) fights for free public transport and is also present in various urban struggles, especially during the Rebellions of June in 2013, uniting a great contingent of young students working for their survival.

Other parts of Latin America have also seen important movements. In Venezuela, Ecuador, and Chile, the poor workers have been searching for forms of popular organization in the neighborhoods and factories. In Peru, the indigenous and peasants initiated various uprisings, such as in 2009 against the conservative government, and have opened and widened the spaces of resistance and rebellion together with a number of other Andean indigenous communities (→ Indigeneity, I/31). In Bolivia, the indigenous people and the peasants showed great strength against the intense exploitation and plundering of their natural resources, such as water, mines, petrol, etc., integrating themselves into the workers' struggles with a long tradition in the Andean country. This sum of confrontations characterizing the class struggles in the Americas (and particularly in Latin America) demonstrate that contrary to an exclusionary vision, both the urban working class and the peasants and indigenous communities have been decisive in these confrontations, presenting rich transversalities between class, ethnicity/race, gender (→ Intersectionality, I/32), generation, environmental struggles, etc. (→ Environmental Justice, II/8).

The important Peruvian Marxist José Carlos Mariátegui was pioneer in presenting these decisive connections between class and ethnicity in Latin America. He demonstrated how some basic values of community-based indigenous production are constituted as values that should be incorporated by socialism (→ I/42). In his words, "[t]he solution of the indigenous has to be a social solution" (Mariátegui 1972, 105). Mariátegui articulated the indigenous question with both the rural proletariat and its urban counterpart. He affirmed that the liberty of organization, the rise of salaries, the reduction of working hours, compliance with workers' rights of protection, all bring the workers and the indigenous closer together toward definitive emancipation. He concluded that the problem is social and economic and that race has an important function (Mariátegui 1969, 1972).

Conclusion

There is a myriad of examples expressing class struggle on the American continent. Their understanding is crucial for emancipation in the Americas. When they amplify to include questions of gender, generation, environmental protection, etc., a rich and polymorphous design of these struggles can be seen. Although if the most qualified sectors of the working class, generating surplus value, can potentially be considered more relevant for class struggle, it is also important to note that class struggles also occurred in different social, political and cultural conjunctures. Thus, also the most precarized sectors of the working class (including the unemployed) can exercise a decisive role on the American continent. Furthermore, throughout the Americas the ethnic and racial dimensions of class struggles are vital (→ Ethnicity, I/25; Race, I/39, Indigeneity).

With regard to the North-South divide of the hemisphere, the U.S. constitutes a decisive space for class struggle, being the country the heart of capitalism. Nonetheless, Latin America has also developed into an exceptional laboratory of class struggle. This situation converts the American continent into an important political space for the struggle between social classes.

Works cited

Antunes, Ricardo. 2011. *O Continente do Labor.* São Paulo: Boitempo Editorial.

———. 2013. *The Meaning of Work.* Chicago, Leiden and Boston: Brill Books/Historical Materialism Book Series.

———. 2014. "The New Morphology of the Working Class in Contemporary Brazil." In *Transforming Classes: Socialist Register 2015*, eds. Leo Panitch and Greg Albo, 178–199. London: Merlin Press.

Armelino, Martín. 2004. "Algunos aspectos de la acción colectiva y la protesta en la CTA y el MTA." *Revista de Estudios sobre Cambio Social* 6, no. 15: 5–33.

Bernardo, João. 2000. *Transnacionalização do Capital e Fragmentação dos Trabalhadores.* São Paulo: Boitempo.

Bialakowsky, Alberto and Ricardo Antunes. 2009. *Trabajo y Capitalismo entre Siglos en Latino America.* Guadalajara: University Press of Guadalajara.

Biondi Guanais, Juliana. 2016. *Pagamento por produção, intensificação do trabalho e superexploração na agroindústria canavieira brasileira. Tese de Doutorado.* Campinas: IFCH-UNICAMP.

Braverman, Harry. 1974. *Labor and Monopoly Capita.* New York: Monthly Review Press.

Casanova, Pablo González. 1984. *Historia del Movimiento Obrero en América Latina.* Mexico: Siglo Veintiuno, Instituto de Investigaciones Sociales.

Chesnais, François. 1996. *A Mundialização do Capital.* São Paulo: Xamã.

Fernandes, Florestan. 2009. *Capitalismo Dependente e Classes Sociais na América Latina.* São Paulo: Global.

Genovese, Eugene. 1976. *A economia política da escravidão*. Rio de Janeiro: Pallas.
Godio, Julio. 1972. *Inmigrantes assalariados y lucha de clases 1880–1910*. Buenos Aires: Tiempo Contemporáneo.
Harvey, David. 1989. *The Condition of Postmodernity*. Oxford: Blackwell.
James, Cyril Lionel Robert. 2013. *Toussaint Louverture: The Story of the Only Successful Slave Revolt in History. A Play in Three Acts*. Durham and London: Duke University Press.
Lora, Guillermo. 1969. *Historia del movimiento obrero boliviano*. La Paz: Los Amigos Del Libro.
Mariátegui, José Carlos. 1969. *Ideologia y política*. Lima: Amauta.
———. 1972. *Peruanicemos al Peru*. Lima: Amauta.
Marini, Ruy Mauro. 2008. *Dialéctica de la Dependencia*. Bogotá: Siglo de Hombre, CLACSO.
Marx, Karl. 1996. 'Capital', Vol. I. In: *Marx and Engels Collected Works, Vol. 35*. New York: International Publishers. Orig. pub. 1867.
Mészáros, István. 1995. *Beyond Capital: Towards a Theory of Transition*. London: Merlin Press.
Moody, Kim. 1998. "Acordo encerra greve em Flint: mas problemas continuam insolúveis." *Revista Lutas Sociais* 4: 155–159.
Panitch, Leo and Greg Albo. 2013. *Socialist Register 2014: Registering Class*. London: Merlin Press.
———. 2014. *Socialist Register 2015: Transforming Class*. London: Merlin Press.
Prado, Caio Jr. 1969. *História Econômica do Brasil*. São Paulo: Editorial Brasiliens.
Praun, Luci. 2016. *Reestruturação Produtiva, Saúde e Degradação do Trabalho*. São Paulo: Papel Social.
Rama, Carlos. 1967. *Historia del movimiento obrero y social latinoamericano contemporaneo*. Montevidéu: Palestra.
Silver, Beverly. 2005. *Forças do trabalho: movimentos de trabalhadores e globalização desde 1870*. São Paulo: Boitempo.
Valencia, Adrian. 2003. *La reestructuración del mundo del trabajo*. México, Itaca: Mexico City University Press.
Van der Linden, Marcel. 2013. *Trabalhadores do mundo: Ensaios para uma historia global do trabalho*. Campinas: Editora da Unicamp.
Van Velden, Jacobus Hermanus Antonius. 2007. *Strikes around the World, 1968–2005*. Amsterdam: Aksant.
Williams, Eric. 2013. *Capitalismo e Escravidão*. São Paulo: Companhia das Letras.

4
CRISIS

Aaron Tauss

The concept of crisis is key to understanding political struggles and economic transformations in the history of the Americas and ongoing developments. Viewed from an Inter-American perspective, economic, financial, and political crises always need to be analyzed in terms of their transnational and hemispheric dimensions. Etymologically, "crisis" comes from the Ancient Greek words *krísis* and *krínō*, which mean "judgment," "election," "dispute" and "to choose," or "to decide." The theoretical and empirical analysis of crises occupied a prominent place in the early works of political economy. Notwithstanding their differences, authors like Jean Charles Léonard de Sismondi, John Stuart Mill, Thomas Malthus, and David Ricardo shared a deep-rooted skepticism about the long-term sustainability and reproductive capacities of capitalism (→ II/2). Similarly, Karl Marx regarded capitalism as an inherently unstable and crisis-prone system of social reproduction. Yet instead of blaming the limits of capitalism on nature (→ II/39), population growth (→ Biopolitics, I/22), competition, or the existence of a *rentier* class of landowners, his critique of classical political economy concluded that "the *true barrier* to capitalist production is *capital itself*" (Marx 1981, 358).

Following the "marginal revolution" in the late 19th century, mainstream economics in its neoclassical guise began to view crisis as a socio-economic and political phenomenon external to capitalism. Based on the assumption that capitalism was a self-correcting and harmonious economic system, the analytical focus was placed on the exchange of commodities in the marketplace and on the social interaction of rational individuals, resulting in general equilibrium (Moseley 2009) (→ Global Commodity Chains, II/12). During the Great Depression of the 1930s, the notion of a crisis-free capitalism was radically called into question. For nearly four decades, the theories of John Maynard Keynes, who analyzed the unstable and volatile character of capitalism, served as the ideological foundation for economic development (→ II/6) in the industrialized world. Following the oil shocks and a stagflation crisis of the 1970s, a neoliberal counter-offensive succeeded in re-vitalizing the discourse on efficient and self-regulating markets and the necessary rollback of the Keynesian welfare state (→ Neoliberalism, II/16; Nation State; II/38). The financial crisis of 2007–2008 and the global recession the year after, however, clearly demonstrated the limits of the neoliberal project based on deregulation, liberalization, and financialization.

Marx's theory of economic crisis

A key starting point for the critical engagement with the concept of crisis remains the conceptual framework Marx first developed in his critique of political economy. A theoretical understanding of the abstract potentials of crisis under capitalism is crucial for the empirical analysis of historical reality and hence for the explanation of actual crises in the Americas. The detachment of the concrete historical process and the rational determination of its underlying relations in an ideal and abstract form is ultimately indispensable for any intellectual comprehension and scientific reproduction of history (Mandel 1978, 13ff). Marx derives the most general account of crisis from the principles of historical materialism, i.e. the historically evolved contradictions between productive forces and the social relations of production. Under capitalism this contradiction expresses itself in the growing antagonism between the tendential socialization of productive forces – resulting from the growing social division of the labor process on the world market – and the increasingly private character of the appropriation of surplus labor and ownership of the means of production. Marx's primary analytical focus was, however, the specific contradictions and crisis tendencies inherent to the capitalist mode of production.

Crises are always form-determined in the sense that they originate from the inherent contradictions and antagonisms of a specific social form. The abstract potential of crisis under capitalism is therefore rooted in the fundamental social forms of the capital relation. In other words, a crisis, which unfolds in a capitalist social formation, always engenders general elements that are related to the specific character of capitalism: private ownership of the means of production, formally free wage labor, private production, commodity exchange in the market, and competition. Marx developed his crisis theory on the basis of commodity production under capitalism and viewed the potential for a crisis as inherent in the commodity form, i.e. in the contradictory relation between use value and value (Marx 1976, 209). This contradiction reproduces itself externally and manifests itself in a modified manner in other social forms such as money, capital, labor power, wages, land, (→ II/15), and knowledge. An analysis of actual capitalist crises must therefore depart from these abstract contradictions inherent in the capitalist mode of production. It must scrutinize the crisis potential of industrial capital and, in addition, analyze the specific character of crises originating independently from financial relations (Marx 1976, 236; see also Caputo Leiva 2012).

There is no generally accepted Marxist theory of crisis, only distinctive approaches analyzing different crisis tendencies of the capital relation (Clarke 1994). Each approach provides crucial abstract-theoretical insights into the unstable character of the capitalist mode of production. However, these approaches can neither foresee the coming of future crises, nor predict the eventual collapse of capitalism. The abstract potential of capitalist crises must therefore always be distinguished from the empirical analysis of actual crises in a specific historical context. It is worth noting that the economic laws of capitalism are always historically overdetermined and mediated by institutions and political and ideological class struggles (→ II/3). In other words, capital accumulation is never a purely economic phenomenon (Jessop 2013). Political and ideological struggles would, however, be incomprehensible and arbitrary without a theory of accumulation and economic crisis under capitalism. The existing Marxist literature distinguishes three main theoretical approaches to crises originating from the circuits of productive capital: 1) The law of the tendency of the rate of profit to fall, 2) Theories of underconsumption, overproduction, and disproportionality, and 3) Profit-squeeze theories.

First, the law of the tendency of the rate of profit to fall focuses on the contradictory relation between productivity increases through permanent technological and organizational transformations of the production process and the accumulation of capital. Marx departs from the basic assumption that the historical tendency to replace human labor through technological innovation leads to a rising organic composition of capital, i.e. an increase of the value of constant capital (means of production) *vis-à-vis* variable capital (wages) due to technological change. Together with the rate of surplus value (the rate of exploitation of labor power), the organic composition of capital determines the profit rate. Assuming a stagnant or lower rate of surplus value *vis-à-vis* a rising organic composition of capital, the profit rate necessarily declines with the growth of the organic composition of capital. In short, Marx argued that the rising productivity of labor and the limitless valorization of capital are incompatible.

The theoretical underpinnings of the law of the tendency of the rate of profit to fall, are, however, fairly weak. Marx failed to demonstrate that the organic composition of capital must necessarily rise faster than the rate of surplus value and thus lead to a falling rate of profit (Marx 1976, 772ff). Therefore, the law of the tendency of the rate of profit to fall does not provide a solid basis for the prediction of the actual development of the profit rate or the definitive collapse of capitalism. It merely explains why capital is forced to permanently re-organize the process of accumulation in light of the rising organic composition of capital as well as to activate distinctive "counteracting factors" such as the intensification of the exploitation of labor, the reduction of wages below their value, the cheapening of the elements of constant capital, the growth of a relative surplus population, foreign trade, or the expansion of fictitious capital (Marx 1981, 317ff).

Second, theories of underconsumption, overproduction, and disproportionality locate the origins of capitalist crises in the contradictions between production and circulation. The analytical focus is placed on effective consumer demand, the overproduction of commodities, and the realization of surplus value (→ Consumerism). A crisis of underconsumption results from insufficient effective demand in the market for the produced commodities. Neither the workers' salaries, nor capital's private consumption are high enough to counter the growing contraction between the production and the realization of surplus value. Commodity capital can no longer be successfully transformed into money capital. A crisis thus occurs due to a faster increase of the productive capacities of capital than of effective consumer demand in the sphere of circulation (Marx 1978, 391, 1981, 615).

Theories of overproduction, on the other hand, locate the roots of crises in capital's productivity gains as a consequence of the progressive development of the productive forces. A crisis of overproduction occurs when industrial capitalists are unable to employ further capital at the average profit rate in order to expand production. Such a scenario is often followed by the devaluation of capital (commodity, money, and means of production) and labor power (rising unemployment). Drawing on Marx's reproduction schemes laid out in Volume II of *Capital* (Marx 1978, 427ff), theories of disproportionality argue that the expanded reproduction of capital is only possible as long as production proportionalities between certain sectors of the economy are upheld. A crisis of disproportionality would hence unfold as a result of a prolonged sectorial disequilibrium in the market.

Third, profit-squeeze theories put their analytical emphasis on the contradictions that emerge from the relation between capital accumulation, wages, and the labor market. They argue that the accumulation of capital leads to a growing demand for labor power and therefore reduces unemployment (Marx 1976, 768ff). Such a development strengthens the political stance of the working class (→ Labor Representation, II/14) and leads to rising wages

(Marx 1981, 360). If the capitalist class fails to counter this tendency with the cheapening of the elements of constant capital through productivity gains, rising wages will eventually provoke a decline in the profit rate. This will not only reduce investments and slow down the accumulation of capital, but also lead to more unemployment, lower wages, and the eventual recuperation of the economy on the basis of rising profits. Wages are ultimately dependent on the dynamics of capitalist accumulation. Critics of the theory argue that the demand for workers only increases if economic growth is stronger than productivity gains. A profit-squeeze crisis would thus only occur, if wages were to grow faster than the productivity rate, and if wage increases were higher than the cheapening of the elements of constant capital.

Financial crises

In his critique of bourgeois economics Marx not only analyzed the crisis tendencies and contradictions of productive capital, but also the abstract potential and the actual concretization of crises, which independently originate from the circuits of interest-bearing capital, as well as their repercussions on the "real" economy (Jessop 2013; Kenway 1980; Lehner 2010). The very distinction between the "real" economy and the financial sector is, however, misleading, as the exchange of commodities under capitalism is always mediated by money (Marx 1976, 181). The potential for a monetary crisis is therefore already present in the buying and selling of commodities, more specifically in the functions of money as means of circulation, store of value and means of payment (ibid, 188ff). A general crisis of overproduction of commodities and insufficient effective demand may thus occur when the Commodity-Money-Commodity (C-M-C) circuit is interrupted through hoarding, an insufficient money supply, or the incapacity of debtors to finalize the purchase of commodities. The role of money becomes even more prominent in the general formula of capital (M-C-M), in which money as circulating and self-valorizing value is transformed into capital. Here money is both the point of departure and the final result (including surplus value) of capitalist production.

The relative autonomization of finance capital occurs when money is not being used as functioning capital in the process of production, but instead as property. With the appearance of credit (created by banks) and fiat money (created by the state), the abstract possibilities of crisis emerge independently from money as capital. Credit and fiat money become fictitious commodities with no value in themselves, yet represent value by assuming the functions of "money as money" and "money as capital." Since credit and fiat money are created by banks and the state, their uncontrolled growth increases the likelihood of crises rooted in the financial sector. The expansion of fictitious capital (e.g. in the form of derivatives) can therefore lead to a crisis of oversupply with potentially destructive consequences for the rest of the economy. Even though fictitious capital has the capacity to extend credit relations and increase the elasticity of finance capital (and capital in general), its growth also intensifies capital's existing contradictions and increases the likelihood and scope of crisis.

Political crises

Since capital's inherent contradictions are not soluble in the abstract, provisional and temporary strategies must be pursued by the dominant social forces in order to implement particular accumulation models and regulatory frameworks according to specific spatio-temporal circumstances. During periods of crisis, different economic strategies and political projects compete over the adequate form of crisis-management and the overall direction of capitalist societalization. Crises may thus be viewed as "complex moments of indeterminacy" (Jessop 2012, 24), in the sense that they provoke the formulation of multiple crisis interpretations offering specific narratives, theoretical approaches, discourses, projects, policy recommendations, and political strategies. Public institutions, private organizations, intellectuals (→ Public Intellectuals, III/18), and the mass media (→ Media Flows, III/35) play a crucial role in this political and ideological struggle.

Whether an economic crisis is temporarily solved through the swift implementation of stabilizing policies or used as an opportunity to address underlying structural causes is contingent upon the existing balance of power between social forces. As the history of capitalism (→ II/2) has shown, economic crises often play a crucial role in re-regulating the process of capital accumulation. Despite their socially destructive consequences, in many cases economic crises serve to stabilize class domination and re-organize capitalist production. An economic crisis therefore does not necessarily lead to political crisis (crisis of hegemony within the power bloc and *vis-à-vis* the subordinate classes) and/or a crisis of the state (a crisis of the state apparatuses). According to Poulantzas (1979), an economic crisis is only politically relevant if it has a real impact on the balance of power, and if it contributes to the radicalization of class struggle (→ II/3).

From the Great Depression to the crisis of Fordism

Turning now to the Inter-American context, numerous economic, financial, and political crises in recent decades have evidenced the underlying contradictions inherent in the capital relation. These episodes illustrated how "violent eruptions" (Marx 1981, 357) were brutally deployed by capitalist classes to re-establish and transform the existing balance of power. Following the profound crisis of global capitalism during the Great Depression in the 1930s and World War II, Fordism (→ II/10) emerged as the dominant regime of accumulation in industrialized capitalist countries. In essence, the Fordist growth model was based on a virtuous cycle of mass production, rising productivity resulting from the Taylorist organization of the labor process, rising incomes, growing consumer demand fueled by rising wages, rising profits, and increased investment in machines and technology for the expansion of mass production. Politically and institutionally, Fordism was regulated and materialized in the Keynesian welfare state, which promoted the expansion of the internal market, full employment, demand management, collective bargaining, a mixed economy, and welfare rights (→ Nation State, II/38).

Internationally, the Fordist accumulation system was held together by the monetary and financial framework of the Bretton Woods institutions (IMF, World Bank, GATT), which coordinated the regulation of relatively independent national economies. In Latin America, the economic and political fallout from the Great Depression and World War II prompted the region's shift to an economic growth model based on import substitution industrialization (ISI) and the formation of developmental national states (→ Development, II/6). The objective of the ISI accumulation system was to decrease the dependence on foreign imports and replace the latter with domestic production. The developmental national state played a crucial supportive role by protecting domestic industry through subsidies, high tariffs on imports, and an elevated exchange rate.

After two and a half decades of economic growth and relative political stability in the north, during the late-1960 and early-1970s the limits of Fordism reared their heads. The productivity increases achieved through technological innovation and the Taylorist organization of the labor process began to wear themselves out in the late-1960s (→ Deindustrialization, II/5). The result was a falling rate of profit. The attempts by capital to respond to this tendency via increased investment in research and development, the organization of production and cost-cutting provoked militant reactions from organized labor determined to preserve the trend of rising wages witnessed since the 1950s (→ Labor Representation, II/14). In addition to its attempted internal solutions to the profit squeeze, capital sought the external solution of putting up prices on saleable goods. Inflation with an economic recession from 1973 (stagflation) prompted a serious internal debate among dominant classes and economists: as the Keynesian remedies popular throughout the previous decades threatened to worsen inflation, monetarist arguments began to gain attraction. Increasingly, concerns for the U.S. dollar's status as the global reserve currency should it continue to devalue, combined with the prevailing desire of the financial industry to lower inflation as a means of increasing financial yields, spurred the emergence of the neoliberal age (Panitch and Gindin 2012).

The rise of neoliberalism as a crisis response

During the 1970s, the intensification of international financial flows (itself in part another strategy on the part of capital to compensate the falling rate of industrial profit) further weakened the capacity of national states to organize economies along Keynesian lines. During and after the crisis of Fordism, hypermobile transnational financial capital successfully established itself as the dominant fraction and the primary driving force behind the global expansion of the world market under neoliberalism (→ II/16).

This emerging global finance-driven accumulation system was consolidated after 1979, when the Volcker Shock spiked interest rates; this not only brought down inflation, it multiplied debt burdens throughout the periphery, particularly in Latin America. This in turn prompted the restructuring of the Bretton Woods institutions, now geared toward prying open peripheral economies, thus facilitating further rent-seeking opportunities for transnational finance capital (→ Transnational Corporations, II/23).

The emergence of the new growth model in the 1980s and 1990s must also be viewed in relation to the profound transformation of capitalist class relations to the detriment of the working-class and organized labor. The power shift paved the way for the progressive dismantlement of the post-war Keynesian welfare state and its transformation into an internationalized competition state (→ Nation State, II/38), which increasingly began to focus its policies on improving the competitiveness of the distinctive capitals (foreign and national) operating within its territory on the global markets. International economic and financial regulatory institutions such as the IMF, the World Bank, and the WTO began to assume a more prominent role in facilitating the transformation of national states (→ State Transformation, II/21) and, (as mentioned above) became key centers for the coordination and the management of neoliberal globalization.

The shift in the balance of economic and political power enabled the internationalization of production, the liberalization of trade, the privatization (→ II/17) of public assets, the smashing of trade unions, the flexibilization of labor markets, and the deregulation of finance. Under neoliberalism, finance capital assumed a dominant role in re-stabilizing the process of capital accumulation and, in combination with internationalization and liberalization, overcoming the barriers established by the nationally oriented, Keynesian capitalist states during the Fordist era (→ Regional Integration, II/18). The massive expansion of fictitious capital – most notably in the form of derivatives – accelerated the internationalization of production on a global scale and shifted the focus of finance capital (and capital in general) to rent extraction through financial innovation, overleveraging, and arbitrage. The increased accumulation of capital in the financial sector was a response to existing valorization problems of industrial capital, but also represented a strategy to stabilize industrial reproduction.

Although the internationalization of financial markets and the massive expansion of derivatives under neoliberalism created new investment opportunities for transnational capital, financialization merely deferred and relocated structural problems and crisis potentials in time and space, as the global financial crisis in 2007–2008 clearly demonstrated (Ivanova 2011). The emancipation of finance capital from extra-economic regulatory control mechanisms facilitated the permanent search for spatio-temporal fixes, yet at the same time it intensified and accelerated capital's tendency of uneven and combined development. Despite its dominant position – not only relative to the other fractions of capital but also with regard to nation-states – financial capital is still materially dependent on the exploitation of the working class, and the production and appropriation of surplus value by industrial capital.

From the ISI model to neoliberal restructuring in Latin America

As the crisis of Fordism (→ II/10) progressively unfolded in North America from the 1960s, Latin America was dealing with the structural contradictions and the inherent crisis tendencies of the ISI accumulation regime and the corresponding regulatory framework institutionalized in the developmental national state (→ Nation State, II/38). The failure of the ISI growth model resulted from the convergence of different, yet interrelated, crisis moments. Under the ISI accumulation regime, Latin America's emerging industrial bourgeoisies had not succeeded in substituting the import of capital goods and thus failed to overcome the technological backwardness and structural dependency of their industries in relation to the dominant capitalist countries. National production of heavy machinery, tools, and other equipment would have required huge investments and the simultaneous expansion of production in consumer and intermediary goods.

The relatively rapid exhaustion of the internal market due to the extreme levels of social inequality (→ II/20) and the concentration of income and wealth turned out to be the main structural obstacles to the expansion of mass consumption (→ Consumerism, I/23) and the realization of surplus value. At the same time, the weak industrial base limited employment opportunities and in combination with the process of urbanization (→ I/45) enabled the expansion of a growing urban industrial reserve army. This in turn depressed wages and encouraged Latin America's capitalists to focus on the production of absolute surplus value through the pursuit of an extensive accumulation strategy. It also discouraged technological and organizational innovation and hence perpetuated the countries' historically low levels of productivity of labor. The import of capital goods from the industrialized countries was contingent upon the availability of a sufficient amount of foreign reserves. Due to the historical trend of deteriorating terms of trade, Latin America's capitalist classes were increasingly forced to sell more raw materials and agricultural goods to the advanced capitalist countries in the north in order to generate the necessary funds for their imports (→ Extractivism, II/9). In addition, state intervention in the economy, primarily to the benefit of national conglomerates, increasingly led to widening fiscal deficits, which generated inflationary pressures and growing levels of foreign and internal indebtedness (Bulmer-Thomas 2003).

In light of the crisis of ISI, from the 1970s to 1990s the vast majority of Latin American countries shifted toward a neoliberal and export-led accumulation strategy (Ocampo 2009; Thwaites Rey 2010). Following the U.S.-backed military coup against the democratically elected communist president Salvador Allende in 1973, Chile became the first laboratory for neoliberal polices (→ Authoritarianism, II/25; Military, II/37). Under the authoritarian aegis of General Pinochet, Chile's policy focus was placed on the liberalization, deregulation, internationalization, and deindustrialization (→ II/5) of the economy, the privatization (→ II/17) of public companies and services, the flexibilization of the labor market, the reduction of direct taxation (→ II/22), and the promotion of competitiveness and entrepreneurship (Duménil and Lévy 2004).

During the 1980s, the regime shifts and the neoliberal restructuring of Latin America's societies were internally pursued by the dominant social forces – in part under military rule – and also externally imposed by the advanced capitalist countries, primarily via transnational financial institutions such as the IMF and the World Bank. In response to the severe debt crisis in 1982, which primarily affected the region's major economies, neoliberal adjustment programs were adapted as part of the conditions that accompanied the international financial assistance packages. In retrospect, national conglomerates, the financial sector, and the export industries were the main beneficiaries of Latin America's neoliberal restructuring. Trade liberalization promoted an influx of foreign direct investment from multinational firms and transnational banks (→ Transnational Corporations, II/23) while opening new markets for primary sector exports. The liberalization of finance and the enhanced access to international credit enabled the expansion of consumerism (→ I/23) as well as private and public indebtedness in Latin America and also accelerated the process of financialization via accumulation through dispossession in the form of land grabbing (→ Land, II/15), the privatization of public goods, or the commodification of intellectual commons (→ II/31).

Over the following decade Latin America's dominant classes succeeded in creating a hegemonic, Washington-backed consensus around neoliberalism, even though structural adjustment in most cases did not produce the expected outcomes. In many cases, the implementation of technocratic neoliberal policies aggravated underlying structural problems. The severe economic and financial crises that wreaked havoc in countries like Mexico, Brazil, Colombia, and Argentina during the 1990s and early 2000s testified to the inherently unstable logic of neoliberal globalization. In particular, the Argentine economic recession and financial crisis of 2001–2002 brutally revealed the inherent contradictions and the unstable character of the financialized model of capital accumulation (Frenkel 2003; Setser and Gelpern 2006). The 1990s in Latin America were also marked by the onset of the "special period" in Cuba, a severe and long-lived economic depression that followed the failure of "real existing socialism" and the collapse of the Soviet Union and the Comecon (Moreno 1998; Ritter 2010) (→ Socialism, I/42). The United States was largely unscathed by these crises, indeed the turmoil and instability in Latin America encouraged a massive outflow of capital to the financial centers in the north and inflated U.S. stock markets and helped finance its growing balance of payments deficits. Latin America's shift to an outward-oriented and export-led accumulation regime also had profound socio-economic consequences. It increased industrial unemployment, exerted downward pressure on real wages, accelerated the concentration of wealth and income, deepened class divides, weakened trade unions, and promoted the growth of informal work and precarious forms of employment such as short-term contracts and subcontracting (Dietz 1995) (→ Informality, II/13).

The Zapatista uprising in Mexico in the mid-1990s and the electoral victory of Hugo Chávez in Venezuela in 1998 marked the beginning of the crisis of neoliberal restructuring and the shift toward progressive politics in the region. The emergence of nationalist, reformist, and neo-developmentalist governments in countries like Brazil, Argentina, Uruguay, Bolivia, and Ecuador during the first half of the 2000s, and the struggle of social movements (→ I/41) such as the landless peasants' movement in Brazil, the workplace takeovers in Argentina, and the indigenous and peasant communities in countries like Ecuador, Bolivia, and Colombia (→ Indigeneity, I/31) challenged the neoliberal hegemony and weakened the political influence of the United States in the region (Gambina and Pinazo 2014; Petras 2011) (→ Interventionism, II/36). In recent years, however, military and civic coups, the region's political roll to the right, and the ongoing crisis in Venezuela have notably curbed the advancement of a progressive agenda and bolstered neoliberal and reactionary forces, which vehemently advocate for the extension of neoliberalism (→ II/16).

The global financial crisis of 2007–2008 in the Americas

In North America, the neoliberal agenda was seriously questioned during the global financial crisis of 2007–2008, which threw the post-Fordist and finance-driven accumulation model into its most severe crisis thus far. The global financial crisis was in essence a crisis of the overaccumulation of financial capital, itself a response to the crisis of Fordism and the deflationary effects of neoliberal restructuring (Jessop 2012, 32). In 2007–2008 a subprime mortgage crisis in the U.S. housing sector rapidly turned into a liquidity crisis of the global financial sector, then into a solvency crisis hitting financial and industrial firms, and from there into a fiscal and sovereign debt crisis. The expansion of high-risk loans and fictitious capital in the form of derivatives artificially inflated asset prices and in combination with securitization, excessive hedging, widespread speculation, and Ponzi schemes, created a massive financial bubble that overwhelmed the capacities of central banks as lenders of last resort.

The sheer size of the asset bubble paved the way toward the socialization of accumulated debts and toxic financial assets at inflated prices. As the crisis dangerously spread and deepened, governments across the world rapidly moved to implement emergency measures such as short-term stimulus packages, quantitative easing, zero-interest-rate policies, and the recapitalization and nationalization of banks, all of which essentially aimed at safeguarding the monetary and financial systems, and protecting the largest banks and companies from going bankrupt. The measures, however, were ultimately ineffective, due to persistent insufficient productive demand and the implementation of austerity policies. A declining wage rate and the increasingly unequal distribution of income and wealth in combination with a re-established profit rate caused growing problems of insufficient aggregate effective demand and deflationary tendencies. Over the past years, the expansion of public and private debt, the increased export of capital to the periphery in search of raw materials, the intensification of primitive accumulation, and the expansion of imperialist wars have emerged as the main strategies to sustain capital accumulation in the post-crisis context.

The emergency measures taken by governments following the 2009 global recession rapidly turned the global financial crisis into a fiscal and political crisis as well as into a crisis of legitimacy and representation. Legislative re-regulatory attempts to rein in speculation and casino-type risk taking were largely undermined by the direct lobbying efforts of finance capital and through crony capitalist links with government officials. To this day, the activities of shadow banking, Ponzi finance, and off-balance sheet transactions go on unabated. The failure of passing meaningful re-regulation of the financial sector has clearly demonstrated that the neoliberal and finance-led growth model based on free trade, deregulation, liberalization, financialization, and private enterprise remains the paradigmatic accumulation strategy and political project.

The financial crisis of 2007–2008 was, however, far more than just a crisis of the neoliberal, post-Fordist regime of accumulation and the corresponding mode of political and institutional regulation. It is organically related to the growing chronic environmental crisis that increasingly threatens the dominance of neoliberalism (Klein 2014; Löwy 2011). Moreover, the current crisis bears upon the relative decline of the United States as an imperial power (→ Geopolitics, II/34). Even though the United States has succeeded in re-organizing its informal empire and its hegemonic position in the era of neoliberalism (Panitch and Gindin 2012), it has continued to lose economic weight and political influence relative to the European Union, Russia and newly emerging regional powers such as China, India, and Brazil.

In comparison with the debt crisis of the 1980s and the economic and financial crises in the 1990s and the early-2000s, the impact of the global financial crisis in Latin America was less severe, yet still significant. The region was primarily affected through the deterioration of trade relations – both in volume and dropping prices of manufacturing goods and commodities – and a drastic decline in domestic production, foreign investment, state revenue, and remittances (→ II/19) from migrant workers living in the United States. After the 2001 global recession, Latin America's neoliberal economies began to intensify the focus of their growth model on the primary export sector (→ Extractivism, II/9). This had largely to do with a commodity boom fueled by the rising demand in East Asia. The financialization of commodity futures, however, also played a major role in inflating commodity prices in the lead-up to the global financial crisis (Ocampo 2009).

Following a sharp decline of commodity prices in 2008, the world's major mining companies began to reduce investment in Latin America. This move had a negative impact on government revenues from the export of raw materials, and in some cases led to budgetary crises, exchange rate problems, and the deterioration in the current account. During the financial crisis and the global recession, the accumulation of foreign reserves proved to be the main strategy of the region's struggling central banks to cushion the decline in export revenues and foreign investment. The financial turbulences of the past years thus clearly showed that Latin America's economies are still heavily dependent on the inflow of capital from the industrialized countries.

The neoliberal and finance-led growth model pursued in the Americas has not only accelerated the expansion of the world market, but has also amplified the contradictions of capitalism (→ II/2). Over the past decades, the neoliberal global restructuring has intensified the social disembedding of market relations through the accelerated commodification of fictitious commodities (→ Neoliberalism, II/16) such as land (→ II/15), money, labor power, and knowledge (Fraser 2014; Polanyi 1944). The reproduction of this growth model would appear increasingly contingent upon a more political, predatory and authoritarian form of capitalism. This very authoritarianism (→ II/25), however, will open new avenues of resistance, as the rise of Occupy Wall Street, the Indignados Movement, and Black Lives Matter has clearly demonstrated over the past years. The likely deepening of economic, ecological, and political crises in the near future will certainly enable the emergence of new social movements (→ I/41), whose political struggles will be aimed at the re-embedding of the market into society and at the revitalization of the quest for a viable alternative to capitalist societalization. A Marx-inspired, theoretical reflection of crisis potentials under capitalism and the critical empirical analysis of actual crisis from an Inter-American perspective can play a crucial role in the conflictual and crisis-prone construction of such a transformative project.

Works cited

Bulmer-Thomas, Victor. 2003. *The Economic History of Latin America since Independence.* Cambridge: Cambridge University Press.

Caputo Leiva, Orlando. 2012. "Crítica a la interpretación financiera de la crisis." In *La crisis capitalista mundial y América Latina: Lecturas de economía política*, ed. Jairo Estrada Álvarez, 37–64. Buenos Aires: CLACSO.

Clarke, Simon. 1994. *Marx's Theory of Crisis.* Houndmills: St. Martin's Press.

Dietz, James L. 1995. *Latin America's Economic Development: Confronting Crisis.* Boulder, CO: Lynne Rienner.

Duménil, Gérard and Lévy, Dominique. 2004. *Capital Resurgent: Roots of the Neoliberal Revolution.* Cambridge, MA: Harvard University Press.

Fraser, Nancy. 2014. "Can society be commodities all the way down? Post-Polanyian reflections on capitalist crisis." *Economy and Society* 43, No. 4: 541–558.

Frenkel, Roberto. 2003. "Globalización y crisis financieras en América Latina." *Revista de la Cepal* 80: 41–54.

Gambina, Julio and Pinazo, Hernán. 2014. "La crisis y las trayectorias de América Latina: Neoliberalismo, neo-desarrollismo y proyectos alternativos." In *América Latina: En medio de la crisis mundial*, ed. Jairo Estrada Álvarez, 89–106. Bogotá: Clacso/Universidad Nacional de Colombia.

Ivanova, Maria N. 2011. "Money, housing and world market: The dialectic of globalised production." *Cambridge Journal of Economics* 35, No. 5: 853–871.

Jessop, Bob. 2012. "Narratives of crisis and crisis response: Perspectives from North and South." In *The Global Crisis and Transformative Social Change.* International Political Economy Series, ed. Peter Utting, Sarah Razavi, and Rebecca Varghese Buchholz. London: Palgrave Macmillan.

_____. 2013. "The North Atlantic financial crisis and varieties of capitalism: A Minsky moment and/or a Marx moment? And perhaps Weber too?" In *Financial Crisis, Labour Markets and Institutions*, eds. Sebastiano Fadda and Pasquale Tridico, 40–59. London: Routledge.

Kenway, Peter. 1980. "Marx, Keynes and the possibility of crisis." *Cambridge Journal of Economics* 4, No. 1: 23–46.

Klein, Naomi. 2014. *This Changes Everything: Capitalism vs. The Climate.* New York: Simon & Schuster Paperbacks.

Lehner, Marcus. 2010. "Marx, money and modern finance capital." *Fifth International Journal* 3, No. 4: 53–128.

Löwy, Michael. 2011. *Ecosocialismo. La alternativa radical a la catástrofe ecológica capitalista.* Buenos Aires: Ediciones Herramienta/Editorial El Colectivo.

Mandel, Ernest. 1978. *Late Capitalism.* London: Humanities Press.

Marx, Karl. 1976. *Capital: A Critique of Political Economy, Volume I.* London: Penguin Books.

_____. 1978. *Capital: A Critique of Political Economy, Volume II.* London: Penguin Books.

_____. 1981. *Capital: A Critique of Political Economy, Volume III.* London: Penguin Books.

Moreno, José A. 1998. *Cuba, periodo especial: perspectivas.* Pittsburgh, PA: Editorial de Ciencias Sociales.

Moseley, Fred. 2009. "Marx, Minsky and Crotty on crisis in capitalism." In *Heterodox Macroeconomics: Keynes, Marx, and Globalisation*, eds. Jonathan P. Goldstein and Michael G. Hillard, 140–150. London: Routledge.

Ocampo, José Antonio. 2009. "Latin America and the global financial crisis." *Cambridge Journal of Economics* 33, 703–724.

Panitch, Leo and Gindin, Sam. 2012. *The Making of Global Capitalism.* London: Verso.

Petras, James. 2011. *Social Movements in Latin America: Neoliberalism and Popular Resistance.* New York: Palgrave Macmillan.

Polanyi, Karl. 1944. *The Great Transformation: The Political and Economic Origins of Our Time.* New York: Rinehart and Company.

Poulantzas, Nicos. 1979. "The political crisis and the crisis of the state." In *Critical Sociology: European Perspectives*, ed. J.W. Freiberg, 357–393. New York: Irvington.

Ritter, Archibald R. 2010. "Shifting realities in special period Cuba." *Latin American Research Review* 45, No. 3: 229–238.

Setser, Brad and Gelpern, Anna. 2006. "Pathways through financial crisis: Argentina." *Global Governance: A Review of Multilateralism and International Organizations* 12, No. 4: 465–487.

Thwaites Rey, Mabel. 2010. "Después de la globalización neoliberal. ¿Qué Estado en América Latina?" *Cuadernos del Pensamiento Crítico Latinoamericano* No. 32, www.fundacion.uocra.org/documentos/recursos/articulos/despues-de-la-globalizacion-neoliberal.pdf

5
DEINDUSTRIALIZATION

Lachlan MacKinnon and Steven High

Scholarly treatments of deindustrialization largely emphasize the local and national aspects of economic and political change in the so-called "industrialized world." Primarily, researchers have explored the contours of these processes in relation to Canada, the United States, Western Europe, and Australia. When comparative studies do arise, these often focus on deindustrialization in the borderlands (→ II/26) of North America and Europe. Such approaches gesture toward an increasing awareness of "trans-nationality" within the field, and express the distinct influence of state and community action on a set of processes traditionally considered the result of macro-economic transition (→ State Transformation; II/29). Tracy Neumann's recent work on deindustrialization in Hamilton, Canada, and Pittsburgh, U.S. is an excellent example of such a focus. Neumann analyzes the intersectional response of municipal and federal actors in each city to reveal a divergent set of transitions to "post-industrial" life (Neumann 2016). The Inter-American approach this Routledge Handbook offers is an opportunity to consider how renewed attention to the North-South relationship of economic change in the Americas might profitably be brought into conversation with a burgeoning "transnational turn" in deindustrialization studies.

Deindustrialization and the Global North

In North America, the devastation of mill and factory towns during the late 1970s and early 1980s prompted a flurry of resistance – both in the form of community-based protest and from scholar-activists. Barry Bluestone and Bennett Harrison, now ubiquitously cited within deindustrialization scholarship, articulated the scope and urgency of the problem. Offshoring and capital flight were at the heart of their analysis; the rapidly globalizing market, they believed, offered companies an opportunity to shift production to areas where lower labor costs and union density would provide a better return on shareholders' investment (Bluestone and Harrison 1982, 6).

In Mexico, the *maquiladora* system expanded in correspondence with these shifts; transnational corporations (→ II/23) increasingly turned to non-unionized, low-waged female workers in Latin America for industrial manufacturing (→ Labor Representation, II/14; Gender and Work, II/11). Ground zero in the transition from Fordism (→ II/10) to "flexible accumulation" strategies, the maquiladoras were often alienating, exploitative, and grim workplaces – but, as authors such as Daniel James and Norma Iglesias-Prieto describe, so did they open up new avenues for economic and gendered resistance on the U.S.-Mexico frontier (Iglesias-Prieto 1997; James 2000). This has created a popular perception, evidenced by the recent election of Donald Trump to the Presidency of the United States and the Brexit decision in Europe, that the Global South has been the great beneficiary of deindustrialization in the North (→ Geopolitics, II/34). In fact, the processes of deindustrialization are much more global than is popularly imagined; indeed, Latin America and the Caribbean have struggled greatly with the decline of employment in basic manufacturing, unionization rates, and economic disparity resulting from the globalized economy of the 21st century.

The first wave of scholarly and political attention to deindustrialization focused on its scale and scope, and issued a clarion call for concerted resistance within the United States. Bluestone and Harrison called for political intervention in the market to offset the impact of industrial closure. Staughton Lynd, outraged at steel mill closures in Youngstown, Ohio, demanded an overhaul of labor legislation to give workers the legal tools to effectively challenge employers' decision to relocate (Lynd 1982, 4). Despite such demands, united resistance did not materialize. Steven High describes the situation in which the groups opposed to plant closures in the U.S., "proved incapable of coming together" as exemplified by the different tactics in which "unions directed their patriotic response at Japanese imports and a buy American strategy" and the "young activists conducted a guerrilla war against capital" which then ultimately "fundamentally weakened the nascent anti-plant shutdown movement" (High 2003, 193).

Deindustrialization continued unabated. Jefferson Cowie, tracing the 20th-century movements of the Radio Corporation of America (RCA), argues that the company wielded the threat of divestment and mobilized to suppress labor agitation. Moving from Camden, New Jersey to Bloomington, Indiana and, ultimately, to Ciudad Juárez, Mexico, the corporation used capital flight as a means of countering workers increasing sense of entitlement and control over investment in their community (Cowie 1999, 4). While Canadian workers were more successful at softening the blow of plant shutdowns, relying as they did on left-nationalist sentiment, hundreds of thousands of industrial workers were still left without work during the 1970s and 1980s (→ Socialism, I/42).

Scholarship was soon re-oriented toward the cultural and representational aftermaths of deindustrialization. As the moment of political and economic crisis (→ II/4) passed, researchers began branching out from the activist economistic focus of earlier works. Jefferson Cowie and Joseph Heathcott's 2003 collection *Beyond the Ruins* marked a significant moment in this shift. The editors remark, "What was labeled deindustrialization in the intense political heat of the late 1970s and early 1980s turned out to be a more socially complicated, historically deep, geographically diverse, and politically perplexing phenomenon than previously thought" (Cowie and Heathcott 2003, 2). The authors in their collection moved beyond the economic impact – the "body count" – of deindustrialization, instead directing attention toward its environmental aftermath (→ Environmental Justice, II/8), racial aspects of decline in American cities (→ Race, I/39), and the transitions in local identities that emerge in response to plant and factory closures.

Others have turned their attention to the aestheticization, appropriation, and commodification of industrial landscapes and experiences that has often occurred in the aftermath of deindustrialization. Sharon Zukin articulates the functional replacement of the industrial mode of production with what she calls the *artistic mode of production*, postulating that the idea of historic preservation serves as a vehicle for removing the idea of the "built legacy of the industrial city from the social matrix of industrial production," and

> [w]hen the lofts that were used for light manufacturing are reduced to being considered as a cultural artefact, the image that their economic function is dead is reinforced. Without such a function, the urban-industrial infrastructure submits to the rules of the "picturesque."
>
> *(Zukin 1982, 180)*

This notion has prompted significant debate. "Smokestack nostalgia," a term coined by Cowie and Heathcott, castigates uncritical representations of a Golden Age of industry. Drawing upon this concept, Tim Strangleman writes, "In our enthusiasm to recognize working-class heritage and find value in it, we also have to be aware of what is potentially problematic there" (2013, 24). On the other hand, oral history accounts of former industrial workers deindustrialized cities and towns throughout North America demonstrate that there *was* something about work in the post-war factories, mills, and mines that many found deeply satisfying. Not only were these jobs often unionized (→ Labor Representation, II/14), with higher wages and benefits than those found within the "post-industrial" service economy, but the ability to challenge aspects of work control on the shop floor, the emergence of work cultures, and a sense of shared identity meant that these recollections cannot *solely* be written off as nostalgic (High and Lewis 2007, 41–2). As Paul O'Hara reminds us, writing of steel production in Gary, Indiana, "There was deep meaning in the processes of steel work and steel production, and though it might not have been the idealized class consciousness that we wish it to have been, its importance and its nuances should not be dismissed" (O'Hara 2011, 14) (→ Class Struggle, II/3).

Industrial ruins have been the focus of many discussions on representation and memory in deindustrialized places. Alice Mah argues that abandoned industrial sites remain connected with the urban environments and communities that surrounds them (2012, 3). Some tension arises between readings of post-industrial ruination that rely largely upon aesthetic or artistic forms of analysis and others that seek to keep the focus on the political and economic processes by which ruination occurs. Tim Edensor defines the aesthetic approach in a 2005 book, *Industrial Ruin*, wherein he explores abandoned sites of British industry. He describes the creative re-use of these sites in the aftermath of industrial production; they take on a transgressive quality, Edensor argues, and represent spaces wherein the normative rules of everyday life are disarticulated (2005, 4). Steven High, critiquing the aestheticization of post-industrial landscapes, has argued that these spaces do *not* exist as disruptive spaces that counter capitalist structural hegemony – but as emblems of its destructive capabilities (→ Capitalism, II/2). Whether the deindustrial aesthetic is communicated through coffee-table booklets filled with images of ruined steelworks and factories or the social media (→ III/41) accounts of middle-class urban explorers is immaterial. High argues that "artists and urban explorers are active participants in the post-industrial transformation, and are thus a 'colonizing arm' of the middle class, there is little doubt that they are implicated as much as we are as scholars" (2013, 149).

The concept of ruination has been extended in recent publications on deindustrialization in North America and Western Europe. *The Deindustrialized World*, an edited collection that emerged from a 2014 conference at Concordia University in Montreal, includes a substantial focus on the ways that people in deindustrializing and post-industrial communities live in and with ruination. Authors examine subjects such as the bodily aftermath of deindustrialization and its impact on workers' health, the role of the state (→ Nation State, II/38) in mitigating industrial closure, and the violation of "moral economies" in deindustrializing regions (High, MacKinnon, and Perchard 2017). Intended as a "step towards the global historicization of deindustrialization," the editors write, "the [articles] in this volume serve to capture the global movements offered by some orthodox international political economy, as well as economic history, of the progressive growth of the global economy and its social benefits" (High, MacKinnon, and Perchard 2017, xx).

Deindustrialization as global history?

The Inter-American approach of this Handbook offers an opportunity to reflect upon this existing body of work, extend recent developments within the literature, and begin to draw connections between how deindustrialization occurs in both North and South America. Developing regions throughout the world, with the exception of Asia, "experienced falling manufacturing shares in both employment and real value added" in recent decades, and Latin America has been one of the hardest-hit areas (Rodrik 2016, 2). The scale of industrial job losses has been staggering. However, an extensive read into the English- and French-speaking secondary literature on deindustrialization in Latin America has identified three significant themes that hold promise for further transnational studies.

The collapse of national industrialization strategies throughout Latin America was prompted by several factors beginning in the 1970s (→ Development, II/6). In contrast with Canada and the United States, deindustrialization in Latin America often went hand-in-hand with targeted campaigns of state violence against workers, trade unionists, and others on the left. Right-wing military dictatorships were at the forefront of many market-oriented reforms that dramatically restructured and curtailed the industrial sectors of Chile, Argentina, and elsewhere (→ Authoritarianism, II/25; Military, II/37). Paramilitaries and death squads systematically targeted trade unionists and political activists during the 1970s and 1980s. Union organizers are counted among the tens of thousands killed, exiled, or disappeared in Chile, Argentina, Columbia, El Salvador, and Guatemala within these years. In Brazil, these reforms were instituted after the end of military rule in 1985 at the behest of organizations such as the International Monetary Fund (IMF) and the World Bank (Buechler 2014, 11). Mark Anner cites the example of the average tariff in Brazil on imported automobiles that dropped from 85 percent in 1990 to 34.3 percent in 1994 as a particularly visible example of this sort of neoliberal restructuring (Anner 2008, 49). Combined with regional trade liberalization (→ Regional Integration, II/18), the resulting collapse of unionization and workers' organizations reveals an alternative political trajectory that would benefit from further study.

Second, neoliberalism (→ II/16) has long provided an explanatory framework for understanding economic and social change within Latin America. Re-examining integrated global approaches, such as dependency theory and world-systems theory, provides an opportunity to link restructuring in the Global South with contemporaneous developments in the "industrialized" world. An emerging neoclassical consensus on regional deindustrialization in Latin America would benefit from closer conversation with radical and other forms of deindustrialization scholarship. The *premature deindustrialization thesis*, which presupposes a natural and progressive character of these processes, perhaps obscures some of the more concrete political and economic reasons for industrial decline.

A significant downtrend in manufacturing employment began to impact Latin America at the same time that Canadian and U.S. firms were beginning to feel the crisis (→ II/4). Chile and Peru were among the first to experience these effects, followed shortly thereafter by other countries that abandoned the development path of "import substitution industrialization (ISI)" and that shifted to trade liberalization and export promotion in the 1990s and 2000s. In Chile, this was directly related to the political and economic atrocities of the Pinochet regime; the dictatorship radically restructured the economy after 1973, putting "industrialization into reverse gear," and reduced industrial employment from 555,000 to 378,000 a decade later. Manufacturing employment in Argentina declined similarly under its military dictatorship, with job losses approaching 10 percent between 1974 and 1985 (Hirschman 1987, 15). This has created multiple forms of grassroots resistance; notably, the "factory-takeover" movement that sprouted in the early 2000s (Ranis 2005, 1–2) (→ Social Movements, I/41) . In Brazil, the most industrialized country in Latin America, 1.7 million manufacturing jobs were lost between 1988 and 1998 (Anner 2008, 38) (→ Social Inequality, II/20). Deindustrialization has also resulted in increased residential segregation in Mexico City, Buenos Aires and other major cities, and economic restructuring has led to the geographic dispersal of jobs, as manufacturing shifted from more highly unionized cities and regions to more peripheral areas (Kanai and Ortega-Alcazar 2009, 490) (→ Urbanization, II/43).

Economic diversification and the development of new industries, such as textiles and automobile production, had characterized much of the growth in Latin America after 1945 (Brady, Kaya, and Gereffi 2011, 205; Hirschman 1968, 2). The import substitute model of state-driven industrialization contributed to the rise of the middle class in many countries (→ Modernization, I/35), but also a growing awareness of economic inequality and mass poverty as the population boomed. In fact, the population of Latin America more than doubled over a thirty-five-year period, from 155 million in 1945 to 388 million in 1980. Massive urbanization (→ I/45), and a shift away from agriculture, meant that the economic growth of these years could not support everyone (Hirschman 1987, 8–9). The collapse of manufacturing employment in many of these industries corresponded with a period of significant state repression of workers, leftists, and intellectuals as neoliberal reforms were enacted and expanded after the 1970s.

Regional trade agreements (RTAs) were a key aspect of this restructuring process (→ Regional Integration, II/18). By the early 2000s, there was a complex and imperfect patchwork of overlapping and competing RTAs throughout Latin America, which affected virtually every country in the region (Brady, Kaya, and Gereffi 2011, 184–5). The impact of these neoliberal-oriented agreements was uneven. Some initially boosted industrial production, while others prompted immediate stagnation or decline. Mercosur, for example, tightened restrictions outside the bloc, which led to lost industrial jobs in some member countries. Industrial employment in Argentina and Uruguay dropped from 31.6 percent and 33 percent of overall employment in 1990, respectively, to under 22 percent in 2002 (Brady, Kaya, and Gereffi 2011, 202). Contrastingly, the North American Free Trade Agreement encouraged U.S. and Canadian companies to shift production to Mexico (Cowie 1999). The rise of Export Processing Zones in Mexico (1.2 million workers), Central America (700,000 workers), and the Caribbean (540,000 workers) has also hurt workers, as these areas were left with far lower rates of unionization (Anner 2008, 39). As early as 2001, however, it seems that Mexican maquiladoras have lost jobs to China and other low-waged producers (de la Garza Toledo 2007, 400; Jenkins and de Freitas Barbosa 2012, 61).

The combination of targeted political violence with economic liberalization and restructuring has battered Latin American trade unions. While these organizations benefited from state support in the 1950s and 1960s, they have been increasingly marginalized. During the

1990s, the decline of unionization ranges from 5 percent in Brazil and Ecuador to more than 50 percent in Honduras, Paraguay and Peru (→ Labor Representation, II/14). The decline of unions in other jurisdictions was also sizable: Argentina (10.8 percent from 1995 to 1999), Bolivia (46.9 percent from 1990 to 1996), Chile (16.9 percent between 1990 and 1998), and Mexico (36.2 percent between 1986 and 1995). Despite pro-labor law reform in some jurisdictions, unions have struggled with the "challenges presented by economic restructuring" and the offshoring of jobs (Anner 2008, 33–7).

Deindustrialization in Latin America accelerated through the debt crises of the 1980s (→ Crisis, II/4). As capital markets were deregulated, foreign direct investment was facilitated while regional capital investments were directed elsewhere. Some scholars have also blamed the "bureaucratic authoritarianism" of military dictatorship for the decline of industry, primarily for spending "enormous resources on inefficient and wasteful state-sponsored industrial enterprises" (Brady, Kaya, and Gereffi 2011, 186). As a result of each of these factors, Rhys Jenkins concludes, "Latin American countries are not experiencing deindustrialization in the same way as was experienced by affluent democracies" (Jenkins 2015, 45).

Other analysts have focused on the place of Latin America within the global economy. Dependency and world-systems theorists "view open trade as detrimental to the periphery and favour protectionism or disengagements for industrialization" (Brady, Kaya, and Gereffi 2011, 187). In this sense, the development of trade dependency has damaged basic industry; economic historians have reached back to the beginnings of European colonization (→ Colonial Rule, I/5) and resulting national independence movements (→ I/10) to find examples. Independence came quickly in former Spanish colonies, more slowly in Portuguese Brazil. The immediate post-independence period saw a great deal of political instability, border wars, and the economic balkanization of an area that had been hitherto economically integrated (Bates, Coatsworth, and Williamson 2007, 918). Mexico was able to resist this trend during the 19th century, as early wool and cotton manufacturers defended their position "better than did the rest of the poor periphery" (Gonzalez, Galvarriato, and Williamson 2008, 758). Even then, Latin America was considered "highly protectionist" as the average tariff rate in 1870 was 24 percent, or four times that which prevailed in Western Europe. Latin American governments relied on customs duties for revenue (Bates, Coatsworth, and Williamson 2007, 930).

Trade liberalization expanded after the 1970s, and by 1990 "almost every political economy in the region was in the process of integration into the global market. The liberalization period constituted a structural adjustment process undertaken under the strong influence of the so-called Anglo-Saxon neoliberal model" (Bogliaccini 2013, 79) (→ Neoliberalism, II/16). Such reforms played an important role in the destruction of industrial jobs and growing income inequality (→ Social Inequality, II/20). This transformational process coincided with the rise of China, reducing the region's ability to compete with cheap imports or secondary markets even further. Deindustrialization was perhaps strongest in "middle income" countries starting with Chile, Argentina and Uruguay where "[o]n average, tariffs were cut by half over the 1970s, and again from an average of 46 percent in 1990 to 12 percent in 1995" (Bogliaccini 2013, 82–3). The deindustrialization debate is particularly heated in Brazil, but also extends to other countries that had developed manufacturing sectors through import substitution and other protectionist measures. Manufacturing was severely affected by the "new competitive pressures brought about by the combination of an overvalued currency, high interest rates and falling tariffs during the 1990s" (Jenkins and de Freitas Barbosa 2012, 68). The 1982 debt crisis was also pivotal. Falling tariff barriers combined with austerity in the public sector, the privatization (→ II/17) of state enterprises and labor reform to enhance labor force "flexibility" (Kanai and Ortega-Alcazar 2009, 487).

Deindustrialization has also emerged as a political rallying cry and a point of academic debate across Latin America. There has been a wide-ranging discussion in recent years over the "nature, scope, and causes" of deindustrialization in the region (Cypher 2015, 617). According to Chong-Sup Kim and Seungho Lee, who have compared the different paths toward deindustrialization in Latin America and Southeast Asia, "acknowledging that deindustrialization is a universal phenomenon that most countries experience at a certain stage of economic development" and "that the factors that cause deindustrialization differ widely across countries, thereby dictating different deindustrialization paths" (Kim and Lee 2014, 65). Export promotion, which coincided with the rise of China as a global industrial superpower, has significantly impacted manufacturers across the region. In Brazil, economists have focused on whether or not the economy was "pushed into a 'premature' stage of deindustrialization due to neoliberal monetary policies" (Cypher 2015, 639). Deindustrialization has also been blamed on the overvaluation of exchange rates, which were the result of a red-hot commodities market (Trindade, Cooney, and Pereira de Oliveira 2016, 275) (→ Extractivism, II/9).

While academic debate surrounding the subject continues, men and women in deindustrializing areas have resisted these processes of global capitalism (→ II/2). Protests regularly accompany plant closings across the Americas, as does the desperate scramble for a potential buyer. These last-ditch efforts sometimes extended to plant occupations and employee or public ownership. In Canada, Steven High writes of the left-nationalist narratives that emboldened opposition to plant closure during the 1970s. In these instances, workers were able to forestall closure and offshoring through an appeal to an imagined national identity that was contracted with the profit-seeking actions of large, foreign-owned multinationals (High 2003) (→ Transnational Corporations, II/23). While community-based protest movements in the United States were not as successful, closure protests at Weirton Steel in West Virginia represent an exception where workers' resistance efforts were temporarily successful in forestalling closure and achieving some measure of workers' control. In 1982, Weirton Steel employees successfully negotiated a purchase agreement with the company; to avoid layoffs, the nearly 24,000 employees entered into an employee stock ownership plan (ESOP) that was overseen by a board of outside directors. Although Weirton would eventually wind down production in the early 2000s, its workers achieved decades of continued production after the negotiation of the ESOP and avoided the degree of economic shock associated with immediate closure and layoffs as experienced in places such as Homestead, Pennsylvania (Martin 2016, 175).

Direct-action solutions were seen mainly in South America in response to capital flight and the threat of deindustrialization. After the crippling economic crisis in 2001, workers in Argentina moved to take control of their workplaces through an expansive factory-takeover movement. On 18 December 2001, workers at the Brukman textile manufacturing plant in Buenos Aires – facing closure – took matters into their own hands by occupying their workplace. Despite several eviction attempts, these workers were successful in maintaining production and – supported by the unemployed movement and leftist political organizations – created a workers' co-operative to continue operations (→ Commons, II/31). Despite these tentative successes, as Marina Kabat writes, the co-operative model of taken factories is an uneasy fit within an overarching policy framework predicated upon the acceptance of capitalist market forces and foreign "structural adjustment" plans (Kabat 2011).

Some Latin American economists have suggested that regional deindustrialization was "premature," and thus different from the "normal" iteration seen in the advanced industrial economies of North America and Western Europe (Jenkins 2015, 45). The *premature deindustrialization thesis* is predicated on the belief, prevalent among neoclassical economists, that the industrial sector "naturally" loses relative weight once an economy matures (Trindade, Cooney, and Pereira de Oliveira 2016, 641) (→ Modernization, I/35). In this view, deindustrialization may "not always be considered a negative phenomenon but rather a natural consequence of the industrial dynamism in a developed economy" (Kim and Lee 2014, 66). The manufacturing sector only serves as the primary engine of growth until "countries reach a certain level of per capita income," at which the manufacturing sector weakens and industrial employment declines. For economists like Moritz Cruz, "de-industrialisation, the sustained decline of manufacturing output in total output and of manufacturing employment in total employment, has long been recognized as a normal, endogenous process in any capitalist economy" (2015, 114). However, should the economy deindustrialize too early, the economy therefore loses its capacity to create jobs, resulting in a "cumulative vicious circle of insufficient growth – low investment – low productivity – high unemployment." Indeed, it can become a "pathological condition" characterized by a slow rate of economic growth, productivity stagnation, and declining investment. The timing of deindustrialization is therefore important.

Deindustrialization as an explanatory framework has regained currency in the region in recent decades as a result of the commodities boom. According to economists Trindade, Cooney, and de Pereira Oliveira, "Booming commodities exports and a very high exchange rate value for the Brazilian real have caused manufacturing exports to fall as a share of total exports, while cheap, imported Chinese manufactures have wreaked some havoc on the domestic industrial base" (2016, 640–1). Economists have also documented the distorting effects of the commodities boom, and the "increased reliance on exports of primary products to generate foreign exchange," in parts of Latin America (Jenkins 2015, 45) (→ Extractivism, II/9). Writing in 2015, Rhys Jenkins makes a distinction between "orthodox" economists who "take a benign view of deindustrialization" and heterodox economists and radical political economists who believe otherwise (2015, 46). Jenkins noted that China has had a three-fold impact on Brazil: one, the importation of cheap Chinese-made commodities into Brazil have reduced the domestic market share of domestically manufactured goods; two, Brazilian manufacturing exports have faced increased competition from China in other markets; and three, Chinese demand for Brazilian raw materials – leading to inflated world commodity prices – has seen the "primarization" of the Brazilian economy (→ Global Commodity Chains, II/12).

The so-called "primarization" of exports is caused, some argue, by the "Dutch disease effect" brought on by the boom in primary commodity prices, leading to a shift in capital from manufacturing to the resource sectors, with the rise of China as a global economic superpower (Jenkins 2015, 43; Kim and Lee 2014, 66). Brazil's iron ore sector is a good example of this, as China now accounts for more than half of the world's iron ore consumption. Jenkins calls this the "primarization of exports" – which can "lead to a form of 'Dutch disease'" what means that the overvalued exchange rate reduces the cost of imported manufactures and makes it more difficult for Brazilian industry to compete in export markets (2015, 45–57; Cruz 2015, 117). Economists note that the Dutch Disease is only found in those countries with abundant natural resources that generate a trade surplus in primary commodities and finance their trade deficits in manufacturing with it (Kim and Lee 2014, 67). The political and social consequences of deindustrialization and the primarization of exports are important, notes Jenkins, as "a shift away from factory employment, where it is relatively easy to unionize and mobilize, to more dispersed workplaces" can mean fundamental changes in "the structure and nature of the working class . . ." and thus causing primarization to possibly

> lead to a strengthening of the position of landlords and mine owners, some of whom may be foreign, while deindustrialization threatens the interests of domestic industrial capital or changes the nature of their activities as they shift from manufacturing into trade and services.
>
> *(Jenkins 2015, 46)*

All agree, competition from China has posed serious challenges to Latin American manufacturers (Jenkins and de Freitas Barbosa 2012, 60). Interestingly, the same set of issues has also arisen in Canada in relation to the negative effects of the commodity boom and Alberta's oil sands development on the country's manufacturing sector (→ Energy, II/7).

The scale and scope of the suffering caused by mine, mill, and factory closures has been enormous. The gales of creative destruction unleashed by capitalism (→ II/2) has contributed to the rise of what Richard Florida calls the creative class and the culture-led regeneration of abandoned industrial zones in some cities (→ Cultural Industries, III/27). Care must be taken that such efforts do not further exploit and marginalize those who have been most impacted by deindustrialization; "disaster" or "slum tourism," often emerging in the aftermath of economic declension, has sometimes been dubbed "economic disaster porn" for its commodification of the lives of working-class residents in places like Detroit, Michigan (Malone 2011). Similarly, the gentrification of former working-class and racialized neighborhoods in inner city areas has further dislocated those who have suffered most from the decline of industry.

Despite these challenges, a residual culture of industrialism often persists in these neighborhoods, cities, and regions. Local arts and media projects have opened up spaces for local residents to remember and mourn what was lost (→ Media Participation, III/36). We will end with Daniel James's account of one such multimedia requiem for closed packing houses in Berisso, Argentina:

> It was mourning for lost loved ones, for lives wasted in the plants, for lives enjoyed, friendship, solidarities, jokes, loves and hates. But it was also mourning for a physical and social space that was lost and with it, perhaps, the possibility of recovering through memory the identities and experiences evoked by the mourning.
>
> *(James 2000, 149)*

Works cited

Anner, Mark. 2008. "Meeting the Challenges of Industrial Restructuring: Labor Reform and Enforcement in Latin America." *Latin American Politics and Society* 50, no. 2: 33–65.

Bates, Robert H., John H. Coatsworth, and Jeffrey G. Williamson. 2007. "Lost Decades: Postindependence Performance in Latin America and Africa." *Journal of Economic History* 67, no. 4: 917–43.

Bluestone, Barry, and Bennett Harrison. 1982. *The Deindustrialization of America: Plant Closings, Community Abandonment, and the Dismantling of Basic Industry*. New York: Basic Books.

Bogliaccini, Juan Ariel. 2013. "Trade Liberalization, Deindustrialization, and Inequality: Evidence from Middle-Income Latin American Countries." *Latin American Research Review* 48, no. 2: 79–105.

Brady, David, Yunus Kaya, and Gary Gereffi. 2011. "Stagnating Industrial Employment in Latin America." *Work and Occupations* 38, no. 2: 179–220.

Buechler, Simone Judith. 2014. *Labor in a Globalizing City: Economic Restructuring in São Paulo, Brazil.* London: Springer.

Cowie, Jefferson. 1999. *Capital Moves: RCA's Seventy-Year Quest for Cheap Labor.* Ithaca, NY: Cornell University Press.

Cowie, Jefferson, and Joseph Heathcott, eds. 2003. *Beyond the Ruins: The Meanings of Deindustrialization*. Ithaca, NY: Cornell University Press.

Cruz, Moritz. 2015. "Premature De-industrialization: Theory, Evidence and Policy Recommendations in the Mexican Case." *Cambridge Journal of Economics* 39, no. 1: 113–37.

Cypher, James M. 2015. "Emerging Contradictions of Brazil's Neo-Developmentalism: Precarious Growth, Redistribution, and Deindustrialization." *Journal of Economic Issues* 49, no. 3: 617–48.

de la Garza Toledo, Enrique. 2007. "The Crisis of the Maquiladora Model in Mexico." *Work and Occupations* 34, no. 4: 399–429.

Edensor, Tim. 2005. *Industrial Ruins: Space, Aesthetics and Materiality*. Oxford: Berg Publisher.

Gonzalez, Rafael Dobado, Aurora Gomez Galvarriato, and Jeffrey G. Williamson. 2008. "Globalization, De-Industrialization, and Mexican Exceptionalism, 1750–1877." *Journal of Economic History* 68, no. 3: 758–811.

High, Steven. 2003. *Industrial Sunset: The Making of North America's Rust Belt, 1969–1984*. Toronto: University of Toronto Press.

———. 2013. "Beyond Aesthetics: Visibility and Invisibility in the Aftermath of Deindustrialization." *International Labor and Working Class History* 84, 140–53.

High, Steven, and David Lewis. 2007. *Corporate Wasteland: The Landscape and Memory of Deindustrialization*. Ithaca, NY: Cornell University Press.

High, Steven, Lachlan MacKinnon, and Andrew Perchard, eds. 2017. *The Deindustrialized World: Confronting Ruination in Postindustrial Places*. Vancouver: University of British Columbia Press.

Hirschman, Albert O. 1968. "The Political Economy of Import-Substituting Industrialisation in Latin America." *Quarterly Journal of Economics* 82, no. 1: 1–32.

———. 1987. "The Political Economy of Latin American Development: Seven Exercises in Retrospection." *Latin American Research Review* 22, no. 3: 7–36.

Iglesias-Prieto, Norma. 1997. *Beautiful Flowers of the Maquiladora: Life Histories of Women Workers in Tijuana*. Austin, TX: University of Texas Press. Originally published in 1985 as *La flor más bella de la maquiladora*.

James, Daniel. 2000. *Dona Maria's Story: Life History, Memory, and Political Identity*. Durham: Duke University Press.

Jenkins, Rhys. 2015. "Is Chinese Competition Causing Deindustrialization in Brazil?" *Latin American Perspectives* 42, no. 6: 42–63.

Jenkins, Rhys, and Alexandre de Freitas Barbosa. 2012. "Fear for Manufacturing? China and the Future of Industry in Brazil and Latin America." *The China Quarterly* 209, 59–81.

Kabat, Marina. 2011. "Argentinean Worker-Taken Factories: Trajectories of Workers' Control under the Economic Crisis." In *Ours to Master and Own: Workers' Control from the Commune to the Present*, eds. Immanuel Ness and Dario Azzellini, 365–81. Chicago, IL: Haymarket Books.

Kanai, Miguel, and Iliana Ortega-Alcazar. 2009. "The Prospects for Progressive Culture-Led Urban Regeneration in Latin America: Cases from Mexico City and Buenos Aires." *International Journal of Urban and Regional Research* 33, no. 2: 483–501.

Kim, Chong-Sup, and Seungho Lee. 2014. "Different Paths of Deindustrialization: Latin American and Southeast Asian Countries from a Comparative Perspective." *Journal of International and Area Studies* 21, no. 2: 65–81.

Laxer, James, and Robert Laxer. 1973. *The Liberal Idea of Canada: Pierre Trudeau and the Question of Canada's Survival*. Toronto: James Lorimer & Company.

Lynd, Staughton. 1982. *The Fight against Shutdowns: Youngstown's Steel Mill Closings*. San Pedro: Singlejack Books.

Mah, Alice. 2012. *Industrial Ruination, Community, and Place: Landscapes and Legacies of Urban Decline*. Toronto: University of Toronto Press.

Malone, Noreen. 2011. "The Case against Economic Disaster Porn." *New Republic*. https://newrepublic.com/article/81954/detroit-economic-disaster-porn

Martin, Lou. 2016. *Smokestacks in the Hills: Rural-Industrial Workers in West Virginia*. Chicago, IL and Urbana: University of Illinois Press.

Neumann, Tracy. 2016. *Remaking the Rust Belt: The Postindustrial Transformation of North America*. Philadelphia, PA: University of Pennsylvania Press.

O'Hara, Paul. 2011. *Gary: The Most American of All American Cities*. Bloomington, IN and Indianapolis, IN: Indiana University Press.

Ranis, Peter. 2005. "Argentina's Worker-Occupied Factories and Enterprises." *Socialism and Democracy* 19, no. 3: 1–23.

Rodrik, Dani. 2016. "Premature Deindustrialization." *Journal of Economic Growth* 21, no. 1: 1–33.
Strangleman, Tim. 2013. "'Smokestack Nostalgia,' 'Ruin Porn' or Working-Class Obituary: The Role and Meaning of Deindustrial Representation." *International Labor and Working-Class History* 84, 23–37.
Trindade, Jose Raimundo, Paul Cooney, and Wesley Pereira de Oliveira. 2016. "Industrial Trajectory and Economic Development: Dilemma of the Re-primarization of the Brazilian Economy." *Review of Radical Political Economists* 48, no. 2, 269–86.
Zukin, Sharon. 1982. *Loft Living: Culture and Capital in Urban Change.* New Brunswick, NJ: Rutgers University Press.

6
DEVELOPMENT

Karin Fischer

"Development" in the modern sense implies the intentional intervention in collective affairs, most often, but not exclusively, by state agencies, according to a standard of improvement. What constitutes an appropriate intervention and how development, as the desirable goal of intervention, is defined, varies over time and space, and according to ideology, culture, and relations of power. Development theory is the negotiation of these issues (Nederveen Pieterse 2010, 3–4).

Following the definition of Nederveen Pieterse, the end of World War II can be taken as a starting point. At that time, "development" emerged as a hemispheric program of the U.S. that involved ideas of social change, and actions to transform the "underdeveloped" people and countries to the south (→ Modernization, I/35). Starting with the Truman era, the main currents of development thinking can be considered anchor points. Modernization theory, the dependency school, the Washington Consensus, and new approaches from the south, all correspond with development periods, during which thoughts and thinkers, the transfer of ideas, and concrete practices were introduced.

Post-war development disputes in Inter-American relations

Development became a worldwide program after the end of World War II, and the United States was at the forefront to define it. The inaugural address of re-elected U.S. president Harry S. Truman (1949) was seminal in this respect. Backed by the internationalists in his administration and in Congress, he proclaimed that the U.S. "must embark on a bold new program for making the benefits of our scientific advances and industrial progress available for the improvement and growth of underdeveloped areas." He offered modern scientific and technical knowledge, because "the material resources which we can afford to use for assistance of other peoples are limited."

In fact, the U.S. did make great funds available, however Latin America remained largely excluded in the immediate post-war period. The U.S. canceled their supply contracts for ores and other strategic raw materials. Latin American exports to the U.S. collapsed. Financial aid almost ceased until the early 1950s, and the same was true for government and private investments, with some exceptions in Mexico and Venezuela. Even after Truman's speech in 1949, economic aid, public and private, as well as military assistance, were channeled to other world regions, mainly to Western European countries, Iran, Korea, and the Philippines. For example, between 1945 and 1960, the Philippines alone obtained more grants than all Latin American countries combined (Niess 1984, 229). Behind this "benign neglect" – as it is often referred to, rather misleadingly – stood a deep conflict between U.S. American and Latin American development planners over economic policies and development strategies (Thorp 1995, 131–135).

The U.S. was above all interested in agricultural and mineral imports. At the same time, and in contrast to their official promotion of free trade, the U.S. foreclosed its market for manufactured goods from the south. Meanwhile, Latin Americans had completely different aspirations. They aimed at building up and diversifying their own industrial facilities, gaining better control of foreign investment flows, and establishing mechanisms to stabilize the world market price for their raw materials. They strongly criticized the U.S. policy of "free trade abroad, protectionism at home." One of the strongest critics of the U.S. dominated, world economic order in general, and the economic policy towards Latin America in particular, was Raúl Prebisch, the second Executive Secretary of the United Nations Economic Commission for Latin America (and the Caribbean) (ECLA, later ECLAC), created in 1948 (FitzGerald 2000).

The political swing began at the end of the Eisenhower administration. With the Cuban Revolution and the alarming anti-Americanism in its "backyard" (→ Revolution, II/44), the U.S. embarked on the "hemispheric crusade for economic development" that foreshadowed the Alliance for Progress (Eisenhower 1960). They felt like Latin America was the place where the United States could lose the Cold War:

> The fate of the world will not be decided in Europe nor in Asia nor in Africa … If Latin America is conquered by totalitarianism, the West is lost. If, on the contrary, victory is gained here, the fate of communism is sealed.
>
> *(Ravines 1965, 136)*

Development as modernization

The intellectual fulcrum of the Alliance for Progress (1961–1971; 1974) was modernization theory. Modernization theories gave the Kennedy team supreme confidence that the United States had found the key to solve the problems of Third World development and win the Cold War (→ Modernization, I/35), by weakening the revolutionary potential (Hickman 2013, 11–12) . It became the basis of the "informal empire" that the U.S. built during the Cold War with the Global South (Ekbladh 2010). For Latham (2000, 6, 53–68), modernization theory and practice constitutes, thus, a reformulation of the Manifest Destiny, and imperialism in more inclusive terms. It clearly bears notions of Western superiority (Guevara et al. 2006, 9). At the same time, modernization was not just "a political instrument" or "a rhetorical tool" to push through U.S. interests in the region. It was, as Latham explains, a "cognitive framework" through which U.S. intellectuals and foreign policy elites interpreted the country's own history and its role in the world. It was, in other words, crucial to U.S. American thinking about both itself and the rest of the world (→ Geopolitics, II/34).

Modernization theorists were convinced that individual economies and societies differ from one another only in the extent and speed of their progress, away from the traditional and into modernity. Schooled in evolutionary and functionalist theory, they used the ideal–typical construction of "traditional" and "modern" development, and conceptualized development as a series of transitions from one stage to the other. In their view, nations travel along a pre-determined track of development, mapped out for them by the forerunners. The measures to be taken to become modern were derived from the United States' own historic experiences of "backwardness," and how it was overcome both after the Civil War and during the Great Depression: through social engineering, comprehensive planning, and state-led infrastructure initiatives (Ekbladh 2010, see Chapters 1 and 2).

The policy prescriptions to transform primitive, subsistence economies into technology-intensive, industrialized economies varied. The economic backwardness theorists recommended a big push of investment (Rosenstein-Rodan 1943), balanced or unbalanced growth (Nurkse 1953; Hirschman 1958), a critical minimum investment effort (Leibenstein 1957), or a takeoff into sustained growth (Rostow 1956). They agreed that it was *American* technical knowledge, capital, and advice which lead to greater production. Political and sociological modernization theorists advised the "westernization" of political structures, values, and habits. Lipset (1960) stated that economic prosperity makes democracy (→ II/32) work, and that, vice versa, democracy favors economic growth. For psychosocial theorists, education (→ I/24), urbanization (→ I/46), and mass media (→ Media Flows, III/35), replace ascriptive status systems, extended kinship units and religious ideologies, and make people either empathic, innovative, and adaptive (Lerner 1958), or competitive and open to new experiences (Inkeles 1966) (→ Biopolitics, I/22).

The modernization theorists were part of the international behavioralist movement in the social sciences which started in the U.S. and penetrated disciplines and academic cultures in other parts of the world (Robin 2001). They were obsessed with "objective" and verifiable results, and made development a quantifiable task. The set of methods included modeling and statistics. Development progress became a number; history, power relations, and normative orders were neglected. One example of this is Gabriel Almond's notion that modernization theory is "governed by professional criteria of evidence and inference." Its critics are denounced as "mere propagandists" (Almond in Wiener and Huntington 1987, 444–468, cited in Leys 1996, 6). The scientification of the social strengthened not only the power of experts, but also the belief that one development model fits all (Latham 2000). Key players in the knowledge/power regime were the Department of Social Relations (DSR) at Harvard University, the Social Science Research Council's Committee on Comparative Politics (CCP), and the MIT Center for International Studies (CIS), where Rostow worked. The formerly very well-funded institutions were all dissolved in the early 1970s when the post-war modernist optimism crumbled (Gilman 2004, Chapters 3, 4 and 5).

A preferred site for the transfer of Western ideas and practices were peasant communities. The aim was for these communities to be "freed" from traditional living, familiarized with modern technology, and immunized against radical socialist or indigenous ideas (→ Indigeneity, I/31). One such example of "guided social change" was the Cornell-Peru Project (Pribilsky 2009). Between 1952 and 1966, the Department of Sociology and Anthropology at Cornell University assumed responsibility for a *hacienda* in the Andean Highlands of Peru. Financed by the U.S. government and a number of foundations, the *hacienda* became a huge research laboratory with 2,250 indigenous people as research subjects. The main goal of the project was, among others, to convince the community to turn to Western biomedicine instead of native healers, and to use DDT to get rid of insect-borne diseases and fertilizers to improve potato yield. Many of the programs of "planned intervention" later fell under Peruvian developmental state agencies, but researchers and advisers "maintained a vested interest in demonstrating a model of conservative land reform that would rival Soviet development" (Pribilsky 2009, 418).

An economic field of action was the transfer of U.S. know-how in the practice of regional planning. The so-called "TVA model" (which stands for Tennessee Valley Authority, Ekbladh 2002), established during the New Deal, is associated with dam building to generate hydropower and management programs. Regional development of the type promoted by the Tennessee Valley Authority became "a favorite technique in the transnational world of modernization" and the dam "both a tool of modernization and the quintessential symbol of modernity" (Bamba 2010, 67). The influence of the TVA model finds its expression in the creation of the Venezuelan Guayana Development Corporation, the Superintendency of the San Francisco River Valley in Brazil, and the Federal Commissions of the Principal River Basins in Mexico (Boisier 1979, see also Hirschman 1967).

The transfer of an American-orchestrated development from above failed, and the promise of catching-up remained unfulfilled, although the modernizing elites in Latin America undertook massive efforts toward import-substituting industrialization. It was then that the radical critics of the still dominant modernization paradigm started their intellectual journey, this time in the opposite direction, emanating from Latin America and traveling up to the north.

Development as dependency

The dependency school, Latin America and the Third World in general's first and distinctive contribution to the field of development studies, challenged the basic assumptions of the modernization paradigm. This contribution being made by theorists from Latin America was not by chance. The continent had enjoyed formal independence for a century, but had not progressed along the development path predicted by modernization theorists.

The analysis of dependency was rooted in the work of early Marxist thinkers of the region, like José Carlos Mariátegui, and critics of ECLA-Keynesianism (→ Socialism, I/42). With the exhaustion of the import-substituting industrialization process, including in the most advanced countries of Latin America, Celso Furtado (1964) and a group of younger economists began to theorize the underlying causes of why domestic industrialization of the periphery was hampered. Over the course of the 1960s, this way of thinking made itself heard within the UN Economic Commission of Latin America, in universities, and finally, in academic communities abroad.

The diffusion of radical critique was shaped by the social movements (→ I/41) and anti-capitalist struggles of the time, both globally and on the continent. In such a context, analysis of dependency corresponded to the "search for new models of explanation, not only in order to comprehend what is happening in Latin America, but also what is happening in the U.S." (Cardoso 1977, 17). Additionally, the anti-revolutionary military regimes which seized power in some Latin American countries (→ Authoritarianism, II/25; Military, II/37), prompted left-wing intellectuals to consider more radical strategies, in order to overcome the systems of domination.

The dependency school shared essential aspects of the modernization paradigm, including the thought that development is an important goal to reach, the focus of which should be on economic growth and state intervention. The *dependentistas*, however, inverted many of the ontological assumptions of modernization theory. Instead of linear thinking toward progress, the neo-Marxist thinkers conceptualized *capitalist* development (→ Capitalism, II/2), and there was nothing else but capitalist development, as uneven. They historicized both development and underdevelopment, and stressed the exploitative and distortive character of capitalist conquest. "Underdevelopment" was neither a country's original state, nor a reflection of its own characteristics. Instead, "underdevelopment is in large part the historical product of past and continuing economic and other relations between the satellite underdeveloped and the now developed metropolitan countries" (Frank 1969, 4).

Dependency theorists predictably questioned the moral teleology of the development project as predicted by modernization theorists and practitioners. In their view, the incorporation of the periphery in the capitalist mode of production made things worse instead of better. Therefore, economic and social development cannot happen through exchange between metropoles and satellites, it can "occur only independently of most of these relations of diffusion" (Frank 1969, 4). On the other hand, Cardoso and Faletto (1979) coined the term associated-dependent development. They argued that capitalist development (economic growth) is possible, but creates an authoritarian and upper-class oriented type of market and society (→ Social Inequality, II/20), based on the alliance between domestic bourgeoisie and foreign capital (on "dependent" or "peripheral capitalism" see Marini 1965). What they had in common was the endeavor to theorize the specific nature of dependent economies.

With regard to the "distorted character" of colonized societies (→ Colonial Rule, I/5), they identified internal political alliances (→ Clientelism, II/29), ideologies, and class structures. They arrived at concepts like structural heterogeneity (Furtado 1964; Pinto 1965; Cardoso and Faletto 1979), marginality (Quijano 1974), and internal colonialism (González-Casanova 1965). Another concept was that of the lumpenbourgeoisie, which lacks, in alliance with foreign capital, the capacity to lead processes of any form of development with greater equity for the popular classes (Frank 1969; similarly but under a different name, see Cardoso and Faletto 1979). The concept of internal colonialism became popular during the U.S. Civil Rights Movement (→ Race, I/39). Addressing the racial division of labor, U.S. theorists characterized African Americans as the internal colony of the United States, and identified them with the exploited masses of the Third World (Dey 2014).

The Marxist journal, *Monthly Review,* played an important role in the transfer of ideas to the United States. It translated and published articles by Frank, Marini, and Quijano. Meanwhile, the work of Paul A. Baran and Paul M. Sweezy, founder of the journal, on "Monopoly Capital" (1966), influenced the dependency theorists. Although Cardoso stated that it "did not reveal anything not already present in the perspective of critical Latin American thought before 1960" (Cardoso 1977, 9), he himself acknowledged Sweezy's interpretation of multinational corporations as "quasi-self-sufficient units of decision and action" (Cardoso 1972, 87) (→ Transnational Corporations, II/23).

Since the early 1970s, disseminating involved reviews, articles, and edited volumes by critical U.S. academics, from Marxist thinkers like *Monthly Review* co-editor Harry Magdoff, to Ronald H. Chilcote, who was radicalized during his fieldwork on U.S. business in Guatemala and Chile (see, for example, Magdoff 1969; Bodenheimer 1971; Chilcote 1974; Kahl 1976). Dependency acquired a specific local approach in the United States. The studies with U.S. origin were (politically) preoccupied with the colonial forms of U.S. foreign aid, CIA interventions, and the practice of U.S. multinationals (→ Interventionism, II36). The reception of the dependency school was confined to left-wing thought collectives; with a few exceptions, mainstream academic journals and discourse could not be reached.

"Development" remained a point of reference for the dependency theorists, but should occur in favor of the subordinated classes. The critical reflection of import-substituting industrialization and its urban bias drew their attention to the agrarian question. Development strategies revolved around food security, basic needs, south-to-south cooperation under the name "collective self-reliance," endogenous development, a temporary delinking from the world market, and concepts of revolutionary strategy (→ Revolution, II/44). However, these visions did not become a reality. Rather, with the neoliberal turn in the 1980s, opposing ideas which did not originate in the region conquered the political stage.

Structural adjustment instead of development: a Washington-based consensus for Latin America

While the 1970s was the decade of the dependency school, the political situation moved in quite a different direction at the beginning of the 1980s (Palma 2009). The debt crisis and power shifts at the international level, and in the U.S. in particular, drove indebted countries to accept neoliberal policy prescriptions in exchange for new loans (→ Neoliberalism, II/16). Conditional lending was not a new concept. Balance of payment issues had already taken Latin American countries to the International Monetary Fund during the 1950s and 1960s, for lack of alternative sources of credit. Yet it was not until the international debt crisis that the International Monetary Fund (IMF) and the World Bank became, with the full support of the Reagan administration, the global authorities of intervention (→ Crisis, II/4). Painful structural adjustment programs were clearly directed toward developing and emerging countries in the Global South, first and foremost in Latin America.

An early bastion of neoliberal development economists was the U.S. National Bureau of Economic Research (NBER) (Fischer 2016). Since the early 1970s, NBER scholars like Jagdish Bhagwati, T. N. Srinivasan, and Anne Krueger had conducted numerous case studies on developing countries to prove that state-led development and import substitution only produces inefficiency and corruption. All soon entered top positions in the World Bank's research department. They first designed the austerity programs which were built on restrictive demand policies, and a radical cutting of public expenditures. In the second stage, the liberalization of trade, finance, and labor markets were to pave the way for an export-led development strategy based on comparative advantages. In their view, "economic principles" like rationality and maximizing own benefits were universals. Hence, there was no need for a specific development theory or model for developing countries. Once the distorting influence of the state was removed (→ Nation State, II/38), it was assumed that the economies would prosper (Balassa 1971; Krueger 1974; Lal 1983).

John Williamson (1990) later coined the term "Washington Consensus" for the neoliberal reform agenda, thereby expressing that it was basically a consensus between Washington-based institutions: the U.S. government, partisan think tanks, and the headquarters of the World Bank and IMF. Nevertheless, a simple outside-in perspective was misleading, as neoliberalism found its way to Latin America through different routes.

At an early stage, and with the help of U.S. foundations, Latin American scholars and business professionals engaged in the founding of neoliberal think tanks. Based in Mexico, Guatemala, Argentina, and Brazil, for example, they introduced neoliberal perspectives, and fought against the post-war development paradigm of import substitution and "statism" (Fischer and Plehwe 2013).

In the 1970s, the military dictatorships of the Southern Cone responded to the economic crisis and social polarization through repressive neoliberal adjustment. From these early cases, only Chile's path to neoliberalism turned out to be durable. The roots of the "success" can be traced back to the mid-1950s when an alliance was struck between the economic faculty of the Catholic University of Santiago and its counterpart at the University of Chicago. The so-called "Project Chile" was conceived as part of Truman's Point Four Program of technical assistance and economic aid to "underdeveloped" countries. The civil cadre that was nominated for high political offices after the coup d'état in 1973, had been trained through the exchange program (Fischer 2009, 309–310).

The transfer of neoliberal ideas to Chile was part of a larger attempt to influence the intellectual climate, economic thinking, and curricula in Latin America. Funded by U.S. universities and foundations, hundreds of Latin American economists received their training in the U.S. After returning to their home countries, they occupied key positions in universities, in the private sector, and within state agencies. In this way, they became important "bridgeheads" for the diffusion and implementation of an ideology of transnational academic and policy circles which was emanating from the United States. The U.S.-trained local "political technocracy," including high officials in the central bank, the treasury, and Ministry of Economy, also facilitated the neoliberal transformation of the 1980s and 1990s. They negotiated the adjustment packages and new loans with the World Bank and IMF staff. In the so-called "policy dialogues," agreements could be reached relatively easily as they had a common base of consensual knowledge and spoke the same language (Teichman 2001).

Today, the neoliberal thought collective throughout the American continent, can rely on a robust organizational infrastructure, such as transcontinental think tank networks. Among the largest are the Virginia based Atlas Network, and the Hispanic American Center for Economic Research headquartered in Washington D.C. Under their umbrella, nearly one hundred think tanks in Latin America perform different tasks such as research, policy advice, campaigning, and dissemination. While the transfer of funds goes from north to south, personnel, ideas, and writings of Latin American neoliberals make their way north. Hernando de Soto, Peruvian economist and think tanker, for example, convinced not only former President Fujimori of his anti-poverty ideas, but also world bankers and politicians in the U.S. His solution was to restructure the legal system to enable proper titling of (informal) properties and businesses, which could then be leveraged and traded, thereby "freeing" the value of the working poor's assets (De Soto 2000).

In the 1990s, poor economic results, currency crises, and popular protest, subsequently led to a revision of the Washington Consensus by its original advocates. The so-called post-Washington Consensus claimed to be more sensitive to social concerns and institutional issues, without deviating from its core beliefs of fiscal discipline, free trade, and private enterprise (Kuczynski and Williamson 2003). Seminal in this respect is the report of two Washington-based think tanks, the Carnegie Endowment for International Peace and the Inter-American Dialogue (→ Pan-Americanism, II/40). They present a "toolkit for equity with growth" which includes social safety nets, workers' rights, and progressive tax reforms (→ Taxation, II/22) (Birdsall and de la Torre 2001, 10–14).

Contemporary developments in development thinking: innovations from the South

Over the course of the 1990s, neoliberalism lost its legitimacy in the eyes of the general public. Social movements (→ I/41) and popular vote, from the bottom up to the middle classes, led to the ascent of center-left or progressive governments since the end of the decade. The reduction of inequality was taken seriously, and the developmental state experienced a renaissance.

Latin American scholars and activists were again at the forefront when it came to developing alternatives to neoliberalism (→ II/16). A philosophical and ethical-political contribution stemmed from indigenous movements (→ Indigeneity, I/31) and organic intellectuals (Gudynas 2011). The concept of *sumak kawsay* or *buen vivir* (living well or collective well-being) is community-centric and embraces a broad notion of well-being in cohabitation with others, and in harmony with nature. *Buen vivir* disciples latch on to former Latin American critics of development such as Arturo Escobar (1995) or Gustavo Esteva (1992, 9) who condemned development as an instrument of domination, "robbing peoples of different cultures of the opportunity to define the forms of their social life." *Buen vivir* presents a radical alternative to development: a new paradigm of social and ecological commons based on a "bio-civilization." Although deeply rooted in indigenous (Andean) knowledge, the vision of collective well-being receives a lot of scholarly attention, and even Marxists join in the debate (see Boron 2013 for a socialist version of *buen vivir*). In the U.S. the debate connects to degrowth and deep ecology movements (→ Environmental Justice, II/8).

With the election of presidents from the political right throughout the Americas during the last couple of years (Macri in Argentine in 2015, Trump in the USA in 2016, Piñera in Chile and Bolsonaro in Brazil in 2018) the wave of center-left governments in the hemisphere came to an end, which will have an impact on the design of development policies in the region advocating for the extension of neoliberalism.

> [The] contrasting political, social and economics projects being implemented in the name of development, more often than not with despairing results, discussions of ideas of development hold a particular sense of urgency in Latin America, one that has given birth to particularly fertile forms of critical development thinking.
>
> *(Carballo 2014, 6, 7)*

For over a decade, the search for post-neoliberal strategies has made Latin America the center of attention for critical development studies. This debate continues to this day, and will likely continue, with a new sense of urgency.

Works cited

Balassa, Bela. 1971. *The Structure of Protection in Developing Countries*. Baltimore: Johns Hopkins University Press.

Bamba, Abou B. 2010. "Triangulating a Modernization Experiment: The United States, France, and the Making of the Kossou Project in Central Ivory Coast." *Journal of Modern European History* 8, no. 1: 66–84.

Baran, Paul A., and Paul M. Sweezy. 1966. *Monopoly Capital. An Essay on the American Economic and Social Order*. New York and London: Monthly Review Press.

Birdsall, Nancy, and Augusto de la Torre. 2001. "Washington Contentious: Economic Policies for Social Equity in Latin America." *Carnegie Endowment for International Peace and Inter-American Dialogue*. http://carnegieendowment.org/pdf/files/er.Contentious.pdf.

Bodenheimer, Susanne. 1971. "Dependency and Imperialism: The Roots of Latin American Underdevelopment." *Politics & Society* 1, no. 3: 327–357.

Boisier, Sergio. 1979. "Regional planning: what can we do before midnight strikes?" *Cepal Review* 7: 133–165.

Boron, Atilio. 2013. *América Latina en la geopolítica del imperialismo*. Bilbao: Hiru Argitaletxea.

Carballo, Ana Estefanía. 2014. "The Opportunity of Latin American Critical Development Thinking." *Alternautas* 1, no. 1: 6–16.

Cardoso, Fernando Henrique. 1972. "Dependency and Development in Latin America." *New Left Review* I, no. 7: 83–95.

———. 1977. "The Consumption of Dependency Theory in the United States." *Latin American Research Review* 12, no. 3: 7–24.

Cardoso, Fernando Henrique, and Enzo Faletto. 1979. *Dependency and Development in Latin America.* Berkeley, Los Angeles and London: University of California Press.

Chilcote, Ronald H. 1974. "A Critical Synthesis of the Dependency Literature." *Latin American Perspectives* I, no. 1: 4–29.

De Soto, Hernando. 2000. *The Mystery of Capital: Why Capitalism Triumphs in the West and Fails Everywhere Else.* New York: Basic Books.

Dey, Dipanker. 2014. "Internal Colonialism." In: *The Encyclopedia of Political Thought*, ed. Michael T. Gibbons, Chichester, UK and Malden USA: Wiley Blackwell. http://ssrn.com/abstract=2562327.

Eisenhower, Dwight D. 1960. "Joint Statement of the President and President Kubitschek of Brazil." *The American Presidency Project.* www.presidency.ucsb.edu/ws/?pid=12105.

Ekbladh, David. 2002. "'Mr. TVA': Grass-Roots Development, David Lilienthal, and the Rise of the Tennessee Valley Authority as a Symbol for U.S. Overseas Development, 1933–1973." *Diplomatic History* 26, no. 3: 335–374.

———. 2010. *The Great American Mission: Modernization and the Construction of an American World Order.* Princeton: Princeton University Press.

Escobar, Arturo. 1995. *Encountering Development: The Making and Unmaking of the Third World.* Princeton: Princeton University Press.

Esteva, Gustavo. 1992. "Development." In: *The Development Dictionary: A Guide to Knowledge as Power*, ed. Wolfgang Sachs, 6–25. London: Zed Books.

Fischer, Karin. 2009. "The Influence of Neoliberals in Chile Before, During, and After Pinochet." In: *The Road from Mont Pèlerin. The Making of the Neoliberal Thought Collective*, eds. Phil Mirowski and Dieter Plehwe, 305–346. Cambridge and London: Harvard University Press.

———. 2016. "Entwicklung im Neoliberalismus." In: *Handbuch Entwicklungsforschung*, eds. Karin Fischer, Gerhard Hauck, and Manuela Boatcă, 79–90. Wiesbaden: Springer.

Fischer, Karin, and Dieter Plehwe. 2013. "The 'Pink Tide′ and Neoliberal Civil Society Formation: Think Tank Networks in Latin America." *State of Nature.* www.stateofnature.org/?p=6601.

FitzGerald, E. V. K. 2000. "ECLA and the Theory of Import Substituting Industrialization in Latin America." In: *An Economic History of Twentieth-Century Latin-America.* Vol. 3. *Industrialization and the State in Latin America*, eds. Enrique Cárdenas, José Antonio Ocampo, and Rosemary Thorp, 58–97. Oxford: Macmillan-Volumes.

Frank, Andre Gunder. 1969. "The Development of Underdevelopment." In: *Underdevelopment or Revolution*, ed. Andre Gunder Frank, 3–17. New York and London: Monthly Review Press.

Furtado, Celso. 1964. *Development and Underdevelopment.* Berkeley, Los Angeles and London: University of California Press.

Gilman, Nils. 2004. *Mandarins of the Future: Modernization Theory in Cold War America.* Baltimore, MD: Johns Hopkins University Press.

———. 2005. "Off the Beach: The United States, Latin America, and the Cold War." In: *A Companion to Post-1945 America*, eds. Jean-Christophe Agnew and Roy Rosenzweig, 426–445. New York: Wiley-Blackwell.

González-Casanova, Pablo. 1965. "Internal Colonialism and National Development." *Studies in Comparative International Development* 1, no. 4: 27–37.

Gudynas, Eduardo. 2011. "Buen Vivir: Today's Tomorrow." Development 54, no. 4: 441–447.

Guevara, Ernesto, María del Carmen Ariet, and Javier Salado. 2006. *Our America and Theirs: Kennedy and the Alliance for Progress: The Debate at Punto del Este. Speeches and Interviews by Ernesto Che Guevara.* Melbourne and New York: Ocean Press.

Hickman, Christopher. 2013. "The Kennedy Administration's Alliance for Progress and the Burdens of the Marshall Plan." *Federal History* 13: 75–98.

Hirschman, Albert O. 1958. *The Strategy of Economic Development.* New Haven: Yale University Press.

———. 1967. *Development Projects Observed.* Washington, DC: Brookings Institution.

Inkeles, Alex. 1966. *The Modernization of Man.* Cambridge, MA: Center of International Affairs, Harvard University.

Kahl, Joseph A. 1976. *Modernization, Exploitation, and Dependency in Latin America: Germani, Gonzalez Casanova, and Cardoso.* New Brunswick, NJ: Transaction Books.

Krueger, Ann O. 1974. "The Political Economy of Rent-Seeking Society." *American Economic Review* 64, no. 3: 291–302.

Kuczynski, Pedro-Pablo, and John Williamson. 2003. *After the Washington Consensus: Restarting Growth and Reform in Latin America.* Washington, DC: Institute for International Economics.

Lal, Deepak. 1983. *The Poverty of "Development Economics."* London: Institute of Economic Affairs.

Latham, Michael E. 2000. *Modernization as Ideology: American Social Science and "Nation Building" in the Kennedy Era.* Chapel Hill: University of North Carolina Press.

Leibenstein, Harvey. 1957. *Economic Backwardness and Economic Growth.* New York: John Wiley.

Lerner, Daniel. 1958. *The Passing of Traditional Society: Modernizing the Middle East.* New York: Free Press.

Leys, Colin. 1996. *The Rise and Fall of Development Theory.* London: Currey.

Lipset, Seymore Martin. 1960. *Political Man: The Social Bases of Politics.* Garden City, NY: Doubleday.

Magdoff, Harry. 1969. *The Age of Imperialism: The Economics of U.S. Foreign Policy.* New York: Monthly Review Press.

Marini, Ruy Mauro. 1965. "Brazilian 'Interdependence' and Imperialist Integration." *Monthly Review* 17, no. 7: 10–29.

Nederveen Pieterse, Jan. 2010. *Development Theory: Deconstructions/Reconstructions.* 2nd ed. London etc.: Sage.

Niess, Frank. 1984. *Der Koloss im Norden. Geschichte der Lateinamerikapolitik der USA.* Köln: Pahl-Rugenstein.

Nurkse, Ragnar. 1953. *Problems of Capital Formation in Underdeveloped Countries.* New York: Oxford University Press.

Palma, José Gabriel. 2009. "Why Did the Latin American Critical Tradition in the Social Sciences Become Practically Extinct? From Structural Adjustment to Ideological Adjustment." In: *The Handbook of International Political Economy*, ed. Mark Blyth, 243–265. New York: Routledge.

Pinto, Anibal. 1965. "Concentración del p"rogreso técnico y de sus frutos en el desarrollo de América Latina." *El Trimestre Económico* 32, no. 125: 3–69.

Pribilsky, Jason. 2009. "Development and the 'Indian Problem' in the Cold War Andes: *Indigenismo*, Science, and Modernization in the Making of the Cornell-Peru Project at Vicos." *Diplomatic History* 33, no. 3: 405–426.

Quijano, Anibal. 1974. "The Marginal Pole and Marginal Labor Force in Latin America." *Economy and Society* 3, no. 4: 393–428.

Ravines, Eudocio. 1965. "Ideology, Intellectuals and the Security of the Hemisphere." In: *Latin America. Polictics, Economics and Hemispheric Security*, ed. Norman A. Bailey, 115–140. New York etc.: Frederick A. Praeger for the Center for Strategic Studies.

Robin, Ron. 2001. *The Making of the Cold War Enemy.* Princeton: Princeton University Press.

Rosenstein-Rodan, Paul N. 1943. "Problems of Industrialisation of Eastern and South Eastern Europe." *The Economic Journal* 53, no. 210/211: 202–211.

Rostow, Walt W. 1956. "The Take-off Into Self-Sustained Growth." *The Economic Journal* 66, no. 261: 25–48.

Teichman, Judith A. 2001. *The Politics of Freeing Markets in Latin America: Chile, Argentina, and Mexico.* Chapel Hill, NC and London: The University of North Carolina Press.

Thorp, Rosemary. 1995. "The Latin American economies: 1939–c.1950." In: *The Cambridge History of Latin America, Vol. 6, 1930 to the Present, Part 1: Economy and Society*, ed. Leslie Bethell, 117–158. Cambridge: Cambridge University Press.

Truman, Harry S. 1949. Truman's Inaugural Address, January 20, 1949. www.trumanlibrary.org/whistle stop/50yr_archive/inagural20jan1949.htm.

Williamson, John. 1990. "What Washington Means by Policy Reform." In: *Latin American Adjustment: How Much Has Happened?*, ed. John Williamson, 5–20. Washington, DC: Institute for International Economics.

7
ENERGY

Maria Backhouse, Anne Tittor, and Fabricio Rodríguez

For thousands of years, human beings have extracted energy for food, transport and processing from solar-based biomass (wood, crops, fibers, etc.), wind, water as well as animal and human muscles. With the emergence of global capitalism (→ II/2), the energy basis of modern societies has undergone a deep transition toward fossil energy – coal, gas, and oil (Moore 2003; Altvater 2006; Mitchell 2011). In 2015, global energy consumption was twenty-five-times greater than in 1800, with fossil fuels contributing the largest share of this exponential expansion (Ritchie and Roser 2018). In 1800, biomass (mainly wood) was the world's main source of energy. Coal came to deliver half of the world's energy demand by 1900, while oil and natural gas have complemented the expansion of fossil fuels since the mid-20th century (Ibid.). In 2015, these three fossil energy sources accounted for 86 percent of the world's total level of primary energy consumption (WEC 2016, 4).

This energy transformation has taken different forms, entangling several regions and histories, causing climate change and producing durable global inequalities. The industrialized Western countries in Europe and North America have become the center of the world economy concentrating and dominating the global flow of fossil energy. Meanwhile, since its colonization (→ Conquest and Colonization, I/7), Latin America has kept its peripheral or semi-peripheral position in the global economy (→ Global Commodity Chains, II/12) – either by relying on the import of, or by becoming increasingly dependent on the export of fossil resources at volatile prices. Generally, the use of energy-related materials is very dominant. According to Haas et al. (2015), the consumption of energy requires almost half of the processed materials flowing into the global economy (c.f. Martinez-Alier 2016, 468). However, the consumption of energy – in all of its forms – is unequally distributed: In 2015, North America was responsible for 21.3 percent of all the energy consumed in the world, with the U.S. accounting for 17.3 percent, Canada for 2.5 percent, and Mexico for 1.4 percent. By contrast, Central and South America accounted for only 5.3 percent of the global share in primary energy consumption (BP 2016, 40).

Until today, many social conflicts all over the Americas are connected to energy. Who is a producer of energy in which territory, and under which conditions, how energy is distributed or exported within the respective country, and who appropriates the benefits are contested questions. This entry takes the political-economic perspective of Political Ecology to explore the issue of "energy" while discussing how the specific materialities of distinct kinds of energy are deeply articulated with societal power relations. It takes a historical perspective and sketches out seven snapshots of different entanglements of unequal energy relations within and beyond the Americas. To conclude, it points at the challenges entailed in the transformation of the dominant energy system via renewable energies.

The concept of energy and its origins from the perspective of political ecology

Etymologically the word "energy" is a Greek compound of *ev* (in) and *ergon* (work or activity), that was probably invented by Aristotle (Smil 2008, 2). He gave the concept "energeia" a kinetic meaning as he stated that every object's existence is maintained by energy. In this view, energy signifies motion, action, work, change. Over nearly two millennia, "energy" was a philosophical generalization, which lacked any serious intent of conceptual redefinition. Yet, the energetic challenges of everyday life led different societies to develop a wide range of technologies. Not only humans and animals, but also machines driven by water and wind contributed to the energizing of societies. The concept of energy, as it is widely understood today, originated in Europe and dates back to the 19th century. As Smil puts it,

> [e]nergy is not a single, easily definable entity, but rather an abstract collective concept, adopted by nineteenth century physicists to cover a variety of natural and anthropogenic (generated by humans) phenomena. Its most commonly encountered forms are heat (thermal energy), motion (kinetic or mechanical energy), light (electromagnetic energy) and the chemical energy of fuels and foodstuffs.
>
> *(Smil 2006, 8–9)*

This abstract concept of energy is part and product of European modernity (→ Enlightenment, I/8; Modernization, I/35). European physicists discovered the idea of metabolism, the equivalence of heat and mechanical energy, and the laws of thermodynamics. Later on, Rudolf Julius Emanuel Clausis deployed the idea of entropy, stating that the energy level of a closed system can only decline, while Albert Einstein formulated the idea that mass is a form of energy. The development of the concept of "energy" is linked to the emergence of capitalism (→ II/2) in Europe. This epochal shift – also called the Industrial Revolution – comprised a transition away from the prime movers, mainly people and animals, to the deployment of inanimate powers, especially coal and oil (Smil 2008, 55).

From the perspective of Political Ecology, the above-discussed definitions of energy are only one part of the story. "Like many other modern abstractions such as 'resource,' 'nature,' 'development,' … and 'education'" (Lohmann and Hildyard 2014, 25), the concept of "energy" is not a politically neutral construction (→ Nature, II/39; Development, II/6; Education, I/24). Following Larry Lohmann and Nicholas Hildyard, a thorough understanding of energy must emphasize the inherent social relations of energy. With the aim of avoiding technological inevitability or deterministic abstractions, an adequate analytical perspective to depict the politically contested, as well as the socially and geographically uneven character of "energy" is required. Therefore, Political Ecology can offer helpful starting points as it is interested in the social hierarchies and power asymmetries that are intertwined with the societal appropriation and production of nature (Escobar 2008; Robbins 2010; Leff 2015; Alimonda et al. 2017a, 2017b). The principal aim is the "politicization" of environmental issues by exposing and analyzing the associated conflicts instead of "naturalizing" conflicts through environmental analysis.

Characteristically, contributions from Latin American Political Ecology (Leff 2015; Alimonda et al. 2017a, 2017b) highlight the extent to which nature was crucial to the formation of a long-lasting mesh of unequal relations of power, territorial subordination, and conflict between the ruling centers of Europe and their colonies (Martín and Larsimont 2017). Building on this historically informed and transnational perspective, this entry deals with the question of how colonial structures are reproduced or restructured across the Americas and within the prevailing energy regime. While drawing on Political Ecology perspectives on the materiality of nature, this entry understands energy as a societal production without denying its physicality. Natural resources like air, wood, biomass, gas, water, sunlight, heat or oil, for instance, have a specific physical quality or materiality, which influences societal relations of energy production and distribution. As Timothy Mitchell argues in his work on the intersecting histories of coal, oil and democracy, the physical materiality of energy resources could favor or impede the workers' struggles for the improvement of social rights (Mitchell 2011) (→ Class Struggle, II/3). Given the materialities of coal, the argument runs, the worker's class could exercise direct control over the UK's most important source and network of energy supply by strikes or blocking the railway line. This put the workers in the position to negotiate major improvements regarding the social rights of the working class. This phenomenon turned out very differently in the case of oil, which was key for industrialization in the U.S. According to Mitchell, the physical qualities of oil, namely high concentration of energy, lightness, and fluidity, made it feasible for large corporations to transport this energy source *via* pipelines and ships. In comparison to coal mining, oil requires a much smaller, globally dispersed workforce, which made transnational distribution systems less vulnerable to strikes and other forms of working struggles.

To be sure, this is not to say that social relations are determined by the physical materiality of natural resources. According to prominent political economists (O'Connor 1988; Moore 2003; Altvater 2006; Clark and Foster 2009), the dominant – currently capitalist – arrangement of social relations structures how energy is produced and distributed. In turn, the dominant energy regime is not exclusively determined by the economy. As discussed in this entry, energy regimes are also challenged and sometimes changed in and through social struggles.

Energy consumption and energy mix in the Americas

The level of global energy consumption is constantly on the rise. Despite warnings about global warming caused by increasing levels of CO_2 emissions (→ Climate Change, II/30), and despite local, national, and global attempts to improve energy efficiency, the world continues to consume higher levels of energy every year. However, the consumption of energy is unequally distributed across the globe. In 2015, for instance, the Americas accounted for 26.6 percent of the world's total consumption of primary energy. This figure represents more than double the share of primary energy consumption in the EU (12 percent) and is slightly higher than that of China (22.9 percent), which holds the largest national share in the consumption of primary energy in the world (BP 2016; Enerdata 2017).

Within the Americas, energy consumption is far from being homogenous. In fact, there are remarkable structural inequalities within and between different regions. In terms of energy consumption per capita in 2014, the average U.S.-citizen used the equivalent of 7.0 tons (t) of oil, an average Canadian 9.4 t, whereas an average Mexican used 1.6 t, which is below the world's average of 1.8 t. While Venezuela (2.7 t), Argentina (2.1 t) and Trinidad and Tobago (15.9 t) are above, Ecuador (1.0 t), Colombia (0.8) and Peru

(0.8), for instance, are below the world's average in terms of energy consumption per capita (BPB 2016).

Since the 1990s, the Americas have experienced an important increase in the level of primary energy consumption per capita, but it has nevertheless remained at 30 percent below the global average. Regarding the total energy mix, oil is the most dominant energy source in North, Central, and South America accounting for 32.9 percent of total energy supply in 2015 (Fischer 2017, 658). In fact, some important producers (U.S., Mexico, Venezuela, Brazil) and consumers (U.S., Brazil) of oil are located in the Americas. In Latin America, in particular, oil and natural gas are the two most important sources of energy. In 2013, oil accounted for 46 percent of the region's primary energy supply (TPES), which is similar to the level exhibited by OPEC countries and higher than the world's average level of 31 percent (IRENA 2016, 12). By contrast, natural gas accounts for 23 percent of Latin America's primary energy supply and is slightly below the global average of 23.8 percent. In Latin America, the use of coal contributes 5 percent of TPES (ibid.), which is comparatively low, considering that coal is the second most important energy source in the world, accounting for 29.2 percent of total primary energy consumption (WEC 2016).

Within South America, the use of nuclear energy has been generally limited to a few countries like Argentina and Brazil. According to the World Nuclear Association (2019), Argentina has three nuclear reactors, which generated 5 percent of the country's electricity in 2017, while only 3 percent of Brazil's electricity was generated by its two nuclear reactors. Argentina is the only country dominating all steps in the production chain including the mining of uranium, its processing, as well as the technical capacities to design and build nuclear facilities. With the aim of strengthening its nuclear capacities for the purpose of electricity generation, Argentina has recently signed cooperation agreements with Russia and looked for investments from China. In North America, nuclear energy is more important. In Canada there are nineteen nuclear reactors which generated 15 percent of the country's electricity in 2017. The U.S. has ninety-eight nuclear reactors, which generated 20 percent of the country's electricity, while in Mexico only 6 percent of the electricity generated in 2017 came from two nuclear plants. Canada is currently the world's second-largest uranium producer – after ceding first place to Kazakhstan in 2009, while the U.S. is the largest uranium and nuclear power importer (World Nuclear Association 2019).

In general, fossil sources (oil, gas and coal) accounted for 74 percent of Latin America's total consumption of primary energy in 2015, which remains below the global share of 86 percent (WEC 2016). Against this backdrop, the Americas exhibit a comparatively high share of renewable energies. The concept of renewable energy encompasses all energy sources from biomass, sun, wind, to water. They are not derived from fossil or nuclear sources and have been used for thousands of years. With renewable energy accounting for 25 percent of TPES in 2013, Latin America is above the global average of 13 percent. Within Latin America, solid biofuels such as wood, sawdust, charcoal, or bagasse (57 percent) and hydropower (31 percent) are the main sources of renewable energy in the region's primary energy mix. These are followed by liquid biofuels i.e. biodiesel on the basis of vegetable oil or ethanol on the basis of vegetable starch/sugar (8 percent), geothermal (3 percent) and other renewable energy sources (IRENA 2016). In relative terms, Central America has the highest share of renewable energy (55 percent of TPES, although around half of it is traditional solid biofuels), followed by Brazil (39 percent of TPES, mainly for end-uses and power generation).

One of the most significant trends in Latin America's energy sector is the rapidly growing importance of electricity. In fact, power generation has more than quadrupled from 1980 to 2013 (ibid., 32). The production of electricity is largely based on hydropower, but natural gas and other renewable sources have gradually gained relevance. While hydropower was responsible for 67 percent of electricity generation in 1990, this share had fallen to 50 percent in 2013. Hydropower is used to different degrees in different countries. It contributes to 100 percent of power generation in Paraguay and about 75 percent in Brazil, Colombia, Venezuela, and Costa Rica. In parallel, natural gas has progressively gained relevance as the most important source of electricity generation in Bolivia, and the second most important in Colombia, Peru, and Venezuela (ibid., 33).

In terms of renewable energy, bioenergy and onshore wind have experienced the highest growth rate in terms of installed capacity since the year 2000 (ibid.). Across Latin America, renewable energy supplies 35 percent of heat demand, nearly one-quarter of which comes from traditional biomass. Some countries in the region rely heavily on renewable sources for industrial heat, including Paraguay (90 percent), Uruguay (80 percent), Costa Rica (63 percent) and Brazil (54 percent).

In 2016, moreover, several countries in the Americas experienced high levels of investment in renewables. Bolivia shows the world's highest level of investment in renewable energy and fuels per unit of GDP. In terms of hydropower investment, Brazil occupies second place, behind China, while Ecuador holds the third place. In terms of the world's total investment in solar and wind power in 2016, the United States held second place, respectively behind China. Notably, the Americas take the global lead in terms of annual investment in biodiesel and fuel ethanol production, whereby the U.S. takes first and Brazil second place respectively (REN 21 2017, 25).

This data portrays the unequal distribution and the diversity of energy sources available for consumption and/or export in the Americas, but they leave the ecological burdens of growing levels of energy consumption unexposed. The extraction, production, export, and distribution of energy is deeply entrenched with socio-environmental conflicts all over the Americas. Countries, in which the export of natural resources plays a dominant role, typically entail a high level of embodied materials, pollution, and energy use per unit of economic output. In this case, the expansion of the economy relies on the physical expansion of exports while the production of energy creates unequally distributed social and ecological risks within each country (Muradian et al. 2012, 560; Martinez-Alier et al. 2016).

Entangled unequal histories of energy flows: reconfigurations and struggles

The focus on the entangled histories of energy flows within and beyond the Americas exemplifies that "energy" is not only a neutral and abstract concept of thermodynamic rules, but involves (neo)colonialism (→ Colonial Rule, I/5; Postcolonialism, I/38), unequal development (→ II/6), transnational power asymmetries, exploitation of labor and nature (→ II/39) as well as social struggles. The following seven snapshots shed light on the entangled and unequal histories of energy flows while showing how energy and social structures are deeply connected.

The carbon lock-in in Canada and the U.S.

Before the carbon age, the direct and indirect energy flows from the Americas to Europe were based on biomass and human labor. Indirect energy flows were (and still are) linked to the deforestation of whole regions and to the exploitation of human labor for mining (Moore 2003). Sugar is an example of direct energy flows; it was the first international traded crop exploiting slaves and simultaneously energized the emerging urban labor forces in the context of industrialization (Mintz 1986). In contrast to Latin America, the U.S. benefited from an early emancipation from its colonial dependence from the British Empire in 1776, also taking advantage of the mercantilist interests of Britain, France, Spain, and the Netherlands, who competed to tap into its good soils and the Great Plains. After the dispossession of the First Nations (→ Indigenous Peoples, I/11) of their land and the construction of the railroads, the land produced very high quantities of grains, which allowed for urbanization (→ I/45) within the country and a remarkable increase in exports to Europe (Krausmann and Fischer-Kowalski 2010, 49). However, compared to Britain, coal was not as crucial to the rise of the U.S. as water (Malm 2016, 259). Waterwheels were central energy sources until the end of the Civil War in 1865, and until 1850, 90 percent of the nation's heat was generated from wood.

With the discovery of large oil reserves in Texas around 1900, the global energy regime was deeply transformed. Until the mid-20th century, the U.S. was the most important producer of oil. The combination of oil, internal combustion engines, aircrafts, a chemical industry with rising wages, the emergence of assembly line production, and cheap energy was crucial to Fordism (→ II/10) and U.S.-American global hegemony. Later on, the automobile, central heating, and meat joined the list of key elements of an energy intensive form of living connected to the "American Way of Life" (→ Consumerism I/23). The U.S. and Canada were host to "the carbon lock-in," which describes the cementation of fossil fuel-based technologies within transport (cars, not trains or bicycles). An entire infrastructure emerged from oil terminals, to petroleum refineries, asphalt plants, road networks, gasoline stations as well as the individual transportation sector while others, especially the train transportation system, lost their importance (ibid. 12).

Brazil and the U.S.: the role of biofuels within a fossil energy regime

The dominance of the fossil regime does not mean that other energy sources – considered in the context of climate change (→ II/30) as renewables – are dispensable. Until today, the share of biomass-based energy in total global final energy consumption is about 14.1 percent (REN 21 2017). Nevertheless, the transition toward a fossil regime in the 20th century did not replace but instead absorbed and integrated renewable energy sources, as illustrated by the case of biofuels.

Biofuels – including animal fats, vegetable oils, and methanol from wood – were humanity's first liquid fuels and powered the early stages of the Industrial Revolution. Around the early 20th century, biofuels were used for the combustion of engines all over the world, given concerns with regard to fuel quality and petroleum depletion (Kovarik 2013). After the emergence of the fossil regime, biofuels vanished until the oil crisis in the 1970s (→ Crisis, II/4), which induced stronger concerns over national energy security. In the 1970s Brazil and the U.S. started, for instance, the production of ethanol as a means to substitute gasoline and simultaneously restructure their agricultural sectors through subsidies. Since then, the Brazilian sugar/ethanol complex has overcome several economic crises (e.g. because of the volatility of the oil market) by state incentives and technological innovations like the flex car. Flex cars can mix ethanol and gasoline depending on the global oil price.

In the context of climate change, ethanol, as all different forms of biofuels, has been reframed as green substitution of fossil fuels, especially within the transport sector (Wilkinson and Herrera 2010). In 2017, with a blending quota of 27 percent and a production of 26.2 billion liters, Brazil was the second-largest global consumer and producer of ethanol after the U.S. (USDA 2017). The Brazilian National Biodiesel Production Program (PNPB) was created in 2004 to promote domestic production, reduce import dependency on oil, to generate jobs and to tackle poverty in the countryside. In 2017, the biodiesel mandate is set at 8 percent and the total biodiesel production is estimated at 4.3 billion liters (ibid.). Nowadays, Brazil is the second-largest biodiesel producer after the U.S. Indeed, 70 percent of Brazil's biodiesel is produced from soybean oil, followed by animal tallow (16 percent), while the rest comes from cottonseed oil and other oil seeds (ibid.).

However, many actors question the sustainability of biofuels. As part of a transnational agro-industrial complex, biofuels generate CO_2 emissions *via* land-use changes (→ Land, I/15) while their production is still dependent on fossil fuel inputs. Furthermore, the production of biofuels is not necessarily inclusive of smallholders but strengthens land concentration and land-grabbing processes (Bernardes and Aracri 2011; Borras et al. 2011; Backhouse 2015). Additionally, the "food-vs-fuel-debate" started in 2007 since growing food prices provoked protests in Mexico ("Tortilla Crisis") and other parts of the world. The corn-ethanol mandate adopted by the U.S. government contributed to this problem as it absorbed scarce grain supplies and pushed up food prices. In response, NGO campaigns and social movements (→ I/41) damaged the seemingly sustainable image of biofuels, which led the EU to reconsider the increase of blending quotas.

Nationalization of oil companies across the Americas as a reaction against U.S. and European dominance

As a means to eradicate external dominance in the domestic hydrocarbon sector, many countries in Latin America opted for the nationalization of the corresponding enterprises. During the first three decades of the 20th century, a few transnational enterprises (→ II/23) backed by the U.S. and other Western governments were able to secure comprehensive concessions for oil exploration and production in many parts of Latin America. From 1912 onwards, British and U.S. investors started drilling for oil in Veracruz, Mexico, on the Atlantic Coast of Nicaragua, and in different parts of Venezuela. By 1932, the Standard Oil Company of New Jersey (Standard Oil, now ExxonMobil) became the largest foreign oil company in the region, acquiring concessions for oil exploration, refining, and transportation in Bolivia, Venezuela, Mexico, Colombia, and Peru (Philip 1982, 43f.; Perreault and Valdivia 2010, 694). A few years later, Royal Dutch/Shell made its entrance into Latin America, acquiring exploration concessions in Ecuador, Guatemala, Colombia, Mexico, and Venezuela, with the latter providing for nearly one third of Shell's global production of oil in 1937 (Philip 1982, 45).

With the emergence of Import Substitution Industrialization (ISI), different Latin American states (→ Nation State II/38) strengthened control over the oil industry, which they regarded as a strategic pillar of *desarrollismo* (→ Development, II/6). This led to a series of nationalization processes. The first state-owned oil enterprise emerged in 1922 in Argentina under the name of YPF (*Yacimientos Petrolíferos Fiscales*). Following this example, Bolivia created its state-owned oil and gas company YPFB (*Yacimientos Petrolíferos Fiscales Bolivianos*) in 1936. As part of a strong national movement to assert economic independence, Mexico nationalized its oil production and founded PEMEX (*Petróleos Mexicanos*) in 1938. Chile created the national oil company *Empresa Nacional del Petróleo* (ENAP) in 1950. After intense political struggles, Brazil created the state-owned company Petrobrás in 1953. This regional wave of nationalization processes reached Ecuador and Venezuela in the 1970s. Although the Venezuelan state had begun exerting significant tax pressure on U.S. companies in 1943 (→ Taxation, II/22), the nationalization of the oil industry was concluded in 1976 with the creation of PDVSA (*Petróleos de Venezuela*) (Prado and Schaposnik 2015, 100).

Pitfalls of rentier politics and the emergence of extractivism

Albeit to different degrees, the nationalization of the hydrocarbon sector led to the proliferation of rentier politics, and delivered the material basis for extractive development models to arise during the 2000s. Tighter state-control over oil, gas, and mineral "rents" – defined as "the difference between revenues and extraction cost" (Barma et al. 2011, 11) – has since led to volatile increases in public revenue but has not automatically served as a development motor. In fact, drawing on the negative economic outcomes of the "Dutch Disease," the problems of the "resource curse," "rent-seeking," and more recently "extractivism" (→ II/9), represent prominent fields of debate across the Americas. The "Dutch Disease" is a commonly cited argument, according to which the accelerated expansion of gas exports in the Netherlands became a "curse" during the 1960s. This one-commodity based, export-oriented economic model induced high levels of currency appreciation and inflation, which, in turn, had a negative effect on the diversification of the manufacturing and industrial sectors (Ross 1999, 306; Peters 2017, 47).

The "resource curse" debate also criticized the political implications of "rent-seeking," given that oil, gas, and minerals provide privileged social groups with vast incentives to compete for control over the state infrastructure to access the national resource base and use it mostly to their own political and economic advantage (→ Social Inequality, II/20). Hence, a substantial part of the debate on "rentier economies" and the "rentier state" links resource extraction with higher levels of corruption, patronage, and clientelism (→ II/29) (Omeje 2010). In this case, the term "rent" is used in a broader sense and makes reference to money transfers from oil consumers (mostly in the Global North) toward rentier states, who use these transfers to stabilize state revenues without due accountability to citizens and tax payers. Venezuela, currently the oil-richest country on Earth holding 18 percent of all confirmed reserves in the world (Fischer 2017, 662), is an outstanding example of a "rentier economy." In 2014, oil represented over 97 percent of the country's export, while oil rents made up 45 percent of the state income and 35 percent of GDP (Peters 2017, 54). Since the beginning of the 2000s, China's demand for Venezuelan oil has grown significantly, hence contributing to the rentist character of the Venezuelan state and its Bolivarian developmental model (Rosales 2016).

Social scientists from Latin America use the term "extractivism" (→ II/9) to conceptualize a problematic developmental model through which resource exporting states become increasingly dependent on volatile market prices and predatory practices of extraction to foster policies of (re-)distribution (Acosta 2009; Gudynas 2015; Svampa 2015). Albeit with different social, political, economic and ecological implications, this kind of model has been adopted by different South American states, including Bolivia, Ecuador, Peru, Colombia, Chile, Argentina, and Brazil, and this regional trend has reinforced Latin America's position as a provider of raw materials (Svampa 2015).

According to Fernando Coronil, the problems of resource extraction are thus better explained as a "neocolonial disease." Because of pre-existing relations of international subordination, he argues, postcolonial states are substantially more vulnerable to the economic and political "traps" of expanding commodity exports than most Western countries (→ Global Commodity Chains, II/12). Additionally, extractive development models tend to reproduce the "relations of colonial dependence between these formally independent nations and metropolitan centers" (Coronil 2008, 19).

Privatization and the economic weight of energy companies across the Americas

During the 1990s, many of the national energy companies were privatized, such as in Bolivia and Argentina (→ Privatization, II/17). In many other cases, although the nation formally owned the enterprises, the influence and profit of international investors were often higher than the decisions and revenues of several states (as in Venezuela or Mexico). Since 2000, a period of high commodity prices driven substantially by China's rapidly rising energy demand motivated different Latin American states to reassert national control of the energy sector (Rodríguez 2018). Nowadays, seven energy companies figure among the world's ten largest firms in terms of revenues (Fischer 2017, 660). Looking at the ten largest companies within the energy sector, two enterprises from the Americas hold prominent positions: Exxon/Mobile holds the fourth and Chevron the tenth place. Both companies are privately owned, stock-market-listed enterprises with headquarters in the U.S.

Nevertheless, National Oil Companies (NOCs) have progressively gained influence in the world energy market. According to the World Bank, about 90 percent of the world's oil and gas reserves and about 75 percent of their exploitation is controlled by NOCs. In the Americas, furthermore, state-owned energy companies have expanded transborder activities, leading to new Inter-American entanglements.

Multilatinas and Caribbean oil diplomacy: contra-hegemonic instrument or authoritarian power base?

The emergence of the *multilatinas* is a noteworthy phenomenon (→ Transnational Corporations, II/23). The three most important examples of state-owned enterprises pursuing deliberate strategies of internationalization (through exports, investment, and joint ventures) are PEMEX from Mexico, Petrobrás from Brazil, and PDVSA from Venezuela. While PEMEX has expanded its operations mainly into the U.S. and European markets, Petrobrás has diversified its operations into the U.S., China, Latin America and given significant attention to African countries including Angola, Nigeria, Mozambique and Tanzania (Satsumi et al. 2017). In fact, the nationalization of the oil and gas industries in Bolivia and Ecuador have respectively led to strong bilateral tensions with Brazil, as different social movements (→ I/41) rejected Petrobrás' policies of intraregional expansion. PDVSA has engaged in overseas operations in Asia and the U.S. but also placed a strong focus on implementing Venezuela's oil diplomacy in the Caribbean and Central America.

Between 2008 and 2016, Venezuela developed a strategy for fueling Caribbean integration (→ Regional Integration II/18), regional industrialization, and new trade flows with its oil. The most important element of the strategy was the creation of Petrocaribe in 2005. The Venezuelan state-owned oil company PDVSA has created fourteen mixed enterprises in eleven Petrocaribe member countries (Aponte García et al. 2015, 89). PDVSA maintains from 60 to 83 percent of the shares in the respective enterprises. Under this umbrella Venezuela sold oil to the companies or states at favorable prices; a part has to be paid directly, another part is given as a long-term credit with a low interest rate, and a certain percentage goes to the ALBA Caribe Fund. The latter has developed eighty-eight projects between 2006 and 2008 in the areas of housing and habitat (32 percent), social aspects (24 percent), urban services (14 percent), and productive sectors (13 percent) in different Central American and Caribbean Countries (Aponte García et al. 2015, 93). For several Caribbean countries, the contribution of these projects to electrical infrastructure has been significant. Oil can be partially paid in services. Cuba, for example, sends medical and educational personnel to Venezuela.

For Nicaragua's president Daniel Ortega, the Petrocaribe initiative and the ALBA process were a key element for economic growth, as Venezuela in 2012 bought almost 50 percent of Nicaragua's beef exports, as well as a high share of milk, beans, and sugar (Martí I Puig and Baumeister 2017, 391). For Ortega's authoritarian regime (→ Authoritarianism, II/25) and practice of repression this mechanism is key, as PDVSA has extended oil loans to an FSLN-owned, private bank for twenty-five years. However, the use of this money is not transparent (Thaler 2017, 165) (→ Clientelism II/29). Venezuela tried to reduce the exposure to price volatility on the world market, to deepen South–South relations and to adapt its own commodity chains and trade networks (Prado and Schaposnik 2015, 97f). In recent years, however, PDVSA has faced serious financial problems in the face of hyperinflation rates, and mounting levels of foreign debt, which have forced Venezuela to develop an oil-backed cryptocurrency called *petro*. The political regime turned out to be incapable of responding to the severe economic and political crisis. This situation has forced almost three million Venezuelans to leave the country in the face of drastically deteriorating living conditions (→ Transnational Migration, I/44).

Resistance movements against transnational large-scale fossil and renewable energy projects

Struggles around energy have usually involved resistance movements fighting against powerful national and transnational energy companies (→ Environmental Justice, II/8). These struggles cut across different energy sectors including hydrocarbons, wind, biomass, and the development of large-scale infrastructures related to the extraction, production, and distribution of energy.

While some countries managed to reverse the privatization tendencies of the 1990s (→ Privatization, II/17), the Americas continued to witness intense resistance against large-scale energy projects. In Bolivia, the struggles between those calling for national control of hydrocarbon resources and revenues, and those calling for regional autonomy and greater local control of oil and gas rents have been intensive (Perreault and Valdivia 2010, 690). In 2003, a conflict over the export of natural gas from Bolivia through a Chilean port to Mexico and the U.S. caused a huge social mobilization known as "the gas war," with a death toll of nearly eighty people killed in the protest. In 2005, road blockades and rising protests demanding the nationalization of the country's natural gas reserves compelled the president to resign (Spronk and Webber 2007). Natural gas has now become the symbol of Bolivian sovereignty and has been declared a natural heritage. In fact, the Bolivian constitution (2009) and a special law (2010) now entitles the *Pachamama* (Mother Earth) with legal mechanisms to protect itself from overexploitation. Nevertheless, the Bolivian state is strongly dependent on the extraction and export of natural gas: hydrocarbons represent Bolivia's single largest source of income, with revenues increasing from $188 million in 2001 to over $1.5 billion in 2007 (Perreault and Valdivia 2010, 696).

A particularly interesting case is the resistance movement against Big Oil (Chevron/Texaco) in Ecuador. In 1993, more than 30,000 indigenous people joined the *Unión de Afectados por las Operaciones de Texaco* (UDAPT) to demand compensation for the irreversible damages caused by Texaco's oil-drilling activities in a sensitive area of the Ecuadorean Amazon (→ Indigeneity, I/31; Social Movements, I/41). The oil company Texaco obtained extraction rights from the Ecuadorean government in 1963 while becoming a subsidiary of the California-based oil corporation Chevron in 2001. In collaboration with research organizations, activist groups, and state bureaucracies, local communities gathered striking evidence of the social and ecological damage caused by Texaco between 1964 and 1993 (Pigrau 2012, 1). Texaco dumped toxic waste into the Amazonian rivers and caused hundreds of oil leakages, which affected 1,500 km of river basins, leading to the destruction of more than 450,000 hectares of Amazonian rainforest. In 2011, an Ecuadorian court sentenced Chevron to pay a US$ 8.6 billion fine for the negligent actions of its daughter-firm Texaco. Since then, Chevron has sued the Ecuadorian government at three international instances. In 2017, the U.S. Supreme Court declared that the available evidence brought against Chevron in this decade-long litigation process was fraudulent. This ruling impedes any judicial measures originating in Ecuador to be legally effective against Chevron in the U.S. (Chevron 6/19/2017).

Another emblematic case is the resistance to hydropower in the context of Belo Monte in Brazil. Since the 1970s the building of the massive hydro-electrical plant "Belo Monte" – the world's third largest – has threatened the Xingu River in the state of Pará, part of the Brazilian Amazon Basin. Massive local resistance and transnational protests stopped the project for nearly three decades. However, in 2010 the project was re-launched, and enforced by the Brazilian government against existing laws and enduring protests. Belo Monte is part of an official plan to convert Brazil into a global energy player through the systematic expansion of hydropower. However, the technical, procedural, as well as the political aspects of this project are highly contested. Belo Monte magnifies the risk of gigantic floods, deforestation, and huge biodiversity losses, which have vast and negative effects on the livelihoods of traditional and indigenous peoples (→ Indigeneity I/31). The construction of the dam, which began in 2011 with large governmental support and financial commitments up to US$13 billion, implied the flooding of 400 square kilometers and the displacement of more than 20,000 people, whose livelihoods have, for centuries, depended upon river navigation and fishing (Rodríguez 2017).

Meanwhile, Brazil does not necessarily depend on hydropower to meet its domestic demand for electricity. Instead, part of the energy-surplus will be either directly exported, or used by Vale (Brazil's mining company) in the extraction, production, and export of aluminum for the global market. The levels of resistance against Belo Monte have thus been impressive, yet costly. While the first turbines began operations in 2016, the resistance movement has split into different groups. There are those who continue to fight the dam, those pledging to seize the opportunities of the financial resources made available by the government, and those who see "the importance of working with local and federal government officials in order to support the needs of dam-affected people" (Klein 2015, 1153).

A last case touches upon resistance to energy-related infrastructures in the context of TIPNIS-IIRSA. The regional initiative *Integración de la Infraestructura Regional Suramericana* (IIRSA) was born in 2000 (→ Regional Integration, II/18), as a multilateral agreement promoted by the Inter-American Development Bank and signed in Brasilia by twelve governments including Argentina, Bolivia, Brazil, Chile, Colombia, Ecuador, Guyana, Paraguay, Peru, Suriname, Uruguay, and Venezuela. The aim was to promote a unified system of transportation, energy, and telecommunication infrastructures (→ Telecommunications, III/42). With the creation of the *Unión de Naciones Suramericana* (UNASUR) in 2009, Venezuela, Brazil, and Argentina increased their political and financial engagement in IIRSA, which led to a series of intraregional conflicts around the development of energy-related infrastructures.

One of the most prominent cases is the construction of a 300 km road, which cuts across Bolivia's *Territorio Indígena y Parque Nacional Isiboro-Secure (TIPNIS)*. Alongside obtaining US$332 million financial assistance from the Brazilian National Development Bank (BNDES), the Bolivian government has argued in favor of the construction of this road to connect national producers with the Chilean and Brazilian markets. In 2011, this project drove more than a thousand indigenous leaders to walk to the capital La Paz and protest against the building of the road. Denouncing critical levels of repression by the national police, the protesters were able to force the Bolivian government to stop the project (Calle and Gomez Goiri 2016). Despite this achievement, the Bolivian Senate passed a national law in August 2017, which paved the way for the construction of the road. The social struggles against this law were soon to re-ignite (Collyns 2017).

Transforming the dominant global energy regime?

The political-economic perspective of Political Ecology sheds light on the social-ecological materiality of energy. The physical quality of energy resources influences its societal appropriation and *vice versa*. However, how energy is entangled with production and consumption relations depends on historical and current conditions. Energy flows are further contingent upon transnational relations of political, economic and social power, which can in turn be affected by social struggles and resistance movements. It is only against this backdrop, that the unequal developments, trajectories, and entanglements of energy flows in the Americas can be analyzed.

This perspective is also useful to evaluate alternative energy systems in the context of the multiple social-ecological crises (→ II/4). The cases of renewable energies underline that the substitution of fossil energy cannot – by itself – bring about social-ecological change. The example of biofuels shows how state incentives boost the expansion of the agro-industrial production of sugar cane, soy or palm oil – a mode of agricultural production, which relies highly on fossil inputs. At the same time, agro-industry is responsible for high levels of land concentration (→ Land, II/15), the dispossession of peasants and indigenous peoples (→ Indigeneity, II/2), while causing high rates of deforestation and biodiversity loss, which add up to one third of global CO_2 emissions. Therefore, if renewable energies – be it biofuels, solar or wind energy – are implemented within the currently existing centralized infrastructures of fossil capitalism, social inequalities (→ II/20), exploitation as well as negative social-ecological impacts are likely to be reproduced.

Nevertheless, the physical materiality of renewable energies driven by the sun, wind and water can open new opportunities for decentralized, democratic, and equitable forms of energy production and distribution (Altvater 2006; Wissen 2016). However, the achievement of such conditions depends on a democratic societal transformation (→ Democracy, II/32), which includes the advancement and protection of workers' rights as well as new consumption relations on a global scale (→ Consumerism, I/23).

Works cited

Acosta, Alberto. 2009. *La maldición de la abundancia*. Quito: CEP Swissaid and Abya-Yala.

Alimonda, Héctor, Catalina Toro Pérez and Martín Facundo. 2017a. *Ecología Política Latinoamericana. Pensamiento crítico, diferencia latino-americana y rearticulación epistémica*. Volumen 1. Ciudad Autónoma de Buenos Aires: CLACSO.

———. 2017b. *Ecología Política Latinoamericana. Pensamiento crítico, diferencia latino-americana y rearticulación epistémica*. Volumen 2. Ciudad Autónoma de Buenos Aires: CLACSO.

Altvater, Elmar. 2006. *Das Ende des Kapitalismus, wie wir ihn kennen. Eine radikale Kapitalismuskritik*. Münster: Westfälisches Dampfboot.

Aponte García, Maribel, Carlos Antonio Àlvarez and Swihart Nayrobi Berra Romero. 2015. "Strategic Regional Public Enterprises and Petroleum Sovereignty: PDVSA, Petrocaribe and the ALBA-TCP." *Revista de Ciencias Sociales* 28, 74–103.

Backhouse, Maria. 2015. "Green Grabbing – the Case of Palm Oil Expansion in so-called Degraded Areas in the Eastern Brazilian Amazon." In *The Political Ecology of Agrofuels*, eds. Kristina Dietz, Bettina Engels, Oliver Pye and Achim Brunnengräber, 167–185. New York: Routledge.

Barma, Naazneen, Kai Kaiser, Tuan Minh Le and Lorena Viñuela 2011. "Rents to Riches?: The Political Economy of Natural Resource-led Development." *The World Bank*. https://openknowledge.worldbank.org/handle/10986/2381.

Bernardes, Júlia Adão and Luís Angelo Aracri Dos Santos. (eds.). 2011. *Novas Fronteiras do Biodiesel na Amazônia: limites e desafios da incorporação da pequena produção agrícola*. Rio de Janeiro: Arquimedes Edições.

Borras, Saturnino M., Jennifer C. Franco, Cristóbal Kay and Max Spoor. 2011. *Land grabbing in Latin America and the Caribbean viewed from broader international perspectives. 14 November 2011 Version*. FAO. www.tni.org/sites/www.tni.org/files/download/borras_franco_kay__spoor_land_grabs_in_latam__caribbean_nov_2011.pdf.

BP. 2016. *Statistical Review of World Energy 2016*. BP. www.bp.com/en/global/corporate/energy-economics/statistical-review-of-world-energy.html.

BPB, Bundeszentrale für Politische Bildung. 2016. *Verbrauch von Primärenergie pro Kopf*. www.bpb.de/nachschlagen/zahlen-und-fakten/globalisierung/52758/verbrauch-pro-kopf.

Calle, Antonella and Mikel Gomez Goiri. 2016. *TIPNIS*, Bolivia: EJ Atlas. https://ejatlas.org/conflict/tipnis, updated on 7/20/2016.

Chevron. 2017. "United States Supreme Court Denies Petition for Review by Lawyer Behind Fraudulent Ecuador Lawsuit." *Chevron press release*, June 19. www.chevron.com/stories/united-states-supreme-court-denies-petition-for-review-by-lawyer-behind-fraudulent-ecuador-lawsuit.

Clark, Brett and John Bellamy Foster. 2009. "Ecological Imperialism and the Global Metabolic Rift: Unequal Exchange and the Guano/Nitrates Trade." *International Journal of Comparative Sociology* 50, no. 3–4: 311–334.

Collyns, Dan. 2017. "Bolivia Approves Highway through Amazon Biodiversity Hotspot." *The Guardian*, August 15. www.theguardian.com/environment/2017/aug/15/bolivia-approves-highway-in-amazon-biodiversity-hotspot-as-big-as-jamaica.

Coronil, Fernando. 2008. "It's the oil, Stupid!" *ReVista. Harvard Review of Latin America*, Fall 2008. 19–20.

Enerdata. 2017. "Global Energy Statistical Yearbook 2017." *Enerdata intelligence and consulting*. https://yearbook.enerdata.net/total-energy/world-consumption-statistics.html.

Escobar, Arturo. 2008. *Territories of difference. Place, Movements, Life, Redes*. Durham and London: Duke University Press.

Gudynas, Eduardo. 2015. *Extractivismos. Ecología, economía y política de un modo de entender el desarrollo y la naturaleza*. Primera edición. Cochabamba Bolivia: CEDIB Centro de Documentación e Información Bolivia.

Haas, Willi, Fridolin Krausmann, Dominik Wiedenhofer and Markus Heinz. 2015. "How Circular is the Global Economy?: An Assessment of Material Flows, Waste Production, and Recycling in the European Union and the World in 2005." *Gornal of Industrial Ecology* 19, no. 5: 765–777.

IRENA, International Renewable Energy Agency. 2016. *Renewable energy market analysis: Latin America*. IRENA: Abu Dhabi. www.irena.org/DocumentDownloads/Publications/IRENA_Market_Analysis_Latin_America_2016.pdf.

Klein, Peter Taylor. 2015. "Engaging the Brazilian state. The Belo Monte dam and the struggle for political voice." *The Journal of Peasant Studies* 42, no. 6: 1137–1156.

Kovarik, Bill. 2013. "History of Biofuels. Chapter One." In *Biofuel Crops. Production, Physiology and Genetics*, ed. Bharat P. Singh, 1–22. Wallingford: CABI.

Krausmann, Fridolin and Marina Fischer-Kowalski. 2010. „Gesellschaftliche Naturverhältnisse. Globale Transformationen der Energie- und Materialflüsse." In *Globalgeschichte 1800–2010*, eds. Reinhard Sieder and Ernst Langthaler, 39–66. Böhlau: Wien/Köln/Weimar.

Leff, Enrique. 2015. "Political Ecology: A Latin American Perspective." *Desenvolvimento e Meio Ambiente* 35, 29–64.

Lohmann, Larry and Nicholas Hildyard. 2014. *Energy, Work and Finance*. Sturminster Newton: The Corner House.

Malm, Andreas. 2016. *Fossil Capital: The Rise of Stream Power and the Roots of Global Warming.* London and New York: Verso.

Martí I Puig, Salvador and Eduardo Baumeister. 2017. "Agrarian Policies in Nicaragua: From Revolution to the Revival of Agro-Exports, 1979–2015." *Journal of Agrarian Change* 17, 381–396.

Martín, Facundo and Robin Larsimont. 2017. "Es posible una ecología cosmo-política?" *Polis Revista Latinoamericana*, 45. http://polis.revues.org/12155.

Martinez-Alier, Joan, et al. 2016. "Changing Social Metabolism and Environmental Conflicts in India and South America." *Journal of Political Ecology* 23, 328–491.

Mintz, Sidney W. 1986. *Sweetness and Power: The Place of Sugar in Modern History.* New York: Penguin Books.

Mitchell, Timothy. 2011. *Carbon Democracy: Political Power in the Age of Oil.* London: Verso.

Moore, Jason W. 2003. "The Modern World-System as Environmental History? Ecology and the Rise of Capitalism." *Theory and Society* 32, 307–377.

Muradian, Roldan, Mariana Walter and Joan Martinez-Alier. 2012. "Hegemonic Transitions and Global Shifts in Social Metabolism: Implications for Resource-Rich Countries. Introduction to the Special Section." *Global Environmental Change* 22, 559–567.

O'Connor, James. 1988. "Capitalism, Nature, Socialism. A Theoretical Introduction." *Capitalism, Nature, Socialism* 1, no. 1: 11–38. www.vedegylet.hu/okopolitika/O%27Connor%20-%20Capitalism,%20Nature,%20Socialim.pdf.

Omeje, Kenneth C. (Ed.). 2010. *Extractive Economies and Conflicts in the Global South: Multi-Regional Perspectives on Rentier Politics.* Aldershot and Burlington, VT: Ashgate.

Perreault, Tom and Gabriela Valdivia. 2010. "Hydrocarbons, Popular Protest and National Imaginaries: Ecuador and Bolivia in Comparative Context." *Geoforum* 41, 689–699.

Peters, Stefan. 2017. "Beyond Curse and Blessing: Rentier Society in Venezuela." In *Contested Extractivism, Society and the State: Struggles over Mining and Land. Development, Justice and Citizenship*, eds. Bettina Engels and Kristina Dietz, 45–68. London: Palgrave Macmillan.

Philip, George. 1982. *Oil and Politics in Latin America.* Cambridge: Cambridge University Press.

Pigrau, Antoni. 2012. *The Texaco-Chevron Case in Ecuador.* Ejolt Factsheet. www.ejolt.org/wordpress/wp-content/uploads/2015/08/FS-42.pdf.

Prado, Eugenia C. and Carmen R. Schaposnik. 2015. "Petrocaribe y ALBA-TCP: propuestas de Venezuela para una nueva integración regional y energética." In *Revista Anales de la Facultad de Ciencias Jurídicas y Sociales* 12: 97–107.

REN 21. 2017. *Renewables 2017 Global Status Report.* Paris. www.ren21.net/status-of-renewables/global-status-report/.

Ritchie, Hannah and Max Roser. 2018. "Energy Production & Changing Energy Sources." *OurWorldInData.* https://ourworldindata.org/energy-production-and-changing-energy-sources, checked on 2/12/2019.

Robbins, Paul. 2010. *Political Ecology: A Critical Introduction.* 2nd ed. Chichester: Wiley-Blackwell.

Rodríguez, Fabricio. 2018. *Oil, Minerals, and Power: The Political Economy of China's Quest for Resources in Brazil and Peru.* Doctoral Dissertation. University of Freiburg.

Rodríguez, Francisco A. 2017. "Belo-Monte Dam, Brazil." *EJ Atlas.* https://ejatlas.org/print/belo-monte-dam-brazil, updated on 2/27/2017.

Rosales, Antulio. 2016. "Deepening Extractivism and Rentierism: China's Role in Venezuela's Bolivarian Developmental Model." *Canadian Journal of Development Studies/Revue canadienne d'études du développement* 37, no. 4: 1–18.

Ross, Michael L. 1999. "The Political Economy of the Resource Curse." *World Pol* 51, no. 2: 297–322.

Satsumi, Lopez-Morales Jose, Roberto Alejandro Gonzalez-Barragan, Andres Maldonado de Luna, Antonio Eduardo Velez-De Alba and Roberto Jose Muller-Jasso. 2017. "Internationalization of State Multilatinas. A Multi-Case Study in the Oil Sector." *International Journal of Business, Economics and Management* 4, no. 4: 65–81.

Smil, Vaclav. 2006. *Energy: A Beginner's Guide.* Oxford: Oneworld Publications.

———. 2008. *Energy in Nature and Society: General Energetics of Complex Systems.* Cambridge, MA and London: MIT Press.

Spronk, Susan and Jeffrey R. Webber. 2007. "Struggles against Accumulation by Dispossession in Bolivia." *Latin American Perspectives* 34: 31–47.

Svampa, Maristella. 2015. "Commodities Consensus. Neoextractivism and Enclosure of the Commons in Latin America." *South Atlantic Quarterly* 114, no. 1: 65–82.

Thaler, Kai M. 2017. "Nicaragua: A Return to Caudillismo." *Journal of Democracy* 28, 157–169.
USDA. 2017. Gain Report. Brazil. Biofuels Annual 2017. GAIN Report Number: BR17006. USDA. São Paulo. https://gain.fas.usda.gov/Recent%20GAIN%20Publications/Biofuels%20Annual_Sao%20Paulo%20ATO_Brazil_9-15-2017.pdf.
WEC. 2016. *World Energy Resources 2016*. London: World Energy Council (WEC). www.worldenergy.org.
Fischer Weltalmanach. 2017. *Energie. Der neue Fischer Weltalmanach 2017. Zahlen Daten Fakten*. Frankfurt: Fischer Taschenbuch-Verlag.
Wilkinson, John and Selena Herrera. 2010. "Biofuels in Brazil: Debates and Impacts." *Journal of Peasant Studies* 37, no. 4: 749–768.
Wissen, Markus. 2016. "Jenseits der Carbon Democracy. Zur Demokratisierung der gesellschaftlichen Naturverhältnisse." In *Transformation der Demokratie – demokratische Transformation*, ed. Alex Demirović, 48–66. 1. Auflage. Münster: Westfälisches Dampfboot.
World Nuclear Association. 2019. Nuclear Power in the World Today. www.world-nuclear.org/information-library/current-and-future-generation/nuclear-power-in-the-world-today.aspx.

8
ENVIRONMENTAL JUSTICE

Lucrecia Wagner

Environmental Justice (EJ) is a concept that connects environmental problems with social justice. It was constituted within the struggles against the unequal distribution of environmental burdens and benefits between different social groups (→ Social Inequality, II/20; Nature, II/39). This concept was born in the United States of America (USA) in the 1980s to denounce the practice and policy that led to some individuals, groups, and communities receiving less environmental protection than others because of their geographic location, race (→ I/39), and economic status. In such cases, risk burdens are localized to specific, often marginalized groups, yet the benefits are generalized across all segments of society (Bullard 1994).

The concept was developed by an emerging movement opposing environmental injustices of different kinds: The actors who are involved in this movement argue that differences of race, economics status, as well as sex, gender (→ Gender Identities, I/28), age and capabilities, among others, are the cause of unequal distribution of environmental impacts. Theory and practice of EJ necessarily includes distributive conceptions of justice, but also embraces notions of justice based in recognition, participation (→ II/41), and capabilities (Bauler n.d.; Schlosberg 2007). The *environmental injustice* term describes the disproportionate imposition of environmental risks to populations who have less financial, political, and informational resources (Acselrad, Amaral Mello and Neves Bezerra 2009).

Environmental racism is one form of *environmental injustice* and the first one to become scandalized. In the USA, mainly African-American, Hispanic, or Native American populations have experienced toxic activities near their neighborhoods (Bullard 2000). The environmental racism and environmental injustice can materialize in so-called *locational blackmail*. This term defines the use of the need for jobs and public revenue to impose polluting practices and setbacks in social rights (Acselrad 2010) (→ Human Rights, I/35).

The emergence of the environmental justice movement

The initial EJ movement sprang from a Warren County protest, in North Carolina. In 1982, this small, predominately African-American community was designated to host a hazardous waste landfill that contained polychlorinated biphenyl (PCB). In response to the state's decision, local people staged a massive protest along with the "National Association for the Advancement of Colored People" and others. More than 500 protesters were arrested, and the site of the disposal facility was not changed. However, following the Warren County protest, people in poor minority communities were inspired to create groups to fight against environmental burdens (→ Social Movements, I/41). By the early 1980s, the *environmental justice movement* developed into a national social and racial protest movement that joined communities across the country together who were seeking social justice and environmental protection (US Department of Energy n.d.). In 1987, the United Church of Christ's Commission on Racial Justice (CRJ) released a report "Toxic Wastes and Race in the United States," the first study that documented the relationship between hazardous waste sites and racial demographics (Bullard et al. 2007).

Joan Martínez Alier (2002) argues that the organized EJ movement is an outgrowth of the Civil Rights movement, and not of previous currents of environmentalism. Some direct collaborators of Martin Luther King were among the 500 people arrested in Warren County. In fact, the Environmental Protection Agency (EPA) of United States highlights that the Civil Rights movement of the 1960s actually sounded the alarm about public health dangers for families and communities in an event preceding the Warren County protest: the Memphis Sanitation Strike, an action to claim fair pay and better working conditions for Memphis garbage workers, in Tennessee (EPA 2019) (→ Labor Representation, II/14). EPA has an office of Environmental Justice, an official space that reports possible violations of environmental laws and regulations.

Similarly, the first visible and widely reported environmental justice mobilizations that emerged and took place in the USA also had clear targets: environmental contamination and its impacts on human health (→ I/29). For example, the Love Canal protest in 1978 where white working-class residents fought against 20,000 tons of toxic chemicals sitting underneath homes and schools and won the relocation of their households (Anguelovski 2015).

Nevertheless, there is a central difference between these two protests: While in Warren County the key issue was environmental racism as Black residents fought – without success – against the filling of a landfill with hazardous waste, in Love Canal the key issue was poisoning due to the use of the area as a toxic landfill prior to the neighborhood's construction. The interaction between various protests as anti-war and anti-nuclear influenced and drove many anti-toxics groups across the USA (Leonard 2008).

Joan Martínez Alier argues that the environmental justice movement could be potentially of great importance provided it learned to speak not only for the minorities inside the USA but also for the majorities outside the USA (which locally are not always defined racially) and become involved in broader issues such as biopiracy and biosafety (→ Biopolitics, I/22), or climate change (→ II/30), beyond local instances of pollution (Martínez Alier 2002, 14). Other perspectives, which are already partially included in the movement are *popular environmentalism* (Martínez Alier 1992), *livelihood ecology* (Garí 2000) and *liberation ecology* (Peet and Watts 1996). All share the preoccupation with the unequal distribution of environmental impacts that emerge from economic growth, as well as the geographical displacement or even destruction of sinks and water sources such as forests, wetlands, rivers, lakes, fountains etc.

The areas where social and ethnic groups who do not have participation on decision-making of the state and the market live, also contain a concentration of a lack of investment in sanitation infrastructure as well as an absence of policies for controlling toxic landfills, habitable risks, desertification and other factors that affect their environmental conditions of life and work (Acselrad, Amaral Mello, and Neves Bezerra 2009) (→ Nation State, II/38). As participation and claims of recognition increased in the environmental struggles, the importance of environmental issues resulted in a process of *environmentalization* of social conflicts (Leite Lopes 2007).

Outside of the USA, the term environmental justice needs reworking to broaden its scope (Martínez Alier 2002). The majority who suffer environmental injustices are peasants, indigenous people (→ Indigeneity, I/31) or also poor without ethnic or racial differences. The problem is that they have no possibility or access to participation and recognition to defend their form of life or demand other types of "development" (→ II/6) in their territories (Schlosberg 2004; Day 2018). Poverty or underdevelopment is therefore conceptualized as capability deprivation (Day, Walker, and Simcock 2016). The sovereignty or autonomy of indigenous peoples and other's communities are very important topics, along with the recognition of the knowledge capacity generated through EJ struggles that emphasizes the need for *epistemic or cognitive justice* (Temper and Del Bene 2016).

Related forms of justice

Deeply related to environmental justice, concepts such as *energy justice* (→ Energy, II/7), *water justice* and *climate justice* (→ Climate Change, II/30) divide the broad topic of the environment into specific issues each with their own challenges. "*Energy justice* emerged as a new crosscutting social science research agenda which seeks to apply justice principles to energy policy, energy production and systems, energy consumption, energy activism, energy security and climate change" (Jenkins et al. 2016, 175). Energy poverty as a form of injustice, and geographic disparities in the risk and incidence of domestic energy deprivation are key components of energy justice (Bouzarovski and Simcock 2017). *Climate justice* highlights the relationship between consequences of climate change and environmental injustices. The climate change politics provides a good framework for practical illustration of the partial and conflicting claims to environmental justice in the literature [...]: debates about distribution of impacts, responsibilities, and distribution of costs and benefits (Ikeme 2003, 200). *Water justice* (Boelens 2015) aims to show that water injustices imply exclusion of vulnerable groups from access to clean water and affordable services, but also from representation in water-control decision-making.

> Although water governance is about institutional configurations, regulations and policy making and implementation, it is also about capabilities, powers and social struggle over access to resources, setting the agenda and discursively framing problems. Water justice, then, is not something that can easily be crafted through tinkering with governance arrangements but requires struggles and continuous renegotiation as part of larger battles for justice and democracy.
>
> *(Vos, Perreault, and Boelens 2018, 188)*

In conclusion, these perspectives have questions and searches in common. One of them is the emphasis on access to decision-making by affected groups (→ Participation, II/42), and another is the struggles that develop to reach this participation. Pellow and Brulle have argued environmental justice scholars need to appreciate "the larger social dynamics of the social production of inequality and environmental degradation" (2005, 3).

Inter-American connections between environmental justice debates and struggles

Jedediah Purdy (2001) has highlighted how this effort to address the relationships among race, poverty, and environmental harm has come to rapid prominence in the USA, connecting the environment with social justice or, on an international scale, the environment with human rights (→ II/35). This movement that fights against LULU (locally unwanted land use) has allowed for projects to be challenged when they cause environmental harm in minority areas where so-called minorities or marginalized populations live (Been 1993). Many communities have been accused of having demands for their own local environment, which has been polemically summarized as NIMBY (not in my backyard), BANANA (build absolutely nothing anywhere near anything) and NOTE (not over there either) (Wester-Herber 2004). But it is important to consider this process as not only how a community opposes an activity in a specific physical place. The most important issue to consider from the EJ perspective is the need to also include the place-identity in the discussion concerning risk, as Misse Wester-Herber has pointed out.

> Risk can be defined in many ways that can range from a strict technical estimate of the probability and magnitude of a negative outcome, to other definitions of risk that include social filters or individual preferences that need not be dependent on a technical calculation.
>
> *(Wester-Herber 2004, 109)*

The relationships between different EJ struggles around the world increased during the 1990s. Robert Bullard, who is recognized as the founder of the environmental justice movement in the USA, documented many of the struggles. He was influential in Brazil in the 1990s as well as also pushing national environmental justice movements in South Africa (Anguelovski 2015). "The civil rights heritage of the environmental justice movement of the USA has also been useful worldwide because of its contributions to non-violent Gandhian forms of struggle" (Martínez Alier 2002, 14), as exemplified in the resistance of the rubber-tappers named "empates" (in Acre, Brazil), among others (Barbosa de Almeida, 2004) (→ Social Movements, I/41). One current of environmental justice that encompass the environmental justice movement from USA with other popular ecologisms can be seen in the convergence between the rural "Third World" notion of the environmentalism of the poor, and the urban notion of environmental justice as used in the USA (Guha and Martínez Alier 1997).

There are other countries where the EJ perspective has won less attention or contain processes with different characteristics. For example, Canada has been noted as a country that does not show such large-scale patterns of racial segregation, either regionally or in urban areas, and also has a different racial history, different discourses and dynamics than in the USA (→ Race, I/39) (Teelucksingh 2002; Haluza-Delay 2007). Nevertheless, there are also studies in Canada inspired by the U.S.-EJ perspective (Fryzuk 1996). Canadian environmental inequality research is dominated by situations involving aboriginal peoples, who are faced with considerable environmental injustice in terms of abrogation of treaties, land rights (→ Land, II/15), resource management and living conditions, and a depreciation of their traditional knowledge (Haluza-Delay 2007). Multiculturalism (→ I/36) hides systemic inequalities, such as the poor infrastructure in many indigenous communities that produce environmental and health risks, including contaminated water. In this sense, the framing and utility of EJ must be sensitive to the Canadian context (Teelucksingh, Poland, and Buse

2016, 3). This situation is shared with other aboriginal and indigenous peoples from Central and South America, and facilitates networks between these peoples (→ Indigeneity, I/31).

The country of South America that has received heavy U.S.-American influence with regards to the environmental justice perspective has been Brazil. The realization of the "United Nations Environmental Conference" in Rio de Janeiro in 1992 (also called the "Earth Summit"), opened a new opportunity for articulation: the "Brazilian Forum of non-governmental organizations (NGOs) and Social Movements for the Environment and Development." This space allowed for discussion of environmental issues in a broader critical debate with the objective to search for alternatives to the dominant development model (→ Development, II/6). It established a dialogue around the construction of common agendas among environmentalist entities and union activists, the movement of landless rural workers (→ Labor Representation, II/14), those affected by dams, community movements on the peripheries of cities, rubber-tappers, extractivists, and the indigenous movement (Acselrad 2010). Previously, the environment had been put on the agenda of the subaltern groups in the 1980s with important social movements like rubber-tappers in Acre State, the Movement of People Affected by Dams ("Movimento de Atingidos por Barragens" – MAB), and the Landless Farm Workers Movement ("Movimento dos Trabalhadores Rurais Sem Terra" – MST), showing the existence of relationships between different movements from diverse countries. The MAB has links with REDLAR (Latin American network against dams and for the rivers, communities, and water), but also includes North American organizations, such as International Rivers, with similar claims and common campaigns (Gómez et al. 2014). The MST is also a member of Via Campesina, an international peasants' movement (→ Social Movements, I/41).

Transnational networks of a global environmental justice movement?

Joan Martínez Alier et al. (2016) claim that there is a global movement for environmental justice. Although almost all conflicts are local and they target specific local grievances, the movement is global because such local events belong to classes of conflicts that appear regularly elsewhere in the world (→ Alter-Globalization, I/3). The authors highlight that the EJ movement raises the conflict issue to a global level through movements' networks that favor connections between local experiences. Another issue is that the same companies act in different countries, depending on the legal and institutional limits that each country has. One interesting source to analyze trans- and multinational corporations (→ II/7) involved in most of the environmental conflicts is the Atlas of Environmental Justice, coordinated by the team of Joan Martínez Alier, with collaboration of different researchers and social movements around the world.

Another important example of EJ networking happened in 1991 in Washington D.C. with the "First National People of Color Environmental Leadership Summit." The meeting furthered the building of a multiracial grassroots movement around environmental and economic justice, with delegates from Puerto Rico, Chile, Mexico and other countries. The summit delegates adopted the "17 principles of environmental justice," as a guide for organizing, and their Spanish and Portuguese translations were used and circulated by NGOs and environmental justice groups at the Earth Summit in Rio de Janeiro (Bullard and Johnson 2000).

A few years later, representatives of EJ movement networks in the United States traveled to Brazil, in 1998, to promote their experience and establish relations with local organizations willing to establish alliances in the resistance to processes of "exportation of environmental injustice" (Acselrad 2010). This alliance included NGOs, workers' unions and university research groups. The objective was to re-work the USA experience but through Brazilian entities, and the results were three volumes of the series "Unionism and Environmental Justice" (IBASE/CUT-RJ/IPPUR-UFRJ 2000, in Acselrad 2010). This process stimulated other university groups, as well as NGOs, unions and social movements to explore this debate. As a result, the "Brazilian Environmental Justice Network" was created, and the definition of a category of *environmental justice* was expanded to include a set of principles and practices that broadened the scope of the complaints beyond the issue of environmental racism (Acselrad 2010). Using a narrow perspective of environmental justice, only in parts of the Caribbean basin and Brazil can a comparable legacy of Afro-American slavery (→ I/18), segregation, and civil rights mobilization be found. Nevertheless, race-based struggles for rights and citizenship (→ II/27) have been going on in Latin America for centuries. "Indigenous identity replicates inherited social hierarchies and has long been a focal point of social justice mobilization" (Carruthers 2008, 5) (→ Indigeneity, I/31). In the Caribbean, the term environmental justice is related to climate justice addressing the vulnerabilities of the agriculture, fisheries, and tourism sectors (Maclennan and Perch 2012).

Another example of a network of environmental justice is Colombia. The "Network for Environmental Justice in Colombia (RJAC)" was launched in 2010 and was designed to promote the optimal use of resources with a human rights perspective. It is coordinated with the "Interamerican Association for Environmental Defense (AIDA)" and other organizations and universities participate in this network. Its objective is to propose solutions to environmental conflicts in Colombia, and to promote a fair and effective implementation of national and international environmental law, including the right to a healthy environment (→ Human Rights, II/35).

"Despite the number of mobilization and resistance events and the 'success' of environmental justice, the voices of the communities have been systematically invisibilized (→ Silencing, III/19). Several people have been victims of repression including persecution, judicialization, threats, disappearance, and murder" (Pérez Rincón 2014, 77). Consequently, Latin America remains at the top of the scale for global killings of land and environment defenders in 2017, and Mexico is now a far more dangerous place for those fighting to protect their land (Global Witness 2018). Additionally, types of violence are not always visible, thus necessitating a multidimensional violence approach (Navas, Mingorria, and González 2018).

Isabelle Anguelovski highlights other problems that the environmental justice movement confronts. One of them is the exposure to harm and risk that exists in the workplace, for instance, the contact with pesticides and hazardous waste. Another problem is the deterioration of poor residents' health (→ I/29) in the "Global South," as a consequence of mercury spills from gold mines, open cast copper and coal mining, oil and timber extraction, deforestation and erosion from mono-cultural farming, and hydroelectric dams devastating millions of hectares (→ Extractivism, II/9). In addition, tons of toxic waste from industry, agriculture, electronic products, and ships to be dismantled, are also being exported to poorer countries (Carmin and Agyeman 2011; in Anguelovski 2015). The environmental justice agenda has now expanded to include environmental initiatives such as urban gardening in marginalized neighborhoods, as well as community farms for socializing and building stronger ties (→ Commons, II/31) (Anguelovski 2015).

One special issue is the environmental justice on the borders between the "North" and the "South" of America (→ Borderlands, II/26), in which Mexico is the main example. Hazardous production processes are transferred from the USA to Mexico through transnational corporations operating maquiladoras (Grineski and Collins 2010) (→ Transnational Corporation, II/23; Regional Integration, I/18). However, studies have found that it is generally economically better-off residents who are exposed to greater densities of industrial hazards, which is the opposite of what is usually found in the Global North. The reason is that this class prefers to live in neighborhoods with civil infrastructure. These studies point to the importance of urban development trajectories in shaping patterns of environmental injustice (Grineski, Collins, and Romo Aguilar 2015) (→ Urbanization, I/45). In this sense, David Carruthers (2008) argues that clear correlations between race or poverty and environmental risk do not typically appear in Latin American cities. In the same sense, other research in Latin America, for example, such as in Chile, aims to show that environmental injustice is not always directed toward minority groups and marginalized peoples, but also includes ignoring and endangering the values, rationales and lifestyles of all persons opposed to the dominant development model (Bustos, Folchi, and Fragkou 2016).

Several research teams from civil society (→ II/28), universities and governments have been creating inventories of environmental conflicts, in order to provide knowledge about the commodities that generate conflicts, the actors involved, the forms of resistance and the outcomes of such conflicts in terms of environmental justice (EJAtlas, OCMAL, OLCA, WRM, among others). The objective of these type of maps is not only to show environmental injustices, but also to demonstrate the success in environmental justice. The maps show whether "transformations," alternatives, or new institutions have arisen from such cases, sometimes described as the *productivity of conflicts* (Melé 2003; Merlinsky 2013). In Latin America, at the civil society level, some conflicts have given rise to new public policy tool, *communities consultations*, which are

> a hybrid institution where non-state and state actors and formal and informal institutions are mobilized. Consultations are a strategic tool of social movements and a contested emergent institution – as different state bodies support or reject their validity – that reclaim the right of affected populations and indigenous peoples to participate, in empowering forms, in high-stake decisions that affect their territories, livelihoods and future.
>
> *(Walter and Urkidi 2015, 1)*

Environmental concerns are deeply woven into the fabric of the Latin American popular mobilization for social justice and equity (Carruthers 2008) (→ Social Inequality, II/20). The problem of the extraction of natural resources is rooted in the colonial history of Latin America with the mining exploration of Potosí as its biggest symbol (Alimonda 2011; Machado Araoz 2013) (→ Colonial Economies, I/4). For this reason, the main discussion related to environmental justice adopts the term *extractivism* (→ II/9) and the major debate is the sense of *development* (→ II/6) (Lang and Mokrani 2012). In addition, there are countries where the EJ perspective is new but there are other names to describe this type of movement or ecological distribution conflicts. For instance, in Argentina the main term used by academia and social movements is *socio-environmental conflicts and movements* (Wagner 2016). The study concerning the Argentinean shantytown "Flammable," was the basis of which Javier Auyero and Debora Swistun created the term "Environmental Suffering" (Auyero and Swistun 2009). The authors show that residents doubt or even deny the harmful impact of pollution on their lives, and it was explained through another term: *toxic uncertainty*. From Chile, Paola Bolados (2016) highlights that concepts of suffering and environmental justice take into account cultural understandings of pollution as a social and cultural fact in permanent construction.

Conclusion

The Environmental Justice movement has amplified in its significance from 1980s to the present. It was started as local movements, with specific incidences and objectives: to denounce and stop activities that generate risks. The movement continued, reaching a broader perspective and organizing networks with organizations in other countries. At the same time, social movements (→ I/41) who had not used environmental language added this "new idiom" to their terms. In this way, the singular similarity of the struggle became visible: the unequal distribution of environmental burdens and benefits.

The environmental justice perspective is not only central for analyzing environmental conflicts, but also other social processes and interactions. It acknowledges the unequal positions of different social actors in and beyond conflicts, including people of different ethnic backgrounds, sex, age, capabilities and gender (→ Intersectionality, I/32). Furthermore, it focuses on the unequal distribution of environmental benefits and costs among different social groups (→ Social Inequality, II/20).

Critical thought and action dedicated to studying these power relationships is key to understanding the management and appropriation of natural resources and their use by different social groups. The concept is not only an analytical tool, but a call to organize and reflect on a sustainable form of human-nature relations (→ Nature, II/39).

Thus, the environmental justice movement attacks the lack of democracy (→ II/32) regarding the prevention of environmental contamination. It claims to extend equal social participation (→ II/41) in decision-making processes. In conclusion, environmental justice also implicates justice regarding different aspects of the environment and beyond. As Giovanna Di Chiro says, it involves the protection of the place where we "live, work and play" (1998).

Works cited

Acselrad, Henri. 2010. "Ambientalização das lutas sociais -o caso do movimento por justiça ambiental." *Estudos Avançados* 24, no. 68: 103–119.

Acselrad, Henri, Cecilia Campello do Amaral Mello, and Gustavo das Neves Bezerra. 2009. *O que é Justiça Ambiental.* Rio de Janeiro: Garamond.

Alimonda, Héctor, ed. 2011. *La Naturaleza colonizada: Ecología política y minería en América Latina.* Buenos Aires: CLACSO.

Anguelovski, Isabelle. 2015. "Justicia Ambiental." In: *Decrecimiento: vocabulario para una nueva era,* eds. Giacomo D'Alisa, Federico Demaria, and Giorgos Kallis, 92–97. Barcelona: Icaria-Antrazyt.

Auyero, Javier and Debora Swistun. 2009. *Flammable: Environmental Suffering in an Argentine Shantytown.* Oxford: Oxford University Press.

Barbosa de Almeida, Mauro W. 2004. "Direitos à floresta e ambientalismo: seringueiros e suas lutas." *Revista Brasileira de Ciências Sociais* 19, no. 55: 33–53.

Bauler, Tom. n.d. "Environmental (in) Justice." *Environmental Justice Organizations, Liabilities and Trade. Mapping Environmental Justice (EJOLT).* www.ejolt.org/2013/02/environmental-injustice/

Been, Vicki. 1993. "What's Fairness Got to Do with It? Environmental Justice and the Siting of Locally Undesirable Land Uses." *Cornell Law Review* 78, no. 6: 1001–1085. http://scholarship.law.cornell.edu/cgi/viewcontent.cgi?article=2495&context=clr

Boelens, Rutgerd. 2015. *Water Justice in Latin America: The Politics of Difference, Equality, and Indifference.* Amsterdam: Inaugural Lecture, University of Amsterdam.

Bolados, Paola. 2016. "Conflictos socio-ambientales/territoriales y el surgimiento de identidades post neoliberales (Valparaíso-Chile)." *Izquierdas* 31: 102–129.

Bouzarovski, Stefan and Neil Simcock. 2017. "Spatializing Energy Justice." *Energy Policy* 107: 640–648.

Bullard, Robert D., ed. 1994. *Unequal Protection: Environmental Justice and Communities of Color.* San Francisco CA: Sierra Club Books.

———. 2000. *Dumping in Dixie: Race, Class, and Environmental Quality*. 3rd ed. Boulder, CO: Westview Press.

Bullard, Robert D. and Glenn Johnson. 2000. "Environmental Justice: Grassroots Activism and Its Impact on Public Policy Decision Making." *Journal of Social* 53, no. 3: 555–578.

Bullard, Robert D., Paul Mohai, Robin Saha, and Beverly Wright. 2007. *Toxic Wastes and Race at Twenty 1987–2007*. Cleveland, OH: Justice and Witness Ministries, United Church of Christ.

Bustos, Beatriz, Mauricio Folchi and Maria Fragkou. 2016. "Coal Mining on Pastureland in Southern Chile; Challenging Recognition and Participation as Guarantees for Environmental Justice." *Geoforum*. http://repositorio.uchile.cl/handle/2250/139660

Carmin, Joann and Julian Agyeman. 2011. *Environmental Inequalities beyond Borders: Local Perspectives on Global Injustices*. Cambridge, MA: MIT Press.

Carruthers, David, ed. 2008. *Environmental Justice in Latin America: Problems, Promise and Practice*. Massachusetts: MIT Press.

Day, Rosie. 2018. "A Capabilities Approach to Environmental Justice." In: *The Routledge Handbook of Environmental Justice*, eds. Ryan Holifield, Jayajit Chakraborty, and Gordon Walker, n.p. London: Routledge.

Day, Rosie, Gordon Walker, and Neil Simcock. 2016. "Conceptualising energy use and energy poverty using a capabilities framework." *Energy Policy* 93: 255–264.

EJAtlas. n.d. "Environmental Justice Atlas (EJAtlas)." https://ejatlas.org/(Accessed on 11 June 2019).

Environmental Protection Agency (EPA). 2019. "How Did the Environmental Justice Movement Arise?." *EPA*. www.epa.gov/environmentaljustice

Fryzuk, Lori Anne. 1996. *Environmental Justice in Canada: An Empirical Study and Analysis of the Demographics of Dumping in Nova Scotia*. Ottawa: National Library of Canada.

Garí, Josep A. 2000. *The Political Ecology of Biodiversity*. Oxford: University of Oxford. DPhil thesis.

Di Chiro, Giovanna. 1998. "Nature as Community: The Convergence of Environment and Social Justice." In: *Privatizing Nature: Political Struggles for the Global Commons*, ed. Michael Goldman, 120–143. New Brunswick: Rutgers University Press.

Gómez, Anahí, Lucrecia Wagner, Beatriz Torres, Facundo Martín, and Facundo Rojas. 2014. "Resistencias sociales en contra de los megaproyectos hídricos en América Latina." *European Review of Latin American and Caribbean Studies* 97: 81–104.

Grineski, Sara and Timothy Collins. 2010. "Environmental Injustices in Transnational Context: Urbanization and Industrial Hazards in El Paso/Ciudad Juarez." *Environment and Planning* 42: 1308–1327.

Grineski, Sara, Timothy Collins, and María de Lourdes Romo Aguilar. 2015. "Environmental Injustice along the US–Mexico border: Residential Proximity to Industrial Parks in Tijuana, Mexico." *Environmental Research Letter* 10, no. 19: 1–10.

Guha, Ramachandra and Joan Martínez Alier. 1997. *Varieties of Environmentalism: Essays North and South*. Delhi: Earthscan, London and Oxford University Press.

Haluza-Delay, Randolph. 2007. "Environmental Justice in Canada." *Local Environment* 12, no. 6: 557–563.

Ikeme, Jekwu. 2003. "Equity, Environmental Justice and Sustainability: Incomplete Approaches in Climate Change Politics." *Global Environmental Change* 13, no. 3: 195–206.

Jenkins, Kirsten, Darren McCauley, Rapahel Heffronb, Hannes Stephanc, and Robert Rehner. 2016. "Energy Justice: A Conceptual Review." *Energy Research & Social Science* 11: 174–182.

Lang, Miriam y and Dunia Mokrani, eds. 2012. *Más allá del desarrollo*. México: Fundación Rosa Luxemburg/Abya Yala.

Leite Lopes, José Sérgio. 2007. "Sobre processos de 'ambientalização' dos conflitos e sobre dilemas da participação." *Horizontes Antropológicos* 12, no. 25: 31–64.

Leonard, Liam. 2008. "The Anti-Toxics Movement." In: *The Environmental Movement in Ireland*, ed. Leonard Liam, 119–129. London: Springer.

Machado Araoz, Horacio. 2013. *Potosí El Origen: genealogía de la minería contemporánea*. Buenos Aires: Mar Dulce.

Maclennan, Michael and Leisa Perch. 2012. "Environmental Justice in Latin America and the Caribbean: Legal Empowerment of the Poor in the Context of Climate Change." *Climate Law* 3: 283–309.

Martínez Alier, Joan. 1992. *De la economía ecológica al ecologismo popular*. Barcelona: Icaria.

——. 2002. *The Environmentalism of the Poor: A Study of Ecological Conflicts and Valuation*. Massachusetts: Edward Elgar Publishing.

Martínez Alier, Joan, Leah Temper, Daniela Del Bene, and Arnim Scheidel. 2016. "Is there a Global Environmental Justice Movement?" *The Journal of Peasant Studies* 43, no. 3: 731–755.

Melé, Patrice. 2003. "Introduction: Conflits, territoires et action publique." In: *Conflits et Territoires, Tours*, eds. Patrice Melé, Corinne Larrue, and Muriel Rosemberg, 13–32. France: Presses universitaires François Rabelais.

Merlinsky, Gabriela, ed. 2013. *Cartografías del Conflicto Ambiental en Argentina*. Buenos Aires: CLACSO-CICCUS.

Navas, Grettel, Sara Mingorria, and Bernardo Aguilar González. 2018. "Violence in Environmental Conflicts: The Need for a Multidimensional Approach." *Sustainability Science* 13, no. 3: 649–660. https://doi.org/10.1007/s11625-018-0551-8.

OCMAL (Mining Conflicts Observatory of Latin America). n.d. *Surge una esperanza común*. In: www.ocmal.org/ocmal/#esperanza-comun (Accessed on 11 June 2019).

OLCA (Latin American Observatory of Environmental Conflicts). n.d. *Conflictos observados*. In: http://olca.cl/oca/enlista02.php?pagn=0&c_sel=11 (Accessed on 11 June 2019).

Peet, Richard and Michael Watts, eds. 1996. *Liberation Ecologies*. London: Routledge.

Pellow, David and Robert Brulle. 2005. *Power, Justice, and the Environment*. Cambridge: MIT Press.

Pérez Rincón, Mario Alejandro. 2014. "Injusticias ambientales en Colombia: estadísticas y análisis para 95 casos." *Ambiente y Sostenibilidad* 4: 65–78.

Purdy, Jedediah. 2001. "Shades of Green." *The American Prospect*. November 14. http://prospect.org/article/shades-green

Schlosberg, David. 2004. "Reconceiving Environmental Justice: Global Movements and Political Theories." *Environmental Politics* 13, no. 3: 517–540.

———. 2007. *Defining Environmental Justice: Theories, Movements, and Nature*. Oxford: Oxford University Press.

Teelucksingh, Cheryl. 2002. "Spatiality and Environmental Justice in Parkdale (Toronto)." *Ethnologies* 24, no. 1: 119–141.

Teelucksingh, Cheryl, Blake Poland, and Chris Buse. 2016. "Environmental Justice in the Environmental Non-Governmental Organization Landscape of Toronto (Canada)." *The Canadian Geographer/Le Géographe canadien* 60, no. 3: 1–13.

Temper, Leah and Daniela Del Bene. 2016. "Transforming Knowledge Creation for Environmental and Epistemic Justice." *Current Opinion in Environmental Sustainability* 20: 41–49.

United Church of Christ/Commission on Racial Justice. 1987. "Toxic Waste and Race in the United States. A National Report on the Racial and Socio-Economical Characteristics of Communities with Hazardous Waste Sites." New York.

US Department of Energy. n.d. *Environmental Justice History*. In: https://energy.gov/lm/services/environmental-justice/environmental-justice-history (Accessed on 11 June 2019).

Vos, Jeroen, Tom Perreault, and Rutgerd Boelens. 2018. "Introduction: Exclusion and Struggles for Co-Decision." In: *Water Justice*, eds. Rutgerd Boelens, Tom Perreault, and Jeroen Vos, 188–192. Cambridge: Cambridge University Press.

Wagner, Lucrecia. 2016. "Conflictos socioambientales por megaminería en Argentina: apuntes para una reflexión en perspectiva histórica." *AREAS* 35: 87–99.

Walter, Mariana and Leire Urkidi. 2015. "Community Mining Consultations in Latin America (2002–2012): The Contested Emergence of a Hybrid Institution for Participation." *Geoforum*. http://dx.doi.org/10.1016/j.geoforum.2015.09.007.

Wester-Herber, Misse. 2004. "Underlying Concerns in Land-Use Conflicts—The Role of Place-Identity in Risk Perception." *Environmental Science & Policy* 7, no. 2: 109–116.

Global Witness. 2018. "New data reveals 197 land and environmental defenders murdered in 2017." Feb, 2. *Globalwitness*. www.globalwitness.org/en/blog/new-data-reveals-197-land-and-environmental-defenders-murdered-2017/

World Rainforest Movement (WRM). n.d. *Acerca del WRM*. In: http://wrm.org.uy/es/

9

EXTRACTIVISM

Paul Bowles and Henry Veltmeyer

Models of economic development (→ II/6) based on natural resource extraction (extractivism) have been the subject of controversy and a source of conflict among states (→ Nation State, II/38), transnational corporations (→ II/23), communities, and the labor movement (→ Labor Representation, II/14) since the early decades of the 20th century – indeed even earlier. In fact, it could be argued (see Girvan 2013) that extractivism was a form of capitalism (→ II/2) that predated industrial capitalism, a system based on the exploitation of labor (the unlimited supplies of surplus rural or agricultural labor), by several centuries. From this perspective capitalism, defined on the basis of the capital-labor relation i.e. as a system used to expand society's forces of production and bring about notable improvements in the social condition of the world's population, has had a relatively short history that can be traced back to the 19th century when the fundamental pillars of the system were constructed.

From the same perspective, what is now understood as "neoextractivism" (the combination of extractivism with a new social policy designed to bring about a more inclusive form of development) is the result of conditions generated in the 1980s within the institutional and policy framework of a "new world order" (free market capitalism, neoliberal globalization) on the periphery of the world system, particularly in parts of Latin America (→ Neoliberalism, II/16). Extractivism or natural resource wealth extraction can be traced back for centuries, but neoextractivism as the latest phase of capitalism has a history of only decades. Extractivism, Gudynas (2017) notes, is not an industry, as some economists claim with their language of "extractive industries," since there is no industrial transformation involved. The insistence on qualifying it as an industry, he adds, is to appeal to the imaginary of large factories with many workers as a means of seeking broad support within the citizenry (→ Civil Society, II/28). For this reason, he argues, both for its conceptual limitations and for its political implications the term "extractive industry or industries" must be abandoned. Hence the term (neo)extractivism is used and reserved as a descriptor of capitalism in its latest phase.

This phase began with the deregulated expansion of capital in the form of foreign direct investment (FDI) under the aegis and dictates of the Washington Consensus (Williamson 1990) particularly in the South American periphery of the world capitalist system. This phase generated conditions, the intensification of natural resource extraction and development, new forces of resistance and class struggle (→ II/3), that exposed the fundamental contradictions of the capitalist system – contradictions that raise new questions and pose a serious challenge for communities, researchers, policy-makers, and corporations alike.

This entry provides a summary of the dynamics associated with this challenge, and the debates – and the Inter-American discussion – generated by the expansion of extractive capital in the neoliberal era of capitalist development. Of central concern is the political economy of natural resource extraction, with a particular focus on the contradictions and development implications of the economic development strategy adopted by an increasing number of countries in the Americas – particularly in the southern cone of South America, and the Andes, and by Canada in North America. Behind this concern, which is essentially intellectual or theoretical, is the more practical and existential concern of the indigenous and non-indigenous communities that are negatively impacted by the operations of extractive capital (→ Indigeneity, I/31).

The concept of extractivism and the Latin-American debate

The theoretical and political discourse on extractivism or neoextractivism (with reference to the use of extractivism by the center-left "progressive" Latin-American regimes in the first decades of the new millennium) refers to a national development strategy which relies on the extraction of natural resources and the export of these resources in primary commodity form. This strategy was not new to Latin America: it was the object of a critique launched from the perspective of "dependency theory," a theory that attributed the lack of development (→ II/6), or the underdevelopment of countries in the region, to an economic structure in which countries on the periphery exported raw materials and primary commodities in exchange for the importation of goods manufactured in the center of the system (Kay and Vergara-Camus 2017) (→ Global Commodity Chains, II/12). With reference to this theory, a number of countries in the region initiated a policy of import substitution industrialization based on the regulation of capital and the protection of domestic firms and producers. However, the installation of a "new world order" based on a program of "structural reforms" (neoliberal globalization) in the 1980s created a counter-dynamic, resulting in a deepening of this relation of dependence on the inflow of "resource-seeking" capital and a corresponding reprimarization of exports.

A description of this process might be described as the new geoeconomics of capital based on the expansion of extractive capital in the region. Looking at the geoeconomics of the capital flows – the predominance of resource-seeking capital and an increasing flow to the South American periphery, a situation was created in which conditions were favorable for a resurgence of extractive capital including a primary commodities boom, and compliant governments were anxious to take advantage of their comparative advantage in natural resources (→ Nature, II/39). Several changes in the global economy, especially the rise of China as an economic power and the expansion of the demand for natural resource, aided and abetted this process, resulting in what has been termed the "new dependency" (Arellano 2010; Borón 2008; Martins 2011; Sotelo 2009).

In the Latin-American context, this new dependency has taken the form of an exploitation of natural resources and the export of primary goods – metals and minerals, agro-food and forest products, hydrocarbons and biofuels (→ Energy, II/7) – on a vast scale (Svampa 2012; Svampa and Viale 2014). Extractive projects typically involve large-scale (often foreign) investments in the acquisition of land (→ II/15) – dubbed "landgrabbing" in the discourse of critical agrarian studies (Borras et al. 2012) – concessions to explore and mine for minerals and metals, and infrastructural development projects undertaken by transnational corporations (→ II/23), and capital-intensive activities that generate little employment beyond the construction stage. Extractivism in this context also requires constant territorial expansion – the extension of the extractive frontier into remote areas where there remain large untapped reserves of minerals and sources of energy and agro-food products – leading to the displacement or destruction of alternative, local forms of production and ways of life. The result, for Svampa and other Latin-American scholars of extractivism (Gudynas 2010, 2011, 2017), is a proliferation of enclave economies and the splintering of indigenous and peasant territories through dispossession: "accumulation by dispossession" in Marxist discourse (Harvey 2003).

In the new millennium, changing conditions resulted in an entirely new dynamic based on the new geopolitics (→ II/34) and geoeconomics of extractive capital. At the political level, the activism of the peasant-based social movements (→ I/41) in the 1990s in the resistance against the neoliberal policy agenda resulted in widespread disenchantment and the rejection of neoliberalism as an economic doctrine and development model (→ Alter-Globalization, I/21). By the end of the decade, neoliberalism was on the defensive and gave way to a succession of "progressive" (anti- or post-neoliberal) regimes oriented toward what has been described as "inclusionary state activism" (the use of resource rents collected in the process of primary commodity exports to fund poverty reduction programs) (→ Nation State, II/38). This development was reflected at the level of theoretical discourse in a discussion regarding "neoextractivism" (Gudynas 2010, 2011; Veltmeyer and Petras 2014).

Under conditions of a primary commodities boom on the world market, and the widespread rejection of neoliberalism in both policy circles and the popular sector, as well as the turn of a number of governments away from neoliberalism toward inclusionary state activism, neoextractivism (together with the reprimarization of exports) became the dominant form of capital accumulation and national development in the region.

There are three main sectors of resource extraction and extractive capital. One is based on the extraction of fossil fuels (oil and gas) (→ Energy, II/7), an industry of particular importance to Mexico, which nationalized the oil industry as far back as the 1930s; Bolivia, which, with the second largest reserves of natural gas in the region (second only to Venezuela), decreed that the country's mineral resources and reserves of natural gas and petroleum "belong to the people" and cannot be alienated – sold or ceded to multinational corporations that dominate the extractive sector and related industries; Ecuador, which turned from the export of bananas to the export of oil in the 1980s and 1990s, and today relies on the extraction of oil for its national development; and Venezuela, where today up to 95 percent of export earnings are based on the extraction and exportation of oil. A second sector relates to the extraction of industrial minerals and precious metals (gold and silver), an old industry that can be traced back five hundred years (→ Colonial Economies, I/4), but that has acquired increased importance over the past two decades in the form of open-pit mining, particularly in traditional mining countries such as Chile, Peru and Bolivia, but also in Argentina, Colombia, Mexico and Brazil, the region's biggest recipient of "resource-seeking" FDI. A third sector might be labeled "agro-extractivism" – the extraction of agro-food and forest products, an activity that can also be traced back centuries, but that has assumed increased importance in recent years in global commodities trade. The most important development in this sector is the conversion of land (→ II/15) from the production of food to the production of energy (→ II/7) in the form of biofuels such as ethanol and soy.

Biofuels, as a source of energy, have turned into a major driving force of capitalist development in South America. In the cases of Paraguay and Uruguay, over 60 percent of the country's arable land is now given over to the production of soybeans for export. In Bolivia, soybean is the most treasured crop in the agricultural sector with over 14,000 producers and 45,000 workers, more than that engaged in the production of coca, the traditional agro-extraction crop. In Argentina, over 19.5 million hectares of farmland, accounting for 18 percent of worldwide soy production, is dedicated to growing soybeans (Giarracca and Teubal 2014, 54–55).

Predictably this dynamic has given rise to new cycles and forms of resistance and repertoires of social protest as well as major social conflicts over territorial rights to land, water, and natural resources (Bebbington 2012; Bebbington and Bury 2013). While the extractive model has assumed its most violent forms in countries governed by forces on the political Right, most infamously in Colombia where mining projects have advanced under the protective shield of paramilitary death squads, the center-left regimes have also embraced the model and found themselves mediating confrontations between extractive capital and socio-environmental movements in the popular sector (see Petras and Veltmeyer 2009) (→ Environmental Justice, II/8). Indigenous territories and communities are at the leading edge of both the extractive capital frontier and the related social conflicts (→ Indigeneity, I/31).

These conflicts, and associated pressures and struggles, generally pit peasant and indigenous movements against the companies in the extractive sector and at times the governments that facilitate their operations (Bebbington and Bury 2013). In this situation, the indigenous and peasant communities in the zones where the sought-after resources are located and extracted are confronting forces and conditions leading to the dispossession of their lands, the loss of livelihoods, the pillage and looting of their subsoil resources, the degradation of the environment and their habitat, and also the privatization (→ II/17), commodification, and pollution of the water on which their livelihoods, health and well-being, not to mention life itself, depend (→ Disaster, II/33). At the same time, while the mining companies made windfall profits as they rode the wave of soaring prices associated with the primary commodities boom, governments came to increasingly depend on FDI for the extraction of their countries' natural resource wealth as well as on the revenues derived from resource rents collected in the process (Cypher 2010; Helbling et al. 2008).

Schools of thought on extractivism

In the debates that have surrounded the question of "extractivism," three schools of thought have emerged. The first school includes advocates of "inclusive growth" or sustainable natural resource development and those who favor and support extractivism as an economic development strategy but see it as an issue of socially responsible development or as a management issue – resource management and management of the inevitable conflicts that extractive capitalism generates.

A second school of thought could be labeled "anti-extractivist," either because extractivism is viewed as fundamentally incompatible with the cultural values placed by indigenous communities and environmentalists on the environment (→ Indigeneity, I/31; Environmental Justice, II/8), as well as the protection of their territorial rights and livelihoods, or because of the deep contradictions of extractive capital with development or post-development in the form of living well in social solidarity and in harmony with nature (→ II/39) (Huanacuni Mamani 2010). This anti-extractivist school brings together both environmentalists and social ecologists who prioritize the environment over and above industrialism and extractivism in any of its forms (regardless of corporate social and environmental responsibility, or pretensions of "sustainability" or social inclusion), (→ Deindustrialization, II/5) as well as Marxist political economists concerned with the contradictions of extractive capital and even development economists concerned about the development implications of what has been described as a "resource curse" (Acosta 2009; Auty 1993; Frankel 2012; Haber and Menaldo 2012).

A third, much smaller school of thought, most notably features Alvaro García Linera, the Vice-President of Bolivia. He is the chief ideologue of "socialism" in the Bolivian context, where socialism (→ I/42) is not seen as an alternative system to capitalism or "a new mode of production that would coexist alongside capitalism" but as a "battlefield between capitalism in crisis and the tendencies, potentialities and efforts to bring production under community ownership and control" (García Linera 2013, 4). He is also a highly respected sociologist who is convinced that it is possible to combine extractivism with both socialism and the indigenous concept of "living well" – *buen vivir* in Ecuador, or *vivir bien* in Bolivia (Gudynas and Acosta 2011). A similar conclusion is reached by the Argentinian sociologist Maristella Svampa on the basis of an examination of the political-ecological studies of such thinkers as Alberto Acosta and Eduardo Gudynas, and a particular focus on their proposals for a transition away from extractive capitalism toward a post-development alternative future. She concludes that this need not mean a halt to all extractive activities, but would prioritize the raising of living standards in a framework of truly sustainable production, or, as argued by García Linera, "increasing communal ownership and control" over productive processes, whether extractivist or nonextractivist, and securing the "social distribution of the resulting wealth" – "to generat[e] wealth [via natural resource extraction] and redistribut[e] it among the population, reducing poverty and extreme poverty" (García Linera 2013, 7) (→ Commons, II/31). In this conception, natural resource extraction would be geared primarily toward endogenous needs rather than externally driven market opportunities, and kept within strict ecological limits. Immediate steps to be taken would include extraordinary taxation (→ II/22) and redistribution of the vast profits accruing to the mining companies, as well as a moratorium on new oil and gas exploration. The success of any transition would hinge on the regional balance of social forces, and upon the steps taken on a global scale to end the use of fossil fuels.

The war over water – the new frontier of resistance to extractivism

Access to safe water for the world's poor has been one of the fundamental problems confronted by the development community for many decades, a problem that has been accentuated in recent years by the extension of the neoliberal policy agenda to the privatization (→ II/17) of the means of social production and the commodification of the productive resources of land and forests, water and waterways, and subsoil minerals and metals. Throughout the 20th century, capitalist development of the forces of production was associated with a process of "accumulation by dispossession" – dispossession of the small-scale rural producer, family farmers or peasants from the land, resulting in a protracted century-long struggle for land (→ II/15). But the return of capitalism in recent years toward an extractive strategy has shifted the class struggle (→ II/3), and the forces of resistance, toward resisting the new enclosures of the global commons (→ II/31), that is, to resist the forces of capitalist development that have been mobilized to privatize and commodify the last remaining element of the global commons: water (Barlow 2009; Barlow and Clarke 2005; Shiva 2002).

A major milestone and turning point of this "development" was the water war in Cochabamba, Bolivia, a series of protests that took place in Bolivia's third largest city between December 1999 and April 2000 in response to the privatization of the city's municipal water supply. The resulting wave of demonstrations and police violence was described as a public uprising against water prices, but it had a significance that reaches well beyond Bolivia, prefiguring as it did what is now regarded as one of the most important battle-places for the world market and the resistance to the advance of extractive capital in the 21st century. The water war in Cochabamba and elsewhere, however, has not settled the issue and the struggle over the privatization of the access to water remains a major issue for both extractive capital and communities around the world who have been denied open and free access to what is not only a major productive resource but a source of life – a fundamental human right (→ II/35).

The dynamics of this struggle, the contestation of water rights and the efforts to strengthen local water control can be traced not only in the Andean countries (Boelens 2008) but also the Mexican and Canadian borders of the U.S. where the demand for water, and a process of water-grabbing, is well underway (Barlow 2009). Canada, with 20 percent of the world's freshwater, is a site of continued interest to global capital and of resistance; bulk water exports were excluded from the 1994 NAFTA Agreement but its replacement by the U.S.–Mexico–Canada Agreement (USMCA) in 2019 has set the scene for potential renewed struggles over the commodification of water notwithstanding the (vague) provisions of the USMCA Side Letter on water. Within the U.S. and Canada too, the emergence of indigenous and other "water protectors," opposing extractive capital's threat to water from infrastructure (such as the Dakota Access Pipeline in the U.S.) as well as from new technologies such as fracking, illustrate the internationalization of the struggles over water (See also Barlow and Clarke 2005).

The Inter-American discussion

While extractivism and the struggles arising from it are common across many Latin-American countries, there are also Inter-American entanglements, connections and parallels, which can be seen from including Canada in the discussion. Firstly, much of the increase in FDI into Latin America, increasingly more of which has been directed to the resources sector has come from Canada. Official figures show that Canada's stock of FDI in Latin America stood at C$2.6 billion in 1990 but increased by over 2000 percent to C$59.4 billion in 2013 (Gordon and Webber 2016, 15). This was four times faster than the rate of growth of FDI from the U.S. and pushed Canada to become the second largest external source of FDI to the region (after the U.S.) between 2007 and 2012 (ibid. 16). Furthermore, the expansion of Canadian capital into the extractive sector in Latin America was strongly encouraged and facilitated by the Canadian state. The state-capital nexus in this process has been such that Canada played the role of what Gordon and Webber (2016) call that of a secondary imperialist power.

While these flows demonstrate Inter-American capitalist entanglements, the process of extractivism in Canada itself exhibits many of the same characteristics as the Latin-American experience. The long commodities boom of 2000–14, led by Chinese demand, gave a huge spur to extractivism in Canada especially in the oil, gas, and minerals (including precious metals, the molybdenum used in steel-making, coal, and potash). The Conservative government at the time encouraged this expansion believing that it would turn Canada into an "energy superpower" (→ Energy, II/7).

While dependency theory in Latin America had questioned the long-term viability of extractivism as a development strategy and pointed to the need for industrialization, Canada had its own history of a similar debate. The staples approach, described by Watkins (2006) as "Canada's most distinctive contribution to political economy," analyzes the impacts of global forces on the export of natural resources from "new countries" such as Canada, characterized by low labor to land ratios. Pioneered by Innis, the staples approach points to how dependence on natural resource exports leads staple economies to be subject to higher volatilities in prices and output, lack control over their own economic resources and destiny, make them dependent on inflows of foreign capital, and shape their political cultures. The data on Canadian FDI presented above suggests that Canadian capital is not as weak and underdeveloped as the staples approach might imply, but the limitations of the extractivist strategy remain important.

For Innis's followers, extractivism was seen as limiting development, placing obstacles in the way of independent economic development and preventing Canada from transitioning to a mature capitalist economy; countries could become caught in a "staples trap" or the "straitjacket of soft capitalism" as Drache (1991, 24) calls it. Of course, economic development was possible; it was just that it had certain limiting characteristics. Just as in the Latin-American case, it was seen as producing enclave economies, structurally only weakly linked to the rest of the economy and incapable of generating widespread industrialization. Canada had sought to develop its own industrial sector behind tariff walls but with the signing of the Canada–U.S. Free Trade Agreement in 1989 and NAFTA in 1994 (→ Regional Integration, II/18), Canada followed the same neoliberal path as Latin-American countries. The commodities boom led to a high value for the Canadian dollar and this further spurred the loss of manufacturing jobs and the increased reliance on commodity exports (→ Deindustrialization, II/5).

Just as in Latin America, this has resulted in multiple conflicts. Three main lines of challenge to the extractivist model can be identified and illustrated by examples from northern British Columbia, a resource rich region on Canada's west coast and which experienced the pull of commodity exports to China in a particularly intense way. The first set of challenges arose from the concerns articulated by the staples approach that extractivist projects provide only limited economic linkages. As an example of this, is the campaign waged by a local NGO, Douglas Channel Watch, in Kitimat (see Bowles and MacPhail 2017). Kitimat was the proposed terminus of the Enbridge Northern Gateway pipeline which would transport oil from the Alberta oil sands to Kitimat for shipping to Asia. But, in a plebiscite held in April 2014, the municipality of 9,000 people voted against the pipeline proposal even though it had been approved by the Federal Joint Review Panel (JRP). Three of the five major arguments used by the NGO directly appealed to the lack of linkages to the rest of the economy and the limited employment benefits for local workers. These arguments drew on the public consciousness the limits of staples development – implicitly a reference to Innis's famous characterization of Canada as being comprised of "hewers of wood and drawers of water" and an important narrative in resource communities. The focus on limited labor impacts has been recognized as having Americas-wide parallels that "inclusionary" policies have sought to partly address. Also Americas-wide is a critique of the way in which labor is incorporated in the extractive sector where it is found; although typically relatively well-paid in the formal sector it has also been the site of protracted labor struggles, and of gendered and racialized workforces (→ Intersectionality, I/32; Gender and Work, II/11); male workers have often dominated direct employment but gendered and racialized employment discrimination, prostitution, and increased domestic and sexual violence are also common at extractive sites (see Jenkins 2014 for the example of mining).

But as in Latin America, new forms of protest and public opposition to extractivism have arisen. One of these concerns the demands for "procedural justice." In the eyes of extractivism's opponents, this has been violated by the ways in which *referenada* and *consultas* have been ignored in many Latin-American countries. In Canada, there are also examples such as that by of the Carrier Sekani Tribal Council (CSTC) which decided to boycott the JRP hearings on the Enbridge Northern Gateway pipeline proposal because they did not feel that they had the resources, human or financial, to compete with the proponent, the world's largest pipeline company. Since they were unable to compete on an equal footing, they believed that to participate in the JRP process would have provided it with an appearance of legitimacy which it did not deserve. The CSTC chose, therefore, to boycott the hearings and join others in pursuing legal action subsequently.

A third type of opposition to extractivism is based on environmental and recognition concerns. That natural resource projects give rise to concerns over environmental impacts is stating the obvious. Recognition draws upon the idea that the values and lifestyles of all residents are recognized and validated, especially those of marginalized groups including indigenous peoples (→ I/11). Recognition can also go beyond this to recognize that alternative non-capitalist livelihoods can be threatened by resource projects. This can include the forms of accumulation by dispossession and the commodification of nature (→ II/39) and labor. As an example of this from northern British Columbia consider the opposition to Petronas's proposal (now withdrawn) for a liquefied natural gas (LNG) terminal at Lelu Island on the northwest coast, an opposition led by First Nations (in this case the Lax Kw'alaams Hereditary Chiefs and community members) but supported by a wide range of other organizations and individuals spanning the both indigenous and settler communities. The concern is that the terminal threatened salmon spawning grounds and this mobilized many, indigenous and non-indigenous, who rely on wild salmon for subsistence and for sharing in non-capitalist forms as well as recreational purposes. These alternative forms of social organization, typically based on local economies, are threatened by industrial resource projects and proponents which do not understand or account for their existence, and lead to opposition as a result (→ Commons, II/31).

Conclusion

Extractivism – a phase of capitalist development (→ II/35) based on the exploitation of raw materials rather than of labor – returned to the Americas as an economic development strategy in the 1980s onwards. In both Latin America and Canada this was driven by a neoliberal policy agenda (→ Neoliberalism, II/16) and led to a reprimarization of the economy (→ Deindustrialization, II/5). The post-neoliberal turn in some of the countries of Latin America left extractivism in place but repackaged it in forms of "inclusive" or "sustainable" development. The reliance on FDI to support extractivism was met in part by increasing FDI from Canada and the U.S. Thus, the new dependency in the southern continent was mirrored by the renewed imperialism from the northern continent (→ Geopolitics, II/34).

Extractivism has generated opposition in both continents and across some common themes. These include the problematic nature of extractivism as an employment generating development model, the adverse environmental consequences which render some areas "sacrifice zones," and the destruction of alternative ways of life. This is especially critical for indigenous peoples (→ Indigeneity, I/31) and their cultures which are threatened by land-based and water-threatening expansions of extractive processes and who are therefore often found as the leaders of resistance to extractivism. Indigenous communities have also linked together across continents and find common cause in their support for the recognition of, and adherence to, the UN's Rights of Indigenous Peoples and especially that regarding the right to free, prior and informed consent (→ Human Rights, II/35). Social movements (→ I/41) and NGOs have also formed information sharing and advocacy alliances across the continents as Canadian-based organizations such as Mining Watch demonstrates (→ Civil Society, II/28). The end of the global commodities boom, rising and organized resistance, together with the increasing severity of global climate change (→ II/30) may point to a relaxation of the reliance on extractivism by states but this is unlikely to be a long-term solution as the logic of capitalist extractivism is to continue to exploit resources until they are gone (→ Capitalism, II/2).

Works cited

Acosta, Alberto. 2009. *La maldición de la abundancia.* Quito: CEP and AbyaYala.

Arellano, Juan Martin. 2010. "Canadian Foreign Direct Investment in Latin America." *Background Paper,* North–South Institute, Ottawa.

Auty, Richard M. 1993. *Sustaining Development in Mineral Economies: The Resource Curse Thesis.* London: Routledge.

Barlow, Maude. 2009. *Blue Gold: The Global Water Crisis and the Commodification of the World's Water Supply.* San Francisco: International Forum on Globalization.

Barlow, Maude and Tony Clarke. 2005. *Blue Gold: The Fight to Stop the Corporate Theft of the World's Water.* New York: The New Press.

Bebbington, Anthony ed. 2012. *Social Conflict, Economic Development and Extractive Industry. Evidence from South America.* Abingdon: Routledge.

Bebbington, Anthony, and Jeffrey Bury. eds. 2013. *Subterranean Struggles: New Dynamics of Mining, Oil, and Gas in Latin America.* Austin: University of Texas Press.

Boelens, Rutgerd. 2008. "Water Fights Arenas in the Andes." *Water Alternatives* 1, no. 2: 48–65.

Borón, Atilio. 2008. "Teorías de la dependencia." *Realidad Económica* 238: 20–43.

Borras, Saturnino, Jennifer Franco, Sergio Gomez, Cristobal Kay, and Max Spoor. 2012. "Land Grabbing in Latin America and the Caribbean." *Journal of Peasant Studies* 39, no. 3–4: 845–872.

Bowles, Paul, and Fiona MacPhail. 2017. "The Town That Said 'No' to the Enbridge Northern Gateway Pipeline: The 2014 Kitimat Plebsicite." *The Extractive Industries and Society* 4, no. 1: 15–23.

Cypher, James M. 2010. "South America's Commodities Boom: Developmental Opportunity or Path Dependent Reversion?" *Canadian Journal of Development Studies* 30, no. 3: 635–662.

Drache, Daniel. 1991. "Harold Innis and Canadian Capitalist Development." In *Perspectives on Canadian Economic Development: Class, Staples, Gender and Elites.* ed. G. Laxer, 22–49. Don Mills: Oxford University Press.

Frankel, Jeffrey A. 2012. "The Natural Resource Curse: A Survey of Diagnoses and Some Prescriptions." *HKS Faculty Research Working Paper Series RWP12-014,* John F. Kennedy School of Government, Harvard University. Cambridge, MA.

García Linera, Álvaro. 2013. "Once Again on So-Called Extractivism." *Monthly Review* 9: 1–9.

Giarracca, Norma, and Miguel Teubal. 2014. "Argentina: Extractivist Dynamics of Soy Production and Open-Pit Mining." In *The New Extractivism.* eds. Henry Veltmeyer and James Petras, 47–65. London: Zed Books.

Girvan, Norman. 2013. "Extractive Imperialism in Historical Perspective: A Caribbean View." Presentation at the Alternative Trade and Development conference, Saint Mary's University, Halifax, 1 November.

Gordon, Todd, and Douglas Webber. 2016. *Blood of Extraction: Canadian Imperialism in Latin America.* Halifax: Fernwood Books.

Gudynas, Eduardo. 2010. "The New Extractivism in South America: Ten Urgent Theses about Extractivism in Relation to Current South American Progressivism." *Bank Information Center.* www.bicusa.org/en/Article.11769.aspx.

Gudynas, Eduardo. 2011. "La izquierda de los límites al nuevo extractivismo." *La Primera* 11 de mayo. www.diariolaprimeraperu.com/online/columnistas/la-izquierda-de-los-limites-al-nuevo-extractivismo_85841.html.

———.2017. "Extractivisms: Concepts, Local Impacts and Spill-Effects." In *Alternative Development Models: Latin American Results and Prospects?* eds. Ronaldo Munck and Henry. Veltmeyer, 37–52. London: Routledge.

Gudynas, Eduardo and Alberto Acosta. 2011. "El buen vivir más allá del desarrollo." *Revista Qué Hacer* 181: 70–81.

Haber, Stephen, and Victor Menaldo. 2012. "Natural Resources in Latin America: Neither Curse Nor Blessing." *SSRN Working Paper*, Oxford Handbook of Latin American Political Economy. Available at SSRN: http://ssrn.com/abstract=1625504.

Harvey, David. 2003. *The New Imperialism*. Oxford: Oxford University Press.

Helbling, Thomas, Valeria Mercer-Blackman, and Kevin Cheng. 2008. "Riding a Wave." *Finance and Development* 45, no. 1: 10–15.

Huanacuni Mamani, Fernando. 2010. *Buen Vivir/Vivir Bien: Filosofía, políticas, estrategias y experiencias regionales andinas*. Lima: Coordinadora Andina de Organizaciones Indígenas – CAOI.

Jenkins, Katy. 2014. "Women, Mining and Development: An Emerging Research Agenda." *The Extractive Industries and Society* 1, no. 2: 329–339.

Kay, Cristóbal, and Leonardo Vergara-Camus. 2017. "Agribusiness, Peasants, Left-Wing Governments, and the State in Latin America: An Overview and Theoretical Reflections." *Journal of Agrarian Change* 17, no. 2: 239–257.

Martins, Carlos Eduardo. 2011. *Globalizacao, Dependencia e Neoliberalismo na América Latina*. Sao Paulo: Boitempo.

Petras, James, and Henry Veltmeyer. 2009. *What's Left in Latin America*. London: Ashgate Publishing.

Shiva, Vandana. 2002. *Water Wars: Privatization, Polution and Profit*. New York: South End Press.

Sotelo, Adrián. 2009. "Neo-imperialismo, dependencia e novas periferias." In *A América Latina e os desafíos da globalizaca*, eds. Emir Sander and Theotonio dos Santos, 327–378. Rio de janeiro: Boitempo.

Svampa, Maristella. 2012. "Resource Extractivism and Alternatives: Latin American Perspectives on Development." *Journal für Entwicklungspolitik (JEP)* 28, no. 3: 43–73.

Svampa, Maristella, and Enrique Viale. 2014. *Maldesarrollo. La Argentina del extractivismo y el despojo*. Buenos Aires: Katz.

Veltmeyer, Henry, and James Petras. 2014. *The New Extractivism*. London: Zed Books.

Watkins, Mel. 2006. "A Staple Theory of Economic Growth." In *Staples and Beyond: Selected Writings of Mel Watkins*. eds. H. Grant and D. Wolfe, 5–29. Montreal: McGill-Queen's University Press.

Williamson, John. 1990. "What Washington Means by Policy Reform." In *Latin American Adjustment: How Much has Happened?* ed. J. Williams, 7–40. Washington: Institute for International Economics.

10
FORDISM

Joachim Becker and Rudy Weissenbacher

The epistemological concept of Fordism is most often used to refer to a) the phase of global capitalism (→ II/2) between 1945 and the crisis (→ II/4) of the 1970s that is euphemistically dubbed the "Golden Age" and b) the political-economic model of accumulation and regulation during this time period. The stability that is ascribed to this period (especially if one compares it to later periods) was safeguarded by strong post-war regulations within the Bretton Woods system which lasted until 1971–73. Of course, stability was the perception of core countries within the *Pax Americana* and seen differently in Kinshasa, Hanoi, or Santiago de Chile. This entry will distinguish between core and peripheral Fordism. Overall Fordism stands for a new social and political-economic formation within the capitalist period, named monopoly capitalism, organized capitalism, or imperialism that left behind liberal industrial capitalism by the turn of the 20th century.

Origins of Fordism

In the early days of monopoly capitalism in the late 19th century, corporate integration of industry and finance in the USA began forming conglomerates and started to homogenize labor and production. What was later known as Fordist production was the overall restructuring process of production in the prime challenger of *Pax Britannica*, exemplified by the Ford Motor Company. Employers needed a compliant and efficient workforce that matched rising productivity. Workers resisted and tried to avoid these early homogenization attempts (→ Labor Representation, II/14). The new "scientific" principles of Taylorism (that led to the conveyor belt and drive system) helped to justify the homogenization of labor which lead to the segmentation of work, divided and alienated workers, and impaired solidarity among them. "[T]he supposedly impartial findings of science tended to confirm the approach of management, not labour. Collective bargaining had little place in a world of technological imperatives and piece-work wages" (Maier 1970, 31). Wages were linked to output and prompted a possible increase of daily earnings (up to a third). Wage differences divided workers even further. Generally, labor supply countered wage bargaining power even if the demand for labor increased. Huge immigration waves came from Europe (and into the factories) (→ Migration, I/15), more women entered the labor market (→ Gender and Work, II/11) resulting in segregation dividing workers along ethnic and gender lines

(→ Ethnicity, I/25). Above all, African-American workers earned only about a third of white workers in 1910 and were not admitted to most American Federation of Labor Unions (AFL) (Meyer 1980, 69–70; Gordon, Edwards, Reich 1983, 119–120, 140, 171; Zinn 1995, 320). Despite rationalization of production, productivity increases seemed limited to the expansion of the workforce at the Ford Motor Company. On the eve of introducing the assembly line (1913) and the infamous five-dollar-a-day wage (1914), Ford faced massive labor turnover and inability to meet demands. "The Ford Company simply had no choice" (Dassbach 1991, 87) than to compensate workers for intensification of work efforts, increase in work tempo, and the degradation of working conditions that transformed mechanics into workers within a few months. The five-dollar wage almost doubled the income for a section of workers by a "profit sharing plan," which led predominantly foreign-born workers to adapt to a disciplined U.S.-American lifestyle and work habits, defined and controlled by the Ford Company's Sociological Department (Meyer 1980, 69). Between the 1890s and the 1920s, homogenization "helped restore stability to the production process and foster renewed control by the employer over production workers" (Gordon, Edwards, Reich 1983, 127). Repression of radicals and campaigns against unions accompanied further segregation of workers in the 1920s, before the depression halted this homogenization (Gordon, Edwards, Reich 1983, 171).

Fordism and Americanism: the Northern – U.S.-centered perspective

In the Interwar Years, Gramsci discussed Fordism from a broader perspective and linked Fordist tendencies with their country of origin, the USA, coining the term "Americanism" (1971, 279). Gramsci transcended the "narrow technological-economic perspective" (Hübner 1990, 122) and regarded the changes in the forms of production and standardized mass production as the change towards a new civilization model and form of hegemony. He underlined that the implementation of the new production model was contingent on the change of behavioral norms, a "new way of life" (Gramsci 1971, 317). It was the regulation that originated in the years fighting the depression that institutionalized capital labor relations (→ Class Struggle, II/3) during the era of the New Deal, and which laid the base for a "new social structure of accumulation" (Gordon, Edwards, Reich 1983, 169). This was a long period of "incubation," as Elmar Altvater (1992, 23) argues, that institutionally complemented the original Fordist productivity increases. The New Deal politics in the U.S. were followed by Keynesian state interventionism in nearly all developed Western capitalist countries (→ State Transformation, II/21). Therefore, only the period after World War II can truly be called the "Fordist" stage of capitalist development (→ II/6).

It was from this broader perspective that the term Fordism was utilized by Michel Aglietta in his founding work of the French regulationist school *A Theory of Capitalist Regulation: The US Experience,* originally published in 1976. In his reformulation of Marxist concepts, Aglietta referred empirically to the U.S. experience, as indicated in the subtitle of the book. Aglietta started his discussion of Fordism with the labor process, which he considered characterized by "semi-automatic assembly line production" (1987, 117). This form of production was gradually transferred from the production of standardized final consumption goods upstream to the production of components. The departments of means of production and consumption goods became more closely linked, causing both consumption and production norms to coevolve (Aglietta 1987, 159). Two commodities – automobiles and standardized housing – came to epitomize this new capitalist era. However, the spread of mass consumption was not only contingent on the generalization of wage labor (→ Consumerism,

I/23), but also on collective bargaining, access to credit for workers, and the public provision of infrastructure. In the USA, the so-called collective consumption (e.g. transport infrastructure) also became of growing importance.

Aglietta did not explicitly discuss the international dimension of Fordism (Aglietta 1987, 32). The key to such a dimension, to which Aglietta attached the term imperialism, is a

> hegemony difficult to exhibit through which one state manages to influence a series of other states to adopt a set of rules that are favourable to the stability of a vast space of multilateral commodity relations guaranteeing the circulation of capital.
>
> *(1987, 32)*

Fordism coincided with U.S. hegemony and its principles were transferred to other areas of the capitalist core. However, even in Western Europe, U.S. Fordism was not simply copied, as the local entities required qualifications. In the case of Japan, the appropriateness of the term "Fordism" for the development model was even more doubtful (Jessop 1992, 54).

The French *régulationist* interpretation of Fordism, maintaining a temporary and regionally limited analysis of the capitalist mode of production, made an impression on the U.S. discussion. "I will recourse to the terminology of the école de regulation," argued Mike Davies in his 1986 book on *Politics and Economy in the History of the US Working Class*, "In contrast to the Anglo-American usage, which conventionally discusses 'Fordism' as a more comprehensive application of scientific management to the labor process" (1999, 106, FN 5).

Peripheral Fordism in the south of the Americas

In the 1970s, "a very productive debate took place on the spatiality of capitalism in relation to the state" (Hadjimichalis 2015, 1) in Paris (→ Nation State, II/38), where régulationists, e.g. Alain Lipietz and Michel Aglietta, discussed with social scientists from other fields, such as Henri Lefebvre, Nicos Poulantzas, and Michel Foucault. The theoretical findings from the Latin American dependency school, e.g. Fernando Cardoso and Enzo Faletto (Becker and Weissenbacher 2015) influenced Lipietz's seminal work. Both understood the global periphery as different "situations of dependency" and varying characteristics of peripheral development within the parameters of global capitalism (→ Development, II/6). Cardoso and Faletto seem to have come to similar conclusions as Poulantzas concerning internal and external class relations at the state level that would coin each national system. They were such fruitful theoretical considerations that they seem to have influenced régulationists when they expanded their framework to the Global South. Alain Lipietz (1987, 78) pointed out that Fordist structures could only be found in some areas of the Global South (including Latin America) and, if they existed, had undergone substantial modifications. In Latin America, the concept of Fordism has been primarily applied to those countries that launched a substantial inward-facing industrialization process after the great crisis of 1929 and continued the imports substitution industrialization and export diversification until the 1970s or 1980s. This pertains primarily to Argentina, Uruguay, Brazil, and Mexico. The term "Fordism" is usually employed in a qualified manner, like "peripheral Fordism" (Lipietz 1987, 78; Conceição 1990, 219–20) or "tropical Fordism" (Faria 1996, 81–3). The differences to the "canonical," i.e. U.S. and West European Fordism, made researchers increasingly refrain from employing the term "Fordism," even in a qualified form, and rather apply analytical categories that were more suited to the local conditions (Quemia 2001, 65). In a largely encompassing regulationist study from the late 1980s, Carlos Ominami, a Chilean economist exiled to France and later Minister of Finance in the Chilean Concertación government, did not apply the term Fordism at all in his study on the crisis in the Third World. His characterization of a "mixed regime" of accumulation (Ominami 1986, 143) is relatively close to Lipietz's and Faria's conceptualizations of accumulation in peripheral Fordism. In a recent comprehensive and comparative study, which argues from the perspective of "historical" and "topological" institutionalism (Bizberg and Théret 2015, 27) and draws on the theory of régulation, many types of Latin American capitalism during the phase of import substitution are identified without reference to Fordism (Bizberg 2015, 42).

In the years of complex inward-looking industrial development, the formation of the salaried work force has been less pervasive and more heterogeneous in Latin American countries than in the core countries. Unprotected or informal forms of employment were more widely spread (→ Informality, II/13) and the coverage of the welfare state tended to be less extensive than in the core countries (→ Nation State, II/38). In the post-Fordist period, forms of unprotected and precarious work expanded significantly in the core states whose social structures adopted some features typical of the peripheries. Faria points out that the institutional arrangement pertaining to the wage relations was closer to "core Fordism" in Argentina and Uruguay than in Brazil and Mexico (2004, 102). Fierce social and distributional conflicts manifested in high rates of inflation, occasionally (particularly in Argentina) in hyperinflation. The spill over of distributional conflicts into escalating inflation was much stronger than in the Fordist core economies, where increasing rates of inflation were registered when the Fordist dynamics showed signs of exhaustion. In countries like Argentina and Brazil, the national currency was questioned as a measure of account, means of payment, and storage of wealth. Thus, the monetary order differed between Fordist core economies and Latin American "peripheral Fordist" economies (Faria 1994).

As Ominami points out, "the slow pace which characterises the transformation of the norms of the salaried workers constitutes one of the main blockades of industrialisation processes which are oriented towards the domestic market" (1986, 155). In a large economy like Brazil, however, a very advanced degree of wage inequality provided a significant market of consumer durables (146). The industrial structure exhibited a certain degree of heterogeneity between sub-sectors exhibiting features of intensive accumulation, like reliance on growing productivity (e.g. cars, chemical goods, machinery), and sub-sectors with features of extensive accumulation (e.g. food, wood products, textiles) (Faria and Estrella 1996, 84 ff.) (→ Deindustrialization, II/5). Among the Latin American economies showing features of peripheral Fordism, the Brazilian industry was the only Latin American one that came close to a relatively complete branch structure. The dependence of machinery imports persisted as a weakness of Latin American peripheral Fordism. Export industries remained relatively limited in scope during those years. Thus, the gaps in the production structure had to be closed by commodity exports (→ Extractivism, II/9). The balance of payments proved to be a recurrent external constraint. Different than Keynesianism, its Southern equivalent, Latin American structuralism or Cepalism, named for its intellectual center of Comisión Económica para América Latina (Cepal), identified the subordinate international insertion of the peripheral economies as a key conditioning factor of their development trajectory and assigned high priority towards modifying it (the classical text of Prebisch 1998 on peripheral development patterns in Latin America). One key ingredient of the Cepal strategy was import substitution. The complex internal development models of Latin America reached social and economic limits that were different from Fordism in the core economies. The social contradictions, partially among the dominant class fractions (→ Class Struggle, II/3), were so fierce that there was a swing towards authoritarianism (→ II/25) (Ominami 1986, 157).

Concluding remarks

Fordism serves as a global catchword for the socio-economic dispensation of the three post-WWII decades. The concept of Fordism was developed with the core countries in mind, particularly the USA. It cannot be simply transposed to the periphery. Altvater's account reflects the difficulties to describe an

> international configuration of national Fordisms in the 'First' and the 'Third' World... There was neither modernization nor just dependency but some kind of dependent modernization or modernized dependency. In any case, the countries of the Third World became subordinate partners within the international division of labor.
>
> *(Altvater 1992, 234)*

It is obvious that the concept of Fordism faces similar difficulties if used in Latin America as the "regulating doctrine" of Keynesianism itself. Ultimately, Latin American structuralism (Cepalismo), which guided economic policies from the late 1940s until the early 1970s, adapted elements of Keynesian analysis in a political-economic context and political practice which differed significantly in the peripheral Latin American states (CEPAL). The subordinate insertion into the international division of labor has made the key difference.

Works cited

Aglietta, Michel. 1987. *A Theory of Capitalist Regulation: The US Experience*. London and New York: Verso.

Altvater, Elmar. 1992. "Fordist and Post-Fordist International Division of Labor and Monetary Regimes." In *Pathways to Industrialization and Regional Development*, eds. Michael Storper and Allen J. Scott, 21–45. London and New York: Routledge.

Becker, Joachim, and Rudy Weissenbacher. 2015. "Changing Development Models: Dependency School Meets Regulation Theory." Paper presented at the International Conference Recherche and Régulation. Paris.

Bizberg, Ilán. 2015. "Tipos de capitalismo en América Latina." In *Variedades de capitalismo en América Latina: los casos de México, Brasil, Argentina y Chile*, ed. Ilán Bizberg, 41–94. México City: El Colegio de México.

Bizberg, Ilán, and Bruno Théret. 2015. "Introducción." In *Variedades del capitalismo en América Latina: los casos de México, Brasil, Argentina y Chile*, ed. Ilán Bizberg, 11–39. México City: El Colegio de México.

CEPAL. ed. n.d. "Raúl Prebisch and the Challenges of Development of the XXI Century." Textos Esenciales: Introduction to Keynes. https://biblioguias.cepal.org/prebisch_en.

Conceição, Octavio, and Augusto Camargo. 1990. "Da crise do escravismo à crise do fordismo periférico no Brasil: uma proposta de periodização sob a ótica regulacionista." In *Desvendando a espuma. Reflexões sobre crise, regulação e capitalismo brasileiro*, ed. Luiz Augusto Estrella Faria, Octavio Augusto Camargo Concção and Teresinha da Silva Bello, 209–222. Porto Alegre: FEE.

Dassbach, Carl. 1991. "The Origins of Fordism: The Introduction of Mass Production and the Five-Dollar Wage." *Critical Sociology* 18, no. 1: 77–90.

Davies, Mike. 1999. *Prisoners of the American Dream: Politics and Economy in the History of the Working Class*. London and New York: Verso.

Faria, Luiz, and Augusto Estrella. 1994. "Uma regulação inflacionária: moeda e dinâmica de preços no Brasil." In *Crise ou regulação?* eds. Jorge Mendonça, Paulo Naketani Passos de and Reinaldo Antonio Caranholo, 135–153. Vitória: Editora Fundação Abel de Almeida.

Faria, Luiz, and Augusto Estrella. 1996. "Fordismo periférico, fordismo tropical y posfordismo: el camino brasileño de acumulación y crisis." *Ciclos en la historia, la economía y la sociedad* 6, no. 10: 73–101.

———. 2004. *A Chave do Tamaho. Desenvolvimento Econômico e Perspectivas do Mercosul*. Porto Alegre: UFRGS Editora and FEE.

Gordon, David, Richard Edwards, and Michael Reich. 1983. *Segmented Work, Divided Workers: The Historical Transformation of Labor in the United States.* Cambridge: Cambridge University Press.
Gramsci, Antonio. 1971. *Selection from Prison Notebooks.* London: Lawrence and Wishart.
Hadjimichalis, Costis. 2015. "Geographies of the state: Nikos Poulantzas and contemporary approaches to state/space." Paper presented at the International Conference Nicos Poulantzas, un marxisme pour le XXI Siecle. Paris.
Hübner, Kurt. 1990. *Theorie der Regulation. Eine kritische Rekonstruktion eines neuen Ansatzes der Politischen Ökonomie.* Berlin: Edition Sigma.
Jessop, Bob. 1992. "Fordism and Post-Fordism: A Critical Reformulation." In *Pathways to Industrialization and Regional Development*, eds. Micheal Storper, and Allen J. Scott, 46–69. London and New York: Routledge.
Lipietz, Alain. 1987. *Mirages and Miracles: The Crisis of Global Fordism.* London and New York: Verso.
Maier, Charles. 1970. "Between Taylorism and Technocracy: European Ideologies and the Vision of Industrial Productivity in the 1920s." *Journal of Contemporary History* 5, no. 2: 27–61.
Meyer, Stephen. 1980. "Adapting the Immigrant to the Line: Americanization in the Ford Factory, 1914–1921." *Journal of Social History* 14, no. 1: 67–82.
Ominami, Carlos. 1986. *Le tiers monde dans la crise. Essai sur les transformations récentes des rapports Nord-Sud.* Paris: La découverte.
Prebisch, Raúl. 1998. "El desarrollo económico de América Latina y algunos de sus principales problemas." In *Cincuenta años de pensamiento en la Cepal. Textos seleccionados. Vol 1*, ed. CEPAL, 63–129. Santiago de Chile: Cepal.
Quemia, Miguel. 2001. "Théorie de la régulation et développement: trajectoires latino-américaines." *L'Année de la régulation. Économie, Instiutions, Pouvoirs* 3: 57–103.
Zinn, Howard. 1995. *A people's history of the United States: 1492 – present.* New York: Harper Collins Publishers.

11

GENDER AND WORK

Olga Sanmiguel-Valderrama

Historically, wealth and income distribution in the Americas, and especially in Latin American and the Caribbean societies, have been highly unequal. Since 2002, nonetheless, some progress has been made to reduce income inequality and poverty in many countries of the region (Andrea Cornia 2014, 7–8) (→ Social Inequality, II/20). However, despite this progress, none has been made concerning wealth distribution. In fact, across the Americas wealth and economic power continues to remain in the hands of a minority – the traditional dominant elites and transnational capital, both of which are mostly controlled by men.

As in other regions of the world, in the Americas, women's socioeconomic status differs from that of men, in particular if they are part of ethnic minorities (→ Race, I/39): they have less wealth and earn lower wages than men, perform most of the unpaid social-reproductive work in the household regardless of whether they have a full-time job or not, constitute most of the sole-heads of households, are overrepresented among poor households, face a sharp gender-based occupational segregation in the labor market, experience much higher rates of sexual harassment and violence in the workplace, in public spaces and inside the home, and consistently face higher unemployment rates than men. Even though class and race remain the main causes of inequality among the societies of the Americas, unpaid work, gender-based discrimination, gender-based violence, and differential treatment remain major impediments to women and their efforts to fully enjoy their human and workers' rights (→ Human Rights, II/35).

Conceptual framework

To understand the notion of "Gender and Work," one must first define the meaning of "work" in the global capitalist economy (→ Capitalism, II/2) and how it has been traditionally divided among genders (→ Gender Identities, I/28), classes, ethnicities (→ II/25), and nationalities. Work encompasses mental, emotional and physical labor done by men, women and children. Much of national and international statistics and discourses refer to work as employment that is work done in exchange of money, goods, or services, whether in the formal or informal sectors (→ Informality, II/13) of the paid economy. Within the conceptual framework of the market (supply and demand of goods and services), classical and neoclassical economics count paid work as generators of wealth and hence as the productive forces of society.

In disputing this understanding, and based on Karl Marx's and Friedrich Engels's distinction between exchange value (commodities produced for the market) and use-value (goods and services produced for self-consumption and need), critical feminist scholars have argued that the unpaid domestic work chiefly done by women – and to a lesser degree by other family members – is a part of the paid economy and should count as productive work. The state (→ Nation State, II/38) or society should not only recognize it as valuable, but somehow compensate those who perform it (Marilyn Waring 1988, 1999; Folbre 2000; Ferguson and Folbre 2000; Ferguson 2004). It is in this domestic space where the previous, present and future generations of workers are created, sustained, and cared for, so that they can devote their time and energy to activities in the so-called public sphere, i.e. paid work in the private and public sectors, education (→ I/24), political participation (→ II/41), etc.

Globally, unpaid social-reproductive work involves not only mothering (pregnancy, birthing, and nurturing children), but also caring for the sick and elderly, and the endless housekeeping chores of cooking, shopping, laundry, cleaning, material and emotional support for family members, among others. In the traditional gendered division of labor, households, and especially mothers, hold the responsibility of fulfilling unpaid social-reproductive work (→ Family, I/26).

Unpaid work includes not only biological and social-reproductive work, but also community work, such as volunteer work in a union (→ Labor Representation, II/14), not-for-profit organizations, religious organizations (→ Religious Beliefs, I/40), community associations, and political mobilizations, e.g. for accessing clean water or child care facilities, support for elderly care, mobilizations against racism, privatization (→ II/17) of public services and lands, or for the conservation of environment (→ Environmental Justice, II/8; Nature, 39), dignifying wages and working conditions, etc. (→ Civil Society, II/28).

Within the frameworks of classical and neoclassical economic theories, the regulatory power of the market also shapes micro-level relations and the division of labor within the household and firms. Performing unpaid reproductive work is considered a choice made by individuals out of love or kinship relations, and is regarded as being an efficient allocation of human capital resources – even if it is unpaid, highly regulated by the state, and pivotal for the working of communities, the paid economy and personal, family and social well-being (Luxton and Bezanson 2006). For feminist critical scholars, however, who undertakes the unpaid reproductive work follows the lines of socially constructed hierarchal systems such as patriarchy, racism, nationalism, the international division of labor, and other forms of discriminations, such as xenophobia, ageism, and classism. In concluding this section, for critical scholars, hence, work is divided between paid, underpaid (unequally paid based on gender, ethnicity, age, and nationality or citizenship (→ II/27; Intersectionality, I/32), and unpaid, mostly performed by women. As Maxine Molyneux (1979, 3–4) argued many decades ago, all these forms of work need to be considered in order to truly understand the world of women and work.

The above framework is particularly important across the Americas because most of the unpaid work is performed by women, which places them at a disadvantage in terms of their time and energy to perform paid work. In the region, the world of paid work is still modeled around "the ideal worker" who is totally committed to his/her career, without care-work obligations. It is usually a male who has a "wife" to perform most, if not all, of the unpaid social-reproductive work (Davis 2000; Drago 2007). In Latin America and the Caribbean, women do between 71 and 86 percent of the total unpaid work that households require, depending on the country. Surveys on the use of time by men and women conducted by eighteen countries in the region show that, on average, women work more hours in unpaid work than men and less paid work than men (Aguirre and Ferrari 2013, 88).

The above framework is also important for a region where 80 percent of total household income comes from paid work. On average, 54 percent of total income for both men and women comes from wages and salaries; while 33.7 percent of men's total income and 23.3 percent of women's is derived from self-employment and profits in the formal and informal sectors of the economy (ECLAC 2015, 33, ECLAC 2016, 39) (→ Informality, II/13). This gap is present in the region even when Latin American and Caribbean women surpass other regions in terms of their likelihood to be "entrepreneurs," often more of a euphemism for being self-employed. In Latin America and the Caribbean, "the gap between the number of male and female entrepreneurs is 24% compared to 43% in Asia and 45% in Europe" (IADB 2017). Therefore, the division of paid and unpaid work between men and women, and the quality of work, wages and benefits are critical for the welfare of most Latin Americans and play a key role in human development (→ Development, II/6) and equality goals for the region by gender, race, and class.

Labor force participation by gender

In Latin America and the Caribbean, during the 20th century, the patriarchal division of labor between men and women – by which men were ideally the breadwinners, while women cared for the household and relatives – was the reality for those who could afford it, which generally excluded racialized peoples. However, due to the region's high levels of inequality (→ Social Inequality, II/20), historically many women and children had to undertake underpaid work for their own survival and that of the family. They did so mostly in the informal sectors of the economy in agriculture, petty commerce, and in the service sector as administrative assistants, nannies, cleaners, laundry workers, household servants, and sex workers. This is particularly true for low-income landless individuals from members of Afro-Latino Americans, indigenous, and migrant communities (→ Indigeneity, I/31; Transnational Migration, I/44).

In fact, during Latin America's export boom of natural resources and commodities in the late 19th century, economic inequality increased due to the concentration of ownership of land in the hands of an elite group of mostly European descendants (Coatsworth 2008, 567–568), as well as lack of access to formal education (→ I/24) for the great majority. Income inequality was at historic levels by the 1920s, and contrary to North America and Europe where welfare state policies lowered income inequality, promoted the "family wage" for most of the 20th century, and provided free access to education, in Latin America and the Caribbean, income inequality persisted and even increased in some countries during the 20th century (Williamson 2015). This feature of Latin America propelled many women to work in informal settings (→ Informality, II/20) and in the formal economy in occupations traditionally associated with "women's jobs" (e.g. teachers, secretaries, bank tellers, etc.). Many of the informal occupations, such as those in petty commerce, however, never made it into government statistics, making women's informal paid work invisible.

During the so-called "lost decade" in the 1980s, as neoliberal policies spread across the continent (→ Neoliberalism, II/16) – including the deregulation of labor relations, the privatization (→ II/17) of social security and public service systems, as well as the promotion of export-led development (→ Development, II/6) and free trade (→ Regional Integration, II/18), family incomes plummeted in the midst of high unemployment levels, especially in the late 1980s and 1990s. During the 1990s, except for Brazil, Panama, Uruguay and Chile, the region experienced growing income polarization and an increase in the number of workers living under the poverty line, despite having a paid job.

Lower family incomes, together with higher levels of education, rapid urbanization (→ I/45), the expansion of female intensive export-oriented production (i.e. agribusinesses, textiles and garments in export-processing zones), and feminist and liberal stands that promote women's economic autonomy and independence, propelled even more women to move into the paid economy, either in their home countries or overseas (→ Transnational Migration, I/44). In the region, female labor force participation (FLFP) has steadily increased in recent decades. In 1980, 36 percent of working women had a paid job. By 2008, more than half of women were in the labor market, 51 out of 100. By 2014, 54 percent of working women had a paid job. By 2016, "in some countries like Bolivia, Brazil, Peru and Jamaica, FLFP exceeds OECD levels" (IADB 2017).

In terms of variations by economic income and age, among women of a childbearing age, FLFP reaches 70 percent (ILO/UNDP 2017). As more economic need is present, women's participation in the labor force is much higher among low-income women (72 percent), followed by high-income women (52 percent), and middle-income women (48 percent) (World Bank 2017). High-income family units have the economic means to reduce members' contributions to unpaid work in favor of wage and salaried employment by contracting out unpaid work (i.e. nannies, cleaners, elderly care, cooked food, laundry services, gardening, etc.), generally hiring low-income racialized peoples.

Although in recent decades the increase in women's labor force participation rates have been impressive, men's participation remains higher: 80 percent on average; 83 percent for low-income men; 78 percent for middle-earning men; and 69 percent for high-income men (World World Bank 2017). These figures, however, hide significant differences within the region. For example, Caribbean countries have had historically high levels of female participation in the labor force, in particular the Bahamas, Barbados and Santa Lucia, where FLFP are similar to those of Canada and the USA. The countries of South America, and to a lesser extent Central America, have seen gains in women's paid labor participation rates since the 1990s (ECLAC (Economic Commission for Latin America and the Caribbean) 2016).

In terms of job quality, women entered the labor market at a time of labor deregulation characterized by a sharp rise of regional unemployment rate (between 1990 and 2002), a substantial shift of labor to the informal sector (→ Informality, II/20), lower rates of unionization and a general weakening of unions (→ Labor Representation, II/14), a shrinkage of the industrial working class, a widening gap in the rate of personal wage growth compared to GDP growth per capita, while the minimum/average wage ratio fell and wage differentials by skill widened (Andrea Cornia 2014, 8–13). The neoliberal deregulation of labor markets legalized what was previously considered to be in violation of legal labor standards, increasing formality but with lower standards. Many nations, including the Andean countries, underwent constitutional and national labor law reforms that lowered labor standards, sometimes contrary to the country's commitment to the International Labor Organization (ILO) conventions (→ State Transformation, II/21). Among these changes are part-time or temporary contracts for permanent positions, the elimination of higher pay for nocturnal work and overtime, firing workers who have worked for more than ten consecutive years for the same firm without compensation or significantly reduced rates of compensation, the proliferation of agencies that supply temporary workers, even for permanent posts, and the privatization (→ II/17) of pension plans and workers' compensation schemes. Also, under the premises of neoliberalism (→ II/16), several countries saw a reduction in well-paid, unionized and stable public-sector employment, due to public administration downsizing and the privatization of public services. The public sector has been traditionally a place where women could find well-paid, secure jobs.

After the shift in the region to progressive governments, known as the Pink Tide, in selected countries such as Argentina, Brazil, Bolivia, Ecuador, Uruguay and Venezuela, public policy began addressing "unemployment, job informalization, falling unskilled and minimum wages, diminishing coverage of social security, and weakening of institutions for wage negotiations and dispute settlements" (Andrea Cornia 2014, 22). These policies together with rising educational achievements contributed to moderate growth in average wages for both men and women and an increase in unionization in countries such as Brazil and Argentina. Most countries of the region increased public social expenditure financed by tax reforms (→ Taxation, II/22) reducing income inequality, albeit income inequality remains one of the highest in the world (Andrea Cornia 2014, 24) (→ Social Inequality, II/20).

Gender, race, age and nationality wage gaps

Although FLFP rates have increased steadily in recent decades in Latin America, and despite the fact that women in various countries, such as Argentina, Brazil, Colombia and Chile, among others, have on average surpassed the educational levels of those of men (with the exception of Bolivia, Haiti and Guatemala) (→ Education, I/24), women are still paid less than men and are concentrated at the lower ranks of the hierarchies in both the formal and informal labor markets. The gender wage gap persists even though "53.7 per cent of economically active women reached ten or more years of formal education, compared with 40.4 per cent for men. In addition, 22.8 per cent of women in the workforce have college education, against 16.2 per cent for men" (Tinoco 2014). The same type of discrimination occurs in fields that require high educational attainment levels. Women "constitute a minority in the field of scientific and technological research and receive less funding than their male colleagues. They also occupy relatively few management positions in the information and communications technologies sector" (ECLAC (Economic Commission for Latin America and the Caribbean) 2016, 77).

Recently, the wage gap has narrowed, mainly due to a decrease in men's formal sector wages, but still, on average, men make 17 percent more than women of the same age and occupation. There are great variations across the region: in Mexico, women earn an average of 20 percent less than men; in Argentina, 12 percent less; and in Brazil, the figure is 25 percent less (Chioda, Garcia-Verdu and Muñoz-Boudet 2011). According to the UN's Economic Commission for Latin America and the Caribbean (ECLAC 2016), among women with more than thirteen years of education the wage gap is higher, as they earn 26 percent less than their male peers. Likewise, Panizza and Zhen-Wei Qiang (2005) found that women are paid less than men in the private and public sectors, but the gap is larger in the private sector. Wage differentials among men and women are attributed to employers' bias toward women, who see them as less committed, less productive due to women's unpaid work in the home, but they are also perceived as being less competent just for being women.

As in other parts of the world, historically in Latin America and the Caribbean the wage gaps exist among ethnicities (→ I/25). Data from across the region show that white men and women have higher wages than women and men from other ethnicities (→ Whiteness, I/46). Indigenous and Afro-descendant women earn the lowest wages, while white men earn the highest. Similarly, "Indigenous men earn 40 to 65 percent less than non-indigenous men" (de Ferranti, et al. 2004, 92) (→ Indigeneity, I/31). A Study by ECLAC in eight Latin American countries concluded regarding labor income:

> The pattern of inequality is clear, situating non-indigenous, non-Afro-descendent men at one extreme of the income scale and indigenous women at the other, regardless of their levels of schooling... non-indigenous, non-Afro-descendent men are followed, in descending order, by Afro-descendent men, non-indigenous, non-Afro-descendent women, Afro-descendent women, indigenous men and, finally, indigenous women.
>
> *(ECLAC 2015, 29)*

Where do women and men work? Segregation of the labor force by gender and race

According to Duryea, Edwards and Ureta (2004, 13) Latin America has the highest levels of occupational segregation by gender in the world. The region has experienced a reduction in the share of manufacturing in total employment, where men have been historically overrepresented, and an increase in services, where women are overrepresented (IADB 4). In Latin America and the Caribbean, 78.1 percent of employed women work in what are considered the three lowest-productivity sectors of agriculture, personal services and commerce (ECLAC (Economic Commission for Latin America and the Caribbean) 2016, 64). These sectors are considered precarious in terms of job security, limited opportunities for mobility and lowpaid, unstable work with little use of technology and innovation.

The export-led model adopted by many countries in the region has not generated enough jobs for the population. An analysis of six countries (Argentina, Brazil, Chile, Colombia, Mexico and Uruguay) concluded that the export-led sector generates between 11 and 24 percent of jobs (ECLAC 2016, 27). In the last decades of the 20th century, the boom in new agricultural export industries (i.e. flowers, fruits, vegetables, and fishery) (→ Extractivism, II/9) created employment for women with low educational levels and usually from rural and minority ethnic backgrounds. However, those jobs are characterized by their precarity, that is, low payment, insecurity, low independent unionization rates (→ Labor Representation, II/14), unsafe working conditions and over-exploitation. Despite their hard work, women employed in export-processing zones do not see much of the financial benefits of this sector of production. Their work is the first link in a global wealth chain, as participants in the production of goods that are then sold by companies around the world (ECLAC 2016, 114) (→ Global Commodity Chains, II/12). The lion's share of profits is concentrated in the service sectors of transportation, distribution and overseas retailing of these products. At the same time, much local production, agricultural or otherwise, is unable to compete with cheaper imports, and as such, many local industries have shut down, adding to local economic dislocation and unemployment.

Unemployment

Rising levels of urban unemployment was a reality for many Latin Americans during the 1980s and 1990s. Historically, precarious jobs have been disproportionally held by women, racial minorities, rural, youth and the poor. Unemployment rates are higher for women than for men, reaching levels of 30 percent in some countries during the 1990s. The average unemployment rate among the poorest women is five times higher than among those women with highest incomes.

Regarding youth, defined as those aged 15 to 29 years old, the region has youth unemployment rates three times higher than adults. One fifth of the 163 million youth work in the informal sector and an equal share are unemployed and not engaged in education or training. According to the ECLAC, the majority of the young people not participating in either the education system or the labor market are women (73 percent) and more than half (55 percent) are engaged in unpaid domestic and care work (ECLAC 2016, 63). For those working, their jobs typically tend to be less rewarding, productive, and more insecure. This is particularly true for youth of low-income backgrounds and for women (OECD/ECLAC/CAF 2016, 23–24). More than two thirds of youth in the region lack college, university or high-level technical education. The absence of prospects for stable economic independence is one reason why many young adults decide to leave their countries of origin in search of better opportunities elsewhere.

Sexual harassment

Sexual harassment and violence against women are another manifestation of discrimination against women in the workplace. Violence and sexual harassment are widespread in the Americas, not only in the workplace, but in other public and private spaces. This issue was recently exposed by the #Metoo movement, which has its origins in the USA in 2017 – Based on reports from different Latin American and Caribbean countries, Aguilar Pereira and Orellana Calderón (2007, 106–107) assert that sexual harassment in the workplace ranges from 4 percent of women in Montevideo to 95 percent of women in Mexico. According to Gaby Oré-Aguilar (1997, 631) "sexual harassment is one of the most tolerated human rights violations against women in Latin American societies" (→ Human Rights, II/35). Most of the victims are women, chiefly young women; however, to a much lesser extent, men also suffer from it.

The toxic environment created by sexual harassment becomes a serious deterrent for women to perform well and advance in organizations. Sexual harassment is a manifestation of the objectification of women, particularly women from minority ethnic and racial groups and young women. Often they are perceived as being objects to be conquered, possessed, subordinated, controlled, exploited, and dominated.

In Latin America and the Caribbean, the objectification of women is culturally normalized, and many times explained as part of sexual innuendos and confused with "love." Consequently, sexual harassment is seen as both inevitable, expected, unaddressed, and highly underreported (Oré-Aguilar 1997). Regulations criminalizing sexual harassment and sexual violence – from provisions in international conventions on women's human rights to national labor and criminal laws – remain largely unenforced due to cultural beliefs and treated with a lack of seriousness by authorities and employers in addressing the problem once a victim reports it. As reporting is not taken seriously, and in many instances, women are stereotyped as provoking it or lying about it, some victims prefer to quit their jobs, transferring if possible, or tolerating it to the extent possible as part of workplace health hazards. Few studies have researched sexual harassment in the workplace in Latin America and the Caribbean, but, given its pervasive presence in other public and private sites, it is safe to assert that it is persistent in the workplace throughout the region.

Migration

During the 20th and present century, millions of Latin American and Caribbean women and men have migrated within their countries of birth, usually from rural to urban areas (→ Urbanization, I/45), as well as internationally (→ Transnational Migration, I/44), as a means of earning a living for themselves and their families. A lack of local economic opportunities, high levels of unemployment for youth, as well as political instability and violence in most of the countries of the region propel both young men and women to move within or beyond the region.

The United States continues to be the main country of destination for Latin American and Caribbean migrant workers. However, in the 1990s, there has been a significant rise in migration to other countries, especially to Spain, other member countries of the European Union and Canada. More recently, especially during the Pink Tide period, and the associated improvement in economic performance in much of the region, the patterns of migration have experienced a shift, characterized by a decline in emigration toward North America and Europe and an increase in emigration between Latin American and Caribbean countries. However, the USA and Europe (chiefly Spain) still remain the principle destination sites for migrants from the region (ILO 2017, 51–56, 92).

Within South America, Argentina, Brazil, Chile, and Colombia have become receiving destinations. In Central America, Belize, Costa Rica, Mexico, and Panama are major receiving countries; and in the Caribbean, the Dominican Republic, Bahamas and Trinidad and Tobago are preferred destinations countries (ILO 2017, 19–55).

Although regional and global economic integration have increased (→ Regional Integration, II/18), making national borders increasingly irrelevant for the movement of capital, goods and services, for workers, national frontiers have become, perhaps more important than ever. For those seeking work, the act of crossing increasingly militarized borders is becoming ever more restricted and dangerous (→ Borderlands, II/26). Ethnicity (→ I/25) and class status (→ Social Inequality, II/20) are important factors for how migrants travel and the degree of danger faced on the journey. Those who can afford an airplane ticket and have a visa, travel with less risk than those who undertake their journey without documents, by either car, train or foot. These migrants must rely on trafficking and smuggling networks to avoid authorities, resulting in many cases of abuse, violence, slavery, death, and other violations of human rights. Most of the victims of traffickers are people of indigenous descent or mix-raced and from rural backgrounds (Sanmiguel-Valderrama 2013).

While in the past, men dominated migration flows, today there is a growing feminization of migration, as more women move to make a living abroad usually to work in jobs in the lower ranks of the service sector. There is however a degree of "brain drain," as skilled female and male workers also leave their countries of origin for better opportunities. Many women are mothers who perform transnational mothering, that is, mothering from afar and abroad. If undocumented, decades could pass before they can see their children again (Hondagneu-Sotelo and Avila 1997) (→ Family, I/26). Immigrant workers not only contribute with their labor to the economic and social growth of countries of destination. They also help reduce poverty in the countries of origin. Latin American and Caribbean countries benefit from their labor by receiving remittances (→ I/19), which in many Latin American and Caribbean countries are one of the main sources of foreign exchange and a foundation of local economic growth and social mobility for their families.

Once migrants cross borders, however, they are often confronted with anti-immigrant hostility and social exclusion. Latin American and Caribbean women's and men's immigration experiences are profoundly shaped by the receiving countries' gender and racist practices, including gender and ethnic occupational segregation in paid work (→ Intersectionality, I/32). The current rampant anti-immigrant sentiments in countries such as the USA and in Europe position Latin American and Caribbean immigrants as second-class non-citizens (→ Citizenship, II/27) without an ability to exercise many of their fundamental human rights (→ II/35), particularly those in irregular or undocumented situations. Women immigrant workers from Latin America and the Caribbean even when holding a bachelor's degree are overrepresented in the lowest ranks of female dominated occupations such as the cleaning industry, domestic work (as nannies, caregivers, and maids) and in restaurant, food processing and hotel services. Male migrant workers are predominantly found undertaking manual labor in agriculture, landscaping, and the construction sectors. Latin American immigrants are devalued and underpaid. They face precarious working conditions, poor occupational safety, health, and social protections, a lack of recognition of their skills and education, and are concentrated in the informal sector of the economy (→ Informality, II/13). If undocumented or trafficked, their vulnerability makes them easy prey for exploitation. They face not only discrimination in employment, but also in housing, education (→ I/24), health (→ I/29) and other services needed for daily life. Their work and sacrifices are, however, the foundations of growth, not only for their employers, but also for many of their countries of origin.

Conclusions

Latin American and Caribbean women, following the global pattern, are still far from reaching their full potential in the labor force. In spite of higher levels of education (→ I/24) than men, as well as impressive labor force participation rates, they are confronted by structural barriers in the labor market which are difficult to overcome: patriarchy, racism, nationalism, classism, and wealth concentration in the region and beyond (→ Social Inequality, I/20), and a lack of local economic opportunities that often force them to migrate (→ Transnational Migration, I/44). For many women their increased involvement in market production is not necessarily emancipatory. Their employment is precarious, and wages are low. Additionally, the disparities between men and women in unpaid work in Latin America persist. The literature on work-family conflict highlights how unpaid social-reproductive work curtails caregivers' time and energies from fully participating in paid work in comparison to someone who does not need to perform unpaid work (e.g. by not being able to have a "flexible" schedule to work overtime or by asking for more leave time or permits so that they can fulfill their care responsibilities). The job market is still shaped by a patriarchal understanding of a male "ideal worker" who has a partner in his private life in charge of all socially reproductive unpaid work, so the paid worker has unlimited flexibility and commitment to perform his job. Hence, employers associate caregivers, particularly women, with being less productive, less committed, and less reliable. For those who assume the unpaid work of families, this results in being overlooked for promotions, full-time positions, wage increases, and managerial positions. Unpaid work hence limits access to the male-modeled job market, and its related benefits.

Accessing managerial jobs, achieving equal pay, desegregation of jobs by occupation, expanding economic opportunities for women, youth, indigenous, Afro-descendants, and the poor, the elimination of sexual harassment and violence against women in the work, public, and domestic domains, and the recognition of their contribution via unpaid work and the implementation of concomitant measures such as access to good quality infant and child care, flexibility in schedules, less restrictive immigration policies, among other measures, would contribute to help women succeed in the paid economy. Paramount to this goal is the imperative that both the private and public sectors formally recognize the high importance of women's contributions to communities and the economy via unpaid social-reproductive work they undertake.

Works cited

Aguirre, Rosario and Fernanda Ferrari. 2013. "Surveys on Time Use and Unpaid Work in Latin America and the Caribbean: Experience to Date and Challenges for the Future." Gender Affairs no. 122. Naciones Unidas Comición para América Latina y el Caribe (CEPAL). December 2013. Santiago de Chile.

Andrea Cornia, Giovanni. 2014. "Income inequality in Latin America: Recent decline and prospects for its further reduction." Macroeconomic Development Series no. 149. Naciones Unidas Comición para América Latina y el Caribe (CEPAL). July 2014. Santiago de Chile.

Chioda, Laura, Rodrigo Garcia-Verdu, and Ana María Muñoz-Boudet. 2011. *Work and Family: Latin American Women in Search of a New Balance*. Washington, DC: World Bank.

Coatsworth, John. H. 2008. "Inequality, Institutions and Economic Growth in Latin America." *Journal of Latin American Studies* 40, no. 3: 545–569.

Davis, Adrienne D. 2000. "Straightening It Out: Joan Williams on Unbending Gender." *American University Law Review* 49, no. 4: 823–849.

de Ferranti, David, Guillermo E. Perry, Francisco H. G. Ferreira, and Michael Walton. 2004. *Inequality in Latin America: Breaking with History?* Washington, DC: The International Bank for Reconstruction and Development/The World Bank.

Drago, Robert W. 2007. *Striking a Balance: Work, Family*. Boston, MA: Dollars and Sense.

Duryea, Suzanne, Alejandra Cox Edwards, and Manuelita Ureta. 2004. "Women in the Latin American Labor Market: The Remarkable 1990s." In *Women at Work: Challenges for Latin America*, ed. Piras, Claudia, 27–61. Washington, DC: Inter-American Development Bank Sustainable Development Department.

ECLAC (Economic Commission for Latin America and the Caribbean). 2015. "Inclusive Social Development: The Next Generation of Policies for Overcoming Poverty and Reducing Inequality in Latin America and the Caribbean." November 2015. Santiago de Chile.

———. 2016. "Equality and Women's Autonomy in the Sustainable Development Agenda." October 2016. Santiago de Chile.

Ferguson, Ann. 2004. "A Feminist Analysis of the Care Crisis." In *La Passió per la Libertat/A Passion for Freedom*, eds. Birulés, Fina and Aguado, Maria Isabel Peña, 293–298. Barcelona, Spain: Publicsciones y Ediciones de la Universitat de Barcelona.

Ferguson, Ann and Nancy Folbre. 2000. "Women, Care and the Public Good: A Dialogue." In *Not for Sale: In Defense of Public Goods*, eds. Anatole, Anton, Fisk, Milton, and Holmstrom, Nancy, 95–108. Boulder, CO: Westview Press.

Folbre, Nancy. 2000. *The Invisible Heart: Economics and Family Values*. New York: The New Press.

Hondagneu-Sotelo, Pierrette and Avila, Ernestine. 1997. "I'M HERE, BUT I'M THERE: The Meanings of Latina Transnational Motherhood." *Gender & Society* 11, no. 5: 548–571.

IADB (Inter-American Development Bank). 2017. "Gender Equality." www.iadb.org/en/topics/gender-indigenous-peoples-and-african-descendants/gender-equality/gender,1926.html

ILO (International Labor Organization). 2017. "Labour migration in Latin America and the Caribbean. Diagnosis, Strategy and ILO's work in the Region." Regional Office for Latin America and the Caribbean. March 2017. Lima.

Luxton, Meg and Kate Bezanson. 2006. *Social Reproduction: Feminist Political Economy Challenges Neo-Liberalism*. Montreal: McGill-Queen's University Press.

Molyneux, Maxine. 1979. "Beyond the Domestic Labour Debate." *New Left Review* 116: 3–27.

OECD/ECLAC/CAF. 2016. Latin American Economic Outlook 2017: Youth, Skills and Entrepreneurship. Organization for Economic Cooperation and Development (OECD), United Nations Economic Commission for Latin America and the Caribbean (ECLAC), and Corporación Andina de Fomento (CAF). October 2016. Paris. http://dx.doi.org/10.1787/leo-2017-en.

Oré-Aguilar, Gaby. 1997. "Sexual Harassment and Human Rights in Latin America." *Fordham Law Review* 66, no. 2: 631–645.

Panizza, Ugo and Christine Zhen-Wei Qiang. 2005. "Public-Private Wage Differential and Gender Gap in Latin America: Spoiled Bureaucrats and Exploited Women?" *Journal of Behavioral and Experimental Economics* (Formerly *The Journal of Socio-Economics*) 34, no. 6: 810–833.

Pereira, Aguilar, Víctor Manuel, Orellana Calderón, and Ligia María. 2007. "Acoso Sexual: Elementos de discusión para la redefinición del fenómeno." *Encuentro* 1, no. 39: 102–122.

RECLAC, FAO, UN-Women, UNDP, ILO. 2013. "Trabajo decente e igualdad de género." Políticas para mejorar el acceso y la calidad del empleo de las mujeres en América Latina y el Caribe. November 2013. Santiago de Chile.

Sanmiguel-Valderrama, Olga. 2013. "Border Enforcement at Family Sites: Social Reproductive Implications for Mexican and Central American Manual Labor in the United States." *Latin American Perspectives* 40, no. 5: 78–92.

Tinoco, Elizabeth. 2014. "Gender Equality: 100 Million Women in Latin America's Labour Force." *International Labour Organization ILO.* March 8. www.ilo.org/global/about-the-ilo/newsroom/comment-analysis/WCMS_237488/lang–en/index.htm.

Waring, Marilyn. 1988. *If Women Counted: A New Feminist Economics.* New York: Harper and Row.

———. 1999. *Counting for Nothing: What Men Value and what Women are Worth.* Toronto: University of Toronto Press.

Williamson, Jeffrey G. 2015. "Latin American Inequality: Colonial Origins, Commodity Booms, or a Missed 20th Century Leveling?" *NBER Working Paper* no. 20915: 1–40. www.nber.org/papers/w20915.

World Bank. 2017. "Gender Data Portal. Latin America and the Caribbean." *The World Bank.* http://datatopics.worldbank.org/gender/country/latin-america-&-caribbean.

12

GLOBAL COMMODITY CHAINS

Daniel Hawkins and Mark Anner

The term "Global Commodity Chains" (GCCs) was popularized in the mid-1990s with the publication of *Commodity Chains and Global Capitalism*, edited by Gereffi and Korzeniewicz (1994). The concept was developed a decade earlier by Terence Hopkins and Immanuel Wallerstein in their seminal study, "Commodity Chains in the World-Economy Prior to 1800" (1986). These authors illustrate how networks of labor and production processes that span states have been a part of global capitalism (→ II/2) for over two hundred years. In the current era of globalization, Gary Gereffi, Miguel Korzeniewic, and Roberto Korzeniewic see a dramatic growth of commodity chains, which they define as "sets of interorganizational networks clustered around one commodity or product, linking households, enterprises, and states to one another within the world-economy" and that "[t]hese networks are situationally specific, socially constructed, and locally integrated, underscoring the social embeddedness of economic organization" (Gereffi, Korzeniewicz, and Korzeniewicz 1994, 2). As such, the GCCs approach seeks to be more than a paradigm for understanding economic relations. It is an imminently political and historical approach that endeavors to explore the dynamics of spatial inequality through a particular form of capitalist expansion. Inequality is associated with unequal power relations between core and periphery nodes along GCCs. In this regard, the GCCs approach builds on a long history of scholarship in the Americas on dependency, world systems, and development (Cardoso and Faletto 1979; Evans 1979; Frank 1967; Palma 1978; Prebisch 1949) (→ Development, II/6).

The GCCs approach, however, shifts the focus of analysis from the state (→ Nation State, II/38) to the role of firms as the organizing agents of capitalism (Bair 2009). This change in perspective expands the point of examination beyond the nation-state as a means of escaping what has been referred to as methodological nationalism (for an overview, see Davis 2015), allowing for a more concrete analysis of the agency of individual entrepreneurs, firms, sectors, and workers in economic development (Topik, Marichal, and Frank 2006). In this way, the implicit lens of imperialism, underpinning the diverse schools of Dependency and World Systems Theory, which presupposes a structural relationship of domination and subordination between a hegemonic state and nations under its control (Palma 1978), is substituted for an examination of the dynamic historical constructs that change over time and across diverse social geographies (Topik and Samper 2006, 119).

Focusing on the agency of firms, instead of the primary role of nation-states in an international zero-sum system, the GCCs approach also builds on the work of scholars such as Gerry Helleiner and Stephen Hymer, both of whom examined the role of multinational enterprises (MNCs) as they looked to take advantage of export-oriented industrialization in developing countries: firstly by integrating less-developed countries into their orbit of international production and supply (of raw materials and industrial goods); and secondly, by the externalization of production via networks of independent enterprises (Bair 2009, 4–5) (→ Transnational Corporations, II/23).

Gereffi and his colleagues, while indebted to the Marxist tradition of the World System Theory, explained the appeal of the GCCs approach in that it allowed for greater analytical breadth, examining macro–micro links between processes that were otherwise perceived as being distinct units of analysis, be they global, national, or local (Gereffi, Korzeniewicz, and Korzeniewicz 1994, 2). Furthermore, they prioritized an approach that investigated the inter-firm networks that linked exporters based in developing countries to the world market, instead of adopting the World System Theory (WST) preference for examining the cyclical dynamics of commodity chains (Bair 2009, 9).

Taking such perspectives into account, the GCCs approach examines how the reorganization of production by MNCs reconfigured the international division of labor so that importance is given not simply to the product produced for the global market, but rather the specific segment of the commodity chain in question, with special emphasis placed on the key owners and operators of each segment (Evans 1997). Notably, product design and marketing are high value segments with higher profit levels and better remunerated employment, whereas the product assembly segment is often of much lower value and with lower remuneration (Dicken 1998).

One important contribution of this foundation work on GCCs was the concept of commodity chain governance structures, understood as "authority and power relationships that determine how financial, material, and human resources are allocated and flow within a chain" (Gereffi 1994, 97). In Gereffi's early work, he makes a distinction between "producer-driven" and "buyer-driven" chains. A producer-driven chain is one in which a MNC's production headquarters plays a central role in controlling the production system. This would be the case in automobiles, aircraft, and electrical machinery. In contrast, buyer-driven chains refer to industries in which large retailers and brand-name merchandizers play the pivotal role in setting up production networks. This form of production and distribution is common in garments, footwear, toys, and consumer electronics (Gereffi 1994).

The research paradigm of the GCCs perspective also differentiates between four dimensions of analysis: input-output structure, which examines how raw materials are transformed into final products; territoriality, understood as the geographical configuration of each commodity chain; governance structure, which explains how key actors in the chain control the actions of other agents and how these lead firms to use their power to appropriate the value produced along the chain; and institutional context that Gereffi introduced at a later date, which describes how the chains are organized and reproduced (Bair 2009; Gereffi 1994).

Transforming and debating concepts

Following the publication of the Gereffi and Korzeniewicz volume, research on GCCs proliferated, as did debates over terms and concepts. The first modification to the concept was provided by Gereffi himself, who joined with other colleagues and argued that the two main forms of commodity chain governance developed in the earlier work were an oversimplification. In fact, they argued that there were five forms of governance: hierarchy, captive, relational, modular, and market – which range from high to low levels of explicit coordination and power asymmetry (Gereffi, Humphrey, and Sturgeon 2005).

At the same time, Gereffi also abandoned the GCCs term and replaced it with Global Value Chains (GVCs). The modification incorporated transaction cost and economic organization into the paradigm (Bair 2009). But more than simply expanding the analytical reach of the concept, the preference for "value chain" over "commodity chain" was made due to the apparent prioritizing of production over consumption in the original term, coupled with its supposed failure to adequately address trade in primary products, services, and information (Dougherty 2008, 32).

Due in part to this more explicitly economic focus, the GVC framework became increasingly mainstream, and the World Bank and other international institutions began to incorporate it in their reports and policy proposals. GVC analysis came to focus on economic and social upgrading along value chains as a path toward development (→ II/6) in the "capturing the gains" framework (Barrientos, Gereffi, and Rossi 2011; Lee, Gereffi, and Barrientos 2003). In 2013, the Organization for Economic Cooperation and Development (OECD), the World Trade Organization (WTO), and the United Nations Conference on Trade and Development (UNCTAD) were using the GVCs approach to analyze trade, investment, and development patterns throughout the world (OECD, WTO, and UNCTAD 2013).

Parallel to these developments, a group of British scholars known as the "Manchester School" built on and critiqued the GCCs and GVC approaches. This group of scholars sought to emphasize the spatial dimensions of production systems that spanned states, using the term "Global Production Network" (GPN). As the GVC approach increasingly emphasized governance and value/transaction costs, the GPN approach sought to re-emphasize embeddedness. In their foundational study on GPNs, Jeffrey Henderson, Peter Dicken, Martin Hess, Neil Coe, and Henry Wai-Chung Yeung (2002) argued that

> GPNs do not only connect firms functionally and territorially but also they connect aspects of the social and spatial arrangements in which those firms are embedded and which influence their strategies and the values, priorities and expectations of managers, workers and communities alike.
>
> *(Henderson et al. 2002, 451)*

The need to place workers and their strategies in the center of the analysis has been pursued by scholars who began looking at the implications of a GCCs approach for labor movements (→ Labor Representation, II/14). For example, Anner finds that production workers in buyer-driven chains in the Americas are likely to build ties with consumer advocacy groups that use symbolic power to shame retailers and brands into addressing worker rights violations in their supplier networks through transnational activist campaigns (→ Social Movements, II/11), whereas workers in producer-driven chains are more likely to target producer headquarters through transnational labor networks (Anner 2011). Other scholars placed emphasis on the impact of value chains on women workers (→ Gender and Work, II/6). Barrientos and her collaborators emphasized how supply chain labor markets "reify and reflect socially constructed gender divisions of labor [that] reflect the socially derived gender division of labor, and are situated at the intersection between productive (paid) and reproductive (unpaid) work" (Barrientos, Dolan, and Tallotire 2003, 1515). The authors argue that GVCs, particularly in sectors such as horticulture, embody a gender-employment pyramid with a male-dominated formal employment segment at the top of the pyramid, and female-dominated informal and reproductive work at the bottom (ibid.).

Despite the conceptual and theoretical reifications and precisions made throughout the years, critique of the GCCs or the GVC analyses has centered on how this approach marginalizes the regulatory spheres in which economic actors undertake their activities and in which such activities are embedded. Indeed, by implicitly prioritizing firm agency and the attributes associated with intra-chain coordination, the GVC approach subverts the degree to which power is developed and maintained in social, political, and legal institutions (Patel-Campillo 2010).

The value chain approach for labor gained further attention when the International Labor Organization decided to discuss the implications at the 2016 International Labor Conference. The ILO opted to use the more generic term, Global Supply Chains (GSCs), in its debate, which it defines as, "cross-border organization of the activities required to produce goods or services and bring them to consumers through inputs and various phases of development, production and delivery" (International Labor Office 2016, 1). At the Conference, the workers' group argued that GSCs have created governance gaps that should be addressed through a new ILO Convention on Decent Work in Global Supply Chains. The worker group from Latin America emphasized that the solution to problems created by GSCs should be addressed through joint liability legislation. The employers' group resisted these proposals, but in the end agreed that the ILO governing body should decide on the right mechanism to discuss ways to address decent work deficits in GSCs, which may include standard setting.

Global value chain analyses in the Americas

In North America, academic and conceptual debates surrounding GCCs and GVCs have been prolific for over two decades. Particularly after the ratification of the North American Free Trade Agreement (NAFTA) (→ Regional Integration, II/18), there was a significant amount of academic attention devoted to studying how heightened economic integration between Canada, the USA, and Mexico would bring about changing patterns of organization and distribution of production, inevitably leading to transformations in the control, appropriation and distribution of value within some of the most affected product chains, such as the automotive and apparel industries (Bair and Gereffi 2003; Sturgeon, Van Biesebroeck, and Gereffi 2008). Further south, however, discussions of this term had languished on the periphery of debates concerning regional economic development. The surge in the mining industry across Latin America, at the beginning of the 21st century attracted significant attention from multilateral institutions and development agencies, however their initial conceptual point of analysis stemmed more from agglomeration economies and industrial clusters than from the GCCs and related approaches (Dussel 2002). Nonetheless, with the mainstreaming of the global value chain paradigm, its incorporation into the discourse and research focus of many development agencies was not long in coming (→ Development, II/6). Latching onto this research paradigm, many studies focused on how to foment economic upgrading as part of Latin-American countries' heightened economic integration (Pietrobelli and Rabelloti 2006; Prochnik 2010).

The increasingly popularity of the GVC research paradigm led to research undertaken by multilateral institutions such as the mentioned WTO, UNCTAD, as well as the Inter-American Development Bank (IDB) and the Economic Commission for Latin America and the Caribbean (ECLAC). However, the diverse publications and reports of these entities, for the most part, have tended to simplify the complexity of the conceptual debates and developments of the past two decades and instead, focus on methodological attempts to measure the extent to which developing countries were participating in GVCs (Blyde 2014; OECD, WTO, and UNCTAD 2013).

Various reports and studies examined the degree to which Latin-American and Caribbean countries were taking advantage of the supposed benefits of the growth in GVCs. Their findings point to two notable geographical trends. Firstly, Central American and certain Caribbean countries have become quite integrated into the regional value chain termed the "American factory" wherein they generally assemble intermediate goods (Durán-Limay and Zaclicever 2013; Stephenson 2013), while Andean and Southern Cone countries, except for Brazil, remain relatively peripheral to such developments (Trujillo, Álvarez, and Rodríguez 2014). Secondly, despite the immersion of many Central American and Caribbean countries in this predominantly regional value chain, the degree of economic upgrading achieved remains either questionable (Hernández, Martínez-Piva, and Mulder 2014) or negligible, depending on the measurement used. In terms of social upgrading (wages and workers' rights), conditions appear to have worsened as a result of integration to these regional value chains due to downward pressure on labor (Anner 2015).

One of the key tendencies of the recent attention being paid to the concept of GVCs in the Americas by institutional and multilateral entities is the way they have stretched the conceptual and theoretical analyses of many of the long-term scholars focusing on GVCs and GPNs so that they fit in with their policy prescriptions grounded in further economic liberalization for the Latin-American and Caribbean region (Demián, Fossati and Lavopa 2013). Despite offering tepid caveats regarding the inherent sectorial differences of GVCs and the significant obstacles to strategies aiming at value-added upgrading, the recommendations for advanced economic development via insertion into these chains remain remarkably homogeneous: greater and easier market access, further tariff reductions (→ Taxation, II/22), as well as other policies designed to improve a country's business environment (Blyde 2014; Stephenson 2013; UNCTAD 2013).

Case studies on GVCs in the Americas

Case studies on GCCs in the Americas have proliferated, adding greater nuance to the existent literature. One of the most notable publications examining the historical development of some of the most important raw material commodity chains in Latin America and their link to the world market was the 2006 book edited by Stephen Topik, Carlos Marichal and Zephr Frank, *From Silver to Cocaine: Latin American Commodity Chains and the Building of the World Economy, 1500–2000*. This seminal work examines the dynamics of a wide array of commodities grown or produced in Latin America and transported to be sold across the world for the past five hundred years. The authors adopt an analytical approach that combines the commodity chain concept with the French *filière* and the Latin-American *circuito commercial* approach as a means of understanding the interactions and relative power of different actors and segments of a commodity chain (Topik and Samper 2006) and how these interactions and power differentials change across time and space. More recent studies have examined the changing integration of the banana industry in terms of production in Central and South America and marketing and sales predominantly in North America (Hough 2012; Riisgaard and Hammer 2011). These studies have highlighted how this industry moved from a vertically integrated production chain, controlled by multinational firms such as Chiquita (→ Transnational Corporations, II/23), toward a vertically "disintegrated" system of production that links MNCs that monopolize the importation and distribution of branded bananas to "a vast array of locally-contracted farmers, domestic plantation owners, and small-scale marketing companies" (Hough 2012, 244). Such global production chain frameworks are then used to examine both the impacts on labor of such MNC-propelled readjustments as well as the new possibilities this offers to novel strategies of resistance whereby banana workers are able to leverage the bipolar nodes of power in the chain by threatening to disrupt, both production at Chiquita plantations as well as consumption via campaigns targeted at Chiquita and retailers selling Chiquita bananas (Riisgaard and Hammer 2011).

Other authors in the region have studied the gradually changing strategies of firms involved in different agro-industrial sectors that have been sources of significant growth in the post-1970s world order, as they attempt to grapple with the vagaries of highly fluctuating exchange rates which significantly impact the feasibility of linking with GVCs and more importantly, upgrading within them (Forero 2012; Salom-Serna and del Pilar Sepúlveda 2012), as well as sustainable development agricultural certification systems which place the greater burden of costs of entry on often small-scale producers, even while the bulk of value-added gains is trapped at the point of sale in the U.S. and European markets (Hawkins 2018).

With the vertiginous growth of the biofuel market in the past two decades, enormous swaths of the Americas have been converted into regions devoted almost singularly to soya, maize, and palm oil production for the local and global markets (→ Energy, II/7; Extractivism, II/9). Unsurprisingly, the GCCs and GVCs frameworks have been adopted to examine the emergence and changing dynamics of this new agro-industrial chain. A CEPAL study from 2010 examined how the biofuel market had considerably reconfigured Argentina's agricultural sector, limiting the conceptual utility of dividing primary, industrial, and service-related activities due to the growing diffusion and entanglement of all these phases, and noting that the key mode for understanding the power differentials within and along each segment of the chain has now become the contract that determines prices, quality, processes, and functional routines (Anlló, Bisang, and Salvatierra 2010, 10).

Keeping within the sectorial context of agriculture, other studies have used the GCCs framework to examine the competitive economic relations between the U.S. and Colombia from within the backdrop of the cut-flower industry (Patel-Campillo 2010), while also critiquing its limitations, such as the GCCs approach having paid scant attention to the regulatory and institutional frameworks that influence and indeed, shape competitive relations.

Conclusion

Suffice to say that the GCCs approach and its conceptual siblings, GPNs and GVCs, have become increasingly prevalent as conceptual and methodological tools to examine the distribution of power and the changing patterns of productive organization and distribution across the Global Political Economy and increasingly across the American Continent. As already outlined, each specific conceptual choice examined here, while loyal to the analytical framework of the commodity chain perspective, does prioritize certain components, actors, or industries. The GCCs approach, for instance, stemming from within the WST tradition, offered the possibility of studying the "macro–micro links between processes that are generally assumed to be discreetly contained within global, national, and local units of analysis" (Gereffi, Korzeniewicz, and Korzeniewicz 1994, 2), while also contending that the GCCs of the post-1970s have fomented organizational forms related to a process of economic integration that is qualitatively different from previous periods of capitalist development (Bair 2009, 10) (→ Capitalism, II/2). The Manchester School promotion of the GPN approach attempted to highlight the spatial and relational nature of GCCs, emphasizing how global networks are also embedded in local and regional ones. Nevertheless, both approaches share a similar methodological approach, focusing on conducting rigorous empirical research on the power dynamics within industries and their interlinked chains. The move toward a more concerted and shared paradigm based on the global value chain perspective gradually attained precedence not only because it expanded the original analytical framework to include transaction costs, but also because it implicitly broadened the conceptual reach of the approach, moving the lens beyond only raw materials and low value-added industries, such as apparel. Various of the most acclaimed proponents of the GCCs and GPN frameworks asserted that the GVC rubric was the most appropriate term to use as it was "the most inclusive of the full range of possible chain activities and end products" (Gereffi, Humphrey, Kaplinsky, and Sturgeon 2001 cited in Bair 2009, 12).

The dimension of governance within the GCCs and the GVC approaches is also qualitatively different although not mutually exclusive. Gereffi's buyer- or producer-driven commodity chain developed within the GCCs framework was later expanded to include the further dimensions of governance, however, as argued by Bair (2009, 13–14), the typology of governance used does not depend overtly on whether one professes to use the GCCs or the GVC analytical framework, but rather on the concrete analytical or theoretical issue that is being highlighted.

Despite this, the change toward the preference for the GVC concept contributed to the mainstreaming of the approach, as many multilateral and developmental institutes began sponsoring and undertaking research into how developing states and specific industries were being integrated into GVCs (→ Development, II/6). For much of the Americas, the GVC approach has been used to examine, on the one hand, the impacts of free trade agreements such as NAFTA (→ Regional Integration, II/18) on the dynamics and cost-benefits within specific sectors of these structural models of integration, and secondly, the consolidation of the mining and agro-industrial sectors across Latin America and how these activities may either promote economic upgrading or, alternatively, perpetuate the structural dependencies noted by proponents of Dependency or World Systems Theory in the 1960s and 1970s (→ Extractivism, II/9). Very much tied into the study area of developmental economics, the GVC approach, particularly in Latin America and the Caribbean, has gained in popularity as a conceptual and methodological tool to examine how specific industrial segments fare in regional or global economic integration processes. This trend points to a degree of academic departamentalization across the Americas that obviously affects the point of focus and the objectives of the multifarious research projects undertaken within the GCCs or GVC approaches. In North America, the GCCs methodology has been widely used by sociologists, economic sociologists and labor studies' scholars, while in Latin America, the multilateral preference for adopting the GVC framework within economic-based studies, and at times, from within Development Economics has limited its inter-disciplinarian reach; and in so doing, perhaps the possibilities such a framework has for contributing to more critical studies on the power relations and their unequal distribution along geographically divided but socially embedded commodity or value chains.

Works cited

Anlló, Guillermo, Roberto Bisang, and Guillermo Salvatierra. eds. 2010. *Cambios estructurales en las actividades agropecuarias. De lo primario a las cadenas globales de valor.* Santiago de Chile: Comisión Económica para América Latina y el Caribe (CEPAL).

Anner, Mark. 2011. *Solidarity Transformed: Labor's Responses to Globalization and Crisis in Latin America.* Ithaca: ILR Press, an imprint of Cornell University Press.

———. 2015. "Social Downgrading and Worker Resistance in Apparel Global Value Chains." In *Putting Labour in its Place: Labour Process Analysis and Global Value Chains*, eds. Kirsty Newsome, Phillip Taylor, and Jennifer Bair, 152–170. Basingstoke: Palgrave Macmillan.

Bair, Jennifer. 2009. "Global Commodity Chains: Genealogy and Review." In *Frontiers of Commodity Chain Research*, ed. Jennifer Bair, 1–34. Stanford: Stanford University Press.

Bair, Jennifer and Gary Gereffi. 2003. "Upgrading, Uneven Development, and Jobs in the North America Apparel Industry." *Global Networks* 2, no. 3: 143–169.

Barrientos, Stephanie, Catherine Dolan, and Anne Tallotire. 2003. "A Gendered Value Chain Approach to Codes of Conduct in African Horticulture." *World Development* 31, no. 9: 1511–1526.

Barrientos, Stephanie, Gary Gereffi, and Arianna Rossi. 2011. "Economic and Social Upgrading in Global Production Networks: A New Paradigm for a Changing World." *International Labour Review* 150, no. 3–4: 319–340.

Blyde, Juan S. ed. 2014. *Fábricas sincronizadas. América Latina y el Caribe en la era de las cadenas globales de valor.* Washington, DC: Banco Interamericano de Desarrollo (BID).

Cardoso, Fernando Henrique and Enzo Faletto. 1979. *Dependency and Development in Latin America.* Berkeley: University of California Press.

Davis, Mike. 2015. "Marx's Lost Theory." *New Left Review* 93: 45–66.

Demián, Dalle, Verónica Fossati, and Federico Lavopa. 2013. "Política industrial: ¿el eslabón perdido en el debate de las Cadenas Globales de Valor?" *Revista Argentina de Economía Internacional* 2: 3–16.

Dicken, Peter. 1998. *Global Shift: Transforming the World Economy.* 3rd ed. New York: Guilford Press.

Dougherty, Michael. 2008. "Theorizing Theory: Origins and Orientations of Commodity Chain Analysis." *The Global Studies Journal* 1, no. 3: 29–38.

Durán-Limay, José and Dayna Zaclicever. 2013. *América Latina y el Caribe en las cadenas internacionales de valor.* Serie Comercio Internacional. 124th ed. Santiago de Chile: CEPAL.

Dussel, Enrique Peters. 2002. *Territorio y competitividad en la Agroindustria en México: Condiciones y propuestas de política para los clusters del limón mexicano en Colima y la piña en Veracruz.* México: Ayuntamiento Constitucional de Isla, Veracruz, Secretaria de Economía de la Universidad de Colima, las Naciones Unidas.

Evans, Peter B. 1979. *Dependent Development: The Alliance of Multinational, State, and Local Capital in Brazil.* Princeton: Princeton University Press.

———. 1997. "The Eclipse of the State? Reflections on Stateness in an Era of Globalization." *World Politics* 50, no. 1: 62–87.

Forero, Jaime Álvarez. 2012. "Estrategias adaptativas de la caficultura colombiana." In *Crisis y Transformaciones del Mundo del Café: Dinámicas locales y estrategias nacionales en un periodo de adversidad e incertidumbre*, eds. Mario Samper and Steven Topik, n.p. Bogotá: Universidad Pontificia Javeriana.

Frank, Andre Gunder. 1967. *Capitalism and Underdevelopment in Latin America.* New York: New York University Press.

Gereffi, Gary. 1994. "The Organization of Buyer-Driven Global Commodity Chains: How U.S. Retailers Shape Overseas Production Networks." In *Commodity Chains and Global Capitalism*, eds. Gary Gereffi and Miguel Korzeniewicz, 95–122. Westport: Praeger.

Gereffi, Gary, John Humphrey, and Timothy Sturgeon. 2005. "The Governance of Global Value Chains." *Review of International Political Economy* 12, no. 1: 78–104.

Gereffi, Gary and Miguel Korzeniewicz. 1994. *Commodity Chains and Global Capitalism. Contributions in Economics and Economic History.* Westport: Greenwood Press.

Gereffi, Gary, Miguel Korzeniewicz, and Roberto Korzeniewicz. 1994. "Introduction: Global Commodity Chains." In *Commodity Chains and Global Capitalism*, eds. Gary Gereffi and Miguel Korzeniewicz, 1–14. Westport: Praeger.

Hawkins, Daniel. 2018. "Working Conditions and Sustainable Coffee in Colombia." In *Decent Work Deficits in Southern Agriculture: Measurements*, eds. Christoph Scherrer and Santosh Verna, 227–250. Muenchen: ICDD; Rainer Hamp Verlag.

Henderson, Jeffrey, Peter Dicken, Martin Hess, Neil Coe, and Henry Wai-Chung Yeung. 2002. "Global Production Networks and the Analysis of Economic Development." *Review of International Political Economy* 9, no. 3: 436–464.

Hernández, René A., Jorge Mario Martínez-Piva, and Nano Mulder. eds. 2014. *Global Value Chains & World Trade: Prospects & Challenges for Latin America.* Santiago de Chile: Economic Commission for Latin America & the Caribe (Eclac).

Hopkins, Terence and Immanuel Wallerstein. 1986. "Commodity Chains in the World-Economy Prior to 1800." *Review* 10, no. 1: 157–170.

Hough, Phillip. 2012. "A Race to the Bottom? Globalization, Labor Repression, and Development by Dispossession in Latin America's Banana Industry." *Global Labour Journal* 3, no. 2: 237–264.

International Labour Office. 2016. *Report IV: Decent Work in Global Supply Chains*. Geneva: International Labour Organization.

Lee, Joonkoo, Gary Gereffi, and Stephanie Barrientos. 2003. *Capturing the Gains*. Manchester: Capturing the Gains.

OECD, WTO, and UNCTAD. 2013. "Implications of Global Value Chains for Trade, Investment, Development and Jobs." Prepared for the G-20 Leaders Summit, Saint Petersburg (Russian Federation), September.

Palma, Gabriel. 1978. "Dependency: A Formal Theory of Underdevelopment or A Methodology for the Analysis of Concrete Situations of Underdevelopment?" *World Development* 6: 881–924.

Patel-Campillo, Anouk. 2010. "Rival Commodity Chains: Agency and Regulation in the US and Colombian Cut-Flower Agro-Industries." *Review of International Political Economy* 17, no. 1: 75–102.

Pietrobelli, Carlo and Roberta Rabelloti. eds. 2006. *Upgrading to Compete: Global Value Chains, Clusters, & SMEs in Latin America*. Washington, DC: Inter-American Development Bank.

Prebisch, Raúl. 1949. *The Economic Development of Latin America and its Principal Problems*. New York: United Nations.

Prochnik, Víctor. 2010. "América Latina en las Cadenas Globales de Valor." *Red Mercosur de Investigaciones Económicas, Serie Policy Briefs* no. 6, April.

Riisgaard, Lone and Nikolaus Hammer. 2011. "Prospects for Labour in Global Value Chains: Labour Standards in the Cut Flower and Banana Industries." *British Journal of Industrial Relations* 49, no. 1: 168–190.

Salom-Serna, Luis Felipe and María del Pilar Sepúlveda. 2012. "Canales de distribución y estrategia de comercialización para la flor colombiana en los Estados Unidos: un marco conceptual." *Estudios Gerenciales* 28, no. 124: 191–228.

Stephenson, Sherry. 2013. *Global Value Chains: The New Reality of International Trade*. Geneva: ICTSD and WEF.

Sturgeon, Timothy, Johannes Van Biesebroeck, and Gary Gereffi. 2008. "Value Chains, Networks and Clusters: Reframing the Global Automotive Industry." *Journal of Economic Geography* 8, no. 3: 297–321.

Topik, Steven, Carlos Marichal, and Zephyr Frank. 2006. *From Silver to Cocaine: Latin American Commodity Chains and the Building of the World Economy, 1500–2000*. Durham and London: Duke University Press.

Topik, Steven, and Mario Samper. 2006. "The Latin American Coffee Commodity Chain: Brazil and Costa Rica." In *From Silver to Cocaine: Latin American Commodity Chains and the Building of the World Economy, 1500–2000*, eds. Steven Topik, Carlos Marichal and Zephyr Frank, 118–146. Durham and London: Duke University Press.

Trujillo, Edgar, Martha Cecilia Álvarez and María Fernanda Rodríguez. 2014. "Inserción de Colombia en las Cadenas Globales de Valor." Ministry of Commerce, Industry and Tourism of Colombia. www.mincit.gov.co/descargar.php?id=71175.

UNCTAD. 2013. "Global Value Chains & Development: Investment and Value-Added Trade in the Global Economy." A preliminary analysis. United Nations.

13
INFORMALITY

Daniel Hawkins

The term "informal sector" has been one of the most hotly debated socio-economic concepts of the past forty-five years. Etymologically, one can only define it with respect to the formal sector as it derives from and is intrinsically defined by its comparison to this term. Taking this cue, it can be understood as all income-generating economic activities not authorized or regulated by the State (→ Nation State, II/38) in social contexts where other similar activities are monitored and authorized (Castells and Portes 1989, 12). Widening this definition to encompass socio-cultural aspects, one can perceive the informal sector as contravening State regulations but not social moral codes (De Soto 1994). But as Portes (1996) says, these definitions are more appropriate for industrialized countries not the Third World. The character of what is informal or formal is always defined in the ever-fluxing relationship between the State and civil society (→ II/28). The informal sector must also be differentiated from the illegal economy. While the first term entails the production, distribution and sale of goods (and services) that are socially perceived and normatively defined as licit, the second involves goods that are deemed illicit.

Uneven capitalist development and urban poverty: the emergence of informality

Petty trade and unregistered work have existed as long as humanity and in Latin America, street commerce was documented and banned in Lima as early as 1594 (De Soto 1994, 75), and their pervasiveness across societies in the Global South became synonymous in the post-World War II period with underdevelopment and urban poverty (→ Development, II/38). This interpretation was quite different from the political economy perspective that examined the effects of the Industrial Revolution in England during the early-to-mid-19th century. In that period, intellectuals such as Simonde de Sismondi outlined the contradiction between the growing productive capacities of industry and agriculture and the stagnant income of the wider population, while other utopian socialists, such as Proudhon and Kropotkin, made emphatic critiques of the urbanization-industrialization processes and their link to urban poverty (→ Socialism, I/42). Marx, while accepting these appraisals, did not agree with their call for a retreat to small-scale agricultural production. Instead, he examined how these two capitalist-impelled processes led to the fragmentation of worker unity, particularly through the growth of the industrial reserve army (IRA) of laborers, which was made up of three distinct modalities: floating, latent, and stagnant, all of which were manifestations of capital's cycles of boom–bust development (Karl 1973) (→ Capitalism, II/2).

The association of capitalism and social exclusion was not part of the liberal philosophical tradition. Adam Smith ignored the problems of social inequality (→ II/20) and labor market distortions as being the side effects of excessive State intervention in the economy. Reformist-minded liberals, such as John Stuart Mill and David Ricardo, were more attentive to the relationship between capital accumulation and social exclusion, however, they argued that the latter resulted not from capitalist exploitation, but rather, that it was a manifestation of unequal opportunities and State action was needed to provide health (→ I/29), education (→ I/24) and vocational training services as a means of overcoming poverty, while ensuring the continuation of a system of work grounded on individual incentives (Hawkins 2011, 141–142).

Fast forward to the post-World War Two era, in the midst of *Pax Americana* capitalist hegemony, much of the nuanced examinations of the systemic, social, and class distortions of industrialization of the past century were sidelined and certain new sociological perspectives, especially those led by Kingsley Davis from the International Urban research group at California's Berkeley University, analyzed the urban problems of industrialization, especially in the U.S., prioritizing their demographic causes (Castells 2006). Other U.S. scholars, for example from the Chicago School (Marshall Clinard, Leo Strole, Ruth Glass, Robert Park, and Lewis Killian, among others), highlighted how cities were becoming focal points of social disorganization, criminality and acculturation (→ Urbanization, I/45). Herein, socio-economic inequality was ignored and immigration came to be perceived as a central process in the formation of what one renowned sociologist, Robert Park, termed the "marginal personality" that was, supposedly, synonymous with many ethnic groups located on the peripheries of urban societies due to their cultural fears and antagonisms (Park 1969) (→ Migration, I/15; Ethnicity, II/25). This cultural-sociological-empiricist perspective, located in the Fordist-Keynesian "wage-based" society of the U.S. (→ Fordism, II/10), completely ignored the multiple inequalities and distortions of the urban labor market as factors of relevance in understanding social exclusion and poverty.

In Latin America, the promise of U.S.-American modernization (→ I/35) had not played out according to plan. The supposed path to development (→ II/6), while successful in spreading the norms and values associated with Western consumerism (→ I/23) and halting fertility rates (Portes 1997), failed remarkably in fomenting wealth creation and its redistribution across the region. During the initial phase of development for the region, conveniently heaped into what Harry Truman had called the Third World during his 1949 inaugural presidential address, policy prescriptions focused on reorienting and modernizing institutions, cultural values and fomenting industrialization. Herein, petty trade and non-factory labor were perceived as being appendages of the supposed backwardness of agrarian societies, where export commodities such as sugar and coffee, with their inherent volatility vis-à-vis world market prices, helped pave the way for authoritarian and populist political leaders (→ Populism, II/43). The resetting of State policies would focus on increasing capitalist development as a means of converting the rural peasant population into urban industrial workers. What was needed, it was contended, was a "Big push" via massive State-led investment programs geared toward the industrialization of these economies. The result would be the gradual elimination of surplus labor and the unstoppable growth of the industrial wage worker. Such perspectives attained considerable prominence with one United States economist, W. Arthur Lewis, receiving the Nobel Prize in Economics for similar contentions (Chen 2012).

By the 1960s, however, it was becoming clear that the wage-based societies of industrialized countries were not being replicated in the underdeveloped countries of Latin America and the Caribbean. Instead, the cities of the Third World were seemingly entrapped by severe and structural labor market segmentations and vast levels of urban unemployment and poverty. Nevertheless, there were a multiplicity of scholarly perspectives regarding the causes of such phenomena. Two Latino sociologists, José Nún and Aníbal Quijano, drew on the work of Marx to understand the high degree of structural and long-term unemployment and the cataclysmic rise of unregulated economic activity in the region's urban centers. Central to their analyses was the concept of the IRA. However, while for Marx, its periodic expansion and decrease depended on the cyclical fluctuations of capitalist development in the core city heartlands of Britain, in Latin America one hundred years later, the internationalization and monopolization of capital and the increasing dominance of constant over variable capital, had led to a reconfiguration of the IRA. There, the primitive accumulation first conceptualized by Rosa Luxemburg, was in abundance and peasants were constantly "thrown" into the orbits of capital wage relations (Quijano 1983, 80). Nonetheless, because of these new tendencies in capital development, this new proletarian class was generally denied wage work and remained caught in limbo on the urban peripheries, coming to form what they referred to as the "marginal mass": a pseudo class expendable to capital with no real impact on the movement of wage levels (Nún 1969; Quijano 1983). While attaining prominence in academic discussions on urban poverty and uneven capitalist development in the region, Quijano and Nún's focus on the vagaries of 20th century peripheral capitalism (→ II/2), rather than on the structural problems facing the unilineal developmental model of Anglo-modernization theorists in much of the Third World, ensured that their work remained on the outskirts of multilateral and inter-State policy discussions of the time. Instead, ever-more attention was being paid to the vast levels of urban unemployment across the underdeveloped world.

From unemployment and underemployment to informality: definitions and policy prescriptions

In this context, the International Labor Organization (ILO) launched its World Employment Program in 1969, which sought to develop a more detailed understanding of the workings of the labor markets of various countries of the South. This Program revolutionized labor market theory and brought together a group of researchers from both North and South, who combined an assorted mixture of theoretical and methodological tools, assuring that their findings would display a broad array of perspectives and policy responses (Chen 2005, 2012). This rethinking of how labor markets evolved and were structured in underdeveloped economies led to a growing consensus regarding the inadequacy of the term "unemployment." An array of new terms soon propped up in the literature as "underemployment," "hidden employment," "visible and invisible underemployment," "urban marginality," etc.

The term "informality" was first used by the British anthropologist Keith Hart in a paper presented in 1971 at the Conference on Urban Unemployment in Africa held at Sussex University. Hart, examining the heterogeneity of economic activity in Accra, Ghana, distinguished between two possibilities for income generation: wage employment and self-employment. While Hart perceived these two types of work to be separate, he highlighted the dynamism and diversity of forms of self-employment (Hart 1973, 68). Indeed, critiquing the practice of poor countries copying industrialized countries' development models, Hart questioned whether the "reserve army of urban unemployed and underemployed" was, rather than being a drain on economic growth, actually a source of untapped potential (Hart 1973, 68). While Hart's work delved into the relation between poverty and informality, he also critiqued the notion that there existed any perfect correlation between the two (Hawkins 2011, 147). Nonetheless, Hart's definition of the vitality of much of informal sector activity was soon lost as the concept became redefined and institutionalized within the ILO bureaucracy as being synonymous with poverty (Portes 1996). The informal sector was taken to refer to an urban "way of doing things" that was very much at odds with the supposed way that industrial-urban development should take place in the Third World. However, there was no easy academic accord regarding the factors that created, reduced or expanded the informal sector. Instead, over the ensuing years, three main schools (or groupings) of thought developed different manners of perceiving informal economic activity.

The dualist perspective

The ILO was the most important institutional actor in developing and promoting the dualist understanding of the informal sector. Initially very empirically grounded, the ILO's World Employment Program undertook four employment missions during the early 1970s: "Towards full employment" in Colombia; "Matching employment opportunities and expectations" for Ceylon (now Sri Lanka); "Employment incomes and equality" in Kenya; and "Employment and income policies" in Iran. All of these programs examined the workings of labor markets and economic activity in the growing urban centers of the underdeveloped world.

Taken together and then institutionalized by the ILO, these four missions came to perceive the informal sector as being highly segmented, unproductive, and caught in the poverty trap (Souza and Tokman 1976). In the Colombian report, Bairoch contended that in the urban settings of Third World countries structural unemployment reached worrying levels. The cause was the transformation in capitalist production which led to the loss of wage-labor opportunities (Bairoch 1976, 66–67). There was no apparent connection between the informal sector and the formal, industrial-urban economy; instead, the informal sector lost any of its fluidity and came to be defined as being easy to enter, generally family-based (→ Family, I/26), small-scale, labor intensive with outdated capital or machinery, hindered by its low productivity, and generally taking place in unregulated and competitive markets (Portes 1996). In 1975, the ILO's Regional Employment Program for Latin America (PREALC) conducted extensive research across four cities of the region (Asunción, Guayaquil, San Salvador, and Santo Domingo), paying particular attention to the labor markets but continuing the dissemination of the view that saw unemployment in the informal sector as being "underemployment" and detached from the modern economy. Often the informal sector, in these studies, was termed the excluded sector (Bairoch 1976, 148) and remained at the bottom layer of economic activities. Contrary to Hart's contention of the potential growth of this sector, the PREALC Director concluded that, due to the oligopolistic market structure, it "offers little scope for the accumulation of capital and thus has little capacity for expansion" (Souza and Tokman 1976, 356).

The legalist perspective

This view, most widely associated with the Peruvian economist Hernando de Soto and the work he and his colleagues undertook at the Institute for Liberty and Democracy in Lima, revolutionized debate concerning the causes and proposed "cures" for the informal sector as well as redefining informality in a positive light as one of the key paths to wealth creation and entrepreneurial spirit. Where the ILO suggested that States were key agents in offering credit and other support services to informal enterprises, as a means of helping them to formalize, the legalists perceived the State and its crony functionaries as being the main culprits for the link between informality and urban poverty. For De Soto, "costly and cumbersome government regulations inhibit the ability of informal entrepreneurs to operate a business and earn a living" (Chen 2005, 20), while informal, generally self-employed merchants, were the true agents of wealth creation, embodying entrepreneurial vigor which had been repressed by a mercantilist State in collusion with industrial giants (De Soto 1994). De Soto's 1994 book, *The Other Path: The Economic Answer to Terrorism* even received acclaim from then U.S. President Bill Clinton and former President George Bush.

According to the legalists, the informal urban sector expanded enormously with the massive rural-urban exodus in most developing countries during the 20th century. With urban formal labor markets swamped, working in the informal sector was, originally, a survival strategy but gradually, it became the only alternative in the face of the model of crony mercantilist capitalism associated with the policies of Import Substitution, especially in Latin America. The legalist perspective shared many of the policy prescriptions of the emerging neoliberal development orthodoxy (→ Neoliberalism, II/16). Its proponents promoted not new laws and State support but rather, mass deregulation, especially of private property rights, creating, instead, a system of "accessible" property rights that would enable informal entrepreneurs to use their legally non-recognized capital. Access to formal credit was key as a means of disentangling the webs of high-interest informal credit lines often run by mafia-type organizations. One of the pillars of the De Soto team's reasoning was the need to grant property titles to the millions of peripheral urban dwellers who had built housing without legal titles and without following regulatory permits. Such dormant capital could be the source of enormous wealth creation if only the State would face reality and legalize such informal settlements. Such a contention was a central feature of the influential work of John Turner (1968), but wrapped in the polemic rhetoric of De Soto, the new sell was much more successful. In the legalist perspective, contrary to the ILO view, the informal sector was neither marginal, nor a sign of poverty but rather, informal actors were the harbingers of new hope for future wealth creation. However, there was no attempt to examine the overlapping of informal-formal activities and although the informal "entrepreneur" was the key agent of change and subject of analysis, informal sector workers did not enter into the legalist analytical framework.

The structuralist perspective

Whereas both the dualist and legalist perspectives separated the informal and formal sectors, the first due to their different development stages and the second due to State exclusion and cronyism, structuralist examinations of informality highlighted the intrinsic links between both economies (Chen 2005). This perspective, associated with but not limited to Marxist political economy, emphasized the manner in which informality was incorporated into specific social relations (Castells and Portes 1989; Fernández-Kelly 2006). This more heterogeneous approach to examining informality introduced into the discussion the illegal economy as a means of differentiating it from the informal economy. While advocates of this perspective differentiated between the formal and informal economies based on the process of production and distribution of goods and services rather than the products sold (Castells and Portes 1989; Centeno and Portes 2006), such a definition could also be stretched to highlight how informal activity used illegal methods to produce legal goods (Cross 2000). Both economies share many operational similarities (they circumvent laws and must avoid detection) and neither can obtain legal protection when transaction agreements are violated, however, the penalties for undertaking informal-illegal activities are vastly different (Cross and Peña 2006).

Perhaps the key difference between the illegal and informal economies and their activities has to do with the concept of social legitimacy. Formal/informal/illegal are not stagnant concepts or realities but depend on normative changes over time. In other words, the key difference between the informal and illegal economies (and the products sold in both) is that the first, while circumventing State regulations, is deemed as socially acceptable by society, while the second is not. The structuralists focus on the link between the economic reconfigurations of the post 1970s and the growth of informality. Herein, as deregulation, privatization (→ II/17), economic liberalization and labor flexibilization have expanded, so too has the informal economy, which increasingly becomes subordinated to the formal economy, as formal employment is gradually replaced with informal and/or non-standard employment as a means of lowering labor costs, squeezing labor rights and simultaneously, ensuring the competitiveness of firms (Carr and Chen 2002; see also International Labor Office (ILO) 2013). For the structuralist approach the mass rural-urban migration of the 20th century was key in generating excess labor supply in developing city centers, however, they argue that such a process led to consequences that were more complex than simply fomenting survival strategies of the populations of the urban poor. Informal enterprises became ever-more important in supporting modern capitalist accumulation (both in terms of production and the reproduction of the labor force), helping to increase formal firm profitability by lowering direct wage costs and reproduction costs of formal workers (Portes 1996, 150) (→ Capitalism, II/2).

A significantly different take on the formal-informal divide seeks not to examine the linkages of one with the other, nor propose new policy paradigms and institutional practices to formalize the informal. Rather, informal activities are perceived as being representations not of underdevelopment but rather explicit resistance against the whole paradigm of Western development and unwanted incursions of the State into the daily practices of local communities across the Global South (Chakrabarty 2000; Escobar 1995). Roughly grouped under post-structural theories or post-colonial perspectives, these perspectives do not explicitly grapple with the term "informal economy" because, epistemologically, this term is seen as being inherently tied to the binary discourse of the West and its developmental models (→ Development, II/6). Instead, they contradict the dualist, legalist, and structuralist understandings of informality as well as their views on why it exists and how to eradicate it. Formality becomes an unwanted objective. What is proposed is a decoupling of local communities from the Western development discourse of growth, consumption and State intervention (for a critique, see Williams and Round 2008).

State capacity is perhaps the central pillar for the analysis of trends within the informal economy (→ Nation State, II/38). While the dualist perspective saw the informal sector as being innately destructive to the State and economic development and the legalist perspective saw the State as being the key agent in fomenting informality, the structuralist take is more nuanced, arguing that the informal economy can be both good and bad for the State and governments. Indeed, informality is determined by the ever-changing relationship between the State and civil society (→ II/28) (Centeno and Portes 2006, 31) and as such, while regulations are important in curtailing or ignoring informality, their actual enforcement is the preeminent factor. In other words, the actions of the State are key to determining not just the extent of informality but also the impacts of informality on different social and economic actors. For structuralists the growth of informalization is not a process that occurs beyond State reach. Instead, it is

> the expression of a new form of control characterized by the disenfranchisement of a large sector of the working class, often with the acquiescence of the state … For the latter, the loss of formal control over these activities is compensated by the short-term potential for legitimation and renewed economic growth that they offer.
>
> *(Castells and Portes 1989, 27)*

From theoretical debate to statistical measurement

The extensive theoretical debate regarding definitions, causes, and the problems/potential of informality has also led to numerous efforts aimed at more precisely measuring the size and trends of informal economic activity. Nevertheless, despite important advances, all these attempts suffer from limitations due, more than anything, to the lack of conclusive national and international data from which to draw. As informal activity is synonymous with a lack of registration and regulation, it is unsurprising that most measurement efforts are based on proxies rather than concrete data bases.

Hart's anthropological-sociological take on informality and specifically, the "informal income opportunities" of individuals within this sector, inspired many of the labor force surveys of Latin American countries to begin measuring the degree of worker marginalization, based on the level of income below the minimum wage and in connection with poverty (Charmes 2012, 105). The second form of measurement of informality was based on the enterprise as an economic unit of analysis and became a central part of many studies and economic surveys conducted by the ILO in Africa and the PREALC team in Latin America (Charmes 2012, 105). Bringing together both definitions and measurements, as was attempted by the ILO in 1993, has led to a broad acceptance that informal sector activities should be distinguished from underground activities due to the fact that tax evasion (→ Taxation, II/22) or avoiding other administrative or social security schemes has not been an explicit act of most informal sector agents. Nonetheless, for data collection purposes, both the non-registration of individuals (in labor and/or social security codes/systems) or the non-registration of enterprises (in fiscal or commercial registers) have become basic elements in defining informality (Charmes 2012, 106). In 2003, there was another tentative effort at statistically defining and measuring informal employment so that it could be included in regular or permanent labor force surveys in different nations. Nonetheless, differences both in their definition and measurement have ensured that both concepts remain far from being mutually exclusive and nor does informal employment include all segments of the informal sector (Charmes 2012, 104).

Later efforts to more precisely measure and collate levels of informal employment led to an expansion of the conceptual tools as it was found that informal employment included non-registered work and protection in the informal sector but also the same factors in the formal economy, i.e. in firms that were formally registered as enterprises (fiscally and commercially) but where at least some workers either had no written contract and/or were not covered (or registered) by labor legislation and social protection systems. In recent years, especially since the ILO developed its Decent Work Agenda, many national labor statistics have come to combine measurements of informality based on the size of an enterprise (generally employing either less than ten or less than five workers) or the percentage of workers' with access to basic social protection services (generally, health, pension, and workplace accident/illness insurance). Nevertheless, measurements of coverage, at least in Latin America, generally do not differentiate between types and levels (Portes 1996, 159) and nor do they distinguish between unprotected workers and the self-employed. However, the ILO does define informal employment as encompassing workers in diverse categories of employment: employers, employees, own-account workers, unpaid family members and members of producer cooperatives (ILO 2013, 3). Of course, attempts to measure informality are not confined to labor market statistics. Indeed, data examining trends in housing informality (UN Habitat 2006) in participation in GDP (ILO and WIEGO 2012; Jütting and Laiglesia 2009) and many other economic sectors are commonplace.

As already mentioned, the inconsistencies and unavailability of data measuring different types of informality makes it difficult to analyze cross-country or inter-regional comparisons and trends. Perhaps the most diffuse measurement category relates to informal employment (non-agricultural). Below recent trends in the size of this measurement can be seen when examining data taken from those countries of the region where data was available. While there is a very timid drop in the regional size of informal employment between 2010–2014, there is also a notable disparity between countries, with Bolivia, Honduras and Guatemala (78.81, 73.31, 71.74 percent of total non-agricultural employment, respectively for 2014) topping the charts, while Uruguay, Costa Rica and Brazil (22.95, 36.89, 37.79 percent of total non-agricultural employment, respectively for the same year) ranking as the countries with the lowest levels of informal, non-agricultural employment (The World Bank IBRD Data Catalog).

The informal economy in the Americas

Without doubt, in the more than forty years of academic preoccupation over the informal economy, the principal socio-geographical reference point has been countries and cities of the Global South. Less attention has been given to examining the trends of informality in industrialized countries such as Canada and the U.S., while Latin American countries have been key focal points for the formulation of both theory, empirical studies, and policy prescriptions concerning the informal sector and the informal economy. The Caribbean, for its part, was initially not given much importance in terms of examining trends in informality due, perhaps, to the small size of the countries in question (but not their population densities), as well as the huge importance migration has played in balancing demographic growth (see Guzmán et al. 2006) (→ Transnational Migration, I/44).

Nonetheless, despite the prevalence of studies on the informal sector in the South, there has been less controversy surrounding the definition and measurement of the informal economy in the U.S. and Canada compared to Latin America and the Caribbean. However, in both these countries informal economic activity and employment are defined and treated differently. First and foremost, the conventional understanding of the informal economy in the U.S. and Canada associate it with the shadow economy, where such activity is undertaken as a means of obtaining income in ways that circumvent government regulation, taxation (→ II/22) and statistical observation (Schneider and Buehn 2018, 3). Herein, often both the actors and agents are differentiated but collectively grouped in this sphere of the economy: illegal traders in the illegal economy (black market), white-collar professionals and low-wage workers looking to supplement their income and avoid tax, or undocumented immigrant workers forced to undertake cash work (Nightingale and Wandner 2011). The more pervasive presence of regulation and the predominance of the wage-based societies in the U.S. and Canada helped to create a more stable social and legal order which has regulated and legitimized property rights and contracts, factors that have helped control legally and socially a significant rise of informality and the "free rider syndrome."

The greater variety of economic organization and levels of development across the Global South have led to more debate concerning aspects of informality (Portes 1996). Furthermore, the much greater size of the informal economy in Latin America and the Caribbean has also led to different policy recommendations compared to those found in the U.S. and Canada. The predominant focus has been on designing policies geared toward "formalizing" (or at least semi-formalizing) the informal, especially small unregistered businesses (or the self-employment) and more recently, informal workers. Mexico and Colombia were perhaps initially the most active countries for implementing policies and programs aimed at reducing the size of the informal sector while also opening up more avenues for State support of informal entrepreneurialism (Otero 1994). Nevertheless, such policies were ineffective, at least on a national scale, with informal work still largely out-ranking formal work in terms of size in both countries. Two relatively recent success stories of employment formalization have come from further South of the continent with the progressive governments of Lula da Silva, in Brazil, and the Kirchners, in Argentina, making significant inroads into labor informality via a combination of social policies that sought to tackle extreme poverty through assistance programs while also increasing wages and generating formal jobs in a period of strong economic growth. Indeed, according to the ILO (2014), between 2003–2012 the percentage of unregistered workers in Argentina dropped by 14.5 percent, while in Brazil, between 2002–2012 the rate fell by 13.9 percent, improvements way beyond those seen in any other country with the important exception of Uruguay where, according to World Bank data, informal employment dropped by 15.9 percent in the five years between 2010 and 2014 (The World Bank IBRD Data).

Another important political and legislative advance in numerous countries across the region has been the relatively widespread ratification of the 2011 Domestic Workers' ILO Convention 189 and Recommendation 201. As of 2018, thirteen Latin American and Caribbean countries have ratified this convention: Uruguay (2012), Bolivia, Ecuador, Nicaragua, and Paraguay (2013), Argentina, Colombia, and Costa Rica (2014), Panama, Chile, and the Dominican Republic (2015), Jamaica (2016) and Brazil (2018). While there is often discord between the ratification and implementation/enforcement of ILO Conventions, the move to promote new laws and policies that seek to make visible and protect such a vast population of previously statistically and politically overlooked domestic workers should not be taken for granted. In Colombia, for example, the National Department for Statistics has estimated that 3 percent of the economically active population works in private households as domestic workers (over 677,000), and 95 percent of whom are women. In recent years, steps have been made to increase these workers' access to the social security system and formalize their rights to some of the legal benefits obtained by all formal employees, for example the biannual payment of a service bonus "*prima de servicios.*"

In the U.S. and Canada, the predominant understanding perceives the informal sector as being dependent on the formal sector and counters the assertion that the informal sector harbors survivalist strategies in marginal urban groups. Nevertheless, more recent research in North America has begun to highlight the growth of non-registered, often digitally based economic and work activity, as a means of supplementing income in periods of adverse employment conditions, especially after the 2008 global financial crisis (Bracha and Burke 2014) (→ Crisis, II/4). The type of dependence between both economies is often perceived as being either complementary (in the case of sub-contracting) or competitive (i.e. unregistered activities with lower labor and production costs) (Harding and Jenkins 1989). In

North America, there has been continual interest in examining the links between informal economic activity and irregular migration (→ Transnational Migration, I/44). In particular, researchers have explored how undocumented migrant communities, excluded from the formal economy, have adapted their lives around work and business activities in the informal economy as a survival strategy, while also being forced to access credit from informal and illegal channels, generating significant risk (Portes and Sensenbrenner 1993).

Despite their definitional differences and the notable size differences of informal economic activity within and across these two socio-geographical regions of the Americas, one point of general agreement relates to the supposed counter-cyclical nature of the informal sector, i.e. most academics contended that the informal sector grew when the economy contracted and decreased in times of economic growth (Carr and Chen 2002). However, more recently, this notion has been challenged (Gasparini and Tornarolli 2009). Indeed, with increased regional economic integration, many studies have begun to reframe the informal economy, highlighting its "hidden enterprise culture" over-and-above its association with "sweatshop labor" (Williams and Nadin 2010, 364). Along the way, the links between both economies have become ever-more permeable and temporal and while the relation between informality and poverty has not subsided, increasingly, scholars have differentiated between informal agents, who may be either "necessity entrepreneurs" (i.e. own-account petty merchants) or "opportunity ones" (366).

Furthermore, the significant transformations of both economic and cultural globalization have led to not only the partial informalization of diverse State apparatuses but also the expansion of transnational communities who, often, work together to circumvent regulations, both in origin and host nations (Itzigsohn 2006). Their efforts to undertake informal transactions can lead to increased costs and as such, they must distribute risk along the social network, using what Portes and Sensenbrenner called "bounded solidarity" (qtd. in Fernández-Kelly 2006, 8).

Furthermore, despite the diversity of definitions and understandings of informality (and the informal sector and informal economy) when associated with First-and-Third World or advanced-developing countries, often the interpretations and policy prescriptions given have more to do with the political spectrums of the scholar in question than any intrinsic difference in the place studied. Neoliberal and conservative scholars see informal agents in a positive light and propose the promotion of private enterprises and the deregulation of the State (→ State-Transformation, II/21); Liberals promote targeted social welfare programs that support the working poor who labor in the informal economy; Marxists and Neo-Marxists perceive informal workers and producers as being in a relation of subordination to multinationals and their global supply chains (→ Global Commodity Chains, II/12) and they propose the adoption of policies that protect their basic rights (Chen 2005, 6).

Conclusion

During the various decades since the term "informal economy" first emerged, a number of important developments have taken place. Over time a gradual re-appreciation of the nature of the informal economy surfaced; its growth, both in developing and industrialized countries, has led to a consensus that sees it as being a permanent feature of capitalist development (Chen 2005) (→ Capitalism, II/2). Such a view has since permeated research and policy initiatives. Whereas initially, research into the informal economy and policy directive follow-ups stressed the need to instigate State-led processes of formalizing the most productive sectors of the informal economy as a means of expanding employment possibilities;

more recently, attention has turned to the effects of informality on informal workers and informal subsistence enterprises, specifically the decent work deficits that permeate the informal economy. This development turned policy attention, particularly at the multilateral level, to the vast "protection gap" that permeates the informal economy. In line with this redirection, in 2002 the ILO published its definitive definition of the informal economy, and more recently it has promulgated the concept and policy initiative of decent work, which goes beyond the formal/informal divide to center on ensuring worker protection and dignified working conditions in all spheres of economic activity.

Works cited

Bairoch, Paul. 1976. *Urban Unemployment in Developing Countries: The Nature of the Problem and Proposals for its Solutions*. Geneva: International Labor Office.

Bracha, Anat and Mary Burke. 2014. "Informal work activity in the United States: Evidence from survey responses." *Current Policy Perspectives*, 2014–1, no. 14–13: 1–48.

Carr, Marilyn and Martha A. Chen. 2002. "Globalization and the informal economy: How global trade and investment impact on the working poor." *WEIGO (Women in Informal Employment Globalizing and Organizing*, 1–28.

Castells, Manuel. 2006. *Problemas de Investigación en Sociología Urbana*. Mexico City, Buenos Aires, Madrid: Siglo XXI Editores.

Castells, Manuel and Alejandro Portes. 1989. "World Underneath: The Origins, Dynamics and Effects of the Informal Economy." In *The Informal Economy: Studies in Advanced and Less Developed Countries*, ed. Alejandro Portes, Manuel Castells, and Lauren A. Benton, 11–37. Baltimore: John Hopkins University Press.

Centeno, Miguel Angel, and Alejandro Portes. 2006. "The informal economy in the shadow of the state." In *Out of the Shadows: Political Action & the Informal Economy in Latin America*, eds. Patricia Fernández-Kelly and Jon Shefner, 23–48. Pennsylvania: Pennsylvania State University Press.

Chakrabarty, Dipesh. 2000. *Provincializing Europe: Postcolonial Thought and Historical Difference*. Princeton: Princeton University Press.

Charmes, Jaques. 2012. "The informal economy worldwide: Trends and characteristics." *The Journal of Applied Economic Research*, 6, no. 2: 103–132.

Chen, Martha. 2012. "The informal economy: Definitions, theories and policies." *WEIGO* (*Women in Informal Employment Globalizing and Organizing*), no. 1: 1–23.

———. 2005. "Rethinking the informal economy: Linkages with the formal economy and the formal regulatory environment." Research Paper no. 2005/10, EGDI and UNU-WIDER, Helsinki.

Cross, John. 2000. "Street vendors, modernity and postmodernity: Conflict and compromise in the global economy." *International Journal of Sociology and Social Policy*, 20, no. 1–2: 30–51.

Cross, John and Sergio Peña 2006. "Risk and regulation in informal and illegal markets." In *Out of the Shadows: Political Action & The Informal Economy in Latin America*, eds. Patricia Fernandez-Kelly and Jon Shefner, 49–80. Pennsylvania: Pennsylvania State University Press.

De Soto, Hernando. 1994. *El Otro Sendero: La Revolución Informal*. Bogotá: Tercer Mundo Ediciones.

Escobar, Arturo. 1995. *Encountering Development. The Making and Unmaking of the Third World*. Princeton: Princeton University Press.

Fernández-Kelly, Patricia. 2006. "Introduction." In *Out of the Shadows: Political Action & The Informal Economy in Latin America*, eds. Patricia Fernández-Kelly and Jon Shefner, 1–22. Pennsylvania: Pennsylvania State University Press.

Gasparini, Leonardo and Leopoldo Tornarolli. 2009. "Labor informality in Latin America and the Caribbean: Patterns and trends from household survey microdata." *Desarrollo y Sociedad*, First Semester: 13–80.

Guzmán, José M., Jorge Rodríguez, Jorge Martínez, Juan Manuel Contreras, and Daniela González. 2006. "The demography of Latin America and the Caribbean since 1950." *Population E*, 61, no. 5–6: 519–576.

UN Habitat. 2006. *State of the world's cities 2006*. London: Earthscan and UN Habitat.

Harding, Philip and Richard Jenkins. 1989. *The Myth of the Hidden Economy: Towards a New Understanding of Informal Economic Activity*. Philadelphia: Open University Press, Milton Keynes.

Hart, Keith. 1973. "Informal income opportunities and urban development in Ghana." *The Journal of Modern African Studies*, 2, no. 1: 61–81.

Hawkins, Daniel. 2011. *The Struggles over City Space: Informal Street Vending & Public Space Governance in Medellín, Colombia, Studien zu Lateinamerika*. Baden-Baden: NOMOS Verlagsgesellschaft.

International Labor Office (ILO). 2013. *Measuring informality: A statistical manual on the informal sector and informal employment*. Geneva: International Labor Office.

———. 2014. Report V (1), "Transitioning from the informal to the formal economy." International Labor Conference, 103rd Session, Geneva.

International Labor Office (ILO) & Women in Informal Employment: Globalizing and Organizing (WIEGO). 2012. *Women and Men in the Informal Economy – A Statistical Picture*. Geneva: International Labor Office.

Itzigsohn, José. 2006. "Neoliberalism, markets and informal grassroots economies." In *Out of the Shadows: Political Action & the Informal Economy in Latin America*, eds. Patricia Fernández-Kelly and Jon Shefner, 81–96. Pennsylvania: Pennsylvania State University Press.

Jütting, Johannes and Juan Laiglesia. 2009. *Employment, Poverty Reduction and Development: What's New? Is Informal Normal? Towards More and Better Jobs in Developing Countries*. Paris: OECD.

Karl, Marx. 1973. *El Capital*. Buenos Aires: Editorial Cartago.

Nightingale, Demetra S. and Stephen A. Wandner. 2011. "Informal and nonstandard employment in the United States: Implications for low-income working families." *The Urban Institute, Brief 20*, August.

Nún, José. 1969. "Superpoblación relativa, ejército industrial de reserve y masa marginal." *Revista Latinoamericana de Sociología*, 5, 178–236.

Otero, Maria. 1994. "The role of governments and private institutions in addressing the informal sector in Latin America." In *Contrapunto: The Informal Sector Debate in Latin America*, ed. Cathy A. Rakowski, 177–197. New York: State University of New York Press.

Park, Robert. 1969. "Human migration and the marginal man." In *The Classic Essays on the Culture of Cities*, ed. Richard Sennett, 131–142. New York: Appleton-Century-Crofts.

Portes, Alejandro. 1996. "The informal economy: Perspectives from Latin America." In *Exploring the Underground Economy*, ed. Susan Pozo, 147–165. Kalamazoo: W. E. Upjohn Institute for Employment Research.

———. 1997. "Neoliberalism and the sociology of development: Emerging trends and unanticipated facts." *Population & Development Review*, 23, no. 2: n.p.

Portes, Alejandro and Julia Sensenbrenner. 1993. "Embeddedness and immigration: Notes on the social determinants of economic action." *The American Journal of Sociology*, 98, no. 6: 1320–1350.

Quijano, Aníbal. 1983. "Imperialism and marginality in Latin America." *Latin American Perspectives*, 10, no. 76: 76–85.

Schneider, Friedrich and Andreas Buehn. 2018. "Shadow economy: Estimation methods, problems, results and open questions." *Open Economics* 1, no. 1: 1–29.

Souza, Paulo and Victor Tokman 1976. "The informal urban sector in Latin America." *International Labour Review*, 114, no. 3: 355–365.

Turner, John C. 1968. "Housing priorities, settlement patterns, and urban development in modernizing countries." *Journal of the American Institute of Planners*, 34, no. 6: 354–363.

Williams, Colin C. and Sara Nadin 2010. "Entrepreneurship and the informal economy: An overview." *SSRN Electronic Journal*, 15, no. 4: 361–378.

Williams, Colin C. and John Round. 2008. "A critical evaluation of romantic depictions of the informal economy." *Review of Social Economy*, 66, no. 3: 297–323.

The World Bank IBRD Data. "Data bank." *The World Bank*. https://databank.worldbank.org/home.aspx.

14
LABOR REPRESENTATION

Kjeld Jakobsen

The very origin of the colonization of Latin American, Caribbean, and North American countries by the Spanish, the French, the Dutch, and the English (→ Colonial Rule, I/5) explains the different models of labor organization and legislature implanted in each country. They basically follow Roman and German law, and the *Common Law*. Law doctrines from different ideologies – Anarchism, Socialism (→ I/42), Christianity (→ Religious Beliefs, I/40), Liberalism and Fascism – provided content for labor legislature in the majority of American countries (Moraes Filho 1978). Despite similar features, each country in Latin America developed with unique dynamics. As a rule, the creation and acknowledgment of unions in the colonies came later, for their appearance was linked to the independence movement (→ I/10). However, since in European countries there was already legislation that regulated union operations, the legalization of labor unions in their colonies in the Caribbean was less vexing than in other American countries.

The creation of unions in the United States was not a peaceful process, instead massive violations of human rights (→ II/35) occurred. The Haymarket Square demonstration in Chicago for a workday of eight hours was met with repression and the unjust death penalty assigned to union activists who sought to establish the celebration of a Labor Day on May 1st. In the 19th century, an act of repression resulted in a hundred deaths and hundreds of injuries when the army cracked down on a national strike by the railroad workers. The steel tycoons of Pittsburgh, the Carnegies, and also Henry Ford, were not regarded as bosses who were favorable to the unions and labor representation. For instance, the Ford Company had a department of entrepreneurial security with hundreds of employees set up to repress union organization.

The institutionalization of worker and social rights, as well as labor structures as we know them today, started in the 1930s. The institutionalization in countries like Brazil generated a consolidated legislation of workers' rights, rules of procedure for labor organization, and a specialized law. Other countries, like the United States, basically institutionalized the rules of union membership. In general, the basic trade union organization was based on the following models: unitary organization by professional category in Argentina, Brazil, Cuba, Uruguay, and the Caribbean; organization by company, unitary, or pluralist in the rest of Latin America; and organization by "locals" in Canada and the United States. Unions in the current Dutch and British colonies are organizations of local origin. In the case of the

French colonies, organizations may be either local or by extension of centers. In the case of Puerto Rico, unions are connected with local confederations, with the "Locals" of international unions, and with the union central of the U.S.: The American Federation of Labor – Congress of Industrial Organizations (AFL–CIO).

In the first half of the 20th century labor legislation was basically aimed at regulating labor relations and minimizing conflicts in growing urban and industrial markets (→ Urbanization, I/45) by means of powerful State mediation (→ Nation State, II/38), particularly in countries farther along in the process of industrialization. In some countries, especially in Argentina, Brazil, and Mexico, the rulers who promoted legislature also aimed to regulate the cooperation of unions and patron organizations with their political parties and the State (→ Populism, II/43). The extent of union freedom and labor rights in agriculture and public service was achieved decades later, however, following the same labor organization model from urban and private workers.

Beyond the efforts in regard to legislation, the self-organization of male and female workers is the main reason for the establishment of real labor representation and labor rights. In the 19th century, most American countries created the first labor organizations on record, the mutual-aid labor associations of Latin America, the "Knights of Labour" associations of North America, or general laying-claims unions influenced by European anarchists and socialists. These associations promoted solidarity among workers by collecting resources to aid the unemployed, the sick and people with burial costs. The *Knights of Labour* was an organization that sought to unify workers so that they value their work. It emerged in the second half of the 19th century in the United States and Canada with an agenda of laying claims related to the reduction of working time, abolition of child labor, etc., but disappeared by the beginning of the 20th century (Murray 1998).

In Central America the first labor organizations appeared in the 1920s from national entities tied to the Central American Labor Center (*Central Obrera Centro Americana* – COCA) and the U.S.-based American Federation of Labor (AFL) (Arriola 1984). Since the appearance of the first unions in Central America and in Mexico, particularly in the farming and mining sectors, after World War II the AFL sought to develop a presence in the region.

This entry presents an analysis of the development and factors that have affected labor representation in the Americas. Over the past century, workers' representation has needed to adapt to the changing economies through Industrial Revolutions, World Wars, and the politics that followed, as well as the expansion of neoliberal capitalism (→ Neoliberalism, II/16). These factors among others had varying effects on the different industries in each country, creating a need for workers to use their collective power to bargain for better conditions.

The institutionalization of trade unions and labor rights

When World War II ended, the beginning of the "30 Golden Years" in the Americas was met with union-entity structures fairly consolidated. The exceptions were some Caribbean countries, particularly Haiti, where union institutionalization did not occur until the 1950s, soon thereafter dismantled during the dictatorship of "Papa Doc." However, in the United States and in Canada, this period marked the apogee of labor power, with high fees, financial resources, and political influence for unions. This union influence could be consolidated into four different areas that highlight the structural and strategic role of the represented economic sector, associated representation of the union, organizational capacity, and institutional influence (McCormick and Hyman 2013). This was also the moment when a series of social-protection measures were introduced, which in the U.S. were characterized by a more liberal and private conception, while in Canada a universal and public conception dominated.

After World War II, three factors have contributed to defining labor and its representation practices in Latin America: the politics of import substitution, the labor organization model controlled by the State, and the ideological dispute of the Cold War. Restrictions on world commerce during the two World Wars stimulated some Latin American countries to follow the model of import substitution industrialization with the aim of overcoming the structural dependency on the capitalist centers.

Few countries achieved the superior phase of import substitution, and when they were able to, bottlenecks often set back economic development, which was the case in Argentina, Brazil, and Mexico. In these three countries, a corporative union-organization model was instituted, in which the State organized, controlled, and regulated the unions. Corporative practices presuppose a strong State capable of obliging the social classes, particularly workers and employers, to cooperate among themselves according to rules established by the State. The State could also maintain rules and influence practices through its power to co-opt and coerce. This model of work relation management was consistent with the necessity to secure "social peace" in the transition from agrarian economies to industrial economies.

Particularly in Mexico, unionism gained strength by associating with the political party who ruled the government: the Institutional Revolutionary Party (*Partido Revolucionario Institucional* – PRI). General Lázaro Cárdenas, the country's president between 1934 and 1940, organized the PRI unions into four sectors: the working class, represented by the Confederation of Mexican Workers (*Confederación de Trabajadores de México* – CTM), then with 1.25 million members; the rural sector, represented by the National Peasants Confederation (*Confederación Nacional de Campesinos* – CNC), with 2.5 million; the popular sector, through the National Confederation of Popular Organizations (*Confederación Nacional de Organizaciones Populares* – CNOP), created in 1942, with 500,000; and the military sectors (→ Military, II/37), represented by 55,000 members. The latter was later dissolved (Villa 1993). Therefore, in order to join the party, one needed to be part of one of the four union organizations; conversely, adhering to one of them meant joining that party. This established the Mexican "*blanco*" corporative norm, where an authoritarian State (→ Authoritarianism, II/25) and social organizations controlled by the PRI battled for influence and for privileges that ended in the hands of their directors.

In Argentina, an organic relationship developed between the government of Juan Perón, his *Partido Justicialista* (PJ), and the labor movement, particularly in the institutionalization of workers' rights and in the resolution of conflicts between employers and employees, with the latter normally being favored (→ Populism, II/43). This relationship was not formally institutionalized like in Mexico, yet still the co-optation of union leaders was an important device used which gave them some influence over government sectors like social security and State companies. The power of labor organizations included their total support for members of the PJ during elections and in the exercise of the government.

Brazil's labor legislation still contains corporative elements, which were inspired by the "Carta del Lavoro" introduced in Italy in 1927 by Benito Mussolini. There were similar attempts of co-opting labor organizations via the Brazilian Labor Party (*Partido Trabalhista Brasileiro* – PTB) founded by Getúlio Vargas in 1945, which not became as dominant as the PRI in Mexico or the PJ in Argentina.

The union's vanguard in each country was defined by its most important sector, whether industry, mining, or agriculture, in addition to the fact that this economic profile deeply influenced each country's labor culture. For example, there is no way of dissociating the labor culture of the Bolivian Workers' Confederation (*Confederación Obrera Boliviana* – COB) from the actions of the miners, or the grand labor demonstrations of Central America from the banana-plantation workers at the Workers United Front of Honduras (*Frente Unitária de Trabajadores* – FUT-H).

Pan-Americanism (→ II/40) also contributed significantly to the development of labor and representation practices in the beginning Cold War period. Agents from the American Institute for Free Labor Development (AIFLD), financed by the U.S. State Department, tried to exclude Communists and other left-wing currents from the labor movement of the Americas. This attempt was meant to make the working class more receptive to capitalism (→ II/2), liberal democracy (→ II/32), and the values of the United States. Additionally, the AIFLD's presence and the participation of the Inter-American Regional Organization of Workers guided the national labor centers to affiliate, and directed the actions of the union training institutes, such as the Labor Cultural Institute (*Instituto Cultural do Trabalho* – ICT) – tied in Brazil to AIFLD.

The Fordist mode of production (→ Fordism, II/10) adopted in the Americas since the first decades of the 20th century established industrial installations, many of bulk size, for assembling products destined for mass consumption (→ Consumerism, I/23), such as kitchen appliances and automobiles, or continual-production goods like steel products and those of the chemical sector. In its infancy, the majority of workers participating in this model did not possess great professional qualifications, as these were not required for working on the assembly lines. Thus the jobs created were a key attraction for land-workers and peasants who left the countryside for the city in the case of Latin America, and for European immigrants who headed to the United States. Brazil, for example, between the 1940s and the 1970s experienced one of the greatest population movements in the world, with migration from the country to the cities reaching thirty million inhabitants (→ Urbanization, I/45). These factors were essential for the creation of unions in the spear-point sectors of the country's economy, such as the automobile sector, and for the formation of the so-called "new labor movement," which beginning in the 1970s, started to alter the character of Brazilian political and social organization.

In the U.S., the nascent industry-worker unions were not well received by the original directors from the craft unions that comprised the majority of the AFL. These individuals did not believe in the possibility of organizing workers without professional qualifications, of which many did not even speak English. Thus, the industrialists created an alternate central union, the Congress of Industrial Organizations (CIO). Finally, in 1955 the AFL and the CIO united (Lichtenstein 1997).

The ascension of unions pervaded industrialization in the Americas. The growth of mining and agriculture provoked demonstrations and important achievements in workers' rights, such as the 13th month's salary (mandatory bonus); judicial security for labor organization and collective negotiation based in International Labor Organization's (ILO) Conventions No. 87 or No. 98; land reform initiatives in Brazil, Bolivia, Chile, among others (→ Land, II/15); in addition to achievements in the area of social protection. Nonetheless, some fractions of the working class such as public servants, small rural producers, and informal workers were excluded from labor organization and from its eventual benefits (→ Informality, II/13).

Labor organization of public servants started to become acknowledged in some countries, as in 1940s Argentina, but the majority launched much later. For example, Canada did not start until 1960. Up until then, the idea was counteracted with the argument that "the Queen does not bargain!" (Heron 2012). That is, State servants should be loyal and not create conflicts, even if for contractual reasons, thus remaining without labor organization and collective negotiation. The ILO Convention No. 151, which reserves the right for collective organization by public servants, was approved only in 1978.

In Central American agriculture major unions were established early, while in countries like Brazil, the first rural workers' unions were not acknowledged until 1950. A particular characteristic of rural unions was that they simultaneously represented wage-earning rural workers, small owners, and subsistence-peasants. César Chávez's and Dolores Huerta's struggle to organize rural workers in U.S. fruit plantations also dates from this period. It culminated in the creation of the United Farm Workers (UFW).

In 1968, the ILO launched their World Employment Program with the aim of contributing to enhance the creation of jobs in developing countries (→ Development, II/6). In this context the "ILO Kenya Employment Mission" (1972) produced a report that, among other aspects, provided the first fundamentals for describing what today we know as "Informal Work," a duality in the job market: the minority of well-employed and well-remunerated workers in the economy's modern sector versus the majority of workers, marginalized by unemployment or underemployment (→ Informality, II/13). The background reasons that provoked this situation were various: intense scientific and technological capital concentration in industrialized countries, which accelerates its productivity indexes and the absence of specific technologies able to increment the comparative advantages of developing countries; destruction of traditional jobs of low competition; preference for urban life and work; concentration of land; among other factors (ILO 1972).

In a similar fashion researchers, like Viktor Tokman and Paulo Renato de Souza, while analyzing the movement of migrants into the big cities of Latin America (→ Urbanization, I/45) found that there were spare laborers who could find neither jobs in the industries nor other structural occupations in urban areas. This contingent of workers, who thickened the cords of poverty in the *favelas* and outskirts of these cities, devoted themselves to informal activities as a means of survival (Souza and Tokman 1980). From these findings, the ILO sketched criteria to define what informal work is and began to classify its main characteristics such as easy-access activities financed with local resources: family property (→ Family, I/26), small-scale operations, intensive work with adapted technology, training acquired outside of the education system, and activity in unregulated and competitive markets.

The structural adjustment programs implemented in Latin America and the Caribbean in the 1980s and 1990s provoked large transformations in the workplace and consequently in labor organization (→ Neoliberalism, II/16). Informal work, which was initially an alternative for the spare workforce during the period of strong growth following World War II, started to take the role of protective "cushion" for workers with formal contracts after the external-debt crisis from the beginning of the 1980s (→ Crisis, II/4). The Employment Program in Latin America and the Caribbean (PREALC) tied to the ILO which worked from 1968 to 1993 and that stimulated the non-agricultural informal section in the region between 1980 and 1990, jumped from 25.6 percent to 30.8 percent, while the percentage of total workers in formal working conditions dropped from 74.4 percent to 69.2 percent with significant reductions of workers in private sectors (ILO 1993). The ILO also found later that out of one hundred new occupations created in Latin America and the Caribbean between 1986 and 1996, eighty of them were informal (ILO 1998).

The growing informalization of national markets has tended to reduce the affiliation rates to unions. Divisions engendered by the Cold War or by more recent representation disputes, mainly for ideological reasons, have also made common actions and the strengthening of labor movements difficult, as well as the ever-larger employment of youth and women who have no interest in affiliating with a union, for they do not see their specific interests addressed by them (→ Gender and Work, II/11).

In smaller countries the statistics regarding union density are not reliable due to the absence of specialized institutions. Extant data derives from self-declared statements from union directors, or from older ILO estimations. Notwithstanding, numbers from a few countries illustrate the difficulties that the labor movement faces today. According to their respective ministries or labor administrations, Canada has a density of 26.6 percent, the United States 11.1 percent, Brazil 17.8 percent, Argentina 37.6 percent, and Uruguay 17.3 percent (ATO (Argentina Trabajo y Empleo) 2018; MTB (Ministério do Trabalho Brazil) 2018; MTSS (Ministerio de Trabajo y Seguridad Social Uruguay) 2018; STATCAN (Statistics Canada) 2018; US DOL United States Department of Labor 2018). In Central America, the average density of represented workers from the seven countries is approximately 7 percent, with forty different union confederations. In the four countries of Andean America, a similar percentile is reached by their twenty union confederations (Jakobsen 2016).

Unions in the "30 Golden Years" of Latin America had their ascension interrupted in the majority of the countries by military coups consolidated in the 1960s and 1970s (→ Military, II/37; Authoritarianism, II/25). These coups, supported by different U.S. governments, leaned on anticommunist sentiment and in the Doctrine of National Security, and they frequently regarded unionism as one of the "enemies" to be controlled, as it was the case in Argentina, Chile, and Uruguay (→ Security, II/45). When the civil-military coup took place in Brazil in 1964, the coup promoters accused João Goulart's government of being a "Labor Republic." Hundreds of Latin American union members were murdered, thrown in jail, or tortured during this period. Even in Colombia, where there were no military coups, the Labor movement paid a high price with regard to human rights (→ II/35) violations, due to thousands of deaths and the disappearance of union leaders. This was the effect of the conflict for almost fifty years, which involved leftist rebel guerrillas, right-wing paramilitary groups, narcotics dealers, and State agents. There were entire regions in Columbia where unions ceased to exist.

The re-democratization of American countries that had submitted to authoritarian regimes coincided with the crisis in the model of import substitution in the region, and the shift in paradigm from Fordism (→ II/10) and Welfare State to new, global production chains (→ Global Commodity Chains, II/23) and Neoliberalism (→ II/12; State Transformation, II/21). In this context, labor movements had to re-conquer their space under a totally different and unknown paradigm; in many cases they never recovered the fortitude they had before the State coups. Even the unions in more industrialized countries like the United States and Canada were impacted by the shift in paradigm and by the ascension in anti-labor attitudes in the entrepreneurial milieu. For example, union density in the U.S., which had reached 35 percent in the 1950s, dropped to 11 percent in the 1990s and has never recovered.

Unionism in the Americas in a global economy

With the respective elections of Margaret Thatcher in England 1979, and of Ronald Reagan in the U.S. in 1980, neoliberalism turned into government programs, resulting in profound privatization (→ II/17) programs, and reductions in both taxes private companies (→ Taxation, II/22) as well as the limiting of labor and social rights for workers.

Neoliberal government programs were adopted by other countries worldwide, particularly by indebted countries in Latin America and the Caribbean. The latter were often forced to structural adjustment by international organizations such as the International Monetary Fund (IMF) and the World Bank, institutions over which the U.S. and its allies had total control. Central aims of these adjustment programs were to facilitate openness to commerce and international investment, to promote the privatization of public companies, and to deregulate social policies – a set of measures that became known as the "Washington Consensus" (Batista 2009). For workers in the Americas and in the Caribbean in the 1980s and 1990s, structural adjustment meant the loss of jobs, the growth of informality (→ II/13), the reduction of State capacity to promote adequate public policy, lessening of social protection, and property and income concentration (→ Social Inequality, II/20). In virtually all countries, labor regulation experienced processes of change in the sense that they adapted to the flexibility of specific labor laws sought after by business people expressly for increasing productivity and profit.

A cornerstone of this adjustment process was the integration of Latin America and the Caribbean on the supply side of the global productive chains controlled by transnational corporations (→ II/23). The region was assigned as export platform for natural resources (→ II/9), in addition to the expansion of services. Attempts to build alternatives gained terrain in the late 1990s and early 2000s through the election of leftist political leaders in many Latin and Central American countries starting. These elected officials adopted initiatives with the aim of diversifying the economy of each country, of integrating them and their energy resources, and of implementing industrial policies. However, pressed by the international economic crisis (→ II/4) and the right-wing reaction, political setbacks have affected the neo-development that has been implemented since then (→ Development, II/6).

Nonetheless, the 2000s have been productive for the labor movement. In addition to the noted paradigmatic shifts, unions in many countries have managed to negotiate better working conditions and salaries. The Uruguayan labor movement, for example, has benefited from dozens of laws favoring workers. However, in countries like Colombia, Guatemala, and Honduras, the violation of human and labor rights continues (→ Human Rights, II/35).

In this new phase of class struggle (→ II/3) in the Americas, there have been attempts, albeit insufficient ones, at adapting labor organizations to the new work-market reality, particularly in so much as it deals with informal, precarious, and flexible work (→ Informality, II/13). The first attempt has naturally been the attempt to organize workers. Since its creation, Bolivia's COB has enabled other social sectors – students, peasants, among others – to affiliate themselves into the Confederation. Still, they kept a minimum union participation of 50 percent; and the Secretary General of the COB should always be a miner, that is, a "proletarian." The Argentinian Workers' Central (*Central de Trabajadores Argentinos* – CTA) establishes in its statutes the possibility of individual affiliation of informal workers' alternative associations, which opens the way for informal workers to be represented.

Informal workers' unions are also accepted by labor confederations in countries like Paraguay, Peru, Guatemala, among others. However, normally one speaks only of the most visible part of informality, which comprises public service providers. Their associations usually fail, for the attempt is made to organize them under the industrial model used for workers with formal job contracts, overlooking the fact that their workplace is mobile, and that their main demand is the power to commercialize their products without restrictions. Nevertheless, in spite of such difficulties, one has increasingly begun to hear about cooperativism, economics of solidarity, social economics, and ways of generating jobs and income for thousands of workers who now live in informality. United and organized, they could obtain better results with their production. The reality is that unions, as of today, face ever growing obstacles such as outsourcing, under hiring, and temporary work, among others, and struggle to continue to represent workers via the traditional organization model that "Fordist" production institutionalized almost eighty years before (→ Fordism, II/10).

The capitalist production paradigm (→ Capitalism, II/2) was profoundly altered with the ascension of Neoliberalism (→ II/16) and the technological changes that enabled the establishment of globalized economies and productions. Financial capital became hegemonic, and currently a little fewer than 700 megabanks and investment funds control 80 percent of global productive chains (→ Global Commodity Chains, II/12). Unions' area of representation, today, barely surpasses the peak of these chains where workers with higher qualification find themselves; the unions represent the workers of companies in the beginning of the chain, if at all. However, unions have distanced themselves more and more from workers of the production net formed under the command of the main companies, who are in turn submitted to increasingly deregulated work conditions.

If history shows that for unions to be effective they had to organize themselves in a way that was coherent with production models of each epoch – like the manufacture aspects of the First Industrial Revolution – there is no reason that the productive chains of today should be different. Surely it will be harder and more complex, since one is speaking of workers' organization and coordination in different productive networks and in the context of deindustrialization (→ II/5).

However, it is evident that the industrial organization model created during the "golden years of capitalism" no longer addresses the needs of workers, and it is the duty of union leaders to adapt to this new conjuncture if they want to avoid their organizations disappearing along with the traditional forms of production.

Works cited

Alexander, Robert J. and Eldon M. Parker. 2004. *A History of Organized Labour in the English-Speaking West Indies.* Westport: Praeger Publishers.

Arriola, Arturo Taracena. 1984. "La Confederación Obrera de Centro América (COCA): '1921–1928'." *Anuario de Estudios Centroamericanos*, 10, 81–93.

ATO (Argentina Trabajo y Empleo). 2018. www.argentina.gob.ar/trabajo.

Batista Jr, Paulo Nogueira. 2009. *Pensando o Brasil (Ensaios e palestras).* Brasília: FUNAG.

ENS (Escuela Nacional Sindical). 2018. www.ens.org.co.

Hayek, Frederick. 1944. *The Road to Serfdom.* London: Routledge.

Heron, Craig. 2012. *The Canadian Labour Movement: A short history.* North Carolina: Lorimer.

ILO (International Labor Office). 1972. *Employment Incomes and Equality: A Strategy for Increasing Productive Employment in Kenya.* Geneva: International Labour Office and United Nations Development Programme. www.ilo.org/public/libdoc/ilo/1972/72B09_608_engl.pdf.

———. 1993. *PREALC 25 Years.* Genebra: OIT.

———. 1998. *Panorama Laboural, 1998.* Lima: OIT.

Jakobsen, Kjeld Aagaard. 2016. *Perfil do Movimento Sindical das Américas.* Unpublished manuscript. São Paulo.

McCormick, Rebecca G. and Richard Hyman. 2013. *Trade Unions in Western Europe: Hard Times, Hard Choices.* Oxford: Oxford University Press.

Moraes Filho, Evaristo. 1978. *O problema do sindicato único no Brasil.* São Paulo: Alfa-Ômega.

MTB (Ministério do Trabalho Brazil). 2018. www.mte.gov.br.

MTSS (Ministerio de Trabajo y Seguridad Social Uruguay). 2018. www.mtss.gub.uy.

Murray, R. Emmett. 1998. *The Lexicon of Labour.* New York: The New Press.

Lichtenstein, Nelson. 1997. *Walther Reuther: The Most Dangerous Man in Detroit.* Chicago: University of Illinois Press.

Souza, Paulo R.C. and Victor Tokman. 1980. "Sector Informal Urbano." In *Empregos, Salários e Pobreza*, ed. Paulo Renato Souza, n.p. São Paulo: HUCITEC.

STATCAN (Statistics Canada). 2018. www.150.statcan.gc.ca/n1/en/subjects/Labour.

US DOL (United States Department of Labor). 2018. www.dol.gov.

Villa, Marco Antonio. 1993. *A revolução mexicana.* São Paulo: Ática.

15

LAND

Anne Tittor

Access to and control over land are key for the history of the Americas and are still an important issue in many current social struggles. Although land is a necessary (pre-)condition for all societies, it is systematically underestimated within social sciences. Without land, there is no agriculture, which is the basis for modern societies; but the meaning of the concept "land" differs between and within societies. Liza Grandia, who studied the enclosure of the land of the Q´eqchi´ people in Guatemala writes, "Although the Q´eqchi´ people have little hope of owning land in their lifetimes, they consider themselves intransitively *owned* by land." In fact the land is also seen "as simultaneously feminine and masculine" and the Q ´eqchi´ people "often refer to it as 'our Father, our Mother'" while referring to "themselves as 'children of the earth' (*laa'o laj ralch'och'*)." She also notes that their language highlights their spiritual relationship to land and soil by connecting the adjective *loq'laj* (sacred) to the word *ch'och'* (land). In Spanish, Q´eqchi´ settlers describe their parcels as "trabajaderos" (places to work). In either language, land is something "not merely to be acquired but to be labored" (Grandia 2012, 117).

The oligarchies in contrast, who have ruled since colonial times (as in Guatemala) (→ Colonial Rule, I/5), perceive land as property and a symbol of power. For companies and investors, land is considered a resource to be exploited. Within the history of capitalism (→ II/2), the expulsion of peasants from their land, the emergence of the "double free laborer," and the commodification of land were essential. Karl Marx, Karl Polanyi, and others have analyzed these dynamics referring to Western Europe, but they occurred in different ways and still exist as an ongoing process within various parts of the Americas.

Traditionally, social sciences comprehend conflicts over land as conflicts of nation-states (→ II/38) over their borders (→ Borderlands, II/26). To understand all land conflicts, which revolve around use, access, and control over certain territories, a broader definition is necessary. When analyzing land conflicts, two different types of conflicts appear. First, conflicts about what was classically called "the agrarian question" or "land question" in terms of land reform, which is a key element of progressive politics. Mainly, the rural poor aim to acquire their own parcels of land to produce their own food. They face opposition from big landowners, who displace them and/or employ them as laborers on their farms and plantations. Marxist authors have discussed this issue as one of proletarianization of the peasantry and have especially been interested in whether the peasants would seek an alliance with the working classes to overthrow capitalism (→ Class Struggle, II/3).

A second kind of land conflict is not so much about agrarian production and structures such as land ownerships and working conditions, but about territoriality. Many of these conflicts include the appropriation of certain areas by transnational enterprises (→ II/23), international investors, the nation-state, or other powerful actors (e.g. paramilitary forces). These appropriations exclude the population using those areas, and modify the forms of land use, which has often led to an entire transformation of the landscape (e.g. for plantations, infrastructural projects, or energy production) (→ Energy, II/7). In recent years, many indigenous and Afro- descendant groups have struggled for territorial rights and an institutionalization of their ancestral forms of land uses, as well as self-determined territorial governance in order to participate in the decision-making process over the form of land uses (→ Indigeneity, I/31), including the use and potential deterioration of waters, soils and changes of landscapes. The current struggles against land grabbing and agro-business expansion are inseparable, and peasants as well as indigenous and Afro-descendant groups are equally affected. Several theoretical approaches can help to develop a systematic understanding of the field: agrarian studies, Marxism, political economy, development studies, and political ecology. Although this entry does not include systematic distinctions between these approaches, these debates emphasize how central land issues are for the Americas.

In the following, the social implications of the appropriation of land during colonialism are briefly resumed, as the resistances against it. The entry will use political economy perspectives on land to provide a background that helps explain the importance of land reforms during the 20th and 21st century for many revolts, revolutions, and progressive governments (→ Revolution, II/44). Even today, the discussion continues as current debates on "land grabbing" and agribusiness as the newest forms of large-scale land acquisitions. Throughout the colonial period until today, transnational and especially Inter-American entanglements have played a key role. The text describes the historical development of certain patterns outlining their connection to current social structures in the Americas.

Geographically the entry will focus, though not exclusively, on Central America as the land question is very important within the region and is linked to several transnational entanglements. In different countries of the Americas, the composition of social classes, especially the percentage of indigenous and Afro-descendant groups and the size of the peasantry differ considerably. In contrast to other areas, Central America is densely populated and land concentration was (and in many countries still is) very high (→ Social Inequality, II/20). Compared to the Conosur for example, urbanization (→ I/45) is less pronounced; in Central America about half of the population lives in rural areas. Most of them depend on agriculture and for many people the question if they have access to land, is a question of getting enough food for them and their families. The land question is inseparable both from the formation of revolutionary movements and from massive violence against them; additionally, violence is shaping many land conflicts between different rural groups. Outside Central America, in countries like Argentina, Chile, Brazil, and Colombia, land concentration is currently increasing and has generated profound, often violent conflicts. Some of these conflicts are resistance against dispossession, but many of them are conflicts against working conditions, which imply health risks due to, inter alia, pesticide use.

Appropriation and access to land as a key dimension in political economy

Within the field of political economy, intensive discussions have taken place about the importance of land for capitalist accumulation (→ Capitalism, II/2). Karl Marx outlines in his treatment of the "so-called primitive accumulation" the crucial importance of the expropriation of the peasantry for the formation of capitalism in a non-capitalist environment. It was the way the so-called "doubly free laborer" was established, who was neither bound to the land nor to any guilds (Dörre 2010, 45). This process is described as an extremely brutal procedure of peasant expropriation, compulsory dispossession of common land (→ Commons, II/31) and expropriation of church estates. Karl Polanyi analyzes the great transformation from feudalist and mercantilist production relations, where land and labor were part of a specific non-market social organization, toward capitalist production relations where money, land, and labor are commodified (Polanyi 1977 [1944], 97f). The state actively has to create a market and to enclose different areas to transform them into (fictive) commodities. As these enclosures that precipitated the market economy of modern capitalism resulted in a social upheaval of the social forces of feudalism, many of the poor and the ruling classes opposed further enclosures.

The processes of commodification and privatization (→ II/17) of land and the forceful expulsion of peasant populations as ongoing processes can also be labeled as "accumulation by dispossession" (Harvey 2004, 74). They include the conversion of various forms of property rights – common, collective, state, etc. – into exclusive private-property rights; suppression of rights to the commons (→ II/31); commodification of labor power and the suppression of alternative, indigenous forms of production and consumption; and colonial, neo-colonial and imperial processes of appropriation of land (Harvey 2004, 74). The analytical framework of accumulation by dispossession and the so-called primitive accumulation have been used by many scholars to analyze land grabs in the Americas (Backhouse et al. 2013; Hall 2013; Spronk and Webber 2007).

Within the discipline of economics, the discussion of land has often been centered on private property of land. This focus itself, privileges a certain Western understanding of land regimes, and for a long time, private ownership property of land was promoted as the most efficient form of land management and was legitimated by the narrative of the "tragedy of the commons" (Hardin 1968). Nevertheless, empirical work has shown that private-property models often fail to address certain problems, whereas commons can effectively work well in case rights and duties are well defined by the involved actors (Ostrom 1990, 20). Departing from intense empirical research, Schlager and Ostrom (1992, 250ff) distinguish between a bundle of rights associated with positions. It makes a great difference whether people are only allowed to use and benefit from an area on a short-term perspective, or if they dispose of the land on a long-term schedule and therefore are responsible for improving it, think about rules and responsibilities for all users, and make collective decisions on it. Therefore, in current research, many authors are not only asking how capitalism appropriates land, but also investigating how collectives and groups have successfully managed to regulate land access and use in the 20th and 21st century. Commons are back on the agenda of social struggles – the perception of land as commons (as well as other goods) is therefore a current strategy to fight against expropriation of land in its colonial and neo-colonial forms (Burger 2001; Finley-Brook and Offen 2009; Monterroso and Larson 2013).

Colonial and anticolonial struggles over land: the dispossession of indigenous communities from their land and the long way to establish their land rights

In colonial times, the appropriation of – in the eyes of the colonizers – "new" lands was at the heart of conquest (→ Conquest and Colonization, I/7). Whereas in the first years the extraction of raw materials, especially silver and gold, was a key motivation for invasion, over the years the entire appropriation of land became equally important. The conquerors settled in the areas they perceived as best lands, whereas the indigenous population was murdered, subordinated, or had to flee into more remote areas (often mountains, very arid areas, or primary forests). By force, the conquerors established big *latifundios* (large landholdings) and enclosed indigenous land, where the autochthonous population had to work for the new landowners (Kay 2001). The *latifundio* depended on the *minifundio* (parcel smaller than required for a family's subsistence), which meant that the family members needed to work on the *latifundio* (Grandia 2012, 117). Until the decades of agrarian reform from the 1960s to the 1980s, this pattern remained a crucial element of the agrarian structure (with the exception of Mexico, which had a successful agrarian reform in the 1930s, see below). The rural population in Latin America suffered several waves of proletarization and pauperization, where increasing numbers of small farmers were transformed into landless peasants. In some countries, landless peasants were offered to care for the farm of someone else and in return were allowed to appropriate a part of the food or cattle products generated. Leasing agreements and labor relations, like contract farming or debt bondage, often went hand in hand with the so-called agrarian modernization (→ Modernization, I/35).

The conquerors perceived the land they "explored" as "Terra Nullis" – empty land that was not owned by anybody and therefore could easily be declared lands of the Spanish, Portuguese, Dutch, or British Empires. They implemented the idea of land ownership and private property on land (and many other items), which did not exist before on the American continent (Stam and Shohat 2014, 18, 28). Indigenous groups perceived land, water, and air as common goods (and goodness) that could not be owned by anybody but rather used by a community according to their collective rules. In many cases, every family had rights to a parcel, to work (on) it and to obtain the products. Additionally, common hunting grounds existed. In Canada and elsewhere, early treaties between First Nations and colonial powers aimed to extinguish Aboriginal titles to facilitate European settlement and establish European legal systems (Wyatt 2008, 173). In all American countries, the colonial myth that there were plenty of "empty" lands at the settlers' disposal to be cultivated, at the same time bringing progress and development (→ II/6) to the country, was dominant throughout a certain period (although the length of that period differs). The U.S. perceived of itself as a "settler state" – a nation formed on independent farmers in rebellion against British authority (Bauerly 2018, 225). Brauerly explains,

> Settler colonial expansion eased the political tension by offering a seemingly endless supply of land for the masses, as private property was articulated as the source of independence, freedom and equality, while producing increased market dependence, diminishing freedom, and reproducing and expanding inequalities.
>
> *(Bauerly 2018, 529)*

The idea of Terra Nullis finds its continuity today for example in Nicaragua in the concept of "national lands." The state has often made decisions about land utilization without consulting the indigenous communities who have been using these areas for centuries (→

Nation State, II/38). There are even two antagonistic concepts of land. In the interpretation of the state, all properties inside its territorial limits that do not have another owner are considered "national lands." In this concept of property, an owner is a person that received a legally recognized title. However, the understanding of many prominent indigenous leaders see the concept of national lands as illegitimate, and argue that the ancestral rights existed before nation-state building (→ I/16) (Williamson Cuthbert 2006, 250). Although indigenous communities received some land titles in the 1930s at Nicaragua's Atlantic Coast, these lands were relatively small and the borders were not clear for the communities themselves. Thus, they continued to perceive of a broader area as their territory (Hale 2006, 21). However, national governments, foreign investors, large landowners, and settlers arriving to the area ignored the practices and land rights of the indigenous communities and appropriated this land for their own purposes. All over the Americas, indigenous people have resisted these developments and have started to build transnational networks among each other, including support from liberation theologians (→ Religious Beliefs, I/40) and civil society (→ II/28) initiatives.

From the 1980s onwards, International Organizations like the International Labor Organization (ILO), the World Bank, and the Inter-American Court of Human Rights have had a key role in institutionalizing indigenous rights. A very important step has been the ILO's *Convention concerning Indigenous and Tribal Peoples in Independent Countries* (Convention 169) from 1989. Additionally, several constitutions have changed: in Canada, the constitution of 1982 established land rights of First Nations, especially concerning forests. In Colombia, the constitution of 1991 was seen as one of the most progressive ones in Latin America as it fully defined indigenous land rights and rights over the use of resources.

Nevertheless, the forward momentum experienced two major setbacks. First, these changes caused a series of conflicts with non-indigenous peasants who did not possess these rights and resulted in a (re)ethnicization of land conflicts (Chavez Chamorro 2002) (→ Ethnicity, I/25; Indigeneity, I/31). This also contributed to an increase of land conflicts between (non- indigenous) peasants on the one side and indigenous and Afro-descendant groups on the other. Second, rural violence intensified again, and in many countries, especially in Honduras, Guatemala, and Colombia, paramilitary groups started to displace indigenous, Afro-descendants, and peasants by force. The title itself did not guarantee for indigenous communities to survive on their own lands (Grajales 2011).

In Nicaragua, the constitution of 1995 established the right for indigenous communities to have their own culture, language, social organization, and different forms of property, including collective rights over land and resources (Art. 5, Nicaraguan Constitution). Nevertheless, the concrete mechanisms to implement the rights were missing. The situation changed with the Awastigni case in September 2001, when the Inter-American Court of Human Rights stated that the Nicaraguan state had violated the rights of a Mayanga community by imposing a logging concession on their lands without consultation. The community was judged to have "customary" land rights based on historical occupation. The state of Nicaragua was forced to develop a legal framework through which indigenous and Afro-descendant groups could claim their land rights (Stocks 2005, 87). This impulse was key for the later development of the law of the demarcation of indigenous and Afro-descendant territorial rights in Nicaragua and many other countries in the Americas.

Within the last three decades, Canada has seen a series of court decisions that have defined and extended Aboriginal rights (Wyatt 2008, 173). The "First Nations Land Management (FNLM) Regime" was introduced to allow First Nations to develop their own laws about land use, the environment and natural resources (→ Nature, II/39) and to take advantage of economic development opportunities with their new land management powers. The growing interest in sustainable forest management from the 1990s onward helped Aboriginal and indigenous knowledge, rights, and practices, to be taken into account – especially if the land claims are within areas with primary, extended, and more or less, intact forest.

Nevertheless, the ways toward indigenous land rights differ between various countries; they are often long, contradictory, and still in process. By comparing the different processes of implementation of territorial rights of indigenous communities in five different Latin American countries (Brazil, Peru, Bolivia, Colombia, Nicaragua), Stocks argues that "time" is one of the biggest obstacles for the implementation of rights (Stocks 2005, 98). Even if the state originally recognizes indigenous rights (→ Human Rights, II/35), multiple claims and interests of diverse actors complicate the realization of these rights. In many countries, the existence of multiple titles for the same piece of land, nontransparent mechanisms of land titling combined with corrupt authorities, complicate the process. Peru and Bolivia face a high number of dissonant laws with regard to indigenous lands (Stocks 2005, 97). In Colombia and Brazil, a relatively clear juridical framework exists for obtaining territorial rights for indigenous groups, but increasing violence is a major obstacle. In Colombia currently, over four million people are internally displaced by violence – despite existing rights on paper. Some groups, like the Mapuche in Chile and Argentina, are still in open conflict over land rights with both states.

The extermination of huge parts of the indigenous populations in many countries of the Americas as well as the continued dispossession of lands are not the only legacy of colonialism concerning land issues in the Americas. The concentration of land in the hands of a few (often direct descendants of the colonizers) is an outcome of coloniality and a key driver of profound conflicts about the use, access, and ownership of land. The territorial forms of land tenure and production like the *hacienda*, *estancia*, and plantation are relics of colonial practices but have retained their relevance in the continued use of forms of territorial control including political power and the command over the labor force – in case of the plantation inseparably linked to enslavement and the transatlantic trade of enslaved people from Africa (→ Slavery, I/18).

Social inequalities along the lines of race and ethnicity structure the access and control over land, not only in Latin America but also within the USA (→ Intersectionality, I/32). U.S. agricultural policy has been a continuity of colonialism in different ways. The colonial and expansionist project of "removing" native people from their lands was driven by U.S. agricultural agendas and policies for wheat cultivation and livestock farming. Its assimilationist coercions via general allotments led to the loss of nearly two-thirds of native lands, between 1887 and 1930, to white homesteaders (Graddy-Lovelace 2017, 82) (→ Whiteness, I/46).

In many cases, the dynamics of capitalism (→ II/2) and state policies did not only cause many social inequalities (→ II/20), but even intensified the social inequalities between different ethnic groups: In the south of the USA in the 1910s, about 90 percent of African-Americans lived in rural areas. Just a decade later, less than half did (Graddy-Lovelace 2017, 84). Those who stayed used their considerable agricultural expertise and experience to farm their own lands, although federal farm policy systematically undermined their endeavors. Structural racism was inscribed in all of the state institutions and in 1982 USDA Civil Rights Commission further chronicled the "Decline of Black Farming in America." Discrimination permeated loan approvals, servicing, and extension. In 1984–1985, at the height of the U.S. farm crisis, USDA lent $1.3 billion to 16,000 farmers – only 209 of them were African-American (Jones and Alston 2009, 15).

In the last decades, however, some shifts in the U.S. agriculture have occurred: while white farmers have retired en masse, a significant number of Latinos (most of them Mexicans) have been able to buy their own farms, practicing a smaller-scale and more diverse crop production compared to the dominant national agricultural model (Minkoff-Zern 2018). Many of these immigrant farmers are peasants from Latin America who had been displaced from their land by international food dumping, agricultural trade policies, and local land conflicts (Minkoff-Zern 2018, 393). They worked as laborers within huge-scale U.S. agriculture, which is completely dependent on cheap immigrant labor concerning the production of fruits and vegetables (→ Transnational Migration, I/44; Informality, II/13). The Latinos have – despite lacking state support – fulfilled their dream of becoming small-scale farmers. Most of them work – not at least because of the difficult access to credit – with limited synthetic inputs and mostly family labor, which allows them to reclaim control over land, their own labor and livelihoods, while also earning a cash income (Minkoff-Zern 2018).

The struggle for agrarian reforms in the 20th and 21st century and the gender asset land gap

Land has been at the center of many uprisings, revolts and even revolutions (→ II/44) The claim for agrarian reform and the unwillingness of politicians to expropriate the influential land oligarchy is one of the key contradictions of Latin America's history. The oligarchies were oriented to export agricultural commodities produced in plantations and huge monocultures – first cacao and sugar, later indigo, coffee, and banana, afterwards cotton and meat and in the last years also soybean and palm oil (→ Extractivism, II/9). They did not only appropriate the land, but also transformed entire landscapes by cutting primary forests. Most conservative forces have favored the expansion of agricultural exports and implemented policies to secure sufficient land and cheap labor available for their activities (Brockett 1998, 2). Specific forms of domination have been developed to produce export crops. Sugar was predominantly produced by enslaved persons (→ Slavery, I/18). The so-called "coffee economies" in the many Central American countries, Colombia, and Brazil were based on non-wage labor and different forms of unfree-labor (→ I/19), indentured or contract workers, debt bondage etc. Often the expansion of export crops resulted in an inadequate food supply for the rural poor.

Large-scale banana production has transformed and entangled large parts of Central America and the Caribbean due to foreign interests and has increased their dependence on the volatile banana price on the world market. Particularly one transnational corporation (→ II/23) – The United Fruit Company, which was established in 1899 in New Jersey – converted land and social structures in specific parts of Costa Rica, Nicaragua, Honduras, Guatemala, Panama, Ecuador, Columbia, Jamaica, and Belize into foreign enclaves (Striffler and Moberg 2003). Their infrastructure, such as streets, harbors, and railways, was built for export, so that these territories were better connected to the banana-importing countries than to the nation-state (→ II/38). The United Fruit Company influenced political decisions including diplomatic and military pressure against recalcitrant governments, supported authoritarian regimes (→ Authoritarianism, II/25), avoided taxes (→ Taxation, II/22), oppressed union organization (→ Labor Representation, II/14) even by mass killings, and exploited its workers. It had managed to build a monopoly in many regions, ruining independent growers and rivals. For decades, it was an archetypical case of a transnational company building their own "banana empire," where they almost exclusively defined working conditions and land use patterns.

Land issues are also tied to different forms of migration (→ I/15). While many members of the land oligarchy were of European descent, some were direct successors of the colonizers. For example, throughout the 18th and 19th century in Guatemala, Costa Rica, and Nicaragua several waves of migration brought French and German landowners to start as coffee growers. With the Haitian Revolution of 1791, around 30,000 refugees fled to Cuba, among them 10,000 Whites. Many of them had been slave owners and coffee growers of French origin and now had an important role in starting the coffee business in Cuba (Lundahl 1982, 32). In Guatemala, Costa Rica, and Nicaragua, landowners of German descent still (or for Nicaragua: again) own big coffee farms.

Within the Mexican Revolution of 1910, the agrarian question was of crucial importance. Peasants who had lost their land due to the expansion of big landowners and foreign investors started to follow Emiliano Zapata and Pancho Villa's rebellion against the Mexican oligarchy with the key demand for agrarian reform. After years of conflict, President Lázaro Cárdenas embarked on an ambitious reform program in 1936 and redistributed more than 49 million acres of land to peasants, which is more than twice as much as the redistributed land from his predecessors combined. His government awarded most of this land to farmers as communal land (*ejidos*) and enabled a rapid increase in food production (Buchenau 2015, 14).

The Mexican Revolution affected several other Central American countries. Combined with the effects of the Wall Street Crash in October 1929 (→ Crisis, II/4), which caused the Great Depression in many countries of the world, several socialist movements (→ Socialism, I/42) formed by workers and peasants started rebellions. In El Salvador, the military brutally repressed the peasant rebellion of 1932, which ended up in a massacre of 10,000 to 40,000 persons. Contemporaneously, Augusto C. Sandino fought against the U.S. military occupation and for land reform in Nicaragua but was finally defeated and killed as well.

While in the 1930s and 1940s more attempts to achieve agrarian reforms were violently defeated, in the 1960s, 1970s, and 1980s, the agenda of reformist and revolutionary forces in the region saw important gains. Two models were influential at the time: The Bolivian Revolution of 1952 and the Cuban Revolution of 1959 (→ Revolution, II/44). The Bolivian Revolution brought about agrarian reform that was only as comprehensive as necessary to contain peasants' unrest and to "secure" investment stability. In contrast, the land reform of the Cuban Revolution expropriated all the big landowners and redistributed land consequently. The threat of communism acted as an incentive to pursue land reform for even many conservative governments. The United States also promoted agrarian reforms on a discursive level with the Alliance for Progress (→ Development, II/6), but in practice only half-heartedly supported them. Wealthy rural elites and their allies resisted land reforms, slowed or blocked them, or later, as was often the case, reversed them. And even when the landlord class could no longer prevent agrarian reform, it often managed to curtail its implementation or even reverse the process with agrarian counter-reforms (Kay 2002) (→ Class Struggle, II/3). This contributed significantly to delay, diminish, and complicate processes of industrialization during the 20th century, and was and still is a key reason for the high amount of rural violence (Kay 2001).

Around the same time as both the Cuban and Bolivian Revolutions, Brazil, Colombia, Venezuela, and Paraguay only had minimal land reforms (Thiesenhusen 1995, 162). After more or less insignificant reforms in El Salvador, Chile, and Nicaragua, who failed to co-opt the peasants, a second wave of mobilization for a wide-reaching redistribution of land followed and created an important pillar for the revolutionary movements. Agrarian reform proposals of progressive governments threatened the control of the land oligarchy catalyzing conservative forces to overthrow governments in Guatemala in 1954 and in Honduras in

1963. And still decades later, agrarian reform was at the heart of social struggles in the 1980s in Nicaragua and El Salvador (Brockett 1998, 1).

The lack of an agrarian reform has contributed to the emergence of many guerilla movements in Latin America: Sandino's army in Nicaragua in the late 1920s; Emiliano Zapata's movement in the 1920s; the FARC in Colombia in the 1960s; the FSLN in Nicaragua; as well as the FMLN in the 1970s in El Salvador; the Shining Path in Peru in the 1980s; and the EZLN in the 1990s in Mexico. Agrarian reform has often been associated with violence. In fact however, it was often the counter-reform and reaction of land owners that caused thousands of deaths: During the agrarian reform in Chile between 1964 and 1973 about half of all lands within the country were expropriated; nevertheless it was not a violent process, as the number of deaths did not pass a dozen (Kay 2001, 223). With the military coup of 1973 however (→ Military, II/37), several thousands of peasants and rural activists were murdered. In El Salvador in the 1970s, large landowners started to organize and pay paramilitary death squads to assassinate peasant union members and terrorize the rural population to avoid agrarian reforms. The land question was one of the most pressing issues that led to the FMLN attempt of revolution and to the military response that caused twelve years of civil war. Within the peace accords, land still was a key issue, but a significant redistribution of land was not established.

In contrast, a far-reaching land reform in Nicaragua was initiated by the Sandinista government in 1980, which started by appropriating the land of the family of the former dictator Somoza (which was almost half of the country's land). Later on, they confiscated all land bigger than 350 hectares in the densely populated Pacific region and 700 hectares in the rest of the country. Furthermore, the state confiscated idle land or land that their owners rented out to other farmers. Originally, the revolutionary government wanted to establish units of state production and agricultural cooperatives to produce food, but later on, they distributed land to individual famers, too. In the decade of the 1980s, around 60,000 rural families received land in collective or individual form (Kinloch Tijerino 2012, 314). In 1988, 50 percent was owned by the state, 42 percent by farmers cooperatives, and only 8 percent by individual landholders (Kinloch Tijerino 2012, 341). Nevertheless, many peasants were not content with the cooperative model and preferred individual titles. Despite the re-concentration of land after 1990, the agrarian reform still has its effects and more rural families than in other Central American countries possess land.

Despite many attempts, the agrarian reforms in Latin America have reached on average about a quarter of those engaged in agriculture. Most agrarian reforms distributed poorer-than average land to richer-than-average peasants (Thiesenhusen 1995, 159). Additionally, they often failed to provide the beneficiaries with credits, technical assistance, fertilizers, improved seeds, and education (→ I/24) needed to improve their situation. Often, this has led to owners selling their land just a few years after they obtained it.

Furthermore, governments have developed a number of strategies to avoid land reforms such as land colonization programs. For decades, poor peasants who cleared (which means deforested) primary forest and established agriculture on it qualified for some sort of land title. Within Guatemala, Nicaragua, and Brazil among others, this was a key mechanism to reduce the pressure for agrarian reform.

In the 1990s, the World Bank started to push for a new type of land reform in Latin America: a market reform. The market reform was supposed to clarify land ownership, make the country more efficient in land registry and bring together "willing sellers and willing buyers." USAID and other donors promoted various land bank projects giving loans to buyers (→ Development, II/6). But older failures in registry, and many unfinished projects caused a huge number of overlapping land claims, some of them dating back to Spanish colonization (Ybarra 2009, 48). Attached to market reform, both environmentalists and economists hoped that constructing new institutions and executing a land titling project in Northern Guatemala would strengthen existing property regimes and increase tenure security. Small farmers would buy into the ownership society only on credit, reinforcing a vision of individual property rights that could only be attained and validated via the market. But the reform had several unintended effects: large landowners, palm oil companies and other agricultural export producers benefited more from increased tenure security and managed to buy much of the land and profited from the fact that small farmers did not make their living in a context of extreme poverty, missing access to credit, and a setting of increasing violence. A considerable part of the land was resold, speculation on the land started and inequalities were reinforced (Grandia 2012, 140; Ybarra 2009, 51).

The market reforms did not solve the problem of the unequal distribution of land. For example, despite five major attempts of agrarian reform in Guatemala (1890s, 1950s, 1960s, 1980s, 1990s), the land distribution there is extremely unequal. In 1950 about 2 percent of the landowners controlled 69 percent of the land; in 1979 2,6 percent of the farms owned 65 percent of land, and in 2003, 3,2 percent controlled 66 percent of the land (Grandia 2012, 118). However during the 1990s, in several Latin American countries, rural movements – many of them indigenous (as the CONAIE in Ecuador) or with a considerable indigenous base (as the MAS in Bolivia) (→ Indigeneity, II/31), landless movements (as the MST in Brazil), or classical peasants movements (as the Movimiento Campesino de Santiago del Estero in Argentina) gained in importance and power. Many of them are organized within the worldwide laborers' network *Via Campesina*; some of the movements mentioned here have played a key role in bringing left governments to power.

Not only were there huge inequalities in land access along the axis of race (→ I/39) and ethnicity (→ I/25), but along gender as well (→ Gender Identities, I/28). All of these different types of reform had severe shortcomings as they failed to decrease the immense gender asset land gap. Often women do not have tenure of land on their own, but only access to land through their male relatives (Agarwal 1998, 204ff). In the 17th and 18th century under the Iberian codified tradition, married women could own, inherit and will property. In case of separation or widowhood, women were entitled to the property they brought into marriage. They had a stronger bargaining power than women in the U.S. at the time (Deere and León 2001). During the 19th century, these patterns were revised, and women gained more rights over their property in the U.S. With the first wave of the women's movement, not only suffrage, but also the enhancement of legal capacities of (married and unmarried women), as well as full property rights were continuously on the agenda (→ Citizenship, II/27).

Over the decades, legal barriers for women to own land have been abolished. Nevertheless, inequalities in land ownership are still very high. In 2000, in Brazil, women owned 11 percent of the land (compared to 89 percent owned by men); in Mexico in 2002, women owned 22.4 percent compared to 77.6 percent owned by men; and in Nicaragua (1995), women had 15.5 percent of land ownership, couples 3.6 percent and men 80.9 percent (data quoted in Deere and Leon 2003, 928).

There are several factors contributing to the gender asset gap concerning land. First, there is male preference in inheritance and marriage. Additionally, often there is a male bias within community and state programs of land distribution. Furthermore, the land marked has a certain gender bias, with women less likely than men to be successful buyers (Deere and Leon 2003, 925). The most common form of land ownership for women is by inheritance, as women are less likely to acquire land through its distribution by communities or the state and via the market. Most land reforms – within both a socialist and a market framework – have failed to distribute land toward women so far.

Land grabbing and current territorial struggles

In the 21st century, land reappeared at the center of several debates, as the number of land-scale acquisitions, often called "land grabbing," increased tremendously on a global scale. Connected to the global food crisis in 2008 and intensified during the world financial crisis of 2008/2009 (→ Crisis, II/4), the investors' interest in land skyrocketed. Consequently, land prices rose, as more and more private companies, new and old oligarchies, and even entire states sought to buy or rent land.

Food insecure states (especially China and the Gulf states) appropriated land overseas in order to secure their own food supply. By doing so, vast numbers of people have been displaced in their host countries (Edelman et al. 2013, 1514). The online platform *Land Matrix* (www.landmatrix.org) started to document all land transaction above a size of 200 hectares (ha) in 2000. Even though the USA is ranked first and Brazil fourth place among the top investors on a global scale, it is China – ranked fifth place – that is at the center of the debate on land grabbing. Their data further indicates that concerning the target countries, in Brazil 3.0 million ha and in Argentina 1.8 million ha (place 10) have been acquired. All over the Americas, deals over 6.0 million ha of land have been made, among which 21 percent have been for food crops, 20 percent for non-food crops, 22 percent for flex crops, and 37 percent for multiple use (as of December 2017).

Scholars and activists expanded their analyses of land grabbing along the course of events, adjoining "green grabbing" (land acquisitions for preservation or "green" energy production including wind parks or biofuels) (→ Energy, II/7), "water grabbing" (capture of water resources), and the financialization of agriculture, while drawing attention to the forms of intertwinement of these processes (Borras et al. 2013; Edelman et al. 2013). With green grabbing, new and uncommon alliances of military and paramilitary agencies with conservation professionals have emerged. Some local people have begun cooperating with new entrepreneurs who are seeking to profit as wildlife operators involving companies who develop forest carbon offset projects or pharmaceutical firms (Fairhead et al. 2012, 250). Other local people have opposed these types of developments and have even lost land access because of them.

Several elements are specific to land grabbing in the Americas. First, foreignization of land ownership is one of the most controversial aspects in Argentina, Brazil, Bolivia, Uruguay, Paraguay and Guatemala, while foreign direct investment in specific value chains have contributed to a restructuring of agriculture according to needs of other countries (→ Global Commodity Chains, II/12). That certain foreign citizens acquire land is a conflictive point in Bolivia and Paraguay (Borras et al. 2013). Second, in difference to other world regions, the companies involved in current large-scale land investments in Latin America and the Caribbean are often not the conventional North Atlantic-based transnational companies (TNCs) (→ II/23), but increasingly (trans)Latina companies, which involve mainly national capital, some in alliance with other Latin American countries, or from outside the region. The greater part of the capital involved in large-scale land investments originates from Argentina, Brazil, Chile, Colombia, Panama, Mexico and Costa Rica (Borras et al. 2013, 412). This contributed to rising land prices and the financialization of agriculture which means new actors involved in agricultural production through forms like sowing pools, more futures on oilseeds, corn, and wheat among others, and a full restructuring of certain production patters according to commodity prices on the world market as recent debates on flex-crops show. With the debate on land grabbing, increasing land concentration is becoming a controversial issue again as well as food sovereignty.

Borras and Franco (2013, 1731) describe four different struggle fronts around global land grabbing and provide a helpful systematization of current land conflicts. They argue that several areas of struggle do not only correspond with different key issues, but with different actors, too. On the one hand, "struggles against expulsion" are dominantly driven by international or national companies and the expelled people address the national state for compensation or to defend their rights to have their land returned. "Struggles for and within incorporation" on the other hand, have a similar actor constellation but the key issues are labor rights in the new (agro-)industrial production. Trade unions often play an important role in these struggles (→ Labor Representation, II/14), which address rent, wage, or terms of exchange e.g. on plantations (Borras and Franco 2013, 1735ff). The third type of struggle – struggles against land concentration and for redistribution and recognition – predates global land grabbing and is underestimated in the current debate. Recognition is always a key issue if indigenous people are claiming land rights (ebd.1738f). The fourth type of struggle, "struggles across overlapping/intersecting geographical and institutional spaces," is the most open category and the least developed. The authors argue that agrarian, labor, and environmental issues overlap.

In contrast to other world regions, especially Europe, the colonial legacy of land ownership structure was never completely broken in Latin America and the Caribbean. Agribusiness sectors, finance, and banking, as well as large landlords are generally in favor of increased land investments and are often among the investors or those who benefit from them. Local communities and their various organizations have varied reactions toward them; some support them, hoping for jobs and modernization (→I/35). But in many parts, social movements (→ I/41), indigenous and Afro-descendant groups (→ Indigeneity, II/31), as well as peasants try to resist these developments. Conflicts over land are therefore an important issue of struggle in the Americas.

Works cited

Agarwal, Bina. 1998. "The gender and environment debate." In *Political Ecology. Global and Local*, eds. Roger Keil, Bell David, Penz, Peter, and Fawcett Leesa, 193–219. New York: Routledge.

Backhouse, Maria, Olaf Gerlach, Stefan Kalmring, and Andreas Nowak. eds. 2013. *Die globale Einhegung – Krise, ursprüngliche Akkumulation und Landnahmen im Kapitalismus*. 1st ed. Münster: Westfälisches Dampfboot.

Bauerly, Brad. 2018. "The agro-industrial state: Early agrarian influence on U.S. state building." *The Journal of Peasant Studies* 45, no. 3: 525–544.

Borras, Saturnino M. Jr. and Jennifer C. Franco. 2013. "Global land grabbing and political reactions 'from below'." *Third World Quarterly* 34, no. 9: 1723–1747.

Borras, Saturnino M., Cristobal Kay, Sergio Gómez, and John Wilkinson. 2013. "Land grabbing and global capitalist accumulation. Key features in Latin America." *Canadian Journal of Development Studies/Revue canadienne d' études du développement* 33, no. 4: 402–416.

Brockett, Charles D. 1998. *Land, Power, and Poverty: Agrarian Transformation and Political Conflict in Central America*. Boulder: Westview Press.

Buchenau, Jürgen. 2015. "The Mexican revolution, 1910–1946." In *Oxford Research Encyclopedia, Latin American History*. Oxford: Oxford University Press. http://latinamericanhistory.oxfordre.com/view/10.1093/acrefore/9780199366439.001.0001/acrefore-9780199366439-e-21?print=pdf.

Burger, Joanna. 2001. *Protecting the Commons: A Framework for Resource Management in the Americas.* Washington, DC: Island Press.

Chavez Chamorro, Margarita. 2002. "Conflictos territoriales o la política de la ubicación. Actores étnicos, re-etnizados y no étnicos en disputa por un territorio en el Putumayo." In *Territorio y Cultura. Territorios de conflicto y cambio sociocultural,* ed. Beatriz Nates, 167–186. Manizales, Colombia: Universidad de Caldas.

Deere, Carmen D. and Magdalena Leon. 2003. "The gender asset gap. Land in Latin America." *World Development* 31, no. 6: 925–947.

Deere, Carmen Diana and Magdalena León. 2001. *Empowering Women: Land and Property Rights in Latin America.* Pittsburgh: University of Pittsburgh Press.

Dörre, Klaus. 2010. "Social classes in the process of capitalist Landnahme. On the relevance of secondary exploitation." *Socialist Studies/Études socialistes* 6, no. 2: 43–74.

Edelman, Marc, Carlos Oya, and Saturnino M. Borras. 2013. "Global land grabs: Historical processes, theoretical and methodological implications and current trajectories." *Third World Quarterly* 34, no. 9: 1517–1531.

Fairhead, James, Melissa Leach, and Ian Scoone. 2012. "Green Grabbing. a new appropriation of nature?" *Journal of Peasant Studies* 39, no. 2: 237–261.

Finley-Brook, M. and Karl Offen. 2009. "Bounding the commons: Land demarcation in Northeastern Nicaragua." *Bull Latin American Research* 28, no. 3: 343–363.

Graddy-Lovelace, Garrett. 2017. "The coloniality of U.S. agricultural policy: Articulating agrarian (in) justice." *The Journal of Peasant Studies* 44, no. 1: 78–99.

Grajales, Jacobo. 2011. "The rifle and the title. Paramilitary violence, land grab and land control in Colombia." *The Journal of Peasant Studies* 38, no. 4: 771–792.

Grandia, Liza. 2012. *Enclosed: Conservation, Cattle, and Commerce among the Q'eqchi' Maya Lowlanders.* Seattle: University of Washington Press (Culture, place, and nature: studies in anthropology and environment).

Hale, Charles R. 2006. "Nociones contenciosas de los derechos sobre la tierra en la historia miskita." In *Demarcación Territorial de la Propiedad Comunal en la Costa Caribe de Nicaragua,* eds. Álvaro Rivas and Rikke Broegaard, 14–37. Managua: CIDCA-UCA. Orig. pub. 1992.

Hall, Derek. 2013. "Primitive accumulation, accumulation by dispossession and the global land grab." *Third World Quarterly* 34, no. 9: 1582–1604.

Hardin, Garrett. 1968. "The tragedy of the commons." *Science. New Series* 162: 1243–1248.

Harvey, David. 2004. "The 'new' imperialism: Accumulation by dispossession." *Socialist Register* 40: 63–87.

Jones, Trina and Antoine J. Alston. 2009. "A case study analysis of African American agriculturists and their perceived future in America." *Journal of Southern Agricultural Education Research* 59: 17–30.

Kay, Cristóbal. 2001. "Estructura agraria, conflicto y violencia en la sociedad rural de América Latina." *Revista Mexicana de Sociología* 63, no. 4: 159–195.

———. 2002. "Why East Asia overtook Latin America. Agrarian reform, industrialisation and development." *Third World Quarterly* 23, no. 6: 1073–1102.

Kinloch Tijerino, Frances. 2012. *Historia de Nicaragua.* 4th edition. Managua: IHNCA-UCA.

Lundahl, Mats. 1982. "A note on haitian migration to cuba, 1890–1934/Nota sobre la migracion haitiana a cuba, 1890–1934." *Cuban Studies* 12, no. 2: 22–36.

Minkoff-Zern, Laura-Anne. 2018. "Race, immigration and the agrarian question: Farmworkers becoming farmers in the United States." *The Journal of Peasant Studies* 45, no. 2: 238–408.

Monterroso, Iliana and Anne M. Larson. 2013. "The dynamic forest commons of Central America: New directions for research." *Journal of Latin American Geography* 12, no. 1: 87–110.

Ostrom, Elinor. 1990. *Governing the Commons: The Evolution of Institutions for Collective Action.* New York: Cambridge University Press.

Polanyi, Karl. 1977. *The Great Transformation: Politische und ökonomische Ursprünge von Gesellschaften und Wirtschaftssystemen.* Wien: Europaverlag. Orig. pub. 1944.

Schlager, Edella and Elinor Ostrom. 1992. "Property-rights regimes and natural resources: A conceptual analysis." *Land Economics* 68, no. 3: 249–262.

Spronk, Susan and Jeffery R. Webber. 2007. "Struggles against accumulation by dispossession in Bolivia." *Latin American Perspectives* 34, no. 2: 31–47.

Stam, Robert and Ella Shohat. 2014. *Race in Translation: Kulturkämpfe rings um den postkolonialen Atlantik.* Münster: Unrast Verlag.

Stocks, Anthony. 2005. "Too much for too few: Problems of indigenous land rights in Latin America." *Annual Review of Anthropology* 34: 85–104.
Striffler, Steve and Mark Moberg. ed. 2003. *Banana Wars: Power, Production and History in the Americas.* Durham and London: Duke University Press.
Thiesenhusen, William C. 1995. *Broken promises. Agrarian reform and the Latin American campesino.* Boulder: Westview Press.
Williamson Cuthbert, Dennis. 2006. "Tipología de conflictos sobre la propiedad comunal en el municipio de Puerto Cabezas." In *Demarcación Territorial de la Propiedad Comunal en la Costa Caribe de Nicaragua,* eds. Álvaro Rivas and Rikke Broegaard, 247–260. Managua: CIDCA-UCA. Orig. pub. 2003.
Wyatt, Stephen. 2008. "First nations, forest lands, and 'aboriginal forestry' in Canada: From exclusion to comanagement and beyond." *Canadian Journal of Forest Research* 38, no. 2: 171–180.
Ybarra, Megan. 2009. "Violent visions of an ownership society. The land administration project in Petén, Guatemala." *Land Use Policy* 26, no. 1: 44–54.

16
NEOLIBERALISM

Dieter Plehwe

The term "neoliberalism" refers to a worldview in support of market liberalism and a political regime conducive to economic freedom. It is grounded in a variety of economic and political schools of thought, notably drawing on German-Swiss ordoliberalism, Austrian economics, and the Chicago School. Neoliberalism is rooted in the liberal tradition of individualism and freedom (→ I/27), but it places an emphasis on economic freedom, property rights, procedural justice, and the rule of law. Ordoliberalism developed by the Freiburg School around Walter Eucken perhaps offers the clearest idea of a neoliberal order. It combines legal and economic doctrines and stipulates state responsibility for the maintenance of a competitive marketplace (Ptak 2009). Neoliberalism is simultaneously ambiguous with regard to the liberal traditions of democracy (→ II/32), basic political rights, not to mention social rights (→ Human Rights, II/35). If traditional liberalism promoted both economic and political freedom of the third estate in opposition to the ruling classes in feudal society (clergy and land owning nobility, first and second estate), neoliberalism emphasized economic freedom vis-à-vis challenges from the working classes (→ Class Struggle, II/3), from socialism (→ I/42), from fascism, but also from political regimes relying on majority vote (parliamentary democracy) and later-on from the welfare state. Neoliberals established a new binary code: individualism versus old and new forms of collectivism (→ Commons, II/31). To this end neoliberals treated right-wing and left-wing ideologies such as traditional conservatism, socialism, communism, or fascism in a similar manner: they are all considered varieties of collectivism because of their support for strong governments that inevitably infringe on the economic freedom of citizens. In general, neoliberalism is best understood as a right-wing turn of liberals in opposition to the left-wing turn of social liberals who embraced the expanding and substantive agenda of political and social rights, the broad vision of equality and social citizenship (→ Citizenship, II/27).

In contrast to traditional liberals and social liberals, neoliberals focused on the perceived tensions between economic and political rights. Social democratic parties and trade unions are considered as big a threat to economic freedom (→ Labor Representation, II/14) as the threat emanating from collectivist movements on the right. Under conditions of free elections, workers, and their representatives can dominate the parliament due to their larger number. In conjunction with majority rule, democracy is considered to potentially lead to the discrimination of property owners, e.g. by way of high taxes and highly progressive tax rates (→ Taxation, II/22). Likewise, workers organized in trade unions can force employers to pay wages above market rates. Against this backdrop, it is possible to comprehend the ambiguity many neoliberals voice with regard to parliamentarian democracy, majoritarian decision making, and basic political rights, such as the freedom of coalition. Neoliberals in fact went so far to distinguish between authoritarian and totalitarian regimes (→ Authoritarianism, II/25). The former are considered a sort of benevolent dictatorship if they are designed to protect economic rights, the latter are considered a sort of servitude because they are designed to destroy economic rights. Walter Lippmann was the first to introduce this notion of totalitarianism, the binary of economic individualism versus collectivism (Walpen 2004, 53). Neoliberals were obviously not concerned about the reverse argument, namely the extraordinary influence of wealthy people in politics and the coercive power of employers in the labor market unless workers are organized in trade unions. To their credit neoliberals never did care to hide the selective affinity of propertied classes, elites, and neoliberal ideas (→ Social Inequality, II/20).

Authoritarian varieties of neoliberalism subsequently played a critical, if ambiguous, role in the history of neoliberalism. The particularly cruel examples of neoliberal dictatorships in Chile under Pinochet in 1973 after the coup d'état against president Allende (and in Argentina after the coup d'état against Isabel Peron in 1976) led many Latin Americans to equate free market economics with dictatorship (Dussel Peters 2006). While this makes sense in a Latin American context, other varieties of more and less democratic neoliberalism should not be overlooked. However, the radicalness and pioneer character of Latin American neoliberalism requires a careful consideration of the variety, as well as of the multidirectional neoliberal transfers between this and other regions.

In public discourse, neoliberalism has been frequently reduced to, and is often misrepresented as a radical free market economics doctrine (benefits of the "invisible hand"). The ideas of neoliberalism as a pure market doctrine are due to the neoliberal propaganda leveled against public property, social regulation, or trade restrictions. Contrary to notions of unregulated markets or anarcho-capitalism, it is crucial to realize that neoliberalism is an ideology developed to direct, or re-direct public policy making based on a clear understanding of the need to protect and support economic freedom. To this end, legal order and enforcement and the repressive capacities of the state are indispensable (State Transformation, II/21; Nation State, II/31).

History of the concept

The term "neoliberalism" was coined in France in 1938 when a group of liberal intellectuals gathered at the Colloque Walter Lippmann in Paris to discuss Lippmann's book, *The Good Society* (Denord 2009). Liberals across Europe and the Americas had long been concerned with the rise of socialism (→ I/42) in Russia, and additionally had to face the increasing emphasis on protectionism and economic planning in Western and Southern societies after the Great Depression (→ Crisis, II/4). But liberal scholars, businessmen, and politicians, also addressed the perceived failure of traditional liberal doctrines to meet the social, political, and economic challenges of the interwar years, in an effort to bring the liberal tradition up to date with the changing circumstances and needs of the time. While neoliberalism was conceived in this dual opposition of collectivism and traditional liberalism in the 1930s, the inherent break with the laissez-faire past has since been frequently downplayed, and even denied, in order to present a continuous history of classical liberalism (e.g. Sally 1998). A linear history of liberalism fails to observe the novelty of both social liberalism and neoliberalism and obscures the key controversies between progressive and right-wing liberals.

While both neoliberals and social liberals agreed on the need to stabilize capitalism (→ II/2) in face of the Great Depression (→ Crisis, II/4), they disagreed on key questions of stability and (social) security. Progressive liberals supported the development of the welfare state and shared notions of social equality; the neoliberals instead supported social inequality (→ II/20) and endorsed "social minimum standards not inimical to private initiative and the market" only as set out in the statement of aims of the Mont Pèlerin Society founded by Friedrich August von Hayek and others in 1947.

In order to conduct the international program to renovate liberalism, a number of think tanks were planned in different countries. The title of the research program, referred to in the minutes of the meeting, selected the term "neoliberalism" over competing terms like "individualism," "positive liberalism," and even "left-wing liberalism." "To be 'neoliberal' was supposed to imply the recognition that 'laissez-faire' economics was not enough and that, in the name of liberalism, a modern economic policy was needed" (Denord 2009, 48). While the interwar efforts were stalled due to the outbreak of World War II, the transnational network design anticipated the organizational dimensions and intellectual ambitions of post-war neoliberalism (Plehwe 2009; Walpen 2004).

After World War II (WWII), the project was resurrected under the umbrella of the Mont Pèlerin Society, founded by Friedrich August von Hayek and the Swiss businessman Albert Hunold in 1947 (for different perspectives cf. Plickert 2008; Walpen 2004). The early Mont Pèlerin intellectuals observed the greatly increased dangers of collectivism due to the expansion of the socialist empire around the Soviet Union, the anti-colonial liberation struggles, and the rise of Keynesianism and the welfare state in the Western world. Only a few countries, such as Germany and Switzerland, featured economic and social policies that were broadly aligned with the neoliberal ideas developed by members of the Mont Pèlerin Society. Economists, namely Wilhelm Röpke, Walter Rüstow, and Alfred Müller-Armack, were key advisors to Germany's economic minister, and later chancellor, Ludwig Erhard, and helped create the original social market economy (Ptak 2009).

Neoliberalism travelled across borders easily as a result of a transnational discussion among intellectuals of different backgrounds and experiences. The resulting worldview combined different schools of (economic) thought, and involved the collaboration of scholars from many different academic disciplines. Apart from the German-Swiss ordoliberal tradition, which had mainly been developed in Freiburg by Walter Eucken, Franz Böhm, Leonhard Miksch and others, and in Geneva (Röpke) during the period of National Socialism, Austrian economists in exile in the United Kingdom (von Hayek), and in the United States (von Mises), as well as local traditions in these and other countries, were among the key pillars of the ongoing debate.

As well as the London School of Economics (LSE) department of Lionel Robbins (Tribe 2009), and the second Chicago School (Van Horn and Mirowski 2009), a French group of early neoliberals contributed to a vibrant intellectual exchange as they banded together around the organizers of the Colloque Walter Lippman, including philosopher Louis Rougier. This dialogue was reinforced by political leaders, such as Italy's President Luigi Einaudi, and journalists such as John Davenport, Henry Hazlitt, Trygve Hoff or George Révay, who worked for magazines like Fortune, Newsweek, Farmand, and Readers Digest. Other members published articles in newspapers like the Wall Street Journal, Neue Zürcher Zeitung, Le Monde and Frankfurter Allgemeine on a regular basis. Due to the range of different formations and perspectives involved in the Mont Pèlerin circles, the evolution of the neoliberal worldview is best characterized as pluralism, confined by a set of neoliberal norms and principled beliefs such as individualism, economic freedom, and the rejection of historical and moral relativism (Walpen 2004). In contrast to a certain amount of intellectual flexibility and diversity of neoliberalism, the ideology has been popularized in rigid ways since the late 1970s. The most prominent example was Margaret Thatcher's "TINA" (There is no alternative) formula. Practical constraint arguments usually invoke the world market and international competition to advocate unpopular reforms. Increasingly furious attacks on the welfare state since the 1970s stand in contrast to the careful discussions of social issues during earlier periods. Popular political representations of neoliberalism as a "pensée unique" (Pierre Bourdieu) and the equation of neoliberal ideology to practical constraint arguments therefore do not capture the complexity and variety of neoliberal thought, or the political flexibility of neoliberal actors.

The analysis of neoliberalism thus requires attention to different, complementary, and sometimes conflicting wings. Scholars have pointed to the Chicago boys in Chile in particular (Valdés 1995). The link between Santiago and Chicago dates back to the 1950s and was a long-term investment from different public and private sources into the transfer of neoliberal ideas. Another major hub of North American influence in Latin America was the Foundation of Economic Education (FEE) in Irvington, New York. Founded and run by radical anti-New Deal business forces, Ludwig von Mises was the most prominent economist at FEE, and also the most prominent neoliberal in multiple Latin American countries, long before the Chicago School gained influence. Unlike the Chicago School mix of rational choice-based theory, monetarism and neoclassical economics, Guatemala's Marroquin University is an important Central American hub for Austrian economics (Ayau 1990). Fischer (2009) has pointed to the local origins of Christian and legal subsidiarity thinking in Chilean corporatism, which became an important part of neoliberal social philosophy, akin to European traditions of ordoliberalism. As early as 1965 Norman Bailey observed militant groups of organized neoliberals in Latin America, which protected president Kennedy on trips to Colombia, Costa Rica, and Mexico, both intellectually and physically (Bailey 1965, 448).

Evolutions of neoliberalism

Many observers regard neoliberalism as an Anglo-Saxon creation of the late 1970s and early 1980s (due to the "revolutions" of Thatcher and Reagan), or point to the "Washington Consensus" of 1989 (Williamson 2003, 2004). However, as already mentioned, the Anglo-Saxon neoliberalism rise to prominence was preceded by the earlier instantiation of Germany's Social Market economy of the 1950s and 1960s (Fischer 2009), and the 1970s Latin American authoritarian varieties of neoliberalism in Chile and Argentina (Plehwe 2011) (→ Authoritarianism, II/25). Typically, American scholars tend to forget the early continental European history of neoliberalism, particularly when distinguishing different phases of neoliberal development. Robinson and Harris (2000) suggest a first "radical" laissez-faire phase linked to Milton Friedman, followed by a structuralist phase (featuring Social Democratic third way politics), and most recently a new type of neoliberal regulation partly informed by criticism of the Washington Consensus (Stiglitz 2002, 2003). Nancy Fraser refers to the era before the recent challenge from the new right ("right-wing populism") as "progressive neoliberalism" (Fraser 2017) (→ Populism, II/43). Contrary to this periodization, neoliberals enjoyed considerable influence in Europe immediately after WWII. Early European history and the history of European integration offer a rich reservoir of regulatory alternatives developed by neoliberals since the time of WWII, including the social market economy and certain aspects of regional integration (Ptak 2009; Wegmann 2002).

Plehwe, Walpen, and Neunhöffer (2006) alternatively suggest distinguishing between a defensive period of neoliberalism, lasting until the 1960s, and a movement phase, during the 1960s and 1970s period of social liberal hegemony constellations, leading up to the contemporary epoch of neoliberal (or right-wing liberal) hegemonic constellations. Some authors suggest a new post-neoliberal era has started, as a result of the global financial crisis in 2007/8, and observe promising initiatives in Latin America in particular (Brand and Sekler 2009). However, given the latest shift to austerity in Europe following the Global Financial Crisis/Great Recession (→ Crisis, II/4), the attacks on the Obama administration's deficit spending (Blyth 2013), and the plans of the Trump administration in the areas of taxation (→ II/22) and regulation, and, last but certainly not least, the replacement of "pink tide" governments in Chile, Argentina, and Brazil by radical right-wing neoliberal governments, it is more likely that neoliberalism has not quite run its course. Because many items on the agendas of neoliberal movements and governments were accomplished between 1980 and 2010 (erosion of planned economies, deregulation, and liberalization resulting in intensified globalization, privatization (→ II/17), limits set on progressive tax regimes, the dismantling of social redistribution schemes, etc., cf. Harvey 2005), the task of neoliberals after the Great Financial Crisis is arguably best understood as defending the status quo in the face of crisis (of 2008, cf. Plehwe 2017).

Transformations of neoliberalism with an eye to the Americas

Despite the origins of neoliberalism being strongest in Europe, the important networks of neoliberal intellectuals across other world regions both deserve more recognition and need greater scrutiny. Latin American scholars, administration officials, and business professionals, for example, played an important role in the global evolution of neoliberalism since its beginnings. Intellectuals from Mexico, Guatemala, Argentina, and Brazil contributed to the formative stage of neoliberal development. Mexico's Gustavo R. Velasco was among the editors of a volume written in honor of Ludwig von Mises (Harper et al. 1971), which also included contributions from Argentina, Guatemala, and Peru. Many think tanks had already been founded by Latin American scholars during the 1950s and 1960s, contributing to the critique of modernization theory (→ Modernization, I/35) and dominant left-wing theories of underdevelopment in the emerging field of development economics (Goodman and Marotz-Baden 1990; Plehwe 2009) (→ Development, II/6).

Neoliberals in Chile played a key role in the transnational battle over development economics and politics, although they represented a rather marginal spectrum of academic positions in the immediate post-war period. The dominant post-war analysis of "underdevelopment" at the time was steeped in heterodox economics, pointing to disadvantageous terms of trade for the South, and underemployment due to the structural power of industrialized countries and capitalist inequality in both the North and the South. Unsurprisingly, neoliberal development economists objected to the basic tenets of the mainstream, which at the time held powerful positions in the United Nations Development Program. The presence of the United Nations Economic Commission for Latin America (ECLA), under the leadership of Raúl Prebisch in Santiago, attracted a high level of attention.

The headquarters of the new school of economic thinkers, which promoted import substitution to industrialize southern countries, was opposed by local conservatives and neoliberal intellectuals alike. Domestic and international advocates of free trade, and critiques of the new theories of development, were reinforced in 1956 by an alliance struck between the Catholic University of Santiago and the University of Chicago. Strong links between local and foreign neoliberals and the Chilean military subsequently developed (→ Military, II/37), mirroring the links between local business conservatives, neoliberals, and the military, which already existed in Argentina (Plehwe 2011).

Military neoliberalism rose to prominence in Chile during the 1970s. Two years after the Allende government was toppled, neoliberal technocrats were placed in key advisory positions. Fischer (2009) distinguishes different phases of neoliberal restructuring in Chile. Initially, the reforms of Allende's socialist government were reversed, followed by what has now become known as "shock therapy." Subsequently, the privatization of social security, labor laws, designed to undermine trade unions and collective bargaining, moved to the top of Pinochet's agenda. Neoliberal reforms in Chile were ultimately consolidated in a new constitution inspired, in parts, by the work of Friedrich August von Hayek.

Argentina is better known for radical neoliberal reforms under President Menem and his finance minister, Cavallo, during the Washington Consensus years, in spite of the radical neoliberal policies adopted during the dictatorship of the 1970s and 1980s. Contrary to the flexible exchange rate regime recommended by Washington Consensus, Argentina introduced a currency board to peg the Peso to the U.S. Dollar. After a short-lived boom during the early 1990s, Argentina's economy crashed due to the overvaluation of the local currency, and the resulting loss of competitiveness of local businesses. Although most of the Washington Consensus priorities have been correctly identified as key items on the neoliberal agenda, the currency board and monetary rigidity clearly went beyond the pragmatic neoliberalism of the Washington Consensus era. The short-lived regime presented a more radical effort to privilege domestic and foreign capital ownership against exchange rate fluctuation and manipulation by the government or central bank. The transnational neoliberal discourse coalition, in support of the currency board solution, can be traced from the time of reinventing this colonial policy instrument in Hong Kong in the early 1980s, to the Argentinean case. While the business and political partners in the various local instances varied, a common group of neoliberal intellectuals contributed the underlying perception of the monetary problems, and the institutional solutions, thus tying the various projects together over time and across space (Plehwe 2011).

Neoliberalism in Latin America has a rich history, combining projects promoted by some of the most ruthless authoritarian regimes, along with democratically elected governments. More recently, neoliberal networks of think tanks feature somewhat stronger social integration perspectives, in addition to the traditional defense of inequality and the dynamics of free market capitalism (Fischer and Plehwe 2013). The macro-economic record of neoliberal economic policies is mixed with pragmatic varieties of neoliberalism clearly yielding better results than more radical projects. Most of the declared goals have not been reached. More than anything, neoliberalism in Latin America consolidated the traditional position of the commodity-exporting countries in the world market (→ Extractivism, II/9).

Conclusion

Despite a rich, nearly eighty-year history since the inception of neoliberal theorizing during the interwar years at the Colloque Walter Lippmann in 1938, neoliberalism remains a rather obscure concept for many reasons. Both the conflation of neoliberalism and corporate globalization and the equation of neoliberalism to specific countries or institutions such as American imperialism or the IMF have conspired to prevent a more comprehensive and adequately analytical discussion. Neoliberalism has become a catchall phrase for many on the left to attack capitalism (→ II/2) and imperialism in general, which levels important differences between social and right-wing liberal approaches to policy making, both in the Global North and in the Global South. This can become truly confusing, for example, if free trade in agriculture is a demand from the South to open up protected markets in the North. Are farmers in the Global South in reality neoliberals? Surely not, because access to protected markets is but one of the means considered to improve the social position of peasants. More contextual information is necessary to assess the ideological leaning of political demands.

A variety of reductions hinder a better understanding of neoliberalism. In Latin America, progressive intellectuals tend to equate neoliberalism to authoritarian rule (→ Authoritarianism, II/25), due to the entanglements of neoliberal intellectuals, especially with Pinochet. Other observers reduce neoliberalism to economic doctrines from post-WWII Chicago, or to Austrian economics as represented by von Mises and von Hayek. Partly due to (the English translation of) Foucault's biopolitics (→ I/22) lectures, ordoliberalism has recently gained a place in the race to the title of true neoliberalism.

An alternative approach, which focuses on networks of neoliberal intellectuals, think tanks, and ideas, is better suited to observe the evolution and transformation of neoliberalism in both time and space. The equation of liberalism and the New Deal makes the use of the right-wing counter concept nearly impossible to use in the United States, where neoliberals call themselves both libertarian and conservative. Instead, a better understanding of the neoliberal realm of thinking in contrast to left-wing (or social) liberal thinking can be considered most useful (against equality, in favor of individualism and competitiveness, in favor of interventionism, in support of capitalist market relations, etc.).

T. C. Marshall once wrote that social citizenship, representing the equality principle, which he thought was in class war with the inequality principle (→ Class Struggle, II/3), was at the heart of capitalist social relations. The violence involved in this class has been particularly harsh in the history of Latin American neoliberalism. Possibly due to the pink tide which followed the great crisis of neoliberal hemispheric integration after the collapse of Socialism (→ I/42), moderate neoliberal perspectives seem to have been growing and gaining ground in Latin America. However, Bolsonaro's success in Brazil in 2018 is once again closer to the harsh versions of authoritarian neoliberalism of the Latin American past (Bruff and Tansel 2018). Always in competition with more collectivist forms of social integration, neoliberal re-regulation must offer more than a simple defense of free markets, as it has done so routinely. Projects that design property rights in favelas to fight poverty, micro-credits, and micro-insurance programs are just a few examples of neoliberal efforts to expand market relations and financialization as an alternative to the welfare state in Latin America and beyond (→ State Transformation, II/21).

Due to the strong interest in Latin America from the United States, and the strong financial support for local neoliberals from U.S., German, and Spanish sources in particular, neoliberal think tanks and networks of intellectuals developed faster and stronger in Latin America than in other regions of the Global South (→ Public Intellectuals, III/18). Under the umbrella of the Atlas Economic Research Foundation, presently headed by the Argentinean, Alejandro Chafuen, the work of neoliberals has been coordinated across borders. Local neoliberals and business professionals have helped build think tanks and even universities, such as Guatemala's Marroquin University and Argentina's ESEADE Business School, in order to spread their ideas of economic freedom and free trade in Latin America, both at home and in neighboring countries.

Neoliberalism is strongly entrenched in Latin American civil society (→ II/28) as a result of fifty years of steadfast organizing. The region's neoliberal networks continue to participate in the battles of today and tomorrow concerning the future direction of Latin American regionalism and development (→ II/6). When the enhanced role of the state is more easily visible during times of protracted crisis (→ II/4), neoliberals will continue their attempt to hide the state behind a semblance of the rule of the law and the market.

Works cited

Ayau, M. 1990. "The War of Ideas in Guatemala." In *Fighting the War of Ideas in Latin America*, eds. John C. Goodman and Ramona Marotz-Baden, 138–146. Dallas: National Center for Policy Analysis.

Bailey, Norman A. 1965. "The Colombian 'Black Hand': A Case Study of Neoliberalism in Latin America." *The Review of Politics* 27, no. 4: 445–464.

Blyth, M. Austerity. 2013. *The History of a Dangerous Idea*. New York: Oxford University Press.

Brand, Ulrich and Nicola Sekler. 2009. "Postneoliberalism: Catch-all Word or Valuable Analytical and Political Concept?" *Development Dialogue* 51: 514.

Bruff, Ian and Cemal Burak Tansel. 2018. "Authoritarian Neoliberalism: Trajectories of Knowledge Production and Praxis." *Globalizations* 16, no. 3: 233–244.

Denord, Francois. 2009. "French Neoliberalism and its Divisions: From the Colloque Walter Lippmann to the Fifth Republic." In *The Road from Mont Pelerin: The Making of the Neoliberal Thought Collective*, eds. Philip Mirowski and Dieter Plehwe, 45–67. Cambridge, MA/London: Harvard University Press.

Dussel Peters, Enrique. 2006. "The Mexican Economy since NAFTA: Socioeconomic Integration or Disintegration?" In *Neoliberal Hegemony: A Global Crotoque*, eds. Dieter Plehwe, Bernhard Walpen and Gisela Neunhöffer, 120–138. New York: Routledge.

Fischer, Karin and Dieter Plehwe. 2013. "The 'Pink Tide' and Neoliberal Civil Society Formation: Think Tank Networks in Latin America." In *State of Nature* www.stateofnature.org/?p=6601#sthash.1uKpHc8i.dpuf

Fischer, Karin. 2009. "The Influence of Neoliberals in Chile Before, During and After the Pinochet." In *The Road from Mont Pelerin: The Making of the Neoliberal Thought Collective*, eds. Philip Mirowski and Dieter Plehwe, 305–346. Cambridge, MA and London: Harvard University Press.

Fraser, Nancy. 2017. "The End of Progressive Neoliberalism." *Dissent*, January 2 www.dissentmagazine.org/online_articles/progressive-neoliberalism-reactionary-populism-nancy-fraser

Goodman, John C. and Ramona Marotz-Baden. 1990. *Fighting the War of Ideas in Latin America*. Dallas: National Center for Policy Analysis.

Harper, Floyd Arthur, Friedrich August von Hayek, Henry Hazlitt, Leonard E. Read, and Gustavo R. Velasco. 1971. *Towards Liberty*. Menlo Park: Institute for Humane Studies Inc.

Harvey, David. 2005. *A Brief History of Neoliberalism*. New York: Oxford University Press.

Plehwe, Dieter. 2009. "The Origins of the Neoliberal Economic Development Discourse." In *The Road from Mont Pelerin: The Making of the Neoliberal Thought Collective*, eds. Philip Mirowski and Dieter Plehwe, 238–279. Cambridge and London: Harvard University Press.

———. 2011. "Transnational Discourse Coalitions and Monetary Policy: Argentina and the Limited Powers of the 'Washington Consensus'." *Critical Policy Studies* 5, no. 2: 127–148.

———. 2017. "Neoliberal Think Tanks and the Crisis." In *Liberalism and the Welfare State*, eds. Roger Backhouse, Bradly Bateman, Tamotsu Nishizawa and Dieter Plehwe, 192–211. New York: Oxford University Press.

Plehwe, Dieter, Bernhard Walpen, Gisela Neunhöffer. 2006. *Neoliberal Hegemony: A Global Critique*. London: Routledge.

Plickert, Philip. 2008. *Wandlungen des Neoliberalismus*. Stuttgart: Lucius & Lucius.

Ptak, Ralf. 2009. "Neoliberalism in Germany: Revisiting the Ordoliberal Foundations of the Social Market Economy." In *The Road from Mont Pelerin: The Making of the Neoliberal Thought Collective*, eds. Philip Mirowski and Dieter Plehwe, 89–138. Cambridge and London: Harvard University Press.

Van Horn, Rob and Philip Mirowski. 2009. "The Rise of the Chicago School of Economics and the Birth of Neoliberalism." In *The Road from Mont Pelerin: The Making of the Neoliberal Thought Collective*, eds. Philip Mirowski and Dieter Plehwe, 139–180. Cambridge and London: Harvard University Press.

Robinson, William I. and Jerry Harris. 2000. "Towards a Global Ruling Class? Globalization and the Transnational Capitalist Class." *Science and Society* 64, no. 1: 11–54.

Sally, Razeen. 1998. *Classical Liberalism and International Economic Order: Studies in Theory and Intellectual History*. London: Routledge.

Stiglitz, Joseph. 2002. *Globalization and its Discontents*. New York: W. W. Norton & Company.

———. 2003. *The Roaring Nineties: A New History of the World's Most Prosperous Decade*. New York: W. W. Norton & Company.

Tribe, Keith. 2009. "Liberalism and Neoliberalism in Britain, 1930–1980." In *The Road from Mont Pelerin: The Making of the Neoliberal Thought Collective*, eds. Hilip Mirowski and Dieter Plehwe, 68–97. Cambridge and London: Harvard University Press.

Valdés, Juan Gabriel. 1995. *Pinochet's Economists: The Chicago School in Chile*. Cambridge: Cambridge University Press.

Walpen, Bernhard. 2004. *Die offenen Feinde und ihre Gesellschaft*. Hamburg: VSA.

Wegmann, Milène. 2002. *Früher Neoliberalismus und europäische Integration*. Baden-Baden: Nomos.

Williamson, John. 2003. "From Reform Agenda to Damaged Brand Name: A short history of the Washington Consensus and suggestions for what to do next," *Finance & Development*, September 2003: 10–13.

———. 2004. A Short History of the Washington Consensus. Paper commissioned by Fundación CIDOB for a conference, "From the Washington Consensus towards a new Global Governance," Barcelona.

17
PRIVATIZATION

Richard Huizar and Fabricio Rodríguez

In its strictly instrumental sense, privatization refers to the transfer of responsibility from state institutions (→ Nation State, II/38) to privately owned companies for the sake of improving the provision of public goods. The central question at stake is whether governments are able to provide quality services regarding water, sanitation, education (→ I/24), health (→ I/29), roads, ports, airports, telecommunications (→ III/42), transportation, security (→ II/45), digital infrastructure (→ Digital Culture, III/28), and/or national defense (→ Military, II/37), or, alternatively, whether private companies can perform better in fully – or partly – delivering these services to the public. Albeit contested, the assumption underpinning privatization processes is that profit-driven organizations can efficiently generate and allocate public goods where governmental capacity is limited (Chong and López-de-Silanes 2012b; Estrin and Pelletier 2018; Megginson and Netter 2001). In that regard, privatization "involves a transfer of ownership: the government bows out and the private sector enters" (Prager 1992, 311). Therefore, the privatization of publicly owned companies is a highly political process reflecting what societies – or the dominant actors in them – believe about the level of involvement the state should have in steering, enabling, or regulating the domestic economy (Whitfield 2001) (→ State Transformation, II/21).

Historically, privatization represents "a countermovement to the growth of government that has characterized much of the post-World War II period in industrial and developing countries" (Bienen and Waterbury 1989, 617). At the outset of the 1980s, a time in which the battle between capitalism (→ II/2) and socialism (→ I/42) was vivid, Margaret Thatcher embraced the concept of "privatization" as the structuring axis of her government. This fact displaced the language of "denationalization," which had thus far prevailed among those proclaiming the retreat of the nation-state from economic affairs (Megginson and Netter 2001, 324). Accordingly, Great Britain experienced the single most influential package of privatization, which has since become a historical blueprint for hundreds of governments to follow suit (Megginson and Netter 2001). Although other governments (Germany under Konrad Adenauer, or Chile under Pinochet's dictatorship) undertook privatization efforts earlier than Great Britain, privatization is generally acknowledged as being an "Anglo-American public policy" (Whitfield 2001, 2). This is further explained by the fact that Washington-based international organizations such as the International Monetary Fund (IMF) and the World Bank adopted privatization policies as the cornerstone of multilateral policy toward the transitioning economies of Eastern Europe and the so-called developing world, particularly during the 1980s and 1990s (Nellis, Menezes and Lucas 2004) (→ Development, II/6).

Partly as a result, Latin America stands out as one of the world-regions in which the adoption of privatization has been most intense. At the same time, Latin America is host to the most active movements opposing privatization, which is considered "the strongest area of citizen dissatisfaction with neoliberalism" (Kingstone, Young and Aubrey 2013, 94) (→ Social Movements, I/41; Neoliberalism, II/16). Critics denounce the nexus between privatization and neoliberalism for its inherent drive "to create better conditions for capitalist accumulation, and in particular by having a minimalist state that places the free market above all other considerations" (Segura 2018). Following Latin America's "left-turn" during the early 2000s, due to widespread disenchantment, privatization policies in Latin America has stalled. However, and beyond its instrumental character, privatization represents a central driver of ongoing political struggles and socio-economic change across the Americas. The rationale of privatization has incited much criticism, as well as stimulated discussion about the social, political, and economic implications of privatization processes in the Americas. This is highlighted in the *privatization-versus-nationalization dilemma* exemplified by the oil sectors of Mexico and Argentina, two cases of central relevance to the privatization wave of the 1980s and 1990s (→ Energy, II/7).

The rationale of privatization – and its discontents

Privatization is an important intervention in state-market-society relations. The choice to privatize or leave particular sectors of the economy in the hands of the government is crucial to the political and economic character and performance of a state (→ Nation State, II/38). The extent to which a society embarks in privatization affects not only the institutional framework but also the structural matrix shaping the outcomes and quality of social, economic, cultural, and environmental policies. As an effect of and response to economic globalization, privatization also affects the extent to which the nation-state is constrained to and capable of accommodating external actors and interests in its domestic market. In the Americas, privatization is the result of political decisions implemented by the means of parliamentary legislation and/or presidential decrees.

Paradoxically, the nation-state is instrumental to its own transformation (→ State Transformation, II/21), representing both the subject and object of privatization. Privatization policies are hence a normative project: They contend that the "entrepreneurial energy" of businesses can not only function as growth-catalysts but also as safeguards to individual rights and liberties regarding access to public goods and services (Kingstone 2010, 46). There are some services, which are generally considered a natural duty of governments, whether at the central, regional, or municipal levels (Roth 1989, 1). Privatization can thereby stretch over, and have distinct, oftentimes problematic, implications in a variety of policy fields including telecommunications (→ III/42), water provision, healthcare (→ Health, II/29), sanitation, security (→ II/45), housing, basic, and/or higher education (→I/24), as well as road and ports infrastructure, among others.

The arguments in favor of privatization are plentiful while its results are contested (Chong and López-de-Silanes 2012a; Kingstone, Young and Aubrey 2013; Prager 1992; Whitfield 2001). In general terms, privatization comes into question when states seek to *first*, enhance public revenues in the face of growing budget constraints, *second*, set up clear and predictable rules to enhance economic efficiency, *third*, eliminate bureaucratic obstacles to profit accumulation, *fourth*, diversify shares and forms of ownership, *fifth*, strengthen the principle of competition while combating public monopoly, and, *sixth*, subject state-owned enterprises (SOEs) to market discipline while diminishing the risk of political interference (Megginson and Netter 2001, 324). Advocates of "privatization" see a natural tendency for citizens to reject the initial stages of policy implementation while embracing its benefits at later stages (Chong and López-de-Silanes 2012b, 1). Others point at the distributional problems generated by privatization policies, even in the cases where positive effects in terms of quality and coverage may arise as a result. As Kingstone et al. (2013, 96) point out, "Privatization has led to improved service and access for some while threatening jobs, raising tariffs, worsening service, and disrupting communities and ways of life for others. These effects foster a diverse set of actors potentially available for mobilization against privatization" (Kingstone, Young and Aubrey 2013, 96).

While the nation-state (→ II/38) is crucial to the creation of enabling legislation, the implementation of privatization can take place at different levels of government. The literature on local governance, for instance, defines privatization as a strategy through which the state shifts its responsibility in public service provision to profit-driven and/or community-based organizations at the subnational level (Rondinelli, Nellis and Shabbir Cheema 1987, 28). These local organizations, the argument goes, represent the broader set of societal interests and may include "farmers' cooperatives, credit associations, mutual aid societies, village development organizations, trade unions, or women's and youth clubs" (Rondinelli, Nellis and Shabbir Cheema 1987, 28). However, criticism against privatization programs is actually rooted in the fact that state-reform generally offers more room for large corporations to take control of large segments of the public sphere. Given the high requirement of capital needed to maintain or rehabilitate large infrastructures in telecommunications (→ III/42), roads, or energy (→ II/7) provision, most local actors are automatically left out of the bargaining equation (Whitfield 2001). Some of the fears associated with privatization include the loss of national sovereignty to the rule of transnational corporations (→II/23), job losses alongside the deregulation of worker's rights as well as the shrinking possibility for social movements (→ I/41) and citizens to hold private actors accountable in case they fail to provide public services.

Privatization in the Americas

In the Americas, privatization – and the different forms of resistance against it – have suffered ongoing and enduring consequences from state-market relations, significantly affecting the lives of citizens within and beyond the Anglo-American sphere. One of the key issues relates to the question of which goods and services should stay in the hands of the government and where can the rationale of private companies contribute to their efficient production and allocation. The answers to these questions are not straightforward as they are largely contingent upon each state's historical, political, societal, economic, normative, and institutional constituencies. Consider for instance the cases of education (→ I/24), health care (→ I/29), or even imprisonment (→ Security, II/45). While European states understand the management of these sectors as the unequivocal task of the public sector, the U.S. has a much different tradition. Critics of school privatization (Ravitch 2013) face much more resistance in the U.S. than they would in Europe.

One of the most disputed fields regarding privatization policies in the U.S. concerns the health care system, which encompasses a largely heterogeneous mix of private networks with limited public engagement (Duggan, Gruber and Vabson 2018) and is substantially different from that of Canada. In fact, both North American countries followed similar pathways to private health care provision until Canada opted for the institutionalization of a universal, publicly funded health care system called *Medicare* in the late 1960s. Since then, Canadian citizens defend their health care system against attempts to privatize, or partially decentralize public responsibility to the private sector. As noted succinctly by Marcia Angell, the realization of the Canadian Medicare system emphasized the visible contrast to the U.S. system. The U.S. system became increasingly expensive leaving tens of millions without proper coverage, 15 percent of the population lacking a means to pay for basic doctor and hospital visits, and medical expenses per person doubling that of Canada (Angell 2008, 916).

One of the main points highlighted by Angell is the fact that profit-driven organizations are not automatically entitled to claim higher levels of efficiency regarding the provision of public services. This argument is further strengthened by the analysis of the U.S. imprisonment system. In this case, U.S. regulations allow public instances to outsource "inherently public" competences such as "punishment" to private companies – a function which scholars of Legal Philosophy believe "should not be privatized since private actors would inevitably fail in performing [it]" (Dorfman and Harel 2013 68). Instead of resolving this particular problem of public concern, privatization ends up exacerbating it. As Farah writes, "Private prisons have no real incentive to rehabilitate prisoners" (2015, n.p.). The higher the rate of incarceration, the higher the profits.

While North American states face specific challenges regarding the question of privatization, Latin America has traditionally taken the role of the policy-taker as opposed to Washington's longstanding position as the policy-maker. In Latin America, as part of the so-called developing world, privatization has taken a specific focus with international organizations promoting their virtues for the sake of good governance, development (→ II/6), and human rights (→ II/35). The IMF's structural adjustment programs are a paradigmatic example and explanation of why privatization is closely tied to the promotion of the "Washington Consensus" (Williamson 2011) – a developmental matrix boosting trade liberalization, economic deregulation, and privatization as the beacons of Western modernity (→ Modernization, I/35).

The World Bank complemented Washington's efforts to promote the hemispheric adoption of these values by indoctrinating Latin American countries on "good governance" (→ State Transformation, II/21). Under this concept, privatization reached the capitals of Latin America as an antidote against fiscal imbalances, as a means of rationalizing the use of limited budgets in the face of increasing debt and inflation, and as a policy-tool for business promotion and economic growth. Consequently, privatization was hailed as a remedy to virtually any developmental malfunctioning caused by the inefficiencies of the state apparatus. These included the provision of basic services like drinking water, sewerage, and sanitation services declared as key priorities under human rights considerations. In spite of strong levels of resistance (Kingstone, Young and Aubrey 2013; Nellis, Menezes and Lucas 2004), the privatization project worked its way through virtually all sectors of public service provision below the southern border of the U.S., where "in Mexico and Chile in the mid-1980s … everything from banks, power plants, and telecommunication systems to roads, water, and transport services … were sold off to the private sector …" and by the next decade "the accumulated privatization revenues in 18 Latin American countries reached 6 percent of gross domestic product (GDP)" (Nellis, Menezes and Lucas 2004, 1).

Privatization, however, carried along many problems. For instance, the promise that the privatization of state-owned companies would increase efficiency and provide cheaper services to the consumer went oftentimes unfulfilled. The reality is that some companies moved from being public monopolies to private monopolies so that consumer prices were locked into the policies of new private monopolies. This was the case of Telmex, Mexico's telephone company. When the telephone company was privatized in 1990, it remained a private monopoly for five years as part of the privatization agreement (Osorno 2015, 61). During the five years after its privatization, domestic consumers continued paying exceedingly high rates for telephone service. While telephone costs may have drastically gone down due to the emergence of newer technologies, the actual benefits of privatization have remained ambivalent.

A different argument applies to the macro-economic notion that privatization would provide badly needed revenues for the state and enhance fiscal capacity in the long-term. For instance, from 1985 to 1998 Mexico obtained over US$26 billion in privatization revenues, and Argentina over US$19 billion dollars from its privatization program from 1990 to 1998 (Wilkie, Aleman and Ortega 2002, 907). Besides generating short-term revenues by selling state-owned companies, there was an additional benefit of saving money by putting an end to the state subsidies previously allocated to state-owned companies. "In the case of Mexico, government subsidies to state-owned accounted for 12 percent of the GDP in 1982; 10 years later the privatized firms had become net tax payers" (Megginson and Kay 2000, 20) (→ Taxation, II/22). These measures further stimulated foreign investment, increased competition, and improved macro-economic efficiency in terms of tax collection, although state performance regarding tax spending was difficult to assess.

One of the greatest challenges was the high number of workers that lost their jobs in the aftermath of privatization. "A study of more than 200 companies in Mexico revealed that roughly half of all the workers lost their job after the government divested its ownership" (Megginson and Kay 2000, 23) (→ Deindustrialization, II/5). Something similar took place in Argentina during the privatization of the national rail company, "when 79 percent of the company's total work force was laid off in 1991 as part of the restructuring of the railroad" (Megginson and Kay 2000, 23). During the 1980s and 1990s, the majority of the Latin American population retained a negative view of privatization. Survey data from 2002 indicates that over 70 percent of Latin Americans did not believe that privatization programs were beneficial to their country (Shirley 2005, 196).

If privatization programs were unpopular among Latin Americans, then, what explains their widespread radius of implementation throughout the region? Given its highly controversial nature, the advancement of privatization must manage a number of problems while generating favorable conditions in the process. One of the most important problems concerns state-labor relations i.e. the opposition of public workers fearing the loss or degradation of jobs and rights (→ Labor Representation, II/14). Teichman (1995), for instance, believes that the stronger the labor sector is in a country, the easier the privatization process becomes as long as the labor sector can be co-opted or repressed by the regime in power. In some cases, a strategy of divide and conquer may proof fruitful. In others, as in the case of authoritarian rules (→ Authoritarianism, II/25), mechanisms of repression have played a key role in the enforcement of privatization. In Chile, for instance, Pinochet's military dictatorship paved the way for one of the most comprehensive privatization reforms in the Americas to take place during the 1980s (Cypher 2004). Against this backdrop, privatization processes further depend on the behavior of veto powers. Support or pressure from important groups such as the military (→ II/37) can also explain the extent to which privatization programs are able to advance (Teichman 1995). Additionally, the presence of a strong executive has been widely instrumental in the enforcement and diffusion of privatization agendas across the Americas. According to Kleinberg (1999), the presence of a strong executive allows for the expansion of privatization programs, especially when the executive branch has more power than congress and the judiciary. In the case of Peru, the authoritarian program of Alberto Fujimori, who is considered a semi-dictator, helped Washington institutionalize long-lasting privatization reforms, which are now useful to other actors seeking economic and political influence in the region (see Rodríguez 2018).

The oil industry: the last frontier of economic sovereignty?

With the spectacular rise of commodity prices at the beginning of the 2000s, different left-leaning governments opted for the nationalization of the oil industry (→ Energy, II/7). This was a political wave which understood the oil sector as a strategic platform for the nation-state to regain sovereign control over subsoil resources (Rosales 2013). China's economic and political rise coincided with a rapidly increasing demand for fossil resources. This new international scenario motivated – volatile – policies focusing on the use of attractive oil revenues for the sake of fostering greater levels of financial independence from external actors (Rodríguez 2018). As a new set of governments embracing trade liberalization and market deregulation have made a come-back to the political arena, the privatization question arises. Will the oil industry become the last frontier of economic sovereignty available to Latin American states? A comparative analysis of Mexico and Argentina – two prominent cases of privatization during the 1980s and 1990s – shows that the privatization of the oil industry is contingent upon several factors. These include *inter alia*: the level of dependency on oil revenues, the extent to which oil is linked to economic nationalism, the way in which labor unions relate to the national elites in power (→ Labor Representation, I/14), and, finally, the extent to which external actors are capable of forcing less powerful states to accommodate their interests.

The cases of Mexico and Argentina are illustrative, because both countries implemented two of the most extensive privatization programs in the region. The outcomes regarding the privatization of the oil industry were however different. In Mexico, privatization was fully implemented during the neo-liberal administration of Carlos Salinas who was in power from 1988 to 1994 (→ Neoliberalism, II/16). In Argentina the administration of Carlos S. Menem, which lasted from 1989 to 1999, was responsible for the nation's deep-ranging privatization program. By the early 1990s both Carlos Salinas and Carlos S. Menem had become the poster children of the Washington Consensus.

However, Mexico and Argentina traveled very different paths regarding oil-ownership. Mexico maintained PEMEX (Petróleos Mexicanos) as a state-owned oil company while Argentina privatized YPF (*Yacimientos Petrolíferos Fiscales*). The primary reason for this outcome has to do with the different levels of each state's dependence on oil revenue. While Mexico was heavily reliant on oil with 39 percent of its total government revenue generated from oil profits in 2006 (INEGI 2009), Argentina was not. In 1991, for instance, when YPF was still state-owned, Argentina only obtained 7.8 percent of its total government revenue from the oil industry (MECON 2009). Thus, during the privatization process YPF represented no game-changer in the landscape of state-owned companies, which the Argentinian government could privatize.

Another reason explaining the different effects that these two similarly intense processes of privatization had on the oil sector was economic nationalism. Defined as "a sentiment, movement, or policy geared to the nationalization of economic resources" (Knight 1994, 138), economic nationalism played a distinctive and decisive role in the national protection of PEMEX in Mexico, as opposed to the privatization of YPF in Argentina. In the case of Mexico, oil has remained a matter of collective identity and pride since the nationalization of the industry in 1938. In 1998, after the far-reaching wave of privatization had taken place, 70 percent of the population believed that oil should remain owned by the state, according to representative data issued by *Latinobarometro n.y*. According to other important reports, this trend was still relevant a decade later (Report CESOP 2008). Unlike PEMEX, Argentina's state-owned oil company did not survive the neo-liberal administration of Carlos S. Menem. Although the majority of Argentinians (54 percent) were in favor of keeping the oil industry under state control in 1995, with the share rising to 61.3 percent in 1998 according to *Latinobarometro n.y*), YPF was finally privatized.

In the case of Argentina, the limited capacity of the state-owned company to provide a stable oil supply was a key factor alongside the strategies pursued by the Menem government to negotiate an agreement with national labor unions. The different degrees to which labor unions could mobilize resistance in Mexico and Argentina are in fact key variables explaining why PEMEX remained a state-owned company while YPF was privatized under Menem. Mexico's oil workers' union, the STPRM (*Sindicato de Trabajadores Petroleros de la República Mexicana*) was in fact a vocal and powerful opponent of the privatization of the oil company. Additionally, the labor union had built a corporatist relationship to the PRI (Revolutionary Institutional Party) since its establishment in 1938. In this corporatist relationship, the oil workers' union provides electoral support and financial support to the PRI and receives political support and protection from the PRI (Camp 2007). Scholars such as Denise Dresser (2009) have argued that the bargaining power of the STPRM and its leadership has increased substantially in the course of its long-term relation with the government.

Menem's relationship to labor unions in the Argentinian oil sector was not as tight, which provided him with other options to enforce privatization measures. Working for YPF provided oil workers with job security, generous economic benefits, and social prestige. In order to downsize the volume of public workforce, the Menem administration implemented a policy of "inducements" and "constraints." The inducements consisted of providing the workers generous severance benefits for those that accepted to retire on a "voluntary" basis. In addition to severance pay, the oil company was willing to retrain the workers in a different profession and hire them as independent contractors if the workers were interested in starting their own business. The constraints included firing those workers that would protest the privatization of the oil company or were not willing to accept the "voluntary retirement" option. Following the company's privatization in July 1993, most of the Argentinian oil workers had accepted the voluntary retirement option. As a result, the level of opposition that is typically expected from a workers' union in the oil sector remained absent in the case of Argentina.

Finally, a central co-determinant in the privatization of oil in Mexico and Argentina was the role played by the IMF and the World Bank. During its financial crisis between December 1994 and January 1995 (→ Crisis, II/4), Mexico was very vulnerable to international pressure as growing debt stress brought the economy very close to default. Thus, the government became heavily reliant on external financial assistance, fearing pressures to privatize its state-owned industries. Surprisingly, the U.S. government and the IMF did not exert pressure on the Mexican government to privatize its oil industry despite the option of enhancing Washington's energy security through greater access to Mexico's oil reserves. In fact, Washington extended financial aid but there were no strings attached to the privatization of the oil sector. In a matter of weeks, the Clinton administration put together a financial rescue package, which totaled US$49.8 billion (Sanger 1995). The Clinton administration did not see the U.S. in the position to force Mexico to privatize PEMEX, because revenues from Mexico's oil exports were used as collateral means of payment (Rubin 1995). From a U.S. perspective, the long-term economic risks of privatizing Mexico's oil sector exceeded the potential benefits.

In Argentina, the circumstances were very different. In this case, the World Bank was key to financing Argentina's national privatization program with the privatization of YPF constituting a central conditionality. As part of the agreement with the Argentinian government, the World Bank gave way for the use of multilateral funding to privatize a wide range of state-owned companies, explicitly including the oil company YPF in its proposal (Huizar, 2019). The Menem administration was particularly welcoming of the World Bank's role in the restructuring of the Argentinian economy. As a result, YPF went private in July 1993, when stocks were sold to domestic and international investors in the Buenos Aires and New York stock markets. As a paradigmatic case of the *privatization-nationalization-dilemma*, the government of Christina Fernández de Kirchner regained control of the nation's oil industry by granting the Argentinian state a 51 percent share of the oil company, which was previously controlled by the Spanish multinational oil company Repsol.

Conclusion

Privatization is often defined and used as a policy instrument through which the public sector gives way for profit-driven organizations to take responsibility in the provision of public goods. Discussions and criticism around the rationale underpinning privatization processes expose the wider implications of privatization as a contested process of social, political, and economic change. This process does not necessarily respond to the agendas of local communities striving for the collective provision of the public good. Privatization responds to a global agenda, which started spreading across the globe in the 1980s, subsequently affecting societies in industrialized and so-called developing countries in very specific ways, depending on the context and sector at stake. For the Americas, privatization constitutes a major field of political struggle between those who believe in the virtues of the market and those who trust the capacity of the state (→ NationState, II/38). In the Inter-American sphere, privatization produces and reinforces an unequal division of labor, which places the North as the policy-maker and the South as the policy-taker. The significance of privatization may not necessarily emerge from its narrow, instrumental definition. For the Americas, as for much of the world, the meaning of privatization materializes at the complex and oftentimes-conflicting conjunctures of economic globalization and its histories and geographies of resistance.

Works cited

Angell, Marcia. 2008. "Privatizing Health Care is not the Answer: Lessons from the United States." *Canadian Medical Association Journal* 179, no. 9: 916–919.

Bienen, Henry and John Waterbury. 1989. "The Political Economy of Privatization in Developing Countries." *World Development* 17, no. 5: 617–632.

Camp, Roderic Ai. 2007. *Politics in Mexico: The Democratic Consolidation*, 5th ed. New York, NY: Oxford University Press.

Chong, Alberto and Florencio López-de-Silanes, eds. 2012a. *Privatization in Latin America: Myths and Reality*. Washington, DC: World Bank and Stanford University Press.

———. 2012b. "The Truth about Privatization in Latin America." In *Privatization in Latin America. Myths and Reality*, eds. Alberto Chong, Florencio López-de-Silanes, 1–66. Washington, DC: World Bank and Stanford University Press (Latin American Development Forum).

Cypher, James M. 2004. "Is Chile a Neoliberal Success?" *Dollars and Sense* 255: 30–35.

Dorfman, Avihay and Alon Harel. 2013. "The Case against Privatization." *Philisophy and Public Affairs* 41, no. 1: 67–102.

Dresser, Denise. 2009. "Foro de Propuestas y Compromisos México ante la crisis: ¿Qué hacer para crecer? Senado de la República Mexicana, LXI Legislatura." January, 29. Mexico City. www.senado.gob.mx/index.php?ver=sen&mn=3.

Duggan, Mark, Jonathan Gruber, and Boris Vabson. 2018. "The Consequences of Health Care Privatization: Evidence from Medicare Advantage Exits." *American Economic Journal: Economic Policy* 10, no. 1: 153–186.

Estrin, Saul and Adeline Pelletier. 2018. "Privatization in Developing Countries: What Are the Lessons of Recent Experience?" *The World Bank Research Observer* 33, no. 1: 65–102.

Farah, Mohammed. 2015. "The Problem with Privatizing Prisons: If Private Prisons Make their Profit from Criminal Society, Its Goes against Business Sense to Reduce Criminality." *JSTOR Daily*, May 15.

Huizar, Richard. 2019 In Press. "Why was Yacimientos Petrolíferos Fiscales (YPF), Argentina's National Oil Company, Privatized?" *The Extractive Industries and Society.*

INEGI (Instituto Nacional de Estadística). 2009. Geografía e Informática, August 17. Mexico City. www.inegi.org.mx/.

Kingstone, Peter, Joseph K. Young, and Rebecca Aubrey. 2013. "Resistance to Privatization: Why Protest Movements Succeed and Fail in Latin America." *Latin American Politics and Society* 55, no. 3: 93–116.

Kingstone, Peter R. 2010. *The Political Economy of Latin America.* London: Routledge.

Kleinberg, Remonda Bensabat. 1999. *Strategic Alliances and Other Deals: State-Business Relations and Economic Reforms in Mexico.* Durham, NC: Carolina Academic Press.

Knight, Alan. 1994. "Peasants into Patriots: Thoughts on the Making of the Mexican Nation." *Mexican Studies/Estudios Mexicanos* 10, no. 1: 135–161.

Latinobarometro. n.y. "Opinion Publica Latinoamericana, 1998-2005, Computer File, Marta Lagos, Principal Investigator." *Latinobarometro.* www.latinobarometro.org/lat.jsp.

MECON (Ministerio de Economía y Finanzas Públicas), Centro de Documentación e Información (CDI). 2009. "Dirección Nacional de Investigaciones y Análisis Fiscal." June 23. Buenos Aires. http://catalogo.mecon.gov.ar/entidad.php?ent=12.

Megginson, William and Stephen J. Kay 2000. "Privatization." *Foreign Policy* 118: 14–27.

Megginson, William L. and Jeffry M. Netter 2001. "From State to Market: A Survey of Empirical Studies on Privatization." *Journal of Economic Literature* 39, no. 2: 321–389.

Nellis, John, Rachel Menezes, and Sarah Lucas. 2004. "Privatization in Latin America. The Rapid Rise, Recent Fall, and Continuing Puzzle of a Contentious Economic Policy." *Policy Brief* 3, no. 1: 1–7.

Osorno, Diego E. 2015. *Slim: el Mexicano mas rico del mundo.* Mexico, D.F.: Vintage.

Prager, Jonas. 1992. "Is Privatization a Panacea for LDCs? Market Failure versus Public Sector Failure." *The Journal of Developing Areas* 26, no. 3: 301–322.

Ravitch, Diane. 2013. *Reign of Error. The Hoax of the Privatization Movement and the Danger to America's Public Schools.* New York, NY: Alfred A. Knopf.

Reporte CESOP (Centro de Estudios Sociales y de Opinión Pública). 2008. *Sector Energético.* Publicación Mensual del Centro de Estudios Sociales y de Opinión Pública de la Cámara de Diputados, LX Legislatura, no. 10, March.

Rodríguez, Fabricio. 2018. *Oil, Minerals, and Power: The Political Economy of China's Quest for Resources in Brazil and Peru.* Doctoral Thesis, Germany. University of Freiburg.

Rondinelli, Dennis A., John R. Nellis, and G. Shabbir Cheema. 1987. *Decentralization in Developing Countries: A Review of Recent Experience*, 4th ed. Washington, DC: The World Bank.

Rosales, Antulio. 2013. "Going Underground. The Political Economy of the 'Left Turn' in South America." *Third World Quarterly* 34, no. 8: 1443–1457.

Roth, Gabriel. 1989. *The Private Provision of Public Services in Developing Countries.* New York, NY and Oxford: Oxford University Press.

Rubin, Robert E. 1995. "Statement of the Honorable Robert E. Rubin, Secretary of the Treasury, Before the House Committee on Banking and Financial Services, U.S. House of Representatives." *U.S. and International Response to the Mexican Financial Crisis: hearing before the Committee on Banking and Financial Services.* U.S. Congress, House, 104th Cong. 1st sess., January 25, 1995.

Sanger, David E. 1995. "Mexican Rescue Plan: The Overview; Clinton Offers $20 Billion to Mexico for Peso Rescue; Action Sidesteps Congress." *The New York Times*, February 1, section A, 1.

Segura, Natalia. 2018. "Neoliberalism Has Vandalized Latin America." *Thruthout.* https://truthout.org/articles/neoliberalism-has-vandalized-latin-america/.

Shirley, Mary M. 2005. "Why is Sector Reform so Unpopular in Latin America?" *The Independent Review* 10, no. 2: 195–207.

Teichman, Judith A. 1995. *Privatization and Political Change in Mexico.* Pittsburgh, PA: Pittsburgh University Press.

———. 2001. *The Politics of Freeing Markets in Latin America: Chile, Argentina and Mexico.* Chapel Hill, NC: The University of North Carolina Press.

Whitfield, Dexter. 2001. *Public Services or Corporate Welfare. Rethinking the Nation State in the Global Economy.* Sterling, VA: Pluto Press.

Wilkie, James W., Eduardo Aleman, and Jose Guadalupe Ortega, eds. 2002. *Statistical Abstract of Latin America.* Los Angeles, CA: Latin American Center Publications; University of California.

Williamson, John. 2011. *A Short History of the Washington Consensus.* New York, NY: Routledge.

18
REGIONAL INTEGRATION

Stefan Schmalz

Most studies of regional integration have historically focused on European integration, which stands out due to its solid supranational institutions, deep economic integration, and cultural exchange, despite ongoing crises. However, during the second half of the 20th century, new cooperation agreements emerged in other world regions, such as East Asia, Sub-Sahara Africa, and Latin America, which were less institutionalized and, in some cases, did not refer to common cultural practices. From a non-Eurocentric perspective, regional integration therefore must be understood as a form of increasing economic, political, and social cross-border interactions such as trade flows, migration networks, and political institutions (Arrighi, Hamashita and Selden 2003, 4–9).

Following this line of reasoning, the first attempts of regional integration in the Americas date back to the beginning of the 19th century. After the independence of most Latin American states, regional integration emerged as an important issue in political debates. In his messages to the Congress of Angostura (1819) and the Congress of Panama (1826), Simón Bolívar emphasized the necessity of regional unity and a continental army to protect America from colonial domination (Mace 1988, 404–405). Nevertheless, the more limited forms of political unification such as Gran Colombia (1821–1831), the República Federal de Centro América (1824–1839) and the Confederación Perú-Boliviana (1836–1839) were unable to remain stable. Conflicting interests between regional creole elites and the "local backwardness of capitalism and technology in relation to the stretch of the empire" (Anderson 1991, 63) equally impeded the development of regional statehood (→ Nation and State Building, I/16). The attempts of deeper political integration were therefore not supported by close economic and social integration.

Similar to the Bolivarian concept (*Bolivarianism*), the precursors of the *Pan-American* idea of regional integration go back to the times of independence. With the pronouncement of the Monroe doctrine in 1823, U.S. policymakers made it clear that the U.S. would regard any attempt by European powers to colonize land or interfere with states in the Americas as an act of colonial aggression. During the late 19th century, however, this anticolonial orientation increasingly turned imperialist. By the 1880s, the U.S. had transformed into a large industrial power and, thus, competed for markets and territories with European countries on a global scale. In this period, regional integration re-emerged on the political agenda with the First International Conference of American States (1889–1890) in Washington. This summit aimed to create a continental customs union, but the Latin American delegates eventually rejected the U.S. proposal of a continental free trade zone (Martí 1955). Notwithstanding, the conference did lay the first seeds of a Pan-American institutional architecture (→ Pan-Americanism, II/40). The eighteen participating states founded the International Union of American Republics, which remained a loose institutional structure, but did not exert any real political influence. Canada was not even involved in these integration efforts, as it was still a member of the Commonwealth and was represented by the British ambassador in the United States (MacKenzie 2016).

Throughout the next decades, *Pan-Americanism* and *Bolivarianism* continued to be the most important ideas of regional integration, thereby influencing further attempts of cooperation in the Americas. Pan-Americanism has always produced an asymmetry between the U.S. and its Latin American neighbors and was often perceived as being a tool of imperialist domination (→ Interventionism, II/36), while Bolivarianism focused on Latin American states and was generally seen as a strategy of the emergent Latin American bourgeoisie to reduce U.S. influence and to build independent institutions and economic structures.

Regional integration after World War II

After World War II, the geopolitical situation changed dramatically. The U.S. turned into the hegemon of the capitalist world system, with the USSR as its main opponent (Hobsbawm 1994, 225–256). During this time, Pan-American ideas re-emerged. The U.S. had a strong interest in integrating its "Latin American backyard" into the capitalist order (→ Capitalism, II/2). In 1948, the Organization of American States (OAS) was founded. Since then, OAS has remained the most important continental organization with up to thirty-four member states. Besides its focus on diplomacy affairs in the Americas, OAS has also become an important player in regional economics: The Inter-American Development Bank was founded in 1959 and, similar to the World Bank, it serves as a source of financing large-scale development projects in Latin America and the Caribbean (→ Development, II/6). Today, the credit volume of the bank is about US$67 billion (2013). The U.S. traditionally holds the largest number of shares in the bank and is effectively able to veto most decisions, together with its Latin American and European allies who are also members of the bank. Unsurprisingly, both OAS and Inter-American Development Bank are perceived as dominated by the U.S. For instance, Cuba was suspended as a member in 1961 as a result of the Cuban Revolution and the OAS initiated the "Alliance for Progress" in order to contain Soviet influence in the Americas. The "Alliance for Progress" was the largest U.S. aid program in the Americas and comprised investment and economic assistance of about US$22.3 billion. However, in most Latin American countries the initiative was perceived as a failure, as it did not achieve its original aim of a more rapid improvement in standards of living (Taffet 2007). The Nixon administration eventually dropped the Alliance of Progress in 1967.

Furthermore, post-war capitalism eventually diverged from earlier forms of capitalism, as it was strongly regulated by a system of capital controls, fixed currency exchange rates, comparatively high import duties, as well as high taxes and state influence on the national level (→ Fordism, II/10). This transformation also had a stark influence in Latin America. After the Great Depression in 1929, a new economic model slowly emerged in most Latin American countries (Donghi Halperin 2005, 361–431). Liberal trade policy was replaced by import substitution with a strong developmental state pushing for industrialization (→ Nation State, II/38). The import-substitution model continued to exist after World War II and developed further throughout the 1950s and 1960s. However, already by the mid-1950s, most Latin American industrial projects began to reach their first limits: The substitution of capital goods and technologically advanced consumer goods turned out to be challenging, as domestic markets were too small and lacked local technological knowledge (→ Deindustrialization, II/5).

In order to overcome these limits, UN-regional commission United Nations Economic Commission for Latin America and the Caribbean (ECLAC), influenced by dependency theory, recommended to create regional trade agreements. In the 1960s, several new regional initiatives emerged: The largest regional agreement was the Asociación Latinoamericana de Libre Comercio (ALALC, 1960), which was comprised of Mexico and most South American states. Likewise, the Mercado Común Centroamericano (MCCA) was founded in 1960, which brought together the Central American states. In 1969, the Andean Community was also formed. All three agreements aimed at economic integration, thereby focusing on cutting customs for specific goods, and fostering economic coordination.

Most scholars agreed that the approach of "closed" or "old regionalism," which was deeply linked to import-substitution politics, was not able to effectively create a regional domestic market (Bulmer-Thomas 2001). The breakdown of the Bretton Woods currency regime and the diverging economic development in Latin America after the 1973 oil crisis were major blows for the import substitution-based trade agreements. Asociación Latinoamericana de Integración (ALADI) (1980), the successor of ALAC, tried to revive this failed model of regional integration, but was proven unsuccessful. Instead, the debt crisis of 1982 created an unstable economic environment (→ Crisis, II/4), which prevented further integration in the Americas.

Neoliberalism and open regionalism

By the late 1980s, both international relations and global capitalism had, once again, undergone a dramatic change. The disintegration of the Eastern bloc ended the Cold War and opened up new possibilities for regional integration. As the most important capitalist core nations had started to embrace neoliberal politics since the late 1970s, they liberalized global trade and investment flows. The U.S. had already embarked on neoliberalism (→ II/16) with the election of President Ronald Reagan in 1981, while Canada's neoliberal turn proceeded much slower beginning in the mid-1980s. Likewise, several Latin American governments changed their economic policies under pressure from the debt crisis from the early 1980s. As a consequence of the "Washington Consensus" (Williamson 1990) privatization (→ II/17), deregulation, and liberalization, Latin American economies transformed significantly. Between 1985–1995, the average import duties dropped by two-thirds. During the 1990s, the average share of foreign trade almost doubled, and the net inflow of foreign direct investment increased fourfold. As a result, Latin America became deeply integrated into global circuits of accumulation, thus strengthening transnational economic activities such as finance, agribusiness, *maquiladora* (export processing) production (→ Global Commodity Chains, II/12), and tourism (Robinson 2008). Consequently, Latin America was among the first world regions that underwent a full-scale neoliberal reorganization of its economy.

Furthermore, the neoliberal turn came along with a new wave of regionalism that shaped global trade (Gudynas 2005, 25). The official World Trade Organization (WTO) website states that by February 2016, some 625 Regional Trade Agreements had been reported to the WTO, with most of them implemented by 1990. Unlike earlier agreements of "closed regionalism" in the Global South, these "open regionalism" treaties were based on generalized liberalization. Thus, they go far beyond the classical content of trade agreements, such as the lowering of duties for industrial products. Open regionalism agreements include lowered duties in the agricultural sector, liberalization of services and investment, establishment of intellectual property rights, and liberalization of government procurement. Moreover, open regionalism is characterized by weak supranational institutions.

In the Americas, two important regional agreements, North American Free Trade Agreement (NAFTA) and Mercado Común del Sur (Mercosur), were created in the early 1990s. Mercosur was founded in 1991 when Argentina, Brazil, Paraguay and Uruguay signed the Treaty of Asunción. At this time, Argentina and Brazil were governed by ultra-liberal presidents Carlos Menem and Fernando Collor de Mello, respectively. Unlike earlier agreements, the creation of Mercosur implied rapid liberalization of intraregional trade (Rattner 2002, 63). Between 1990 and 1994, intraregional trade doubled, and competition intensified. In the following years, however, trade conflicts between Brazil and Argentina escalated, as Brazilian transnational capital quickly expanded into other markets and outcompeted local companies. After 1999, Mercosur experienced a deep crisis (→ II/4) as Brazil (1999) and Argentina (2001) suffered from financial crises and devalued their currencies.

NAFTA (1994), an agreement between the U.S., Canada, and Mexico, was the blueprint for later attempts of Pan-American integration in the Americas. Similar to Mercosur, NAFTA imposes the overall liberalization of goods, capital, and service markets, but comprises neither effective social and environmental clauses nor strong supranational institutions. Moreover, the treaty's infamous Chapter 11 strongly strengthens the private sector in comparison to public agents through investor-to-state arbitration. NAFTA is also a highly asymmetric mode of integration: While most sectors of Canada's high-wage economy had already been integrated into U.S.-dominated value chains for several decades (Panitch 1981), NAFTA turned out to be a serious challenge for Mexican companies. In most sectors, Mexican companies were not able to compete with U.S. businesses. Only a few Mexican transnational corporations (TNCs) (→ II/23) were able to establish themselves successfully in the North American market. Most Mexican industrial companies integrated into a subordinate position in regional value chains (Robinson 2008, 107). Consequently, even though the official tone of Latin American policy makers suggested that open regionalism would operate as a "stepping stone to the world market" (Malcher 2005, 109), both NAFTA and Mercosur treaties were part of a project to foster neoliberal hegemony, since they created transnational political, social, and economic structures that were dominated by a transnational neoliberal power bloc (Scherrer 2001, 585; Schmalz 2013).

Divergent approaches after the left turn

NAFTA was the starting point for a larger project of integration. The U.S.-led initiative for the Free Trade Area of the Americas (FTAA) aimed to liberalize trade and investment in the Americas in order to create the world's largest free trade zone with more than 800 million consumers and thirty-four member states. The negotiation process for FTAA began in 1994. The first drafts of the agreement resembled NAFTA, as it included issues such as liberalization of investment and services and investor-to-state arbitration. However, at the beginning of the 2000s, social movements (→ I/41) that had spread throughout Latin America increasingly challenged neoliberal hegemony. As a consequence, leftist governments such as Chávez in Venezuela (1998), Lula da Silva in Brazil (2002), Kirchner in Argentina (2003), Vázquez in Uruguay (2004), and Morales in Bolivia (2005) were voted into office.

Due to this left turn, FTAA eventually failed at the Summit of Mar del Plata 2005 (Moniz Bandeira 2006, 26). The U.S. government reacted with several bilateral agreements such as the U.S.-Chile agreement (2004), U.S.-Peru agreement (2005), the CAFTA-DR agreement (2005) with Central America, and the U.S.-Colombia (2012) agreement. These trade areas were also an attempt to undermine resistance to free trade in Latin America. For instance, the announcement of trade talks between U.S. and Colombia led to a quasi-breakdown of the surviving Andean Community when Venezuela withdrew from the alliance.

The left governments started to create opposing projects: In 2003, a new Argentinean-Brazilian axis emerged that, in its potency, resembled the neoliberal axis of the early 1990s. Its main objective was to reshape Mercosur to a "social Mercosur." By 2003, through the "Objetivos 2006," it had adopted a new orientation. One of the main aims of the Objetivos 2006 was to accelerate the creation of EU-like supranational institutions, such as a parliament, a commission, and a court of justice. The Objetivos 2006 also outlined the goal of proactive regional industrial policy, thus harking back to the spirit of closed regionalism. Finally, South American governments agreed on FOCEM (Fondo para la Convergencia Estructural del Mercosur), a structural convergence fund of about US$100 million, with the small member states of Paraguay and Uruguay set to be net receivers. Another important measure was the enlargement of Mercosur, with Venezuela (2013) and Bolivia (2015) accepted as full members (Agramont Lechín 2015). However, due to Brazil's unwillingness to provide the project with sufficient resources, intensified conflicts between member states, and a general decline of the importance of Mercosur vis-à-vis new trading partners in Asia, the idea of a "social Mercosur" never materialized. Consequently, the project has made no meaningful progress until today.

As a result of this period of stagnation, Brazil and Venezuela pushed the Unión de Naciones Suramericanas (UNASUR) agreement forward, which was comprised of all South American states. In particular, the project of UNASUR involved policy fields, which had been neglected by Mercosur, such as finance, energy (→ II/7), and security (→ II/45) (Serbin 2009). After two years of preparation, the South American states finally agreed on the foundation of the Banco del Sur in September 2009, with starting capital of about US$7 billion. The major task of the bank is to finance infrastructure projects in South America. The member states of Banco del Sur, however, do not include all countries; Chile, Colombia, and Peru are not participating in the project. Since its implementation, UNASUR has pushed forward some important initiatives, such as the free movement of its citizens for up to three months in the area. In general, the Brazilian led-initiatives Mercosur and UNASUR helped to strengthen regional ties, but did not create a stable South American block.

Some more radical left-wing governments founded the Alianza Bolivariana para los Pueblos de Nuestra América (ALBA) as a counter-project to FTAA in 2005, with Venezuela as its driving force. Member states include Venezuela, Cuba, Bolivia (2006), Nicaragua (2007), Dominica (2008), Saint Vincent and the Grenadines (2009), Antigua and Barbuda (2009), Surinam (2012), St. Lucia (2013), Granada (2014), as well as Saint Kitts and Nevis (2014). ALBA took advantage of the commodity boom before 2013. The framework of flexible integration built the core of solidarity-based trade in energy resources for goods and services, and the cooperation between state-owned enterprises through import duty reductions on goods (Muhr 2013). Ideologically, ALBA refers extensively to Bolivarianism. However, ALBA is inspired by *Chavismo* which effectively turns Bolivarianism into a leftist concept. In line with Venezuelan socialism of the 21st century, ALBA does not only focus on regional independence, but also on the empowerment of the subaltern classes (→ Socialism I/42; Class

Struggle, II/3). ALBA is primarily project oriented, thus, it is based on projects such as the energy pact Petroamérica, the trade agreement Tratado de Comercio de los Pueblos, and different measures in social policy, e.g. education (→ I/24) and health (→ I/29). In addition to several individual agreements, e.g. the South American television channel Telesur (→ Television, III/43), the member states also aim for stronger financial integration. For instance, member states introduced a virtual regional currency for foreign trade named the Sucre in 2010. The manifold of initiatives has led to a significant rise in common trade between member states and to welfare gains such as the complete elimination of non-literacy in some member states. However, the agreement also has led to contradictions. For example, member states can simply withdraw from ALBA, as the coup d'état in Honduras (2009) and the election of former socialist Lenin Moreno in Ecuador (2017), who later allied with right-wing political forces, demonstrated, as well as territorial fragmentation between member states.

Generally, the diverging attempts of regional integration after the left turn can be perceived as projects of different transnational social forces to create political, social, and economic structures, with FTAA and comparative bilateral agreements pushed forward by a transnational neoliberal social bloc, Mercosur/UNASUR by a Social Democratic axis, and ALBA by more radical left-wing social forces (Schmalz 2013).

Perspectives

Regional integration in Latin America is facing severe challenges as contradicting projects emerge. From a historical perspective, FTAA can be seen as inspired by Pan-Americanism (→ I/24), and ALBA and Mercosur/UNASUR influenced by Bolivarianism. In fact, it seems to be that both historical projects are running out of steam. First, the left turn is reaching an end. Argentina voted for the neoliberal Macri government in late 2015 and the Brazilian congress firstly impeached left-wing president Rousseff in 2016 and in 2018 voted for far-right president Jair Bolsonaro. Also, Venezuela's government is under severe pressure. Thus, both UNASUR and ALBA have lost momentum, as most conservative governments are seeking closer relations to the U.S. For instance, the U.S., Chile, Peru, and Colombia have established the trade bloc Pacific Alliance in 2012. Thus, several South American countries are already ignoring the strategic option of exclusive trade negotiations in the UNASUR. Second, the rise of (East) Asia and China markets is challenging both Bolivarianism and Pan-Americanism. In particular, the rise of China as an economic power has led to a reorientation of trade in South America (Gallagher 2016, 41–63). China has already replaced the U.S. as the most important export market for several South American nations. In comparison to these new ties, intraregional trade flows in both Latin America and the Americas are getting weaker, undermining any attempt of closer economic integration. Therefore, it is likely that the recent wave of regional integration in the Americas has come to an end.

Works cited

Agramont Lechín, Daniel. 2015. "Bolivia mira hacia el sur. El ingreso al Mercosur y la política exterior de Evo Morales." *Nueva Sociedad* 259: 15–26.

Anderson, Benedict. 1991. *Imagined Communities: reflections on the Origin and Spread of Nationalism.* London and New York: Verso.

Arrighi, Giovanni, Takeshi Hamashita, and Mark Selden. 2003. "Introduction: The Rise of East Asia in Regional and World Historical Perspective." In *The resurgence of East Asia: 500, 150 and 50 year perspectives*, eds. Giovanni Arrighi, Takeshi Hamashita, and Mark Selden, 1–17, London: Routledge.

Bulmer-Thomas, Victor. 2001. "Regional Integration in Latin America and the Caribbean." *Bulletin of Latin American Research* 20, no. 3: 360–369.
Donghi Halperin, Tulio. 2005. *Historia contemporánea de América Latina*. Vol. 6. Madrid: Editorial Alianza.
Gallagher, Kevin. 2016. *The China Triangle. Latin America's Boom and the Fate of the Washington Consensus*. Oxford and New York: Oxford University Press.
Gudynas, Eduardo. 2005. "Desde la integración blanda y el comercio rígido al regionalismo autónomo." *Ecuador Debate* 65: 21–38.
Hobsbawm, Eric. 1994. *The Age of Extremes*. New York: Vintage Books.
Mace, Gordon. 1988. "Regional integration in Latin America: A Long and Winding Road." *International Journal* 43, no. 3: 404–427.
Malcher, Ingo. 2005. *Der Mercosur in der Weltökonomie: eine periphere Handelsgemeinschaft in der neoliberalen Globalisierung*. Baden-Baden: Nomos.
Martí, José. 1955. *Argentina y la Primera Conferencia Panamericana. Ordenación y prólogo por Dardo Cúneo*. Mexico: Ediciones Transición.
MacKenzie, David. 2016. "Before the UN: Early Canadian Involvement with International Organizations." In *Canada and the United Nations. Legacies, Limits, Prospects*, eds. Colin McCullough, and Robert Teigrob, 18–43, Montreal and Quebec: McGill-Queen's Unversity Press.
Moniz Bandeira, Luiz Alberto. 2006. "Brazil as a Regional Power and Its Relations with the United States." *Latin American Perspectives* 22, no. 3: 12–27.
Muhr, Thomas, ed. 2013. *Counter-Globalization and Socialism in the 21st Century: The Bolivarian Alliance for the Peoples of Our America*. London and New York: Routledge.
Panitch, Leo. 1981. "Dependency and Class in Canadian Political Economy." *Studies in Political Economy* 6: 7–33.
Rattner, Hentique. 2002. *Mercosul e ALCA. O Futuro Incerto dos Países sul-americanos*. São Paulo: Editora da Universidade de São Paulo.
Robinson, William I. 2008. *Latin America and Global Capitalism. A Critical Globalization Perspective*. Baltimore: Johns Hopkins University Press.
Scherrer, Christoph. 2001. "'Double Hegemony?' State and Class in American Foreign Economic Policymaking." *Amerikastudien* 46, no. 4: 573–591.
Schmalz, Stefan. 2013. "Regional Integration in the Americas." In *Transnational Americas. Envisioning Inter-American Area Studies in Globalization Processes*, ed. Olaf Kaltmeier, 17–34, Trier and Tempe: WTV/Bilingual Press.
Serbin, Andrés. 2009. "América del Sur en un mundo multipolar: es la Unasur la alternativa?" *Nueva Sociedad* 219: 145–156.
Taffet, Jeffrey F. 2007. *Foreign Aid as Foreign Policy: The Alliance for Progress in Latin America*. London and New York: Routledge.
Williamson, John. 1990. "What Washington Means by Policy Reform." In *Latin American Adjustment: How Much Has Happened?* ed. John Williamson, 224–244, Washington, DC: Institute for International Economics.

19
REMITTANCES

Christian Ambrosius, Barbara Fritz, and Ursula Stiegler

In the general conception, remittances are financial transfers usually sent by (national or international) migrants to support relatives back home (→ Transnational Migration, I/44). Beyond monetary transfers, there are also remittances in kind (in the form of goods or services) and so-called "social remittances" (ideas, identities, practices, social capital, see Levitt 1998). Monetary remittances have grown extraordinarily since the 1990s, both worldwide and in the Americas. Although remittances to Latin America temporarily declined as a result of the U.S. financial crises in 2007–08 (→ Crisis, II/4), they recovered after 2010 and reached a new height in 2014 (Ratha, Eigen-Zucchi and Plaza 2016). Whereas the United States are by far the world's largest sending-country since emigration from Mexico and Central America is largely concentrated there, Mexico was the fourth largest receiver of remittances (more than US$25 billion) in 2014, after India, China, and the Philippines (12). Concerning the economic relevance in relative terms, remittances in Mexico account for around 2.5 percent of the Gross Domestic Product (GDP), while in smaller countries with large diasporas, like Haiti, Honduras, and El Salvador, they summed up to more than 15 percent of the GDP in 2014 (ibid). Next to remittances from the U.S., many South American countries such as Bolivia, Ecuador or Peru receive remittances from sizable diasporas in Europe, with Spain being the most important destination country for Latin American emigrants in Europe (Ratha, Eigen-Zucchi and Plaza 2016). Globally, South-South remittances amount for a third of total remittances (11). Within Latin America, important South-South corridors of migration and remittances corridors exist between Nicaragua and Costa Rica, Haiti and the Dominican Republic, Central America and Mexico, Peru and Chile, and Paraguay and Argentina, among others (ibid). In view of the above, remittances have become an important topic in the flows of wealth from country to country. Research on remittances is often viewed from two perspectives, either by an "optimist" or "critical" view concerning their development potential.

The "optimists": remittances as a tool of bottom-up development finance

Motivated by their strong rise, remittances have increasingly been "discovered" as a potential source of capital for development (→ II/6) in the international policy discussion. Most of the leading international organizations have dedicated flagship reports to the nexus between migration, remittances, and development raising the question whether remittances would become a new "mantra" (Kapur 2004) in the development discourse that responds to the search for a "third communitarian way" of development between pure market-liberalism and state-led development strategies (cp. de Haas 2010).

This shift in policy discourse has been accompanied by academic research that has highlighted several channels through which remittances can have positive effects on the home countries and contribute to poverty reduction. Many of these works build on insights of the New Economics of Labor Migration (Stark and Bloom 1985), where the transnational family – rather than the individual migrant – is put at the center of analysis (→ Family, I/26). In this perspective, remittances provide an insurance function for families staying behind through the diversification of household income and enable receiving households to undertake investments into human or physical capital. Studies have found empirical evidence that receivers of remittances spend a larger share of their income on education (→ I/24) (e.g. Hanson and Woodruff 2003), health (→ I/29) (Amueda-Dorantes, Pozo and Sainz 2007) and entrepreneurship (e.g. Woodruff and Zenteno 2007); and that remittances function as informal insurance in the case of economic crisis (→ II/4), natural disasters (→ II/33), or household shocks.

Beyond the direct effects of remittances at the household levels, other authors have emphasized indirect effects of remittances on the economies via consumption spillover (Durand, Parrado and Massey 1996), the stabilization of exchange rates (e.g. Singer 2010), and via the development of the financial sector (e.g. Ambrosius and Cuecuecha 2013; Ambrosius, Fritz and Stiegler 2014). Moreover, collective remittances sent by home town associations for community projects have been praised as an important mechanism through which migrants may generate positive development in the wider community (e.g. Duquette-Rury 2014). The most well-known initiative of this kind is the Mexican Three-for-One Program, where Mexican governments at the municipal, state and federal level match each dollar sent by migrants for community projects in their home towns. Although dwarfed by the amount of private remittances, social spending out of the program ranked second in terms of total size after the national anti-poverty program in Mexico (Duquette-Rury 2014).

Beyond its economic effects, a number of studies have emphasized that migrants are potentially important actors for processes of democratization in their home countries (→ Democracy, II/32), either via the transmission of social values and political beliefs (Barsbai, Rapoport, Steinmayr and Trebesch 2017), or by debilitating local clientelistic ties through an external source of revenue (Escribà-Folch, Meseguer and Wright 2015). In the case of Mexico, scholars have claimed that migration and remittances played a role in debilitating the dominance of the traditional Partido Revolucionario Institucional (PRI) party by undermining clientelism (→ II/29) (Pfutze 2012) and that remittances are associated with lower corruption (Tyburski 2012).

"Critical" perspectives: do remittances sustain old and create new dependencies?

Whereas in Latin America many governments and social scientists have joined optimistic discourses about the development potential of remittances and there is an increasing number of initiatives to capitalize on that potential, there are also many critical voices in the region and beyond. Skeptics point toward the unfulfilled promises and the remittances' (potential) negative implications. On a macroeconomic level, it has been argued especially that remittances may lead to a loss in international competitiveness through the appreciation of the exchange rate (e.g. Amueda-Dorantes and Pozo 2004). On the micro level, expectations that remittances transform into so-called "productive" investments are often disappointed as large parts of remittances are spent for daily consumption as they basically replace or complement other household incomes (Binford 2003; Canales 2006; Cortina, de la Garza and Ochoa-Reza 2005).

Some authors have criticized that remittances reduce incentives for productive investment of resources in the countries of origin and do therefore not represent a source of capital for development (Chami, Fullenkamp and Jahjah 2003). Moreover, even if remittances contribute to lessen poverty, their effect on inequality can be ambiguous, depending on whether richer or poorer individuals migrate (Acosta, Calderón, Fajnzylber and Lopez 2008) (→ Social Inequality, II/20). Finally, social scientists with a critical perspective on globalization see migration and remittances as the negative outcome of neoliberalism (→ II/16). Authors like Delgado Wise and Covarrubias (2008) argue that remittances are mere results of strangled economic and social development rather than a tool for growth and well-being. In their view, these flows help sustain the fragile socioeconomic situation of the migrants' country of origin, expanding the asymmetries between north and south and exacerbating phenomena such as employment insecurity (→ Informality, II/13), poverty, and social marginalization. Instead of altering structural development constraints, remittances, according to that view, at best constitute a palliative against the deteriorating socioeconomic situation of the population caused by failed macroeconomic structural policies (Canales 2006, 2008). Moreover, remittances might accelerate the retreat of the welfare state by replacing public with private mechanisms of self-insurance (Doyle 2015; Ambrosius 2016) (→ State Transformation, II/21).

The financing of community projects in the spirit of the Three-for-One project has also been subject to critics. On the one hand, the program has been prone to political capture. Meseguer and Aparicio (2012) provide qualitative evidence for the strategic use of the program by elected officials. Municipalities that share partisanship with higher levels of government are more likely to benefit from the political bias of the program (Aparicio and Meseguer 2012). On the other hand, spending for the Three-for-One project could be cross-financed at the expense of spending on other items or for other regions (Ambrosius 2016; Simpser, Duquette-Rury, Hernández Company and Ibarra 2016). Whereas "optimists" have praised remittances as catalysts for democratization and political accountability, some political scientists have taken an opposite view. For example, Ahmed (2012) observes higher corruption in countries that receive remittances and draw parallels to other forms of unearned foreign income that provokes rent-seeking behavior by governments.

Critical perspectives on the effects of remittances in countries of origin also emphasize that monetary flows cannot be separated from the broader phenomenon of migration and its implications. For example, feminist theorists have analyzed how emigration affects the organization of social relations of reproduction in countries of origin along care chains (Hochschild 2000; see Herrera 2005 for an application to the Ecuadorian context) (→ Gender and Work, II/11). While women in the north employ the low-wage services of migrant domestic workers for their reproductive economy, migrants' absence at home is compensated either by other women who receive even lower wages or by remaining family members (→ Family, II/26) In this sense, international migration reproduces class-relations and global social inequalities (→ II/20) in which the value ascribed to the reproductive economy decreases and is often unpaid at the end of the chain.

Conclusion: conceptual and methodological challenges in research on remittances

Empirical studies have amassed overwhelming evidence that remittances reduce poverty and provide an important mechanism of insurance for transnational households. Most of these studies depart from the observation that income from remittances tends to be more stable than revenue earned at home. At the same time, the decline of remittances as a result of the U.S. financial crisis, and the restrictions on immigration together with the menace of taxing remittances by populist governments in the north (→ Populism, II/43; Taxation, II/22), exposes the vulnerabilities of a model that relies on remittances as a counter-cyclical insurance mechanism. A main research agenda for the years to come will be the consequences of stricter immigration rules and threats of deportation for Latin American countries that rely heavily on remittances (→ Transnational Migration, I/44), and where migration and remittances have functioned as an important social valve in the context of economic restructuring and market reforms (see Garcia Zamora 2017 for an assessment of the Mexican case).

While few question the beneficial effects of remittances on poverty indicators at the household level, no consensus exists on their macroeconomic, institutional, and social effects. On the one hand, polarized views on their outcomes reflect in differing models of economic development along the traditional cleavages of neoclassical/liberal versus heterodox or structuralist economic theories. On the other hand, grasping the broader effects of remittances in receiving countries poses several conceptual and methodological challenges to researchers. First, from a theoretical viewpoint, a distinction of the effects of migration from those of remittances is artificial, since decisions on migration and remittances are closely related. In particular, a discussion over the use of remittances – i.e. investment versus consumption – misses the point stated by the New Economics of Labor Migration that emigration of one or more families already constitutes an investment by the transnational family, whereas remittances can be seen as a return on this investment. Second, it is empirically challenging and often impossible to disentangle the effects of remittances and migration (Clemens and McKenzie 2014). Frequently, forces may operate in opposite directions. For example, migration might be motivated by poverty, whereas remittances tend to alleviate income constraints. Positive and negative effects may therefore cancel out in an aggregate view. Finally, wider economic effects are strongly dependent on country contexts. Accumulated research on migration and development both theoretically and empirically gives evidence for the fundamentally heterogeneous nature of migration and its financial counter face, the remittance flows. Their contingency on temporal and spatial analysis forbids any simplistic assertions on remittance-development interactions (see also de Haas 2010).

Remittances may have positive effects on the standard of living of migrants' families and on the economy of the emigration country, depending on the circumstances. It is important to note that the "remittance euphoria," that goes along with the perception of self-development "from below" through transnational migrants and their money sent home, shifts attention away from the relevance of structural constraints and the important role governance by the state and other actors may play in shaping favorable conditions for economic and social development (→ II/6) in the Global South.

Works cited

Acosta, Pablo, Cesar Calderón, Pablo Fajnzylber, and Humberto Lopez. 2008. "What Is the Impact of International Remittances on Poverty and Inequality in Latin America?" *World Development* 36, no. 1: 88–114.

Ahmed, Faisal Z. 2012. "The Perils of Unearned Foreign Income: Aid, Remittances, and Government Survival." *American Political Science Review* 106, no. 1: 146–165.

Ambrosius, Christian. 2016. "Do Remittances Crowd-In or Crowd-Out Public Expenditure?" Annual Conference of the International Political Economy Society. Durham, NC.

Ambrosius, Christian and Alfredo Cuecuecha. 2013. "Are Remittances a Substitute for Credit? Carrying the Financial Burden of Health Shocks in National and Transnational Households." *World Development* 46 (June): 143–152.

———. 2016. "Remittances and the Use of Formal and Informal Financial Services." *World Development* 77 (January): 80–98.

Ambrosius, Christian, Barbara Fritz, and Ursula Stiegler. 2014. "Remittances for Financial Access: Lessons from Latin American Microfinance." *Development Policy Review* 32, no. 6: 733–753.

Amueda-Dorantes, Catalina and Susan Pozo. 2004. "Workers' Remittances and the Real Exchange Rate: A Paradox of Gifts." *World Development* 32, no. 8: 1407–1417.

Amueda-Dorantes, Catalina, Susan Pozo, and Tania Sainz. 2007. "Remittances and Healthcare Expenditure Patterns of Population in Origin Communities: evidence from Mexico." *Integration and Trade Journal* 27: 159–184.

Aparicio, Francisco Javier and Covadonga Meseguer. 2012. "Collective Remittances and the State: The 3×1 Program in Mexican Municipalities." *World Development* 40, no. 1: 206–222.

Barsbai, Toman, Hillel Rapoport, Andreas Steinmayr, and Christoph Trebesch. 2017. "The Effect of Labor Migration on the Diffusion of Democracy: Evidence from a Former Soviet Republic." *American Economic Journal: Applied Economics*. www.aeaweb.org/articles?id=10.1257/ap.20150517&&from=f.

Binford, Leigh. 2003. "Migrant Remittances and (Under)Development in Mexico." *Critique of Anthropology* 23, no. 3: 305–336.

Canales, Alejandro I. 2006. "Remesas y Desarrollo En México. Una Vision Critica Desde La Macroeconomía." *Papeles De Población* 12, no. 50: 171–196.

———. 2008. *Vivir Del Norte. Remesas, Desarrollo y Pobreza En México*. México City: Consejo Nacional de Población.

Chami, Ralph, Connel Fullenkamp, and Samir Jahjah. 2003. *Are Immigrant Remittances Flows a Source of Capital for Development?* Working Paper 03/189. IMF Working Paper. Washington, DC: International Monetary Fund.

Clemens, Michael A. and David J. McKenzie. 2014. "Why Don't Remittances Appear to Affect Growth?" https://papers.ssrn.com/sol3/papers.cfm?abstract_id=2457194.

Cortina, Jerónimo, Rodolfo de la Garza, and Enrique Ochoa-Reza. 2005. "Remesas: límites Al Optimismo." *Foreign Affairs En Español* 5, no. 3: 27–36.

Delgado Wise, Raúl and Humberto Márquez Covarrubias. 2008. "Capitalist Restructuring, Development and Labour Migration: The Mexico-US Case." *Third World Quarterly* 29, no. 7: 1359–1374.

Doyle, David. 2015. "Remittances and Social Spending." *American Political Science Review* 109, no. 4: 785–802.

Duquette-Rury, Lauren. 2014. "Collective Remittances and Transnational Coproduction: The 3 × 1 Program for Migrants and Household Access to Public Goods in Mexico." *Studies in Comparative International Development* 49, no. 1: 112–139.

Durand, Jorge, Emilio A. Parrado, and Douglas S. Massey. 1996. "Migradollars and Development: A Reconsideration of the Mexican Case." *International Migration Review* 30, no. 2: 423–444.

Escribà-Folch, Abel, Covadonga Meseguer, and Joseph Wright. 2015. "Remittances and Democratization." *International Studies Quarterly* 59, no. 3: 571–586.

Garcia Zamora, Rodolfo. 2017. *El Retorno de Los Migrantes Mexicanos de Estados Unidos a Michoacán, Oaxaca, Zacatecas, Puebla, Guerrero y Chiapas 2000–2012*. Zacatecas, Michoacán: Miguel Ángel Porrúa.

Haas, Hein de. 2010. "Migration and Development: A Theoretical Perspective." *International Migration Review* 44, no. 1: 227–264.

Hanson, Gordon H. and Christopher Woodruff. 2003. "Emigration and Educational Attainment in Mexico." www.childmigration.net/files/Hanson_2003.pdf.

Herrera, Gioconda. 2005. "Mujeres ecuatorianas en las cadenas globales del cuidado." In *La migracuón ecuatoriana. Transnacionalism, redes e identidades*, eds. Gioconda Herrera, Maria Christina Carrillo, and Alicia Torres, 281–304. Quito: FLACSO.

Hochschild, Arlie Russel. 2000. "Global Care Chains and Emotional Surplus Value." In *On the Edge: Living with Global Capitalism*, eds. Anthony Giddens and Will Hutton, 130–146. London: Jonathan Cape.

Kapur, Dev. 2004. "Remittances: The New Development Mantra?" United Nations Conference on Trade and Development, G-24 Discussion Papers.

Levitt, Peggy. 1998. "Social Remittances: Migration Driven Local-Level Forms of Cultural Diffusion." *International Migration Review* 32, no. 4: 926–948.

Meseguer, Covadonga and Francisco Javier Aparicio. 2012. "Supply or Demand? Migration and Political Manipulation in Mexico." *Studies in Comparative International Development* 47, no. 4: 411–440.

Pfutze, Tobias. 2012. "Does Migration Promote Democratization? Evidence from the Mexican Transition." *Journal of Comparative Economics* 40, no. 2: 159–175.

Ratha, Dilip, Christian Eigen-Zucchi, and Sonia Plaza. 2016. *Migration and Remittances Factbook 2016: Third Edition*. Washington, DC: World Bank Publications.

Simpser, Alberto, Lauren Duquette-Rury, José Antonio Hernández Company, and Juan Fernando Ibarra. 2016. "The Political Economy of Social Spending by Local Government: A Study of the 3×1 Program in Mexico." *Latin American Research Review* 51, no. 1: 62–83. 10.1353/lar.2016.0013.

Singer, David Andrew. 2010. "Migrant Remittances and Exchange Rate Regimes in the Developing World." *American Political Science Review* 104: 307–323.

Stark, Oded and David Bloom. 1985. "The New Economics of Labor Migration." *The American Economic Review* 75, no. 2: 173–178.

Tyburski, Michael D. 2012. "The Resource Curse Reversed? Remittances and Corruption in Mexico1: The Resource Curse Reversed?" *International Studies Quarterly* 56, no. 2: 339–350.

Woodruff, Christopher and Rene Zenteno. 2007. "Migration Networks and Microenterprises in Mexico." *Journal of Development Economics* 82, no. 2: 509–528.

20
SOCIAL INEQUALITY

Olaf Kaltmeier and Martin Breuer

The Americas are considered one of the most socially unjust regions in the world. This can be seen in a comparative view of the Gini coefficient of income and wealth distribution. The Gini coefficient is a statistically determined value that measures unequal distributions between extreme values of 0 and 1. In terms of income or wealth distribution, a value of 0 means that the wealth or income in a given unit (here mostly: nation-states) is evenly distributed among all citizens, while a value of 1 means that all wealth/income is concentrated in the hands of a single person. In the 1990s, the Gini coefficient of income distribution in Latin America was 0.522 and 0.477 in the U.S., while it was 0.342 in Western Europe and 0.412 in Asia. Only on the global level is this distribution even more unequal.

This inequality was highlighted by the grassroots movement Occupy Wall Street and the non-governmental organization (NGO) OXFAM pointing out the unequal distribution and accumulation of wealth of the top one percent of the richest people. Since 2015, the richest one percent of the world's population has more wealth than the other 99 percent. Translating these bare numbers to real people, it can be said that the richest eight men (gender is also meaningful) have as much wealth as the 3.6 billion people, or half of the world's population account (Oxfam International 2017). In this context, especially entrepreneurs from the IT sector score high in the billionaire rankings worldwide, including U.S.-American billionaires Bill Gates (Microsoft), Jeffrey Preston Bezos (Amazon), Mark Zuckerberg (Facebook), Travis Kalanick (Uber), and Brian Chesky (Airbnb). At the same time, financial speculation in particular has promoted extreme wealth, think of the U.S. investor George Soros. Large conglomerates have also contributed to hyper-wealth as in the case of Carlos Slim in Mexico, who, according to Forbes, was the richest man in the world in 2007, 2010, and 2011.

In the Americas, the issue of social inequality was and is at the center of political debate whereby both vertical inequalities regarding the distribution of income and wealth as well as horizontal inequalities regarding the discrimination and marginalization of specific ethnic, religious, or other social groups are thematized (→ Intersectionality, I/32). The societal acceptation of social inequality is based on the underlying normative system. In the U.S., the foundational narrative from "rag to riches" is a key element of the self-perception of the U.S. as a land of opportunities, where failure (and thus poverty) is often attributed to the individual shortcomings and not to social structures.

Hereby, questions regarding the social justification and historical explanation of inequalities are at stake: What degree of inequality is considered as socially just and economically purposeful? What degree of social mobility, access, and opportunity is necessary and how should society, economy and states regulate social inequalities? Beyond these normative aspects, the analysis and interpretation of social inequality is intrinsically related to questions of social structure and of class analysis. In Latin America – due to the influence of Dependency Theory (→ Development, II/6) – Marxist conceptions of class that are related to ideas of class struggle (→ II/3) are still often used, whereas in North America, descriptive (post-) Weberian class concepts dominate.

In social theory the exclusive use of income as an indicator for social inequality has been criticized as too narrow. Newer research also focuses on non-monetary forms of capital such as cultural or social capital (Bourdieu). Another more complex measurement is the Human Development Index (HDI) of the United Nations that includes access to social services of defined social groups, often national populations, and thus can be used as an indicator of social welfare, which includes factors such as education (→ I/24), health (→ I/29), life expectancy, and per capita income.

In regard to social inequality this index is of particular interest, as it makes the living standard of defined social groups, usually nation-states (→ I/38), comparable. In the Americas, there is a striking North-South divide with regard to human development: In the first half of the 1990s, the U.S. was considered to be the second-highest ranked country in terms of human development. In the following years, its ranking dropped dramatically hovering between rankings of 40 and 30. In 2018, Canada (0.926) and the USA (0.924) were ranked 12th and 13th on a global scale, while the Latin American countries of the Southern Cone ranked 44th (Chile, 0.843), 47th (Argentina, 0.825), and 55th (Uruguay, 0.804). Socialist Cuba (0.777) occupies a remarkable 73rd place, while the countries of the Andean region are located in the middle rankings and Central America – with the exception of Costa Rica (0.794) – can be found in the bottom third of the rankings of 189 countries (United Nations Development Program 2018).

However, when reading this data, it is important to not perceive national territories as homogenous regarding the level and structures of social inequalities. On the contrary, there are immense regional disparities inside particular nation-states (→ I/39): while the HDI of Vitacura, the rich neighborhood of Santiago de Chile, corresponds to that of Japan or the Netherlands, the index of rural areas with a high proportion of Mapuche population corresponds to the HDI of Botswana or Mongolia. Within the U.S., there is also a remarkable North-South divide in the sense that the ex-slave-holder states have a significantly lower HDI, for example Mississippi with 0.866 – a similar rate to Uruguay.

These statistical findings hint to the importance of intersectional analysis (→ Intersectionality, I/32) that includes aspects such as race (→ I/39), ethnicity (→ I/25), gender (→ Gender Identities, I/28), disability and age, which allows for tackling the interconnectedness of vertical and horizontal inequalities. In Bolivia, for example, 74 percent of the indigenous population were considered poor at the end of the 20th century, with Ecuador at 87 percent and in Peru 62.8 percent (→ Indigeneity, I/31), while the same measurements for the respective white and mestizo population are significantly lower.

The political question of overcoming injustices as well as generating more social cohesion arises, in particular, in the empirical assessment and historical dimensions of social inequality. From a liberal perspective, the main focus was on modernization (→ I/35) and development (→ II/6). Simplified, this theory maintains that more development helps to overcome poverty. This idea is ultimately reflected in the Millennium Development Goals (MDG), which aimed to halve global poverty by 2015. However, this approach focuses more on poverty reduction and access to political participation than to questions of wealth and income redistribution.

Structuralist approaches have suggested that in order to revert extreme social inequality, the state must promote policies that prioritize income and land redistribution as a means of transforming existing social structures. This dimension of redistribution is, in a sense, inherent in the concept of social inequality insofar as it is a relational concept that, for example, always considers poverty in relation to wealth. As such, this position promotes policies that attempt to improve social mobility, reduce income inequalities, and regulate the inheritance of wealth.

Another approach to overcome social inequality is addressing the issue of recognition. In the multicultural policies of the 1990s, group rights – especially those of the most disadvantaged indigenous and Afro-American groups – were recognized and efforts to reduce their discrimination were undertaken via policies that promoted affirmative action (→ Multiculturalism, I/36). Although socioeconomic differentiation has begun in these groups, it remains questionable whether a limited recognition policy like affirmative action can overcome structural relationships of social inequality. However, in this context the question of special – often collective (→ Commons, II/31) – land rights of indigenous peoples is of high importance, as it guarantees their access to and ownership of land (→ II/15), especially when it comes to natural resources of this land like water, minerals, and hydrocarbons.

In addition, social inequalities are closely related to opportunities for social participation and the development of individual abilities. This aspect has been recently highlighted by scholars such as Joseph Stieglitz, Thomas Piketty, and Amartya Sen vis-à-vis the growing inequality in the U.S. The condition of the democratic system also depends on the degree of social cohesion (→ Democracy, II/32) and the possibility (and level) of political participation (→ II/41), moving beyond the formal guarantee of universal suffrage.

Dealing with social inequality means examining class relations and the social structures in society which are deeply rooted in history and shaped by the inner logic of the capitalist accumulation process. The deep colonial structure of American societies has especially marked the historical development of social inequalities in the hemisphere (→ Postcolonialism, I/38). This legacy, for example, has created a concentration of land ownership that has by far the highest rate worldwide. In the 1990s, the Gini coefficient for land ownership was 0.81 in Latin America, and 0.72 for the U.S. (Davies, Shorrocks, Sandstrom and Wolff 2007, 13). Within these areas, the most unequal societies in terms of the distribution of agricultural land are Colombia followed by Chile, Brazil, and Paraguay.

Economic development and social inequality: from late 19th century to the Great Depression

During the late 19th and early 20th centuries, the rapid industrialization in the U.S. as well as the integration of Latin American economies into the capitalist world market were decisive in the restructuring of social and economic relations in American societies, which in turn impacted the shaping of social inequalities throughout the region. The accelerating accumulation process and the shifting economic conjunctures, as well as the booms and busts of different economic sectors inserted an increased social mobility both up- and downwards for ever larger segments of the populations. This transformation partially reconfigured the social structures that had been inherited from colonial times and also altered social realities in the peripheral regions, where different forms of semi-servile and servile labor, as well as forms of debt bondage, continued to exist (→ Unfree Labor, I/19). However, the long-lasting colonial structures and the deeply embedded racial and ethnic hierarchies continued to determine the social positions and opportunities of people throughout the Americas (→ Ethnicity, I/25; Race, I/39; Gender Identities, I/28).

In Latin America, the Caribbean, and the Southern U.S., the extreme inequality of land distribution is rooted in the hacienda and plantation system (→ Colonial Economies, I/4). The huge hacienda estates of the Andean countries and the Southern Cone and the plantation system of Brazil and the Caribbean, formerly based on slave labor (→ Slavery, I/18), stayed intact far into the 20th century, cementing an extremely unequal distribution of land in the region. In the northern U.S. and Canada, land was more equally distributed between the white population due to the history of settler colonialism, where indigenous peoples were driven from their lands. In sum, the social structures throughout the Western Hemisphere around 1900 were deeply shaped by horizontal inequalities resulting from colonial heritage.

Furthermore, in the 19th century both parts of the hemisphere, although in a very heterogeneous pattern of regional distribution, received a huge migration influx from Europe as well as from Asia (→ Migration, I/15). The incoming migrants were seeking a better life in the Americas, escaping poverty in their home countries. Their arrival altered the social structures of the receiving societies profoundly and permanently. At the same time the last independent indigenous peoples of the Americas were militarily defeated, expropriated, their people killed or forced into reservations in the Southern Cone and the U.S. (→ Indigenous Peoples, I/11). In other South and Central American countries, indigenous peoples were displaced into less accessible regions of the different nation-states. Comparable data regarding income and property inequality or land distribution around 1900 is rare throughout the Americas. Furthermore, the regional differences between the nation-states as well as within the particular countries were huge.

In Latin America, a new dynamic was created when the creole elites implemented the so-called import-export system producing cash crops for the growing world market like coffee (Mexico, Brazil, Colombia, El Salvador, Guatemala), sugar (Caribbean, Brazil), rubber (Peru, Brazil and Colombia), cacao (Ecuador), bananas (Costa Rica, Honduras, Guatemala, Ecuador, Colombia), as well as wool (Peru), wheat (Chile), and meat (Argentina) (Topik and Marichal 2006) (→ Global Commodity Chains, II/12; Extractivism, II/9).

This agricultural expansion was connected to processes of land grabbing, where indigenous and mestizo subsistence and small holder communities were driven from their lands. The often violent restructuring of the agrarian sector was followed by a process of the proletarization of the rural population. Additionally, the increase in mining activities, especially in the Andes (tin in Bolivia, copper and potassium nitrate in Chile), as well as the beginning of the oil economy in Venezuela (→ Energy, II/7) led to a growing demand for labor (→ Extractivism, II/9). This demand in most Latin American countries was partially satisfied by immigration from Europe and Asia during this period, the latter also in the context of the coolie trade, where contract workers from Asia worked under fierce conditions on the plantations in Peru and Cuba and the railroad construction sites (→ Unfree Labor, I/19). However, disintegrating indigenous and mestizo rural communities also served as a "reserve army" for rural and urban labor markets.

Although Latin America remained predominately rural, urbanization began in in the first decades of the 20th century including the emergence of a urban working class; these new proletarians were mostly employed in the transport and construction sectors of the export economy (Hall and Spalding 1986). But the economic boom did not lead to more social equality, instead there was an increase in inequality in the whole region (Thorp 2012, 16).

In the United States, as well as in Canada, however, social transformation in the decades around the early 1900s differed in many aspects from the southern parts of the hemisphere, with crucial consequences for the shaping of social inequalities. The closure of the inner frontier and the expansion of middle-sized farms throughout the country led to a more equal distribution of land. At the same time this expansion meant the final subjugation and expropriation of the indigenous peoples across North America, who were driven from their ancestral lands and forced onto reservations. Additionally, rapid industrialization process took off, especially during the first decades after the Civil War, making the U.S. the world's largest economy by around 1880.

Mark Twain coined the term the Gilded Age for the last decades of the 19th century pointing, on the one hand, to the rising wealth in society and, on the other, to the harsh living conditions and poverty of a large proportion of the population behind the shining facade. Between 1880 and 1930, a financial and industrial elite emerged in the U.S., including the rise of the famous business tycoons of U.S.-American history, such as Rockefeller and Vanderbilt, who built huge enterprises and accumulated enormous wealth. On the other end of the social strata, a modern working class emerged, employed by the fast-growing manufacturing facilities, transport sector and construction sites. Immigration from Europe and Asia skyrocketed during the decades around 1900 (→ Migration, I/15), and with the end of slavery (→ I/18) in the Civil War, people of African descent began migrating from the Southern States to the industrial centers of the North. All this led to the making of a U.S.-American working class, which was divided by ethnic and racial differences.

There is hardly any comparable data on social inequality during the Gilded Age, as the national income tax system was not put in place until 1913 (→ Taxation, II/22). For 1913, when the first national income tax system was installed, Piketty and Saez estimate that one percent of the population received about 18 percent of the total income (2003, 12). Just between 1910 and 1929, the proportion of income of the richest tenth rose from 33.9 percent to 39 percent, whereas the share of the poorest tenth fell from 3.4 percent to 1.8 percent, within the same time span (Kolko 1969, 22).

During the Progressive Era, in the first decade of the 20th century, federal governments tried to limit the economic and political influence of the economic elites. Furthermore, for a short period, the rising tax rate during the First World War, stemmed the growth of social inequality in the U.S. However, by 1929 the Gini coefficient regarding income distribution had reached 0.48 (Atkinson, Hasell, Morelli and Roser 2017, 57), making this period one of the highest in social inequality in U.S. history. On the other hand, the first decades of the 20th century represent the advent of the era of accelerated urbanization (→ I/45) and mass consumption in the U.S. (→ Consumerism, I/23), where unprecedented technological progress improved the living standards of the poorer layers of society, even if they became poorer in relative terms.

For liberal thought, the social position of an individual was primarily related to her or his personal abilities rather than one's position of social standing inherited by birth. Based on the protestant work ethic and an individualistic interpretation of freedom, the idea of individual social upward mobility restricted the implementation of state social security programs in the U.S. In this light, the social marginalization of the Afro-American population and Chicanos was often interpreted through a racist discourse connecting it to a supposed racial inferiority of ethnic minorities rather than explaining it as the outcome of colonial history.

In Latin America, the Mexican Revolution (1910–1920) was the most important and successful attempt to alter the social order from below (→ Revolution, II/44). Under the slogan "Tierra y Libertad," poor peasants, many of them indigenous, fought for access to land, resulting in the indigenous question being put back on the political agenda with ripples felt in other parts of Latin America. In Mexico and the Andean countries, the discourse of Indigenismo advocated for a national integration of the indigenous population, aiming to overcome horizontal group inequalities (→ Indigeneity, I/31). In 1928, Peruvian Marxist, José Carlos Mariátegui, published his famous *Siete ensayos de interpretación de la realidad peruana* which reflected on the social structure and inequality emphasizing the social marginalization of the indigenous peoples. His work is one of the most important Latin American contributions to Marxist theory, postulating the indigenous population to be the revolutionary subject struggling to overcome injustice and exploitation (→ Class Struggle, II/3).

These intellectual reflections on social inequality were always bound back to social realities and around 1900, the countryside, especially, became the key place for subaltern struggles for social justice in the Americas. During this historical period social inequalities rose and the social structure was further differentiated as a modern urban working class emerged. Even though the quest for social justice was at the base of manifold subaltern struggles of the time, the concentration of wealth in the hands of small groups of elites reached a peak throughout the hemisphere in the 1920s.

Leveling social inequality? - industrialization processes and new deals

The world economic crisis (→ II/4) of the 1930s set in a new conjuncture of shaping social inequalities in the Americas lasting until the 1970s. The Wall Street Crash of 1929 and the economic decline in the U.S. led to vast economic repercussions worldwide, and Latin America was especially affected. Economies in the southern part of the hemisphere had become successively more dependent on their northern neighbor regarding capital imports and the export of commodities during previous decades. Thus, the decline of the U.S. economy put an end to the Latin American export boom. Unemployment in the urban centers throughout the hemisphere became endemic during the 1930s. This long-lasting economic crisis pushed the political critique of the economic model of laissez faire capitalism, as well as the exorbitant social inequalities the model had created, with far-reaching repercussions in the economic theory and political practice of the time.

As such, the 1930s marked a change in macro-economic policies across the Americas. From the 1930s onwards, for nearly four decades, nation-states began taking a more prominent role in the regulation of markets, promoting public investments and welfare programs and implementing redistribution policies, especially regarding the taxation of income and property (→ Nation State, II/38). Programs like Fordism (→ II/10), a term initially coined by the Italian Marxist thinker Antonio Gramsci after the U.S.-American industrialist Henry Ford, allowed a social state to politically regulate mass-production in Taylorist fabrication processes as well as mass-consumption markets (→ Consumerism, I/23).

In the U.S., this transformation is linked to the New Deal policy of the Roosevelt administration, which paved the way for far-reaching social policy programs and the progressive taxation (→ II/22) of higher incomes. In Latin America, many states applied the strategy of Import Substitution Industrialization (ISI) aiming to overcome structural dependency to the capitalist centers and develop a fully-fledged industrial economy and society – the rise of the "developmental" state. Both political models were at the basis of the Golden Age of Capitalism, as Hobsbawm termed it, in the Americas, which included historically high growth rates and the rise of the middle classes. However, Latin America and the U.S. followed different patterns, regarding the restructuring of social inequalities.

In Latin America, the larger national economies of Argentina, Brazil, Mexico and Colombia began implementing the ISI model in the 1930s, while Central American countries and other Andean nations tended to endorse the ISI strategy later in the 1960s (→ Development, II/6). With the industrialization efforts, the urban working classes also grew in size, as formal labor relations expanded. Already in the 1960s in much of Latin American, more people were employed in industrial production and services than in agriculture. While the majority of the new jobs were created in the formal sector, the proportion of informal workers in the cities in relative terms "shrank, slowly but steadily, during the period of import substitution industrialization" (Portes and Hoffman 2003, 50). Thus, between 1960 and 1980, the industrial working class reached its highest percentage of the population as well as political importance. In a parallel manner, there was an expansion of the middle class due to the growing state bureaucracy and an emerging managerial class. Nonetheless, as Latin American population growth was high at this time, the economic growth rates and the newly created formal employment relations were not sufficient to integrate the fast-growing labor force into the formal labor market. The informal urban proletariat grew in real terms and the rising slums around the big Latin American cities were a notorious sign of this (→ Informality, II/13).

In rural areas, the extreme inequality of landownership was at the center of political, academic and public debate. Even though in many countries, labor and agrarian reforms ended the semi-feudal labor relations that had existed up until the early years of the century, redistribution of land in most cases was rather insignificant. Thus, the Latin-American agrarian reforms of the 1960s and 1970s did not bring about a fundamental redistribution of land (→ II/15), but rather, a modernization of the agricultural structure in existing conditions of inequality. Exceptions are the agrarian reforms in the context of revolutionary processes such as in Mexico 1911, Bolivia 1952, Cuba 1959, Peru after 1968 and later in Chile under Allende in 1972.

Concerning the upper layers of society, the traditional oligarchies in commerce and landed property – the so-called *comprador bourgeoisie* – lost importance while a new state bound middle class emerged, which found employment in the growing public sector and also in the management of the transnational corporations (→ II/23) who had extended their activities across much of Latin America. There is no reliable data for the mid-20th century regarding income distribution, as country statistics in most Latin American countries only began during the 1970s, however recent research estimates that income inequality in Latin America increased between the 1920s and 1970s (Williamson 2015, 338). This means that the region did not experience the leveling of income inequality which the U.S. and Western Europe witnessed during this period. In the 1970s, the estimated aggregate Gini of Latin America and the Caribbean was at 0.48 (De Feranti 2004, 55). Even though social structures were profoundly transformed during the ISI period, especially due to rapid urbanization (→ I/45), the emerging working class, a growing middle class employed in the new state bureaucracy, and also the beginning insertion of women into the labor market (→ Gender and Work, II/11), inequality levels stayed stable or even increased.

In the U.S., the breakdown of the economy reduced the total income, causing the impoverishment of the lower layers of the income strata. The Roosevelt administration tried to respond to the social, economic, and political implications of the crisis with the New Deal policy, introducing minimal wages and advancing state investments. However, the results were modest, and unemployment remained high during the 1930s. The crisis was finally overcome with the expansion of industrial production in the context of the buildup of the Allied military force and the entry of the U.S. into the Second World War in 1941. This set the start for a long-lasting boom of industrial production, which only dampened in the 1970s (Junker 2004, 133–138). Especially, during wartime, women – as well as Chicanos – were included into the formal labor market (→ Latinidad, I/33).

By 1947, the Gini income coefficient was at 0.38 points according to the Federal Reserve Bank of St. Louis (FRED 2019), which indicates that income after WWII was more equally distributed compared to 1929, the year before the Wall Street Crash, where the Gini coefficient was at 0.48. This trend in equal distribution of income in the U.S. endured until 1968, when the Gini coefficient reached its 20th century low at 0.35. Thus, the postwar years represent the period in U.S.-American history with the lowest historical level of income inequality. During the 1950s, the new middle class emerged in the U.S. and real income wages increased by 80 percent (Berg 2004, 154). However, this relative increase of social equality regarding income distribution and the rising living standards of large shares of the population did not lead to an end of the social and economic discrimination of Black and Latino people as well as immigrant communities throughout the U.S. Social inequality in the U.S. maintained its ethnic and racial dimension.

In the 1960s, President Johnsons declared the "War on Poverty" in the context of his Great Society program, expanding the welfare state with housing programs and monetary help for people living in poverty, aiming especially at the poor Black urban population. Between 1960 and 1970, the percentage of people living under the poverty line was reduced from 22.4 percent to 12.6 percent, while within the Afro-American population the poverty rate declined from 55.1 to 31 percent (Berg 2004, 167). However, these statistics have to be treated with care, as the measurement of the "poverty line" especially in regard to the growing median income level changed over time. While in 1959 the poverty line was at 59 percent of the median income, in 1980, only people with less than 35 percent of the median income were considered poor (Balzer et al. 2013, 123). During the 1970s, poverty rates slowly declined further while income inequality started to increase slightly again. By the 1980s, deindustrialization (→ II/5) and neoliberal restructuring as well as the cutting of social welfare programs put an end to this development (→ State Transformation, II/21).

The transformation of social structures and the issue of social inequality was at the center of scholarly reflection throughout the Americas during the mid-20th century. Economics as an academic discipline became of paramount importance for political thought and practice in the context of the Cold War and systemic competition. At this time, the dominant approaches of Keynesianism in the U.S. and its Latin American variant of Structuralism proposed a demand-oriented economic policy. Mass consumption and rising living standards of the majority of people were considered a first condition for economic growth and systemic stability (→ Consumerism, I/23) and the state was seen as the key agent to manage this development process, actively intervening with public investment and redistribution policies in the economy (→ Development, II/6).

With the expansion of the state apparatus and the university system across the hemisphere, economic research into social inequality increased consistently, especially alongside the questions of income, property and land distribution. Poverty was discussed internationally not only as a social or political problem but also as an obstacle to economic growth. The question of how to overcome poverty in the Americas became an issue of Inter-American entanglement, as U.S. area studies programs and development cooperation provided expertise and funding to Latin American countries, exporting ideas on how to "reform" the societies of the southern neighbors (→ Modernization, I/35).

This was bound back and embedded in the political struggles of the time. Throughout the western hemisphere, the period between the Great Depression and the 1970s was the heyday of the labor movement (→ Labor Representation, II/14), struggling for better wages and better working and living conditions. In the U.S., after the Second World War, labor union membership reached its highest historical level (around one third of the working population was organized in trade unions) and even in the 1970s, it came to about one fourth (Stepan-Norris and Southworth 2010, 235). During these years, U.S.-American unions achieved a considerable increase in wages and better working conditions. However, the question of horizontal inequalities was raised by the Civil Rights Movement in the U.S. (→ Social Movements, I/41), which set out to overcome the social, political, and economic discrimination of Black people.

In Latin America, the level of union membership also rose in the decades after WWII (→ Labor Representation, II/14). Nonetheless, the industrial proletariat when compared to the U.S. remained much smaller, with few exceptions such as Argentina. Instead the composition of the working class was marked by the informal urban proletariat (→ Informality, II/13). The political consciousness of the informal proletariat was formed more in *barrio* movements then in labor unions, the social struggles in the neighborhoods aimed to guarantee the access to water or electricity and were directed to urban bureaucracies rather the employers.

In the sphere of politics, revolutionary movements throughout the hemisphere advocated for socialism (→ I/42) demanding to end social injustice, to overcome inequalities and all forms of exploitation. In Cuba, the means of production and land was nationalized after the Revolution of 1959, completely transforming the social structure and distribution of wealth and income in the country. The Cuban Revolution, on the one hand, provided a blueprint to follow for the Latin American radical political left (→ Revolution, II/44). On the other hand, for the liberal political and economic elites in the Americas, Cuba served as the negative example, which had to either be eliminated completely or at the very least, contained to the Caribbean island by any means.

Against this background, different governments in the hemisphere tried to push forth reform-oriented policies as a means of pacifying social conflict. In the case of the U.S., the control and pacification of social struggles in Latin America also became a central goal of foreign policy, relying on development cooperation (e.g. the Alliance for Progress) as well as the backing of right-wing military dictatorships (→ Authoritarianism, II/25; Military, II/37).

During the phase of ISI, many Latin American governments intended to pacify class struggles through the inclusion of the working class into a corporatist state system. This tendency of "co-government" of labor unions and governments can be illustrated by Bolivia after the Revolution of 1952, in the "perfect dictatorship" of the PRI (Partido Revolucionario Institucional) Government in Mexico, and in Argentina's Peronismo. Populism (→ II/43) was used as a class-integrating mechanism, applying anti-imperialism, and nationalism as a unifying ideology.

From the 1950s to the 1970s, Latin American governments also tried to implement agrarian and tax reforms (→ Land, II/15; Taxation, II/22). Both types of reform projects were meant to implement distribution policies which could assist the nation-states to more effectively manage social inequality and social struggles, relying on U.S. support for these reforms. However, Latin American economic elites managed to successfully undermine or evade these reform projects and maintain their privileges (Thorp 2012, 160). In the U.S. during this time, the tax system especially, served to reduce inequality. Tax rates for incomes over US$400,000 per family were at 91 percent in 1950 and at 77 percent in 1964 (Tax Foundation n.d.), figures which nowadays seem out of reach even for social democratic political programs.

The neoliberal turn and rising inequalities

With the cooling down of the world economy in the 1970s and the advent of neoliberal macro-economic policies in the U.S. and Latin American countries during the 1980s, the tendency of slowly declining social inequalities in the hemisphere was reversed (→ Neoliberalism, II/16). The decades leading up to the new millennium saw an increase in social inequalities. This period also witnessed a profound transformation of political and economic thought regarding social inequality in the Americas. Neoclassical economics replaced Keynesianism and Latin American Structuralism as the hegemonic economic theory, rejecting state interventions and welfare programs as counterproductive to economic growth. The free play of market forces was seen as most efficient in creating a just society through the "trickle-down" effect, with far-reaching consequences for state economic policies and thus social inequalities. Cuts in company and high-income-earning individual tax rates as well as fiscal austerity and supply-side economic policies reinforced the concentration of income and wealth in the hands of the upper layers of society.

In Latin America, the 1970s witnessed the spread of right-wing military dictatorships (→ Authoritarianism, II/25). In Argentina (1976–1983), Brazil (1964–1985), Chile (1973–1990) and many other countries of the southern part of the hemisphere, right-wing military governments violently repressed the labor movement and the political left (→ Military, II/37), and their demands for the redistribution of property. Thus, military dictatorships defended the interests of the economic elites and prevented further redistributive policies. The transformation of the Chilean society and economy under the military dictatorship (1973–1990) is the emblematic example of non-democratic neoliberal restructuring. Countries such as Argentina, Peru, and Colombia were also subject to far-reaching structural adjustment programs (→ State Transformation, II/21).

With the Latin American debt crisis from 1981 onwards, harsh stabilization and adjustment programs (referred to as structural conditionalities) were implemented in many countries of the southern part of the hemisphere in reaction to the crisis (→ II/4): the privatization of public companies, the deregulation of the economy, processes of deindustrialization and new forms of production and labor management (via outsourcing) that led to a disintegration of the formal working class. Portes and Hoffman (2003) have shown how the number of workers in the public sectors of Latin American countries declined consistently from the 1980s on. Furthermore, the formal proletariat has been shrinking, while at the same time the class of petty entrepreneurs and informal workers have grown. In the 1970s the average Gini coefficient of income distribution for Latin America was at 0.484, while in the 1980s it rose to 0.508, and during the 1990s reached 0.522 (De Ferranti et al. 2004, 55).

Since the 1980s, deindustrialization (→ II/5) has set in in the United States and Canada. New jobs have been created, especially in the service sector, and unionization has decreased since the 1970s. The social structure of the U.S. has also been altered by migration, especially from Latin American countries but also from other continents (→ Transnational Migration, I/44). In general, population has grown rapidly during these years.

Regarding the distribution of income, in 1970 the Gini coefficient was at 0.353, but in 1990 it increased to 0.396, and in 2000 it increased again to 0.433 (FRED 2019). In the southern parts of the U.S., inequality was even higher than in the north. The neoliberal policies have especially favored income from capital, while at the same time deindustrialization, decreasing trade union coverage, and the fast-growing working population has debilitated the bargaining position of the workers.

Regarding the academic and public reflection on social inequalities, the last decades of the 20th century brought with them a rupture with the ideas of the previous decades. Against the backdrop of the economic crisis of the 1970s, corporatist ideas of Fordism (→ II/10), and a necessary level of social equity and cohesion guaranteed by the state, lost influence. Neoclassical economists, such as Milton Friedman, argued that the welfare programs, e.g. of the Johnson administration in the U.S., had been inefficient, slowing down economic growth and thus counterproductive to poverty reduction in the first place. Instead of transfers and economic redistribution, the focus of the discussion moved to education (→ I/24) and equality of opportunity. One example in this context is the focus of the *Economic Commission for Latin America and the Caribbean* (ECLAC) on the idea of *equidad*, in the sense of equity of opportunity, instead of economic and social equality (Ocampo 2000). Group inequalities – in the context of Multiculturalism (→ I/36) – were especially highlighted and arguing that members of marginalized ethnic minorities should have as many opportunities for personal careers as members of the white middle classes (→ Whiteness, I/46).

On the one hand, multiculturalism, claiming the cultural diversity of society and emphasizing the value of marginal groups and non-hegemonic culture, can be seen as a reaction to the far-reaching ethnic and racial inequalities in the Americas. On the other hand, multiculturalism had its heyday during decades in which income and wealth inequality increased, without consistently improving the relative economic position of the ethnic minorities. This was to a certain point also the case in Latin America. However, in Latin America from the 1980s on indigenous movements emerged in various countries, which not only fought for cultural recognition but also for political participation and especially land rights (→ Indigeneity, I/31; Social Movements, I/41).

Since the 1980s, development cooperation in international politics has concentrated more on individual factors of development (→ II/6) and civil society (→ II/28) than on strengthening state administration and infrastructure. The HDI has represented this turn to "human development," which is aimed at capacity building in poor sectors of Latin American countries enabling people to escape poverty through personal initiative and reclaiming their individual human rights (→ II/35). In general, sums for development cooperation in Latin America decreased during the Washington Consensus years, while international institutions such as the World Bank and the International Monetary Fund emphasized the importance of private capital investment for poverty reduction combined with the fiscal austerity of governments.

While in the U.S. and Canada economic growth rates were high during the 1990s, this did not lead to a decrease in economic inequalities. On the contrary the neoliberal restructuring of state policies and the deindustrialization and digitalization led to a growing class divide in society. In most Latin American countries, in general the last two decades of the 20th century was a time of economic recession. Neoliberal adjustment programs did not lead to an economic upturn after the failure of the ISI model. Especially for the working classes in Latin America, the 1980s and 1990s were marked by decreasing real incomes and declining living standards. The disillusion with the results of neoliberal adjustment at the end of the century created the basis for new political approaches to inequality in the new millennium.

Great recession, pink tide, and social polarization

At the beginning of the 21st century, almost all Latin American countries faced an astonishing boom of leftist governments advocating a renunciation of neoliberal economic policies (→ Neoliberalism, II/16). The climax of this boom, the so-called "Pink Tide," was in the mid-2000s with the governments of Hugo Chávez in Venezuela, Ignacio "Lula" da Silva in Brazil, Rafael Correa in Ecuador, Néstor Kirchner in Argentina, and Evo Morales in Bolivia (→ Socialism, I/42). With these governments, there was a more active social policy, which was particularly successful in the fight against poverty especially through indirect cash transfer social welfare programs such as "Bolsa Família" in Brazil. In the context of a favorable economic cycle with high economic growth rates, left-wing governments were able to increase social spending and legislate higher minimum wages. This resulted in a significant upward mobility in the middle class, while the poorer sections of the population benefited from special support measures. The Gini coefficient regarding income inequality in Latin America fell from 0.53 in 1995 to 0.48 in 2015 (Messina and Silva 2018, 12). Even in Chile – due to the continuity of neoliberal economic policies, a rather moderate representative of the "Pink Tide" – social policy programs were applied under the government of Michelle Bachelet that managed to decrease poverty rates to 7.8 percent in 2013 (Larrañaga and Rodríguez 2015, 17).

The U.S. instead was hit hard by the financial crisis of 2007–8 and the following Great Recession, and especially people from the middle and lower classes were affected by the crash of the housing bubble (known as the Subprime crisis), increasing the number of homeless people. In reaction, the Obama administration introduced state-run programs to revitalize the economy (American Recovery and Reinvestment Act and Labor Day) and to reduce unemployment. The federal government also tried to improve the human development of lower and middle classes by the introduction of public system of health-insurance, which became known as Obamacare.

Despite all the successes, the sustainability of the socio-political support programs of the left-wing governments still awaits the verdict of history. It is becoming apparent that the reduction of social inequality is based on the reduction of poverty numbers and this could be achieved by the left-wing governments to a large extent only on the basis of state subsidy and cash transfer programs. However, there has been few significant measures for the social redistribution of wealth. In many cases, the state programs have been financed in the course of the so-called neo-extractivism by revenues that resulted from the increased export of raw materials – from oil to soy to palm oil (→ Extractivism, II/9). Since the price erosion of commodities around the 2010s and the resulting economic crisis (→ II/4), entire segments of society which had seen their fortunes rise in recent decades, appear to be falling back into the lower classes.

Paradoxically, the number of billionaires has grown in this same period of the left-wing governments massively and the top 10 percent have hardly been affected by social decline after the commodity boom. Especially in the last two decades, the number of billionaires has increased significantly. From 2008 to 2016, an increase in the super-rich (or technocratic: high-net-worth individuals – HNWI) in Latin America has risen from just under 420 to nearly 560 (Capgemini 2017). In North America there is a HNWI-population of 5.7 million individuals (5.3 million in the U.S.) with a HNWI-worth of US$19.8 trillion. In 2015, the number of billionaires was 2473 with an average net wealth of US$3.1 billion (Wealth-X 2016, 2, 16). Latin American billionaires are richer than their fellow billionaires in other regions of the world (Mexico with an average net wealth of US$6.2 billion). In the U.S., the top 10 percent of earners took more than half of the country's total income in 2012, the highest level recorded since the government began collecting the relevant data a century ago (Piketty and Saez 2003; Piketty, Saez and Zucman 2016). Some scholars speak of a tendency toward the re-feudalization of the social structure as the middle class vanishes and the polarization between the one percent of the richest against the 99 percent of the rest is similar to pre-revolutionary France (Kaltmeier 2018).

Since the 1990s, contemporary economic conjuncture and social polarization have been based on hyper-accumulation on the liberalized financial markets and the economy of the information age. Nevertheless, despite the global dynamics of the post-Fordist financial market-driven regime, there are regional differences. While in the U.S. and Canada more than 70 percent of social wealth is based on monetary values and 30 percent on non-financial assets, this ratio is reversed in Latin America (28.7 percent to 71.3 percent) (Credit Suisse Research Institute 2016, 146). This corresponds to the high Gini rates for land concentration.

In the U.S., similarly to many Western European Countries, one important factor for growing social inequality is the shrinking of the middle class. The share of incomes for those in the bottom half of the U.S. population stagnated and declined from 20 percent in 1980 to 12 percent in 2014. By contrast, the top one percent's share of income grew from 12 percent in 1980 to 20 percent in 2014. From the 1970s to the 1990s, the growing income gap can be attributed to wage growth of top earners, but since the 1990s it is attributed to the financial market-activities favoring the wealthy who can afford to engage in financial investment (Piketty, Saez and Zucman 2016). In Latin America the crisis of the middle class can be also attributed to de-industrialization (→ II/5), the fragmentation of an educated working class, the informalization of labor (→ Informality, II/13), and the shrinking of state bureaucracy.

Of special interest for the understanding of social inequality is the intersection of race/ethnicity and class (→ Intersectionality, I/32). In the U.S., the wealth gap between White and Black families nearly tripled from $85,000 in 1984 to $236,500 in 2009 due to the patterns of inheritance, the access to higher education, and racial discrimination (Shapiro, Meschede and Osoro 2013). After the Great Recession, the wealth gap between whites and blacks has grown because the median-wealth of whites is thirteen times higher than the wealth of blacks and ten times higher than the wealth of Hispanics (Kochhar and Fry 2014). The transfer of wealth to the next generation points to a fundamental problem of American societies, which has not been effectively addressed even in the left-wing government phase: insufficient taxation (→ II/22) of wealth (in Latin America in 2013 it was just 3.5 percent of the total tax receipts) as well as the low or even missing inheritance tax.

However, there are significant differences in the national distribution of billionaires in Latin America. In 2014 Brazil, with sixty-one billionaires, is the country with the most billionaires, followed by Mexico with twenty-seven and Chile with twenty-one. A similar regional distribution can also be seen with regard to millionaires in Latin America. By far the most millionaires in Latin America are to be found in Brazil and Mexico, followed by Chile, Colombia, Argentina, and Peru. Fewer millionaires are found in the central Andean countries such as Ecuador and Bolivia, the Guyanas, and in Uruguay, which is known for its social system.

While there are deep historical roots in the formation of a money-aristocracy in the former countries, individual countries in the region have also been subject to rapid historical growth. In Bermuda, for example, the number of billionaires increased from four to seven between 2013 and 2014. Thus, this island has the highest spatial concentration of billionaires in the world. None of these billionaires, however, were born in Bermuda. Here the extreme concentration of wealth is based on HNWI-immigration to avoid paying tax. The relation of these tendencies and influences have significant impacts on the growth of fiscal paradises and their political practices as recent scandals, such as those surrounding the Panama papers, come to light.

The social distance between the cosmopolitan elites (→ Cosmopolitanism, III/5) and the excluded, which the urban sociologist Loïc Wacquant (2007) also called "urban outcasts," is also growing in spatial terms. On the one hand, with the growth of slums, favelas, and other poor neighborhoods, a forced segregation (Wacquant 2007) can be seen; on the other hand, new forms of elite self-segregation, such as gated communities or bunker architecture (→ Urbanization, I/45), have emerged. The super-rich are concentrated in the chic neighborhoods of cosmopolitan metropolises. The lower classes are increasingly made "waste" for the process of capitalist accumulation (Bauman 2004) and are subject to violence in the hyper-ghetto as well as new forms of punitive regulation of poverty (→ Security, II/45). The meritocratic capitalist value system is increasingly replaced by a new-rentier value form (→ Capitalism, II/2). In general terms, it seems that social inequality has reached such a high level of polarization that the idea of society itself can increasingly be put into question.

Conclusion

In the historical longue durée, social structures in the Americas are characterized by multiple forms of high social inequalities (→ Intersectionality, I/32), whereby group inequalities regarding race (→ I/39) and ethnicity (→ I/25) and gender (→ Gender Identities, I/28; Gender and Work, II/11) are especially prevalent. In the middle decades of the 20th century, the New Deal policy and the post-World War II boom significantly reduced income inequalities in the U.S. The expansion of industrial production strengthened the bargaining power of the working class as well as the consequent taxation (→ II/22) of high incomes played a crucial role in redistribution. In Latin America, during this period, governments tried to implement ISI policies including tax and land reform, with only modest success in reducing inequalities. With the economic crisis of the 1970s, neoliberal adjustment programs initiated a period with fast-growing wealth in the hands of a small elite on the one side and stagnating or even falling real incomes of the working class on the other (→ Neoliberalism, II/16). In the new millennium, the center-left governments of the Latin American Pink Tide tried to soften the social inequalities by channeling state revenues of primary good exports to the poor. Even though this policy achieved reducing poverty, it did not alter the structural inequality of land and property distribution.

The extreme concentration of wealth in the hands of a small elite came to the forefront of public debates when the financial crisis (→ II/4) of 2007–8 hit the world economy. Since then, the question of tax evasion by transnational corporations (→ II/23) and rich individuals has been broadly discussed, claiming a necessity for improving social cohesion. However, the distribution of income and wealth throughout the Americas has reached a historical high, even surpassing the situation at the end of 1920 prior to the Great Depression. The ebbing of the Pink Tide in Latin America and the tax reform of the Trump administration, favoring again the rich, are signs that current government policies will not aim at overcoming social inequalities.

Works cited

Atkinson, Toni, Joe Hasell, Salvatore Morelli, and Max Roser. 2017. "The Chartbook of Economic Inequality." *Institute for New Economic Thinking at the Oxford Martin School*. www.chartbookofeconomicinequality.com/.

Balzer, Sarah, Tina Lorenz, Victoria Sawadsky, and Christine Schulz. 2013. "Vom Tellerwäscher zum Millionär?" In *Soziale Ungleichheit in den Amerikas: historische Kontinuitäten und sozialer Wandel von der Mitte des 19, Jahrhunderts Bis Heute*, ed. Olaf Kaltmeier, 117–132. KLA Working Paper Series No. 9. Köln.

Bauman, Zygmunt 2004. *Wasted Lives: Modernity and Its Outcasts*. Cambridge: Polity.

Berg, Manfred. 2004. "Liberaler Konsens und gesellschaftliche Polarisierung: Die Innere Entwicklung, 1945–1975." In *Länderbericht USA: geschichte, Politik, Wirtschaft, Gesellschaft, Kultur*, eds. Peter Lösche and Hans Dietrich Loeffelhoz, 153–171. Frankfurt: Campus.

Capgemini. 2017. "*World Wealth Report 2017*." Campini Financial Service. www.capgemini.com/de-de/wp-content/uploads/sites/5/2017/09/worldwealthreport_2017_final-3.pdf.

Davies, James, Anthony Shorrocks, Susanna Sandstrom, and Edward Wolff. 2007. "The World Distribution of Household Wealth." *University of California, Santa Cruz: Center for Global, International and Regional Studies*. https://escholarship.org/uc/item/3jv048hx.

De Ferranti, David, Guillermo E. Perry, Francisco H. G. Ferreira, and Michael Walton. 2004. *Inequality in Latin America: Breaking With History? World Bank Latin American and Caribbean Studies*. Washington, DC: World Bank. http://documents.worldbank.org/curated/en/804741468045832887/Inequality-in-Latin-America-breaking-with-history.

Federal Reserve Bank of St. Louis (FRED). 2019. "Income Gini Ratio of Families by Race of Householder, All Races." Economic Research Federal Reserve Bank of St. Louis, May 21. https://fred.stlouisfed.org/series/GINIALLRF.

Hall, Michael M. and Hobart A. Spalding. 1986. "The Urban Working Class and Early Latin American Labour Movements, 1880–1930." In *The Cambridge History of Latin America*. Vol. 4: c.1870 to 1930, ed. Leslie Bethell, 325–366. Cambridge: Cambridge University Press.

Junker, Detlef. 2004. "Weltwirtschaftskrise, New Deal, Zweiter Weltkrieg, 1929–1945." In *Länderbericht USA: Geschichte, Politik, Wirtschaft, Gesellschaft, Kultur*, eds. Peter Lösche and Hans Dietrich Loeffelhoz, 129–152. Frankfurt: Campus.

Kaltmeier, Olaf. 2018. *Refeudalización. Desigualdad Social, Economía y Cultura Política en América Latina en el temprano siglo XXI*. Bielefeld and Guadalajara: Bielefeld University Press, Universidad de Guadalajara.

Kochhar, Rakesh and Richard Fry. 2014. "Wealth Inequality Has Widened Along Racial, Ethnic Lines since End of Great Recession." *Pew Research Center*. www.pewresearch.org/fact-tank/2014/12/12/racial-wealth-gaps-great-recession/.

Kolko, Gabriel. 1969. *Besitz und Macht. Sozialstruktur und Einkommensverteilung in den USA*. Frankfurt am Main: Suhrkamp.

Larrañaga, Osvaldo and María Eugenia Rodríguez. 2015. "Desigualdad de Ingresos y Pobreza en Chile 1990 a 2013." *Programa de las Naciones Unidas para el Desarrollo – Chile. Documento de Trabajo*. www.cl.undp.org/content/chile/es/home/library/poverty/documentos_de_trabajo/desigualdad-de-ingresos-y-pobreza-en-chile-1990-2013.html.

Mariátegui, José Carlos. 2011. *Siete ensayos de interpretación de la realidad peruana*. Barcelona: Diferencias. Orig. pub. 1928.

Messina, Julián and Joana Silva. 2018. *Wage Inequality in Latin America: Understanding the Past to Prepare the Future*. Washington, DC: World Bank Group. http://documents.worldbank.org/curated/en/501531515414954476/Wage-inequality-in-Latin-America-understanding-the-past-to-prepare-for-the-future.

Ocampo, José Antonio, NU. CEPAL. 2000. *Equidad, desarrollo y ciudadanía*. Colombia: Alfaomega. http://hdl.handle.net/11362/1655.

Oxfam International. 2017. "An Economy for the 99%." Oxfam Briefing Papers. www.oxfam.org/en/research/economy-99.

Piketty, Thomas and Emmanuel Saez. 2003. "Income Inequality in the United States, 1913–1998." *Quarterly Journal of Economics* 68, no. 1: 1–39. https://eml.berkeley.edu//~saez/TabFig2017prel.xls.

Piketty, Thomas, Emmanuel Saez, and Gabriel Zucman. 2016. "Distributional National Accounts: Methods and Estimates for the United States." NBER Working Paper 22945. www.nber.org/papers/w22945.

Portes, Alejandro and Kelly Hoffman. 2003. "Latin American Class Structures: their Composition and Change during the Neoliberal Era." *Latin American Research Review* 38, no. 1: 41–82.

Shapiro, Thomas, Tatjana Meschede, and Sam Osoro. 2013. "The Roots of the Widening Racial Wealth Gap: explaining the Black-White Economic Divide." Research and Policy Brief. Brandeis University Institute on Assets and Social Policy. http://health-equity.lib.umd.edu/4120/1/racialwealthgapbrief.pdf.

Shorrocks, Anthony, James B. Davies and Rodrigo Lluberas. 2016. "*Global Wealth Report*." Credit Suisse Research Institute. www.credit-suisse.com/corporate/de/research/research-institute/publications.html.

Stepan-Norris, Judith and Caleb Southworth. 2010. "Rival Unionism and Membership Growth in the United States, 1900 to 2005: A Special Case of Inter-Organizational Competition." *American Sociological Review* 75, no. 2: 227–251.

Tax Foundation. 2013. "U.S. Federal Individual Income Tax Rates History, 1862–2013." https://taxfoundation.org/us-federal-individual-income-tax-rates-history-1913-2013-nominal-and-inflation-adjusted-brackets.

Thorp, Rosemary. 2012. "A Historical Perspective on the Political Economy of Inequality in Latin America." In *The Oxford Handbook of Latin American Political Economy*, eds. Javier Santiso and Jeff Dayton-Johnson, Oxford: Oxford University Press. doi: 10.1093/oxfordhb/9780199747504.013.0006.

Topik, Frank and Carlos Marichal. 2006. *From Silver to Cocaine: Latin American Commodity Chains and the Building of the World Economy, 1500–2000.* Durham and London: Duke University Press.

United Nations Development Program. 2018. Human Development Reports. New York City. http://hdr.undp.org/en/composite/trends.

Wacquant, Loïc. 2007. "Territorial Stigmatization in the Age of Advanced Marginality." *Thesis Eleven* 91, no. 1: 66–77. https://doi.org/10.1177/0725513607082003.

Wealth-X. 2016. "World Ultra Wealth Report." *Wealth-X.* www.wealthx.com/report/the-wealth-x-world-ultra-wealth-report-2015-2016/.

Williamson, Jeffrey G. 2015. "Latin American Inequality: Colonial Origins, Commodity Booms or a Missed Twentieth-Century Leveling?" *Journal of Human Development and Capabilities* 16, no. 3: 324–341.

21
STATE TRANSFORMATION

Tobias Boos and Ulrich Brand

The debate concerning the state in the Western Hemisphere and how to understand its transformations is an example of the entangled history of the Americas and the transfer of certain (predominant) knowledge subjected to societal development – especially the Eurocentrism of state development and its conceptualization (→ Nation and State Building, I/16; Nation State, II/38). The theorizing of the state has always taken place against the background of real historical developments and, therefore, within a periodization of state development and state theory. Six periods can be defined with focus especially placed on the last three in the second half of the 20th century.

The state in Latin America can be organized around three analytical axes. First, any discussion of state transformation must consider the transformation of social relations and how they condense and crystalize in the institutionalized forms of the state apparatus and state discourses. Therefore, socio-economic, cultural and bio-physical (→ Biopolitics, I/22) structures and processes must be considered, as well as related societal relationships of the forces and discourses (like "*progress*") that produce domination and subordination (→ Modernization, I/35), i.e. the historically constitutive and transforming conditions of the state over time. This is of particular interest given the strong dependency of Latin American political economies from the world market and the role of commodities for (world) capitalist dynamics (→ Capitalism, II/2); Zavaleta also called this constellation a *determinación dependiente* (1986). Since the *conquista* (→ Conquest and Colonization, I/7), the interests in Latin America's material wealth, exploited via direct force or the law of value and respective politics has been an important factor in structuring global capitalism. The entangled Inter-American relations among particular societies and states cannot be simplified as those between the United States and Latin American societies. What has to be considered are both global dynamics and the exchange and interlinked history between different Latin American countries, as they reveal highly uneven development dynamics within Latin America itself (→ Development, II/6).

Second, a basic element of any theorizing of the state in Latin America is its different roles in society. On the one hand, there is a structural heterogeneity and the remaining importance of different modes of production. On the other hand, there is also the overall weakness of the bourgeoisie – with the exception of Chile, Cuba, and later Mexico – and a weak "civil society" (→ II/28) in the sense of more or less state-independent organizing.

Therefore, the state plays a much greater role in the economy and society, i.e. in the historical imposition of capitalism and the nation. It is a "productive force" for itself (Zavaleta Mercado 1986 cit. in Cortés 2012). Linked to this is the tendency to authoritarian rule (→ Authoritarianism, II/25), clientelism (→ II/29), as well as open and structural violence, especially albeit not exclusively, exercised by the state.

Third, concentrated in the field of political thinking, especially within state theory, the Eurocentric legacy with is universalizing claims has had a strong historical and modern pertinence, which includes little recognition of Latin American intellectual production in the Global North (Vega Camacho 2010, 127) (→ Public Intellectuals, III/18). Such Eurocentrism can be countered within the paradigm of Inter-American Studies and its understanding of multi-layered processes and transnationalization, as well as the multiplicity and simultaneity of knowledge production.

State transformation in the Americas

Creole leviathan and oligarchy state (19th century – 1920s)

State-building after independence at the beginning of the 19th century took place under conditions of the legacy of the colonial administration and a contested process between the conservative and liberal elites (→ Nation and State Building, I/16). Nevertheless, the republican states (with the exception of Brazil as a monarchy between 1756 and 1889) were not democratic at all. Their main function was the securing of power and social positions of local elites. The 19th century largely consisted of global expansion of liberal capitalism under the predominance of Great Britain, giving rise to the so-called *Pax Britannica* (Cox 1987, Chapter 5), i.e. the ability of the British government to formulate the major rules for global trade and finance and enforce it via its economic and military power. Latin America's role was as a provider of natural resources, i.e. minerals, agricultural products, and cowhides, and later meat and wheat (→ Extractivism, II/9). Until around 1850, and given the political instability, capitalist development in Latin America was slow. This changed mid-century with the global expansion of capitalism and increased interests in Latin American exports, especially in the Southern Cone. However, especially in the Andean countries and in the south of Mexico a plurality of economies was maintained, as what the Bolivian philosopher René Zavaleta Mercado (1986) later called *sociedad abigarrada* (overlapping society).

One main motivation for political independence was that the creoles did not want to continue being disadvantaged by the Spanish and Portuguese elites, which were debilitated themselves due to the political developments in Europe (especially through the Napoleon Wars after the French Revolution). Moreover, from an Inter-American Studies perspective, the Monroe Doctrine (1823) was decisive as it condemned further European aspirations in the American hemisphere (→ Pan-Americanism, II/40). The U.S. ambition to establish itself as the sovereign of the Americas was expressed explicitly later in the 1904 Roosevelt Corollary (→ Interventionism, II/36).

Two axes of state (forming) dynamics were important. First, right after political independence, complex processes of state formation and the creation of a certain political and social cohesion started. They had been articulated with fierce conflicts among centralizing and federalist forces. The convergence of interests between strong local rural elites, especially the landowners and commercial bourgeoisie, was essential for the formation of state institutions, as trade (through cities) had to be administrated. Consequently, the state was designed for the elite's purposes, initially recognized from the outside as independent, but did not have much legitimation within their territories. State-building and nation-building went hand in hand at this time as state histories were invented (→ Memorial Culture I/14; Memory Politics, I/34). This constellation was called the *Creole Leviathan* (Kaplan 1981): While primarily responding to the interest of the elites and agrarian oligarchy, the state did not care about domestic markets and democratic rights (→ Democracy, II/32), and the constitutions and the institutional systems were largely copied from Europe. Additionally, given the weak bourgeoisies, the state and local institutions had already taken a leading role and the political culture and practice of *caudillismo* – the prominent role of a political leader – and *clientelismo* (→ Clientelism, II/29) emerged.

For the second axis, the Mexican Revolution (1910–17) was the turning point of Latin American politics and thinking (→ Revolution, II/44). Together with the Russian Revolution, it was the emancipatory point of reference at the time. The power of the bourgeoisie was actually put into question and led to the genuinely progressive 1917 Mexican constitution. However, despite the concessions to peasants and workers, the nation remained a creole state.

Import-substituting industrialization and the developmental state (1930s - 1960s)

The economic crisis from 1929 was an abrupt end of the liberal world market and Latin America's subaltern inclusion as a commodity exporter (→ Crisis, II/4). National governments and the elites were forced to alter their economic strategies and turn toward the domestic markets and industrialization. Later within the Economic Commission for Latin America (ECLAC), economists around Raúl Prebisch formulated a new economic strategy that was later called structuralism, which was close to Keynesian ideas at this time (Rodríguez 2006). The state should intervene in the economy (partially through nationalizations of key industries) in order to overcome structural social and economic deficits (→ Development, II/6). The main objective was to gain more independence from the world market and develop internal markets; the means were fortifying the national industrialization processes and substituting imports – the state should play a more active role in the economy. Subsequently, populist regimes with a high degree of legitimacy and capacity to mobilize the masses came into power (→ Populism, II/43), such as Getúlio Vargas in Brazil, Lázaro Cárdenas in Mexico, and Juan Domingo Perón in Argentina. The governments expressed the influx of the formerly excluded masses into the sphere of political representation. Together with internal migration and, in some countries, industrialization, this led to a class compromise between the industrial bourgeoisie, the (new) urban working class and their trade unions, as well as a new state bureaucracy.

However, there are major difference between the shaping of the different populist states. For example, the Bolivian Revolution in 1952 certainly resounded with the strong demand for participation (→ II/41) and self-determination (Oliver Costilla and Pimmer 2014, 40–42). A momentous entanglement started in January 1949. After the Cold War had just begun and the U.S. entered shortly thereafter in Korea in its first hot conflict, U.S. president Harry Truman declared that the world was divided into developed countries and those which were developing (→ Development, II/6). The "era of development" was a powerful discourse and practice, institutionalized in "development aid," or U.S.-based international organizations like the World Bank or the IMF (Sachs 1992) (→ Geopolitics, II/34). However, discourses and practices of development were highly welcomed as *desarrollismo* in Latin American countries, since the promise was economic growth and well-being of the people, as well as the maintenance of the elite's leading positions.

Many years later, the Latin American School of Development (overview in Kay 1989) discussed this period intensively. Protagonists like Cardoso and Faletto (1979) stressed the socio-political factors in the creation of an internal market and alliance with the (new) working class. The state appears for the first time as a regulatory authority which is why this "developmentalist populism" – as Cardoso and Faletto termed it – was sometimes interpreted as the first hegemonic state form in Latin America.

The *dependista* debate is also a case in point for intellectual entanglements that are the conditions of knowledge production. Santiago de Chile was a site of intense debates, as many of the protagonists fled into exile and went to Chile because of the expansion of research funding etc. under the Allende administration (Beigel 2010).

Counter-insurgency state and bureaucratic-authoritarian state (1960s – 1980s)

The 1960s experienced emerging social struggles and a growing importance of critical thinking around the world (→ Class Struggle, II/3). The Cuban Revolution beginning in 1959 became the overwhelming political event at the time that highly influenced political and social thinking (→ Revolution, II/44). U.S. president John F. Kennedy tried to respond to this event with the Alliance for Progress (1961), combing the powerful discourse of development together with the U.S. objective to fight influence of the Soviet Union in "underdeveloped" countries. At the same time, post-war capitalism entered into a crisis (→ II/4), i.e. Fordism (→ II/10) in the capitalist centers. Consequently, the economic model of import substitution, sometimes called peripheral Fordism, was also under pressure due to descending world market prices (with the exception of oil), inflation, and foreign trade deficit.

Parallel to this, authoritarianism (→ II/25) grew in order to deal with the growing contestation and crisis. The economic policy of the Brazilian military government after the *coup d'état* in 1964 was largely oriented at the model of import substitution. In contrast, Chile became the earliest neoliberal laboratory in 1973 after the military coup against the Allende government (→ Neoliberalism, II/16). Promptly, countries like Uruguay and Argentina followed and imposed openly neoliberal politics. The famous "Chicago Boys," a group of economists that gained strong influence under the Pinochet regime, represents the increased influence of the U.S. on the intellectual field during these years. The authoritarian regimes can be seen partly as an attempt of the Latin American bourgeoisie and imperial forces to limit further democratization processes and also as a response to the revolutionary movements emerging all over Latin America.

In contrast to the U.S.-American and European experience of the 1960s, social movements (→ I/41) and upheavals were not answered by an opening up of state and social institutions, but in fact led to the most repressive regimes in the region in some cases. Although without overturning state institutions in Mexico, the Institutional Revolutionary Party (PRI) made a sharp authoritarian turn under the Díaz Ordaz administration (1964–70) and responded in 1968 with the massacre of about 300 students in the Tlatelolco square. Consequently, Rui Mauro Marini (1978) called the state during this time *estado de contrainsurgencia* [counter-insurgency state], with origins in the altered geopolitical strategy of the United States (→ Geopolitics, II/34); the transformation of the Latin American bourgeoisie and its imperialist integration; and the (radical, even revolutionary) mass movements. He analyzed the counter-insurgency state as dominated by the executive authorities, which were composed by military forces (→ Military, II/37) and dominant economic forces at this time i.e. the monopoly capital.

Yet, Guillermo O'Donnell (1973), with his concept of the "bureaucratic-authoritarian state," most prominently theorized the state transformation processes at the time. He argued in this early work that this state formation had its roots in the preceding populist regimes (→ Populism, II/43), its public policies, and the governing political elites. State bureaucracy played a central role in these governments, due to the continuing modernization (→ I/35) and differentiation of society accompanied by technocratization and formation of a group of technocratic-administrative public servants.

Debates since the late 1970s: transition and transformation

From the end of the 1970s onwards, the continent experienced a return to democracy (→ II/32) (Ecuador 1978/79; Peru 1980; Bolivia 1982; Argentina 1983; Uruguay 1983/84; Brazil 1985; Chile 1989/90; Paraguay 1992). Two paradigmatic debates epitomize crucial aspects and dynamics regarding the transformation of the state at that time: Most prominently, the (1) so-called transition paradigm; and (2) the discussion of a group of (former) socialist intellectuals of Latin American on transformation processes.

The first debate shows continuities with research on authoritarianism embodied by G. O'Donnell (1979). This body of literature essentially focused on state institutions in the strict sense, the negotiation between (state) elites, and how contradictions between them lead to the transition processes (O'Donnell, Schmitter and Whitehead 1986). This transition paradigm represents another example of the superimposing of approaches from a U.S. context upon Latin American research traditions, which up to this point had been strongly influenced by materialist and structure-oriented approaches. The research context developing around the "Latin American Program" at Woodrow Wilson Center in Washington in the 1970s was the key to this transition, both personally and institutionally.

The underlying question guiding this research was: "How to accompany the transition to democracy scientifically?" This also clarifies why their studies sometimes read like manuals. Furthermore, the experience of the Latin American dictatorships explains the strong normative bias and uncritical assessment of the potentials of institutions in liberal democracy. Besides the famous critique by Carothers (2002) calling for the *End of the Transition paradigm*, there was also an interesting critique by O'Donnell himself (1995 cit. Ansaldi 2007, 32), who indicated in an interview that their analyses were too politicized and state-centered, as many intellectuals had an affinity to the governing administration or were even incorporated. This clearly shows how a certain paradigm and its research agenda could relate to political power relations, societal developments, and existing research traditions (the dependency theory) (→ Development, II/6). In addition to O'Donnell's self-criticism, the transition paradigm failed to take into account struggles from below (→ Social Movements, I/41), as well as external factors such as world politics and the world market.

A second major discussion about state transformation developed parallel to these debates. Cortés (2012) claims that one of the most intriguing debates can be found back in the late 1970s. Due to the authoritarian regimes in most of the Latin American countries, many intellectual were driven into exile. Paradoxically, this prepared the ground for prolific exchange and debates between prominent leftist intellectuals, as they were received in the same research institutions as e.g. the Universidad Nacional Autónoma de Mexico.

These experiences of the so-called *gramscianos argentinos* can be considered paradigmatic (Burgos 2004; Burgos and Pérez 2002). Confronted with authoritarian regimes and the increasingly obvious limitations of the strategy of armed struggles by the guerrilla movements, they began to review their notion of revolution (→ II/44) as a path to socialism (→ I/42) by shifting the focus to democracy (→ II/32). They proposed a reading of Gramsci's integral state, which emphasized the role of intellectuals and proposed an affirmative reading of the concept of civil society (→ II/28). They argued for the necessity of a new contractualism and pact, in combination with an intellectual and moral reform to assure a democratic system and the construction of state institutions (Burgos 2004, 303–321). Their shift to an "*abordaje predominantemente institucional*" (309) was also expressed in their active participation of the first democratic governments which succeeded the military dictatorships. Furthermore, Burgos (314) singled out as important factors for this shift the transitions processes in Europe, i.e. Spain, Portugal and Greece and the debates on Eurocommunism.

Neoliberalism and its state (1980s - 1990s)

Neoliberalization had already begun during the dictatorships and further deepened in the 1980s, parallel to the reintroduction of liberal democracies. Due to high external debts, unfulfilled strategies of "indebted industrialization" and *plata dulce* [easy money] for upper and middle classes were accompanied by the sharp reorientation of the U.S. government toward neoliberalism in 1981. These policies culminated in the outbreak of an economically and socially disastrous debt crisis and the imposition of the "Washington consensus": privatization (→ II/17), opening of economies, shrinking of state budget, etc. (Williamson 1990). The consequence was a further destruction of social networks and an informal neo-colonization (→ Postcolonialism, I/38).

For Cortés (2012), critical state analysis almost came to its end with the neoliberal counter revolution. Within the academic debate, a new way of thinking in institutions and governance became predominant. However, history did not come to its end, as the U.S.-American conservative Francis Fukuyama (1992) prominently claimed. Contradictorily, the "abandonment" of the state also opened up spaces for social experiments and utopian discourses went hand in hand with the construction of concrete alternatives (→ Utopia, III/23). Due to a further rollback of social achievements and neoliberal globalization and regional integration (→ II/18) initiatives in the mid-1990s [North American Free Trade Agreement (NAFTA) or the Initiative for a Free Trade Agreement for the Americas (FTAA), movements across the continent, like the indigenous movements in Mexico, Bolivia, and Ecuador (→ Indigeneity, I/31) and others (e.g. the landless movement *Movimento dos Trabalhadores Rurais Sem Terra* in Brazil, the *piqueteros* in Argentina), started to resist against neoliberalism. Most prominently, these debates and organizational processes acquired an emblematic role model prior to the 500th anniversary of the beginning of the Conquista: the 1994 upheaval of the Zapatistas in Chiapas, Mexico.

Clearly, societal perspectives on processes of democratization played an important role, and an autonomous perspective on society, state, and struggles became quite prominent. Creative experiments on the foundation and institutionalization of different forms of society focused on the non-considered spaces, *los no lugares de la politica* (Tapia Mealla 2008), and social movements (→ I/41), as well as on processes of self-organization that were considered to be the core of a "new social protagonism" to transform society (Colectivo Situaciones 2012). Here, state transformation was not the main issue as social transformation is understood as distanced from and in opposition to state institutions, as paradigmatically expressed in Holloway's call to "change the world without taking power" (2002). Transformations were not about transforming existing (state) institutions, but inventing and building a completely new types of social institutions, which unfolded in everyday practices and subjectivities.

Variegated dynamics: authoritarian neoliberalism, estado neo-desarrollista, and the decolonization of the State (2000s – present)

Despite its differences, it makes sense to speak of a new phase of capitalist development in Latin America beginning in 2000 (→ Capitalism, II/2). A main reason for this has been the changing world market constellation due to the increase of commodity prices that have enabled a development model that has been later called "extractivism" (→ II/9) and/or "neo-extractivism" (Gudynas 2009; Svampa 2012). Since the turn of the millennium, the dynamics again illustrate the material foundations and necessity for reproduction of the state and the impact of world market dynamics on Latin America. The strong economic growth and the redirected foreign policies of the U.S. toward the Middle East and Asia has led to more space for state action in all countries (Petras and Veltmeyer 2015).

However, nations within Latin America have capitalized on this expanded national and regional room for maneuvering quite differently. On the one hand, in Mexico, Columbia, Peru, and Central America, neoliberal-conservative governments have expressed a deepening of the processes since the 1990s. Inspired by Polanyi's work, Rhina Roux (2012) calls the process during the 1990s in Mexico a great transformation toward authoritarian neoliberalism that split with the social pact founded through the Mexican Revolution. On the other hand, the "pink tide" (Barrett, Chavez and Rodríguez-Garavito 2008; Sader 2011; Webber and Carr 2013) started with the victory of left-wing governments in Venezuela (1999), Bolivia (2006), and Ecuador (2007), as well as center-left governments in Chile (2000), Brazil (2002), Argentina (2003), Uruguay (2004), Paraguay (2008). Debates about the character of "post-neoliberalism" (Brand and Sekler 2009; Yates and Bakker 2014) accompanied this rapidly changing constellation.

Without a doubt, the state – in its authoritarian or progressive orientation – is "back": in real politics (where it never left) and in political theory and debates. Given the complexity of the situation, viewpoints about the state have become variegated and three distinct perspectives can be distinguished. The first perspective argues that the progressive governments in Latin America have canalized and monopolized the transformational potentials created in the previous years by the social movements from below and turned them into state-led development strategies from above.

A second perspective of the debate has a quite different understanding of the state. Against the background of neo-extractivism, the most prominent position is the revival of neo-developmentalism (Ferrer 2010; Webber 2010; Féliz 2012). It emphasizes the regained room to maneuver for the national state. A certain key issue has become the question of potentials and limitations of state-driven transformation processes (Thwaites Rey 2012). Some authors and politicians interpret the current transformation processes in Latin America as revolutionary processes to socialism (→ I/42) led by the state – a "socialism of the 21st century" proclaimed by Hugo Chávez in 2005 (García Linera 2011). While neo-developmentalist thinking again puts the state in control of socio-economic transformation, a third political and intellectual shift takes a much broader approach by claiming to "de-center" (Tapia Mealla 2010) the state. The actions of vast indigenous mobilizations (→ Indigeneity, I/31), especially in Bolivia and Ecuador, in the overturning of neoliberal governments has led to constitutional processes aimed at defining the state on an entirely new basis. This new constitutionalism led by the popular classes points to a re-foundation of the state, new institutions and territorialities, and pluralization of legal forms and subjectivities (De Sousa Santos 2010, 72) in form of a plurinational state (Acosta and Martínez 2009; Tapia Mealla 2010). In sum, regardless of the stance taken, the socio-political developments unquestionably reinserted the state back to the center of debate. However, it also has become clear that to overcome rather pointless dichotomies, "conceptual transitions" are required to rethink transformational strategies and the role of the state in its departure from the current socio-political context (Thwaites Rey and Ouviña 2014; Acosta and Brand 2017).

Outlook

This tentative overview of a highly complex debate shows that theorizing the state and its transformations cannot be thought of as independent from real historical, socio-economic, and cultural developments. Quite the contrary: putting the debates in their socio-historical contexts discloses the societal issues they currently attempt to solve. Latin American thinking has always been entangled with other forms and sites of knowledge production, especially from the Global North and its often universalizing claims, made especially by modernization theory (→ Modernization, I/35), but also, and all too often, by critical thinking.

A further and more intensified work of the "translation" of theories and concepts out of their contexts into other ones is needed (e.g. Jenss and Pimmer 2014). For instance, the concept of *la sociedad abigarrada* [multi-faceted society] provokes to rethink "Northern" societies and their states by acknowledging that multi-layered social relations also exist beyond formal politics and the market economy. Also, the central issue of the plurinational state raised by the Latin American debates could be proven highly relevant for societies outside Latin America.

Additionally, critical and non-institutionalist state analyses especially enables us to better understand why and how it is so difficult to change the state and cultural political economy, even in times of progressive governments. Such a perspective is of utmost importance in times when right-wing forces are fighting back (see elections of Mauricio Macri in Argentina in 2015, Donald Trump in the U.S. in 2016 and Jair Bolsonaro in Brazil in 2018).

Perspectives from the Global South clearly reveal the international character and constantly intertwined histories of the state as well. Given the fact that in Latin America, social structures and relationships of forces – especially class relations – were always highly internationalized (→ Social Inequality, II/20), this can also be applied to the state and its theorizing. Such a perspective – to understand the state as a social relation embedded within society – stands in contrast to the usual Weberian conceptualization of the state, as basically an autonomous entity and a national state. However, future research might go a step further by aiming to understand the internationalized and multi-scalar character of the state and how "the international" is articulated locally.

Finally, further reflection is needed of the question from Thwaites Rey and Ouviña (2014) asking if whether the analytical instruments tackling the post-colonial state are sufficient for considering both the conditions for emancipatory transformations that deal with the state in some way and, at the same time, the entry points and potential to transform it.

Works cited

Acosta, Alberto, and Esperanza Martínez. 2009. *Plurinacionalidad, Democracia en la Diversidad.* Quito: Abya-Yala.

Acosta, Alberto, and Ulrich Brand. 2017. *Salidas del Laberinto Capitalista. Decrecimiento y Postextractivismo.* Icaria: Barcelona.

Ansaldi, Waldo. 2007. *La Democracia en América Latina, Un Barco A la Deriva.* Buenos Aires: Fondo de Cultura Económica.

Barrett, Patrick, Daniel Chavez, and César Rodríguez-Garavito. 2008. *The New Latin American Left: Utopia Reborn*. London: Pluto Press.
Beigel, Fernanda. 2010. "Dependency Analysis: the Creation of New Social Theory in Latin America." In *The ISA Handbook of Diverse Sociological Traditions*, ed. Sujata Patel, 189–200. Los Angeles: SAGE.
Brand, Ulrich, and Nicola Sekler. 2009. *Postneoliberalism: A Beginning Debate*. Vol. 51, *Development Dialog*. Uppsala, Sweden: Dag Hammarskjöld Foundation.
Burgos, Raúl. 2004. *Los Gramscianos argentinos*. Buenos Aires: Siglo XXI de Argentina Editores.
Burgos, Raúl, and Carlos Pérez. 2002. "The Gramscian Intervention in the Theoretical and Political Production of the Latin American Left." *Latin American Perspectives* 29, no. 1: 9–37.
Cardoso, Fernando Henrique, and Enzo Faletto. 1979. *Dependency and Development in Latin America*. Berkeley: University of California Press.
Carothers, Thomas. 2002. "The End of the Transition Paradigm." *Journal of Democracy* 13, no. 1: 5–21.
Colectivo Situaciones. 2012. *19 & 20: Notes for A New Social Protagonism*. New York: Autonomedia.
Cortés, Martín. 2012. "El Leviatán criollo. Elementos para el análisis de la especificidad del Estado en América Latina." In *El Estado en América Latina: Continuidades y rupturas*, ed. Mabel Thwaites Rey, 93–116. Santiago de Chile; Buenos Aires: CLACSO.
Cox, Robert W. 1987. *Power, Production, and World Order*. New York: Columbia University Press.
De Sousa Santos, Boaventura. 2010. *Refundación del Estado en América Latina: Perspectivas Desde Una Epistemología del Sur*. Lima: Instituto Internacional de Derecho y Sociedad.
Féliz, Mariano. 2012. "Neo-Developmentalism: Beyond Neoliberalism? Capitalist Crisis and Argentina's Development since the 1990s." *Historical Materialism* 20, no. 2: 105–123.
Ferrer, Aldo. 2010. "Raúl Prebisch y el dilema del desarrollo en el mundo global." *Revista CEPAL* 101: 7–15.
Fukuyama, Francis. 1992. *The End of History and The Last Man*. New York: Free Press.
García Linera, Álvaro. 2011. *Las Tensiones Creativas de la Revolución: La Quinta Fase del Proceso de Cambio*. La Paz: Vicepresidencia del Estado Plurinacional.
Gudynas, Eduardo. 2009. "Diez tesis urgentes sobre el nuevo extractivismo." In *Extractivismo, Política y Sociedad*, ed. Jürgen Schuldt et al., 187–225. Quito: CAAP/CLAES.
Holloway, John. 2002. *To Change the World Without Taking Power*. London: Pluto Press.
Jenss, Alke, and Stefan Pimmer. 2014. *Der Staat in Lateinamerika*. Münster: Westfälisches Dampfboot.
Kaplan, Marcos. 1981. *Aspectos del Estado en América Latina*. Mexico City: Mexico City University Press.
Kay, Cristóbal. 1989. *Latin American Theories of Development and Underdevelopment*. London: Routledge.
Marini, Ruy Mauro. 1978. "El Estado de Contrainsurgencia." *Cuadernos Políticos* 18: 21–29.
O'Donnell, Guillermo. 1973. *Modernization and Bureaucratic-Authoritarianism*. Berkeley: University of California Press.
O'Donnell, Guillermo. 1979. "Tensions in the Bureaucratic-Authoritarian State and the Question of Democracy." In *The New Authoritarianism in Latin America*, ed. David Collier, 285–318. Princeton, New Jersey: Princeton University Press.
O'Donnell, Guillermo, Philippe C. Schmitter, and Laurence Whitehead. 1986. *Transitions from Authoritarian Rule: Latin America*. Baltimore: Johns Hopkins University Press.
Oliver Costilla, Lucio, and Stefan Pimmer. 2014. "Konfigurationen von Staatlichkeit in Lateinamerika." In *Der Staat in Lateinamerika*, eds. Alke Jenss and Stefan Pimemr, 34–58. Münster: Westfälisches Dampfboot.
Petras, James, and Henry Veltmeyer. 2015. *Power and Resistance: US Imperialism in Latin America*. Boston: Brill Academic Pub.
Rodríguez, Octavio. 2006. *El Estructuralismo Latinoamericano*. México City: CEPAL/Siglo XXI.
Roux, Rhina. 2012. "México: despojo universal, desintegración de la república y nuevas rebeldías." *Theomai* 26: 13–26.
Sachs, Wolfgang. 1992. *The Development Dictionary*. London: Zed Books.
Sader, Emir. 2011. *The New Mole: Paths of the Latin American Left*. New York: Verso.
Svampa, Maristella. 2012. "Resource Extractivism and Alternatives: Latin American Perspectives on Development." *Journal Für Entwicklungspolitik* 28, no. 3: 43–73.
Tapia Mealla, Luis. 2008. *Política Salvaje*. La Paz: Muela del Diablo.
———. 2010. "El estado en condiciones de abigarramiento." In *El Estado: Campo de Lucha*, eds. Álvaro García Linera, Raúl Prada, Luis Tapia, and Oscar Vega Camacho, 95–152. La Paz: Muela del Diablo.
Thwaites Rey, Mabel. 2012. *El Estado en América Latina: Continuidades y Rupturas. Santiago de Chile*. Buenos Aires: CLACSO.

Thwaites Rey, Mabel, and Hernán Ouviña. 2014. "Staatlichkeit in Lateinamerika revisited. Die Dimension des Widerspruchs." In *Der Staat in Lateinamerika*, eds. Jenss, Alke and Stefan Pimmer, 59–84. Münster: Westfälisches Dampfboot.

Vega Camacho, Oscar. 2010. "Al sur del Estado." In *El Estado: Campo de Lucha*, eds. Álvaro García Linera, Raúl Prada, Luis Tapia, and Oscar Vega Camacho, 127–165. La Paz: Muela del Diablo.

Webber, Jeffery R. 2010. "Latin American Neostructuralism: The Contradictions of Post-Neoliberal Development." *In Historical Materialism* 18, no. 3: 208–229.

Webber, Jeffery R., and Barry Carr. 2013. *The New Latin American Left*. Lanham: Rowman & Littlefield Publishers.

Williamson, John. 1990. "What Washington Means by Policy Reform." In *Latin American Adjustment: How Much Has Happened?*, ed. John Williamson, 7–20. Washington, DC: Institute for International Economics.

Yates, Julian S., and Karen Bakker. 2014. "Debating the 'Post-Neoliberal Turn' in Latin America." *Progress in Human Geography* 38: 62–90.

Zavaleta Mercado, René. 1986. *Lo Nacional-Popular en Bolivia*. Mexico City: Siglo XXI.

22
TAXATION

María Fernanda Valdés

There are multiple definitions for the term "taxes," but most commonly taxes are defined as compulsory payments exacted by the state, for which nothing is received directly in return. Thus, taxes have two distinct characteristics: their obligatory nature and their non-reciprocal character. The obligatory nature means taxes are not a voluntary payment, therefore no one can refuse to pay them. The non-reciprocal character means that taxes do not confer any direct individual entitlement to specific goods or services in return, or what is technically named the absence of a direct quid pro quo between the taxpayer and the authority. These two characteristics distinguish taxes from other kinds of fiscal revenues, such as charges, fees, and contributions. There are many gray areas in reference to the categorization of the aforementioned state revenues (→ Nation State, II/38). Charges, fees, and contributions are all considered to be payments from the private sphere to the public, matched by certain goods or services in return. However, while fees and charges tend to be voluntary in nature, at least in theory, contributions are compulsory in many countries.

Having determined the meaning of "taxation," and the way in which taxation differs from other sorts of fiscal revenues, it next becomes necessary to understand its chief categorizations. Taxes are often classified according to their subject matter, for example, taxes imposed on property are classified as property tax, while taxes on personal income are called personal income tax. Taxes can also be classified depending on the authority imposing and collecting said taxes, therefore there are central (federal), regional, and local taxes as well.

One of the most widely known classifications of taxation is that of direct versus indirect taxation. In a purely legal sense, a direct tax is a tax which is imposed directly on the taxpayer and paid directly by the persons (corporations or individuals) on whom the tax is imposed. A direct tax cannot be shifted by the taxpayer to someone else, as is the case of income taxation on corporations or individuals. An indirect tax is paid to the government indirectly via an intermediary from the person who bears the ultimate burden of the tax. A widely known indirect tax is the value-added tax (VAT), the tax a customer pays to a retail store, which ultimately winds up in government hands.

Although this legal definition is largely accepted, the taxonomy is decidedly contested, particularly in the field of economics. From an economic standpoint, the possibility of shifting exists for all taxes, as the person who bears the tax is usually not the person who has the legal responsibility to account for the tax. For example, economists know that it is not necessarily the firm that bears the corporate income tax (Atkinson 1977). On the contrary, its cost can be shifted to the consumers via higher prices of their products.

The roles of taxation

Taxation is vital to the functioning of the modern state (→ Nation State, II/38). Not only do taxes generate revenues used to pay for public services such as education (→ I/24), health (→I/29), and infrastructure, taxation also plays at least two important societal roles that go beyond being merely a method of payment for public goods. Firstly, as has been clearly stated by Mann (1949), taxation plays a vital role in shaping societies. This is because taxation can work as a form of "social control," which can lead to a "correction of socially undesirable human behaviors, readjustment of economic power between social groups and classes, and combating the social abuses of capitalism" (1943, 226). The extraction of tax revenue by the state has such an enormous influence on the societal organization of nations that Schumpeter argued the study of the social processes behind taxation is one of the principal lenses for observing society (Swedberg 1991). In fact, more recent studies, such as those pioneered by Piketty (2014), have shown that simply looking at tax variables over time can explain important characteristics of societies, such as changes in income distribution both nationally and internationally (→ Social Inequality, II/20).

Secondly, taxation plays an imperative role in state-building (→ Nation and State Building, I/16). It can, for example, provide finances for creating military and state agencies (→ Military, II/37) although this is not the only state-building role since these expenses can be financed by other means, such as debt, or, in the case of resource-rich countries, natural resource royalties (→ Extractivism, II/9; Nature II/39). What is most unique about taxation is that in order to be able to tax, authorities must build administrative and enforcement apparatuses (Tilly 1985), such as tax laws and courts. Taxation also stimulates demands for representation (Goldscheid, Hickel and Schumpeter 1976), something that is not likely to occur with other forms of revenue. During the second half of the 18th century, North American colonies rebelled against the taxes imposed by an English government in which they had no voice (→ Independence Movements, I/10). This rebellion rallied behind the slogan "no taxation without representation," which accentuates the important role taxation can play in the creation of a representative government (→ Democracy, II/32; Participation, II/41). Thus, it is clear, as Margaret Levi declared, the history of state revenue production is the history of the evolution of the state (1988).

Taxation in the Americas

Important characteristics of the modern tax systems in the Americas shape the societies in which people live. There are two factors that habitually emerge when comparatively analyzing tax systems: the level of revenue, and the structure of the tax system. In terms of revenue, a great deal of heterogeneity exists on the continent. Countries such as Brazil, Argentina, Uruguay, and Canada, collect amounts higher than 30 percent of GDP in taxes. On the other hand, in the other remaining countries, collection seldom reaches levels higher than 21 percent. Many countries have never reached levels higher than 22 percent in their independent history, as is the case for Colombia, the Dominican Republic, Ecuador, El Salvador, Guatemala, Honduras, Mexico, Nicaragua, Panama, Paraguay, Peru, and Venezuela.

The under-taxation seen in some countries is highly correlated with the society its citizens live in. Although there is no such thing as a universally "optimal" tax burden, one can easily see that with such low levels of taxation, it is very difficult to offer basic public services such as education (→ I/24), health care (→ Health, I/29), and security (→ II/45). Furthermore, the relevant state-building role of taxation discussed above is difficult to achieve with low levels of taxation. In fact, since the 1960s, sufficient levels of taxation have been recognized as a prerequisite to development (→ II/6) (Kaldor 1963). Thus, the under-taxation of many countries on the continent may impose significant limits to their development as nations.

In relation to the structure of the tax system, a significant degree of heterogeneity in the Americas is evident as well, but it is also possible to clearly differentiate between two groups with highly distinctive tax structures. On one hand, there is Canada and the United States, referred to as "the North," and, on the other hand, the countries of the South, meaning the rest of the continent, from Mexico down to the Southern Cone. Countries in the South rely heavily on indirect taxes, such as taxes on consumption, which make up about half of their overall tax revenues. Meanwhile, according to data from the UN-Organization for Economic Co-operation and Development (OECD) and the United Nations Economic Commission for Latin America and the Caribbean (CEPAL), Canada and the U.S. only collect shares equal to 23 percent and 17 percent of their total revenues, respectively (OECD and CEPAL 2016). To compensate for the lower share of indirect taxes, countries in the North depend more heavily on direct taxes from income and profit. Canada and the U.S. collect half of their tax revenues from these sources, while the rest of the continent collects an average of 30 percent of total revenues from these taxes.

Perhaps the most remarkable distinction between the tax structures of the two groups are their revenues from personal taxation. While most of the income and profit taxes collected in the North are from personal income tax (with an average of 32 percent and 44 percent of total tax revenues in Canada and the U.S. respectively), countries in the South have proven to be "allergic" to personal taxation (Tanzi 2000). These countries collect an average of 10 percent of their total tax revenues from personal taxation. Even in countries in the South where the role personal income tax is the largest, their revenue as a percentage of their GDP is still less than one third of those of Canada and the U.S. Prime examples are Mexico and Uruguay, which collect 3 percent and 2.9 percent of their GDP from personal income tax respectively, while Canada collects 11.3 percent and the U.S. collects 9.8 percent. At the other extreme, some countries, such as Colombia, collect as little 0.2 percent of their GDP from personal taxation. Until very recently, there was no tax on personal income at all in some countries, such as in Uruguay until 2007, while in others this tax was rescinded for certain periods of time, as was the case in Ecuador at the end of the 1990s and in Bolivia there is no personal income tax.

The tax system of a country is a factor that, as noted above, can work as a lens to understand the society. An examination of the structure of tax systems can reveal clearly existent inequalities within societies (→ Social Inequality, I/20). The tax structure is thus one of the factors explaining why, and evidencing how, people in the South live in very unequal societies. In countries that are highly dependent on indirect consumption taxes but rely very little on personal income tax, which is considered to be the redistributive tax par excellence, there is little room for redistribution. In fact, a commonly quoted study of the OECD (2008) shows that Canadian and U.S.-American tax systems reduce inequality by 3.7 and 4.4 Gini points. Meanwhile, similar exercises on the rest of the continent find that most of the tax systems do absolutely nothing to improve income inequality. In several countries, such as El Salvador, Colombia, the Dominican Republic, Peru, Bolivia, Nicaragua, and Honduras, among others, they even have the opposite effect: they increase inequality (Cubero and Hollar-Vladkova 2010; Goñi, López and Servén 2011).

The structure of the tax system also determines the possibility of accumulating income and wealth at the top. An excessive accumulation at the top may not only have strong effects on society, but more significantly, it can have harmful influences on the quality of democratic institutions (Stiglitz 2012) (→ Democracy, II/32). Recent studies on the distribution of income at the top in Latin America, showed the following countries to be leaders in income and wealth accumulation at the top, with the wealthiest one percent accumulating 20.45 percent of all income in Colombia (World Wealth and Income Database), 22–26 percent in Chile (Fairfield and Jorratt 2014), and 25 percent in Brazil (Souza, Medeiros and de Castro 2014). These values are higher than the 20 percent seen in the U.S., and more than twice of that seen in Canada, which was estimated at 10 percent in the last decade (World Wealth and Income Database).

Gender gaps are an integral part of these socioeconomic inequalities, and recent evidence suggests that taxation as a reflection of society reveals, creates, and reproduces gender inequalities too (→ Gender Identities, I/28). Although the study of gender dimensions in taxation is embryonic and relatively new both in Latin America and in the rest of the continent, empirical studies show that there are implicit tax biases against women in most countries (including Latin American countries). These biases exist when the regulations established in the tax legislation, due to social arrangements and prevailing economic behavior, have different implications for men and women (Rodriguez and Aguila 2018). These biases may be behind the important gender inequalities found particularly in "the South."

So how did such different tax structures develop historically and, as a consequence, vastly different societies? According to the historical study of Sokoloff and Zolt (2007), during the 19th century there were no major differences in the national tax structures between the South and the North, with both of them relying primarily on trade and excise taxes. However, while U.S. and Canadian local governments developed widespread social programs, such as public schools, sanitation, and infrastructure, mainly financed through direct taxes such as taxes on property and income, the rest of the continent did not follow suit. The authors emphasize that since in Canada and the U.S. direct taxation traces back to the 17th and 18th centuries, it was not technical, administrative, or resource constraints that prevented the other countries from following the same path. Instead, they argue that given the already existing high levels of inequality, economic elites in most countries in the South were reluctant to pay higher direct taxes to expand social investment and services – services they could procure privately for themselves and their families (→ Class Struggle, II/3). Thus, it seems that inequality is not only the result of our tax systems, but also the cause of them.

Recent historical developments also contributed to increase this reliance on indirect taxation in "the South." The 1980s and 1990s, which coincided with the period when Latin American countries completed their round of "neoliberal" reforms (→ Neoliberalism, II/16), exemplifies this. The neoliberal agenda of privatization (→ II/17), deregulation, physical austerity, and liberalization, increased the reliance on indirect taxation in three important ways. Firstly, the agenda made the tax on trade, which was a favorite source of tax revenues in the South, more difficult, particularly after the World Trade Organization (WTO) agreements. Secondly, as countries eased their restrictions on Foreign Direct Investment (FDI) and other kinds of investment, competition for capital attraction increased incentives to start a "race to the bottom" among the countries in "the South." As a result, many dismantled certain types of taxes, particularly direct taxes. This "race to the bottom" was intensified by the existence of tax havens that facilitate abusive tax practices and enable individuals and companies to escape their tax liabilities. When trade could no longer be taxed extensively, and corporations as well as high income individuals did not pay their fair share of income taxes due to the "race to the bottom," the tax burden was habitually shifted onto ordinary citizens, usually in the form of indirect taxes, such as VAT. Lastly, countries of the South are well-known as crisis-prone countries (→ Crisis, II/4). The 1980s and the 1990s were years of strong economic turbulence for the South, as it suffered the debt crisis of the 1980s, which was followed by the devastating financial crisis of the 1990s. In the midst of crisis, most Latin American countries turned to international financial organizations such as the International Monetary Fund (IMF) for financial assistance, and the IMF and other "Washington consensus" organizations usually conditioned loans to a series of reforms, including tax reforms with a strong bias toward indirect taxation.

It is important to note that even though the heterogeneity in terms of taxation is significant in the Americas, there are signs of convergence. In terms of collection levels, Latin American economies, which – with only a few exceptions – had always collected too little, have experienced an increase in tax collection since the 1990s that is greater than has been seen in any other region in the same period (Corbacho, Fretes Cibils, and Lora 2013). Latin American countries have now achieved tax burdens comparable to, or higher than, those that once prevailed in the so-called industrialized countries until the Great Depression in the 1930s, and the Second World War (Tanzi 2013). Although much of this increase in collection was caused by unprecedented favorable external economic conditions, particularly from the commodity boom that inflated tax revenues in the region (Valdés 2016) (→ Extractivism, II/9), there are also countries where tax efforts have been categorically exemplary (Cornia 2014).

In terms of structure, there seems to be a catching-up effect: although countries of the South still seem allergic to personal income taxes, the incidence of taxation equalizing income improved in the last decade in all eleven of the Latin American countries for which comparable data is available, according to a study by Cornia et al. (2011). There seem to be more progressive tax reforms in recent years and, while some reforms have resulted in great social and political instability (as was the case in Ecuador when an attempt to raise taxes on inheritances and real estate in 2015 almost ended in a coup), most reforms have developed smoothly. This is important in a region where, as has been noted by Bermeo (2009), dramatic attempts to reverse economic inequality with the use of taxation or any other redistributive tool, may pose a sharper threat to the durability of a formal democracy than the economic inequality itself.

Despite this catching-up effect, there is a new panorama in the continent characterized by economic slowdown in the South driven particularly by falling prices of commodities and political polarization and instability. In the United States, there is a new government which is attempting to reduce taxes while initiating an important expenditure expansion program. Taxation as both a cause and reflection of society tends to adapt to new contexts, thus important changes in taxation can be expected in the upcoming years as a reflection of new societal realities.

Works cited

Atkinson, Anthony Barnes. 1977. "Optimal Taxation and the Direct versus Indirect Tax Controversy." *The Canadian Journal of Economics/Revue Canadienne d'Economique* 10, no. 4: 590–606.

Bermeo, Nancy. 2009. "Does Electoral Democracy Boost Economic Equality?" *Journal of Democracy* 20, no. 4: 21–35.

Corbacho, Ana, Vicente Fretes Cibils, and Eduardo Lora. 2013. *Recaudar no basta: los impuestos como instrumento de desarrollo*. 1st ed. Washington: Banco Interamericano de Desarrollo.

Cornia, Giovanni Andrea. 2014. *Falling Inequality in Latin America: Policy Changes and Lessons*. Oxford: WIDER Studies in Development Economics.

Cornia, Giovanni Andrea, Juan Carlos Gómez-Sabaini, and Bruno Martorano. 2011. "A New Fiscal Pact, Ta Policy Changes and Income Inequality. Latin America During the Last Decade." *WIDER Working Paper 2011/070*. United Nation University-WIDER. www.wider.unu.edu/publication/new-fiscal-pact-tax-policy-changes-and-income-inequality.

Cubero, Rodrigo and Ivanna Hollar-Vladkova. 2010. "*Equity and Fiscal Policy: The Income Distribution Effects of Taxation and Social Spending in Central America*." IMF Working Paper 10/112. Washington, DC: International Monetary Fund.

Fairfield, Tasha and Michel Jorratt. 2014. "Top Income Shares, Business Profits, and Effective Tax Rates in Contemporary Chile." ICTD Working Paper.

Goldscheid, Rudolf, Rudolf Hickel, and Joseph Alois Schumpeter. 1976. *Die Finanzkrise des Steuerstaats: Beiträge zur politischen Ökonomie der Staatsfinanzen*. Frankfurt am Main: Suhrkamp.

Goñi, Edwin, Humberto López, and Luis Servén. 2011. "Fiscal Redistribution and Income Inequality in Latin America." *World Development* 39, no. 9: 1558–1569.

Kaldor, Nicholas. 1963. "Will Underdeveloped Countries Learn to Tax?" *Foreign Affairs* 41, no. 2: 410–419.

Levi, Margaret. 1988. *Of Rule and Revenue*. Berkeley, CA: University of California Press. www.jstor.org/stable/10.1525/j.ctt1pngtk.

Mann, Fritz Karl. 1949. "Re-Orientation through Fiscal Theory." *Kyklos* 3, no. 2: 116–129.

OECD. 2008. *Growing Unequal? Income Distribution and Poverty in OECD Countries*. Paris: OECD, Organization for Economic Co-operation and Development.

OECD and CEPAL. 2016. *Revenue Statistics in Latin America 2015*. Paris: Organization for Economic Co-operation and Development.

Piketty, Thomas. 2014. *Capital in the Twenty-First Century*. Cambridge, MA: Harvard University Press.

Rodriguez, Corina and Nigolás Aguila. Forthcoming. 2018. "Gender bias of regressive taxation in Latin America. Overview and exploration for the Argentine case." In *Rethinking Taxation in Latin America: Reform and Challenges in Times of Uncertainty*, ed. Jorge Atria, Constantin Grol and María Fernanda Valdés, Palgrave Macmillan, 161–185. Basingstoke: Palgrave Macmillan.

Sokoloff, Kenneth L. and Eric M. Zolt. 2007. "Inequality and Taxation: Evidence from the Americas on How Inequality May Influence Tax Institutions." SSRN Scholarly Paper ID 985831. Rochester, New York: Social Science Research Network.

Souza, Pedro H. G. F., Marcelo Medeiros, and Fabio Avila de Castro. 2014. "Top Incomes in Brazil: Preliminary Results." SSRN Scholarly Paper ID 2511314. Rochester, New York: Social Science Research Network.

Stiglitz, Joseph Eugene. 2012. *The Price of Inequality*. New York, London: W.W. Norton & Company.

Swedberg, Richard. 1991. *The Economics and Sociology of Capitalism*. Princeton, NJ: Princeton University Press.

Tanzi, Vito. 2000. "Taxation in Latin America in the Last Decade." In *Taxation in Latin America in the Last Decade*. Stanford. Conference Paper for the *Fiscal and Financial Reforms in Latin America*. www.siepr.stanford.edu/conferences/FFReform_LA/Tanzi_Taxation_in_LAC.pdf.

Tanzi, Vito. 2013. "Tax Reform in Latin America: A Long-Term Assessment." Paper to be presented at the XXV Regional Seminar on Fiscal Policy. *ECLAC Santiago de Chile*.

Tilly, Charles. 1985. "War making and state making as organized crime." In *Bringing the State Back In*, eds. Peter Evans, Dietrich Rueschemeyer, and Theda Skocpol, 169–187. Cambridge: Cambridge University Press.

Valdés, María Fernanda. 2016. "Reducing inequality in Latin America: the role of tax policy." In *Entangled Inequalities: Exploring Global Asymmetries*, ed. Sergio Costa. London: Routledge.

World Wealth and Income Database. N.Y. "*World Inequality Database*." https://wid.world/.

23
TRANSNATIONAL CORPORATIONS

Katiuscia Galhera, Scott B. Martin, and João Paulo Cândia Veiga

Transnational corporations (TNCs), sometimes referred to as multinationals in everyday parlance, are firms "with the power to coordinate and control operations in more than one country, even if they do not own them" (Dicken 2015, 115). However, TNCs are also characterized by "*direct* production and generally direct business activities abroad" (Ietto-Gillies 2005, 8), usually via ownership and control of assets or direct management of personnel overseas, even if just as buyers. Yet, there is no accepted universal or legal definition of the term (Ruggie 2017), nor supranational legal frameworks to recognize and regulate the cross-national boundary activities of TNCs.

In today's global economy, they are networks within networks as they embed complex interconnections, transactions, trades, and social relations in different national institutions. Still, pathways of TNCs evolution are diverse and complex, involving newcomers and late-comers, as well as "born globals." Also, a typology of transnational corporations may encompass everything from the simple addition of an international or product division to a formerly domestic company's actual structure (→ Global Commodity Chains, II/12), to the firm's organization on a worldwide geographical basis, or global grid/matrix structures that includes both product and structure division, and dual reporting (Dicken 2015). For management studies, the TNC is the natural outgrowth of the multi-divisional hierarchically organized corporation that came to dominate the economy of northern countries, and subsequently expanded overseas. TNCs are the primary agents of Foreign Direct Investment (FDI), especially since the end of World War II (Dicken 2015; Ietto-Gillies 2005).

Historical backdrop, evolution of the term and efforts at regulation and control

The term "transnational corporation" has evolved over time, however the precise birth of the phenomenon to which it refers is difficult to determine. For instance, debate still centers on whether or not trading companies in the 17th, 18th, and 19th centuries, like the British and Dutch East India Companies which engaged in import, export, procurement, and sub-contracting of goods and merchandise abroad for shipment to foreign markets, were true TNCs or more appropriately can be considered their precursors (→ Colonial Economies, I/4). Concerns about practices in what would now be called TNCs in the extractive and mining sectors date as far back as the colonial period. Both are related to the debate on the dependency of the economic model of agro-mineral or primary export in colonial or postcolonial settings to the United States and the United Kingdom as well as the role which the dominant ruling classes in Latin America have played in this region (e.g., the United Fruit Company in Central America and its support for dictatorships, or International Telephone and Telegraph's involvement in the 1973 coup against the then democratically elected Chilean president Salvador Allende) (→ Authoritarianism, I/4). These early TNCs were seen by critics as fostering "enclaves" that did not benefit and were not linked to the national economy. Politically, they were often seen as agents or adjuncts of U.S. or European imperialism.

The post-World War II and *Pax Americana* with U.S. hegemony and economic expansion around the world also constituted early versions of post-war TNCs (Ietto-Gillies 2005). By the 1950s, the term "Multinational Corporations" (MNCs) was mainstreamed as the definition of a company that hierarchically coordinates semi-autonomous national subsidiaries in a liberalizing world in which interventionist states regulate flows of finance, investment, and trade. MNCs had no choice but to adapt to national regulations in setting up their supply networks, procuring finance, and developing products, particularly in the burgeoning manufacturing sector and whether they moved across boundaries in the capitalist West or in the developing and postcolonial world (→ Global Commodity Chains, II/12). The distinction with TNCs – a term that came into vogue in the 1970s – initially within the United Nations system – lay in the notion that multinationals were increasingly seen as transcending the control and coordination of all nation-states (→ II/38), both host and home, thus moving beyond the confines of nation-states and boundaries and escaping regulation given the absence of a global or international regime governing their activities.

The expansion of TNCs within the Global North and into the Global South occurred in the context of the Marshall Plan, European integration beginning with the European Steel and Coal Community (→ Regional Integration, II/18), Japanese reconstruction, the Alliance for Progress in the Americas (→ Modernization, I/35), and more informal or bilateral arrangements connecting Europe to the newly decolonized sub-Saharan Africa, or the United States to allied states in East and Southeast Asia. While American firms predominated, they were quickly emulated by competitors from various countries in Europe and Japan. Within the context of interventionist domestic states within a liberal international trading regime whose combination Ruggie (1982) termed "embedded liberalism" (embodied in the General Agreement on Tariffs and Trade and the International Monetary Fund), traditional export-oriented investment in agricultural and mining commodities was increasingly supplemented, among the range of TNC sectors, by "jumping over the tariff wall" to produce for protected overseas markets in the manufacturing, and later, service sectors.

Agencies and practitioners within the complex of the United Nations system, then under the influence of the Non-Aligned movement and Third World nationalism, coined and popularized the term TNC. Some scholars followed their lead, although making some analytical distinctions. However, the most common pre-existing term was MNCs (Moran 2009).

Amidst calls in the United Nations General Assembly for a New International Economic Order, a more critical perspective on TNCs and efforts to develop a binding code of conduct took shape by the early 1970s. The United Nations Conference on Trade and Development (UNCTAD) took shape in 1964. In 1974, the United Nations Center on Transnational Corporations (UNCTC) was created as a specialized agency under resolution LVII of United Nations Economic and Social Council (ECOSOC) only to be disbanded later. For almost two decades there were unsuccessful efforts to generate consensus on a binding code of conduct to regulate TNC activity. The term "transnational corporations" is usually associated with the UN systems' efforts during this time period (Moran 2009) and remained the term of art after the UNCTC was disbanded, with some of its activities folded into UNCTAD. The broader context was that of concern not only about the negative impacts on economic development (→ II/6) but also the way in which direct investment by TNCs was implicated in abuses such as perpetuation of apartheid in South Africa, the forced marketing of infant formula in development countries by manufacturers such as Nestlé, as well exposés by the Church Commission of the U.S. congress about the involvement of U.S. corporations in overseas covert activities by the Central Intelligence Agency (CIA). There was also much critical analysis emerging in the North that highlighted the way in which TNCs seemed to be undermining the sovereign state and interstate system even from the point of view of home countries – an example is Richard J. Barnet and Ronald E. Müller's (1974) *Global Reach: The Power of Multinational Corporations*. For this reason, International Organizations increasingly believed that TNCs operations must be more strictly regulated by sovereign states and UN agencies (→ Nation State, II/38).

As a mainstream reaction to the efforts to regulate TNC investment, the Organization for Economic Co-operation and Development (OECD) launched the voluntary *OECD Guidelines for Multinational Enterprises* in 1976 with principles and standards for responsible business ethics. A year later the International Labor Office within the International Labor Organization (ILO) launched the Tripartite Declaration of Principles concerning Multinational Enterprises and Social Policy in 1977. In the same year, the voluntary Sullivan Principles started promoting Corporate Social Responsibility (CSR) of TNCs to combat apartheid peacefully in South Africa, particularly through affirmative action in hiring – these might be defined as one of the very first models of CSR.

From the point of view of academic studies of development, an influential perspective in the late 1970s and 1980s was that of the study of TNC-state bargaining. One of its main exponents is Professor Gary Gereffi (1983), who in his early studies was still influenced by dependency theory (→ Development, II/6). One of this literature's contribution is the obsolescing bargain concept under which the balance of power changes to the host state, with sunken costs through time for the firm seeking forms of FDI, i.e. once an investment is made, the bargaining leverage gradually tends to shift away from the foreign company, so that the host government can extract concessions, attach performance conditions, tax remittances, and otherwise regulate TNC activity. Within this broader perspective, both sociologists and political scientists paid attention to manufacturing and industrial policies as well development policies toward valuable commodities such as copper and oil, ranging from nationalization to joint venture projects with nationally owned natural resource firms to various forms of taxation (→ II/22) or regulation.

In the mid-1980s and through the 1990s, complexities and variations of hierarchical coordination were noted and theorized in business and management studies. Some examples are the split and organization of firms at the industry level, different mechanisms of governance of TNCs, and innovation dynamics in corporations (De Marchi et al. 2014). In some ways, these studies were connected to Porter's typology of corporations based on degrees of control and varieties of headquarters-subsidiary relations (Porter 1986). A new direction, influenced initially by world systems theory and the work of Immanuel Wallerstein, was presented in the publication of *Commodity Chains and Global Capitalism* (Gereffi and Korzeniewicz 1994) in the mid-1990s that started an important debate on the venues where TNCs organize their chains (→ Global Commodity Chains, II/12). Of particular importance was a typology of economic upgrading for developing countries and locations, distinguishing among product, process, and functional forms of upgrading.

In the policy world, UNCTAD launched the first World Investment Report in what became an annual series in 1991, spotlighting a different new trend or policy issue each year in FDI and development, as well as disseminating data and research on TNCs and their evolution. Around this time, private codes of conduct for social and environmental standards in TNCs began to proliferate, usually as company- or sector-specific codes and labels. One example is the Responsible Care program, launched after the Bhopal disaster in 1984. By the end of the 1990s, policy activism influenced by the critical movement against neoliberal globalization (→ Alter-Globalization, I/21) moved toward the setting of social minimum standards of global scope, such as the ILO's core standards and Convention on the Worst Forms of Child Labor. These became points of references for activists seeking to turn CSR pledges into more binding commitments. Yet at the same time and with a different emphasis more in consonance with the CSR movement, in 1999, the Global Compact was launched as a voluntary initiative to support UN Goals. It was a sharp move away from binding codes and toward an ambitious effort at voluntarism, criticized by skeptics as based on a simple dissemination of "best practices" through the publication of business case studies instead of fostering effective mechanisms of transparency, accountability, and reporting. Indeed, few if any companies were ever kicked out of the Compact, except if they stopped reporting publicly on their CSR activities or flouted its principles in practice.

In the 2000s, UNCTAD became more policy oriented, shining a light on issues such as MNCs from the South, diverse forms of upgrading (i.e. social and technological) involving TNC linkages with local companies, cross-border mergers and acquisitions and their implications for development, and other emerging policy challenges of particular relevance to the Global South.

In 2011, John Ruggie published the relevant UN document *Protect, Respect, and Remedy: Framework and Guiding Principles* that would become the "ground zero" for efforts to establish treaties on business and human rights (→ II/35), currently ongoing. Ruggie's critical perspectives on TNCs further developed the notions of power, authority, and relative autonomy (Ruggie 2013).

After the Rana Plaza disaster in 2013, a successful binding multi-stakeholder agreement to restrict and regulate TNC buyers and their local manufacturing suppliers around health and fire safety issues was developed by trade unions, NGOs, and buyers. Also, top-down experiences of private agreements between companies and Global Union Federations – international federation of unions organized by sectors or occupational categories – started to have a more bottom-up design. International or Global Framework Agreements (IFAs/GFAs) usually have a strong top-down design, as they are mostly negotiated in closed meetings in home countries of TNCs, although IFAs are expected to empower the rank and file in overseas operations as well as, in some instances, in the supply chains of TNCs. New initiatives or a new generation of IFAs have a more bottom-up design, as they involve workers from the workplace and the participation of other union organizations to promote a sense of ownership and belonging for workers in TNCs. Since 2015, a new binding document, called Protocol to the Legally Binding Instrument to Regulate, in International Human Rights Law, the Activities of Transnational Corporations and other Business Enterprises, has been under negotiation to regulate the operations of TNCs – a rare case of international negotiations to tackle non-state actors' obligations in providing international human rights (OHCHR 2018).

Theoretical debates and evolution

Major debates regarding TNCs evolved over time, involving diverse theories, concepts, units of analysis, schools, paradigms, and organizations, such as the dichotomy between development and dependency for peripheral countries (→ Development, II/6); a capitalist transnational class exploiting workers and peasants worldwide (→Social Inequality, II/2); a division between core and periphery in a world system; postcolonial studies takes on the international division of labor (→ Postcolonialism, I/38); the (new) international division of labor; triple alliance among state, TNCs and big domestic businesses; embedded autonomy of states promoting national development; global commodity chains (→ II/12); and varieties of capitalism (→ II/2).

One of the earlier, more sophisticated, and variegated debates on dependency theory in its various strands was developed in the1960s. The United Nations Economic Commission for Latin America and the Caribbean (ECLAC) developed concepts and analyses of political economy (or economic policy) from a developmentalist perspective, favoring state intervention to foster industrialization and urbanization (→ I/45). The general paradigm was that Latin America could surpass and overcome its underdevelopment by industrialization, and for that goal the process would consist of import substitution industrialization (ISI) and a cross-class alliance that would keep foreign capital at bay and "renegotiate" the terms of dependency on nationally favorable terms.

However, different critical perspectives on the same issue were developed by different schools of thought. Andre Gunder Frank (1978) in *Dependent Accumulation and Underdevelopment* argued that Latin American underdevelopment is a product of its integration to the world economy and this generates "development of underdevelopment" for dependent countries. In this sense, TNCs would be mere tools for the maintenance of underdevelopment in Latin America. Cardoso and Faletto (1979), in *Dependency and Development in Latin America*, had a "historical-structural" analysis of how foreign capital is internalized within domestic class structures and pacts of domination, studied historical evolution, and developed typologies by country and sub-regions of "situations of dependency" based on type of sector and national ownership. For Cardoso and Faletto, with the example of Brazil, there could be a stunted but real (quantitative) economic growth with TNCs through the "internalization of the internal market" and what Cardoso later called "associated dependent development."

Still from the 1960s on, the transnational capitalist class (TCC) or class beyond frontiers theory developed the idea of an international capitalist class and their related powerful corporations exploiting workers, peasants, and other groups through extraction of surplus value, based on dialectical Marxist assumptions (Sklair 2001). High-level managers of TNCs, moving seamlessly across national boundaries within their companies or sometimes between companies, would be an example par excellence of such a transnational class, with interests and loyalties weakly tied to nation-states (→ Social Inequality, II/20).

World systems theory, from the 1970s, had a focus on the global system, and the concept of (international) division of labor is central for understanding the theory. The two varieties of world systems – world-empires with large bureaucracies and an axial division of labor, and the world economy in its various historical carnations with, in the contemporary period, a developed industrialized core and an undeveloped raw-materials-exporting periphery – are based on an endless accumulation of wealth by capitalists (Wallerstein 1974). Later developments of the theory introduced the semi-periphery (for instance, Brazil and Argentina) as an intermediate level of analysis. In this regard, TNCs would be tools for the accumulation process of the core of the systems. In terms of Latin America, while some authors such as Frank and Gills (1993) reaffirmed Wallerstein's first ideas on exploitation and value transfer from peripheries to the center of capitalism, postcolonial authors reused the division of labor to explain systems of coloniality, including gender (Lugones 2016) (→ Gender Identities, II/28).

The international division of labor (IDOL) as a concept emerged in the 1970s and developed further in the 1980s in the context of the Newly Industrializing Countries (NICs). Theories around the IDOL also offer new perspectives and frameworks *vis-à-vis* dependency and world-system theories, such as Haggard's (1990) take on how NICs in East Asia were able to move up in the global economy through export-oriented industrialization, partnering with, and in some cases in tension with, U.S. and European TNCs, through interventionist but market-friendly states. This stood in contrast to the static determinism of the IDOL, in which industrial societies specialized in manufactured products, while Latin America, Africa, and Asia specialized in primary products, especially after the post-war period. In the new international division, activities have changed, but not the overall structure of the world capitalism: industrial societies specialize in capital and expertise, while most countries in Latin America, Africa, and Asia specialize in the provision of cheap labor and natural resources.

Peter Evans in his book *Dependent Development* (2018), borrowed from Cardoso's concept of "associated, dependent development" when describing Brazil in his concept of a "triple alliance" of TNC, domestic resources, and state capital leading to rapid industrialization, but with income concentration that would then contribute to capital accumulation and structural change in the semi-periphery. TNCs (the author calls them multinationals), then, would be agents/actors contributing to dependent development in the periphery. Later on, Evans (1995) developed the concept of "embedded autonomy," which theorizes the developmentalist state (with the example of South Korea) – a concept discussed by other analysts of development strategy particularly in East Asia. In Evans' work, Brazil and India fall short as only "intermediate states" with mere pockets of the state having the right mix of relative autonomy from the capitalist class with ties to the dynamic business sector to promote national development through industrial policy and exports.

The global commodity chains' (GCC) perspective (→ II/12) also has a clear imprint of world systems theory, but it is more empirical (1994). GCC analysis focused on particular sectors and countries, taking into account different relations of power and bargaining. At the early 2000s, GCC concept was melded with the business school/management perspective of global value chains (GVCs), and the latter term became dominant. These ideas also influenced policy debates at national and multilateral organizations on issues such as competitiveness in policy, small and medium-size enterprises (SMEs) promotion of links to TNCs, local upgrading, and national business systems, among others.

Since the 1990s, the varieties of capitalism (VoC) literature from the North (positing for instance sector-coordinated vs. liberal vs. nationally coordinated/social democratic models) has influenced the understanding on TNCs in several ways, particularly whether they reflect the distinctive home country VoCs (e.g., German vs. U.S. vs. Japanese TNCs) as they spread overseas. Debate has emerged in this decade in Latin America about whether there is a single or multiple VoCs in evolving Latin American post-market reforms. On the one side, Schneider (2013) argues that hierarchical capitalism throughout the region involves a retreat of the state and dominance of big domestic groups in services and light manufactures with increased TNC domination of the most dynamic sectors. On the other side, Bizberg (2019) argues instead for market-centric (e.g. Chile and Mexico) versus state-centric VoC (e.g. Brazil and Argentina) and distinguishes these varieties by their more or less forceful or absent policies toward FDI and TNCs when trying to promote domestic firms and their internationalization and/or links to foreign firms.

Shifting empirical terrain of TNCs with globalization and neoliberalism/economic opening

Transnational corporations' history and evolution usually follow the changing nature of import-substituting industrialization. Latin American newly industrialized economies (NIEs) or NICs had similar patterns of ISI: from commodity exports (Mexico 1880–1930, Brazil 1880–1930), going through primary import-substituting industrialization (Mexico 1930–1955, Brazil 1930–1955), secondary ISI (Mexico 1955–1970, Brazil 1955–1968), and diversified export promotion and continued secondary ISI (Mexico 1970–, Brazil 1968-) (Dicken 2015). This means that the sectoral composition and focus of TNCs and FDI, and nature of relationships such as those captured by the triple alliance, changed overtime. Secondary ISI dynamics, especially the drain of resources (→Extractivism, II/9) and crises of "deepening" the productive structure, were seen by some scholars such as Guillermo O'Donnell as contributing to dictatorships in the region (→ Authoritarianism, II/25).

Nationalities of TNCs' ownership investing in Latin America diversified over time, with U.S. and European TNCs joined by firms from Korea and Taiwan (especially in sectors such as electronics and clothing) as well as China, which has become a leading trade and investment partner with the region of Latin America (Gallagher and Porzecanski 2010). China as a partner is controversial as on one hand, there is concern about perpetuating a traditional IDOL with China by buying commodities and financing infrastructure, and on the other hand, there was concern earlier in the century that China was surpassing export zones in northern Latin America and taking away jobs.

Multilatinas (Latin American multinational or transnational corporations) arising from large or dynamic regional economies (especially Brazil, Mexico, and Chile) have frequently emerged with state assistance, for instance, with the support of the National Bank of Economic and Social Development/Banco Nacional de Desenvolvimento Econômico e Social (BNDES), for the Brazilian multilatinas. Other promoters of multilatinas' expansion were processes of regional integration (→ II/18), such as the Southern Common Market (Mercosur), and/or investment overseas, for instance, Natura's expansion, Vale in Africa and Canada, Mexican firms' (like CEMEX, Herdez, and Grupo Chedraui) investment in U.S. production and sales. Still, while developing countries were headquarters to less than 10 percent of the world population of TNCs in 1990, by 2005 they were 23 percent, especially due to the rise of China as a global player (Ietto-Gillies 2005). Multilatinas usually have close ties to the state and oligopolistic positions in markets, although not so much in most technologically dynamic activities (Schneider 2013).

TNCs' interrelation with states and governments may be verified through domestic policies designed to attract FDI (→ State Transformation, II/21), as the role of the state or governments is central for the setting up or development of direct production, sales, and/or distribution activities. Devaluation of a country's currency to make exports competitive, export trade policy measures, easier entry and sending of profit remittances, and regional trade arrangements are some examples of state or governmental intervention to attract FDI. Of particular importance as tactics of countries to attract FDI and stimulation of export industries is the Export Processing Zone (EPZ) model in light manufactures, especially in Mexico and Central America and in parts of South America as well as in much of Asia and Africa. EPZs might take different formats, such as *maquiladoras* and free trade zones. Of course, this process does not follow automatically, and much EPZ activity is locally owned and producing inter-firm for MNC buyers. Thus, most of trade is intrafirm or involves GVCs. Most importantly, a significant share of global commerce is intrafirm trade, which raises the whole problem of transfer pricing (under-invoicing in high-tax jurisdiction and over-invoicing in low-tax ones), and difficulties of the state in taxation (→ II/22), which even the EU is still trying to manage (e.g., questioning Irish policies to attract FDI by lowering tax rates).

A shifting composition of FDI includes increasing shares in services (including commerce, business services, and finance), with a big increase in export agriculture and mining with Chinese demand in the 2000s, and a lesser relative share in manufacturing. Recently, with the rise of China as a global player in the economy, there is a constant concern about the return of Latin America to the periphery of the world economy.

As a probable legacy of market reforms and neoliberalism (→ II/16), in Latin America there are less coherent and systematic policies toward FDI and generally speaking less concern about the nationalities of ownership. FDI is frequently seen as a better and less mobile resource than financial/portfolio capital. For instance, Walmart faces domestic opposition and policy constraints entering South Africa and India, but not in Brazil or Mexico. Of concern are not just local retailers, but also local agricultural producers and manufacturers, and whether they will also lose business as TNCs engage in global sourcing of what they sell locally. Some Latin American countries in certain sectors and in certain ways still constrain and regulate FDI besides promoting their own firms overseas, although this may vary depending on the government. As examples, Brazil pushed for licensing of generic medicines and the automotive regime, thus generating complaints by the U.S. at the World Trade Organization (WTO), and Chile kept the National Corporation of Copper in Chile (Corporación Nacional del Cobre de Chile, or CODELCO) as a state-owned business with foreign capital partners in the country despite its neoliberal orientation. Still, ties of big Mexican firms to the state are more indirect and less based on a coherent development strategy or industry policy, and many have to do with sweetheart privatization (→ II/17) (Slim and Telmex) or with traditionally protected domestic markets (like El Rey de la Tortilla Maseca). Some countries, such as Costa Rica in the case of Intel and other IT activities, have tried to develop dynamic networks of supply and spinoffs, as well as promote human capital formation of high-skilled engineers and other personnel around the presence of TNCs.

Conclusion

It is interesting to note that although this is an entry about TNCs on the American continent, most major debates are located in the North, with the notable exception of the UN ECLAC (CEPAL) and most contributions to dependency theory. The many major theoretical debates regarding TNCs discuss for example the fraught relationship between development and dependency at CEPAL, the theory of a transnational capital class exploiting and expropriating workers and peasants (→ Social Inequality, II/20), the world-system and postcolonial theories (→ Postcolonialism, I/38), the concept of a new IDOL (in world systems, transnational capital class and postcolonial theories), a triple alliance – among TNCs, state and national capital – the debate on GVCs (and derived concepts) (→ Global Commodity Chains, II/12), and VoC (→ II/2). Finally, TNCs act as active agents fostering processes of globalization and neoliberalism/economic opening (→ Neoliberalism, II/16; State Transformation, II/21), especially in the Americas.

Old debates about TNCs and their impacts on development (→ II/6) are still very relevant, albeit in new ways: Do they crowd out domestic investments? Are they better or worse as employers? Do they contribute to environmental and social policy through CSR and diffusion of such norms (→ Environmental Justice, II/8), or are they contributing to a "race to the bottom?" Can domestic firms partner with them productively for economic and social upgrading? Is it a good use of tax dollars to subsidize *multilatinas* overseas, and how and whether should they be linked to states' foreign economic policies? What is their impact on social and economic inequality within and across countries?

These questions should not just be analytically or normatively debated, but also considered and deliberated for concrete policy. Across the political spectrum, one is less likely to get black and white answers to these questions than in the 1960s or 1970s. At the same time, the unbridled enthusiasm for foreign investment associated with the heyday of neoliberalism has also faded, sometimes giving way to a more hard-headed look at when, how, and where to attract, regulate, and try to locally embed FDI, trying to maximize its positive development impact while minimizing its downside. In many ways, financial capital, with its footloose, often speculative character as well as volatility, has replaced TNCs and FDI as the source of greatest criticism for those examining the ills of contemporary globalization since at least the turn of the current century.

With the "pink tide" of the early 21st century there seemed to be a bit more attention to these issues, but some movement to the right across much of the region means these issues are not central to policy agendas of many regional governments, except for certain left or center governments. Most cases show that this policy is seen more of as a "business as usual," pragmatic set of policies shaping FDI, the attraction of which is mostly seen as a strong policy goal.

Returning to earlier developments, as the enthusiasm with TNCs faded, concerns to control and regulate their operations globally with multilateral binding instruments increased. After the failure of the The Multilateral Agreement on Investment (MAI) negotiated among members of the OECD in the 1990s – a framework intended to grant corporations unconditional rights to engage in direct and indirect investment around the world provoking criticism from civil society groups and some developing countries – the treaty negotiations were aborted in 1998, close on the heels of the controversy over the North American Free Trade Agreement that began in 1994 and amidst debates in the North over China's entry into the WTO and granting of permanent, normal trading relations with a still state-dominated economy. What is next? The multilateral treaty on business and human rights under negotiation could be one answer (→ Human Rights, II/35). Instead of constraining and regulating corporate behavior, TNCs would come under the oversight of a centralized body, albeit one with fewer restrictions and more attention to social standards than was true of the still-born code of conduct pursued by UNCTC in the 1980s and early 1990s.

Works cited

Barnet, Richard J., and Ronald E. Müller. 1974. *Global Reach: The Power of Multinational Corporations*. New York: Simon and Schuster.

Bizberg, Ilan. 2019. *Diversity of Capitalisms in Latin America*. Vol. 49 Switzerland: Palgrave Macmillan.

Cardoso, Fernando Henrique, and Enzo Faletto. 1979. *Dependency and Development in Latin America*. Berkeley and Los Angeles: University of California Press.

De Marchi, Valentina, Eleonora Di Maria, and Stefano Ponte. 2014. "Multinational firms and the management of global networks: Insights from Global Value Chain studies." *Advances in International Management* 27, no. 463: 486.

Dicken, Peter. 2015. *Global Shift: Mapping the Changing Contours of the World Economy*. Vol. 7th edition. New York: The Guilford Press.

Evans, Peter. 1995. *Embedded Autonomy: States and Industrial Transformation*. Princeton: Princeton University Press.

———. 2018. *Dependent Development: The Alliance of Multinational, State, and Local Capital in Brazil.* Chichester: Princeton University Press [Orig. pub. 1979].

Frank, Andre Gunder. 1978. *Dependent Accumulation and Underdevelopment.* London: Palgrave Macmillan.

Frank, Andre Gunder, and Barry K. Gills. 1993. *The World System: Five Hundred Years or Five Thousand?* New York: Routledge.

Gallagher, Kevin, and Roberto Porzecanski. 2010. *The Dragon in the Room: China and the Future of Latin American Industrialization.* Stanford: Stanford University Press.

Gereffi, Gary. 1983. *The Pharmaceutical Industry and Dependency in the Third World.* Princeton: Princeton University Press.

Gereffi, Gary, and Miguel Korzeniewicz. 1994. *Commodity Chains and Global Capitalism.* Westport: Praeger.

Haggard, Stephan. 1990. *Pathways from the Periphery: The Politics of Growth in the Newly Industrializing Countries.* New York: Cornell University Press.

Ietto-Gillies, Grazia. 2005. *Transnational Corporations and International Production: Concepts, Theories and Effects.* Cheltenham: Edward Elgar Publishing Limited.

Lugones, Maria. 2016. "The coloniality of gender." In *The Palgrave Handbook of Gender and Development: Critical Engagements in Feminist Theory and Practice*, ed. Wendy Harcout, 13–33. London: Palgrave Macmillan.

Moran, Theodore. 2009. "The United Nations and transnational corporations: A review and a perspective." *Transnational Corporations* 18, no. 2: 91–112.

O'Donnell, Guillermo. 1973. *Modernization and Bureaucratic Authoritarianism: Studies in South American Politics.* Berkeley: University of California Press.

OHCHR. 2018. *Legally Binding Instrument to Regulate, in International Human Rights Law, the activities of Transnational Corporations and other Business Enterprises.* United Nations Human Rights – Office of the High Commissioner. www.ohchr.org/documents/hrbodies/hrcouncil/wgtranscorp/session3/draftlbi.pdf.

Porter, Michael E. 1986. "Competition in global industries: A conceptual framework." In *Competition in Global Industries*, ed. Michael E. Porter, 15–60. Boston: Harvard Business School Press.

Ruggie, John Gerard. 2011. *Guiding Principles on Business and Human Rights: Implementing the UN "Protect, Respect and Remedy" Framework.* Genf: UN Human Rights Council.

———. 2013. *Just Business: Multinational Corporations and Human Rights* (Norton Global Ethics Series). New York: W.W. Norton & Company.

———. 2017. "Multinationals as global institution: Power, authority and relative autonomy." *Regulation & Governance* 12, no. 3: 1–17.

Schneider, Ben Ross. 2013. *Hierarchical Capitalism in Latin America: Business, Labor, and the Challenges of Equitable Development.* New York: Cambridge University Press.

Sklair, Leslie. 2001. *The Transnational Capitalist Class.* Oxford: Blackwell.

Wallerstein, Immanuel. 1974. *The Modern World-System I Capitalist Agriculture and the Origins of the European World-Economy in the Sixteenth Century.* New York and London: Academic Press.

PART II

Geopolitics and Governance in the Americas

Edited by

Olaf Kaltmeier and Eleonora Rohland

BIELEFELD UNIVERSITY

24

INTRODUCTION

Geopolitics and Governance: Inter-American Spaces of Entanglement

Olaf Kaltmeier and Eleonora Rohland

Until very recently, processes of Inter-American exchange, transfer, interdependence and entanglement seem to have increased continuously. The latinoization of the United States during the latter half of that 20th century has deeply changed the country's demographics and cultural politics. The U.S.-Mexican border is still the most crossed border in the world, although politically questioned and profoundly shaped by violence. Cross-cultural media flows shape consumer cultures, both in the North and South of the continent; capital interest fuels geopolitical imaginaries of hemispheric integration while the drug and arms trade (and their prevention) are other examples of the multiple forms Inter-American relations can take. In this volume, on *Geopolitics and Governance* of the Handbook these relations together with the latinoization of the U.S., sub-regional integration, and the growing importance of borderlands as "transfrontera contact zones" (Saldívar 1997) allow for reflecting upon the use of spatial categories from several different but related angles.

The actual (and rather persistent) *spatial turn*, which (re-)ignited debates about space in the humanities was initiated by many critical geographers – from Edward Soja to Doreen Massey to David Harvey – who were also influenced by French post-structural thinkers. Their main point was the critique of the "despatialization of social theory up to the 1960s" (Soja 1989, 39). While Soja did not initially posit the spatial turn as a Kuhnian paradigm shift, it has, in the meantime, acquired some of that significance (Döring and Thielmann 2009, 7).

Debates about space in area studies and history started soon after in the 1990s. Both disciplines tended to perceive areas, and in particular the nation-state, as a kind of closed-off container. This was particularly criticized in the debate between the approaches of comparative and transnational history, which was led more or less hotly in the U.S. and Germany at the time (e.g. Paulmann 1998; Tyrrell 1991) and which tried to move beyond the realm of the nation-state and toward global history. In this context, postcolonial scholars were most vocal in their criticism of the essentialization of Euro- or western-centric concepts and suggested acquiring a new perspective of connected histories with a more reciprocal relationship between nations, in particular in the (post-)colonial context (Chakrabarty 2000; Mignolo 2000; Subrahmanyam 1997). During the early 2000s, the two French historians Bénédicte Zimmermann and Michael Werner suggested overcoming the limitations of comparative history with their approach of *histoire croisée* (entangled history), however this approach was still operating within the European context (Werner and Zimmermann 2002, 2006). Entangled history (or histories) was then taken up by postcolonial scholar Shalini Randeria (2009) and a group of scholars at the Center for InterAmerican Studies (CIAS) at Bielefeld University. (Kaltmeier 2013, 2017; Raussert 2017) who reinforced the argument that flows of ideas, knowledge, and "civilization" were not a one-way street from metropole to (post-) colony, but that they were bidirectional and became mixed into new and hybrid forms, a process called *mestizaje*, in the Latin American context.

From these debates on the reconceptualization of space five particular points have been developed for the rethinking of Inter-American Area studies (Kaltmeier 2012). First, space is constituted through interactions, both between humans and with the environment. Space is thus a relational configuration that is in a constant process of becoming. Praxeological theories of space, such as Martina Löws' sociological approach, have introduced spacing, arranging artifacts in space, and synthesis, the combination of spatial ensembles into geographical imaginaries, as central spatial practices.

Second, space is to be understood as an area of diversity. If it is formed through interrelations, it must be based on plurality. Space is thus constituted from a variety of perspectives, formed by actors with culturally, politically, socially, and spatially different loci of enunciation. These arise not only from the geopolitical localization but also from the overlapping of fields of social practice characterized by different norms and logics of action. Thus, in space, different and often conflicting narratives, imaginations, and histories are present at the same time. In short: "Space and diversity are always mutually constituted" (Massey 2005, 32).

Third, conflict is inherent in space. Places of memory, temporal-spatial fixes of capital, material spatial appropriations, land grabbing, colonization, and geographical imaginations reveal how certain groups inscribe the political into space. A special conflict arises because the material, physical-geographical space is confined to the earth's surface and its subsoil. In this regard, group identities are often related to the marking of antagonisms in space: i.e. "from here" vs. "from there;" left vs. right; and socially elites "from above" vs. the common man/woman "from below." Conflicts are particularly strong when spatial claims overlap or when the same place or space is imagined in different ways.

Fourth, space is open, and not a closed container. There can be a superposition of spaces, and interaction can even overlap with different horizons of interaction in a single place as Massey (2005) has argued with the image of a "global sense of place." This, space is not to be conceived of as a static unit, but in terms of constant becoming. As a result, shifts – for Laclau and Mouffe (2014) "dislocations" – can give rise to new sentences as well as new articulations and interdependencies. There is always a moment of emergence. Through this spatial openness, political development paths, and thus historical processes are open and pluralistic.

Fifth, this implies a new relationship between space and history. The historiography of (European) modernity is still characterized by a discourse of linear progress and development. This has implications for the recognition of political-cultural difference. The anthropologist Johannes Fabian has identified a "denial of coevalness" in the modern interaction with other, mainly non-European cultures, which leads to a constructed cultural Other that is denied the recognition of simultaneity and is located on a underdeveloped precursor of the Occidental process of civilization (Fabian 1983; see also Chakrabarty 2000). Politically, this denial of simultaneity translates into a "war on difference and ambivalence" which, as Zygmunt Bauman points out, is led by the nation-state in particular. The recognition of plurilocality, pluriculturalism and ambivalence implies a reorientation of the spatio-temporal coordinates of historiography. This is neither to be done in the forms of a self-contained meta-history, nor in local regional histories. Instead, according to Randeria and Conrad (2002), the term "shared history" better encompasses this relationship between space and history because it can be understood two-fold. First, it indicates a history that is divided between center and periphery, rich and poor, "developed" and "underdeveloped" due to power asymmetries and social inequality. Second, it literally signifies that this is also a shared history and although there are different epistemological viewpoints and experiences, the common articulator is a globally entangled history within the capitalist world system, where center and periphery can only be understood in a process of mutual becoming.

Relying on these insights of the recent discussion on space in social theory, the concept of entanglement seems to be particularly fruitful to direct new research. Entanglement becomes a central approach with which to analyze transfers and flows of goods, people, knowledge, ideas, plants, animals, and other natural resources between regions. In our approach an area or region is not a given entity, instead it can only be described as a field of interaction and exchange that is relevant to the actors. The constructedness of areas and their relations to others is highlighted by focusing on mutual observation, comparison, competence, interdependence, and interplays. In this way, entanglement also addresses power asymmetries without the schematics of older dependence theories.

On the whole then, three heuristic approaches toward a framework of the space of entanglement have been proposed. First, the concept of *flows* allows for addressing the transregional mobilization and circulation of people, objects, biota, commodities, resources, ideas, and media and their impact in the construction of an Inter-American space of entanglement. This expands Manuel Castells' influential concept of a space of flows, which only focused on informational flows in the context of technological innovation (Castells 1996), to encompass any kind of objects of exchange or transfer that might constitute a specific space of entanglement. Also, in transnational anthropology (Appadurai 1996; Clifford 1997) the methodological approach to follow the itinerary of a given person, artifacts, or concept was proposed as a conceptual shift from "roots to routes" (Clifford 1997). The flow-approach thus allows for describing border-crossing dynamics and processes of deterritorialization as well as the intersection of local, national, regional, and transregional horizons of interaction that become relevant in the context of geopolitics and governance in the Americas. Cross-border flows not only lead to deterritorialization (inter alia; Deleuze and Guattari 1987; García Canclini 1995), but also to the liquefaction of social structures (Bauman 2006) and a change in perception of locality, territoriality, and nationality (Appadurai 1996; Massey 1994). A further research desideratum is to investigate how these multiple flows, understood as entangled dynamics, form new area structures; that is, to what extent do cross-border economic, migratory, and communicative spaces contribute to the material and imaginary foundations of the Americas as spaces of entanglement. And yet there is clearly no linear development of flows, as some proponents of a modernization theory based on societal acceleration might like to argue. Therefore, flows acquire different velocities and that their entanglement may reverse rather suddenly and become disentangled.

While flows form the individual threads within spaces of entanglement, a wider lens is required to take into account larger parts of the "fabric" of those spaces in order to understand the interaction of geopolitical and governance factors. As this wider lens, we propose the concept of *geopolitical imaginaries*. This topic allows for developing theories of articulation and entanglement of several spatial fragments (including different *flows*) into a more complex understanding of space and its representation (Epple and Kramer 2016; Gregory 1994). Geopolitical imaginaries are never static and homogeneous, but are subject to political cycles and negotiation processes, and characterized by changing constellations of actors. In this context, the entanglement of different discourses plays a role in the construction of these spatial imaginations. However, the focus is on the multiple ways these geopolitical imaginaries circulate and how they are used strategically in political communication, or in other words, how geopolitical imaginaries themselves become concepts that circulate in flows. In this regard, the experiences of Latin American Cultural Studies scholars and their analysis of medialized urban imaginaries are required (e.g. García Canclini 1995).

Clearly, *flows* themselves as well as *geopolitical imaginaries*, which are constituted by those flows, may involve both material as well as immaterial aspects and social construction. However, a third dimension should be added that has so far largely been absent from the debate on entanglement and geopolitical imaginaries. The dimension of the environment is a centered spatial concept which addresses the surroundings or conditions in which a person, animal, plant, or other agent lives or operates. However, the environment is not meant as a stage that humans "act upon." Rather, an earth system science understanding of the *biosphere* is meant, of which humans have been and are part of, and with which they have always been deeply (culturally) entangled, which also includes the climate system (Adeney Thomas 2014; Rockström et al. 2009). Such an integrated understanding is not only indispensable in order to grasp the geopolitical and governance implications of border-transcending climatic extreme events, the routes of neobiota-diffusion (Mosena 2018), and its regulations by global climate change politics or biodiversity regimes. From Christopher Columbus to our times, *geopolitical imaginaries*, the expansion and contraction of American empires and national politics have gone hand in hand with the material realities of the Columbian Exchange, of resource extraction, and environmental pollution and degradation (Crosby 1986; Grove 1996).

These heuristic spatial approaches of *flows*, spatial fixes in *geopolitical imaginaries* and the *environment* lead by no means to a description of the Americas as an integrated space without conflict. Spaces of entanglement are never smooth. Instead they are highly fragmented, incoherent, and shaped by uneven power relations through time.

The global sphere of Inter-American entanglements

The constitution of regional, areal, and trans-areal spaces, based on transboundary flows, in the Americas has produced various geopolitical imaginaries throughout history that are constantly changing (on the concept of the imaginary see e.g. Appadurai 1996; Buitrago, Petersen, Tyrell and Wehrmann 2016; Mignolo 2008; Petersen 2018; Pike 1992) (→ Geopolitics, II/34). These imaginaries mark moments when attempts at political integration or demarcation were made, their discursive negotiation and historical legitimation, and the constitution of social identities. In this respect, imaginaries represent a striking key to understanding the scope and intensity of dynamics of regional interdependency. Geopolitical imaginaries are based on different, often competing discourse traditions and actor strategies and make use of a wide variety of political, economic, social, and cultural patterns of interpretation. The function of geopolitical imaginaries is to establish territorial and trans-territorial validity claims, to produce the idea of local, national and transnational communities, and the asymmetrical links within the Americas, as well as to conceptualize the relations between individual regions and nations.

The geopolitical invention of the Americas through the act of European colonialism also meant the annihilation of different autochthonous worldviews of those peoples that since 1492 have been called "indigenous." The conquest did not only establish new forms of dominance and colonial rule, but also multiple ethnocides, the destruction of histories, and of the material and cultural worlds of the conquered. America is a "New World" in a double sense, first for the Europeans as a utopian projection, and second for the indigenous populations in terms of a colonial new world order. Apart from the forms of colonial rule and unfree labor, there were – beginning with the argument of Bartolomé de las Casas on the human nature of the indigenous – prototypic discourses on human rights (→ II/35). Therefore, Serge Gruzinski (2010) writes, "Mundialization rhymes with mobilization," pointing out that in the 17th century, a transnational space of political communication (→ II/42) was formed, marked by dynamics of politicization that cannot be grasped in the local or regional container.

In the same way, the multiple processes of decolonization in the 18th century have to be put into a broader, trans-Atlantic framework. The beginning of what Hobsbawm (1992) called the age of Revolution (Revolution, II/44) was made in 1764 and '65, when the English parliament passed several acts to raise revenue in its thirteen North American colonies in order to finance the aftermath of the Seven Years' War. The subsequent resentment of colonial subjects at being treated as second-rate Englishmen without representation in parliament in Westminster became the source of the American Revolution (1765–1783) and the independence of the thirteen British colonies as the United States of America (Israel 2017; Klooster 2009; Palmer 1959). With regard to the Americas as a space of entanglement, this liberation movement had far-reaching effects across the continent as well as on the other side of the Atlantic in Europe, involving economic flows (goods, tax monies) but also, and crucially, flows of ideas and people.

The American Revolution ignited the French Revolution in 1789, which with its ideas of *liberté, égalité, fraternité* flared back to the Americas by way of the French Caribbean sugar colony of Saint Domingue in 1791. While the question of the equality of enslaved Africans had remained an unsolved issue in and after the American Revolution in North America, it was at the center of events in majority black Saint Domingue (Israel 2017). For white (*criollo*) elites in the Americas, the Haitian Revolution was a double shock as it overturned the world order of white supremacy on the one hand, and the fact that formerly enslaved Africans were capable of founding the second independent republic in the Americas (1804) and governing themselves, on the other. The Enlightenment ideas of the American and French Revolutions had also flowed to the South American continent where they sparked the liberation movements from the Spanish crown in the viceroyalties of New Granada, Peru, Rio de la Plata, and New Spain between 1809 and 1826 (Rinke 2012).

The revolutionary independence movements of the late 18th and early 19th century spelt the end of colonial governance structures and the beginning of modern nation-states in the Americas (→ Nation State, II/38). These nation-building processes were accompanied by violent wars of independence, which by force of circumstance, pushed the evolving nation-states to form their own military (→ II/37) to defend their national security (→ II/45). In particular in the slave-holding Southern United States, the Haitian Revolution, and the refugees it created triggered an atmosphere of heightened racial anxiety among the white planter élite who feared a race war in the South. As a consequence, more restrictive legislation regulating the lives of free people of color and enslaved Africans was introduced in an attempt to suppress revolts and to maintain local and national security (Matthewson 2007; Paquette 1997).

In the extended aftermath of the Haitian and the French Revolutions, U.S.-American internal and foreign politics became uncomfortable with the influence these events may have on their own nation, and thus in 1823, President James Monroe formulated what became known as the Monroe Doctrine. It forbade any form of European intervention, colonization, or transfer of colonial power in the Americas and stated that any attempt at transferring European political systems to the western hemisphere would be considered an act of aggression by the U.S. government. Seeing themselves as the natural leaders of the western hemisphere, American politicians from the first decades of the 19th century onwards included the Caribbean – Cuba and Puerto Rico in particular – and the as yet unexplored American West into their geopolitical imaginaries (→ Borderlands, II/26).

When in 1898 war broke out between Spain and Cuba, U.S. Americans watched the unfolding conflict closely and with an increasing public thrust to enter the war. These U.S.-American attitudes toward Cuba and Cuban independence evolved within the general atmosphere of high imperialism and ideas of the "civilizing mission" of the United States (Pérez 1998). Even though the U.S. tried not to convey the image of being an imperial power, it secured the right to keep troops in Cuba after the capitulation and withdrawal of the Spanish in 1899. Again, the argument of security (→ II/45) (including decidedly racist overtones) and a paternalistic attitude of chaperoning the Cuban liberation process was used as a justification for intervening in Cuban independence. After Cuban protests against this behavior, the U.S. forced the acceptance of the Platt-Amendment (1901) as part of the Cuban constitution which effectively made Cuba a protectorate of the United States. Puerto Rico and the Philippines were further territories that came under U.S. imperial influence after 1898, the year that marked the United States entry into the race for Empire.

The idea that the Western hemisphere is an American one, with the U.S. as its protecting power has shaped transnational relations throughout the 20th century until today. The ugly face of this U.S.-imaginary expressed itself as interventionism (→ II/36) in Honduras (1903), in the Dominican Republic (1903; 1914; 1916–1924), in Columbia and Panama (1903–1914; 1925), in Cuba (1906–1909; 1912; 1917–1922; 1933), in Nicaragua (1912–1925; 1926–1933), in Mexico after the revolution (1913–1919), and in Haiti (1914–1934). With the beginning of the Cold War era, U.S.-American interventions and secret service actions were in particular directed against communist revolutionary movements (→ Revolution, II/44) the U.S. perceived as a threat to Western capitalism such as the Government of Jacobo Árbenz in Guatemala (1954), the Cuban Revolution (1959), the coup d'état against elected socialist president Salvador Allende in Chile (1973), the Contra War in Nicaragua, and the invasion in Grenada in 1983. Not taken into account are the actions of the CIA and secret service forces in other Latin American countries (→ Military II/37). Especially in the 1970s and 1980s, the U.S. pursued the anti-communist doctrine of national security (→ II/45), tolerating or even supporting the establishment of authoritarian military dictatorships (→ Authoritarianism, II/25) that neglected basic citizenship (→ II/27) rights and systematically violated human rights (→ II/35) (Niess 1986; Smith 1996; Westad 2005).

However, the imaginary of an integrated Western hemisphere was also supported by the promotion on Inter-American integration (→ Pan-Americanism, II/40). Early visions of Pan-American integration fostered by Simón Bolívar at the Congress of Panama in 1826 were not realized at the time. The first international conference on American states in Washington 1889/90 was the starting point for regular Inter-American conferences, culminating in the foundation of the Organization of American States (OAS) in 1948.

Besides these state-driven processes of Inter-American integration, there were also several dynamics of Inter-American entanglement in different social fields, from cultural production to sports and grassroot politics. In the era of global neoliberalism and the triadic distribution of the world market between Europe, Asia (first Japan, later China), and the U.S., economic integration became an important driver for Inter-American integration. This found its expression in regional trade agreements, such as the NAFTA between Canada, the U.S., and Mexico established in 1994. Other visions of a hemispheric free-trade area have not been realized due to protests by Latin American civil society and a significant turn to the left at the end of the 1990s, which created new Latin American intergovernmental organizations such as Unasur (Union of South American Nations) and Alba (Bolivarian Alliance for the Peoples of Our America). However, despite the left turn and the subsequent right-wing roll-back in North and South America, with "America first" slogans in the USA after the election of Donald Trump in 2017, the existing forms of regional economic cooperation have been partly renegotiated without having been substantially put into question. "America" – or better – "U.S. America first" is also a result of the reemergence of cultural geopolitics (→ II/34) after the end of the Cold War that Samuel Huntington described in the controversial terms of a "clash of civilizations" (1993) – a geopolitical concept against Islamic extremism that gained ground after 9/11 and that Huntington also turned against Latino immigration in the U.S. (2004).

These processes of Inter-American institutionalization and the evolution of its corresponding legal regimes must be seen in a broad political-cultural context, which includes not only the liberalization of flows of goods but also the fight against poverty, sustainable environmental policy, good governance, human rights issues, and cultural rights. Despite intergovernmental claims to regulation, these institutional dynamics of integration are only the surface of extensive Inter-American interdependency dynamics, focusing on simultaneous, complementary, or even countercultural forms of community building (Faist and Kivisto 2007; Pries 2008) as well as the emergence of transnational political cultures, communication spaces, and transversal consumer cultures in the contemporary global network society. In order to grasp the complexity of these societal, cultural, political, legal, and economic phenomena of interconnectedness in the Americas, this *Routledge Handbook* underlines the threefold entanglement of the macro-level of strategies of state and supranational actors with the meso-level of social movements, non-governmental organizations (NGOs), and other actors of the civil society (→ II/28), and with the micro-level of everyday experience and communication.

The national sphere of Inter-American entanglements

While in modernity the "state was the master of space" (Osterhammel 1998), this relationship has increasingly proven problematic in the face of the profound changes in political-spatial concepts in connection with the forced transnationalization processes since the mid-1970s. In the course of the "velocity revolution" (Virilio 2008), the consequent "space-time compressions" (Harvey 1990) and "information technology innovations" (Castells 1996), transnational migratory movements in the "age of migration" (Castles and Miller 2009), and the global exchange of information, goods, services, and capital speak of a de-territorialization or the "shrinking of space." Nevertheless, this does not mean that the nation-state (→ II/38) has lost its function completely. In regard to a multiple set of practices and discourses of governance and geopolitics, the national sphere remains of supreme importance.

In this sense the nation-state is not a fixed entity, or as French political philosopher Michel Foucault puts it, "The state is not a cold monster; it is the correlative of a particular way of governing" (2008, 6), and these ways of governing are not predetermined by the form of the state, instead they depend on the temporal-spatial-cultural contexts these practices and discourses are embedded in. Questions of governance or governmentality (Foucault 2008), that is, unequal sociopolitical relationships of power were at the center of these studies from which the concept of entanglement evolved. In other words, for postcolonial scholars it is and has been much more common to think about how systems of governance such as democracy (→ II/32) or authoritarianism (→ II/25) and modes of political participation (→ II/41) through civil society (→ II/28) have been entangled in (post-)colonial contexts, than what role geopolitical factors might have played in such entanglements.

Furthermore, the nation-state is not nationally limited. Instead it is a relational phenomenon based on the mutual observation in a world system, with its first incarnations developed in Western Europe after the Westphalian peace treaty that in 1648 was generalized and transferred to the rest of the world in forms of material and discursive (also internal) colonization. It is by no means the case that the development of nation-states is solely a Western phenomenon that diffused into the peripheries. For example, the historian Benedict Anderson (1983) pointed out that Latin American national state formation in the first half of the 19th century was much more powerful and earlier than in many parts of Europe.

While the nation-state is often presented in its self-imagination for example via maps as an integrated political space, the negotiation of the political in peripheral areas also points to how democracy (→ II/32) and citizenship (→ II/27) are exposed here. Especially the postcolonial state shows a Janus face in this regard. On the one hand, the political inclusion of citizens in a civil society (→ II/28) is demanded, which turns out to be more embryonic in terms of real political participation (→ II/41). Clientelism (→ II/29) and populism (→ II/43) – especially important in Latin American regimes of the 1930s and 1940s – have served in several cases as a tool to hide the gap of promised and real participation. Surprisingly, it seems that populist forms of governance have celebrated a revival nearly 100 years later.

On the other hand, despite the overarching promise of inclusion, the state excludes large sections of the population from the sphere of political participation. In democratic regimes, for example, certain groups of the population, such as ethnic minorities, migrants, illiterates, the poor, and women, have, in part formally and sometimes de facto, been excluded from civic rights. In the U.S., segregation and Jim Crow laws are believed to have been examples until the end of the 1960s, but new forms of exclusion have been addressed by the Black Lives Matter – movement. In Latin American countries, on the other hand, the de facto exclusion of the indigenous population until the middle or even the end of the 20th century is also an example. In addition, crude bio-political interventions such as slum-clearance acts promote the development of peripheral areas of the state, which are characterized by the suspension of citizenship. The postcolonial historian Partha Chatterjee (2006) has shown how the poor and marginalized population is excluded from the sphere of civil society (→ II/28), but then acquires agency through the exercise of suffrage and as a target group of (inter-) national government welfare programs as a "political society" from state borders to national policies. Special forms of the delimitation of political rights and citizenship are found in authoritarian regimes (→ II/25), particular in those military dictatorships that arose in the context of the Cold War to contain the communist threat of national liberation movements.

Since the 1980s, borders have been conceived of as spaces that stand out from the existing geopolitical territories and have their own rationalities. Worth mentioning here are the works on interstate border areas, such as they are paradigmatically expressed in the U.S.-Mexican borderlands (→ II/26). Undoubtedly, the crossing of the border is a neuralgic point in migrant itineraries as the example of the U.S.-Mexican-Mexican border shows. The more than 7,000 km-long border is controlled by a 3,000 km-long border fence built according to the Secure Fence Act 2006 – which was extended by Donald Trump – and by high-tech border police, such as the Border Patrol in the operation Gatekeeper (→ Security, II/45). Although this border came to represent not only a national boundary but also the chasm between the "Global North" and the "Global South," after the end of the block confrontation it is still the world's most crossed border. The multitude of border crossings can be explained by trans-migration, as the migrants periodically return to their original communities and remittances have become one of the main sources of funding for development programs in their home villages. In addition, contacts are maintained via modern communication media such as telephone, email, Skype, and social media networks such as Facebook. The migration process is unfinished and open, so that trans-migrants do not live here or there, but in the in-between. All of these changes require a new understanding of space. The cross-border dimension has been worked out in the academic literature on migration, using the example of the U.S.-Mexican-Mexican borderlands. According to these works, borders always have something in common and can be understood as a "transfrontera contact zone" or as *nepantla*. Boundaries act as geopolitical hinges. They are central to the development of cross-border, transnational social spaces that do not coincide with the established territorial spaces.

The biosphere of Inter-American entanglements

As stated at the beginning of this introduction, the Handbook's concept of entanglement challenges the outdated separation between "nature" and "culture." The increasing cognitive dissonance that results from this divide was recently pointed out by literary scholars Nathan Hensley and Philip Steer, noting that "the schism between ecological and postcolonial approaches continues to play out as a split tradition, one concerned with non-human or 'natural' actors … and the other with human – that is sociopolitical – ones" (Hensley and Steer 2019, 5–6). By explicitly including material culture and ecological approaches into the conception of spaces of entanglement, this *Handbook* is trying to offer a solution to unite these two traditions that are highly relevant for the Americas.

The entanglement of geopolitics and governance with the biosphere lies at the heart and at the beginning of the post-Columbian history of the Americas. Environmental historian Alfred Crosby was the first scholar to point to the colossal, global circulation of plants, animals, pathogens, and humans that Columbus' "discovery" had set in motion. The Columbian Exchange as well as Crosby's and a few others' follow-up publications (Crosby 1986; Grove 1996; McNeill 2010; Rohland 2019; White 2017; Zilberstein 2016) laid the groundwork for considering "nature" (→ II/39) or natural resources and the emergence of colonial empires in the Americas as entangled factors. Here, the introduction of neobiota occurred in terms of an "ecological imperialism" and became an integral part of the political process of colonization and the establishment of colonial rule. Beyond this intentional transformation of ecosystems through the introduction of neobiota, there are also complex forms of unintentional diffusion that – nevertheless – are related to the process of colonization (Mosena 2018). Nature in its evolving understandings has been part and parcel of Europeans' geopolitical imaginaries in the Americas (→ Geopolitics II/34). Pre-Columbian cosmologies that understood humans as part of a complex, interconnected, and animate universe in which deities would communicate through natural phenomena or appear in animal form (Bastian and Mitchell 2004; Ortiz Fernández 1947) were suppressed and silenced.

In early colonial times natural extreme events, or disasters (→ II/33), were initially perceived by Europeans as signs of the Christian god's wrath and as a cause for repenting. However, this religious perception of disasters did not preclude the close observation of nature. What is more, because the environment and climate Europeans encountered during the 16th and 17th centuries in the Americas was so strange and unfamiliar, they relied on indigenous peoples in order to learn about the return frequency and seasonality of extreme events (Rohland 2019; Schwartz 2015).

A contentious point in the governance of disasters was the issue of security. In particular in the slave societies of the Caribbean and the U.S. South, the structural and social disruption that went hand in hand with disasters such as hurricanes, volcanic eruptions and earthquakes increased white anxieties of slave uprisings and the overthrow of the precarious social order that could only be maintained with regimes of violence (Mulcahy 2006; Smith 2012).

Structurally, the entanglement between disaster and social order and/or national security (→ II/45) has continued throughout history, as the case of Hurricane Katrina in 2005 has starkly shown (Rohland 2017). The routes of Hurricanes in the Caribbean create entangled risk-scapes that have particular regimes of governmentality due to their embedding in different political contexts – from national regimes (Mexico, U.S., Cuba, etc.) to European overseas-ruled territories (Martinique, Guadeloupe, etc.) (Bohle 2018).

A concept that has deeply influenced the governance of the natural environment is the idea of "wilderness" that stems from the differentiation between cultivated "civilized" nature and its uncultivated "other." It gained enormous traction and became part of the geopolitical imaginary of the Westward Expansion in North America between 1830 and 1870 (Culver 2012; Nash 1967). This process also resulted in an immense land grabbing and a privatization of the commons (→ II/31) – in turn, fueling the process of capitalist accumulation and industrialization in Western Europe and North America.

With the evolution and rise of the natural sciences during the mid- and late 19th century, the understanding of nature in the sense of our natural (non-human) environment has changed radically. In the United States, the acceleration of scientific knowledge and the industrial revolution went hand in hand with a recognition of environmental depletion, in particular with regard to wood and deforestation. During the second half of the 19th century, naturalists George Perkins Marsh and John Muir noted the negative human impact on the environment. During this era, "wild" nature came to be seen as on the retreat and as in need of protection leading to the establishment of National Parks, first in the USA and later in Canada and Latin American countries, in particular Argentina, Chile, Brazil and Mexico under the government of Lázaro Cárdenas in the 1930s (Gissibl, Höhler, and Kupper 2012; Hardenberg, Kelly, Leal and Wakild 2017; Wakild 2011; Kaltmeier 2020).

Some of the environmental degradation environmentalists were observing during the second half of the 19th century, was due to industrialization's changing energy regimes to fossil fuels. Coal mining was on the rise, especially in the Appalachian Basin and in the Powder River Basin of Wyoming and Montana (Jones 2010) and quickly became a geopolitical factor entangled in trade and technological development. The largest deposits of coal in Colonial New Spain were located in New Mexico, Texas, and Louisiana, all of which became U.S. American states during the 19th century. In Mexico, U.S.-dependent companies were involved in coal mining south of the Rio Grande at the beginning of the 20th century. While Chile, Argentina, and Colombia were all exploiting their national coal deposits, the involvement of U.S. American and European companies in the already global coal trade shows how environmental, geopolitical, and during the 20th century increasingly, national and energy security questions became entangled with resource extraction (Wendt 2016). This situation was of course compounded by the discovery and exploitation of oil fields in North and South America from the mid-19th century onwards (Black 2000; Cote 2013) as well as in Mexico since the first half of the 20th century and Venezuela and Ecuador since the mid-20th century. In some countries, the importance of the extraction of one natural resource became so important that it became the basis for the construction of the rentier nation-state (Coronil 1997), often also creating complex networks of clientelism (→ II/29).

From the beginning, European resource extraction in the Americas clashed with indigenous perceptions of the indivisibility of the earth/land (→ Commons, II/31) and earth as a living organism. Resource extraction went hand in hand with an encroachment on and violation of indigenous land rights, in particular during the 20th century, when the scale of oil extraction and hydro-power projects increased exponentially (Cote 2017; Orellana 2005). The geopolitics of capitalist (and neo-extractivist) energy extraction and national energy security have, and have thus had, an evident connection with issues of environmental justice, environmental vulnerability, social inequality, and racism, which underlines our argument about the biospheric component of entanglement. Examples of this nexus range from the Dakota Access and Keystone XL Pipelines in the USA, to the Arco Minero Orinoco in Venezuela, to oil extraction in the Peruvian Amazon, to the hydroelectric dams Ralco in Chile and Belo Monte in Brazil.

The often violent conflicts that ensued around land use and land rights also spell one limit of the neo-extractivist development model that the resource-rich Latin American countries such as Venezuela, Bolivia, Ecuador, Brazil, and Argentina have employed since the beginning of the 21st century to sustain their social policies (Burchardt and Dietz 2014). Currently, not only society, policy, or economics themselves but also "nature" (→ Nature, II/39) and environment set the limit for this model of advancing the state and society.

Recently, the (Western) concept of nature-as-separate-from-humans has in fact become obsolete through the discussion about the Anthropocene (Chakrabarty 2009; Crutzen and Stoermer 2000; Steffen, Grinevald, Crutzen, and McNeill 2011). This is a new geological epoch identified by geologists, in which humans have become a planet-altering force, by their sheer numbers and their interference with the deep layers of the earth's crust as well as the higher atmosphere. The fact that humans are now shaping the planet spells the actual end of the nature/culture divide (Chakrabarty 2009) and, with regard to this Handbook's approach, exemplifies the ultimate entanglement – or acts as a reminder that the separation of "man and nature" as imagined from the Enlightenment onwards, had in fact never taken place.

An intense debate about the concept of the Anthropocene ensued within (and outside of) the Humanities, focusing on the term "Anthropocene" one the one hand, and on the starting date of this new epoch, on the other (e.g. Bonneuil and Fressoz 2016; Davis and Todd 2017; Haraway 2015; Whyte 2017). One of the dating proposals that gained significant scholarly attention focused on the Americas and was introduced by geographers Simon Lewis and Mark Maslin who suggested that the Anthropocene should start in 1610, when, according to their ice-core data, a global slump in CO_2 levels occurred (Lewis and Maslin 2015). Lewis and Maslin connected this low to the mass death of American indigenous populations (→ Indigenous Peoples, I/11) at the hands (and diseases) of Europeans and the consequent reforestation of formerly agriculturally used lands during the 16th century. This proposal has since been contested by members of the Anthropocene Working Group based on contradictory ice-core and land-use data (Zalasiewicz et al. 2015).

The above entanglement between resource extraction, land and energy use and societal development, all of which have contributed to the factors that make up the Anthropocene, shows the complexity of scale that geopolitics and governance have reached during the 20th and 21st centuries. The often conflicting interlocking between the local and the global scale may be most clearly exemplified by climate change governance (→ Climate Change, II/30) since the 1990s. In the aftermath of the end of the Cold War, aiming to streamline economic development and protection of the environment globally, the 1992 Earth Summit in Rio de Janeiro was organized. It built on the notion of sustainability as developed in the

1987 Brundtland Report (World Commission on Environment and Development 1996 (1987)) and was also the moment at which the United Framework Convention on Climate Change (UNFCCC) was opened for signatures. Beyond its impact on global environmental policies, the Earth Summit was also a case in point for the emergence of a global civil society (→ II/28) that did not believe only in politics to solve the problems of the global biosphere.

The current global youth climate movement (including Fridays For Future, School Strike for Climate, Youth for Climate and Youth Climate Strike), the discussions around indigenous earth politics with concepts such as "buen vivir," as well as multiple environmental justice movements almost a generation onwards from the Earth Summit can be seen as taking climate consciousness, questions of sustainability and the urge for political action to a new level. This clearly has to do with the shrinking window of time within which action to reduce carbon emissions adequately is still possible (IPCC 2018). The coming decade will be crucial in showing whether this impulse by (young) people and movements around the world will gain enough traction and support from other sectors of (national) civil society to pressure governments to act on climate and to implement the policies necessary to cope with human-made ecological crises and their multiple impacts.

Works cited

Adeney Thomas, Julia. 2014. "History and Biology in the Anthropocene: Problems of Scale, Problems of Value." *The American Historical Review* 119, no. 5: 1587–1607.

Anderson, Benedict. 1983. *Imagined Communities: Reflections on the Origin and Spread of Nationalism*, London: Verso.

Appadurai, Arjun. 1996. *Modernity at Large: Cultural Dimensions of Globalization*, Minneapolis, MN: University of Minnesota Press.

Bastian, Dawn. E. and Judy K. Mitchell. 2004. *Handbook of Native American Mythology*, Santa Barbara, CA: ABC-CLIO.

Bauman, Zygmunt. 2006. *Liquid Fear*, Cambridge, NJ: Polity Press.

Black, Brian. 2000. *Petrolia: The Landscape of America's First Oil Boom*, Baltimore, MD: Johns Hopkins University Press.

Bohle, Johannes. 2018. "Hurricane-Riskscapes and Governmentality." *Erdkunde* 72, no. 2: 125–134.

Bonneuil, Christophe and Jean-Baptiste Fressoz. 2016. *The Shock of the Anthropocene: The Earth, History, and Us*, London, Brooklyn and New York, NY: Verso.

Buitrago, Clara, Mirko Petersen, Paul-Matthias Tyrell and Dorothea Wehrmann. 2016. "From Ideas to Concepts: (Geo-)Political Imaginaries." *Forum for Inter-American Research* 9, no. 1: n.p.

Burchardt, Hans-Jürgen and Kristina Dietz. 2014. "(Neo-)extractivism – A New Challenge for Development Theory from Latin America." *Third World Quarterly* 35, no. 3: 468–486.

Castells, Manuel. 1996. *The Information Age: Economy, Society, and Culture, Volume 1: The Rise of the Network Society*, Oxford and Malden, MA: Blackwell Publishers.

Castles, Stephen and Mark Miller. 2009. *The Age of Migration*, 4th ed. Houndsmills: Palgrave Macmillan.

Chakrabarty, Dipesh. 2000. *Provincializing Europe: Postcolonial Thought and Historical Difference*, Princeton, NJ: Princeton University Press.

———. 2009. "The Climate of History: Four Theses." *Critical Inquiry* 35, no. 2: 197–222.

Chatterjee, Partha. 2006. *The Politics of the Governed: Reflections on Popular Politics in Most of the World*, New York, NY: Columbia University Press.

Clifford, James. 1997. *Routes: Travel and Translation in the Late Twentieth Century*, Cambridge, NJ: Harvard University Press.

Coronil, Fernando. 1997. *The Magical State: Nature, Money, and Modernity in Venezuela*, Chicago, IL: University of Chicago Press.

Cote, Stephen. 2013. "A War for Oil in the Chaco, 1932–1935." *Environmental History* 18, no. 4: 738–758.

Cote, Stephen. 2017. "Oil in the Andes." *Oxford Research Encyclopedia of Latin American History*. http://oxfordre.com/latinamericanhistory/view/10.1093/acrefore/9780199366439.001.0001/acrefore-9780199366439-e-427#acrefore-9780199366439-e-427-div1-1.

Crosby, Alfred. 1986. *Ecological Imperialism: The Biological Expansion of Europe, 900–1900*, Cambridge, NJ: Cambridge University Press.

Crutzen, Paul J. and Eugene F. Stoermer. 2000. "The 'Anthropocene'." *International Geosphere-Biosphere Program (IGBP) Newsletter* 41, no. May: 17.

Culver, Lawrence. 2012. "Manifest Destiny and Manifest Disaster: Climate Perceptions and Realities in United States Territorial Expansion." In *American Environments. Climates – Cultures – Catastrophe*, eds. Christof Mauch and Sylvia Mayer, 7–30. Heidelberg: Universitätsverlag Winter.

Davis, Heather and Zoe Todd. 2017. "On the Importance of a Date, or Decolonizing the Anthropocene." *ACME, an International Journal for Critical Geographies* 16, no. 4: 761–780.

Deleuze, Gilles and Félix Guattari. 1987. *A Thousand Plateaus: Capitalism and Schizophrenia*, Minneapolis, MN: University of Minnesota Press.

Döring, Jörg and Tristan Thielmann. (ed.) 2009. *Spatial Turn: Das Raumparadigma in den Kulturen – Und Sozialwissenschaften*. Bielefeld: Transcript.

Epple, Angelika and Kirsten Kramer. 2016. "Globalization, Imagination, Social Space: The Making of Geopolitical Imaginaries." *FIAR* 9, no. 1: 41–63.

Fabian, Johannes. 1983. *Time and the Other. How Anthropology Makes its Object*, New York, NY: Columbia University Press.

Faist, Thomas and Peter Kivisto. 2007. *Citizenship: Theory, Discourse and Transnational Prospects*, Oxford, UK: Wiley-Blackwell.

Foucault, Michel. 2008. *The Birth of Biopolitics: Lectures at the Collège de France 1978–1979*, New York, NY: Pallgrace Macmillan.

García Canclini, Néstor. 1995. *Hybrid Cultures: Strategies for Entering and Leaving Modernity*, Minneapolis, MN: University of Minnesota Press.

Gissibl, Bernhard, Sabine Höhler and Patrick Kupper. 2012. *Civilizing Nature. National Parks in Global Historical Perspective*, New York, NY: Berghahn Books.

Gregory, Derek. 1994. *Geographical Imaginations*, Cambridge and Oxford: Blackwell.

Grove, Richard. 1996. *Green Imperialism: Colonial Expansion, Tropical Island Edens and the Origins of Environmentalism 1600–1860* (Reprint edition), Cambridge, NJ: Cambridge University Press.

Gruzinski, Serge. 2010. *Las cuatro partes del mundo. Historia de una mundialización*, Mexiko: Fondo de Cultura Económica.

Haraway, Donna. 2015. "Anthropocene, Capitalocene, Plantationocene, Chthulucene: Making Kin." *Environmental Humanities 6*, 159–165.

Hardenberg, Wilko Graf von, Matthew Kelly, Claudia Leal and Emily Wakild. (ed.) 2017. *The Nature State: Rethinking the History of Conservation*. New York, NY: Routledge.

Harvey, David. 1990. *The Condition of Postmodernity: An Enquiry into the Origins of Cultural Change*, Oxford, UK: Blackwell.

Hensley, Nathan and Philip Steer. 2019. *Ecological Form: System and Aesthetics in the Age of Empire*, New York, NY: Fordham University Press.

Hobsbawm, Eric. 1992. *The Age of Revolution, 1789–1848*, New York, NY: Vintage Books. Orig. pub. 1962.

Huntington, Samuel P. 1993. "*The Clash of Civilizations?*" *Foreign Affairs* 72, no. 3: 22–49.

Intergovernmental Panel on Climate Change (IPCC). 2018. "Special Report: Global Warming of 1.5° C." *IPCC*. www.ipcc.ch/sr15/.

Israel, Jonathan. 2017. *The Expanding Blaze: How the American Revolution Ignited the World, 1775–1848*, Princeton, NJ: Princeton University Press.

Jones, Christopher. 2010. "A Landscape of Energy Abundance: Anthracite Coal Canals and the Roots of American Fossil Fuel Dependence, 1820–1860." *Environmental History* 15, no. 3: 449–484.

Kaltmeier, Olaf. 2012. *Politische Räume jenseits von Staat und Nation*, Göttingen: Wallstein.

———. (ed.) 2013. *Transnational Americas: Envisioning Inter-American Area Studies in Globalization Processes*. Trier and Tempe: WVT/Bilingual Press.

———. 2017. "Doing Area Studies in the Americas and Beyond. Towards Reciprocal Methodologies and the Decolonization of Knowledge." In *Area Studies at the Crossroads: Knowledge Production after the Mobility Turn*, Katja Mielke and Anna-Katharina Hornidge, (Hg.) 47–67. New York, NY: Palgrave Macmillan.

Kaltmeier, Olaf. 2020. *National Parks from North to South: An Entangled History of Conversation and Colonization in Argentina*. Trier and Tempe: WVT/Bilingual Press.
Klooster, Wim. 2009. *Revolutions in the Atlantic World: A Comparative History*, New York, NY: New York University Press.
Laclau, Ernesto and Chantal Mouffe. 2014. *Hegemony and Socialist Strategy*, London: Verso.
Lewis, Simon and Mark Maslin. 2015. "Defining the Anthropocene." *Nature* 519, 171–180.
Massey, Doreen B. 1994. *Space, Place and Gender*, Minneapolis, MN: University of Minnesota Press.
———. 2005. *For Space*, London: SAGE Publications Ltd.
Matthewson, Timothy. 2007. "George Washington's Policy toward the Haitian Revolution." *Diplomatic History 3*, no. 3: 321–336.
McNeill, John. 2010. *Mosquito Empires: Ecology and War in the Greater Caribbean, 1620–1914*, New York, NY: Cambridge University Press.
Mignolo, Walter. 2000. *Coloniality, Subaltern Knowledges, and Border Thinking, Local Histories/Global Designs*, Princeton, NJ: Princeton University Press.
———. 2008. *The Idea of Latin America*, Malden, MA: Blackwell.
Mosena, Alexander. 2018. "Reconstructing the Historical Spread of Non-Native Plants in The North American West from Herbarium Specimens." *Flora (Jena)* 242, 45–52.
Mulcahy, Matthew. 2006. *Hurricanes and Society in the British Greater Caribbean, 1624–1783*, Baltimore, MD: Johns Hopkins University Press.
Nash, Roderick. 1967. *Wilderness and the American Mind*, New Haven, CT: Yale University Press.
Niess, Frank. 1986. *Der Koloß im Norden*, Köln: Pahl-Rugenstein.
Orellana, Marcos. 2005. "Indigenous Peoples, Energy and Environmental Justice – The Pangue/Ralco Hydroelectric Project in Chile's Alto Bio Bio." *Journal of Energy and Natural Resources Law* 24, no. 4: 511–528.
Ortiz Fernández, Fernando. 1947. *El Huracán, su Mitología y sus Símbolos*, 1st ed. Mexico City: Fondo de Cultura Económica.
Osterhammel, Jürgen. 1998. "Die Wiederkehr des Raumes. Geopolitik, Geohistorie und historische Geographie." *Neue Politische Literatur* 43, 374–395.
Palmer, Robert. R. 1959. *The Age of the Democratic Revolution*, Princeton, NJ: Princeton University Press.
Paquette, Robert L. 1997. "Revolutionary Saint Domingue in the Making of Territorial Louisiana." In *A Turbulent Time: The French Revolution and the Greater Caribbean*, eds. David Barry Gaspar and David Patrick Geggus, 204–225. Bloomington, IN: Indiana University Press.
Paulmann, Johannes. 1998. "Internationaler Vergleich und Interkultureller Transfer. Zwei Forschungsansätze zur europäischen Geschichte des 18. bis 20. Jahrhunderts." *Historische Zeitschrift* 267, no. 3: 249–685.
Pérez, Luis A. 1998. *The War of 1898: The United States and Cuba in History and Historiography*, Chapel Hill, NC: University of North Carolina Press.
Petersen, Mirko. 2018. *Geopolitische Imaginarien. Diskursive Konstruktionen der Sowjetunion im peronistischen Argentinien (1943–1955)*, Bielefeld: Transcript.
Pike, Frederick. B. 1992. *The United States and Latin America: Myths and Stereotypes of Civilization and Nature*, Austin, TX: University of Texas Press.
Pries, Ludger. 2008. *Transnationalisierung der sozialen Welt. Sozialräume jenseits von Nationalgesellschaften*, Frankfurt a.M.: Suhrkamp Verlag.
Randeria, Shalini. 2009. *Vom Imperialismus zum Empire. Nicht-westliche Perspektiven auf Globalisierung*, Frankfurt a.M.: Suhrkamp.
Randeria, Shalini and Sebastian Conrad. (ed.) 2002. *Jenseits des Eurozentrismus. Postkoloniale Perspektiven in den Geschichts- und Kulturwissenschaften*. Frankfurt a.M.: Campus.
Raussert, Wilfried. 2017. *The Routledge Companion to Inter-American Studies*, New York: Routledge.
Rinke, Stefan. 2012. *Lateinamerika und die US. Eine Geschichte zwischen Räumen – von der Kolonialzeit bis heute*, Darmstadt: WBG.
Rockström, Johan, Will Steffen, Kevin Noone, F. Åsa Persson, Stuart Chapin III, Eric F. Lambin, Timothy M. Lenton, Marten Scheffer, Carl Folke, Hans Joachim Schellnhuber, Cynthia A. Björn Nykvist, Terry de Wit, Sander Hughes, Henning van der Leeuw, Sverker Sörlin Rodhe, Peter K. Snyder, Robert Costanza, Uno Svedin, Malin Falkenmark, Robert W. Louise Karlberg, Victoria J. Corell, James Hansen Fabry, Brian Walker, Diana Liverman, Katherine Richardson, Paul Crutzen, and Jonathan A. Foley. 2009. "A Safe Operating Space for Humanity." *Nature* 461, 472–475.

Rohland, Eleonora. 2017. "Adapting to hurricanes. A historical perspective on New Orleans from its foundation to Hurricane Katrina, 1718–2005." *WIRES Climate Change* 9. https://onlinelibrary.wiley.com/doi/epdf/10.1002/wcc.488.

Rohland, Eleonora. 2019. *Changes in the Air: Hurricanes in New Orleans from 1718 to the Present*, Oxford and New York, NY: Berghahn Books.

Saldívar, José David. 1997. *Border Matters: Remapping American Cultural Studies*, Berkeley, CA: University of California Press.

Schwartz, Stuart. B. 2015. *Sea of Storms: A History of Hurricanes in the Greater Caribbean from Columbus to Katrina*, Princeton, NJ: Princeton University Press.

Smith, Peter H. 1996. *Talons of the Eagle: Dynamics of U.S.-Latin American Relations*, Oxford, UK: Oxford University Press.

Smith, Simon D. 2012. "Storm Hazard and Slavery: The Impact of the 1831 Great Caribbean Hurricane on St Vincent." *Environment and History* 18, no. 1: 97–123.

Soja, Edward W. 1989. *Postmodern Geographies: The Reassertion of Space in Critical Social Theory*, London, UK: Verso.

Steffen, Will., Jacques Grinevald, Paul Crutzen and John McNeill. 2011. "The Anthropocene: Conceptual and Historical Perspectives." *Philosophical Transactions of the Royal Society A: Mathematical, Physical and Engineering Sciences* 369, no. 1938: 842–867.

Subrahmanyam, Sanjay. 1997. "Connected Histories: Notes towards a Reconfiguration of Early Modern Eurasia." *Modern Asian Studies* 31, no. 3: 735–762.

Tyrrell, Ian R. 1991. "American Exceptionalism in an Age of International History." *American Historical Review* 96, no. 4: 1031–1055.

Virilio, Paul. 2008. *Negative Horizon*, New York, NY: Continuum.

Wakild, Emily. 2011. *Revolutionary Parks: Conservation, Social Justice, and Mexico's National Parks, 1910–1940*, Tucson, AZ: University of Arizona Press.

Wendt, Helge. 2016. Coal Mining in Cuba: Knowledge Formation in a Trans-Colonial Perspective. In *The Globalization of Knowledge in the Iberian Colonial World*, ed. Helge Wendt, 261–296. Berlin: Edition Open Access.

Werner, Michael and Bénédicte Zimmermann. 2002. "Vergleich, Transfer, Verflechtung. Der Ansatz der Histoire croisée und die Herausforderung des Transnationalen." *Geschichte und Gesellschaft* 28, no. 4: 607–636.

Werner, Michael and Bénédicte Zimmermann. 2006. "Beyond Comparison. Histoire Croisée and the Challenge of Reflexivity." *History and Theory* 45, no. 1: 30–50.

Westad, Odd Arne. 2005. *The Global Cold War: Third World Interventions and the Making of Our Times*, New York, NY: Cambridge University Press.

White, Sam. 2017. *A Cold Welcome. The Little Ice Age and Europe's Encounter with North America*, Cambridge, NJ: Harvard University Press.

Whyte, Kyle. 2017. "Indigenous Climate Change Studies: Indigenizing Futures, Decolonizing the Anthropocene." *English Language Notes* 55, no. 1-2: 153–162.

Zalasiewicz, Jan., Colin N. Waters, Anthony D. Barnosky, Matt Edgeworth Alejandro Cearreta, Erle C. Ellis and Alexander. P. Wolfe. 2015. "Colonization of the Americas, 'Little Ice Age' climate, and Bomb-Produced Carbon. Their Role in Defining the Anthropocene." *The Anthropocene Review* 2, no. 2: 117–127.

Zilberstein, Anya. 2016. *A Temperate Empire: Making Climate Change in Early America*, Oxford: Oxford University Press.

25
AUTHORITARIANISM

Alke Jenss

Authoritarianism continues to be a pressing topic in the Americas. This can be seen in claims protestors voice on the streets, in decisions taken in parliaments, in more or less authoritarian measures implemented through state policies (→ Nation State, I/38), and in academic knowledge production. Figures like U.S. President Donald Trump or Jair Bolsonaro in Brazil represent what has been called a new wave of "*antiprogresismo*" in the Americas (Stefanoni 2018). This entry aims to disentangle different strands of discussion within each and across (Latin) American research communities, focusing on and relating to the general notion of authoritarianism. Three perspectives have been used to explain and interpret the different forms of authoritarianism: common historical grounds where concepts flow from one context to the other, comparative analysis, and an entanglements perspective have each shed light on different phases and aspects of these debates over the last five decades.

During the 20th century, the production of knowledge on the state and authoritarianism in the Americas was always intertwined with the political question of how to possibly transform the asymmetries that limited broader participation (→ II/41) in politics through fixating on extremely unequal social relations (→ Social Inequality, II/20). The rich history of debate has focused on state-society relations, historical conditions, and the link of authoritarian politics with capitalist economy (→ Capitalism, II/2). A look at the history of this debate on authoritarianism from an Inter-American perspective with reference to 20th century military dictatorships in Latin and Central America (→ Military, II/37), as well as focusing on more recent examinations that compare single case studies of formal democracies with authoritarian traits helps to provide a basis for highlighting the entanglement of political realities and knowledge production at its center.

Authoritarianism: a common historical frame for an Inter-American discussion

There are many examples of transferring concepts and meanings flowing from one context to the other. However, two historical prerequisites of the debate on authoritarianism exist in Latin America: colonialism and dependency. During colonialism (→ Colonial Rule, I/5), this asymmetrical integration of colonies and semi-colonies into an emerging capitalist world system had rested on – utterly authoritarian – modes of unfree labor (→ I/19). Yet, colonial power relations along constructions of racial difference (→ Race, I/39) were perpetuated and made it almost impossible for certain social segments to ascend to power (Quijano 2000). Constructions of racial hierarchies continued and still fundamentally shape political life in the Americas; the exclusionary political systems have their roots in colonial social relations (→ Inter-ethnic Relations, I/12). The second, Latin America's long-lasting asymmetrical integration into the world market is characterized by dependency approaches of the 1960s and 1970s that presented authoritarian elements of government as a result of their historical and very particular integration into the world market (see Marini 1991) (→ Development, II/6). Dependency approaches exposed how social policies in Latin American postcolonial states were structurally limited i.e. because the fiscal dependence on raw material rents would not allow for more than selective policies (→ Taxation, II/22), and this dependence had its roots in colonialism's fixing of trade relations (→ Colonial Economies, I/4). Galeano (2003) famously describes how in independence, one raw material would be replaced by the next once its role for the world market subsided and prices fell. Cycles of demand and demise of rubber, coffee, or oil determined the economic structure of different countries (→ Extractivism, I/9). Dependency scholars pointed to the limitations for social mobility. This was due in part to the structural limits on economic transformation. Capital dependence, for instance, hardly allowed for the investments necessary to establish economic sectors with higher paid jobs, even during the 1960s, when import-substituting policies prevailed.

As a result of these unequal social relations, the political regimes remained exclusionary, often rigidly closed off to those outside a small dominant class fraction. Their authoritarian traits were clear – from truncated electoral processes to open military takeovers. The experience of colonialism and particularly integration into the world economy have clearly constituted common markers of the "Latin American" debate on authoritarianism (→ Postcolonialism, I/38). However, this common ground for debate does not deny that configurations in each country may differ considerably. Forms of organization and institutionalization, participation and exclusion, access to decision-making processes, means of government all differed greatly in time and space. Each state presented different forms of authoritarianism, because its actual shape depended on internal factors; the external factors (such as "dependence") assumed relevance *in relation to* the contradictions within each society (Cardoso and Faletto 1976, 22); different contextual, historical conditions remained decisive for the shape of the political form (Thwaites Rey 2010, 24).

Read against this background, historical authoritarian regimes such as the dictatorship of Porfirio Díaz, who governed Mexico from 1876–1880 and 1880–1911 up to the Mexican Revolution (→ II/44), and similar regimes of that era played a decisive role for expanding capitalist modernization against resistances (→ Modernization, I/35), and in terms of selective mechanisms of political participation (→ II/41) (loyalty against partial social mobility and protection). The complex state party rule which ultimately was the result of the Mexican Revolution can likewise not be understood without putting its authoritarian and coercive mechanisms in relation with changes in social relations, emerging middle classes, and the limits to these changes; they have been termed an example of a passive revolution, an authoritarian "domestication" of forces struggling for radical change (Morton 2011).

Authoritarianism was not limited to "Latin" America. In the U.S., the authoritarian undercurrents of history have once again surfaced and have been studied from Latin American and U.S. scholars alike. Katznelson (2014) has described how the U.S. New Deal (after 1933) combined democratic representation and welfare (→ Democracy, II/32) with antidemocratic mechanisms of coercion, as a reaction to what was perceived as a world in severe political and economic crisis (→ II/4), international trade conflicts and competition. Apart from fearing that U.S. parliamentary democracy might be too soft to compete with fascist regimes in Germany or Japan, inducing an arms race that made the U.S. military grow exponentially, the political order of the U.S. South and its violent system of racial hierarchy severely limited democratic developments and the enjoyment of rights (→ Human Rights, II/35). Katznelson sees an "anti-liberal white populism" as a distinct characteristic of the U.S. South's order (2014, 23) (→ Whiteness, II/46), yet this organization of hierarchies, of democratic rights around constructions of race, points to similarities with Latin American postcolonial states and the wider relations of global economy (Quijano 2000).

Peronism in Argentina, and similar governments and the opposition to them today still serve as cultural and political reference points, for example through figures such as Eva Perón (→ Populism, II/34). These, however, differed from military dictatorships that spread through Latin America in the 1970s, as Peronism, despite authoritarian tendencies, did integrate broad sectors of society into its social and developmental project. In contrast, the debate in the 1970s revolved around how to differentiate Latin American authoritarianism from European fascism, in terms of the validity of a "European" concept in Latin American contexts (Zavaleta 1979). European experiences provided a background for Latin American debates (Martuscelli and Svampa 1993, 7). In which ways could the military dictatorships gripping Argentina, Uruguay, Chile, and many others in the 1970s, be understood as fascist regimes or Bonapartism? To what extent did they have to be distinguished from European developments? Did not modalities of domination and government or elements as *Caudillismo* or *Caciquismo* have to be grasped via a more thorough socio-historical analysis? Neither did the Latin American regimes have mass support behind them, nor did the regimes include the mass mobilization of extremist party members (Cardoso 1978, 42). Social relations were quite different from those of European societies (see, for example, CEREN 2007, originally published in 1973). The "fascism" label mismatched Latin American realities, and the discomfort with a simple transmission of "European" labels to the Latin American context led to further debate.

Guillermo O'Donnell (2009, 15–59) proceeded to understand the military dictatorships in the *Cono Sur* as historically specific forms of "bureaucratic-authoritarian state" (republished 2009, 15–59) (→ Nation State, II/38). He stressed that the state as a power relation presented elements of "structural complicity" with certain class fractions (→ Class Struggle, II/3). This is a clear reference to the notion of "structural selectivity," coined by Nicos Poulantzas and Claus Offe, from European state theory. O'Donnell argued that this held true for Latin America as much as for the European state. Yet beneath a "cacophony of mismatched strategies, failures and always partial and precarious achievements" (O'Donnell 2009, 19), state institutions contributed to the reproduction of unequal social relations, via law, and, in case of a crisis of domination, via violence. These crises emerged when society did not perceive the state as a "servant to the common good" anymore – quite obviously a recurrent theme in the Americas.

Norbert Lechner, another prominent voice in the authoritarianism debate, however, criticized instrumentalist ideas about the state with "catastrophic" political consequences (Lechner 1981, 7). Lechner, who had accompanied the government of Allende's Unidad Popular in 1970s Chile until the U.S.-backed military coup in 1973, coined the term "technocratic authoritarianism" for the post-coup dictatorship, linking the military's hurry to make all elements of society "functional for capitalist modernization" and liberalization to its recourse to extreme authoritarianism (Lechner 1981, 4). He saw the contradictions in the state's task "to organize dominant groups, atomize dominated groups, and at the same time bring all of them together in an order" (Lechner 1981, 7). Again, this seems to be a dialogue with critical European state theory emerging around the same time (first published in 1978, Poulantzas 2002).

Concepts flowed between contexts, particularly for the *Cono Sur*, to make sense of the military takeovers in Chile (1973–1990), Argentina (1976–1983), Uruguay (1973–1985), Bolivia (1971–1982) and a decade earlier, in Brazil (1964–1985). Precisely in this vein, Fernando Cardoso (1978) called for a differentiation between cases, i.e. an authoritarian Mexico dominated by the Partido Revolucionario Institucional (PRI), and the extremely authoritarian military dictatorships of the *Cono Sur*. In his opinion, these differences had to be reflected in the conceptual debates. These should distinguish between the "state" as an expression of capitalist relations of forces, in an abstract Marxist sense, and that of the "regime." The state, Cardoso argues, assumes similar functions across Latin America, but coexists with a great variety of regimes. The latter is concerned with the formal norms that define the workings of political institutions and the political relation between the governing and the governed (Cardoso 1978, 44–45). These regimes became the catalysts of a highly exclusionary development (Martuscelli and Svampa 1993, 6).

The degree of exclusion of parts of society from the possibility to shape policies, the role of the executive versus the legislature, the relation of the executive to the military (→ II/37), and the latter's role and protagonism, the role and existence of political parties, and means of cooptation or representation toward interest groups are all factors that need to be analyzed (Cardoso 1978, 46ff.). Following Cardoso, social interest groups in authoritarian regimes sometimes serve as "*anillos burocráticos*" ["bureaucratic bands"] for a top-down articulation rather than independent pressure groups anchored in civil society (→ II/28). Mexico and Brazil, to him, seem to have a common history of weak civil society organizations, yet Mexico remained a non-military regime, stable, exerting control over a range of organizations with which it seemed to be in constant negotiation (1978, 49).

The discussion of similarities and degrees of authoritarianism calling for differentiation was indeed taken up within the U.S., and in dialogue with the Latin American colleagues, i.e. in the Joint Committee on Latin American Studies of the American Council of Learned Societies and the Social Science Research Council from 1975 onwards (Collier 1978). It also pointed at overcoming the dichotomy between a supposedly "democratic West" and an authoritarian non-Western world (Guilhot 2005, 120).

The 1980s brought democratizing processes in countries like Argentina, Brazil, Uruguay, pushed in part by growing movements for democracy (→ II/32), newly strengthened indigenous movements (→ Indigeneity, I/31) in countries like Ecuador, and a new academic focus on democratic transition (→ State Transformation, II/21). While the authoritarian state disappeared from many research agendas, scholars increasingly focused on transition topics such as the institutionalization of political pluralism, social dimensions of citizenship (→ II/27) and the search for new principles of social cohesion despite the still palpable effects of an authoritarian political culture (Martuscelli and Svampa 1993, 5–6).

One attempt at analyzing these post-dictatorship states, much-noticed in Latin America and translated into Spanish, was the argument for a new "competitive authoritarianism" by Levitsky and Way (2004). They and others argued that transition literature had been too optimistic in reading the regimes of the 1990s simply as incomplete in their transition from the National Security regimes toward democracy (2004, 159), and that instead, one could sense discontent and uncertainty. They call this authoritarianism despite relatively free elections, universal suffrage, a free press (→ Freedom of Expression and Censorship, III/29) and the relative liberty of government from the military (Levitsky and Way 2004, 162). Yet the universal rules were violated sufficiently, regularly, and severely enough to create an uneven game between the governing and all forms of opposition. Regimes abused state resources, inhibited adequate space for the opposition in the media (→ Media Participation, III/36), and used threats, persecution, detentions, and homicides to discourage opposition politicians and journalists (see Tapia Fernández 2015). These authors understood that democracy had not displaced authoritarianism, but instead, "the authoritarian became a general characteristic which could subsist within democratic political regimes" (Lesgart 2003, 129), that would continue to weaken social struggles. Levitsky and Way (2004, 163) criticize O'Donnell's notion of "delegative democracies," as it trivialized the authoritarian traits of those regimes that based their legitimacy on minimally competitive and transparent elections, but sometimes even expanded their authoritarianism by not respecting institutional norms, circumventing accountability, or concentrating power in the executive (again) (O'Donnell 1994, 7–15). This applied, for example, to the Peru of Fujimori after 1992. O'Donnell, however, contributed to a more differentiated picture of U.S. and Latin American authoritarianism when he stressed how in both the southern U.S. and parts of Brazil, Peru, or Argentina, state bureaucracies coexisted with privatized circuits of power, unwritten rules, personalism, and clientelist mechanisms (→ Clientelism, II/29), which he called subnational "brown areas" (1993).

Comparison: analysis of authoritarianism in different, separated contexts

In the 2000s, studies on democracy and the state clearly diversified. The political arena opened up around the beginning of the 2000s, and new actors forced themselves on the political scene after two decades of neoliberal restructuring (→ Neoliberalism, II/16) paralleled by democratization processes (→ State Transformation, II/21). Organizations self-identifying as indigenous, as defending women's rights, and as eminently urban came together and reorganized social movements (→ I/41). As political practice precedes literature on the state, and democracy, authors based in countries with processes of political transformation, such as Argentina, Bolivia, or Ecuador, began to re-focus on the state after an almost 20-year hiatus (Cortés 2012, 93). The topics they embraced were the dynamic relation between states and social movements, the possibilities of changes within the institutional ensemble, or what has been called new constitutionalism (Gargarella and Courtis 2009).

Another new strand of literature on emerging authoritarianism links the discussion of a new relation between state and social movements to the "new extractivism" debate (→ Extractivism, II/9). It discusses the relative leadership of social movements vis-à-vis the state. This new "developmental" state, which has not been able to overcome its (fiscal) dependence on extractive sectors such as the export of oil, has been criticized for increasingly authoritarian measures toward those parts of society that question this dependence. In Bolivia for instance, widespread, violently repressed protests against water privatization took place (→ Privatization, II/28), mainly in Cochabamba. Labeled the "Water War" in 2000, it led to radical shifts in the relations of forces and thus, to significant changes within the state ensemble. Many expectations rested on Evo Morales, who had been a coca growers' union spokesperson and became the country's first self-identifying indigenous president. Bolivia's new constitution deconstructed a number of normalized discriminations; re-emerging social policies considerably reduced inequality (→ Social Inequality, II/20). Nevertheless, the movement-turned party Movimiento al Socialismo (MAS) presents authoritarian and clientelist traits itself (→ Clientelism, II/29), particularly when local contestation against infrastructure projects emerged in protected areas. The "compensating state" aims to create delicate balances between its concessions to global capital and its quest to regulate it; its dilemma lies between promoting mining and absorbing its social effects (Gudynas 2012). Others, however, have presented Bolivia as a case where forms of dispersal, indigenous forms of political articulation, and a diversity discourse overcame some types of structural authoritarianism (Zibechi 2009).

Literature on authoritarianism during the 2000s was increasingly written by authors based in those Latin American countries where political continuity reigned. As a topic in its own right, it remained urgent in those countries where authoritarian elements kept shaping the daily experience. It was discussed in studies on the related topics of counterinsurgency in Colombia (Franco Restrepo 2009), militarization in Mexico (Fazio 1996; Rodríguez Rejas 2010), political violence in Guatemala (Argueta and Kurtenbach 2017; Figueroa 1990) and the relation between authoritarianism and non-state actors in Honduras (Gutiérrez 2013). These strands of debate mainly focus on single case studies and together form a comparative perspective.

Work on the outsourcing of violence from the state toward paramilitary groups as an element of authoritarianism in democracy, often focused on the emblematic case of Colombia. Franco Restrepo (2009) linked his analysis of an active dispersion of violence by the Colombian state, pushed by particular dominant social sectors, to counterinsurgency policies originating in the U.S. military and taken up by the broad political discourse in Colombia. The central motive in this discourse was to fight an alleged "internal enemy" moving within a sea of civil society (→ II/28), a motive which resulted in a war against political activists presented as guerrilla fighters, and shielded the political regime from transformation via the outsourcing mechanism. This low-intensity warfare became increasingly common and is by no means understudied in countries such as Colombia, Guatemala, or Southern Mexico (Aristizábal 2007; Gutiérrez 2011). Other academics focus on "*formas paraestatales*" as alliances between legal and illegal economic sectors and actors, constantly moving back and forth between deinstitutionalization and re-institutionalization (Estrada and Moreno 2008, 30). These para-institutional forms expand the margins of maneuvering for governments, as the state does not necessarily confront social protest directly. It can relegate a repressive response to para-institutional elements and simultaneously, downplay its own involvement in what the authors have called "criminal capitalism." This argument, which Estrada and Moreno (2008) base on the Colombian case, in some ways resembles the scenario of an "authoritarian etatism" discussed by Greek state theorist Poulantzas (2002). The debate in Mexico has focused more on militarization, stressing the new protagonist role in parliament and on the streets assumed by the military and marines in a supposed fight against drugs (Fazio 1996; Rodríguez Rejas 2010), which includes both pressure and help from the U.S.

When comparing temporally, the debate increasingly differentiates between "old" and "new" authoritarianism. "Old" is characterized by openly military or civil-military rule, a coup, and the destitution of at least part of the democratic institutions. The military coup in Honduras can be read as an example of the "old" authoritarianism in recent times. International observers were blinking with disbelief when the Honduran military sent then President Zelaya, who had promoted a decidedly moderate social democratic agenda, off to exile in a helicopter and took over (Cruz 2010). "New" authoritarianism is quite different in its measures and protagonists. It is non-military, but an agglomeration of lawfare, cooptation, and manipulation to reduce democracy to its formal minimum. Its effects resemble those of the "old" military authoritarianism in that numerous political activists are killed or incarcerated, but such killings are often not as easily attributed to the state as during the military regimes of the 1970s. The killings of black youth in Brazil caused by a *mano dura* approach to security (→ II/45) continued through phases of democratization in the 2000s (Costa Vargas and Alves 2013).

The historic shift from dictatorship to more flexible forms of rule, "competition and circulation among elites" can be partially related to a shift in U.S. foreign policy toward the promotion of polyarchy – which entailed active influence in political affairs toward the outcome of a stable consensus for "neoliberal global capitalism," but claimed that dictatorships had been left behind (Robinson 2013, 230). It was precisely Latin American scholars such as O'Donnell, who had sought refuge in the U.S. during the military dictatorships and contributed to more Inter-American perspectives. However, later these ideas fed into new U.S.-foreign policies of "democracy promotion," as they did not scrutinize liberal state concepts anymore (Guilhot 2005, 123).

Apart from U.S. involvement and despite the historic faltering of dictatorships, authors concerned about a more thorough democratization stress the very limited possibilities of social change within representative democracy, where the greater questions were already fixed per mercantile relations. Robinson has carved out how the (documented) U.S. support for dictatorships such as Somoza in Nicaragua (1970s) or Pinochet in Chile turned into an intervention to more subtly ensure consent to liberal economic policies (2013, 231). These interventions prevented radical outcomes of struggles for democracy and more fundamental changes to existing power relations through the funding and fostering of civil society organizations attuned to the liberal economic agenda (→ Civil Society, II/28). In that vein, some argue that the new security consensus throughout the North and South American continent, with the global threat of terrorism as leitmotiv also served to evade greater change. From these debates stems a strand of discussion arguing for a "democratization of democracy," which could not remain within the tight scope of representative democracy. The latter had lost its already limited capacities for redistribution within capitalism (→ II/2) (for example, De Sousa Santos 2004, 50; Robinson 2013). In these globalized or transnational spaces, fundamental decisions such as for or against open-pit mining, are often not open to democratic decisions, despite the existence of formal participatory institutions (→ Participation, II/41) (Pérez Ricart 2018; Sandoval 2017).

Some speak of a "new authoritarianism" in Mexico, for instance. "New" because the long decades of state party rule by the PRI were often referred to as "the perfect dictatorship," and now authoritarian elements appear within a model of at least apparent changes in power. "New" also because the parliamentary panorama has indeed diversified and requires techniques of cooptation in democratic contestation. Yet, people refer to this as *alternancia*, without a real chance for change (Anguiano 2010). The new authoritarianism is linked to the absence of law in the face of escalated violence, to state-crime collusion, and to vast gray zones in which it is unclear which role the state, and which role crime assumes (Osorio 2009; Roux 2011). However, the idea of a linear transition free of violence, of a PRI-dominated "soft dictatorship" to a still defective democracy, and the associated underestimation of the role of violence during the PRI years, has been criticized. Mexico has often been presented as a more civil exception (see, for example, Cardoso 1978, 52), yet this perception has inhibited a more thorough analysis of the use of coercion (Pansters 2012, 8).

Traveling concepts and entangled authoritarianisms

Entanglement perspectives on authoritarianism have often stressed the U.S.-Latin American relations, particularly the historic U.S. involvement in military operations, anti-democratic takeovers of power, and the fostering of economic liberalism (at the cost of democratic politics and human rights) (→ Interventionism, II/36; Human Rights, II/35). The presence and influence of the U.S. military in the region alone is much more pronounced now than it was during the debates led by O'Donnell, Cardoso, or Zavaleta. Greater numbers of soldiers trained in the U.S. School of the Americas, a reactivated Fourth Fleet and thus U.S. Navy presence in Latin American waters, the admitted U.S. involvement in the Honduras military coup in 2009, and U.S. secret service involvement in Mexican surveillance, are all examples of authoritarian, militarized practices which aim at curtailing more radical political change. These efforts to influence public opinion in Latin America, including the U.S. position on Latin American elections (→ Political Communication, II/42), are closely related to the U.S.'s own authoritarian undercurrents visible in the rise of xenophobic denigration of undocumented and documented U.S. Latino residents (→ Transnational Migration, I/44; Latinidad, I/33).

An entanglement perspective in authoritarianism is necessary, as security (→ II/45), authority, or democracy (→ II/32), are topics often discussed in relation to the state, and less through a transnational lens. Authoritarian elements expressed in the denial of rights to certain social groups are related to both ethnocentrism (→ Ethnicity, I/25) and extremely unequal economic relations in both Americas (→ Social Inequality, II/20). (Class) privilege has been secured partly through identity categories, limiting democracy (→ Intersectionality, I/32). When looking at the interdependence and hybridization of different notions and practices through interchanges, new meanings produced under these circumstances should not just be considered, but also an awareness of a perspective that understands contextualized differentiation *in relation to* the transnational scale. This is why this text has stressed that a clearly "Latin American" debate on authoritarianism assumed a common framework, yet knowledge on the authoritarian state also traveled from Latin American scholars to the U.S. and vice versa.

Political violence has been more prominent in the Latin American debate. First, political violence is discussed as one expression of the authoritarian state, and is continuously linked to its historical importance as well as its integration into the broader economic system. This kind of violence has not disappeared, despite emerging as seemingly apolitical social violence (Pearce 2010). It is articulated with law (Calveiro 2008, 30), not in opposition to it. On its historical role, Calveiro (2008) stresses that violence as an element of politics is necessarily based on "authoritarian structures" that have normalized repression and political assassinations with state participation. This normalization says Calveiro, was already moored in colonial relations and did not disappear with independence (2008, 32). An understanding of the authoritarian state was key to grasping how armed conflict escalated in various contexts in the 20th century, and what role the anti-state violence of guerrilla organizations played. Armed groups oscillated between focal groups and movements more broadly embedded in society, but their alliances with other political forces remained limited. In some cases, their own militarization reproduced precisely those hierarchical and authoritarian relations they had vowed to fight (34–35). One example might be the FARC guerilla in Colombia. As described above, the notion of low-intensity warfare in turn received much attention in the Latin American debate.

Second, *disruption* and *displacement* are two notions of eminent importance in the emerging debates on authoritarianism. This speaks to the Americas as a single space yet also stresses the region's entanglements within global capitalist economy, without which authoritarianism cannot be understood. Simply, political violence is embedded in the authoritarian implementation of economic policies which follow the requirements of global economy. Escobar (2004), as one of many, stresses the links between selective inclusion (in political participation) and forced displacement as a symptom of global economy. In these contested territories, political participation is necessarily exclusive, and in tendency, the relation between state and social pressure groups is characterized by political violence. Entire social sectors seem to be not only excluded from benefits of the current economic model, but increasingly the target of displacement and other forms of violence, as they are potential sources of unrest. Toward the North, new discussions link authoritarian security policies to infrastructure studies, when Cowen (2014) questions the contradictions between increasingly transnationalized security provisions (→ Security, II/45) along the supply chain (→ Global Commodity Chains, II/12). Citizenship (→ II/27) and labor struggles (→ Class Struggle, II/3) still appeal to a rather national state frame and are perceived as threats because of their potential power to disrupt the transnational flow of goods. The threat of disruption turns into a cause for preventive coercion.

Third, there is a broad body of literature emerging on the selectivity of authoritarian responses along racial and class distinctions. These studies are often based in policing studies and assume an entanglement perspective, with respect to their presentation of the loci of enunciation (Costa Vargas and Alves 2013; Hönke and Müller 2016). This newer work is oriented toward presenting the security paradigm – a state supposedly defending its people from attacks – as a logic which models society around particular ideas of order and blocks political articulation as such (→ Participation, II/41). There is particularly extensive work on the dissemination of global policing concepts and crime control policies from the North toward Latin Americas, but also on the Americas as a place of knowledge production on crime policies (Hönke and Müller 2016). Studies explore how the so-called "drug war" fighting paradigm from the U.S. Drug Enforcement Administration (DEA) took root within Latin America (Pérez Ricart 2018) or how global crime control policies led to (re)militarization (Gutiérrez Rivera 2015). The majority of these works stress that the process removed security and crime policies from democratic debate in both Latin America and the U.S., thus contributing to new forms of authoritarianism, where hardliner policies are practically set as standard and inhibit political activism from taking place. This authoritarianism of the 21st century is based on a minimal definition of democracy, a mere formality. Authoritarian entanglements take place via police and military trainings for Mexicans in Colombia, via the removal of highly political questions into a non-debatable transnational legal space, via the takeover of presidential campaigns all over the continent by the same manipulative methods (Bloomberg Business Week 2016).

All three are expressions of "the immense structural inequalities of the global political economy [that] cannot easily be contained through consensual mechanisms of social control" (Robinson 2013, 234). Recurring economic crises (→ II/4) escalate this. While this obvious failing of a generalized consensus on economic liberalism seems to invoke calls for political change and democratization, the actual rise "of an ultra-right in many countries and the specter that it will pursue a project of twenty 1st century fascism points to the dangers of more generalized coercive forms of social control" (Robinson 2013, 234). In 2019, Brazil is an example of this *anti-progresismo*, with a president (and a majority of the electorate) actively vindicating dictatorship, glorifying violence, and belittling all essence of a democratic system (Stefanoni 2018). Much more than in the 1970s, parts of the societies in the Americas seem to perceive this extreme form of rule based on hierarchized difference, political violence and deeply undemocratic mechanisms as a form of renewal against a status quo in crisis.

Final discussion

Summarizing some general elements, the rich history of debate on authoritarianism was presented as an Inter-American debate where its common ground revolved around the effects of colonialism (→ Colonial Rule, I/5) and dependency (→ Development, II/6) on democracy (→ II/32) and authoritarianism. The Latin American discussion of the authoritarian-bureaucratic state in terms of the military dictatorships of the 1970s was a regional debate where notions flowed and were valued against empirical evidence from different contexts (→ Military, II/37). Beneath the debate on authoritarianism there was always a deeper discussion about different understandings of the state (→ Nation State, II/38), combining European theories with Latin American concepts. In more recent discussions, the debate has centered on single case studies of formal democracies, in which nonetheless, authoritarian traits characterize the state. Their comparison is across space and time. Coercion is de- and re-institutionalized, dispersed toward formally non-state actors, or framed as necessary within crime control. Aiming at a more explicit entanglement perspective, apart from mentioning the authoritarian U.S. involvement in Latin American politics, contributes to reactivating the notion of political violence as an integral element of coercion, and stresses the role of the capitalist world system (→ Capitalism, II/2) for authoritarianism – more clearly, the necessity of authoritarianism in the face of a highly exclusionary system. Another strand of debate focuses on the role of police in cementing selectively authoritarian elements in democracy, often based on constructions of racial and class differentiations (→ Race, I/39; Social Inequality, II/20). In general, this undermines political articulation of large parts of societies (→ Participation, II/41). The Inter-American debate shows that authoritarianism is not a thing of the past, nor is it relegated to openly military regimes. Instead, a lively debate continues about new forms of authoritarian democracy.

Works cited

Anguiano, Arturo. 2010. *El Ocaso Interminable. Política y Sociedad en el México de los Cambios Rotos.* Mexico City: Ediciones Era.

Argueta, Otto and Sabine Kurtenbach. 2017. "Guatemala: National fragmentation, local cohesion." In *Peacebuilding in Deeply Divided Societies: Rethinking Political Violence*, eds. Fletcher Cox and Timothy Sisk, 33–64. London: Palgrave Macmillan Cham.

Aristizábal, José G. 2007. *Metamorfosis. Guerra, Estado y globalización en Colombia.* Bogotá: Ediciones desde abajo.

Bloomberg Business Week. 2016. *How to Hack an Election.* New York City: Bloomberg.

Calveiro, Pilar. 2008. "Acerca de la difícil relación entre violencia y resistencia." In *Luchas Contrahegemónicas y Cambios Políticos recientes de América Latina*, eds. Margarita López Maya, Pilar Calveiro, and Nicolás Iñigo Carrera, 23–46. Buenos Aires: CLACSO.

Cardoso, Fernando. 1978. "Sobre la caracterización de los regímenes autoritarios en América Latina." In *El Nuevo Autoritarismo en América Latina*, ed. David Collier, 39–62. Princeton: Princeton University Press.

Cardoso, Fernando and Enzo Faletto. 1976. "Die notwendigkeit einer umfassenden analyse von entwicklung." In *Abhängigkeit und Entwicklung in Lateinamerika*, eds. Fernando Cardoso and Enzo Faletto, 15–38. Frankfurt and Main: Suhrkamp.

CEREN. 2007. "Seminario internacional sobre estado y derecho en un período de transformación (1973)." *OSAL* 8: 211–233.

Collier, David. 1978. *El Nuevo Autoritarismo en América Latina.* Princeton: Princeton University Press.

Cortés, Martín. 2012. "El Leviatán criollo. Elementos para el análisis de la especificidad del estado en América Latina." In *El Estado en América Latina: Continuidades y Rupturas*, ed. Mabel Thwaites Rey, 93–116. Buenos Aires: CLACSO.

Costa Vargas, Joao and Jaime Amparo Alves. 2013. "Geographies of death: An intersectional analysis of police lethality and the racialized regimes of citizenship in Sao Paulo." In *New Racial Missions of*

Policing: International Perspectives on Evolving Law-Enforcement Politics, ed. Paul Amar, 37–62. Oxon: Routledge.

Cowen, Deborah. 2014. *The Deadly Life of Logistics: Mapping Violence in Global Trade*. Minneapolis: University of Minnesota Press.

Cruz, José Miguel. 2010. "Estado y violencia criminal en América Latina. Reflexiones a partir del golpe en Honduras." *Nueva Sociedad* 226: 67–84.

De Sousa Santos, Boaventura. 2004. *Reinventar la democracia: Reinventar el Estado*. Quito: Ediciones Abya-Yala.

Escobar, Arturo. 2004. "Development, Violence and the New Imperial Order." *Development* 47: 15–21.

Fazio, Carlos. 1996. *El Tercer Vínculo. de la Teoría del Caos a la Teoría de la Militarización*. México.

Figueroa, Carlos. 1990. "Guatemala – el recurso del miedo." *Nueva Sociedad* 105: 108–117.

Franco Restrepo, Vilma Liliana 2009. *Orden Contrainsurgente y Dominación*. Bogotá: Instituto Popular de Capacitación/Siglo del Hombre Editores.

Galeano, Eduardo. 2003. *Las venas abiertas de América Latina*. Buenos Aires: Siglo XXI.

Gargarella, Roberto and Christian Courtis. 2009. *El Nuevo constitucionalismo latinoamericano. Promesas e interrogantes. Políticas Sociales*, 153. Santiago de Chile: CEPAL.

Gudynas, Eduardo. 2012. "Estado compensador y nuevos extractivismos. Las ambivalencias del progresismo sudamericano." *Nueva Sociedad* 237: 128–146.

Guilhot, Nicolas. 2005. *The Democracy Makers: Human Rights and the Politics of Global Order*. New York: Colombian University Press.

Gutiérrez, Carlos. 2011. La guerra como 'continuum.' Le Monde Diplomatique, Colombian version (El Diplô) Nr. 86.

Gutiérrez, Lirio. 2013. *Territories of Violence*. New York: Palgrave Macmillan.

Gutiérrez Rivera, Lirio. 2015. "Security and remilitarization in the name of democracy: The impact of global crime control policies in Honduras." CMI Working Paper WP 2015:10.

Hönke, Jana, and Markus-Michael Müller. 2016. *The Global Making of Policing: Postcolonial Perspectives*. London and New York: Taylor & Francis Ltd.

Katznelson, Ira. 2014. *Fear Itself: The New Deal and the Origins of Our Time*. New York: Liveright.

Lechner, Norbert. 1981. "State and Politics in Latin America." LARU Working Paper 31, Ontario, Canada: Latin American Research Unit (LARU).

Lesgart, Cecilia. 2003. *Usos de la transición a la democracia: Ensayo, ciencia y política en la década del 80*. Argentina, Rosario: Homo Sapiens.

Levitsky, Steven and Lucan Way. 2004. "Elecciones sin democracia. El surgimiento del autoritarismo competitive." *Estudios Políticos* 24: 159–176.

Marini, Ruy Mauro. 1991. *Dialéctica de la dependencia*. 11th ed. México D.F.: Ediciones Era.

Martuscelli, Danilo and Maristella Svampa. 1993. "Notas para una historia de la sociología latinoamericana." *Revista Sociología* 8, no. 23: 1–17.

Morton, Adam David. 2011. *Revolution and State in Modern Mexico: The Political Economy of Uneven Development*. Boulder, CO: Rowman & Littlefield Publishers.

O'Donnell, Guillermo. 1993. "On the State, democratization and some conceptual problems." Kellogs Institute Working Paper.

———. 1994. "Delegative Democracy." *Journal of Democracy* 5, no. 1: 55–69. Washington, Johns Hopkins University Press.

———. 2009. *El Estado burocrático autoritario 1966–1973: Triunfos, derrotas y crisis*. 1st ed. Buenos Aires: Prometeo Libros.

Osorio, Jaime. 2009. "México frente a América Latina: El nuevo autoritarismo." In *El Estado mexicano. Historia, estructura y actualidad de una forma política*, ed. Gerardo Ávalos Tenorio, 109–126. México City: Universidad Autónoma Metropolitana Unidad Xochimilco.

Pansters, Wil. 2012. "Zones of state-making: violence, coercion and hegemony in twentieth-century Mexico." In *Violence, Coercion, and State-Making in Twentieth-Century Mexico: The Other Half of the Centaur*, ed. Wil Pansters, 3–39. Stanford: Stanford University Press.

Pearce, Jenny. 2010. "Perverse State Formation and Securitized Democracy in Latin America." *Democratization* 17, no. 2: 286–306. doi: 10.1080/13510341003588716.

Poulantzas, Nicos. 2002. *Staatstheorie. Politischer Überbau, Ideologie, Autoritärer Etatismus*. Hamburg: VSA-Verlag.

Quijano, Aníbal. 2000. "Coloniality of Power, Eurocentrism and Latin America." *Nepantla: Views from South* 1: 533–580.

Pérez Ricart, Carlos 2018. "El papel de la DEA en la emergencia del campo policial antidrogas en América Latina." *Foro Internacional* 231, no. 1: 5–48.

Robinson, William. 2013. "Promoting Polyarchy: 20 years later." *International Relations* 27, no. 2: 228–234.

Rodríguez Rejas, María José. 2010. "El Proceso de Militarización en México: Un caso ejemplar." In *América Latina: Estado y Sociedad en Cuestión*, ed. José María Calderón Rodríguez, n.p. Mexico City: Editorial Edimpo.

Roux, Rhina. 2011. "Ausencia de Ley. El Desmoronamiento del Estado Mexicano." In *Violencia y Crisis del Estado. Estudios sobre México*, ed. Jaime Osorio, 63–84. México City: UAM-Xochimilco, Depto de Ciencias Sociales.

Sandoval, Juan Manuel. 2017. "U.S.-México border states and the U.S. military-industrial complex. A Global Space for expanding transnational capital." *Regions & Cohesion* 7, no. 1: 87–121.

Stefanoni, Pablo. 2018. "Antiprogresismo Un fantasma que recorre América Latina." *Nueva Sociedad*. http://nuso.org/articulo/antiprogresismo/

Tapia Fernández, José 2015. "¿Democracia delegativa o autoritarismo representativo? Hacia un nuevo autoritarismo en América Latina." *De Política, Revista de la asociación Mexicana de ciencias Políticas* 3, no. 4/5: 81–110.

Thwaites Rey, Mabel. 2010. "El Estado en debate: De transiciones y contradicciones." *Crítica y emancipación* 2, no. 4: 9–24.

Zaremberg, Gisela, Marcela Torres Wong, and Valeria Guarneros. 2018. "Descifrando el desorden: Instituciones participativas y conflictos en torno a megaproyectos en México." *América Latina Hoy* 79: 81–102.

Zavaleta, René. 1979. "Nota sobre fascismo, dictadura y coyuntura de disolucion." *Revista Mexicana de Sociología* 41: 75–85.

Zibechi, Raúl. 2009. *Bolivien. Die Zersplitterung Der Macht*. Hamburg: Nautilus.

26
BORDERLANDS

Paul-Matthias Tyrell

"Borderland(s)" is a concept used in various lines of research, where different meanings are attributed to it. As Johnson and Graybill (2010) observed from a North American perspective, the label of borderlands scholarship can refer to heterogeneous fields of research as a focus on certain geographic areas (like for example the U.S. southwest), U.S.-American Mexican history, Mexican migration (→ Transnational Migration, I/44), or interest in cultural hybridity (→ I/30) and identity. Yet even these examples, while prominent, are but a small segment of the research working with the concept of borderlands. Indeed, borderland research originates from all over the Americas and the geographic range of its topics stretches from the North to the South Pole. Equally wide are thematic fields concerned with the topic: Among the scholars interested in borders and borderlands are anthropologists, biologists, economists, geographers, historians, international lawyers, philosophers, political scientists, sociologists, but also those interested in cultural, environmental and many other kinds of studies. Additionally, many heterogeneous approaches, methods, and methodologies across several academic disciplines exist to manage the term borderland(s).

Therefore, no single definition can be applied to the concept, which would be meaningful across the entire field of borderland research. Even within single disciplines, definition attempts are confronted with numerous challenges. One complication is the existence of a considerable number of similar terms, which often overlap in their meaning. Such terms are for example frontier, edgelands, middle ground, transborder community/region, border landscape, or border region/zone. Furthermore, border research is almost by definition a multi-lingual endeavor, yet key vocabulary is often difficult to translate with exactly the same connotations, which sometimes adds to the confusion. While, for example, the French "frontière" means a border region or land, the term "frontier" relates most generally to a moving zone of settlement (Brunet-Jailly 2010, 1). This understanding of frontier is mostly due to the influence of Frederick Turner's famous "Frontier Thesis" (Turner 1965).

The many difficulties with the term borderland are also one of the reasons why some researchers prefer to use the pluralized term, "borderlands" or "borderland(s)." Already in his pioneering research effort *Borderlands Sourcebook*, editor Ellwyn R. Stoddard explains the pluralized use as "a reminder that the multidisciplinary approaches contain slightly varied designations of what constitutes the region or its people." And that "[b]y avoiding the monistic terms 'a border' and 'the borderland' (singular) except when a single discipline or framework is being employed, the term 'Borderlands' reflects a collection of unique overlays – with some similarities and some differences being manifest in each" (Stoddard 1983, 5).

Against this backdrop a small selection of approaches, which are chosen for their variety and which are by no means meant to give a complete overview of the field can be discussed that illustrates some problems and pitfalls connected with the term. To this end a short summary of the history of borderland research since it started to be the object of systematic research close to the beginning of the 20th century is necessary as is also a synopsis of different approaches to define the term borderland(s).

The history of borderland research

For the most part of the 20th century, border research was mostly a matter for the disciplines of political geography, law and international relations, and to a lesser degree of economic theory. Against this backdrop, Friedrich Ratzel's *Politische Geographie* (1903) is regarded as the earliest systematic attempt to approach border and borderlands from a theoretical point of view (Newman and Paasi 1998, 189). Ratzel considered the state as an organic entity (→ Nation State, II/38). In this logic he considered borders as a peripheral (but important) organ of the state. Therefore, borderland was considered a place of interstate struggle and conflict. Even though there were some exceptions, which stressed the connective character of border, the notion of a borderland, as a space of conflict, remained influential (see Minghi 1963, 407–413). In the Americas this kind of thinking was among others prominently adapted and further developed by Ellen Churchill Semple (1911).

Especially in the United States, this development happened against the backdrop of the tremendous influence of Frederic Turner's aforementioned "Frontier Thesis." Turner's argument was that the democracy (→ II/32) of the United States was formed by the so-called pioneer experience and was first published as an essay called "The Significance of the Frontier in American History" in 1893. He argued that western settlement shaped the cultural traits of U.S.-American society and made it distinctive from European society. This essay later became the first chapter of his book *The Frontier in American History*. Turner's thesis had a tremendous impact on his contemporaries and remains discussed and criticized until today. His line of thinking was further developed by Herbert Eugene Bolton, who managed to move beyond Turner's Anglo-Saxon centric perspective. Especially with *The Spanish Borderlands* (1921) Bolton widened the perspective to include the impact of Spanish colonialism into the research on the frontiers (→ Conquest and Colonization, I/7). Popularized by this title, borderlands became a term connected with the parts of today's United States, which originally were claimed by Spain (Bannon 1970). However, in the historical research tradition started by Bolton, borderlands referred thus to a special sub-type of frontier in more or less one political and historical context. Therefore, the analytical contribution of this approach to the understanding of borderlands remained at the time limited.

After the Second World War, the research interest on borders declined and remained relatively low until the 1970s. One important reason for the lack of interest was the association of the topic with classical geopolitics (→ II/34), which was considered tainted due to its association with imperial warmongering in general and National Socialism in particular. Furthermore, borders were perceived as being "physical and static outcomes of the political decision-making process, to be described rather than analyzed" (Newman 2006, 145). The 1980s, however, saw a number of publications which revitalized the topic of borderlands and took it beyond the disciplines that were traditionally interested in borders. One of the earliest landmarks of this development was the *Borderlands Sourcebook* (1983), whose main editor, the sociologist Ellwyn R. Stoddard, also helped to establish the *Journal of Borderland Studies*. Along with Journals like *Estudios Fronterizos* (first issue in 1983) and *Frontera Norte* (first issue in 1989), this provided an important institutionalized resource for border studies. Stoddard (1988) also published the pioneering study *Maquila* on the Mexican border industry in 1987. In the same year Gloria Anzaldúa's book *Borderlands – La Frontera: The New Mestizia* was published. This very influential semi-autobiographical and partially poetic work contributed greatly to the opening of the borderland research for cultural studies and brought it together with an agenda for anti-racism, feminism, and LGBT rights (→ Gender Identities, I/28). Building on such foundations, border studies experienced a massive boost in the 1990s. This boost was not limited to an increased number of publications. It also included numerous institutionalizations in border studies like the International Boundary Research Unit (IBRU) in Durham, the Association of Borderlands Scholars in New Mexico, and the Geopolitics Research Center at the University of London (Newman and Paasi 1998, 187).

While the reasons for this boost were numerous, arguably three stood out. Firstly, a number of events, processes, and changes on a global level came together and highlighted the potential in border studies: The end of the East-West conflict lead to the establishment of a number of new states (and thus borders). Meanwhile, progress in European integration, free trade agreements like the North American Free Trade Agreement (NAFTA), and the acceleration of "globalization" in general highlighted changes in the understanding of borders (and in consequence borderlands) (→ Regional Integration, II/18). In regard to the latter, many scholars embraced border studies to challenge the powerful narrative of a globalized "borderless" world (→ Cosmopolitanism, III/5). Secondly, the rise of post-structural, feminist, and cultural studies not only changed the perspective on borders and borderlands, but also found in it a very fertile ground for its approaches (→ Borders, III/3). Numerous political geographers and other scholars started to argue that all boundaries are socially constructed. Attention should be paid to boundary-producing practices and questions of identity and power relations (Newman and Paasi 1998). Thirdly, before these developments, one specific case of a borderland sparked so much research interest, that it developed into some kind of locomotive, which pulled all borderland research with it: The research on the U.S.-Mexican border. This specific topic became so important for the entire field of research, that in the mid-1990s Robert R. Alvarez, Jr. argued that the U.S.-Mexican "border has become the icon and model for research into other borders as well as for the elaboration and refinement of the boundaries of several salient concepts and their referents" (Alvarez 1995, 449). This picture remains generally true in the new millennium. As of 2009 for example, 56.2 percent of all articles published in the *Journal of Borderland Studies* since its inception had dealt with the U.S.-Mexican border (Brunet-Jailly 2010, 13). Certainly, there is no equivalent in any other, equally as well-known or institutionalized approach to one specific national border anywhere in the world (Sadowski-Smith 2014, 22).

However, despite of its undeniable prominence, even during the pioneering phase it was far from being the only border in the Americas that sparked academic interest. One other example is the Araucanía region, a borderlands between Chile and the Mapuche-nation as well between Chile and Argentina, which was already subject to some noteworthy academic interest in the early 1980s (e.g. Villalobos et al. 1982; Villalobos and Rodríguez 1989) (→ Inter-ethnic Relations, I/12; I Indigeneity, I/31). But, the extent and impact of the research on the U.S.-Mexican border has certainly surpassed work on other regions in the Americas until today.

The reasons why the U.S.-Mexican border could attract that much research interest were numerous and included reasons founded in academic and public interest. Among the academic reasons, the most important one was likely that the U.S.-Mexican border was (and is) not only perceived as an especially strong inequality in power, economics, and human conditions (Alvarez 1995, 451) (→ Social Inequality, II/20), but also of the place of numerous academically interesting interactions between both sides of the border. Among the not purely academic reasons was that questions strongly related to the U.S.-Mexican border (Latin American Immigration, NAFTA and free-trade-related economic concerns) rose in prominence for the U.S.-American public, which undoubtedly helped gather resources for related studies. Furthermore, in the 1980s and 1990s, the borderland became the topic of a wave of Chicano and Chicana literature, poetry, and art (Alvarez 1995, 461) (Latino Media, III/33). This sparked considerable research interest. Especially influential were the works of Americo Paredes (1915–1999), which not only inspired later generations of Chicano and Chicana artists but was also subjected to a number of enlightening analysis. One important underlying theme, which interested artists, recipients and researcher alike, were questions of identity (→ Latinidad, I/33). Among the metaphorical and artistic approaches, the numerous works of Guillermo Gómez-Peña deserve special recognition, which explored the border culture in many groundbreaking poems, performances and other artistic approaches (1996).

These events took place during a time of dramatic loss of life in the U.S.-Mexican borderland, where hundreds of migrants died every year as they attempted to cross the border, (→ Transnational Migration, I/44) as well as the continuing militarization of the border by the United States Government (→ Military, II/37; Security, II/45). Moreover, many crimes, including the exceptionally cruel murders of hundreds of women on the Mexican side of the border (especially around Ciudad Juárez) since the 1990s, added a grim and urgent note to these academic and artistic developments.

Interest in different kinds of borderlands continued in the new millennium. Among other things, the changes in security policies after 9/11 became an important topic in borderland studies (Paasi 2011, 213). Especially for Canadian border studies, security policies had a strong impact since the United States literally started from one day to the other to reinforce a border, which had a very high degree of permeability before. For many Canadians, the border suddenly became a central factor in everyday life, which resulted in a lot of research interest. Until today (2018), each year numerous new publications and academic events have provided proof of the ongoing importance of the topic, as borderlands research keeps innovating and reinventing itself.

Approaches to define borderland(s)

When Oscar Martínez wrote "a borderland is a region that lies abject to a border" (Martínez 1994, 5) he not only wrote a definition, but probably pinned down what most people, not directly involved with borderland studies, would describe as a borderland. This definition also goes well together with most classical borderland research, as it does with many post-modern approaches that often (but not always) assume an implicit social-spatial relationship to an international border. However, the influence of post-modern and post-structuralist thinking in the revival of borderland studies in the 1980s and 1990s meant that the naturalized understanding of borders and borderland was challenged. But even with a more abstract, relational, and constructivist understanding of space, for many borderland scholars the different kinds of international borders and, to a lesser degree, borders within states (between provinces, municipalities etc.) remained relevant (→ Nation State, II/38). This is also true for the notion that borderlands in one way or another describe a region, even if approached from a cultural perspective. McKinsey and Konrad (1989), for example, defined borderlands as a "region jointly shared by two nations that houses people with common social characteristics in spite of the political boundary between them." In his more recent work on borderland culture and the U.S.-Canadian borderland Konrad argues that "Borderlands culture … is the imagined, produced and re-produced meaning ascribed to living in a border zone or region" (2014, 42).

The aforementioned Robert R. Alvarez refers to regional and international borders as well, despite approaching borderlands from an anthropologist perspective. He states, "I designate the 'borderlands' as a region and set of practices defined and determined by this [the U.S.-Mexican but probably international borders in general] border that are characterized by conflict and contradiction, material and ideational" (Alvarez 1995, 448). Even the recent attempt to analyze borders as "mobile" by Amihat-Szary and Girault (2015, 5) pays reference to the fact that for all the impact of technology, the border has not yet disappeared from our landscapes.

Borderlands can also be defined as a historical phenomenon in very specific circumstances. Building on foundations laid by Herbert Eugene Bolton, the historians Adelman and Aron for example develop the term "borderland" in opposition to the terms "frontier" and "bordered lands." In this research framework, borderlands are part of a historical development, in which during the 18th and early 19th century "fluid and 'inclusive' intercultural frontiers yielded to hardened and more 'exclusive' hierarchies." In this context, they reserve the term borderland for contested boundaries between colonial domains in North America (Adelman and Aron 1999, 815–816). Thus, in their definition, borderland becomes a way to describe a historical era in which geographical boundaries intruded on a prior borderless world (→ Nation and State Building, I/16).

As can be deduced from these examples, international borders remain a central point of reference for approaching the term borderlands. However, to define a borderland by its connection to a border (international or otherwise) includes several follow-up questions, most prominently: Where are the borders/limits of the borderland, i.e. how deep does a borderland reach into each of the bordering states? Categories that are employed for statistical or legal purposes often define the borderland as a territory including all counties (or other administrative units) directly connected to the border or use a certain distance from the border. While unsatisfying from an analytical point of view, the potential relevance of such definitions for both the life of the border people and for research regarding them should be taken into account. For example, since the Mexican government grants U.S. tourists VISA-free access for three days to a border zone (defined as an area between 20 to 30 kilometers of the U.S. border, depending on the location) such regulations have a real impact on the economy and, thus, the lives of the people, despite being somewhat arbitrary.

A more analytical definition to determine the limits of a borderland has been offered by the aforementioned Martínez, who argues that these limits depend "on the geographical reach of the interaction with the 'other side.'" Therefore, "some borderlands are physically small because foreign influences are confined to the immediate border area; others are large because such influences penetrate far beyond the border zone" (1994, 5). Another suggestion to deal with the problems of the limits of borderlands is offered by Michiel Baud and Willem van Schendel (1997), who identify three essential regional units of analysis for border studies: the border heartland, the intermediate borderlands, and the outer borderland. Their measuring instrument is the influential strength of the border felt in an area. Thus, in a time of a border crisis an entire country might be at least shortly embraced by the (outer) borderland. This basic notion, that a borderland can grow to encompass much larger spaces, can also be found in different argumentative contexts (e.g. Balibar 2004, 219).

However, there have been important attempts to disentangle the notion of borderland from borders as state made territorial demarcations. This view was prominently taken by Gloria Anzaldúa, whose notion of borderlands became one of the guiding metaphors of Chicana/o studies and also centrally shaped the emergence of transnational and hemispheric perspectives in U.S. American Studies (Sadowski-Smith 2014, 22). While she did not completely abandon the geographical notion, she moved the definition of "borderlands" to another level in the preface of *Borderlands – La Frontera: The New Mestizia* in which "[t]he actual physical borderland that I'm dealing with in this book is the Texas-U.S. Southwest/ Mexican border. The psychological borderlands, the sexual borderlands and the spiritual borderlands are not particular to the Southwest." She continues,

> In fact, the Borderlands are physically present wherever two or more cultures edge each other, where people of different races occupy the same territory, where under, lower, middle, and upper classes touch, where the space between two individuals shrinks with intimacy.
>
> *(Anzaldúa 2007, 19)*

This means *borderland* can also be used as a metaphor in many heterogeneous ways, further adding to the complexity of the term. However, building on the motives and ideas that Anzaldúa introduced, and embracing this very complexity has proved to be a fruitful path. When, for example, José David Saldívar attempted to remap the American cultural studies in the late 1990s, he described the borderland as a "social space of subaltern encounters" where forcefully separated people negotiate with each other, thereby manufacturing new relations, hybrid cultures and multiple-voiced aesthetics (1997, 13–14). Thereby he put forward what has become central in border studies, "The omnipresence as well as the permeability of borders, their interrogation, negotiation, appropriation and invalidation in contexts wider than geopolitical" (Andres 2015, 8).

Conclusion

Not only an attempt to find an interdisciplinary definition is a very challenging endeavor but also that there are certain pitfalls within the singular disciplines. As only one example for the many difficulties relating to the concept, the question where the "borders of the borderland" can be found (and thus how borderland(s) are related to space) has created controversy. This very question implies of course that certain universal features of a borderland(s) can be found. Such an assumption might seem to be questionable at times, even though it is often assumed in borderland research (and certainly adds to the appeal of the concept). But while borderland researchers must be careful in approaching the term, borderland research remains a highly relevant topic. Borderlands intrigue as highly dynamic entities, constantly changing both on a macro and a micro level, reflecting dynamics both in the metropolis and the periphery. Furthermore, borderlands are firmly linked to many core issues of modern societies, such as migration (→ Transnational Migration, I/44), supranational integration and disintegration of supranational institutions (like the European Union, NAFTA) (→ Regional Integration, II/ 38), security (→ II/45) concerns, and economic development (→ II/6), to name just a few. Therefore, it stands to reason that borderland(s) will remain an important topic for the foreseeable future and even more approaches, methods and research questions will be included, further adding both to the complexity and potential of the term.

Works cited

Adelman, Jeremy and Stephen Aron. 1999. "From Borderlands to Borders: Empires, Nation-States, and the Peoples in between in North American History." *The American Historical Review* 104, 3: 814–841.

Alvarez, Robert R., Jr. 1995. "The Mexican-Us Border: The Making of an Anthropology of Borderlands." *Annual Review of Anthropology* 24: 447–470.

Amihat-Szary, Anne-Laure and Frédéric Girault. 2015. "Borderities: The Politics of Contemporary Mobile Border." In *Borderities and the Politics of Contemporary Mobile Borders*, eds. Anne-Laure Amilhat-Szary and Frédéric Girault, 1–19. Basingstoke: Palgrave Macmillan.

Andres, Julia. 2015. *¡Cuéntame algo! Chicana Narrative Beyond the Borderlands.* Trier: Wissenschaftlicher Verlag Trier.

Anzaldúa, Gloria. 2007. *Borderlands: La Frontera: The New Mestiza.* 3rd ed. San Francisco: Aunt Lute.

Balibar, Étienne. 2004. *We, the people of Europe? Reflections in Transnational Citizenship.* Princeton: Princeton University Press.

Bannon, John Francis. 1970. *The Spanish Borderlands Frontier 1513–1821: Histories of the American Frontier.* New York: Holt: Rinehart and Winston.

Baud, Michiel and van Schendel Willem. 1997. "Toward a Comparative History of Borderlands." *Journal of World History* 8, 2: 211–242.

Bolton, Herbert E. 1921. *The Spanish Borderlands: A Chronicle of Olad Florida and the Southwest.* New Haven: Yale University Press.

Brunet-Jailly, Emmanuel. 2010. "The State of Borders and Borderlands Studies in 2009: A Historical View and a View from the Journal of Borderlands Studies." *Eurasian Border Review* 1, 1: 1–17.

Guillermo, Gómez-Peña. 1996. *The New World Border: Prophecies, Poems & Loqueras for the End of the Century.* San Francisco: City Lights.

Johnson, Benjamin H. and Andrew R. Graybill. 2010. "Introduction: Borders and Their Historians in North America." In *Bridging National Borders in North American: Transnational and Comparative Histories*, ed. Benjamin H. Johnson and Andrew R. Graybill, 1–29. Durham and London: Duke University Press.

Konrad, Victor. 2014. "Borders and Culture: Zones of Transition, Interaction and Identity in the Canada-United States." *Borderlands Eurasia Border Review* 5, 1: 41–57.

Martínez, Oscar J. 1994. *Border People: Life and Society in the U.S.-Mexico Borderlands.* Tucson: University of Arizona Press.

McKinsey, Lauren and Victor Konrad. 1989. *Borderlands Reflections: The United States and Canada.* Orono: University of Maine Press.

Minghi, Julian V. 1963. "Boundary Studies in Political Geography." *Annals of the Association of American Geographers* 53, 3: 407–428.

Newman, David. 2006. "The Lines that Continue to Separate Us: Borders in Our 'Borderless' World." *Progress in Human Geography* 30, 2: 143–161.

Newman, David and Anssi Paasi. 1998. "Fences and Neighbors in the Postmodern World: Boundary Narratives in Political Geography." *Progress in Human Geography* 22, 2: 186–207.

Paasi, Anssi. 2011. "Borders." In *The Ashgate Research Companion to Border Studies*, ed. Doris Wastl-Walter, 213–229. Farnham, Surry: Ashgate.

Ratzel, Friedrich. 1903. *Politische Geographie oder die Geographie der Staaten, des Verkehres und des Krieges.* 2nd ed. München: Oldenbourg.

Sadowski-Smith, Claudia. 2014. "The Centrality of the Canada-U.S. Border for Hemispheric Studies of the Americas." *Forum for Inter-American Research.* 7.3. http://interamerica.de/volume-7-3/sadowski-smith/

Saldívar, José David. 1997. *Border matters: Remapping American Cultural Studies.* Berkeley, CA: University of California Press.

Semple, Ellen C. 1911. *Influences of Geographic Environment, On the Basis of Ratzel's System of Anthropo-Geography.* New York: Henry Holt and Company.

Stoddard, Ellwyn R. 1983. "Overview." In *Borderlands Sourcebook: A Guide to the Literature on Northern Mexico and the American Southwest*, eds. Ellwyn R. Stoddard, Richard L. Nostrand, and Jonathan P. West, 3–5. Norman: University of Oklahoma Press.

Stoddard, Ellwyn R. 1988. *Maquila: Assembly Plants in Northern Mexico.* El Paso, TX: Texas Western Press.

Stoddard, Ellwyn R., Richard L. Nostrand, and Jonathan P. West. 1983. *Borderlands Sourcebook: A Guide to the Literature on Northern Mexico and The American Southwest.* Norman: University of Oklahoma Press.

Turner, Frederick Jackson. 1965. *Frontier in American History*. New York: Holt, Rinehart and Winston.

Villalobos, Sergio, Carlos Aldunate, Horacio Zapater, Luz María Méndez, and Bascuñán Carlos. 1982. *Relaciones Fronterizas en la Araucanía.* Santiago: Ediciones Universidad Católica de Chile.

Villalobos, Sergio and Jorge Pinto Rodríguez. 1989. *Araucanaia: Temas de Historia Fronteriza.* Temuco: Imprenta Universidad de La Frontera.

27
CITIZENSHIP

Manuela Boatcă

Prevailing social scientific definitions view citizenship as a modern institution for the distribution of civil, political, and social rights (→ Human Rights, II/35) meant to counterbalance social inequalities (→ II/20) among members of the same polity. For a long time, citizenship was considered to reflect changes occurring in Western societies in the wake of the French and U.S.-American Revolutions (→ Revolution, II/44) and to be directly derived from the industrialization of the Western world and the subsequent processes of urbanization (→ I/45) and secularization accompanying it (Turner and Hamilton 1994). As a result, sociologists analyzed the institutionalization of citizenship as part of a sequence of social change characterizing modern, democratic societies (→ Modernization, II/35; Democracy, II/32). As a modern institution, citizenship was considered a mechanism of inclusion through which particularities of birth such as ethnicity (→ I/25), status, or gender (→ Gender Identities, I/28) play an ever-smaller part in deciding an individual's social mobility once all citizens are equal before the law. However, in a global perspective, citizenship has been shown to function as a mechanism of exclusion along race (→ I/39), class, and gender lines from the moment of its institutionalization (Brubaker 1992; Korzeniewicz and Moran 2009; Shachar 2009). When seen from the Americas, the emergence of citizenship rights is revealed to be not only the result of modernity, the French and U.S.-American Revolutions, and industrialization, but also, and more importantly, premised on colonialism (→ Colonial Rule, I/5), the Haitian Revolution, and the institution of chattel slavery (→ I/18). This article traces the different moments in the theorization of citizenship from nation-state (→ II/38) to global perspectives before turning to citizenship as viewed from the Americas and coloniality as "the underside of modernity" (Dussel 1996; Quijano 2000).

Citizenship: nation-state perspectives

German sociologist and national economist Max Weber viewed citizenship as an institutionalized association of an autonomous status group (*Stand*; literally, *estate*) of *individual* burghers subject to the same law and traced it back to the ancient Greek *polis* and the medieval Occidental city (Weber 1978 [1922], 1240). For him, the revolutionary innovation differentiating the central and northern European cities from all others had been the principle that "city air makes man free": slaves or serfs (→ Unfree Labor, I/29) employed for wages in the city soon became free from obligations to their master as well as legally free (→ Freedom, I/27). Consequently, in time, status differences between free and unfree city dwellers gave way to the equality of individual citizens before the law. For a long time, the link Weber established between the emergence of the medieval Occidental city as an association of free citizens and the rise of the rational urban middle class in the West received little attention as an explanation for the development of rational, industrial capitalism (→ II/2). Instead, Weber's interpretation of the origin of capitalism in the Protestant ethic prevailed (Isin 2005, 35). Since full membership in the ecclesiastic community was the prerequisite for urban citizenship, the fully developed ancient and medieval city of the West was first and foremost a sworn confraternity of individual burghers (Weber 1978 [1922], 1246).

This type of argument still dominates sociological scholarship on the emergence of modern patterns of social stratification as well as of democratic ideals in the West. Thus, Weber's interpretation of citizenship as a distinctly Western institution

> inaugurates a social science tradition where the origins of 'city,' 'democracy,' and 'citizenship' are etymologically traced to the 'Greek,' 'Roman,' and 'medieval' cities and affinities between 'ancient' and 'modern' practices are established and juxtaposed against oriental societies – Indian, Chinese and Islamic – as societies that failed to develop citizenship and hence indigenous capitalism.
>
> *(Isin 2013, 117)*

In the process, discontinuities and differentiations within the West are overlooked or ignored. The separate elements leading up to the emergence of citizenship in the West are not dealt with in terms of their relational significance to one another, but rather are treated as a to-do list. Inevitably, such a procedure systematically encounters incomplete assignments and rudimentary developments everywhere outside the West, where a whole different set of sociopolitical, economic, and cultural elements was at play.

In the mid-20th century, Weber's idea that the equality of citizens before the law represented an overcoming of particularities of birth became central to T. H. Marshall's sociology, who considered the "modern drive toward social equality" the latest phase in the evolution of citizenship (Marshall 1977) (→ Modernization, I/35). Extrapolating from the development of the British social welfare system, Marshall saw this evolution as proceeding from the granting of civil rights in the 18th century, through that of political rights in the 19th century and up to the concession of social rights in the 20th century. He defined citizenship as "a status bestowed on all those who are full members of a community" (Marshall 1977, 92). Its development was seen as tending towards an increase in the number of persons on whom the status is bestowed – and thus towards equality. In his view, citizenship therefore was the opposite of social class, which in turn only generated inequality (→ II/20). He thus advocated the extension of citizenship as the principal political means for reconciling the contradictions between formal political equality and the persistence of social and economic inequality under a capitalist system (→ II/2) based on class divisions. Marshall writes, "The equality implicit in the concept of citizenship, even though limited in content, undermined the inequality of the class system, which was in principle a total inequality." He continues,

> National justice and a law common to all must inevitably weaken and eventually destroy class justice, and personal freedom, as a universal birthright, must drive out serfdom. No subtle argument is needed to show that citizenship is incompatible with medieval feudalism.
>
> *(Marshall 1977, 93)*

Drawing explicitly on Marshall's work, U.S. sociologist Talcott Parsons referred to the institutionalization of the basic rights of citizenship as an egalitarian tendency of modern societies, in which universalistic norms gradually replace earlier particularistic solidarities of ethnicity (→ I/25), religion (→ Religious Beliefs, I/40), and regional origin (Parsons 1965, 1966). In his view, this tendency stood for a shift from societies based on ascriptive criteria to societies based on achievement criteria, and the decisive thrust for its implementation had come from the French Revolution, which "demanded a community that included *all* Frenchmen and abrogated the special status of the *privilegiés*. The central concept was *citizenship*, the claim of the *whole* population to inclusion" (Parsons 1971, 79, emphasis in the original).

Parsons thus offered a textbook example of an Occidentalist conceptualization of citizenship as traceable to a single historical event, the French Revolution, as well as limited – both in its context of emergence and its scope – to continental France and its (white) population (→ Whiteness, I/46), not the French colonies and their inhabitants in the Caribbean. Although his focus was on the U.S. case and its special role in the institutionalization of basic citizenship rights, Parsons considered it legitimate to extrapolate from Marshall's model, centered on Britain. The reason lay precisely in viewing the French Revolution as a common tradition of both contexts, and thus of a broader modern West (Parsons 1965, 1016). He therefore took Marshall's sequence of citizenship rights to reflect not only a rough temporal series, but also a type of hierarchy of institutional steps towards the main aim of the French Revolution, the equality of membership status. Parsons viewed the French Revolution as having furthered civil rights, many of which had already been institutionalized in English and American law, as well as political rights, which he, like Weber, dated back to the ancient Greek polis. In turn, social rights had become important only in the mid-19th century and had started being implemented in the 20th (Parsons 1971). At the same time, Parsons echoed Weber's emphasis on confraternity as a basis for claims to equality when stressing that the French Revolution's slogan "embodied the new conception of community. *Liberté* and *Egalité* symbolized the two foci of dissatisfaction, political authoritarianism, and privilege. *Fraternité* referred primarily to the broader context of belonging, 'brotherhood' being a primordial symbol of community" (Parsons 1971, 79f.). Again, both these accomplishments and the disparities that they addressed were presented as internal to a minimally defined West.

Following Weber's analysis of the Western city, Parsons also traced the solidary social community of modern societies back to the Christian community of faith. He pointed out that, in its secular modern form, however, the pattern of societal community had only been partially and unstably institutionalized in the 19th century: in France, both the aristocracy and the Catholic Church maintained considerable privileges, while in Britain, franchise was extended only from 1832 on and aristocracy remained strong (Parsons 1971). In this case, he also noted that there had been several exceptions to the United States' claim of being a *voluntary* association of citizens, the clearest of which had been the case of enslaved Africans (→ Slavery, I/18), who had been brought to the U.S. by force and had long been barred from inclusion in the political community (Parsons 1965). However significant, these provisos were nevertheless coined in the language of "survivals" of an older system on its way to a modern society, in which privilege would play an ever-smaller part. As an "exception," the case of enslaved Africans also did not appear to warrant an inquiry into its structural impact on racial inequality in the U.S. (→ Social Inequality, II/20). The most consequential aspect of Parsons' analysis of the institutionalization of citizenship in the Western world was therefore contained in his statement that the "critical issue of 'privilege' was actually the hereditary ascription of status, which conflicted with the standards of either achievement or equality, or both" (1971, 80).

At the end of the 20th century, Bryan Turner's critical synopsis of the scope of approaches to citizenship from Max Weber through T. H. Marshall and Talcott Parsons signaled the exhaustion of citizenship as a relevant concept in a world increasingly characterized by supranational entities and allegiances (1990, 1993). Turner held both onto the central components of Weber's Occidentalist analysis and the evolutionary thrust of Marshall's British-centered account. In his view, citizenship was

> an essentially modern institution which reflects the profound changes which have occurred in western societies following the democratic revolutions in France and America and as a consequence of broader, more general social changes associated with the industrial revolution, such as urbanization and secularization.
>
> *(Turner and Hamilton 1994, np)*

He therefore envisaged an ideal/typical historical trajectory, whereby citizenship "evolves through the establishment of autonomous cities, develops through the emergence of the nation-state in the eighteenth and the 19th centuries and finds its full blossoming in the welfare states of the 20th century" (Turner and Hamilton 1994, np). Following Parsons' equally evolutionary notion that the development of citizenship involved a shift from particularistic to universalistic values, Turner concluded that, with globalization, the importance of citizenship might decline in favor of a more universalistic notion of human rights (→ II/35). He notes, "Whereas citizenship as a doctrine has been a progressive feature of western societies in terms of universalistic values behind the welfare state, human-right concepts can be seen as a progressive paradigm which is relevant to a world-system" (Turner 1993, 470).

By taking the autonomous city-state of Western Europe as the locus of emergence of citizenship, such approaches reinforced the notion of a linear trajectory leading from ancient Greece and Rome to revolutionary France and Western-style democracy (→ II/32). By concentrating on how the allotment of citizenship levelled ethnic differences and appeased social conflict within nation-states, they provided accounts of the emergence of citizenship internal to nation-states (→ II/38), while at the same time disregarding the importance of supranational and transregional factors in the development of citizenship as nation-state protection. At most, the transnational dimension of citizenship was seen as deriving from recent developments like the formation of supranational entities such as the European Union, the increasing codification of human rights norms in the context of the emergence of new states, and the movement of migrant and refugee populations (Isin and Turner 2002; Mackert and Müller 2000) (→ Transnational Migration, II/44). Treatment of citizenship from a Weberian perspective thus assumed that global issues with respect to citizenship only have to be taken into account in the era of globalization, but not in the context of the historical emergence of citizenship or at any other moment outside the present. In these accounts, the U.S. (and Canada, when explicitly mentioned) represented merely the latest phase in the evolution of citizenship as an institution, but had played no particular role in its emergence, while Latin America and the Caribbean were not even considered.

Citizenship: global perspectives

It was only in the 1990s that the historical development of the institution of citizenship would be cast in a global perspective. In his acclaimed "Citizenship and Nationhood in France and Germany" (1992), Rogers Brubaker argued that "the division of the world's population into a set of bounded and mutually exclusive citizenries" (1992, 22) was in itself a neglected aspect of the development of the state system (→ Nation and State Building, I/16). In stating that globally, "citizenship is a powerful instrument of social closure, shielding prosperous states from the migrant poor" (1992, x), he pointed to the paradox that a shift from the national to the global perspective made apparent: the fact that citizenship is "internally inclusive" – i.e., it extends rights to all those defined as citizens – at the same time that it is "externally exclusive" – i.e., it restricts the access of non-citizens to the same rights. Thus, citizenship is both an instrument of closure and an object of closure, "a status to which access is restricted" (1992, 31). By analyzing citizenship in terms of status and its corresponding mechanism of status closure, Brubaker operated a momentous change in the common conceptualization of citizenship as an institution of modern societies for which social mobility is viewed as characteristic. The double function of citizenship as an instrument and object of social closure, he argued, had been present ever since the French Revolution, which had created both the nation-state and its logical corollary, nationalism, in the same breath. "A nation-state is a nation's state, the state of and for a particular, bounded, sovereign nation to which foreigners, by definition, do not belong..." Brubaker continues, "By inventing the national citizen and the legally homogeneous national citizenry, the Revolution simultaneously invented the foreigner. Henceforth citizen and foreigner would be correlative, mutually exclusive, exhaustive categories" (1992, 31).

The subsequent generalization of the principle of citizenship allocation in the modern world meant that every person ought to have the citizenship of at least one state. Yet, as Brubaker pointed out, this development stands in sharp contrast to the institution of citizenship in both the ancient Greek polis and medieval towns, where the possession of citizenship was not a given, but a privilege, and the lack of citizenship was no anomaly. By contrast, every state today ascribes citizenship to certain persons at birth through either right of blood (*jus sanguinis*) or right of soil (*jus soli*) arrangements, or a combination of both. This mechanism, as Brubaker noted, was both "a striking exception to the secular trend away from ascribed statuses" and proved that "the state is not and cannot be a voluntary association. For the great majority of persons, citizenship cannot be but an imposed, ascribed status" (1992, 32).

Brubaker's analysis of citizenship as social closure therefore broke with previous approaches in several important respects. On the one hand, the focus on the idea of citizenship as membership ascribed at birth prompted the unfamiliar view of the modern state as structurally different from a voluntary association, and of both as different from the institution of citizenship in ancient Greece and feudal Europe. Thus, his analysis explicitly emphasized the discontinuities, rather than the continuities in the historical trajectory of citizenship in the West (see also Joppke 1994). On the other hand, both the ascription of citizenship and his historical and comparative analysis of the German case convincingly illustrated that the institution of citizenship was not essentially democratic. Instead, showing how German legislation had first proclaimed equality of all before the law, yet had codified membership of the *Stände* and their corresponding inequalities, prompted Brubaker to speak of the "pre-national, pre-democratic quality" (1992, 51) of the development of citizenship in Germany. His approach therefore remains very much within the realm of a historical-comparative analysis and an almost exclusive focus on Europe and North America. The consequences that exclusion through citizenship has had for the non-Western world both during colonial times and today, as well as of the ways in which European colonial possessions have influenced the development of their respective politics of citizenship allocation, remain unaddressed.

The externally exclusive dimension of citizenship has been recently explored in some detail in connection to its role in the maintenance and reproduction of global inequalities (→ Social Inequalities, II/20). Drawing in part on Brubaker's notion of citizenship as both an instrument and an object of closure, legal scholar Ayelet Shachar focused on how the intergenerational transfer of citizenship ascribed at birth resembles the intergenerational transfer of property at a global scale. According to her, birthright citizenship, whether ascribed under the *jus soli* or the *jus sanguinis* principles, functions as a kind of inherited property that restricts membership in well-off polities to a small part of the world population (Shachar 2009). As such, both inherited property and birthright citizenship grant legitimate title bearers the unconditional right of entry on the one hand ("the gate-keeping function" of citizenship) and restrict access to scarce resources (e.g. land in the case of property, a welfare system in the case of citizenship) on the other (Shachar 2009, 35). More importantly, however, she notes that both inherited property and birthright citizenship are automatically transferred from one generation to the next. Although widely criticized in relation to both institutions, the hereditary transmission of privilege has been largely dismissed as feudal and inequitable with regard to property, and yet maintained and even reinforced with regard to citizenship (Shachar 2009).

Thus, both in its gate-keeping and in its opportunity-enhancing functions, citizenship is shown to bear striking similarities to the feudal entail, a legal means of restricting future succession of property to the descendants of a designated estate owner practiced in medieval England. As such, the entail offered a tool to preserve land in the possession of dynastic families by entrenching birthright succession, while forbidding future generations to alter the estate inherited from their predecessors. By analogy, the entail of citizenship helps preserve wealth in the hands of designated heirs of membership titles – the state's citizens – by allocating political membership at birth in dramatically different opportunity structures (Shachar 2009, 38ff.). To use an Inter-American example: For a girl born in 2019 in Haiti, one of the poorest countries in the world, the chances of surviving to age five, having access to clean water, or getting an education are incomparably lower than for a baby born at the same time in Canada, where chances for boys and girls on all these counts are nearly identically high. Contrary to an entire Occidentalist tradition of citizenship theory from Weber through Marshall and up to Turner, citizenship and gender (→ Gender Identities, I/28), the most decisive factors accounting for these extreme inequalities between individuals in poor and rich countries in the 21st century, are both statuses ascribed at birth. Moreover, the paradigmatically modern and universal institution of citizenship is shown to derive from a feudal and very particular arrangement regulating the transfer of property in medieval England.

By insisting that the birthright transmission of political membership represents a "blind spot" of citizenship theory with considerable implications for the global distribution of scarce resources, Shachar convincingly de-emphasizes the contrast between *jus sanguinis* and *jus soli* arrangements, both of which rely on birthright ascription. Although less explicitly, she thus makes a similar case as Korzeniewicz and Moran (2009), who argued that the institutionalization of citizenship did ensure the relative social and political inclusion of the population of Western European nation-states (→ II/38), yet it also accounted for the selective exclusion of colonized or non-European populations from the same social and political rights.

Coloniality of citizenship

A global perspective thus reveals that the institutionalization of citizenship rights in Western nation-states coincided with the legal (and physical) exclusion of populations racialized as non-European, non-White and non-Western from social and cultural rights (→ Race, I/39; Whiteness, I/46). Additionally, the Western construction of gender in the course of the European colonial expansion (Lugones 2007; McClintock 1995; Oyěwùmí 1997; Stoler and Cooper 1997) has shaped the modern/colonial institution of citizenship since it came into existence (→ Gender Identities, I/20). Inside and outside the West, citizenship rights were granted to women only gradually, while men and women of "other" regions were engendered along colonial lines. The notion of coloniality of power and its subsequent theorizations in an Inter-American context (Quijano 2000; Mignolo 2000; Lugones 2007, 2008) have been instrumental in demonstrating how the structural distribution of unequal and engendered citizenship rights have provided a crucial component of modernity/coloniality (Boatcă and Roth 2016) (→ Postcolonialism, I/38).

Citizenship's twin mechanisms – the inclusion of members of the polity and the exclusion of constructed others – became apparent in the very first consequences of the French Revolution in continental France and its Caribbean colony of Saint-Domingue. Slavery (→ I/18) – viewed as encompassing all forms of unfree labor from Antiquity to the Middle Ages – was the very prototype of unfreedom against which the French revolutionary ideal of liberty was projected in 1789. The granting of citizenship as the basis for the universal equality of political and social rights in a modern social order was therefore seen as an expression of liberty (i.e., the opposite of slavery) and as the mark of civilization. As such, citizenship was to be acquired gradually as the result of a civilizing process. In the immediate aftermath of the French Revolution, citizenship rights were thus only granted to male property owners, whose ability to pay taxes and military tribute (→ Taxation, II/22; Military, II/37), i.e., contribute to the maintenance of social order, qualified them as "active citizens." Women, foreigners, and children were in turn defined as "passive citizens" and denied all political rights (Blackburn 1988, 198; Wallerstein 2003, 653f). In the case of women, this was considered a temporary provision, to be remedied by further educational measures. Yet this logic only applied to continental France.

In the French Caribbean colony of St. Domingue, where the revolution of the enslaved led by Toussaint L'Ouverture resulted in the abolition of slavery in 1794, race (→ I/39) took precedence over property as a criterion for the granting of citizenship. Since not all whites were property owners, but relatively many free "mulattos" were, the French colonial assembly included the former in the right to vote even before this was accomplished in continental France. However, it excluded both enslaved people and "mulattos" from franchise after a series of heated debates (Blackburn 1988, 183ff). The argument used by both the white planters and the poor whites of St. Domingue at the close of the 18th century was that enslaved people and free "mulattos" were not part of "the nation" and could therefore not become citizens. The underpinning logic attests to the coloniality out of which the institution of citizenship emerged: through this "externalization of race" (Stam and Shohat 2012, 29), France reinstated in the colonies the slavery that the revolution had just abolished in the metropole, effectively defining those racialized as non-white out of the political community of the nation. In 1802, Napoleon officially reinstated slavery as an institution in France's colonies, thus cementing the divide between metropole and colony.

The history and discourse of modernity were thus premised on the reinforcement of coloniality, to which citizenship became instrumental. Thus, there emerged a dual pattern of hierarchization of difference according to racial and ethnic criteria, both of which were moreover gendered (e.g. depicting indigenous men as feminized and lacking Occidental masculinity while positioning enslaved Africans as hypermasculine, threatening, and thus to be controlled). In turn, the respective gender positions have been racialized and ethnicized along colonial patterns. The image of the White virtuous woman and "mother" of the race/nation – and later housewife – to be monitored and protected from black male aggression, or of the sexually threatening, eroticized and permanently available black female body accordingly deprived of (the right to) protection and motherhood were thus created. It is at this juncture of gender, race, and ethnicity (→ Intersectionality, I/32) as products of the colonial crucible that the institution of citizenship is revealed to be a key element in the maintenance of the coloniality of power of the modern/colonial world system (Mignolo 2000). It is to the specific mechanisms of its functioning throughout the history of the system that we can refer as the coloniality of citizenship (Boatcă 2016; Boatcă and Roth 2016).

Citizenship: from institution to act

At the very moment of its emergence as a modern institution for the provision of universal rights (→ Human Rights, II/35), citizenship was creating systematic particularisms that provided rights to some while denying them to (colonial) others. From the 18th century onward, the provision of formal citizenship rights would accordingly be a mere foil against which "acts of citizenship" (Isin and Nielsen 2008) by individuals, social movements (→ I/41), and political organizations would attempt to wrest citizenship rights away from dominant groups and extend them to excluded ones not only in theory, but also in practice. This was done successfully sometimes, but by far not always.

The "unthinkable" Haitian Revolution (Trouillot 1995) is a case in point. St. Domingue's first constitution as the independent republic of Haiti following the revolution (→ II/44) aimed at erasing precisely the differences that had made racial hierarchization possible. To that end, it ruled that all Haitians, including white women and members of naturalized ethnic groups such as Germans and Poles living on the island were to be referred to by the generic term "black," thus turning the term into a political rather than a biological category (Fischer 2004, 233). The Haitian constitution of 1805 thus seized upon the abovementioned mechanism of deriving a universal term by generalizing from a particular one, but in so doing reversed the prevailing hierarchy (→ Race, I/39; Whiteness, I/46). It thereby crafted a

> radically new concept of citizenship: that only those denoted as 'black' could be citizens, revalorizing what had been stigmatized. Yet 'black' was defined expansively – unlike 'white' – to mean those that rejected both France and slavery, meaning that even a 'white' could be defined as black as long as he or she repudiated the logic of racial slavery that intended that only 'whites' should rule and Africans should serve.
>
> *(Horne 2015, 102)*

Both in France, which had lost its richest and most productive colony when Haiti became independent, and in the recently emerged United States, where slave-holding elites deemed slavery indispensable to the Southern economy, the Haitian Revolution sparked fears that abolition, peasant-based land reform (→ Land, II/15), and egalitarianism would spread across the Caribbean and the U.S. South. Britain, which had lost control of its main trading market in enslaved people with U.S. independence, feared that Jamaica would follow suit. From 1789 to 1815, dozens of uprisings of enslaved and indigenous peoples occurred across the hemisphere (→ Indigeneity, I/31), from Bermuda in 1791 through Spanish Louisiana and St. Lucia in 1795 to the 1798 Revolt of the Tailors in Brazil and the 1810 rebellion in Mexico. The Haitian Revolution thus created a general crisis for the system of chattel slavery (→ I/18) that paved the way for its collapse (Horne 2015, 10). At the same time, it prepared the ground for claims to, and later implementation of *jus soli*, or birthright citizenship in the United States and most of the Americas.

In the United States, fears of a further increase in the number of free African Americans prompted pressures for either colonization or voluntary emigration from the mainland. The American Colonization Society, founded in 1817 and committed to the expatriation of African Americans, had established the West African colony of Liberia by 1821, where free Blacks were supposed to settle. In turn, proponents of emigration called for African Americans to leave the United States for closer locales such as Haiti or Canada, arguing that African Americans could not expect recognition of their rights as citizens, despite having proven their belonging through their labor and the construction of a black public culture (Jones 2018, 37).

In fact, as soon as 1804, Jean-Jacques Dessalines, the first ruler of an independent Haiti, had offered African Americans in the United States material help in order to emigrate to Haiti. By 1824, Haiti's president Jean Boyer made good on this offer by dispatching "fifty thousand weight of coffee" to New York that African Americans there could sell so as to "facilitate the emigration" to Haiti (Horne 2015, 23). From 1824 to 1826, more than 6,000 African Americans took Boyer up on his offer and settled in what is today's Dominican Republic. What became known as the "Haitian emigration" was followed by smaller numbers of immigrants once the Haitian government stopped paying for the travel costs.

In 1838, William Yates' legal treatise "Rights of Colored Men to Suffrage, Citizenship, and Trial by Jury" opposed both the emigration and the colonization pressures by arguing that free African Americans could not be removed from the borders of the United States. At its core, Yates maintained, citizenship was a claim to place, to enter, and remain within the nation's borders (Jones 2018, 4). His plea, however, targeted free black people exclusively, and was meant to encompass neither Native Americans nor enslaved black people, both of whom Yates explicitly excluded from claims to citizenship.

The tensions inherent in pitting one excluded group against another would become immediately apparent with the U.S. Supreme Court's 1857 ruling, in Dred Scott v. Sandford, that people of African descent, whether free or enslaved, could never be American citizens. The eleven-year-long legal battle had been initiated by an enslaved man and his wife on account of having spent years in federal territory, where slavery was prohibited. While the phrase "Dred Scott" became shorthand for the broader struggle over race and rights in which African Americans claimed to be citizens of the United States (Jones 2018, 128), the court's final ruling against Dred and Harriet Scott propelled the United States toward Civil War. The Civil Rights Act of 1866 finally established birthright citizenship to all persons born in the United States regardless of "race, color, or previous condition of slavery or involuntary servitude" (Civil Rights Act 1866). In 1868, the 14th Amendment to the U.S. constitution overturned the Dred Scott v. Sandford ruling, by stating that citizenship applied to "all persons born or naturalized in the United States, and subject to the jurisdiction thereof." Tellingly for the underlying racial colonial legacies, the 14th Amendment however denied citizenship to Native Americans, obviously "born" in the United States, because they were subject to the jurisdiction of their tribal governments (→ Indigeneity, I/31). Congress did not grant citizenship to Native Americans on reservations until 1924, 56 years later.

The acquisition of citizenship through *jus soli*, or birth on the state territory, became the rule throughout the Americas, as more colonies gained independence from Europe in the 19th century (→ Independence Movements, I/10). Although it was the older principle, originating in medieval England, in which "true and faithful obedience" to the sovereign was owed by a subject from birth (Shachar 2009, 114), *jus soli* suited the constitutions of newly independent Latin American and Caribbean states more than the French revolutionary principle of *jus sanguinis*, or citizenship through ancestry, which was only adopted in Haiti. In the case of the young republics in Spanish America, which maintained the traditional *jus soli*, the formal decision to continue the principle of the Cádiz constitution was matched by strategic concerns. In the colonial empire, the quality "born in America" differentiated and disadvantaged the *criollos* versus the *peninsulares*. After independence, the same principle was turned against the former masters.

> By keeping the *jus soli*, all those born in Spain were permanently excluded from membership in the respective nation states, and even the relocation of a family to Spain led to the loss of political civil rights from the next generation onwards.
>
> *(Schwarz 2013, 20 my translation)*

In parallel fashion, the British tradition of *jus soli* was implemented in both the United States and Canada – the only two countries in the Global North that to this day still grant automatic citizenship to children born to non-citizen parents – as well as in its Caribbean colonies.

At the same time, the definition of national citizenship went hand in hand with the invention of the Other within the nation. Leaders of independence movements and nation-state builders in South America and the Spanish Caribbean conceived of the subject of rights in the European tradition and in contradistinction with the native population – in the case of continental Spanish America – and with Blacks – mainly in Brazil and the Caribbean (Mignolo 2014). As Santiago Castro-Gómez (2000) has pointed out, creating the identity of the modern Latin American citizen legally anchored in a constitution involved the simultaneous production of a counterpart from which that identity could be measured and affirmed as such and that would make viable the modern project of governability. The Venezuelan constitution of 1839 stated, for example, that citizens could be only married men, over 25 years old, who could read and write, who owned real estate and who practiced a profession that generated annual income of more than 400 pesos. In that understanding, the disabled, homosexuals, and dissidents fell just as much short of the economically profitable and socially compliant national subject, as women, the illiterate, non-whites, or the enslaved. Castro-Gómez explains, "The acquisition of citizenship is … a filter through which only those are allowed to pass, whose profile fits the type of citizen required by the project of modernity: male, White, paterfamilias, Catholic, property owner, literate and heterosexual…" and people who do not fit this profile "remain outside the 'lettered City' …, sentenced to punishment and therapy by the same law that excludes them" (Castro-Gómez 2000, 149).

The construction of the imaginary of "civilization" necessarily demanded the imaginary of "barbarism" anchored in abstract systems of a disciplinary nature. National constitutions, schools (→ Education, I/24), hospitals (→ Health, I/29), prisons, and guidebooks were in charge of emphasizing the universal norm, isolating, or treating deviation, and preparing the young generation for the role of the citizen as defined by Occidental standards (Boatcă 2016, 99). Especially in those parts of Latin America that had previously been central to the Spanish empire before the 18th century, and which still had a sizable indigenous population such as Mexico, Central America, and the Andean region, the inculcation of Western norms through public education was part of extensive policies of cultural assimilation that was largely built on modified versions of the former colonial policies (→ Indigeneity, I/31). In contrast, in Argentina, Chile, and Uruguay, as well as in the Unites States, where no successful "de-Indianization" was deemed possible, the virtual physical extermination of the natives and the conspicuous absence of Afro-descendants from state discourse silenced the question of the political participation (→ II/41) and social enfranchisement of the non-White population for decades after independence (Quijano 2006b, 199ff) (→ Silencing, III/19).

Indigenous groups were considered obstacles to projects of national integration and modernization (→ I/35) in the Americas throughout the 19th and first half of the 20th century. Formal political rights tended to be restricted on the basis of race, education, property, gender, and literacy, resulting in highly unequal forms of citizenship and reproducing longstanding inequalities (→ II/20) (Meltzer and Rojas 2014). Significant change occurred the 1970s and 1980s, as indigenous organizations emerged in Mexico and the Andean region and quickly became powerful political movements (→ Social Movements, I/41). The Zapatistas' uprising in Mexico, alongside the constitutional reforms in Bolivia and Ecuador in the 1990s that reframed the understanding of democracy (→ II/32) and equal rights and included the recognition of collective property rights and of the multicultural character of society (→ Multiculturalism, I/36) are "acts of citizenship" through which rights that are only granted on theory are still wrested away from dominant groups and redistributed in actual practice to the excluded. Attempts to transform citizenship from a legal status to a process of granting rights are central to Latin American social movements to this day. In the Andes, they culminated in the creation of a new type of indigenous citizenship and the election of Evo Morales as the first indigenous president in 2006 (Meltzer and Rojas 2014).

Concluding remarks

Universal systems of national citizenship throughout the Americas today can be seen as the outcome of long historical struggles in which enslaved and indentured workers (→ Slavery, I/18; Unfree Labor, I/19), women (→ Gender Identities, I/28), indigenous peoples (→ I/11), peasants, migrants, and refugees (→ Transnational Migration, I/44) have both challenged regimes of exclusionary citizenship and negotiated with states (→ Nation State, II/38) and with existing citizenries for inclusion. This was formulated particularly clearly in the Zapatista's first declaration from the Lacandon Forest, which expounded on the long history of struggle accumulated over hundreds of years, including

> first against slavery; then in the insurgent-led war of Independence against Spain; later in the fight to avoid being absorbed by North American expansion; next to proclaim our Constitution; next to proclaim our Constitution and expel the French from our soil; and finally, after the dictatorship of Porfirio Diaz refused to fairly apply the reform law, in the rebellion where the people created their own leaders.
>
> *(First Declaration from the Lacandon Jungle, 1994, quoted in Mignolo 2002)*

In taking up positions as citizens and claiming fundamental human rights (→ Indigeneity, II/35), formerly excluded indigenous, enslaved, and indentured people – and their descendants – have played a crucial part in contesting these exclusions, broadening the scope of freedom (→ I/27), and performing new embodiments of citizenship. Today, however, citizenship remains both an inclusionary and an exclusionary process. Modern forms of citizenship are tied to histories of expulsion of indigenous and aboriginal groups across the Americas, alongside far-reaching systems of slavery, indentureship, and their associated global migrations. Citizenship, moreover, remains embedded in local contexts of practice that are deeply implicated in ongoing processes of emancipation (Sheller 2014, 284). The reconceptualization of citizenship from a global perspective sheds new light on the workings of the institution of modern citizenship from its very emergence in the context of the French Revolution and reveals the crucial role of the Americas in its development. On the one hand, the gradual extension of citizenship rights from propertied white males to all white males and to white women accounted for the development of low inequality within continental France as of the 18th century. On the other hand, the categorical exclusion of Saint-Domingue's black and mulatto population from French citizenship, irrespective of their property status, ensured the maintenance of high inequality between France and Saint-Domingue/Haiti, as well as between other Western colonial powers and their colonial possessions more generally. It thus becomes clear that the entail of property that Shachar (2009) used as an analogy to the entail of citizenship was a colonial entail meant to preserve inherited property, both in the form of material goods proper and of *rights to* goods, state support, social services, and infrastructure in the hands of the (racially, ethnically, and geopolitically) designated heirs to the Western colonial enterprise for several centuries. The Americas and the world are still contesting this legacy.

Works cited

Blackburn, Robin. 1988. *The Overthrow of Colonial Slavery, 1776–1848*, London: Verso.

Boatcă, Manuela 2016. *Global Inequalities Beyond Occidentalism*, London: Routledge.

Boatcă, Manuela and Julia Roth. 2016. "Unequal and gendered: Notes on the coloniality of citizenship." *Current Sociology* 64, no. 2: 191–212.

Brubaker, Rogers. 1992. *Citizenship and Nationhood in France and Germany*, Boston: Harvard University Press.

Castro-Gómez, Santiago. 2000. "Ciencias sociales, violencia epistémica y el problema de la 'invención del otro'." In *La colonialidad Del Saber: Eurocentrismo Y Ciencias Sociales. Perspectivas latinoamericanas*. ed. Edgardo Lander, 145–162. Buenos Aires: CLASCO.

Dussel, Enrique D. 1996. *The Underside of Modernity Apel, Ricoeur, Rorty, Taylor, and the Philosophy of Liberation*, New Jersey: Humanities Press.

Fischer, Sibylle. 2004. *Modernity Disavowed: Haiti and the Cultures of Slavery in the Age of Revolution*, Durham: Duke University Press.

Horne, Gerald. 2015. *Confronting Black Jacobins: The US, the Haitian Revolution, and the Origins of the Dominican Republic*, New York: New York University Press.

Isin, Engin. 2005. "Citizenship after orientalism: Ottoman citizenship." In *Challenges to Citizenship in a Globalizing World: European Questions and Turkish Experiences*. eds. Fuat Keyman and Ahmet Icduygu, 31–51. London: Routledge.

———. 2013. "Citizenship after orientalism. Genealogical investigations." In *Comparative Political Thought: Theorizing Practices*. eds. Freeden, Michael and Andrew Vincent, 120–135. London: Routledge.

Isin, Engin and Bryan S. Turner. 2002. "Citizenship studies: An introduction." In *Handbook of Citizenship Studies*. eds. Engin F. Isin and Bryan S. Turner, 1–10. London: Sage.

Isin, Engin and Greg M. Nielsen. 2008. *Acts of Citizenship*, London and New York: Zed Books.

Jones, Martha S. 2018. *Birthright Citizens: A History of Race and Rights in Antebellum America*, Cambridge: Cambridge University Press.

Joppke, Christian. 1994. "Toward a new sociology of the state: A review essay." *Archives Européennes De Sociologie* 36, no. 1: 168–178.

Korzeniewicz, Roberto Patricio, and Timothy Patrick Moran 2009. *Unveiling Inequality: A World-Historical Perspective*, New York: Russell Sage Foundation.

Lugones, Maria. 2007. "Heterosexualism and the colonial/modern gender system." *Hypatia* 22, no. 1: 186–209.

Mackert, Jürgen and Hans-Peter Müller, eds. 2000. *Citizenship. Spziologie der Staatsbürgerschaft*. Berlin: Springer VS.

Marshall, Thomas Humphrey. 1977. *Class, Citizenship and Social Development: Essays*, Chicago: University of Chicago Press.

McClintock, Anne. 1995. *Imperial Leather: Race, Class and Sexuality in the Colonial Context*, New York and London: Routledge.

Meltzer, Judy, and Cristina Rojas 2014. "Transformations and imaginings and practices of citizenship in Latin America." In *Routledge Handbook of Global Citizenship Studies*. eds. Engin F. Isin, and Peter Nyers, 253–264. New York: Routledge.

Mignolo, Walter D. 2000. *Local Histories/Global Designs. Coloniality, Subaltern Knowledges, and Border Thinking*, Princeton: Princeton University Press.

———. 2002. "The Zapatistas's theoretical revolution: Its historical, ethical, and political consequences." *Review* 25, no. 3: 245–275.

Mignolo, Walter D. 2014. "Who speaks for the 'human' in human rights?" In *Human Rights from a Third World Perspective: Critique, History and International Law*. ed. José-Manuel Barreto, 44–64. Newcastle: Cambridge Scholars Publishing.

Oyěwùmí, Oyèrónkẹ́ 1997. *The Invention of Women: Making an African Sense of Western Gender Discourses*, Minneapolis: University of Minnesota Press.

Parsons, Talcott. 1965. "Full citizenship for the Negro American? A sociological problem." *Daedalus* 94, no. 4: 1009–1054.

Parsons, Talcott. 1971. *System of Modern Societies*, New Jersey: Prentice Hall.

Quijano, Aníbal. 2000. "Coloniality of power and Eurocentrism in Latin America." *International Sociology* 15, no. 2: 215–232.

———. 2006a. "El 'Movimiento Indígena' y las Cuestiones Pendientes en América Latina." *Review. Journal of the Fernand Braudel Center* 29, no. 2: 189–220.

———. 2006b. "Estado-nación y movimientos indígenas en la región Andina: Cuestiones abierta." *OSAL, Observatorio Social de America Latina* 6, no. 19: 15–24.

Schwarz, Tobias. 2013. *Policies of Belonging: Nationale Mitgliedschaft und Zugehörigkeit in Lateinamerika*, Colon: Kompetenznetz Lateinamerika.

Shachar, Ayelet. 2009. *The Birthright Lottery: Citizenship and Global Inequality*, Harvard: Harvard University Press.

Sheller, Mimi. 2014. "Performances of citizenship in the Caribbean." In *Routledge Handbook of Global Citizenship Studies*. eds. Engin F. Isin and Peter Nyers, 284–295. New York: Routledge.

Stam, Robert and Ella Shohat. 2012. *Race in Translation: Culture Wars Around the Postcolonial Atlantic*, New York: New York University Press.

Stoler, Ann Laura and Cooper, Frederick. 1997. *Tensions of Empire: Colonial Cultures in a Bourgeois World*, Berkeley: University of California Press.

Trouillot, Michel-Rolph. 1995. *Silencing the Past: Power and the Production of History*, Boston: Beacon.

Turner, Brayan S. 1990. "Outline of a theory of citizenship." *Sociology* 24, no. 2: 189–217.

———. 1993. "Outline of a theory of human rights." *Sociology* 27, no. 3: 489–512.

Turner, Brayan S. and Peter Hamilton. 1994. *Citizenship Critical Concepts*, London: Routledge.

Wallerstein, Immanuel. 2003. "Citizens all? Citizens some! The making of the citizen." *Comparative Studies in Society and History* 45, no. 4: 650–679.

Weber, Max. 1978. *Economy and Society. An Outline of Interpretive Sociology*, eds. Guenther Roth and Claus Wittich, Berkeley: University of California Press. Orig. pub. 1922.

28
CIVIL SOCIETY

Laura Macdonald

Civil society is one of the most frequently used but also most elusive concepts in the contemporary study of politics and society in the Americas. Jan Aart Scholte defines civil society as "a political space where voluntary associations explicitly seek to shape the rules (in terms of specific policies, wider norms, and deeper social structures) that govern one or the other aspect of social life" (2001, 4). While analytically distinct from both the state (→ Nation State, II/38) and the market, in practice these lines are often blurred. There are widespread debates, however, about the assumptions behind this definition – whether individuals' participation in these associations are actually uncoerced, how civil society organizations (CSOs) actually relate to the state and the market, and where organizations like political parties fit into this definition (Foley and Edwards 1996, 38). How individuals and groups answer these questions depends a great deal on where they are located, as well as on their underlying theoretical assumptions.

The "modern" idea of civil society as disseminated in elite circles in both the Global North and Global South has its roots in the ideas of the Scottish Enlightenment (→I/8) in the 1700s but faded into intellectual obscurity for centuries. It was revived in Latin America and Eastern Europe between the 1960s and 1980s, and then further spread to North America and other parts of the world in diverse political and economic contexts. It has become a virtually universal analytical touchstone in discussions of democracy (→ Democracy, II/32) and democratization in the Americas and refers to a diverse range of entities including non-governmental organizations (NGOs), professional associations, environmental groups (→ Environmental Justice, II/8), unions (→ Labor Representation, II/14), and faith-based associations (→ Religious Beliefs, I/40). However, the assumptions underlying its deployment vary dramatically from place to place across the hemisphere, and Eurocentric conceptions of civil society are being continuously challenged by more local and indigenous approaches (→ Indigeneity, I/31) that are more reflective of the lived experiences of the citizens of the Americas (for a critical discussion of the limits of the concept see Alvarez et al. 2017).

The story of the uses and abuses of "civil society" in the Americas reveals a much more complicated and rich conception of how ideas travel across time and space. Canadian anthropologist Anna Tsing (2005) offers a valuable approach to interpret the transnational flow of ideas related to civil society. Tsing adopts the metaphor of "friction" to describe how ideas initially developed in one location react when received in another location. "Friction" refers to "the awkward, unequal, unstable and creative qualities of [global-local] interconnection across difference" (Tsing 2005, 4). These interconnections mean that supposedly global forms constantly interact with the local and, in the process, are transformed by their contact with stubborn local realities (Calvert 2016). Tsing's theoretical approach examines how "universals and particulars come together to create the forms of capitalism (→ II/2) with which we live" and focuses on the "uneven and awkward links" between the global and the local (Tsing 2005, 4). Similarly, in the context of globalization, ideas about what civil society consists of, how it works, and what role it plays in processes like democracy and development (→ II/6) are constantly debated and contested by both "global" and "local" actors. The idea has traveled back and forth between the Global North and Global South for centuries, and in the process has generated new interpretations in diverse settings.

Intellectual origins of civil society – north and south

The term "civil society" is originally a product of Western philosophical thought, related to fundamental rethinking of modern society occurring in Western Europe in the late 18th century. One of the most prominent early contributions was Adam Ferguson's 1767 *On the History of Civil Society* (2011) (he derived the term from the Latin *societatis civilis*). Ferguson referred to civil society as an ordered, peaceful society, governed by the rule of law that was emerging in Northern Europe. This society, in his view, was characterized by increased social complexity and more "refined manners," in contrast with the more unified and warlike, but also more vigorous societies upon which classic republican ideals were based (Foley and Hodgkinson 2003, ix). Ferguson conceptualized civil society as a sphere separate from the state (→ Nation State, II/38), rather than as the *polis* as a whole. He, and later liberal thinkers, worried that increased specialization, wealth, and refinement would undermine the civic virtue that was necessary to sustain a great nation (Foley and Hodgkinson 2003, xiii). His approach to the concept was vague, but his contribution to this liberal view of civil society also defined it as part of the slow evolutionary process of civilization that was gradually reducing the role of violence in Western societies (Keane 1998, 117).

Influenced by Ferguson, Hegel's 1820 *Elements of a Philosophy of Right* laid out the idea that civil society represented an ethical ideal, the realm in which human beings find ways to work together and shape themselves through ethical norms. Ultimately, however, for Hegel only the state could represent universal interests, since civil society inevitably expressed particularistic interests and individual needs (Foley and Hodgkinson 2003). Marx retained this idea that civil society represented the realm of special interests and inequality (→ Social Inequality, II/20) but viewed Hegel's conception of the universal state as a mask for the oppressive nature of social relations under capitalism (Foley and Hodgkinson 2003, xiv).

The use of the term "civil society" became less prominent in European political philosophy after the early 1800s, but later thinkers continued to contemplate the implications of the organizational and complexity of industrial society. Alexis de Tocqueville (2000 [1835/40]) provided one influential and optimistic approach in his classic work, *Democracy in America.* He was astounded by the propensity of Americans to form associations and remarked, "Nothing deserves more attention than the intellectual and moral associations in America … In democratic countries the knowledge of how to combine is the mother of all other forms of knowledge; on its progress depends that of all the others" (cited in Berman 1997, 401). De Tocqueville thus believed that a vigorous associational life could counteract the destabilizing tendencies of industrialization and urbanization (→ II/45) and permit democratic participation (→ II/41) of ordinary (white male) citizens (→ Citizenship, II/27; Whiteness, I/46), while counteracting the threat of the tyranny of the majority (Howell and Pearce 2001, 43). These ideas were adopted by later theorists of civil society, particularly in the United States.

This liberal understanding of the concept of civil society was resurrected in Central and Eastern Europe in the 1970s and later traveled to Latin America in the 1980s. Eastern European theorists seized upon the work of earlier liberal theorists and applied it to their own reality: civil society was seen as the Achilles heel of totalitarian regimes (→ Authoritarianism, II/25), while citizens' struggles to create and expand civil society were viewed as the best tool to promote democratic change. The goal was to create solidarity among numerous self-governing civil associations that would pressure the state from outside and eventually undermine the political basis of Communist rule (Keane 1998, 20). Maintaining some of the themes from earlier liberal thought, this version insisted on the importance of the complete analytical separation of state and civil society and conceptualized the latter as a sphere of freedom (→ I/27), self-expression, and self-organization.

In contrast, a more radical concept of civil society had already traveled to Latin America in the mid-1960s, primarily through exposure of radical left intellectuals to the work of Italian Communist Antonio Gramsci, produced in Fascist prisons in the 1930s. This understanding of civil society differed in important ways from the liberal assumptions of the Eastern European intellectuals. Like Marx, Gramsci viewed civil society as a conflictual terrain made up of cultural institutions that primarily served to entrench the role of the dominant class (→ Class Struggle, II/3). The rule of the capitalist class was preserved through the ideological hegemony that was established in civil society, between the state and the economy through trench-like structures that preserved the "outer ditch" of state power. Through this analysis, Gramsci developed a sophisticated portrayal of the nature of class power in advanced industrial societies, and he attacked the Bolshevik strategy of seizing state power through violent struggle (what he called "war of maneuver"). He advocated, instead, for a "war of position" within civil society to gradually undermine the power of the state and the capitalist system (Keane 1998, 15). Gramsci's approach also rescued the realm of culture from the economistic and deterministic assumptions of orthodox Marxism.

Gramsci's work would be taken up widely by the left in many parts of Latin America, beginning with the translation of his work into Spanish by Argentine intellectual José María Aricó in the 1960s; Aricó also established a publishing house, *Pasado y Presente*, to disseminate Gramsci's work and that of other critical Marxist scholars (Allen and Ouviño 2017). Gramsci's ideas were popular among the Latin American left for various reasons: they allowed intellectuals and activists to move away from the orthodoxy and vanguardism of the Communist party without giving up their socialist principles (→ Socialism, I/42); they also provided a framework in which Latin Americans could explore the historical specificity of their own societies, and the ways in which state-society relations differed there from those in Europe or the United States. His approach to civil society and the distinctions he made between political and civil society and the state offered a more sophisticated reading than that offered by Leninist or Stalinist orthodoxy where the line between state and civil society was eradicated (see Mignolo 2012).

As well, by the 1980s, Gramsci's work opened up a way to think about the struggle for democracy (→ II/32) where "[t]he strengthening of civil society was seen as paramount to the building of democracy, a view reinforced by the fact that the theoretical critique of the authoritarian state had led … to a critique of statist conceptions of politics" (Dagnino 1998,

39) (→ Authoritarianism, II/25). According to Evelina Dagnino, the dominant reading of Gramsci within the Latin American left brought together three different tendencies: "a renovative critique of traditional Marxism, an emphasis on the building of democracy with its correlated strengthening of civil society, and, in the interstices of these two, a new approach to the relationship between culture and politics" (Dagnino 1998, 39–40). This approach embraced a more pluralistic, diverse, egalitarian and horizontal relationship between actors in civil society, in contrast with more orthodox versions. An important distinction between this approach and the version that was predominant in Eastern Europe was the insistence upon the idea of civil society that interacted and overlapped with state action, in contrast to the view that civil society at least ideally existed in opposition to and distinct from the state (Dagnino 1998, 41). In addition, these Latin American authors maintained a sharp focus on the forms of inequality that permeated civil societies in capitalist societies (→ Social Inequality, II/20; Capitalism, II/2).

Finally, another version of civil society emerged in the United States in the late 1980s and early 1990s, influenced by earlier U.S. liberal pluralist theory (cf. Almond and Verba 1963; Dahl 1961) and particularly inspired by the work of De Tocqueville. The most influential writer in this school was Robert Putnam (1993, 1995)). Like De Tocqueville, Putnam championed a depoliticized and benevolent view of civil society associations as the wellspring of democracy in northern Italy and the United States. Putnam argued that social trust and social capital are nurtured in the informal institutions of everyday associational life (Howell and Pearce 2001, 47) in which "social capital, as embodied in horizontal networks of civic engagement, bolsters the performance of the polity and the economy, rather than the reverse: Strong society, strong economy; strong society, strong state" (Putnam 1993, 176). His work champions individual, voluntary participation in "networks of civil engagement," and reprises the liberal analytical separation of state and society and the normative valuation of civil society as a realm of self-expression and individual liberty. This approach largely ignored forms of class, race (→ I/39), gender (→ I/28), ethnicity (→ I/25) and other axes of oppression that permeate society and limit individuals' capacity to exercise their democratic privileges.

This liberal pluralist approach became dominant among Western donors to Latin America in the context of democratization and neoliberalization in the 1980s (Macdonald 1997; Howell and Pearce 2001) (→ Neoliberalism, II/16). In the eyes of Western international financial institutions (IFI), civil society (specifically NGOs), represented an alternative to delivery of services through state institutions, seen as inherently corrupt and inefficient. Brazilian social scientist Bernardo Sorj argues that these IFIs came to see NGOs as allies in the development of a transnational agenda designed to break the political monopoly of the nation-state (→ II/38) (Sorj 2007). Sorj claims that Latin American social philosophy has always been deeply influenced by international debates, as a result of the fact that the elite and middle classes have also taken as a point of reference practices and ideologies that come from outside of the region. He argues that Western-influenced approaches to Latin American civil society fail to integrate local political traditions, by, for example, promoting the liberal idea of civil society as independent from the state, an idea that clashed with Latin American realities (Sorj 2012, 4). Nevertheless, it must be recognized, as Tsing's (2005) perspective suggests, that Western actors and their Latin American allies were not able to unilaterally impose their narrow conception of civil society. Instead, as Tsing suggests, popular Latin American actors creatively engaged in dialogue with some aspects of the Western civil society paradigm, while rejecting those that did not reflect their local situations (→ Popular, I/37).

Evolution of civil society in Latin America

The context in which civil society was eventually embraced in Latin America was very different from the European sites in which the concept initially arose. It is also important to recognize the enormous diversity in social and political experiences in the region, which means civil society is interpreted in different ways in response to local realities. Any attempt to generalize about the region thus risks losing out on local and national diversities (Sorj 2012, 1). Leonardo Avritzer argues that the Western version of the concept could not make its way to Latin America early on because the social processes that gave rise to the idea did not yet exist outside of the West. He argues that as a result of the impact of Spanish and Portuguese colonialism (→ Colonial Rule, I/5), the differentiation between the household economy and the private sphere, which occurred in early modern Europe, did not occur until the early 20th century. Especially in rural areas, the vast power attached to private forms of political control like the *hacienda* kept in place strong personalistic and clientelistic ties and limited space for the establishment of egalitarian relationships and differentiation between the private sphere and the state (Avritzer 2006, 36).

In addition, the persistence of religious and patriarchal relationships curtailed the exercise of individual rights. The Western concept of civil society was also alien to the indigenous worldview that prevailed in many parts of the region (→ Indigeneity, I/31). Indigenous perspectives reject the artificial division of state and society and rested upon the defense of collective and communal rights (→ Commons II/31), in contrast to the liberal individualism of the Western approach. Guatemalan Mayan theorist Gladys Tzul Tzul argues, for example, that in indigenous societies, there is no separation between the domestic sphere, where reproduction is organized, and political society, which organizes public life. These are complementary domains, as embodied in communal indigenous government (cited in Zibechi 2018). Tzul understands the indigenous commons as the strategies of men and women who manage, self-regulate, and defend their territories on a daily basis (Tzul Tzul 2015, 129).

On the other hand, the renovation of the Latin American church in the 1960s under the influence of liberation theology gave rise to new forms of popular organization and assertiveness on the part of the poor that stimulated the emergence of new CSOs (Oxhorn 2006, 78) (→ Religious Beliefs, I/40). Civil society thus was imbricated with the state and religious practices in a way that was largely distinct from European traditions.

The rapid process of industrialization and urbanization (→ I/45) that occurred in much of Latin America during the middle decades of the 20th century also was not conducive to the development of civil society discourses, since these processes were led by populist regimes (→ Populism, II/43). These regimes developed new forms of interest mediation based on top-down corporatist principles. Individuals were politically incorporated into the state through corporatist bodies (primarily unions) (→ Labor Representation, II/14) that regulated their participation in politics. Early forms of political participation (→ II/41) were thus collective in form rather than individual and were based on the fusion of state and society rather than the separation of the two spheres (Collier and Collier 1991; Silva and Rossi 2018, 7–8). This period was followed by the forceful "disincorporation" of popular sector actors by bureaucratic authoritarian military regimes in most countries of South America (→ Authoritarianism, II/25). Although corporatist forms remained in place in some countries like Brazil and Argentina, unions lacked the capacity to defend the interests and rights of their members. However new forms of organization emerged based on demands for basic civil and political rights (→ Social Movements, I/41).

The 1980s and 1990s brought about a new period of simultaneous democratization (partly because of civil society pressures) and adoption of neoliberal economic principles (→ Neoliberalism, II/16) based upon *laissez faire* principles. Despite democratization, the early years of this period were not encouraging for the development of strong and autonomous CSOs. Neoliberalism was first adopted by the Pinochet dictatorship of Chile, under the influence of the so-called "Chicago boys," U.S. economists like Milton Friedman, who used Chile as a testing ground for their radical beliefs. Subsequently, these ideas spread after the debt crisis (→ Crisis, II/4) broke out in the early 1980s and newly elected democratic regimes were required to adopt neoliberal policies in order to qualify for new loans. As a result, countries throughout the region adopted economic policies that favored foreign investors and local elites, at the expense of both economic growth and the social rights of the poor and middle-class majorities. In order to impose these ideas, neoliberal technocrats advocated policies that effectively neutralized or sidelined domestic critics, whether by governing through surprise, deception, the manipulation of crises, as well as outright repression (Macdonald 2017, 57). In the short to medium term, these processes undermined the potential for more democratic and participatory models of governance. Labor unions (→ Labor Representation, II/14), the primary form of interest representation for popular sectors, were repressed and lost their power of representation because of the decline of formal sector jobs as the result of labor flexibilization and trade liberalization (→ Informality II/13).

In the longer term, however, the impact of neoliberalism and International Monetary Fund (IMF) structural adjustment programs on the poor led to the re-emergence of civil society throughout the region. While neoliberal reformers thought they had vanquished popular opposition through their attacks on labor unions, a diverse group of other forms of social organization emerged that eventually overturned neoliberal governments through electoral means and put in place new "post-neoliberal" governments in most countries of the region (Macdonald and Ruckert 2009). These new social movements included organizations representing indigenous peoples (particularly important in the Andean countries of Ecuador and Bolivia) (→ Indigeneity, II/31), women, the urban informal sector, peasants, environmental activists (→ Environmental Justice, II/8) and other disenfranchised groups that had suffered the effects of neoliberalism (see Stahler-Sholk, Kuecker and Vanden 2008; Silva 2009).

Latin American analysts often view civil society as an ambiguous terrain. Aldo Panfichi, for example, reflecting on the development of civil society in South America in the late 20th century, emphasizes the importance of civil society as a space where actors struggle to recuperate elements of the liberal tradition that were present in the period of formation of new republics in the 19th century but that were rejected by governing elites for most of their history (Panfichi 2001, 2). These new emerging actors were struggling to revive or create instances of autonomy, self-organization, and democracy (→ II/32) in this context. He insists, however, that it is important not to idealize civil society since it can be the site of inequality (→ II/20), and exclusionary and non-democratic practices. Civil society in the Latin American context is frequently "a complex, and heterogeneous reality, composed of actors, practices and institutions representing divergent interests" (Panfichi 2001, 3, my translation).

The emergence of post-neoliberal governments in most countries of Latin America, particularly in South America, has created new opportunities but also new challenges for civil society. Civil society was an important force in creating these new governments, and new forms of political participation became available once democracy was in place. For example, participatory budgeting emerged at the local level in Brazil and spread to other parts of the region, including Rosario and Buenos Aires in Argentina (Avritzer 2009, 182) and created opportunities for civil society actors to demand accountability and shape public spending (→ Participation, II/41).

The forms of participation of civil society in these new left regimes differs considerably, however, depending on the form of regime. Avritzer (2009) describes three forms of participation in the region. The first, a form of "direct, non-institutionalized participation," is the form that was more common during protests against neoliberalism, for example the *caracazo* in Venezuela and the *cacerolazo* in Argentina. These protests have continued in places like Mexico and Honduras, where neoliberalism (→ II/16) remains prevalent, but succeeded in overturning governments in many countries in South America. He calls the second case a form of "institutionalized participation," which emerged in countries like Brazil, Chile and Uruguay where the crisis of representation of the 1980s and 1990s did not destroy the existing political system. Instead, governments of the left came to power, and implemented policies that promoted a degree of re-incorporation of civil society and political participation that led to more inclusive social policies. Finally, he describes the case of Venezuela as a form of "top-down semi-institutionalized participation" in which the socialist regime of Hugo Chávez promoted a certain degree of citizen participation (→ Socialism, I/42), for example in the "Bolivarian Circles," but this participation was linked to unconditional defense of the president.

Other analysts have emphasized the tensions that remained between state and civil society under these post-neoliberal governments, and the distinct forms of relationships that were cultivated. As noted by Stahler-Sholk, Vanden and Becker (2014, 6), different movements have made distinct choices about how they will relate to political parties and governments, ranging from the Mexican Zapatista model of complete autonomy, to the uneasy relationship between the landless peoples' movement in Brazil with the Workers' Party (PT) that governed between 2003 and 2016, to the close relationship between Venezuelan social movements and the Chavista state. Indigenous movements have been among the main protagonists and beneficiaries of the shift to the left (→ Indigeneity, I/31), but they also maintain sometimes fraught relationships with new radical governments in Bolivia (where Evo Morales is the country's first indigenous president) and, especially, in Ecuador under the leftist technocratic leadership of Rafael Correa. Feminists have been critical about the tendency of new leftist leaders in places like Bolivia, Ecuador, and Nicaragua to take advantage of women's support for progressive policies while maintaining in place many patriarchal and homophobic policies and supporting social conservatism (Lind 2013) (→ Gender Identities, I/28). Finally, it is important to note the continued prevalence of neoliberal governments in several countries of the region, including Mexico and Colombia, in which civil society movements remain outside of the state and continue to battle for basic political and social rights.

Civil society in the North America

While Latin Americans picked up on some aspects of the European tradition of civil society, with greater affinity for more critical perspectives, U.S. and Canadian views largely preserved the more liberal interpretation closer to the original version. In the United States, a particular "civil society discourse" permeates discussion of the phenomenon. According to Jeffrey Alexander and Philip Smith, even though differences emerge among various perspectives, they are united by a "democratic code" drawn from liberal individualist and civic republican theory that specifies the appropriate actors, institutions, and social relationships that are appropriate in a democratic society. U.S. actors see the country as the "closest approximation of a democratic society," and therefore "[h]ere, if anywhere, we would expect to see the discourse of civil society in its most pristine form" (Alexander and Smith 1993, 161).

The practices of civil society in the United States are related to the country's escape from colonial rule (→ I/5), and early adoption of democratic institutions as well as relatively equal social structures compared to the feudal structures that continued to shape both Europe and Latin America (→ Social Inequalities, II/20). The types of associations described by De Tocqueville in the 1830s were frequently commented on by subsequent observers, both domestic and foreign. A British visitor in the 1890s, James Bryce, commented that "associations are created, extended, and worked in the United States more … effectively than in any other country" (cited in Skocpol, Ganz and Munson 2000, 527). Social scientists since the 1960s have provided more systematic evidence to support this type of claim, documenting Americans' singular propensity to participate in voluntary groups. Papered over in much of this idealized view of U.S. civil society are the ideologies that categorized African Americans, indigenous people and women as unsuitable and ineligible for full democratic citizenship (→ II/27) for many years, and their exclusion from many of the groups described by these commentators (Arneil 2006).

This literature, like the work of Putnam described earlier, provides a nostalgic and romantic view of the U.S.-American past. Moreover, civil society is viewed as a spontaneous phenomenon, in which groups emerged within small local communities, and individuals formed groups within their cohesive neighborhoods outside of politics. This strand of thought is particularly associated with conservative political traditions in the United States where local community associations are viewed as springing up from below, in opposition to federal government action.

Skocpol et al. take issue with this view of U.S. civil society as characterized by dispersed and unconnected local organizations; instead they insist that U.S. history was shaped by widespread moral crusades, labor unions (→ Labor Representation, II/14), farmers' groups (→ Social Movements, I/41), and associations of veterans, women, social reformers, as well as recreational groups and fraternal societies which attracted hundreds of thousands or millions of members (2000, 529). Overall, they argue, "nearly three-quarters of the U.S. membership associations that grew very large before 1940 … developed federated organizational arrangements that resembled the representative, three-tiered institutions of U.S. governments" (2000, 532). This federal structure gave organizations opportunities for leverage within the U.S.-American political system. As well, the dynamism and mobility of U.S. society meant that translocally organized associations were appealing to people on the move, permitting nationwide cooperation and coordination of activities. The U.S. government's system of checks and balances created incentives and openings for these groups to pressure the state and achieve many of their objectives. Of course, as E. E. Schattschneider warned in his 1960 work *The Semisovereign People*, from the beginning, the system was weighted toward the interests of a small minority when he wrote, "the flaw in the pluralist heaven is that the heavenly chorus sings with a strong upper-class accent" (1960, 65).

Another version of the liberal approach emerged in Canada, where individualism was less predominant in the national political culture, particularly in Quebec. According to Jenson and Phillips (1996), the post-war citizenship regime that governed the relationship between state and society, recognized both individual and collective rights (Jenson and Phillips 1996,

116). The challenge coming from the nationalist movement in Quebec prompted the federal government to use the state to promote a pan-Canadian national identity. The state promoted social equity and a strong civil society as a means to promote national identity. In the post-war period and especially beginning in the 1960s the Canadian federal state provided considerable funding to advocacy groups in civil society as part of the project of promoting social justice and national unity. This citizenship regime came under strain, however, in the 1990s, with the adoption of neoliberal policies and cutbacks for intermediary associations. According to Jenson and Phillips, neoliberalism (→ II/16) promoted a reconstruction of the citizenship regime to foster the role of individual responsibility rather than collective rights (Jenson and Phillips 1996, 119). This challenge to civil society culminated in the cutbacks in funding under the Harper government (2006–2015), although the Trudeau government elected in 2015 reversed some of this tendency.

Conclusions: Civil society dialogues across the Americas

Civil society is a malleable concept that has been transported across the Atlantic and manifested in diverse ways in the various nations of the Americas. The view of civil society as analytically and normatively distinct from the state (→ Nation State, II/38) and as a sphere in which individual identities and freedoms flourish (→ Freedom, I/27) has achieved greater traction in the northern countries of the hemisphere. A more critical view took hold in Latin America, in which civil society is viewed as heavily shaped by the state and by unequal relations of power. In the context of globalization, international financial institutions and NGOs have heavily promoted the liberal Western version in Latin America. As Tsing's (2005) concept of friction implies, however, powerful actors within the global system are not able to unilaterally impose their ideas on passive peripheral actors. Instead, local actors often creatively adapt and respond to those ideas and shape them to their own uses.

In addition, ideas about civil society have not moved only in a North-South direction. Critical interpretations of civil society have also traveled northward and were shared in sites like the Hemispheric Social Alliance, where social movements from across the Americas united in opposition to the U.S.-led Free Trade Area of the Americas (FTAA), launched in Miami in 2004 (→ Alter-Globalization, I/21). In alliance with new left-wing governments in Latin America, civil society actors were able to defeat the FTAA project (Saguier 2007). Transnational movements continue to engage with the concept of civil society and to develop new practices of interpretation and critique. One of the most important challenges to liberal notions comes from indigenous movements (→ Indigeneity, I/31) and decolonial theorists (→ Postcolonialism, I/38) who reject many of the epistemological and normative assumptions behind the concept, while also strategically engaging with it in a creative fashion. These new interpretations of civil society are also fruitful for re-examining the historical interpretations of civil society, its uses and abuses, in the northern countries of the region. Civil society remains an essential concept within discussions of democracy (→ II/32) and citizenship (→ II/27) in the Americas.

Works cited

Alexander, Jeffrey C. and Phillip Smith. 1993. "The Discourse of American Civil Society: A New Proposal for Cultural Studies." *Theory and Society* 22, 151–207.

Allen, Nicolas and Hernán Ouviño. 2017. "Reading Gramsci in Latin America." *NACLA Report on the Americas*, May 26, https://nacla.org/news/2017/05/28/reading-gramsci-latin-america.

Almond, Gabriel A. and Sidney Verba. 1963. *The Civic Culture: Political Attitudes and Democracy in Five Nations*. Princeton: Princeton University Press.

Alvarez, Sonia E., Jeffrey W. Rubin, Millie Thayer, Gianpaolo Biaocchi, and Agustín Laó-Montes. 2017. *Beyond Civil Society: Activism, Participation and Protest in Latin America*. Durham: Duke University Press.

Arneil, Barbara. 2006. *Diverse Communities: The Problem with Social Capital*. Cambridge: Cambridge University Press.

Avritzer, Leonardo. 2006. "Civil Society in Latin America in the Twenty-First Century: Between Democratic Deepening, Social Fragmentation, and State Crisis." In *Civil Society and Democracy in Latin America*, eds. Carlos H.Waisman, Richard Feinberg, and Leon Zamosc, 35–57. New York: Palgrave Macmillan.

———. 2009. "La nueva izquierda, la crisis de Representación y la Participación Social en América Latina." *La 'Nueva Izqierda' en América Latina: Derechos Humanos, Participación Política y Sociedad Civil*, eds. Cynthia J. Arnson, et al., 177–190. Washington, DC: Woodrow Wilson International Center for Scholars.

Berman, Sheri. 1997. "Civil Society and the Collapse of the Weimar Republic." *World Politics* 49, no. 9: 401–439.

Calvert, Julia. 2016. *Reclaiming Domestic Agency: International Investment Agreements and the Defence of Policy Space in Latin America*. PhD dissertation, Ottawa: Carleton University. Political Science.

Collier, Robert and Ruth Berins Collier. 1991. *Shaping the Political Arena: Critical Junctures, the Labor Movement, and Regime Dynamics in Latin America*. Princeton: Princeton University Press.

Dagnino, Evelina. 1998. "Culture, Citizenship, and Democracy: Changing Discourses and Practices of the Latin American Left." In *Cultures of Politics Politics of Cultures: Re-visioning Latin American Social Movements*, eds. Sonia E. Alvarez, Evelina Dagnino and Arturo Escobar, 33–63. Boulder: Westview.

Dahl, Robert. 1961. *Who Governs? Democracy and Power in an American City*. New Haven: Yale University Press.

De Tocqueville, Alexis. 2000. *Democracy in America*. Chicago: University of Chicago Press. Orig.pub. 1835/40.

Ferguson, Adam. 2011. *An Essay on the History of Civil Society*. Cambridge: Cambridge University Press.

Foley, Michael W. and Bob Edwards. 1996. "The Paradox of Civil Society." *Journal of Democracy* 7, no. 3: 38–50.

Foley, Michael W. and Virginia A. Hodgkinson. 2003. "Introduction." In *The Civil Society Reader*, eds. Virginia A. Hodgkinson and Michael W. Foley, 7–14. Hanover: University Press of New England.

Howell, Jude and Jenny Pearce. 2001. *Civil Society and Development: A Critical Exploration*. Boulder: Lynne Rienner.

Jenson, Jane and Susan D. Phillips. 1996. "Regime Shift: New Citizenship Practices in Canada." *International Journal of Canadian Studies* 14, 112–135.

Keane, John. 1998. *Civil Society: Old Images, New Visions*. Stanford: Stanford University Press.

Lind, Amy. 2013. "Latin America's Left Turn: What's in it for Women?" *Al Jazeera Opinion*, www.aljazeera.com/indepth/opinion/2013/03/2013326101350284530.html.

Macdonald, Laura. 1997. *Supporting Civil Society: The Political Impact of NGO Assistance to Central America*. Basingstoke, UK and New York: Macmillan and St. Martin's Press.

———. 2017. "Neoliberal Governance in Latin America." In *The Handbook of South American Governance*, eds. Christopher Wylde and Pia Riggirozzi, 56–69. London and New York: Routledge.

Macdonald, Laura and Arne Ruckert, eds. 2009. *Post-Neoliberalism in the Americas: Beyond the Washington Consensus?*. New York: Palgrave Macmillan.

Mignolo, Walter D. 2012. "Latin America: Between Revolution and Decoloniality." In *The Postcolonial Gramsci*, eds. Neelam Srivastava and Baidik Bhattacharya, n.p.. New York: Routledge.

Oxhorn, Philip. 2006. "Conceptualizing Civil Society from the Bottom Up: A Political Economy Perspective." In *Civil Society and Democracy in Latin America*, eds. Richard Feinberg, Carlos H. Waisman, and Leon Zamosc, 59–84. New York: Palgrave Macmillan.

Panfichi, Aldo. 2001. Sociedad civil y gobernabilidad democrática en los Andes y el Cono Sur: una vision panorámica al fin del siglo XXI. Paper prepared for delivery at the 2001 meeting of the Latin American Studies Association, Washington DC.

Putnam, Robert. 1993. *Making Democracy Work: Civic Traditions in Modern Italy*. Princeton: Princeton University Press.

———. 1995. "Bowling Alone: America's Declining Social Capital." *Journal of Democracy* 6, no. 1: 65–78.

Saguier, Marcelo I. 2007. "The Hemispheric Social Alliance and the Free Trade Area of the Americas Process: The Challenges and Opportunities of Transnational Coalitions against Neo-Liberalism." *Globalizations* 4, no. 2: 251–275.

Schattschneider, Elmer Eric. 1960. *The Semisovereign People: A Realist's View of Democracy in America.* New York: Winston.

Scholte, Jan Aart. 2001. "Civil Society and Democracy in Global Governance." *CSGR Working paper 65/01.* http://wrap.warwick.ac.uk/2060/1/WRAP_Scholte_wp6501.pdf.

Silva, Eduardo. 2009. *Challenging Neoliberalism in Latin America.* Cambridge: Cambridge University Press.

Silva, Eduardo and Federico M. Rossi. 2018. "Introduction: Reshaping the Political Arena in Latin America." In *Reshaping the Political Arena in Latin America: From Resisting Neoliberalism to the Second Incorporation*, eds. Eduardo Silva and Federico M. Rossi, 3–20. Pittsburgh: University of Pittsburgh Press.

Skocpol, Theda, Marshall Ganz, and Ziad Munson. 2000. "A Nation of Organizers: The Institutional Origins of Civic Voluntarism in the United States." *American Political Science Review* 94, no. 3: 527–546.

Sorj, Bernardo. 2007. "Pueden las ONGs reemplazar el estado? Sociedad civil y Estado en América Latina." *Nueva Sociedad*, no. 210: 126–140. http://nuso.org/media/articles/downloads/3445_1.pdf.

———. 2012. *Ocho tesis sobre la sociedad civil en América Latina.* Working Paper no. 8. Rio de Janiero: Centro Edelstein de Investigaciones Sociales.

Stahler-Sholk, Richard, Glen David Kuecker, and Harry E. Vanden, eds. 2008. *Latin American Social Movements in the Twenty-First Century: Resistance, Power, and Democracy.* Lanham: Rowman and Littlefield.

Stahler-Sholk, Richard, Harry E. Vanden, and Marc Becker. 2014. "Introduction: New Directions in Latin American Social Movements." In *Rethinking Latin American Social Movements: Radical Action from Below*, eds. Richard Stahlor-Sholk, Harry E. Vanden and Marc Becker, 1–17. Lanham: Rowman and Littlefield.

Tsing, Anna. 2005. *Friction: An Ethnography of Global Connection.* Princeton: Princeton University Press.

Tzul Tzul, Gladys. 2015. "Sistemas de gobierno comunal indígena: la organización de la reproducción de la vida." *El Apantle: Revista de Estudios Comunitarios* 1, no. 1: 125–140.

Zibechi, Raúl. 2018. "Los pueblos en defensa de la vida y el territorio: contra-poder y autodefensa en América Latina." *Estado del Poder 2018, Transnational Institute.* http://longreads.tni.org/es/estado-del-poder-2018/vida-y-territorio/.

29
CLIENTELISM

Tina Hilgers

In the Americas, relationships based on exchanges of goods and services for loyalty have existed for centuries. The word itself that is used to describe them – clientelism – can be traced to ancient Rome, where prominent men were patrons to groups of supporters, known as *clientela*. Clientelism is now commonly understood as political parties discretionally dispensing public resources to poor individuals in return for their vote. It is considered endemic in Latin America and the Caribbean, but also exists in the United States and Canada. Most analyses focus on the supply side of clientelism through parties and bureaucracies, arguing that candidates should court the vote with policy platforms and bureaucrats should distribute public resources according to the rules, rather than buying support and ruling undemocratically (→ Democracy, II/32). Studies looking at the demand side depict clientelism as a survival strategy and an expression of citizenship (→ II/27) where economic opportunities and political accountability are scarce, because the poor can use it to articulate demands, produce responsiveness, and access resources (→ Participation, II/41). Despite the latter arguments, the literature and the public generally view clientelism negatively, and politicians use it to undercut the activities of their opponents, especially regarding social programs and subsidies for the poor, which they describe as large-scale efforts to buy votes.

There are tensions in the production of knowledge about clientelism as well that underscore the reproduction of exclusionary systems. Meso-level scholarly analyses consider clientelism detrimental to the health of democratic institutions, and politicians use the word to create a negative impression of pro-poor policies. The former assume that, absent clientelism, formal institutions would be stronger and better able to meet the needs of all citizens, and the latter, that citizens should not rely on the state. Micro-level analyses, however, see clientelism as symptomatic of meso- and macro-level systemic inequalities that would have to be addressed before clientelism could become unnecessary (→ Social Inequality, II/20). From this perspective, institutionalist analyses skirt the real problem and the politicization of the word clientelism is normatively untenable. This entry examines knowledge production about clientelism by considering positivist and interpretivist studies, transfers of meaning across time and space, and entanglement with other political practices. It concludes with a discussion of the transnationalization of clientelism and its relevance to Inter-American practices.

Comparisons of clientelism

How clientelism is analyzed depends on the researcher's epistemological position. A number of political scientists have used comparison to identify the general conditions under which clientelism emerges and recedes, as well as the strategies of the political parties and brokers supplying clientelistic resources. The underlying assumption is that if the immediate causes of clientelism are discovered, its solution will appear. A small group of sociologists, anthropologists, and geographers has identified how clientelistic relationships occupy specific places. They are interested in understanding particular instances of how clients live these relationships, and then in critically linking their functions to larger societal structures.

Two political science contributions that stand out in adding to our knowledge of how and why parties use clientelism are Kitschelt and Wilkinson (2007) and Stokes et al. (2013). Kitschelt and Wilkinson (2007) draw on the quality of economic and political development (→ II/6) to explain that programmatic politics – parties campaigning with policy promises applicable to all constituents and applying these by the book upon winning – is more likely than clientelism where ethnocultural cleavages are weak and apolitical institutions regulate political power and the distribution of economic wealth. The shift from clientelism to programmatic politics occurs as the electorate becomes wealthier and, therefore, too expensive to purchase. Stokes et al. (2013) concur with this point in their analysis of brokers who use knowledge of local communities to bring votes to parties. Brokers in poor communities distribute (and pocket) party resources, monitoring recipients to make sure that they remain loyal to the party at the poll booth, and the parties rely on these brokers because, although an inefficient use of resources, they help to ensure electoral success. When wealth and education (→ I/24) levels increase, parties can dispense with brokers because voters become too difficult to monitor and too expensive to buy, but easier to inform through non-personalistic mechanisms. These studies – based on cases from across developed and developing areas, including the Americas – go a long way toward explaining why contemporary parties and politicians continue to engage in clientelism.

Nonetheless, interpretivists argue that general models offer only a partial view of clientelism, which should be seen as a place-based phenomenon. For them, the content of clientelistic relationships depends on the place (geography) in which they occur, on the place (power) of the actors involved, and on the place (agenda) of their critics. Local market structures, institutional configurations, and traditions affect clientelism making generalization across space and time difficult. Evaluations of clientelistic relationships also depend on the position of the actor: clients interpret them as a useful mechanism for constructing accountability and identity, while patrons see them as ways to target scarce resources and care for (or control) the population. Citizens without access to a patron, socioeconomically or politically powerful actors outside the ruling party or coalition, and journalists, however, criticize clientelism as corrupt. The fabric of clientelism depends, then, on where it occurs and on who is experiencing it.

Auyero's (2001) seminal, ethnographic work in Buenos Aires, Argentina, shows how members of a poor community negotiate the reality of poverty with the help of Peronist party brokers (→ Populism, II/43). Residents face any number of challenges in their daily lives, as family members lose jobs or fall ill, or as routine needs including food must be met, and neither the state nor the market can be relied upon to solve problems. The brokers, who live in the same community, are present to laugh and cry with, to propose solutions, to use party networks to come up with a job, or necessary medication. Brokers and clients form a family that, together, attends rallies and other party events – interstices of enjoyment in the drudgery of slum life.

Auyero's analysis of clientelism in this marginalized community gives it meaning as a material and psychological survival mechanism and as a position from which to critique social, political, and economic structures that create an intractable situation for the poor.

Research in the slums of Kingston, Jamaica, also allows Sives (2010) and Jaffe (2015) to highlight the mechanisms of survival and identity, but through a clientelism marked by violence. The island's two major political parties began to construct inner city social housing in the 1960s and 1970s, allowing occupants to live rent free in return for electoral support. Rival party leaders encouraged gangs to protect their respective party's turf, funneled resources to residents through gang leaders, and shielded the leaders from prosecution for illegal activities. Although residents have lived in fear of the constant violence, party and gang affiliation have also been an element of identity construction. In a racialized society that views young, poor blacks as inherently criminal (→ Race, I/39), party and gang seem the only way to build a powerful sense of self.

Based on a historical revision of New York's infamous Tammany Hall, Golway (2014) describes clientelism as a mix of corruption and repression with social work and social policy. Nineteenth and early 20th century Irish immigrants were poor, unemployed, and seen as criminals by New York society. Tammany Hall's Democratic Party machine ruled the immigrants with an iron fist, its leaders grew wealthy from extortion, and judges, police, and politicians were in alliance, ensuring impunity for their own. But Tammany's ward captains and district bosses were also familiar with the deprivations suffered by their constituents; they talked and listened, provided services, found jobs, and made sure that their people turned out to the polls. Ultimately, Tammany politicians were instrumental in bringing about reforms including the minimum wage and workers' compensation, giving their clients formal rights (→ Human Rights, II/35). Tammany was emblematic of urban politics in 19th century United States (→ Urbanization, I/45). Irish immigrants constituted significant minorities in cities including New York, Boston, Chicago, Buffalo, Pittsburgh, St. Louis, New Orleans, and San Francisco (→ Migration, I/15). They lived in misery, but by voting en bloc to support their patrons, managed to take over municipal politics by the late 1800s (Bocock 1894). Members of state legislatures representing European immigrants became central actors in pushing the reform agenda to improve social justice of the early 1900s (Huthmacher 1962). Reformism was, at least partially, built on clientelism.

In the above examples, policy regimes, formal and informal institutional configurations, market structures, and identity intersect in various ways to generate different realities of clientelism. And, while experts, journalists, and opposition politicians portray clients as unwitting victims, clients lucidly assess their place in the world and their options for survival (Auyero 2001). These details give meaning to exploitation, but, through their attention to the everyday lives of the poor, highlight the broader, structural sources of exploitation underlying the specific problems inherent in clientelism.

Transferring meaning

The place-based changes in meanings of clientelism are also evident in its adaptation to historical shifts in social and market structures and political contexts. In traditional societies, kin, fictive kin, and entire communities engaged in exchanges or gifting to redistribute resources and create lasting social and political ties (→ Family, I/26). As social organization increased in complexity, exchanges tied domestic and colonial peripheries to centers; as bureaucracies grew, they were used to fill administrative positions; with the advent of mass suffrage, they linked parties and their constituents; and with the increasing cost of election campaigns, they tied donors to candidates.

For example, in the United States, the practice of exchanging goods and services for votes at the grassroots seems to have decreased, but the term clientelism is now applied to a higher level of analysis with different stakes. Traces of the kind of clientelism practiced through Tammany Hall remain in contemporary New York, Chicago, and Boston, but are not comparable to the scale of these activities in the 19th and early 20th centuries. At the same time, the scale of favor-creating resources moved around among elites has increased – in the U.S. as elsewhere – and analysts are using clientelism to describe such exchanges. Thus, the discretional allocation of public resources to loyal individual voters or their organizations is "retail clientelism," while large campaign donations are "wholesale clientelism" (Fox 2012, 194). Campaign donors provide resources to electoral candidates, who, once in office, demonstrate loyalty by supporting the donors' interests legislatively. Donors are, then, wholesale buyers of the votes in entire constituencies. In the Canadian case, too, clientelism is applied beyond the traditional patron-client dyad, to governments giving patronage positions to supporters and interest groups having special relationships with certain legislators. Based on this, the entire political structure of the eastern provinces is argued to be clientelistic (MacLeod 2006).

Accounts of clientelism across the ages do show certain constants and changes. The exchange partners generally occupy different levels in a status hierarchy but are mutually dependent – the lower status party needs resources, while the higher status one requires power derived from having a number of followers or allies. Changes come in the types of resources needed by the lower status party and the kinds of negotiations that can be envisioned. For example, peasants need land (→ II/15), land titles, seeds and fertilizer, tools, and technical advice (Lapegna 2016), while the urban poor need jobs, transportation and other urban services (→ Urbanization, I/45). Both need food and shelter, but other differences are apparent. Bureaucrats, on the other hand, primarily need information and protection to help career advancement (Grindle 1977), while politicians need money. In all cases, competition among patrons confers negotiating power on clients. In rural areas where a single patron holds the land, peasants have little power, but in urban communities where a number of individuals and political parties vie for community leadership, the poor have choices (Montambeault 2015). Micro-level analyses have identified that, in authoritarian regimes with highly centralized power (→ Authoritarianism, II/25), clients have few means to pressure patrons, but, in democratic regimes with competitive elections, they can negotiate the quality of the clientelistic exchange because they can seek out alternative patrons offering better conditions. Nonetheless, contextual and temporal changes are not always straightforward as they sometimes involve the entangling of different meanings and practices.

Entanglement

Over time, contexts and uses change, so that the meanings and practices of different behaviors and actors become entangled. Clientelism per se comes to take on new meanings, new actors are pulled into clientelistic dynamics, and the term clientelism is used politically to criticize particular policies (→ Political Communication, II/42).

In the Latin American and Caribbean region, the idea that "clientelism" is a pejorative has traveled to the lowest levels of the socio-political hierarchy. It is to be expected that savvy political elites will deny engaging in these exchanges, but even grassroots leaders tend to make such claims. In interviews in Mexico City with people attached to several political parties, officials, militants, and social organization leaders (→ Social Movements, I/41) insisted that clientelism was an authoritarian practice they did not use. However, observations of their interactions with constituents revealed the usual exchanges. Most did not attempt to hide these dynamics, taking for granted that there was a difference between what they understood as authoritarian clientelism and what they deemed necessary to mobilize the poor.

This understanding of mobilization tactics is not limited to traditional power elites. When marginalized ethnic groups (→ Ethnicity, I/25) or class sectors gain access to political office, they may change policy directions and develop participatory processes (→ Participation, II/41), but also replicate familiar political practices. Irish immigrants to the United States were first controlled through clientelism and then, as their leaders took political office, began to use it to control others. The 2005 election of the indigenous union leader Evo Morales to the Bolivian presidency signaled the taking of power by indigenous peoples (→ Indigeneity, I/31) and the popular classes and led to a host of institutional and policy reforms. Among these was the nationalization of the hydrocarbon industry (→ Energy, II/7), income from which has been used to bankroll social programs that require political loyalty of the recipients (Makaran 2016). In Mexico, the opposition Democratic Revolutionary Party (PRD) firmly opposed the existing regime's clientelistic practices, championing the right to independent political participation of the poor. Since winning Mexico City's first democratic elections in 1997, however, it has generated its own clientelistic network (Hilgers 2008). In all three cases, the new forces in power felt they had to cement organic support for their work in office using clientelism.

For their part, international organizations and aid donors aim to undermine clientelistic hierarchies (→ Development, II/6), but do become ensnared in domestic social orders. Rio de Janeiro's Favela Bairro (1994–2008) is a well-known favela-upgrading project that brought infrastructural and social programs to the city's poor communities. Improvements generally included street paving, drainage and sewerage, childcare and recreational center construction, and investment in technical training for employment. The Inter-American Development Bank (IDB) provided several loans for Favela Bairro, judging it to be a development program that fit its goals of improving lives and enhancing transparency and accountability. Bank officials were unaware that drug gangs were appropriating some of the projects, using them to reinforce their positions in the favelas (Gay 2012). The gangs had managed to insert themselves as brokers between residents and politicians because the state was historically unwilling to establish a direct presence in the favelas (Arias 2006) (→ Security, II/45).

Politicized uses of the term clientelism have entangled it with redistributive public policies. It is not unusual for opposition politicians and pundits to label programs such as Brazil's Bolsa Familia or Mexico City's monthly subsidies for the elderly and aid for primary school supplies (→ Education, I/24), clientelistic. The programs are targeted at entire sectors of the population and distributed such that they go directly to recipients, without the intervention of a middle layer of local officials, so that resources are a public right and processes are transparent. Opposition politicians nonetheless characterize the programs as clientelistic, using the logic that the state is creating a dependent population that will necessarily vote for its benefactors (→ Nation State, II/38). Regular intertwining of the term clientelism with this type of redistributive program affects the meaning of both the concept and the policy in public understanding.

Final discussion

There is wide agreement that clientelism exists, in varying degrees, across the Americas, but debates continue about how to study it and what it means. Much knowledge about the retail variant of clientelism is produced from the ostensibly objective perspective of the analyst, but fails to account for the client's view of an intrinsically unequal world in which clientelism may be the only available mechanism for accessing the state (→ Social Inequality,

II/20; Participation, II/41), the market, and their resources. How this world is structured and clientelism is used, is context-dependent and involves diverse actors.

The character and role of new actors makes clientelism relevant to Inter-American studies and debates when regarding the impact of links between international and domestic actors – especially through examinations of transnationalized clientelism. Transnationalized clientelism in the Americas includes banks, organizations, donors, and businesses, whose activities affect, and are affected by, the clientelistic exchanges of domestic actors. International actors, such as the IDB in the above case of favela upgrading, are sometimes unwittingly pulled into local dynamics that they do not support. At other times, however, the type of activity usually undertaken by international agencies, donors, or governments necessarily involves relationships of power that reflect clientelistic dynamics. Thus, international non-governmental organizations enter Latin American communities with resources and skills needed by the locals which in turn causes the locals to express gratefulness and deference, conferring status on NGO staff which then allows NGO staff to organize the locals as they see fit. While such international organizations may work in what they consider to be the best interest of local communities, their socio-political role is not unlike that of the patron (Leonard et al. 2010) (→ Development, II/6). As Inter-American linkages expand in the global era, the transnationalization of traditional modes of exchange becomes more frequent.

In the case of economic interests, the production of transnationalized clientelistic exchanges is often less benign. Canadian mining companies, for example, have built a significant presence in Latin America since the early 1990s (→ Transnational Corporations, II/23). Governments give them privileged status to exploit natural resources (→ Extractivism, II/9), at the expense of local populations and ecosystems (→ Nature, II/39), and to use the local police for protection from opponents, in return for the tax wealth they provide (→ Taxation, II/22). Governments can then invest these resources in social programs, which are sometimes captured by local party brokers and used to gain the political support of voters (see Studnicki-Gizbert 2016, also Bebbington and Bury 2013). Future research is needed to further investigate the interrelationships between external and domestic actors and how these reproduce or transform clientelism.

Works Cited

Arias, Enrique Desmond. 2006. *Drugs and Democracy in Rio de Janeiro: Trafficking, Social Networks, and Public Security*. Chapel Hill: University of North Carolina Press.

Auyero, Javier. 2001. *La Política de los pobres. Las Prácticas Clientelistas del Peronismo*. Buenos Aires: Manantial.

Bebbington, Anthony and Jeffrey Bury, eds. 2013. *Subterranean Struggles: New Dynamics of Mining, Oil, and Gas in Latin America*. Austin: University of Texas Press.

Bocock, John Paul. 1894. "The Irish Conquest of our Cities." *The Forum* April 1894, 186–195.

Fox, Jonathan. 2012. "State Power and Clientelism: Eight Propositions for Discussion." In *Clientelism in Everyday Latin American Politics*, ed. Tina Hilgers, 187–211. New York: Palgrave Macmillan.

Gay, Robert. 2012. "Clientelism, Democracy, and Violence in Rio de Janeiro." In *Clientelism in Everyday Latin American Politics*, ed. Tina Hilgers, 81–98. New York: Palgrave Macmillan.

Golway, Terry. 2014. *Machine Made: Tammany Hall and the Creation of Modern American Politics*. New York and London: W.W. Norton & Company.

Grindle, Merilee Serrill. 1977. *Bureaucrats, Politicians, and Peasants in Mexico: A Case Study in Public Policy*. Berkeley and Los Angeles: University of California Press.

Hilgers, Tina. 2008. "Causes and Consequences of Political Clientelism: Mexico's PRD in Comparative Perspective." *Latin American Politics and Society* 50, no. 4: 123–153.

Huthmacher, Joseph J. 1962. "Urban Liberalism and the Age of Reform." *The Mississippi Valley Historical Review* 49, no. 2: 231–241.

Jaffe, Rivke. 2015. "Between Ballots and Bullets: Elections and Citizenship in and Beyond the Nation-State." *Citizenship Studies* 19, no. 2: 128–140.
Kitschelt, Herbert and Steven I. Wilkinson, eds. 2007. *Patrons, Clients and Policies: Patterns of Democratic Accountability and Political Competition.* New York: Cambridge University Press.
Lapegna, Pablo. 2016. *Soybeans and Power: Genetically Modified Crops, Environmental Politics, and Social Movements in Argentina.* New York: Oxford University Press.
Leonard, David et al. 2010. "Does Patronage Still Drive Politics for the Rural Poor in the Developing World?" *Development and Change* 41, no. 3: 475–494.
MacLeod, Jeffrey. 2006. "Nova Scotia Politics: Clientelism and John Savage." *Canadian Journal of Political Science* 39, no. 3: 553–570.
Makaran, Gaya. 2016. "La figura del llunk'u y el clientelismo en la Bolivia de Evo Morales." *Revista Antropologías del Sur* 5: 33–47.
Montambeault, Françoise. 2015. *The Politics of Local Participatory Democracy in Latin America: Institutions, Actors, and Interactions.* Stanford: Stanford University Press.
Sives, Amanda. 2010. *Elections, Violence and the Democratic Process in Jamaica: 1944–2007.* London: Ian Randle.
Stokes, Susan C., Thad Dunning, Marcelo Nazareno, and Valeria Brusco. 2013. *Brokers, Voters, and Clientelism: The Puzzle of Distributive Politics.* New York: Cambridge University Press.
Studnicki-Gizbert, Daviken. 2016. "Canadian Mining in Latin America (1990 to present): A Provisional History." *Canadian Journal of Latin American and Caribbean Studies* 41, no. 1: 95–113.

30
CLIMATE CHANGE

Franz Mauelshagen and Andrés López Rivera

Climatic changes have occurred many times in the Earth's history. In the last ten thousand years, human activities such as deforestation, rice-growing, pastoral agriculture may have already caused minor modifications to the atmosphere. However, only in the latter half of the 20th century has the sum of human activities become the *dominating* cause for climate change, the reason being massive release of greenhouse gases (GHGs) into the atmosphere (IPCC 2015; IPCC-WG1 2013). It must be emphasized from the start that there are enormous differences in GHG emissions between different countries and peoples with different lifestyles around the world. Such differences are apparent across the Americas. Differences between major and minor emitters, North and South, industrialized economies and emerging economies, rich and poor characterize the political geography of climate governance in the Americas.

Political and physical geography are also entangled with regard to the unequal challenges of adapting to climate change. The Americas are stretched out between the poles, from the Arctic circle in the North, all the way down to Cape Horn at more than 55° South. Climates are tropical and humid in Amazonia, semi-arid and desert on subtropical plateaus, as well as cool and dry in Canada and Patagonia. These climates will change in many different ways challenging the adaptive capacities of societies (→ Nature, II/39). For example, rainfall has increased in south-east Brazil, Paraguay, Uruguay, and the Argentinian Pampas, while it has decreased in southern Chile, southwestern Argentina and southern Peru. Climate change threatens the existing variety of ecological species, particularly in the rich and diverse environment of the Amazon rain forest, while glaciers are melting in the Andes and in parts of North America. Sea-level rise will accelerate coastal erosion and enhance flooding almost everywhere, with small islands in the Caribbean being particularly threatened. Natural hazards such as hurricanes will more severely, and potentially also more frequently, hit the Caribbean, the Gulf of Mexico, and the U.S. East Coast (→ Disaster, II/33). In addition to all these challenges, the adaptive capacities vary as much across the Americas as do the regional and local impacts of climate change (IPCC-WG2 2014, chapters 26 & 27). Adaptation to climate change is as complex an issue of climate change governance as climate mitigation or protection by means of the reduction of GHGs, and it will gain importance with the accelerating and self-enhancing process of global warming.

In the following, our focus is climate change mitigation, much less adaptation policies. This is due to the Inter-American character of our survey, which creates an emphasis on international contexts and institutions, and to the historical pathways of international climate governance, which have put mitigation policies into the foreground.

International climate change governance

The greenhouse effect is basic to the knowledge and politics of anthropogenic climate change. While certain gases block some of the incoming short-wave solar radiation, others capture some of the long-wave radiation reflected from the surface of the Earth, the latter of which are called greenhouse gases. The greenhouse effect has been known since the early 19th century (Archer and Pierrehumbert 2011), and by the late 19th century, scientists began thinking that industrial mass burning of fossil fuels might enhance the natural greenhouse effect (Weart 2003). However, uncertainties remained about how much of the released GHGs from industrial activities really accumulated in the atmosphere, until Charles Keeling developed a reliable and widely recognized method to measure atmospheric carbon dioxide in the late 1950s (Howe 2014). Measurements began during the International Geophysical Year (IGY 1957–8) at the Mauna Loa Observatory (Hawaii) and in other places. In less than a decade of measurements, the results were widely accepted as proof that CO_2 levels in the atmosphere were increasing rapidly.

Atmospheric CO_2 measurements proved crucial to the politicization of climate change. Founded on the scientific study of atmospheric chemistry and effects of its variability on the global climate system climate change developed slowly as a policy field centering on the question of GHG emission reductions. Much of the science of global warming and its early politics took shape in the USA, which started pushing for coordinated international action around the mid-1980s. Back then the *Montreal Protocol on Substances that Deplete the Ozone Layer*, signed in 1987 (effective from 1989), was seen as a model for international cooperation on anthropogenic climate change, though the latter is an incomparably more complex issue.

Following these beginnings, the second stage in international climate change governance saw the establishment of the Intergovernmental Panel on Climate Change (IPCC) in 1988, which was given the main task to frequently provide summaries of the state of climate science. The first Assessment Report of the IPCC confirmed that climate change was clearly dominated by anthropogenic GHG emissions, *not* by natural variability in the climate system, and, in response, called for concerted international action. In 1992, the United Nations Framework Convention on Climate Change (UNFCCC) was drafted and signed during the Earth Summit in Rio de Janeiro. Ratified by 197 member states of the UN, the UNFCCC has become the charter of international climate change governance. With it, the signatory states recognized that climate change is a "common concern of humankind" (preamble, §1), and that it requires maximum participation in mitigation action by reducing GHG emissions. Based on an inventory of national GHG emissions, which at the time excluded emissions from land use, it also recognized that the common goal of controlling climate change implied different responsibilities for different countries, which is reflected in the classification of parties and their commitments: Annex I is a list of 43 parties classified as industrialized countries and "economies in transition" (EiTs, all former centrally planned economies, which had belonged to the Soviet Union and the Eastern Bloc before 1990) committed to reduce emissions; Annex II is a smaller list of 24 countries from Annex I (all members of the OECD) accepting the additional commitment to provide financial and technical support to EiTs and developing countries for, both, mitigation and adaptation purposes. Among American countries only the USA and Canada are listed on Annex I and II. Last but not least, the UNFCCC also created an institutional structure (e.g. a secretariat) and, most important, the Conferences of the Party (COP) as a framework for continuous international negotiations about specifying the commitments that the members of the UNFCCC had generally agreed upon.

After Rio, a third period in the history of climate change governance began, characterized by the purpose to design an international treaty that would define binding emission reduction targets for the parties of the UNFCCC. The Kyoto Protocol, adopted in 1997, established three flexibility mechanisms to reduce GHG emissions as well as the costs of climate protection policies: (1) international emission trading (IET) among Annex I countries, in other words industrialized nations; (2) a Clean Development Mechanism (CDM) through investment in renewable energies and new technologies (→ Energy, I/7), which was meant to foster technology transfer to, and emission reductions in, developing countries (→ Development, II/6); (3) a Joint Implementation (JI) mechanism, which allowed industrial nations to reduce their emissions by (co-)investment in emission reduction projects in other Annex I countries (Gupta 2014, 78–97).

All these Kyoto mechanisms had little or mixed success over the years and have often been criticized as ineffective. In particular, intergovernmental emission trading failed to create the desired price signal to make emission trading attractive (Edenhofer and Jakob 2017, 76–7). The greatest problem with the Kyoto Protocol was its scope. In 2011, total emissions by all the countries who had ratified it, which did not include the USA and other major emitters, only amounted to 13 percent of global GHG emissions. Excluding developing nations from binding emission reductions had become questionable, not least because China, India, and Brazil, with their booming economies, had turned into major absolute emitters. However, in the negotiations after Kyoto, China, and India continued to resist committing to binding emission cuts, arguing that responsibility for climate change is still predominantly with traditional Western industrialized countries, as historically accumulated emissions were showing, and that they needed to protect their sovereignty – a particularly sensitive issue in all climate negotiations with regard to the historical experience of previous European/Western colonial dominance. Combined with the position that U.S. governments have held onto more or less continuously after the Millennium turn, that they themselves would not accept an international treaty on emission cuts without the inclusion of China and India, this led to a deadlock in the post-Kyoto process, which became painfully noticeable in Copenhagen (COP 15) in 2009.

The deadlock in international climate change governance that had been reached in the course of the post-Kyoto negotiations was broken in 2015 by the Paris Agreement. The old differentiation between industrialized and developing countries was overcome in an agreement (1) to limit climate change at 2°C above pre-industrial levels, if possible, even at no more than 1.5°C, obliging (2) *all* parties to propose GHG emission reductions in what has been called Nationally Determined Contributions (NDCs). These two pillars of the agreement were to be supported by a third one, namely (3) a number of flexible multilateral mechanisms such as the possibility to implement new emission trading schemes, financial support of the Green Climate Fund (GCF) to assist developing countries in adaptation and mitigation practices (→ Development, II/6), and the REDD+-mechanism (Reducing Emissions from Deforestation and Forest Degradation), which seeks to compensate states for economic loss from forest protection (Edenhofer and Jakob 2017, 77–9). Yet, reaching the Paris Agreement came at a price. Giving up the top-down approach of defining emission reduction targets for each country based on scientific calculations of remaining carbon emission budgets for a 2°C+ climate and replacing it, instead, by the NDC approach has left open whether the sum of proposed emission reductions will indeed add up to an effective total. At this point of the post-Paris process, the NDCs are far from meeting either the 2°C or 1.5°C targets.

Nevertheless, the Paris Agreement is a major caesura in global climate change governance and "a step change in multilateral efforts to address climate change" (Luterbacher et al. 2018, 13). The new system is now frequently characterized as *polycentric*, a term introduced by Elinor Ostrom and endorsed by a number of her followers (Cole 2015; Ostrom 2010a). Soon after the post-Kyoto process had experienced its greatest setback in Copenhagen 2009, Ostrom argued that the multiple benefits that emission reductions produce at diverse levels of social self-organization (individual, family, small groups, local, regional, state) encourages a polycentric approach to collective action on climate change. Pointing to existing initiatives from the local to transnational levels involving a variety of authorities from different domains of governance she predicted "that a polycentric system for coping with global climate change is emerging and is likely to expand in the future" (Ostrom 2010b, 555).

Climate change governance and the Americas

Anthropogenic climate change positions American territories and their citizens in very diverse ways with regard to, both, their contribution of GHGs and their (expected) exposure to the risks involved with climate change. Emissions reflect, at least to some degree, the enormous diversity of environments, economic wealth, and lifestyles, which can be found across the American continent. The major per capita *and* absolute emitters of CO_2 are namely the USA and Canada (the only American countries listed in Annex I and II of the UNFCCC). Both are in the North, and both were pioneers of industrialization, which is why their historical responsibility exceeds that of all other American countries. Nevertheless, there are other *major per capita emitters*, which are *not* major absolute emitters; Curaçao (NL), Trinidad and Tobago, the Malvinas (Falkland Islands) (UK), the Bahamas, Bermuda (UK), Martinique, and the Cayman Islands (UK) are all islands with relatively small or even tiny territories and with populations living a western lifestyle.

Most countries in North and South America are medium range per capita emitters. Some countries in this group have relatively high absolute emissions due to large territories and populations. Brazil and Mexico are leading this category, followed by Argentina and Venezuela, the greatest Latin American oil producer (→ Energy, II/7). Chile, Colombia, Peru, and Ecuador are next in the list, but emit less than half the Argentinian totals.

However, the overall picture looks different if GHG emissions from agriculture, forestry, and other land use (AFOLU) are included (→ Land, II/15). That applies even more in the Americas than elsewhere, because AFOLU GHG emissions share nearly 40 percent of all GHG emissions in Latin American countries, which is far above the global average (Calvin et al. 2016, 615). Still, there are significant differences between countries. AFOLU GHG emissions are particularly high in Brazil, Argentina, and Columbia, while in Mexico energy production and industry dominate the pattern. One reason for this is the Amazon rainforest, which spreads across as many as nine countries. It has been called the "lungs of the Earth" due to its enormous importance as a carbon sink and because of this, climate change has further politicized its protection.

The United States of America

Lyndon B. Johnson was the first chief executive to mention the evolving danger of increasing atmospheric CO_2 in a "Special Message to the Congress on Conservation and Restoration of Natural Beauty" (Johnson 1965). General concerns about environmental conservation and changes in the atmosphere continued in the 1970s under the Nixon Administration and precipitated in the *National Climate Program Act* (NCAP), signed into law by President Jimmy Carter in 1978 (Henderson 2016). The law supported basic and applied research as well as building an infrastructure for climate services that would help to adapt to climatic changes.

The issue of emission reductions, however, slowly came into the foreground in the wake of the 1970s energy crisis (→ Crisis, II/4; Energy, II/7). Throughout his presidency, Carter was deeply concerned with national energy supply and was looking to reduce dependence on oil imports. Alternatively, he planned to intensify the use of coal, natural gas, nuclear power, and solar energy. However, in April 1979, a report prepared for the U.S. Department of Energy by the independent JASON group warned against the long-term consequences of rising atmospheric CO_2 levels and questioned the option of intensifying coal consumption. Carter's Science Advisor, Frank Press, asked the National Academy of Sciences for a second opinion. The resulting Charney Report, issued in July 1979, confirmed the JASON assessment and climate model calculations, which estimated mean global warming from a projected doubling of CO_2 levels in the 21st century at 2–3°C (Charney et al. 1979). The JASON and Charney Reports are evidence of a basic scientific consensus on climate change that was already forming in the late 1970s and early 1980s (Oreskes, Conway and Shindell 2008). However, the different reports reflect different approaches and recommendations for solving the problem.

When Ronald Reagan was sworn into office in January 1981, his administration was very reluctant to address the issue of climate change and funding for climate science was cut (Oreskes, Conway and Shindell 2008, 133, 135–6). However, recently declassified documents show that the second Reagan administration developed a more constructive position on matters of global environmental concern and even accepted a leadership role in international governance. From the point of view of national interest, U.S. leadership seemed desirable in order to avoid harming the economy through merely unilateral environmental regulations. In other words, international negotiations and treaties were welcomed as a means to avoid putting the U.S. economy at a disadvantage on global markets. This is precisely what motivated the U.S. government to take "a crucial leadership role in securing agreement to the Montreal Protocol" to protect the ozone layer and in establishing the IPCC (Wampler 2015). Combining global climate governance with national economic interests became the default setting of all U.S. governments in international climate negotiations that followed. These early neoliberal origins also created a governance model that gives precedence to market mechanisms over taxation in fostering emission reductions (→ Neoliberalism, II/16; Taxation, II/22). George H. W. Bush, who took office in 1989, signed an amendment to the Clean Air Act in 1990, which improved monitoring of air quality and proposed the first cap-and-trade system as an economic incentive to reduce emissions (Mast 2019, 83). His administration also helped negotiate the United Nations Framework Convention on Climate Chang (UNFCC) during the Rio summit in 1992. But Bush senior is also remembered for stating that the American "way of life is not negotiable" (Latour and Porter 2017, 27) (→ Consumerism, I/23).

Looking back, circumstances to achieve an internationally binding agreement on CO_2 emissions were perhaps never more favorable than in the decade right after the end of the

Cold War. The UNFCCC was ratified under the new Democratic president Bill Clinton in 1992 and Clinton announced his Climate Change Action Plan soon afterwards in 1993 (Mast 2019, 154). However, based on bipartisan agreement, the U.S. Senate did not ratify the Kyoto Protocol. Prior to the Kyoto climate summit, senators from both parties had passed by unanimous vote the "Byrd-Hagel Resolution," which stated that an international agreement under the UNFCCC on emission reductions would have to include commitments for emerging emitters from the non-Annex I group of countries (basically, China, India, and Brazil) and was not to harm the economy of the U.S. (Mast 2019, 187–9). Clinton himself more or less agreed with these conditions, and his administration made no effort to involve China and India in preparatory negotiations to reach an agreement. In the end, signing the Kyoto Protocol was a mere symbolic act that Clinton made before he left office.

The 1990s saw the rise of climate change denialism, and it gained even more ground in the U.S. public and among Republicans during the following decade (Oreskes and Conway 2010), making bipartisan agreement on issues of climate governance increasingly less likely. After only a few months in office, George W. Bush stated that he considered the Kyoto Protocol "fatally flawed in fundamental ways." While initially supporting another research initiative for clarification of remaining uncertainties, allegations surfaced,

> that political officials in the Bush administration pressured scientists to refrain from speaking to media, edited their work in ways that altered the content, or simply refused to release the findings of scientific research that supported policy approaches inimical to the administration's ideological preferences.
>
> *(Mast 2019, 209)*

When Barack Obama became president in 2009, the legacies of the Bush years – the Iraq war, the "war against terrorism," and an economic crisis (→ II/4) – put climate second rank on his agenda. Still, in the early stages of his presidency, Obama supported a new cap-and-trade bill drafted by the U.S. Climate Action Partnership, which failed despite several attempts to organize bipartisan support. This was partly due to successful public pressure built from within circles of the rising Tea Party movement. When Democrats lost their majority in the House of Representatives in 2010, environmental protection became a policy issue of partisan nature, as exemplified by the unanimous Republican vote for Resolution "HR 910," which blocked the Environmental Protection Agency (EPA) from regulating GHGs under the Clean Air Act based on scientific findings that they endangered public health (→ Health, I/29). Lacking a majority, Obama's climate, energy, and environmental policies became reduced to regulatory action in accordance with existing legislation. The EPA's Green Power Plan of 2015 met the resistance of 27 states filing suit against the Agency. In the international arena, the Obama administration played a much more cooperative role than the previous Bush junior administration. After negotiations in Copenhagen 2009 on a binding post-Kyoto agreement failed mainly due to China and India refusing to accept clearly defined emission reduction targets, the U.S. initiated bilateral talks with China, leading to an agreement on greenhouse gases in 2014, and which paved the way to the Paris Agreement in 2015.

Following the Obama years, the wheel of history was once again turned back by president Donald Trump, a declared climate change denialist, who on June 1, 2017 announced withdrawal from the Paris Agreement. Generally, Trump's foreign policy is a right-wing version of some more long-term tendencies in U.S. international policies that have evolved since the end of the Cold War. These tendencies are (1) to act as the only remaining superpower, often disregarding the interests of others, even allies; (2) to take unilateral military

(→ II/37) action independent of United Nation mandates; and (3) growing distrust in political cooperation within the established institutional frameworks of the UN or even NATO. These trends were already visible in Bush junior's attitude toward international cooperation – not only with regard to climate change. In sharp contrast with previous Republican administrations in the 1980s, more recent conservative U.S. leadership has terminated the consensus that successful response to climate change is founded on confidence in scientific knowledge and commitment to international cooperation. This consensus had been upheld throughout the 1990s into the 21st century but has since been lost somewhere along the way.

Latin America and the Caribbean

Climate governance in Latin American and Caribbean countries is embedded in cross-sectoral policies, which interlink domestic policymaking with UNFCCC processes. Policy initiatives specific to climate change grew apace with the post-Kyoto negotiations, as developing states became more assertive in international efforts to reduce greenhouse gas emissions. The "Climate Change Laws of the World" database evidences that it was from 2007 onwards that specific legislation on mitigation and adaptation was introduced in several countries of the region. However, current advances in climate policy build upon pre-existing governance arrangements in climate-related sectors, in particular energy and diverse environmental issues (→ Energy, II/7; Nature, II/39). Preliminary policies include, first and foremost, hydropower development, which lies at the heart of Latin America's low-carbon energy matrix, as well as – albeit sparsely and with mixed success – biodiversity conservation, forest protection, risk management, and urban planning (→ Urbanization, I/45). These policies were, in general, not initially aimed at reducing GHG emissions; in fact, some of them predate the emergence of global warming as a policy issue. Yet, this pre-existing policy framework provided a basis for a number of Latin American countries to position themselves as leaders among developing states, as climate negotiations were moving beyond the Kyoto Protocol and toward the Paris Agreement.

Prior to the Kyoto Protocol, Brazil was arguably the only prominent international player from the region, drawn to climate governance by its hosting of the United Nations Conference on Environment and Development ("Earth Summit"), where the UNFCCC was established, as well as by an increasing global concern about the Amazon rainforest. In the early 2000s Latin American states began to enhance their engagement in UNFCCC negotiations. In 2005, Costa Rica and Papua New Guinea, on behalf of the Coalition of Rainforest Nations, put forth an initiative to reduce emissions from deforestation and forest degradation called RED (for Reducing Emissions from Deforestation in Developing Countries) and later REDD+ (for Reducing Emissions from Deforestation and Forest Degradation and the role of conservation, sustainable management of forests and enhancement of forest carbon stocks in developing countries) (Pistorius 2012). In 2007, Ecuador launched the Yasuní-ITT (Ishpingo, Tambocha, and Tiputini) initiative, a proposal to leave 20 percent of its oil reserves untapped in exchange for international financial compensation. Mexico, for its part, orchestrated the adoption of the Cancun Agreements at COP16, thus assuring the continuation of UNFCCC negotiations, in the aftermath of the troubled Copenhagen accords. Peru hosted the COP20 and guaranteed its successful completion, thereby paving the way for the Paris Agreement in 2015.

The renewed political engagement of Latin American states in global climate governance was mirrored by domestic commitments. The initial thrust came from ambitious pledges to cut greenhouse gas emissions. In 2007, Costa Rica reaffirmed its well-established green credentials pledging to become carbon neutral by 2021. In 2008, Peru was the first developing country to announce a zero-deforestation pledge to be attained by 2021. Brazil followed suit in 2009, announcing a deforestation reduction target of 80 percent by 2020 (Edwards and Timmons Roberts 2015, xvi). These initial pledges were backed by the adoption of national legislations on climate change. Brazil was the first developing country to adopt a climate change law in 2009, followed by Mexico in 2012. Meanwhile, in the Andean region, Bolivia and Ecuador were delineating an alternative approach to climatic and environmental issues – partly in discrepancy with the UNFCCC – drawing upon the indigenous notions of "good living" and Pachamama or Mother Earth (→ Indigeneity, I/31). Ecuador's 2008 constitution enshrines Pachamama and recognizes the "rights of nature." In a similar vein, Bolivia's 2012 Mother Earth Law sets a legal framework to "live well" in harmony with nature (→ II/39).

All these developments intervened in a political and economic context marked by the rise of left-leaning governments across the region, on the one hand, and the enhancement of commodity-led economic growth – driven by a commodity price boom in the period 2003–13 – on the other (Ocampo 2017; Svampa 2015). Thus, while a reawakening of environmental and climate change concerns was taking root in political agendas, a carbon-intensive development model was exacerbating the region's reliance on primary exports and "extractivism" (→ Development, II/6; Extractivism, II/9).

The prospects of low-carbon development in Latin America have been supported by pre-existing favorable conditions and policy advances, especially in the energy sector (→ Energy, II/7). Latin America's power sector stands out as the least carbon-intensive in the world thanks to its reliance on hydroelectricity. Hydropower became the region's main source of electricity generation in the wake of the 1970s oil crisis, as OPEC's oil embargo sparked off unprecedented investments in hydroelectric dams. Hydropower currently accounts for 50 percent of electricity generation in the whole region (IRENA (International Renewable Energy Agency) 2016, 15). Investments in large hydroelectric projects are still soaring, especially in Brazil, Ecuador, and Peru. The reliance on big hydro, however, poses its own dilemmas in the face of climatic changes. On the one hand, it is highly vulnerable to the effects of global warming, particularly to alterations in precipitation patterns and glacier retreat. On the other hand, big hydroelectric plants bring about adverse climatic impacts, as their construction is connected to carbon dioxide emissions, alterations in river connectivity, and forest loss (Rosa et al. 2004). Investments in non-hydropower renewables are also on the rise, above all in Brazil, Mexico, and Chile. Bioenergy and onshore wind are the non-hydro renewables that have registered the greatest increase since 2000 (IRENA (International Renewable Energy Agency) 2016, 12).

Beyond hydropower and other renewables, a carbon neutral future depends upon a fossil fuel phase out. Latin America holds 20 percent of the world's oil reserves and 4 percent of its natural gas reserves (OLADE (Organización Latinoamericana de Energía) 2017), hence, the imperative to leave untapped fossil fuels underground, regardless of whether these are for export or domestic consumption (Edwards and Timmons Roberts 2015, 17). Ecuador's landmark Yasuní-ITT initiative was a ground-breaking proposal in this direction. The initiative, which was launched by president Rafael Correa at the UN General Assembly in 2007, derived its name from the ITT oilfields located in the Yasuní National Park in the Ecuadorian Amazon. The main proposition of the proposal was to leave one-fifth of the country's confirmed oil reserves underground in exchange for international financial compensation, equivalent to half of the expected oil revenues. The funds were to be invested in development projects and renewable energies. It was estimated that the Yasuní-ITT initiative would have avoided the emission of up to 407 million tons of carbon dioxide into the atmosphere (Larrea 2009). However, following a controversial and irresolute international campaign, the Yasuní-ITT initiative was terminated in 2013 on the grounds that it failed to gather the requested funds from international donors. Ultimately, the initiative's termination led to the emergence of a social movement (→ I/41) opposing the government´s decision to open up one of the world's most biodiverse areas to oil exploitation (López Rivera 2017).

Forestry is another crucial sector of Latin American climate governance as it is crucial to tackle the region's main source of GHG emissions, namely land use change and agriculture (→ Land, II/15). From the 1970s onwards, initial advances were made in this policy sector with the creation of protected areas for biodiversity conservation and forest protection. Following the Latin American debt crisis of the 1980s (→ Crisis, II/4), these policies were given a renewed impulse by the so-called "debt-for-nature swaps," an international initiative pioneered in the Americas linking environmental protection to debt relief. Debt-for-nature swaps consist of a transaction whereby a debtor country commits to invest in environmental – or climate-related – programs in exchange for debt forgiveness. The United States and U.S.-based NGOs (primarily, Conservation International, The Nature Conservancy, and World Wildlife Fund) were the largest donor-creditors of these kinds of agreements in the late 1980s and throughout the 1990s. Pioneering projects were implemented in Bolivia, Costa Rica, the Dominican Republic, and Ecuador (Greener 1991). Costa Rica figures as a successful case of debt-for-nature swaps, as 5 percent of its debt was reduced in the initial phases of the initiative, from 1988 to 1990. Protected areas now cover 26 percent of the country's land area (Edwards and Timmons Roberts 2015, 153).

Debt-for-nature swaps were an early international mechanism for the inclusion of forests in climate policy, foreshadowing what was to become REDD+ (Green 2018, 249). REDD+ was proposed at the UNFCCC with the objective of reducing net emissions from deforestation and forest degradation in developing countries. The main thrust of the proposal is to financially reward developing countries for "avoided deforestation;" a scheme that goes is beyond the Kyoto Protocol's CDM. The CDM contemplated the emission of carbon credits for afforestation and reforestation, but not for avoided deforestation. Put simply, under the CDM developing countries were paid for planting forests but not for keeping forests standing. By including avoided deforestation in climate finance, REDD+ provides an incentive for developing countries to enhance emission reductions through forest management, especially in Latin America, a region that holds half of the world's tropical forests (Castro, Hogenboom and Baud 2016, 1). As of 2015, the region featured the greatest number of REDD+ projects globally, with a total number of 61 projects in 21 countries, the bulk of which are situated in Brazil, Mexico, and Peru (Nhantumbo and Camargo 2015, 14). However, the upsurge of REDD+ projects is undermined by the fact that policy interventions are fraught with setbacks, chiefly disputes over the ownership of carbon rights and land tenure. Indigenous and other forest-dependent communities are the main affected populations in this regard (Sikor et al. 2010) (→ Indigeneity, I/31).

Brazil is at the crux of forest-based mitigation policy as it holds around 60 percent of the Amazon rainforest. Brazil entered a REDD+ partnership in 2008 through the creation of the Amazon Fund, a voluntary mechanism to channel international contributions for projects to reduce deforestation. The Amazon Fund has introduced a climate finance component to the policies that have been implemented under the Action Plan for the Prevention and Control of Deforestation in the Legal Amazon since 2004 (Edwards and Timmons Roberts 2015, 85–86).

The outcome of these forest-based mitigation policies has been a success. Between 2005 and 2013, Brazil registered a 70 percent decline in deforestation (Nepstad et al. 2014). One of the key measures driving this progress was the creation of protected areas and indigenous reserves, which grew 68 percent in the period between 2004 and 2012 to cover 47 percent of the Brazilian Amazon region (Nepstad et al. 2014, 1118). Thus, deforestation was brought to a historical low allowing Brazil to report a 39 percent reduction of total GHG emissions between 2005 and 2010. However, under Jair Bolsonaro's presidency, climate policy prospects are uncertain. Recent data indicates an increase in deforestation while environmental protection is being dismantled (Freitas Flavio et al. 2018).

Running counter to the REDD+ consensus, a small number of countries in the region have been opposing or questioning its initial market-based logic, notably Bolivia, Cuba, and Venezuela. Bolivia is an ambivalent case in this respect. On the one hand, it was among the first countries to support REDD+ and it features the longest running carbon offset initiative, the Noel Kempff Climate Action Project, which has been active since 1997 and has since been turned into REDD+ (Green 2018, 249). On the other hand, Bolivia's president Evo Morales has openly accused REDD+ of the "commodification of nature" and putting the burden of climate change on developing countries. Hence, as an alternative to REDD+, the Bolivian government has put forth the "Sustainable Forest Life" proposal as a non-market mechanism for climate change mitigation and adaptation. The proposal put forth a joint mitigation-adaptation mechanism relying on alternative sources of funding that ensures the "non-marketization of forests" (Müller, Pacheco and Montero 2014).

In sum, Latin America's climate change governance, as illustrated by its energy sector and its deforestation policies, is gaining in significance. Other wide-raging policies are being progressively implemented across the region, including carbon taxes (→ Taxation, II/22) and initial steps toward a phase out of fossil fuel subsidies (ECLAC 2015). Domestic advances coincide with an increasing presence in international governance. Indeed, in UNFCCC negotiations, Latin American countries have found their own voice, albeit in a fragmentary fashion. The G77 bloc seems to be giving way to fragmented negotiating groups, which partly correspond to regional integration (→ II/18) in Latin America and the Caribbean. Prominent among these are: the BASIC (Brazil, South Africa, India, and China) bloc; the Bolivarian Alliance for the Peoples of Our America (ALBA); the Independent Association of Latin America and the Caribbean (AILAC); and the Alliance of Small Island States (AOSIS). These groupings were at the center of the negotiations leading to the Paris Agreement.

Following the Paris Agreement, many countries in the region have reaffirmed their commitments as expressed in their (intended) NDCs. However, in spite of favorable pre-existing conditions and significant advances, the region remains on a path of unsustainable growth based on extractivism (→ II/9). Thus, Latin American countries are being constantly confronted with a climate policy paradox as images of a carbon neutral future clash with carbon-intensive growth models. The Economic Commission for Latin America and the Caribbean is lapidary in its assessment when it writes, "The existing production structure and type of infrastructure, the predominant low-innovation technological paradigm, the political economy framework of economic incentives and subsidies, and the public/private goods consumption matrix all feed into an environmentally unsustainable growth path" (ECLAC (Economic Commission for Latin America and the Caribbean) 2015, 10). In this context, the region's main challenge in the future will be to forge alternative paths of sustainable development, which will have to be backed by ambitious NDCs as regards climate policy (→ Development, II/6).

The climate movement in the Americas

The UNFCCC came into being at the 1992 Earth Summit amid an unprecedented gathering of some 1500 civil society organizations from all over the world. At the time, climate change was emerging as a prominent object of social activism alongside other enduring environmental issues, such as air and water pollution, biodiversity loss, and deforestation. An incipient climate movement was discernible in the NGO landscape, deriving from a broad base of environmental organizations whose advocacy agendas included climate change (Lipschutz and McKendry 2011). Prominent among these was the umbrella group Climate Action Network (CAN), a transnational advocacy network created in 1989 by major U.S. and European NGOs. The Earth Summit, hosted by Brazil in Rio de Janeiro, provided the occasion for northern NGOs to strengthen their ties with the incipient environmental movement in Latin America, which began to flourish in the wake of democratization (→ Social Movements, I/41). A major outcome of these exchanges was the creation of the regional network, CAN Latin America, including organizations from Brazil, Chile, and Mexico (CAN 2014, 18). These initial undertakings laid the groundwork for the formation of civic linkages bridging North–South divides, thereby enhancing joint advocacy in the emerging global regime for climate change.

Since its inception, the UNFCCC has provided a global forum for civil society actors working on climate change (Raustiala 2001). The number of admitted NGOs has increased steadily from 163 at COP1, in 1995, to 1866 at COP21 in 2015. However, NGOs occupy disparate advocacy positions within the UNFCCC. On the one hand, "insider" NGOs influence international negotiations providing expertise or serving as private regulators in climate governance projects (Green 2018; Gulbrandsen and Andresen 2004). On the other hand, "outsider" NGOs and social movement organizations mobilize at the fringes of climate negotiations and usually find themselves in asymmetric relations with major NGOs. The insider-outsider divide is often a North–South divide, with U.S. and Canadian NGOs engaging in donor-like relationships with their Latin American counterparts (see, e.g., Lewis 2016). However, there are also increasing exchanges among grassroots organizations and social movements from the Global South and the Global North which do not fit in conventional understandings of northern and southern NGOs. In this sense, the insider-outsider distinction is a more accurate description of the disparate positions that transnational civil society organizations and social movements occupy vis-à-vis the global climate change regime.

In the Americas, REDD+ is an illustrative case of longstanding insider-outsider cleavages in the climate movement. The expertise developed by U.S.-based NGOs in the area of carbon sinks, particularly in the framework of debt-for-nature swaps, conferred them an authoritative position in the operationalization of REDD+ (Green 2018). A constellation of U.S.-based NGOs, including the World Wildlife Fund, Conservation International and The Nature Conservancy, are implementing projects across the region along with other private actors including companies from the fossil fuel industry (Kill 2015; Klein 2014). As of 2015, it was estimated that 36 percent of REDD+ projects globally were being developed by NGOs (Nhantumbo and Camargo 2015, 15). These NGO-led projects have generated popular resistance, especially from indigenous peoples and other forest-dependent communities. The lines of conflict revolve around land tenure, indigenous territories, carbon rights, and the commodification of nature (see Kill 2015; redd-monitor.org). The Amazon indigenous peoples are an illustrative case of resistance. When REDD+ projects started to become implemented in the Amazon rainforest, the Coordinator of Indigenous Organizations of the Amazon River Basin (COICA) launched the "Indigenous REDD+ Alternative" calling for the recognition and protection of indigenous territories, public finance to reduce deforestation, and an end to extractivism and consumerism (COICA 2013).

The opposition to REDD+ is one of the points of contention of an alternative climate movement that has been taking shape in parallel summits at the fringes of UN climate conferences. Already at the Rio Earth Summit, a parallel NGO forum united environmentalists, grassroots organizations, indigenous peoples, and peasant groups from around the globe to put together the Alternative Non-Governmental Agreement on Climate Change. Latin American organizations such as COICA, Acción Ecológica, and La Vía Campesina figure prominently in these incipient southern-led mobilizations. When the post-Kyoto climate negotiations began to gain momentum, these Latin American organizations were crucial for the articulation of a global climate justice movement. In fact, many of the core ideas of this movement (e.g. post-extractivism, ecological debt, and *buen vivir*) are rooted in the indigenous, agroecological, and eco-socialist foundations of Latin American environmentalism (Martinez-Alier, Baud and Sejenovich 2016).

The climate justice movement became global in the wake of COP15 in 2009. In the run-up to the Copenhagen conference, which was expected to produce a new global climate change agreement, civil society groups formed activist networks demanding "climate justice." Prominent among these were Climate Justice Now! and Climate Justice Action. However, at COP15, civil society organizations were excluded from the main negotiations and faced increasing disenfranchisement (Fisher 2010). The general malaise translated into protests that, ultimately, increased the salience of COP15's alternative climate forum or Klimaforum (Chatterton, Featherstone and Routledge 2013; della Porta and Parks 2014). This wave of discontent was backed by leftist governments in Latin America. In 2010, the Bolivian government organized the World People's Conference on Climate Change as a response to the controversial Copenhagen Accord. The summit was attended by social movements around the globe and state delegations from the Global South (Aguirre and Cooper 2010). Its outcome declaration called upon the international community to recognize the universal rights of Mother Earth, to establish an international tribunal for climate justice, and to redress the "climate debt" owed to the Global South. In a similar vein, albeit with less success, Venezuela organized a Social Pre-COP in 2014, in preparation for COP21. These state-sponsored gatherings provided a forum for transnational civil society organizations seeking a voice in climate change governance. However, the paradox is that these very states rely on extractivist economies and are fraught with socio-environmental conflicts.

In the United States the climate movement gathered unprecedented momentum in the run-up to COP21. Interestingly, a crucial mobilizing force was given by newly formed activist networks, namely 350.org and Avaaz. These were the organizers of the People's Climate March, which took place in September 2014 during the UN Climate Summit in New York. The march, which was replicated in many other cities around the globe, is considered to be the largest in the history of the U.S. climate movement and a milestone in the global campaigning on climate change (Jacobs 2016, 319). These global movements were crucial during COP21. The Paris Agreement bears the imprint of climate justice activism: it puts forth a human rights-based approach, it provides for the creation of a platform for indigenous peoples and local communities, and it prompts the establishment of a gender action plan.

Entangled through climate change

The Americas provide a highly diverse landscape, which positions countries differently with regard to their historical contributions to global warming through GHG emissions, their vulnerability to climate change, and their capacity to adapt to it. There is a historical North–South divide, manifest in the UNFCCC's categorization of low emitters (predominantly in Latin America) and major emitters (the USA and Canada). Historical responsibility for global warming is predominantly in the North due to its long history of industrialization and fossil fuel burning. However, there are entanglements between carbon-based economies across the North–South divide, as proven in the case of Venezuela, a provider of primary commodities (fossil fuels) for carbon-intensive advanced industrial production. Generally speaking, differences in GHG emissions between the North and the South reflect differences in economic development and industrialization as well as long-existing tensions between rich(er) and poor(er) countries. Bridging this divide, at least to some extent, is the climate justice movement – an entanglement of resistance and ideals in response to the political stalemate that has hampered the advancement of global climate governance more than once.

The diversity seen in the landscape of climate change governance across the Americas is embedded in the global and regional entanglements produced by anthropogenic climate change – that is as, both, a phenomenon and a political problem. Climate and the atmosphere are natural systems that enclose the Earth as a whole. As such, they have become a source of all kinds of entanglements between states and their people. On the one hand, the atmosphere and the Earth's climate are universal features connecting different parts of the world at various geographical scales. Neither one belongs to a single country or group of nations, which is why they are frequently referred to as "global commons" (→ Commons, II/31). On the other hand, and at the same time, they are very diverse features of the Earth system and, therefore, create local differences that matter to human practices of interacting with these natural systems. For example, meteorological and climatological hazards vary geographically, which also means that their changing in frequency and/or severity as a consequence of climate change affects people differently in different places, making questions of responsibility and justice even more urgent. All human activities producing GHGs potentially affect activities of all other humans around the world, which creates a bond between societies that was absent prior to the discovery of global warming and its predominantly anthropogenic causation.

Political action on climate change, be it mitigation or adaptation policies, has further enhanced the entanglements between countries not just in the Americas, and will continue to do so in the future. Through legislation and other measures, political action converts climate change from a physical process and a scientific fact into a great variety of social facts that establish new relations between people. For example, large forests, such as the Amazon, have become carbon stocks for the world as a whole. Mechanisms such as REDD+ allow countries to profit from forest protection, as they create economic incentives operating against traditional economic incentives for forest exploitation. In this regard, as well as in many others, CO_2 has become a force for entanglements between countries and people in different parts of the world that did not exist before. Climate change governance itself is an emergent and still emerging expression of these multiple entanglements.

Works cited

Aguirre, Jessica Camille and Elizabeth Sonia Cooper. 2010. "Evo Morales, Climate Change, and the Paradoxes of a Social-Movement Presidency." *Latin American Perspectives* 37, 4: 238–244.

Archer, David and Raymond T. Pierrehumbert, eds. 2011. *The Warming Papers: The Scientific Foundation for the Climate Change Forecast*. Hoboken: Wiley-Blackwell.

Calvin, Katherine V., Robert Beach, Angelo Gurgel, Maryse Labriet, and Ana Maria Loboguerrero Rodriguez. 2016. "Agriculture, Forestry, and Other Land-Use Emissions in Latin America." *Energy Economics* 56: 615–624.

CAN (Climate Action Network-International). 2014. *Small Window, Bright Light: A History of Climate Action Network*. Beirut: Lebanon.

Castro, Fábio de, Barbara Hogenboom, and Michiel Baud. 2016. "Introduction: Environment and Society in Contemporary Latin America." In *Environmental Governance in Latin America*, eds. Fábio de Castro, Barbara Hogenboom, and Michiel Baud, 1–25. London: Palgrave Macmillan.

Charney, Jule G., D. Akio Arakawa, James Baker, Robert E. Bert Bolin, Richard M. Dickinson, Cecil E. Goody, Henry M. Leith, Carl I. Wunsch Stonunel. 1979. *Carbon Dioxide and Climate: A Scientific Assessment*. Washington, DC: National Academy of Sciences.

Chatterton, Paul, David Featherstone, and Paul Routledge. 2013. "Articulating Climate Justice in Copenhagen: antagonism, the Commons, and Solidarity." *Antipode* 45, 3: 602–620.

COICA. 2013. "Indigenous REDD+ Alternative. Indigenous Territories of Harmonious Life to Cool the Planet." *Directive Council of COICA*. https://theredddesk.org/resources/indigenous-redd-alternative-indigenous-territories-harmonious-life-cool-planet.

Cole, Daniel H. 2015. "Advantages of a Polycentric Approach to Climate Change Policy." *Nature Climate Change* 5, 2: 114–118.

ECLAC (Economic Commission for Latin America and the Caribbean). 2015. *The Economics of Climate Change in Latin America and the Caribbean: Paradoxes and Challenges*. Santiago de Chile: UN ECLAC.

Edenhofer, Ottmar and Michael Jakob. 2017. *Klimapolitik*. München: C. H. Beck.

Edwards, Guy and J. Timmons Roberts. 2015. *A Fragmented Continent: Latin America and the Global Politics of Climate Change*. Cambridge: MIT Press.

Fisher, Dana R. 2010. "COP-15 in Copenhagen: How the Merging of Movements Left Civil Society Out in the Cold." *Global Environmental Politics* 10, 2: 11–17.

Freitas Flavio, L. M., Gerd Sparovek, Göran Berndes, et al. 2018. "Potential Increase of Legal Deforestation in Brazilian Amazon after Forest Act revision." *Nature Sustainability* 1, 11: 665–670.

Green, Jessica F. 2018. "From Green to REDD: Protean Power and the Politics of Carbon Sinks." in *Protean Power*, eds. Peter J. Katzenstein and Lucia A. Seybert, 246–263. New York: Cambridge University Press.

Greener, Laurie P. 1991. "Debt-for-Nature Swaps in Latin American Countries: The Enforcement Dilemma Comment." *Connecticut Journal of International Law* 7: 123–180.

Gulbrandsen, Lars H., and Steinar Andresen. 2004. "NGO Influence in the Implementation of the Kyoto Protocol: Compliance, Flexibility Mechanisms, and Sinks." *Global Environmental Politics* 4, 4: 54–75.

Gupta, Joyeeta. 2014. *The History of Global Climate Governance*. Cambridge: Cambridge University Press.

Henderson, Gabriel. 2016. "Governing the Hazards of Climate." *Historical Studies in the Natural Sciences* 46, 2: 207–242.

Howe, Joshua P. 2014. *Behind the Curve: Science and the Politics of Global Warming*. Seattle: University of Washington Press.

IPCC. 2015. *Climate Change 2014: Synthesis Report. Contribution of Working Groups I, Ii and Iii to the Fifth Assessment Report of the Intergovernmental Panel on Climate Change*. Geneva: IPCC.

IPCC-WG1. 2013. *Climate Change 2013: The Physical Science Basis Working Group I Contribution to the Fifth Assessment Report of the Intergovernmental Panel on Climate Change*. Cambridge: Cambridge University Press.

IPCC-WG2. 2014. *Climate Change 2014: Impacts, Adaptation, and Vulnerability (Final Drafts)*. Cambridge: Cambridge University Press.

IRENA (International Renewable Energy Agency). 2016. *Renewable Energy Market Analysis: Latin America*. Abu Dhabi: IRENA.

Jacobs, Michael. 2016. "High Pressure for Low Emissions: how Civil Society Created the Paris Climate Agreement." *Juncture* 22, 4: 314–323.

Johnson, Lyndon B. 1965. "Special Message to the Congress on Conservation and Restoration of Natural Beauty, February 8, 1965." *LBJ Presidential Library*. www.lbjlibrary.net/collections/selected-speeches/1965/02-08-1965.html.

Kill, Jutta. 2015. *REDD: A Collection of Conflicts, Contradictions and Lies*. Montevideo: WRM.

Klein, Naomi. 2014. *This Changes Everything: Capitalism vs. The Climate*. New York: Simon and Schuster.

Larrea, Carlos. 2009. *Yasuni-ITT Initiative: A Big Idea from a Small Country*. Quito: Ministerio del Ambiente de Ecuador, UNDP Ecuador.
Latour, Bruno and Catherine Porter. 2017. *Facing Gaia: Eight Lectures on the New Climatic Regime*. Cambridge: Polity Press.
Lewis, Davis. 2016. "Abandoned Pasts, Disappearing Futures: Further Reflections on Multiple Temporalities in Studying Non-Governmental Organisation Worlds." *Critique of Anthropology* 36, 1: 85–92.
Lipschutz, Ronnie D. and Corina McKendry. 2011. "Social Movements and Global Civil Society." in *The Oxford Handbook of Climate Change and Society*, eds. John S. Dryzek, Richard B. Norgaard, and David Schlosberg, 369–383. Oxford: Oxford University Press.
López Rivera, Andrés. 2017. "Chronicle of a Schism Foretold: The State and Transnational Activism in Ecuador's Yasuní-ITT Initiative." *Environmental Sociology* 3, 3: 226–236.
Martinez-Alier, Joan, Michiel Baud, and Héctor Sejenovich. 2016. "Origins and Perspectives of Latin American Environmentalism." In *Environmental Governance in Latin America*, eds. Fábio de Castro, Barbara Hogenboom, and Michiel Baud, 29–57. London: Palgrave Macmillan.
Mast, Jerald C., ed. 2019. *Climate Change Politics and Policies in America: Historical and Modern Documents in Context*. Santa Barbara: CA: ABC-CLIO.
Müller, Robert, Pablo Pacheco, and Juan Carlos Montero. 2014. *The Context of Deforestation and Forest Degradation in Bolivia: Drivers, Agents and Institutions*. Bogor, Indonesia: CIFOR.
Nepstad, Daniel, David McGrath, Claudia Stickler, Ane Alencar, Andrea Azevedo, Briana Swette, Tathiana Bezerra, et al. 2014. "Slowing Amazon Deforestation through Public Policy and Interventions in Beef and Soy Supply Chains." *Science* 344, 6188: 1118–1123.
Nhantumbo, Isilda and Marisa Camargo. 2015. *REDD+ for Profit or for Good? Review of Private Sector and NGO Experience in REDD+ Projects*. London: IIED.
Ocampo, José Antonio. 2017. "Commodity-Led Development in Latin America." In *Alternative Pathways to Sustainable Development: Lessons from Latin America*, eds. Gilles Carbonnier, Humberto Campodónico, and Sergio Tezanos Vázquez, 51–76. Leiden: Brill.
OLADE (Organización Latinoamericana de Energía). 2017. *Anuario de Estadísticas Energéticas*. Quito, Ecuador.
Oreskes, Naomi and Erik M Conway. 2010. *Merchants of Doubt: How a Handful of Scientists Obscured the Truth on Issues From Tobacco Smoke to Global Warming*. New York: Bloomsbury Press.
Oreskes, Naomi, Erik M. Conway, and Matthew Shindell. 2008. "From Chicken Little to Dr. Pangloss: William Nierenberg, Global Warming, and the Social Deconstruction of Scientific Knowledge." *Historical Studies in the Natural Sciences* 38, 1: 109–152.
Ostrom, Elinor. 2010a. "A Long Polycentric Journey." *Annual Review of Political Science* 13: 1–23.
———. 2010b. "Polycentric Systems for Coping With Collective Action and Global Environmental Change." *Global Environmental Change* 20, 4: 550–557.
Pistorius, Till. 2012. "From RED to REDD+: The Evolution of a Forest-Based Mitigation Approach for Developing Countries." *Current Opinion in Environmental Sustainability* 4, 6: 638–645.
Porta, Donatella Della and Louisa Parks. 2014. "Framing Processes in the Climate Movement." In *Routledge Handbook of the Climate Change Movement*, eds. Matthias Dietz and Heiko Garrelts, 19–30. New York: Routledge.
Raustiala, Kal. 2001. "Nonstate Actors in the Global Climate Regime." In *International Relations and Global Climate Change*, eds. Urs Luterbacher and Detlef F. Sprinz, pp. 95–118. Cambridge: MIT Press.
Rosa, Luiz Pinguelli, Marco Aurelio Dos Santos, Bohdan Matvienko, Ednaldo Oliveira Dos Santos, and Elizabeth Sikar. 2004. "Greenhouse Gas Emissions from Hydroelectric Reservoirs in Tropical Regions." *Climatic Change* 66, 1: 9–21.
Sikor, Thomas, Johannes Stahl, Thomas Enters, et al. 2010. "REDD-plus, Forest People's Rights and Nested Climate Governance." *Global Environmental Change* 20, 3: 423–425.
Svampa, Maristella. 2015. "Commodities Consensus: Neoextractivism and Enclosure of the Commons in Latin America." *South Atlantic Quarterly* 114, 1: 65–82.
Wampler, Robert A. 2015. "U.S. Climate Change Policy in the 1980s." *Nacional Security Archive*, December 2. https://nsarchive2.gwu.edu/NSAEBB/NSAEBB536-Reagan-Bush-Recognized-Need-for-US-Leadership-on-Climate-Change-in-1980s/.
Weart, Spencer R. 2003. *The Discovery of Global Warming*. Cambridge: Harvard University Press.

31
COMMONS

Juan Camilo Cárdenas

The Americas have developed, over centuries of transformation of its landscapes and peoples, diverse historical and intellectual paths regarding the problem of the commons and their use. These distant views have resulted from paths of conquest and colonization (→ I/7) that have brought with them different traditions regarding property, ownership, and the roles of self-governance, markets, and the state (→ Nation State, II/38), while encountering rather diverse ecological, cultural, and economic systems already in place. The histories of occupation, transformation and vindication in the territories that could fall in the category of commons are unsurprisingly attached to the intellectual traditions that influenced the legal and policy actions over five hundred years since the encounter between Europe and the Americas. What is seen as the "commons" in the Americas today is the result of contestation between imported public policies mostly from the liberal economic project of the Enlightenment (→ I/8), the indigenous struggles for their territories (→ Indigenous Peoples, I/11; Land, II/15), and the ecological conditions of these territories in the region (→ Nature, II/39).

Vastly different epistemologies include such contrasting ideas as the economic efficiency argument in the natural resource economics school, influenced by the modern European and North American intellectual tradition, to the concept of "good living" (*Buen Vivir*), which emerged from the South American indigenous discourse as an alternative to the growth model in economics (→ Indigeneity, I/31; Development, II/6). Bridges between these ideas could potentially create a link between the notion of ecosystem services in the more recent tradition of socio-ecological systems and the concept of territory from the indigenous viewpoint. From these different paths, an evolution of the concept of the commons can be formed toward a notion of shared territory. In this view, self-governance becomes a critical and necessary strategy for filling the gaps in the challenges of sustaining a healthy, decent and productive life for families and communities where neither the state nor the market have been successful.

The commons can be considered as more than just land under an arrangement of ownership by many. As shared territories, these commons often involve multiple layers of boundaries depending on the many ecological services they provide for their occupants, such as firewood or food, to neighboring communities, such as watershed services, and to people in far places, who, for example, may benefit from the conservation of life and cultures. These commons as shared territories also face the problematic constitutional conundrum in the Hispanic Americas that continues to declare the subsoil as belonging to the nation-state, while allowing through decentralization and devolution the possibilities of communities to exert their rights of use and ownership over the land. The North American legal tradition, however, considers the landowner as the proprietor of the resources beneath its land. The implications of this conundrum emerge often in the persistent tensions between the political and economic interests of those in power with dire needs for fresh financial resources coming from royalties generated in extractive industries (→ Extractivism, II/9), and the multiplicity of cultural and economic expressions in regions with frequent movements of civil resistance to these extractive activities (→ Social Movements, I/41). In many cases, these tensions involve indigenous groups, precisely where most of the modern expressions of commons have emerged or survived.

These conflicts and concerns highlight a need for constructing a better framework for understanding the problem of the commons that incorporates a diversity of paths, and permits a more adaptive institutional approach that includes the ecological, cultural, and legal frameworks that determine the fate of the territories shared by a large number of rural communities in the Americas today. As a starting point, the available schools of thought that have contributed so far to the study of the commons can offer valuable elements to this transition ahead. Through a review of what the concept of the commons has meant in several of these traditions, it is possible to explore the possibility of creating these bridges between concepts that might turn out to be rather compatible. The experience of the Americas, as it turns out, is a unique opportunity for building these bridges. The indigenous struggles throughout the region have been accompanied by a rise in the development of new political discourses and concepts of ownership, property rights, and development (→ II/6) that confront the essentially western tradition in the political and public policy model of land occupation that has governed the Americas in its most recent centuries of independence from colonial rule (→ Land, II/15). If these possible dialogues are to be fruitful, a new view must emerge for how the commons as a concept generates well-being, inclusion, and sustains the diversity of life and cultural forms and is not seen as a hindrance for development and a barrier to modernization (→ I/35).

This chapter does not include the cases of other important commons such as those within the intellectual property rights arena. For those interested, the work of Yochai Benkler (2002, 2006) is a mandatory read in this regard. Peer production and open access to software, artistic creations and other forms of easily replicable goods are spaces where the commons lens also applies. Likewise, the focus on rural territories will also mean excluding the case of urban commons for which there are less available data at country levels. As surveyed by Robson and Lichtenstein (2013) and the special issue of the *Journal of Latin American Geography* they guided, much of the research in Latin America on the commons continues to be rural, with a few mentions to the growing importance of the urban-rural interactions. These urban-shared resources will continue to grow in importance, including the Americas and would deserve a separate text that goes beyond the space and scope here.

The commons in the western law and economic tradition

The economic approach to the commons emerged from the application of mathematical modeling used to search for solutions of dynamic optimization when extracting a renewable resource. When property rights were assigned to one single owner of the resource (e.g. fish, trees), and an infinite horizon was assumed for those property rights and it was in the interest of the owner to maximize rents, the optimal decision was to sustain equal rates of extraction and regrowth. If a discount rate was assumed for future benefits and costs, this would adjust the extraction rate accordingly. However, in some cases, those resource units are available to several individuals and when no property rights were defined, it meant that either resource user could extract those units and reduce their availability to others, affecting also the renewability of the stock. If an individual were to balance their private average cost against the private marginal benefit of the extraction, the sum of the effort and extraction levels by all individuals involved would create a situation of overexploitation, depleting the stock sooner than what the single owner solution would prescribe.

For the second half of the 20th century the discussion about renewable natural resources was concentrated around this dichotomy (non-ownership vs. single ownership). The seminal article that synthetized this simplistic approach was written by Garret Hardin (1968), using precisely the concept of the commons and describing the situation of multiple users having access to a shared resource as a tragedy because of the lack of property rights over its ownership. By no individual ownership of property, he meant that something belonging to all meant belonging to no one. This in turn implied that no ownership of an asset meant its mismanagement. From there, it was easy to argue that declaring and assigning private property rights over such assets would align the interests of the owner with the best possible use of the land (→ II/15), given they would be the residual claimant of all consequences, good and bad, of the decisions on how to use the asset. Alternatively, Hardin also included the possibility of assigning property rights to the state to guarantee its best social use. However, at this point in time in the west, the Cold War had created an intellectual environment against the notion of having a collective access to natural assets and praised instead the private property solution as a protection against the notion of collectivization.

The reader can quickly confirm through a word search in the collection of digitalized books by Google how the use of the term "commons" has evolved over the last two hundred years. Considering this search involves the English-speaking printed press, which means, at least for the start of that period, the English tradition emerged from the 18th-century scholarship where the idea of ownership and property rights was critical to the functioning of society (Waldron 2004, Section 2). Out of the Scottish Enlightenment (→ II/8), private or individual property emerged as the key solution during that western tradition when dealing with the problem of managing widely scarce resources, land being the prominent example. The last two centuries saw private ownership as the solution to the socialist and communist proposals and the natural modernization response to the enclosures of land during the previous centuries in Europe. The commons was perceived as the collectivization of assets through expropriation from those who owned them, or as the lack of ownership, that is, open access. No middle grounds existed for a group of people owning and managing these shared resources. In fact, the term "commons" has meant essentially open access, i.e. absolute lack of property rights (Hardin 1968, 1244).

Such seminal articles were thus critical in those moments of political contestation between the capitalist West (→ Capitalism, II/2) and the socialist proposal as an alternative (→ Socialism, I/42). However, the following three decades from the 1960s to the 1990s saw a revival in the use of the term commons, not coincidentally with the seminal work, *Governing the Commons* (Ostrom 1990). Ostrom's work was targeted at responding to the conjecture that when multiple users shared a resource, and without individual property rights, a solution to the overexploitation problem could emerge from the definition of rules and various mechanisms through which individual users could restrain themselves from depleting it. Tapping into the literature on the local provision of public goods and by searching for cases around the world, she was able to review evidence that such situations of common-pool resources could be sustained for centuries. Most of Ostrom's work focuses on local, small-scale, commons as rightly pointed out by Harvey (2011) while also criticizing Hardin's analysis of the global problem of population with a local metaphor of the pastures.

Harvey, however, highlights the problem of ownership of livestock instead of focusing on the access to the open pasture, in his Marxist approach. In his view, the recognition of the surplus value created, in this case, by joint forces of those producing from the commons, urban or rural, should recognize more ownership rights to the latter, the common labor, than to those controlling the access to the shared resources.

In the subsequent years, Ostrom also begun to deepen into the more micro level through other methodological approaches, including a dialogue with the behavioral and experimental economics community who had been exploring the individual mechanisms through which markets could function efficiently, but also the conditions under which public goods could not be provided privately. Borrowing from experimental psychology and game theory and engaging in a rich collaboration with James Walker and Roy Gardner, seminal works emerged in the following years. These studies were based on a robust number of laboratory experimental results exploring the circumstances in which self-governance could emerge (Ostrom 1992; Ostrom, Gardner and Walker 1994), and that could explain the successes and failures reported in the field studies in Ostrom (1990). This collaboration triggered a vast line of research extending the experimental conditions in various dimensions. These experimental variations included changing the parameters of the economic production function of the resource; exploring static and dynamic renewable resources; testing different institutional mechanisms to explore how cooperation could emerge, including endogenous and external monitoring and sanctions; trying different asymmetries in the endowments and participation of the individuals in the sharing of costs and benefits of the commons; or taking these experiments outside of the lab into the field.

A major contributor to the progress made over the last five decades since the conjecture by Hardin has been the behavioral revolution (See Cárdenas 2016 for an overview of the role of this revolution for the case of natural resources). Game theory, laboratory, field experiments and psychology have joined forces with economics to provide better accounts of how humans understand and solve the problems of cooperation or collective action that are intrinsic to the commons. Models based on preferences for reciprocity and fairness, for instance, can account for part of the cooperative behavior observed in laboratory experiments (Falk, Fehr and Fischbacher 2002). The replication of laboratory experiments in the field has also enriched the understanding of cooperation in these controlled settings when other contextual factors enter into play, beyond the purely economic incentives (Cárdenas and Ostrom 2004). The further exploration through evolutionary game theory can also enrich the understanding of how boundedly rational agents may end up at equilibria of cooperation (Cárdenas, Mantilla and Sethi 2015).

The approaches to the problem of the commons mentioned so far essentially base their analysis on an individual that interacts with others regarding the use of shared resources. Any further element of consideration in the analysis is added to the model in the form of transforming the motivations or incentives, intrinsic, or material that affect the choice set and the preferences of the decision maker. This methodological individualism, it should be clear, does not mean that these approaches consider the resource users as selfish. It only means that the analytical unit is the individual and therefore the analysis of decisions and outcomes is based on studying how these agents choose among possible alternatives of action. This will create a stark contrast to the approaches where the community is the prominent analytical unit, and in opposition to the dominant role of the individual in economics that is highly influenced by the liberal tradition. The economic liberal tradition of looking at the commons problem from the standpoint of the individual, while the new perspective from the Latin American social movements, including the "*buen vivir*" approach bases its analytical unit on the community, will impose a great challenge for those discussing the future of the commons for the 21st century in the Americas.

The commons from indigenous and Afro-descendants perspectives in the Americas

The law and economics tradition came to the Americas through the European liberal school by having large impacts in the republican projects in the region (→ Nation and State Building, I/16), but also in the well-being of the indigenous communities already occupying these territories. The creation of the first independent republics in the northern, central, and southern sub-regions of the continent brought the assigning of property rights to the land with severe consequences to the already struggling forms of communal occupation of the territory. The surviving indigenous peoples (→ I/11) and the newly created Afro-descendant territories emerging from the end of slavery (→ I/18) provide today a complex array of institutional arrangements in the territories that have been conserved or regained through the different struggles to defend their identities and rights.

The closest census data to the year 2010 suggests that about 8.3 percent of the Latin American population declare themselves indigenous (CEPAL 2014, 37). This percentage is higher to that estimated for the North American region, with less than 2 percent in the United States and less than 5 percent for the Canadian case, with 500 and 600 tribes of First Nations identified, respectively. However, the variation across countries is substantial. In the case of Latin America, there are much higher rates of indigenous population in some areas such as Bolivia (62.2%), Guatemala (41%), and Peru (24%). The total estimated indigenous population in the Latin American region adds up to almost forty-five million people, whereas the North American native population is less than seven million people (→ Indigeneity, I/31).

Additional to the demographic dimension, one should add land occupied by ancestral communities today. A valuable source at www.landmarkmap.org/provides a graphical illustration of the percentage of land under indigenous or community property rights for the countries in the Americas, given the best possible data available (Dubertret and Wily 2015). This source illustrates not only the percentage of indigenous population by nation, but also the countries that have ratified Convention No. 169 of the International Labor Organization (ILO), the Indigenous and Tribal Peoples Convention, concerning Indigenous and Tribal Peoples in Independent Countries entering into force on September 5, 1991. In terms of indigenous lands, countries with significant shares of their territory under declared or recognized communal lands to indigenous or Afro-descendant communities include Canada (43.9%), Mexico (52%), Bolivia (33.6%), Brazil (23%), Colombia (33.9%), and Peru (34.8%). Roughly speaking, about 22.5 percent of the territory in North, Central and South America is recognized as communal land, without including the Caribbean where there is no available data.

The Caribbean deserves a particular mention in this sense as there are fewer documented studies on the existence and persistence of commons or shared territories in this region. As mentioned by McIntosh and Renard (2010), the islands have ignored the possibility of self-governed institutions for the management of the territories and their resources when considering development. The plantation system that dramatically transformed the islands has had a major impact on how land is regarded and local groups find little opportunity to base their livelihoods on common-pool resources and through shared ownership of the land (→ Plantation Literature, III/15). A particular arrangement of "family lands," which convey some ideas of common ownership, could represent one of the few relevant cases of commons in the Caribbean, and is often seen by the government and business community as counter-productive to development (McIntosh and Renard 2010, 164).

Today, a diverse configuration of human occupation by individuals declare themselves as indigenous and often setup self-governed management practices for their shared territories. They have devised alternative property rights and rules to access their resources based on group access arrangements as opposed to private property regulations. According to the numbers available, around 850 million hectares of the Americas could be considered as under some kind of communal or indigenous property rights arrangement, although some countries do not have reliable data on this regard. Of these, Canada accounts for almost half with 399 million hectares.

Because of the diversity of histories, a simplified version of the "indigenous" approach to the shared territories is not conceivable. Ecological conditions, linguistics traditions and particular paths of dependence from the starting point of the encounter with the Europeans have created a diverse set of models of occupation of the territory. In fact, the archaeological evidence over the last half century has questioned the idea that the pre-Columbian Mesoamerican political systems were politically and economically similar (Feinman 2018, 2) as previously accepted by scholars. This evidence suggests that the diversity of arrangements ranged from autocratic centrally governed to more collectively managed systems.

Five centuries later, the persistence of this diverse set of governance arrangements remains. In Colombia alone, more than one hundred different indigenous peoples exist today with a diversity of rules and norms regarding their use of their shared territories (Arango and Sánchez 1998). Some of the more hierarchical structures of the political systems in Mesoamerica or the Andes show stark contrasts with the decentralized systems of the northern part of South America or the Amazon. With the arrival of the Europeans, the clash between existing practices and the legal schemes generated a multiplicity of practices regarding the use of the territory that translated into the expulsion of groups in some cases, fragmentation and privatization (→ II/17) of lands in others, and for some cases the maintaining and even recovery of communal rights over land. Yet, several commons managed by indigenous communities have survived these threats, experiencing both successes and failures as indigenous groups have tried to adapt to market forces and modernity (Richards 1997).

Despite the diversity in the histories of commons in different areas of the Americas, some elements shared by many of these groups help to demonstrate the perspective of indigenous rural communities in the Americas. Among one of these shared elements is the notion of "territory." The main struggle of indigenous groups over the past few centuries, in fact, has been focused on the problem of recovering access to land. A common notion of "territory" for many indigenous groups has at least two important features. One, it involves a more comprehensive approach to the biophysical components of the space occupied by a community. The subsoil, in this perspective, would be an integral part of the commons, and the relationships among components such as forest coverage, water streams, and fauna, all play a determinant role in how the commons is understood and managed (→ Nature, II/39). Secondly, when analyzing the common space, the relations between these biophysical components and the social system of humans occupying the territory is also integral. A great deal of institutional arrangements among indigenous and ancestral communities derive their reasoning from an interpretation of natural laws and knowledge about the biophysical world. Traditions or customs based on the knowledge of biological dynamics have created mechanisms for adapting the economic systems to the ecological conditions. For example, extensive research has been compiled on the taboos used for the protection of species. Several indigenous groups in South America, for instance, have declare sacred patches of land where no extraction activity or use of its species is allowed, using religious mechanisms for its enforcement (Colding and Folke 1997, 2001).

Another element of territory for several of these indigenous groups involves a groups-based rights approach instead of one that is individually based. A territorial view of the problem views the group as an analytical unit and not the individual as the sole decision maker. This implies that governance in these territories involves creating and sustaining effective endogenous mechanisms for conflict resolution within the groups. In this territorial view, different types of "resources" are part of the common space and should be managed as a whole. Trees, animals and water are considered so intimately connected that rules and norms within the community also require rules and norms that integrate their management simultaneously. As Escobar (2015) eloquently states, "Within relational worlds, the defense of territory, life and the commons are one and the same."

A considerable number of new social movements (→ I/41) in Latin America, from the bottom up, are creating alternative views on development (→ II/6), and at the same time reinventing the meaning of the commons away from the traditional English Enlightenment interpretation (Esteva 2010, 65). Pleyers describes a substantial number of these political actions from the past ten years and how within the Latin American region, the role of an ecological view of the social problems is permeating these struggles (2018, 147) (→ Environmental Justice, II/8). Commons as territory has, in this new tradition, a more complex meaning than commons as solely land. Furthermore, identity and territory are inseparable in the territorial view by indigenous peoples. As most indigenous movements have based their political agendas precisely on defending or recovering back their territory, their struggle for identity is tightly linked to the occupation of territories. Thus, for instance, the struggles in Brazil for the recognition and titling of land for its more than 3,500 Quilombos is heavily linked to the role of preserving the identity of Afro-Brazilian communities. Similar claims have been made in the case of indigenous groups in the Amazon, or Afro-Colombian communities on the Pacific coast of Colombia, where almost six million hectares have been titled since 1995.

In contrast, the regulatory approach to the law and economics of land consistently separates these components. In the tradition carried over from European legal views, subsoil, and soil can be separated in the assignment of property rights. The Latin American tradition, inherited from the Castellan law in Spain, spread throughout the region the notion that the subsoil with all its mineral resources would, by constitutional mandate, belong to the state whereas the land on top could be privatized. This conflict of ownership between state and private parties has created, not surprisingly, several of the existing conflicts between local communities and extractive industry efforts by government and private investors (→ Extractivism, II/9).

Recent constitutional developments in the region have heightened tensions between the national interest in the gas revenues and the regions' claims of autonomy (Uprimny 2014) (→ Energy, II/7). These tensions are spreading over a large extension of the Americas, and substantially more for the case of Central and South America. The Environmental Justice Atlas (www.ejolt.org/) illustrates the rather high frequency of these conflicts in the Latin American case. Largely, these conflicts have a common thread in the overlap between extractive industries and the threats to biological and cultural diversity surrounding them (→ Nature, II/36). Yet, for most of these projects, the constitutional problem remains. The national governments have discretionary power over the mineral resources in the subsoil and make good use of the royalties from their extraction for funding programs and policies of national strategic interest, using the legal Spanish and French precedent as a means to maintain the subsoil as discretionary to the central government, a clear contrast to the North American case.

However, for many of these local communities with either more traditional or ancestral views of the environment or more modern ecological approach to these ecosystems, the interactions between subsoil elements (e.g. aquifers) and the topsoil vegetation, as well as soil productivity are key to sustaining the ecosystem services for these communities. Furthermore, for several of these cases the flow of non-direct use benefits transcends those within the communities. Most shared territories base their sustainability on the preservation of certain key interactions or flows between the subsoil and other key components such as surface water and vegetation.

Consistent with the separation in this regulatory approach, the creation of separate legal and economic frameworks for each of the components has also created complications when addressing the challenges of sustaining the commons. For a long time, the economics of natural resources has been separated into different epistemological compartments that analyzes soil, forests, water, or minerals with various models of optimization. Only recently has the "ecological economics" approach and more recent "socio-ecological systems" proposals become popular in that both of these approaches are more proactive in highlighting interactions between components and showing their importance when negotiating land conditions.

Meanwhile, the legal frameworks are still highly influenced by the practice of separating resources. Most countries have legislation for forests that are not interconnected or in coordination with legislation for water, fisheries, or for conserving biodiversity. Therefore, it is not surprising to find legislation favoring the replacement of diverse species forests with single species plantations with negative impacts in terms of protecting endangered species or water resources (→ Columbian Exchange, I/6).

The western economic approach to the commons problem has at least two dimensions. One based on property rights, and another based on the "resources" in question. Regarding the former, the approach to the commons problem originated in the inefficiencies associated with open access to shared resources. Long before Garret Hardin (1968) posed the question of the tragedy, many philosophers had argued that the lack of property rights or ownership to a resource may drive its misuse and lack of management, draining its possibilities to generate well-being. This approach during the 18th century led a movement to dismantle the commons in the United Kingdom whereas in Germany and Switzerland, those shared forests and pastures evolved into stronger or more sophisticated arrangements. With respect to water in Spain, the still standing institution of the water tribunals in Valencia is an example of an institution to self-govern water as a commons that has lasted a millennium.

Another approach coming from the western tradition is that of the more recent economic problem based on the separation of resources involved. The commons problem, triggered by various debates in the middle of 20th century, involves the analysis of the nature of the resource in question as well as the economic production function in the extraction and its renewability. Forests, fisheries, water, wildlife each have a set of particular models that involve the rate of growth of the resource, cost function based on effort, and payoffs based on the units extracted at a particular market price (Pearce and Turner 1990, 244).

Final discussion: From "shared resources" to "shared territories"

There are major opportunities in comparing the various approaches reviewed in this chapter. One view comes from the western conventional economic model based on a single-resource bioeconomics and the assignment of property rights. A further expansion of this view, best exemplified by the "ecological economics" tradition, highlights a more systemic view of ecosystem functions, in which multiple goods and services provide benefits to society, including benefits from conservation rather than extraction of resources. Nevertheless, these views are related to a positivist approach to the problem of conservation of nature. In this approach the challenge of the commons is reduced to the definition of institutional arrangements to optimize the economic value of the flow of ecological goods and services to the users' group.

Meanwhile, an alternative anthropological view can be used to explain how indigenous communities seek a model of occupation and resistance to maintain their cultural systems in their territory (→ Indigeneity, I/31). In such models, nature and culture are inseparable and codetermine each other. Here too, defining a system of governance for the land that is compatible with the cultural values is prerequisite for success. However, success is not defined by a single measure such as economic flows, but through multiple objectives including the sustaining of cultural values, social cohesion, or biodiversity (→ Nature, II/36).

However, alternative objectives along the lines of the "good living" (*buen vivir*) model are bringing attention to the indigenous social movement (→ I/41) and creating a common goal of success that moves away from the conventional view of economic development (→ II/6). Possibilities for bridging between rather different views could expand with new ideas emerging from different paths. Svampa (2015) illustrates one of the attempts to build bridges when highlighting the resurgence of the commons question and its possible compatibilities with the "*buen vivir*" model of development. Also, Arturo Escobar (2015) makes the case for bridging the notion of the "*buen vivir*" (good living) with the idea of "commoning" by Bollier and Helfrich (2015). The possibility of such dialogue could come from understanding that the sustaining of the commons as shared territory will be key to support the cultural system, and that the cultural system would serve the purpose of providing the platform for the self-governance of such shared territory.

The concept of shared territory comprises all the biophysical components and interactions with the people that are occupying it with the possibility of sustaining life and a decent, fair and productive livelihood to those living within it. Under this notion of "shared territory," physical boundaries might become blurry and depending on temporal and spatial dynamics, they might also vary. This presents possible contradictions with the conventional view of assigning property rights over land (→ II/15) in contemporary times based on physical static lines. Maintaining the physical boundaries in terms of land might be necessary, as these territories are adjacent to other forms of private land, based on state or private initiatives and purposes.

However, the flows of ecological services that cross these boundaries everyday will require more creative approaches to address the problems of externalities. The conventional economic approach will argue that the assignment of private property rights to these flows and direct bargaining between the parties should solve the problem. In this Coasian bargaining solution, the party affected by the negative externality and the generator of the damage would arrive at an optimal level of damage because the former would be interested in paying the latter an amount to reduce the damage that is at least as costly as the damage itself. On the other hand, the generator of the damage would be interested in paying the affected party an amount to allow them to create the damage, as long as the payment still makes it worth receiving the benefits from the action that creates the damage. This economic approach could also argue that creating the right pricing through Pigovian taxes could also solve the problem (→ Taxation, II/22). In the Pigovian tradition, a tax equivalent to the economic damage to society by the last unit of the externality would reduce the incentives for continuing the activity that creates the damage. With the right calculation of the tax, based on correct estimations of the marginal damage to society, the optimal level of the externality would be achieved. In both solutions, an optimal level of damage would emerge. A level of damage above or below would be socially efficient under this perspective because of the opportunity costs of "too much" or "too little" of the externality.

However, inevitable transaction costs and difficulties in measuring the monetary values of these flows will pose severe challenges to this problem. When neither the state (→ II/38) nor the market (→ Capitalism, II/2) can solve the problems, self-governance must come to the table and offer solutions in terms of norms, agreements, conventions, and endogenous monitoring, and sanctioning to preserve these flows for the benefit of the group.

Another important challenge that must be addressed are the threats from outside these shared territories and outside their cultural systems. The extractive industries continue to attract the attention of investors and national governments that are eager to generate fresh revenue sources to respond to the social needs of their voters (→ Extractivism, II/9). The persistent inequality in the Americas is asking those in office to respond with social public spending to protect the rights of the poor and reduce these gaps (→ Social Inequality, II/20). Royalties from extractive activities are a rapid source of such fiscal resources and are politically difficult to forego or ignore. At the same time, the pursuit of these resources is increasingly creating tensions between national governments and local indigenous groups and environmental movements (→ Environmental Justice, II/8). Not surprisingly, many of the tensions emerging in the Americas involve major projects for natural resource extraction and the threats to the cultural or biological wealth of indigenous communities affected.

A new approach to the commons that responds to the challenges of the Americas will require an understanding of how identity creates the glue for sustaining the self-governance mechanisms for a successful management of these shared territories, as well as a better understanding of the ecological connections of the biophysical components in each ecosystem (→ Nature, II/39). A new commons as shared territory and beyond commons as shared land will combine the cultural identity within a socio-ecological approach. The constitutions in the region have been increasingly strengthened through a rights-based approach (→ Human Rights, II/35) that includes the voices of the indigenous and ancestral groups. Their claims over land have gained legitimacy and recognition, though not without difficulties and, on occasion, violence. Nevertheless, the region today has a healthy number of territories under indigenous communal management from which lessons could be derived about their particular processes. Movements around identities also create tensions as they exacerbate sentiments of exclusion and discrimination by outsiders, while claims for reparation by insiders. This should be a major undertaking by those studying and proposing strategies in favor of indigenous and Afro-descendant shared territories so that the benefits from identity-based self-governance for those within the group do not imply exacerbating the costs for those outside while increasing the ecological, economic, and political redistribution, badly needed in a region that still has to overcome the damages created by the encounter of cultures more than five centuries ago.

Works cited

Arango, Raúl and Enrique Sánchez. 1998. *Los pueblos indígenas de Colombia 1997: desarrollo y territorio*. Bogota: Unidad Administrativa Especial de Desarrollo Territorial.

Benkler, Yochai. 2002. "Coase's Penguin, or, Linux and 'The Nature of the Firm.'" *Yale Law Journal* 112, no. 3: 369–446.

———. 2006. *The Wealth of Networks: How Social Production Transforms Markets and Freedom*. New Haven: Yale University Press.

Bollier, David and Silke Helfrich. 2015. *Patterns of Communing*. Amherst: Commons Strategy Group and Off the Common Press.

Cárdenas, Juan-Camilo. 2016. "Human Behavior and the Use of Experiments to Understand the Agricultural, Resource, and Environmental Challenges of the XXI Century." *Agricultural Economics* 47, no. 1: 61–71.

Cárdenas, Juan-Camilo, César Mantilla, and Rajiv Sethi. 2015. "Stable Sampling Equilibrium in Common Pool Resource Games." *Games* 6, no. 3: 299–317.

Cárdenas, Juan-Camilo. and Elinor Ostrom. 2004. "What Do People Bring into the Game? Experiments in the Field About Cooperation in the Commons." *Agricultural Systems* 82, no. 3: 307–326.

CEPAL. 2014. "Guaranteeing Indigenous People's Rights in Latin America. Progress in the Past Decade and Remaining Challenges." URL=www.cepal.org/en/publications/37051-guaranteeing-indigenous-peoples-rights-latin-america-progress-past-decade-and.

Colding, Johan and Carl Folke. 1997. "The Relations Among Threatened Species, their Protection, and Taboos." *Conservation Ecology* 1, no. 1: n.p.. www.consecol.org/vol1/iss1/art6/.

———. 2001. "Social Taboos: 'Invisible' Systems of Local Resource Management and Biological Conservation." *Ecological Applications* 11, no. 2: 584–600.

Dubertret, Fabrice and Liz Alden Wily. 2015. "Percent of Indigenous and Community Lands." *LandMark: The Global Platform of Indigenous and Community Lands*. www.landmarkmap.org.

Escobar, Arturo. 2015. "Commons in the Pluriverse." In *Patterns of Communing*, David Bollier and Silke Helfrich, n.p. Amherst: Commons Strategy Group and Off the Common Press.

Esteva, Gustavo. 2010. "From the Bottom-Up: New Institutional Arrangements in Latin America." *Development* 53, no. 1: 64–69.

Falk, Armin, Ernst Fehr, and Urs Fischbacher. 2002. *Appropriating the Commons: A Theoretical Explanation*. CESifo Working Paper Series 474. München: CESifo Group Munich.

Feinman, Gary M. 2018. "The Governance and Leadership of Prehispanic Mesoamerican Polities: New Perspectives and Comparative Implications." *Cliodynamics* 9, no. 2: 1–39.

Hardin, Garrett. 1968. "The Tragedy of the Commons." *Science* 162, no. 3859: 1243–1248.

Harvey, David. 2011. "The Future of the Commons." *Radical History Review* 109: 101–107.

McIntosh, Sarah and Yves Renard. 2010. "Placing the Commons at the Heart of Community Development: Three Case Studies of Community Enterprise in Caribbean Islands." *International Journal of the Commons* 4, no. 1: 160–182.

Ostrom, Elinor. 1990. *Governing the Commons: The Evolution of Institutions for Collective Action*. Cambridge and New York: Cambridge University Press.

———. 1992. "Covenants with and without a Sword: Self-Governance is Possible." *American Political Science Review* 86, no. 2: 404–417.

Ostrom, Elinor., Roy Gardner, and James Walker. 1994. *Rules, Games, and Common-Pool Resources*. Ann Arbor: University of Michigan Press.

Pearce, David and Kerry Turner. 1990. *Economics of Natural Resource and Environmental Economics*. Baltimore: Johns Hopkins University Press Baltimore.

Pleyers, Geoffrey. 2018. *Movimientos sociales en el siglo XXI*. Buenos Aires: CLACSO.

Richards, Michael. 1997. "Common Property Resource Institutions and Forest Management in Latin America." *Development and Change* 28, no. 1: 95–117.

Robson, James P. and Gabriela Lichtenstein. 2013. "Current Trends in Latin American Commons Research." *Journal of Latin American Geography* 12, no. 1: 5–31.

Svampa, Maristella. 2015. "Commodities Consensus: Neoextractivism and Enclosure of the Commons in Latin America." *South Atlantic Quarterly* 114, no. 1: 65–82.

Uprimny, Rodrigo. 2014. "The Recent Transformation of Constitutional Law in Latin America: Trends and Challenges." In *Law and Society in Latin America*, ed. Cesar Rodriguez Garavito, 105–123. London and New York: Routledge.

Waldron, Jeremy. 2004. "Property and Ownership." *The Stanford Encyclopaedia of Philosophy* https://plato.stanford.edu/archives/win2016/entries/property/.

32
DEMOCRACY

Jonas Wolff

Democracy is one of those essentially contested concepts that, in W. B. Gallie's famous dictum, "inevitably involve endless disputes about their proper uses on the part of their users" (1956, 169). Combining the Greek words for "people" (*demos*) and "to rule" (*kratein*), democracy literally means to rule by the people. Here the conceptual disputes start: Which entity constitutes "the people"? (In Ancient Greece it was, of course, a tiny minority of free, native, and male citizens.) What does "to rule" mean? (In today's liberal democracies it does not include collective control over the means of production.) How are the people to rule itself? (Directly or indirectly, or by consensus or majority decisions?) Are there any constitutional preconditions of democracy (that enable a people to rule itself) that are outside the reach of the very exercise of democracy (that is, not subject to the rule of the people)?

Gallie's crucial insight that turns his argument about democracy being essentially contestable into an important academic and political intervention is the following: The internal complexity of the very concept of democracy makes it impossible to identify, by way of systematic reasoning, one "correct" or superior conception of democracy. There is simply no single, somehow logically deducible answer to any of the above questions. Still, empirically speaking, democracy is not always actually contested and, at any given point in time, one particular understanding of the concept may be hegemonic. Thus, any specific conception of democracy is always *contestable* in principle, but it may well become *decontested* – that is, taken for granted and assumed common sense status – in a given socio-historical context.

In this sense, the long 1980s (between the late 1970s and the early 1990s) were not simply the years during which most Latin American countries moved from authoritarian to democratic regimes (→ Authoritarianism, II/25). They were also characterized by important ideological shifts that included the decontestation of democracy in terms of a limited, liberal, representative, and market-oriented conception (→ Capitalism, II/2). This conceptual development enabled, and was further consolidated by, the almost region-wide establishment of democracy (see Smith 2011). Furthermore, the convergence of a narrow, Dahlian notion of democracy as polyarchy was actively supported by the U.S. government (Robinson 1996) and also characterizes the scholarship on the transitions to democracy in Latin America (Guilhot 2005, chapters 3–4; Munck 2012, 5) (→ State Transformation, II/21).

Recent years, however, have seen a significant revival of contestation of democracy across the region associated with the so-called leftist turn in Latin America. Like the previous period of decontestation, these ongoing disputes over the parameters of democracy encompass internal struggles over the transformation of democracy within Latin American countries (Cheresky 2006; Dargatz and Zuazo 2012; Escobar 2010), conceptual disputes over the meaning of democracy at the level of Inter-American relations (Heine and Weiffen 2015; Legler, Lean and Boniface 2007; Whitehead 2008), as well as a renewed academic interest in enrichments of, and outright alternatives to, liberal democracy (Arditi 2005; Avritzer 2002; Cameron, Hershberg and Sharpe 2012; Lissidini, Welp and Zovatto 2014; Wolff 2013). To large extent, political developments and related academic debates in the Americas can be read as processes of contestation and decontestation of democracy. In the meantime, a new dynamic of contesting democracy has emerged from the recent turn to the political Right in various American countries, e.g. in Argentina with the election of Macri in 2015, Trump in the USA in 2016 and Bolsonaro in Brazil in 2018.

Democracy in Latin America

With the processes of (re)democratization that started in the late 1970s, democracy became a key topic of major comparative studies and academic debates on Latin America and has remained high on the agenda ever since (see Borón 2003; Domínguez and Shifter 2008; Mainwaring and Scully 2010; O'Donnell and Philippe 1986). Of course, the history of democracy in the region is much older. One prominent way to summarize this history is to recount Latin America's experiences with different kinds of democratic rule since the early 20th century, which mostly failed until the most recent wave of democratization during the long 1980s that inaugurated this remarkable period in which democracy became the almost uncontested norm across the region (Munck 2012, 3; Smith 2011, 17–71).

Scholarly interest in democracy, by and large, evolved in response to these political developments. In the 1960s and 1970s, when scholars addressed the issue of democracy rather indirectly through the lenses of modernization theory or the dependency paradigm (→ Modernization, I/35), studies particularly aimed to explain the failure of democracy in Latin America (→ Clientelism, II/29). From the 1980s onwards, academic interest shifted from explaining democratic transitions to understanding the consolidation of democracy, investigating the limitations, deficits, or, more generally, the quality of Latin America's democratic regimes (see the overview in Munck 2012). It is in this latter context that the previously mentioned decontestation of democracy can be observed. Politically, the experience with brutal repression and economic failure of the military dictatorships (→ Military, II/37) and/or with intense political violence led a broad range of political actors and social forces to converge on an essentially liberal understanding of democracy. These particularly included elites and middle classes that were traditionally fearful of the "populist," if not anti-capitalist, results of mass democracy (→ Populism, II/43), as well as leftist organizations and popular sectors that had traditionally downplayed "bourgeois" political and civil rights as merely formal illusions. Global developments – most notably the decreasing attraction and collapse of real existing socialism (→ I/42) – significantly added to this.

The academic debate generally followed this trend. As Gerardo Munck has noted, scholars that studied the transition to, the consolidation of, or the quality of democracy

> largely converged on a conceptualization of political regimes in terms of the procedures regulating access to the highest political offices in a country and of democracy as, at the very least, a type of regime characterized by mass suffrage and electoral contestation.
>
> *(2012, 5)*

The "intellectual journey of Guillermo O'Donnell" (Guilhot 2005, 123) is a good example of this. When it comes to research on democracy in Latin America, the late Argentine political scientist is probably the most influential scholar (and a genuine Inter-American scholar in his experience with both U.S. and Latin American academia). In addition to his leading role in the landmark study on *Transitions from Authoritarian Rule*, O'Donnell has made important contributions to most democracy related debates on Latin America since the mid-1970s and has coined key concepts such as "delegative democracy," "horizontal accountability," "low-intensity citizenship," and the "brown areas" of the rule of law. What is interesting about O'Donnell in the context of the present entry is that his evolving work reflects the shifting perspectives on democracy in the region.

O'Donnell's early studies on bureaucratic authoritarianism in the 1970s were characterized by a critical engagement with modernization theory, which was significantly influenced by dependency theory, structuralist approaches (→ Development, II/6), and class analysis (→ Social Inequality, II/20). From the late 1970s onwards, however, he theoretically adopted an increasingly actor and elite-centered perspective and began to normatively reassess the value of "bourgeois" democracy (see Guilhot 2005, 123–133). Analyzing democratic transitions, he explicitly adopted a procedural definition of liberal democracy and argued that mobilization for democracy should deliberately stop short of demands that would threaten the bourgeoisie (O'Donnell and Philippe 1986, 8, 27).

At the same time, O'Donnell's work also shows how the convergence of a fairly specific conception of democracy, paradoxically, led to an explosion of competing conceptual innovations intended to grasp the complexities of political regimes and developments in the region. On the one hand, the *limited fit* between the ideal type concept of liberal democracy and the actual shape of Latin American democracies led scholars to invent diminished subtypes of democracy, such as O'Donnell's "delegative democracy," in which weak horizontal accountability makes for virtually omnipotent presidents (see Collier and Levitsky 1997). On the other hand, the *limited scope* of a procedurally defined concept of liberal democracy proved problematic, given that pervasive social inequalities, the confluence of economic and political power, and the socio-geographically selective enforcement of the rule of law effectively limited even the exercise of core liberal rights. Hence, O'Donnell's argument that in most Latin American countries, even if the political regimes are democratic in procedural terms, significant "brown areas" exist that are characterized by "low-intensity citizenship" (see O'Donnell 1999) (→ Citizenship, II/27).

Based on his distinction between a democratic regime defined in procedural terms and democracy or a democratic state in a broader sense, in his latest work O'Donnell increasingly moved away from narrow, institutionalist perspectives. In doing so, he could relate to many of the issues that had long troubled the diverse critics of the liberal mainstream perspective (see, for instance, Avritzer 2002, 27–35; Borón 2003, 227–262). For example, O'Donnell's contribution to the United Nations Development Program (UNDP) project *Democracy in Latin America* brought forward the notion of a "citizens' democracy" based on effective, civil, and social citizenship (see PNUD 2004). Thereby, O'Donnell became a part of the revival of conceptual debates on democracy that have taken place throughout the Americas since the turn of the century. Still, this renewed debate has moved beyond O'Donnell's critique of the limits of liberal democracy and democratic statehood in Latin America (for instance, the contributions by Fernando Calderón, Catherine Conaghan, and José Nun in PNUD 2004).

Just as the narrowed conceptual debate on democracy in the 1980s and early 1990s reflected the actual path of the democratic transitions, the revival of conceptual contestation since the late 1990s has been directly related to actual processes of political struggle and policy experimentation that challenges the limits of liberal, representative democracy in Latin America. Starting with the introduction of participatory budgeting in Porto Alegre (since 1989), through political experiments and academic debates, participatory forms of democracy have thrived throughout the region (see Avritzer 2002; Cameron et al. 2012; Lissidini et al. 2014) (→ Participation, II/31). In a broader sense, waves of citizen protests and social movements (→ I/41) have led to debates about "immediate" forms of democracy (see Cheresky 2006) and new types of "societal accountability" (Smulovitz and Peruzzotti 2000). Indigenous movements (→ Indigeneity, I/31) and their call for collective rights and indigenous autonomy have meant a further "postliberal challenge" to democratic regimes in the region (Yashar 2005). Finally, the rise of anti-neoliberal movements (→ Alter-Globalization, I/21) and the so-called leftist turn produced by them has led to a renewed debate about the relationship between democracy and capitalist development (Escobar 2010) (→ Capitalism, II/2). In a few countries, most notably in Bolivia and Ecuador, these trends have culminated in Constituent Assemblies assigned to profoundly transform the democratic regimes at hand (see Dargatz and Zuazo 2012).

In short, these contested attempts to deepen, or *democratize*, democracy in Latin America have implied significant "postliberal" moves that do not aim to replace, but rather move past mainstream conceptions of liberal, representative democracy (see Arditi 2005; Wolff 2013). In this sense, highly diverse contemporary contestations of democratic theory and democratic practice still share a series of overall features. First, they criticize elitist and institutionalist democracy and stress the role of ordinary citizens and the public space, particularly the contentious collective action by marginalized groups. Second, they do not reject representative institutions, but rather respond to the frequently discussed crisis and limits of representation by emphasizing direct/plebiscitarian and participatory/non-electoral mechanisms. Third, they expand the notion of citizenship (→ II/27), most notably in terms of indigenous collective rights as well as social and economic rights. Finally, the limited reach of neoliberally transformed democracy is challenged through an emphasis on the role and responsibility of the state (→ Nation State, II/38) vis-à-vis the economy and socioeconomic development (→ II/6).

These elements can be observed, perhaps most clearly, in the case of Bolivia. Since the late 1990s, a wave of protests led by indigenous and social movements had challenged the so-called "pacted democracy" (*democracia pactada*) and the neoliberal consensus that united the political elites sustaining it (→ Neoliberalism, II/16). These protests prepared the ground for the election of the country's first indigenous president, Evo Morales, in late 2005. The Morales government not only turned away from neoliberal economic policies and significantly expanded the role of the public sector in the economy, but actually initiated a profound transformation of democracy (Wolff 2013; Zegada et al. 2011). This transformation, as enshrined in the country's new constitution adopted in 2009, broadens and hybridizes Bolivian democracy by officially recognizing three types of democratic rule: "direct and participatory," "representative," and "communitarian." The former is particularly expressed in a series of direct democratic mechanisms, as well as in the far-reaching right to social control that is to be exercised by "organized civil society" (→ Civil Society, II/28) The latter specifically refers to the collective right of indigenous peoples to make use of their own norms and procedures when exercising or delegating political authority (→ Indigeneity, I/31). Certainly, this transformation of democracy is far from settled and the actual implementation of the new constitution is still another matter (Mayorga and Zuazo 2015). Nonetheless, the Bolivian example vividly shows the extent to which social movements in Latin America have succeeded in opening up the conceptual debate on what democracy might mean in contexts in which a narrow, liberal conception appears overly formal and elitist.

Democracy in Inter-American relations

Democracy has long been a key issue in Inter-American relations, at least since Theodore Roosevelt's 1904 Corollary to the Monroe Doctrine established "chronic wrongdoing" in the Western Hemisphere as a legitimate cause for U.S. intervention (→ Interventionism, II/36), followed nine years later by Woodrow Wilson's infamous announcement "to teach the South American republics to elect good men." In 1936, the Inter-American Conference for the Maintenance of Peace in Buenos Aires recognized the "common likeness" of the American republics "in their democratic form of government" and declared "unqualified respect for their respective sovereignties and the existence of a common democracy throughout America," before condemning any intervention "in the internal or external affairs" of other states (United States Government Printing Office 1943) (→ Pan-Americanism, II/40). These quotes effectively illustrate the dual role of democracy *as a common but contested reference* in Inter-American relations. On one hand, in terms of official declarations, for most of the 20th century, most governments self-identified their countries as democratic, which enabled an agreement on representative democracy as a common, region-wide standard (as in the 1948 Charter of the Organization of American States). On the other hand, U.S. governments have generally considered their country as holding a special position to judge and, if need be, help correct the (un)democratic state of affairs in its "backyard." The worldview that has traditionally informed U.S. policymakers implies that the United States – as the shining city upon a hill and the cradle of democracy – is both capable of and entitled to promote the spread of democracy in Latin America and elsewhere (even if, historically speaking, U.S. policy in the region has rarely amounted to anything one could plausibly call democracy promotion). While somehow self-evident from Washington's perspective, this U.S. attitude has understandably led most Latin American governments to emphasize the principle of nonintervention whenever talking about democracy throughout the 20th century.

With the almost region-wide establishment of representative democracy during the long 1980s and the end of the Cold War, this tension temporarily seemed to have finally dissolved (→ Geopolitics, II/34). By and large, Latin America's elected governments now shared an interest in creating mechanisms for the joint defense of democracy against domestic threats. In 1991, the Organization of American States (OAS) adopted Resolution 1080 on "Representative Democracy," which was followed by further democracy related agreements (including the 1991 Santiago Commitment and the 1992 Washington Protocol) and enabled a series of collective responses to (attempted) coups in the region (see Legler et al. 2007). Ironically, when this process of strengthening hemispheric democracy norms culminated in 2001 with the adoption of the Inter-American Democratic Charter, the decay of the temporary regional consensus had already set in (Heine and Weiffen 2015, chapter 3).

However, this collective dimension of democracy promotion and protection in the Americas is only part of the story. At the same time that the OAS moved toward strengthening its democracy related norms and practices, the U.S. likewise expanded and professionalized its unilateral policies of democracy promotion. While the OAS was largely focusing on the relatively uncontested protection of representative democracy against outright domestic threats, U.S. democracy promotion has been more actively engaged in shaping the very kind of democracy that was becoming established in the region. As William Robinson (1996) has forcefully argued, U.S. democracy promotion since Ronald Reagan has deliberately aimed at promoting "low-intensity democracies" across Latin America that would be compatible with the persistence of highly unequal internal and international socioeconomic relations in the new era of neoliberal globalization (→ Social Inequality, II/20; Neoliberalism, II/16). In terms of the conception of democracy, scholars have observed that U.S. democracy promotion was generally guided by an elitist, formal, and market-oriented model that emphasizes institutional checks and balances, civil liberties, and private property rights. Given the previously mentioned region-wide convergence on liberal democracy (cum neoliberal restructuring), this practice was relatively uncontested for some time, at least among the region's elites. This dramatically changed when the domestic tides in many Latin American countries increasingly turned against "neoliberalism" and actually existing democratic regimes.

The new struggle over democracy that has characterized Inter-American relations since the turn of the century is multi-dimensional. With the election of a series of more or less leftist presidents since the first electoral victory of Hugo Chávez in Venezuela in 1998, domestic challenges to liberal democracy *within* Latin American countries scaled up to become an issue of Inter-American relations. More specifically, the emergence of governments that claim to represent a participatory alternative to liberal democracy has led to a revival of the contestation of U.S. interference in the name of democracy (Wolff 2016) and a decreasing conceptual consensus at the level of Inter-American relations (Whitehead 2008). The aggressive turn of U.S. foreign policy under the George W. Bush administration – which included contested support for the ultimately failed coup against Chávez in 2002 – has certainly contributed to this. As a consequence, U.S. democracy promotion policies in countries such as Bolivia, Ecuador, and Venezuela have faced outright resistance, while debates in the OAS have become increasingly polarized between the U.S. and its allies, and the anti-imperialist critics of liberal, representative democracy. These conceptual disagreements – which are intimately connected with conflicts of power and interest – have characterized important debates within the OAS. Most notably, they have contributed to the failure to find common Inter-American responses to coups (as in Venezuela 2002 and Honduras 2008) or to political developments that some governments, but not others, consider a coup (as in Paraguay 2012 or in Brazil 2016), or see as a gradual backsliding of democracy (as in Venezuela under the Chavista governments) (see Heine and Weiffen 2015). As Neil Burron has noted, the political backdrop of these developments is the reemergence of "a struggle over the meaning of democracy – and who possesses the legitimacy to promote it" (2012, 12).

Most different views have emerged in regard to Cuba, which was suspended from the OAS in 1962. While member states such as Bolivia, Ecuador, Nicaragua, and Venezuela demanded the immediate readmission of Cuba to the organization, the U.S. and Canada considered the democratic principles of the OAS to inhibit such a move. In the end, the 2009 General Assembly of the OAS struck a compromise that lifted the suspension of Cuba's membership, while making its future participation in the organization dependent on a process of dialogue "in accordance with the practices, purposes, and principles of the

OAS" (Organization of American States 2009). In this way, the conceptual struggle about how these principles, including those relating to democracy and human rights (→ II/35), are to be interpreted and applied to Cuba, could be postponed until Havana would formally request to start such a dialogue – a request "that was unlikely to be forthcoming" (Heine and Weiffen 2015, 139).

In the context of Inter-American relations, Canada has traditionally occupied a special place. In terms of its democratic regime, the country is the only one with a parliamentary system, in contrast to the presidentialism that characterizes political regimes in the U.S. and across Latin America. Furthermore, Canada has traditionally remained at the margins of regional affairs and, in fact, joined the OAS as recently as 1990. Since then, Canada has followed the U.S. in increasing its involvement in democracy promotion in Latin America. In contrast to the U.S., Canadian democracy promotion has been characterized by a cooperative and multilateral approach, a rather social democratic conception of democracy with a stronger grassroots tradition of working through NGOs. In recent years, however, Canadian development cooperation, including its support of NGOs, has been increasingly "aligned with the foreign policy of the state and the interests of Canadian multinationals" (Burron 2012, 5) (→ Development, II/6; Transnational Corporations, II/23)

Conclusion

A rich debate about the proper meaning of democracy is in itself a good indicator of a democratic state of affairs. In this sense, the revival of the contestation of democracy that can be observed throughout the Americas since the turn of the century can be seen as a signal of democratic progress regarding both the internal affairs of Latin American countries and Inter-American relations. However, this positive conclusion must be qualified in two important regards.

First, democracy – whatever its specific shape – depends on a balance between conflict and consensus. This, in particular, concerns the case of conceptual contestation of democracy. Given the essential contestability of democracy, the absence of any serious conflict over the meaning and implementation of democracy means that relevant voices are silenced and important alternatives concealed (→ Silencing, III/19). Yet, such contestation also needs to be limited by some general agreement on basic (democratic) rules of the game, if conflict is not to turn violent and threaten the very opportunity structure that enables an open debate over democracy. Disagreement over democratic principles is probably not the most important, and certainly not the only, controversy that is driving political conflict in the region. Still, whether in the context of the coups against Chávez in Venezuela (2002) and Zelaya in Honduras (2008), during the heavily contested constitutional reform process in Bolivia (2008), in the contemporary political crises in Brazil and Venezuela (2016), or in the campaign that led to the electoral victory of Donald Trump in the U.S. (2016), the lack of a basic consensus over the legitimate constitution and exercise of political power has clearly contributed to societal polarization. Relatedly, the clash of competing conceptions of democracy and human rights (→ II/35) at the level of Inter-American relations has yet to produce a meaningful political dialogue on this issue, but has already weakened those multilateral institutions that are key fora in which such conceptual conflicts can be carried out in cooperative ways.

Second, it is one thing to say that the strengthening of voices that call for direct, participatory, or communitarian types of democracy is a good sign for democracy. But this does not imply that the actual transformations of democracy that are, at least partially, driven by such calls are necessarily successful by any democratic standard. In fact, there is rather widespread disillusionment with the different attempts to move beyond liberal, representative democracy in the region. If for different reasons, few observers would see contemporary Brazil or Venezuela (to name but two) as hopeful examples of democratic experimentation. Especially the election of Jair Bolsonaro in Brazil in 2018 stands for the advance of a new type of political discourse from the Right throughout the Americas, which openly devalues liberal norms and democratic institutions and justifies the past and possibly future political violence. Yet, what is important for the purpose of this entry is that none of the different problems that these countries currently face is plausibly caused by the actual introduction of participatory and/or plebiscitary institutions or to the strengthening of socioeconomic and/or collective rights. One might rather argue the problem is, in fact, that the promise of transforming democracy by democratic means has not been taken seriously enough by the respective governments. Yet, of course, this argument is as contested as is the normative premises on which it is based.

Works cited

Arditi, Benjamín, ed. 2005. *Democracia post-liberal? El espacio político de las asociaciones*. Barcelona: Anthropos.

Avritzer, Leonardo. 2002. *Democracy and the Public Space in Latin America*. Princeton, New Jersey: Princeton University Press.

Borón, Atilio A. 2003. *Estado, capitalismo y democracia en América Latina*. Buenos Aires: CLACSO.

Burron, Neil A. 2012. *The New Democracy Wars. The Politics of North American Democracy Promotion in the Americas*. Farnham: Ashgate.

Cameron, Maxwell A., Eric Hershberg, and Kenneth E. Sharpe, eds. 2012. *New Institutions for Participatory Democracy in Latin America. Voice and Consequence*. New York: Palgrave Macmillan.

Cheresky, Isidoro, ed. 2006. *Ciudadanía, Sociedad Civil y Participación Política*. Buenos Aires: Miño y Dávila.

Collier, David and Steven Levitsky. 1997. "Democracy With Adjectives. Conceptual Innovations in Comparative Research." *World Politics* 49, no. 3: 430–451.

Dargatz, Anja and Moira Zuazo, eds. 2012. *Democracias en Transformación: ¿Qué hay de nuevo en los Estados andinos?*. La Paz: Friedrich-Ebert-Stiftung.

Domínguez, Jorge I. and Michael Shifter, eds. 2008. *Constructing Democratic Governance in Latin America. Third Edition*. Baltimore: Johns Hopkins University Press.

Escobar, Arturo. 2010. "Latin America at a Crossroads. Alternative Modernizations, Post-liberalism, or Post-development?" *Cultural Studies* 24, no. 1: 1–65.

Gallie, W. B. 1956. "Essentially Contested Concepts." *Proceedings of the Aristotelian Society* 56: 167–198.

Guilhot, Nicolas. 2005. *The Democracy Makers: Human Rights and International Order*. New York: Columbia University Press.

Heine, Jorge and Brigitte Weiffen. 2015. *21st Century Democracy Promotion in the Americas: Standing Up for the Policy*. Abingdon: Routledge.

Legler, Thomas, Sharon F. Lean, and Dexter S. Boniface, eds. 2007. *Promoting Democracy in the Americas*. Baltimore: Johns Hopkins University Press.

Lissidini, Alicia, Yanina Welp, and Daniel Zovatto, eds. 2014. *Mecanismos de democracia directa y participativa en América Latina*. Ciudad de México: UNAM.

Mainwaring, Scott and Timothy R. Scully, eds. 2010. *Democratic Governance in Latin America*. Stanford: Stanford University Press.

Mayorga, Fernando and Moira Zuazo. 2015. "Democracia intercultural y ciudadanía multicultural en el Estado plurinacional." In *Democracia participativa e izquierdas: Logros, contradicciones y desafíos*. eds. Anja Minnaert and Gustavo Endara, 317–382. Quito: FES-ILDIS.

Munck, Gerardo L. 2012. "The Origins and Durability of Democracy." In *Routledge Handbook of Latin American Politics*. eds. Peter Kingstone and Deborah J. Yashar, 3–20. New York: Routledge.

O'Donnell, Guillermo. 1999. *Counterpoints: Selected Essays on Authoritarianism and Democratization*. Notre Dame: University of Notre Dame Press.

O'Donnell, Guillermo and C. Schmitter Philippe. 1986. *Transitions from Authoritarian Rule. Tentative Conclusions about Uncertain Democracies*. Baltimore: Johns Hopkins University Press.

Organization of American States. Resolution on Cuba AG/RES. 2438 (XXXIX-O/09). June 2009. San Pedro Sula, Honduras. www.oas.org/39ag/documents/AGRES-2438E.doc.

PNUD (Programa de Naciones Unidas para el Desarrollo). 2004. *La Democracia an América Latina. Hacia una democracia de ciudadanas y ciudadanos. El debate conceptual sobre la democracia*. Buenos Aires: Alfaguara.

Robinson, William I. 1996. *Promoting Polyarchy. Globalization, United States Intervention and Hegemony*. Cambridge: Cambridge University Press.

Smith, Peter H. 2011. *Democracy in Latin America: Political Change in Comparative Perspective. Second Edition*. Oxford: Oxford University Press.

Smulovitz, Catalina and Enrique Peruzzotti. 2000. "Societal Accountability in Latin America." *Journal of Democracy* 11, no. 4: 147–158.

United States Department of State. 1943. "Declaration of Principles of Inter-American Solidarity And Cooperation, Buenos Aires, December 21, 1936." In *Peace and War. United States Foreign Policy 1931–1941*, 351–352. Washington, DC: Department of State Publication.

Whitehead, Laurence. 2008. "The Fading Regional Consensus on Democratic Convergence." In *Constructing Democratic Governance in Latin America*. Third Edition, eds. Jorge I. Domínguez and Michael Shifter, 13–38. Baltimore: Johns Hopkins University Press.

Wolff, Jonas. 2013. "Towards Post-Liberal Democracy in Latin America? A Conceptual Framework Applied to Bolivia." *Journal of Latin American Studies* 45, no. 1: 31–59.

———. 2016. "Negotiating Interference: U.S. Democracy Promotion, Bolivia, and the Tale of a Failed Agreement." *Third World Quarterly* 38, no. 4: 882-899. DOI: 10.1080/01436597.2016.1153418.

Yashar, Deborah J. 2005. *Contesting Citizenship in Latin America: The Rise of Indigenous Movements and the Postliberal Challenge*. Cambridge: Cambridge University Press.

Zegada, María Tereza, Claudia Arce, Gabriela Canedo, and Alber Quispe. 2011. *La democracia desde los márgenes. Transformaciones en el campo político boliviano*. La Paz: CLACSO.

33
DISASTER

Eleonora Rohland and Virginia García-Acosta

A disaster is usually characterized by its suddenness, its short-onset timeframe (though droughts or multi-year wars may equally qualify as disasters), its disruptiveness for human communities, and by its material, environmental, and economic scope (IFRC 2018). The historical perspective on the study of disasters has shown, however, that the factors that make hazards disastrous for human societies, are in fact embedded in processes of socio-natural entanglement that evolve over time, and that materialize in specific ways in a specific space and time. In this perspective, natural hazards (→ Nature, II/39) can act as triggers that often lay bare problematic societal structures (Oliver-Smith 1996, 303, 2002, 25). Clearly, disasters can be "natural" (i.e. caused by geological and/or meteorological forces) or "human-made" (i.e. technical disasters, such as nuclear accidents, shipwrecks, oil spills, war etc.). In this entry "natural" disasters will be the focus, as the specific geographical, geological, and climatic setting of the Americas makes them inherently hazard-prone landmasses – more so than the Eurasian continent. And together with this hazard-prone setting of the Americas, specific indigenous mythologies and cultures of disaster (Anderson 2011; Bankoff 2003) have evolved over time.

The Pacific coast lines of both continents and Central America are in fact the rims of two large tectonic plates, the North American and the South American plates, that bound on the Pacific and the Nazca plate. However, the smaller Juan de Fuca, Cocos and Caribbean plates should not be underestimated. The tectonic movements of those plates cause earthquakes along their boundaries, across the American continent, most notably in California, Mexico, Guatemala, Peru, and Chile (Keller, DeVecchio and Blodgett 2015, 46–8, 58). The collision of the Caribbean and the Pacific plate some fifteen million years ago led to the formation of volcanic islands in the Archipelago. Further, still active volcanos lie along the backbone of the Andes and belong to the Pacific Ring of Fire, an arc of fault lines along which three quarters of the world's active and dormant volcanos are placed (ibid, 125; Lavell et al. 2014, 229). North, Central and South America have vast interior plains and are drained by large river basins such as the St. Lawrence, the Mississippi, the Amazon, the Paraná and the Bravo, or Grande River. All of these larger and smaller rivers have been the lifelines of human settlements with individual flood regimes that indigenous as well as colonial and modern societies have adapted to in different ways.

Apart from the geological and hydrological hazards, there are specific meteorological and climatic phenomena that have become hazardous for human societies. For example, tornadoes mainly affect the southeast and central states of the United States but may reach as far north as Canada and as far south as Mexico, while hurricanes most strongly affect the Caribbean archipelago, the Circum-Caribbean states along the Gulf of Mexico and the Pacific coast of Mexico and the Central American states.

As continents on a north to south axis, North, Central, and South America are subject to the whole spectrum of climatic zones from polar, through continental to tropical. While there is a large variety of local climates that bring with them their own local hazards in combination with topography and geological situation, the most characteristic, large-scale (in fact, global) climatic phenomenon that has had a strong influence on past and present societies of the Americas, is the El Niño-Southern Oscillation, also known by its acronym ENSO. The El Niño component was first observed and identified off the coast of Peru in the 1890s. It is the term for the irregularly occurring reversal of the Ocean currents and is thus part of the natural climatic variability, when warm water flows in from the north along the Pacific coast of South America. These changes cause fish and bird species to migrate and evaporation from the warm sea surface causing heavy rainfall that is essential to Peruvian desert ecosystems. For human societies, all of these changes could impact food regimes, livelihoods, and property by destroying crops and settlements or by the decline of certain animal species. As this phenomenon usually occurred around Christmas, Peruvian Fishermen called it El Niño – the Christ Child (Grove and Adamson 2018, 3–4; see also Caviedes 2001). The atmospheric pressure component, the Southern Oscillation, was discovered in the 1920s and only after the mid-20th century was it connected to the ocean current pattern. The Southern Oscillation is a shifting pressure relationship between the Indian and the Pacific Ocean. In other words, the whole phenomenon is called El Niño-Southern Oscillation, with El Niño being the warm eastern Pacific extreme of the pattern and La Niña being the cold current extreme of the phenomenon.

Both, El Niño and La Niña years are associated with extreme weather phenomena across the Americas. For example, El Niño cycles are associated with devastating and long-lasting droughts in Mexico, Central America and the southwestern United States, and with torrential rainfall on the Peruvian Coast and the Andes. La Niña cycles, on the other hand, are associated with climatic conditions that are conducive for hurricane-formation in the North Atlantic. While the Pacific off the coast of Peru is unusually cold during La Niña years, the Gulf of Mexico and Caribbean Sea tend to be warmer than usual, which enhances conditions for hurricanes to form in the North Atlantic (Malaizé et al. 2011, 2; Smith 2007). While it is accepted that ENSO is one of the factors that modulate the climate and its interannual variations, little progress has been made in analyzing the association between its presence and the specific societal contexts in which it arises, i.e. between the factors that control weather and climate and the degree of cumulative vulnerability of societies, which are affected by certain effects of El Niño (mostly floods and droughts) and which, together, shape the social construction of disaster risks (Lavell and Brenes 2008).

"Disaster" – A brief conceptual history

Those physical, geographical, and meteorological aspects of the hazards that are characteristic for the Americas are but one side of the story, however. How do natural hazards turn into "disasters," how did human societies through time cope with them, adapt to them, perceive and build them into their religious, cultural, and socio-economic lives?

In the light of the briefly outlined, often-violent physical environment of the Americas, many indigenous cultures developed their mythology around those phenomena (→ Indigenous Peoples, I/11). Among North American First Nations, mythology of a primordial flood event, as it is known in other cultures around the globe, abounds (Bastian and Mitchell 2004, 97–8). Peter Watson in his *Great Divide* makes a compelling case for those myths being the remnants of "disaster memories" of three major coastal flood events caused by glacial melting around 11,000 years ago. These events affected people around the globe and caused human societies to migrate and may also account for the existence of those flood stories throughout North American Native mythology (2013, 23–41). Apart from floods, thunder, winds and whirlwinds in particular, had taken shape as deities in North American Native mythology. For example, among the peoples of the upper plains, whirlwinds were imagined as a female figure or as ghosts. In the mythology of the peoples of the northeast woodlands, thunder was also thought of as a human-like god or as thunderbirds. Together with rain, they were considered beneficent deities (Bastian et al. 2004, 216, 197, 193).

In the area of the Circum-Caribbean, mythology strongly centered around the figure of the deity huracán, also known under the variants "hunrakán," "yuracán," "yerucán," and "yorocán" (Pérez 2001, 17). In all of those cultures, the term was the actual name of a powerful and malevolent god capable of large-scale destruction.

For example, among the pre-Hispanic Maya in the Yucatán Peninsula, a hurricane was perceived as a battle between *chacs*, or rain gods. In this epic showdown, the evil *chac* (the destroyer), who had malevolent intentions toward humans and their environment, was confronted by the good *chac* (the protector) who had benevolent intentions. The physical manifestations of the hurricane, winds and rains, were the by-product of the energy expended, the "sweat of the gods." In the Maya perspective, post-hurricane dry seasons occurred because the good *chac*, having expended so much force in celestial combat, required a lengthy period of recuperation (Konrad 1985, 321).

With regard to earthquakes, several myths and legends have arisen and are part of the region now known as Latin America. Two examples exist with the first being the "Legend of the Five Suns," which is one of the best-known Mesoamerican versions of the creation of the world. It says that the Earth has gone through five different periods since its inception, each governed by a Sun that is destroyed at the end of that period. The last of those stages corresponds to the Fifth Sun, the Sun of movement, which would end because of earthquakes. This is the reason why earthquakes were scrupulously recorded systematically in pictographic writing in many pre-Hispanic and early colonial codices and annals (Anonymus 2008 [1885]) (→ Language, I/13). Second, in Peru, the cult of the *Señor de los Milagros* (Lord of the Miracles), which unifies the indigenous, Afro-descendant, and white parts of the population in imploring him for his protection against earthquakes. The figure of the *Señor de los Milagros* has its roots in the ancient god Pachacamac or "Lord of the Earthquakes," the pre-Hispanic deity that was thought to control nature (Rostorowski 2002).

The terms "disaster" and "catastrophe" as well as their compounds "natural disaster" and "natural catastrophe" came to the Americas with the European colonists. Also, the term *calamidad* was in use in Spanish as well as the English "calamity." In Spanish this last term seems to disappear toward the end of 18th century, while in English the expression is still in use during the 19th century. The term "catastrophe" originally derives from Greek antiquity, where it had a particular place in drama theory, meaning "upheaval," "end," or *dénouement* (Massard-Guilbaud 2002, 12; Mauelshagen 2015, 173). Only in the course of the 19th century did "catastrophe" lose its drama-theoretical meaning and gradually become synonymous with "misfortune" or "harm." It took until the mid-19th century until such "harm" was conceived of in connection to natural hazards.

The compound "natural catastrophe" – more commonly used in German, *Naturkatastrophe* – only started appearing at the beginning of the 20th century, and only by the 1970s had it established itself as the term for disastrous events with a natural (rather than human) cause. The career of "natural catastrophe," or *Naturkatastrophe*, is closely linked with the history of the term "revolution" (Latin, *revolutio*), which is the Latin translation of the Greek *katastrophé*. In the 18th century, "revolution" was adopted by the developing field of geology and came to be used to describe upheavals in nature. However, once "revolution" (→ II/44) started being employed in political and societal contexts, the resulting lexical void was filled by the newly emerging meaning of "catastrophe" (Groh, Kęmpe and Mauelshagen 2003, 16–7).

The English term "disaster" (in the Romance languages, *désastre* (French), *disastro* (Italian) and *desastre* (Spanish) also derives from astrology, meaning literally "bad star," or "unfavorable aspect of a star." This original connotation points to the ancient perception that "fateful turns of events" could be caused by certain constellations of the stars (Hoad 1993, 126; Schenk 2007, 12). In fact, to attribute the presence of natural phenomena as well as disasters associated with them to a superhuman, supernatural or divine origin, has been a constant throughout the history of mankind.

Such metaphysical interpretations of the causation of calamitous "natural" events continued in the early modern (Catholic) Christian perception of disasters as divine punishment. It is important to note that, as opposed to the Judeo-Christian case, a conception of extreme events as punishment from god did not exist, in pre-Hispanic Mesoamerica (García-Acosta 2017a). According to the early modern Christian perception, humans were responsible for their own misfortune, bringing the "wrath of God" upon themselves by behaving sinfully. This pattern of perception has been aptly called *peccatogenic*, as opposed to the 21st-century counterpart of *anthropogenic* causation of disastrous events in nature (Juneja and Mauelshagen 2007, 17). An Anglo-American term related to this context, which, at the latest since Hurricane Katrina, became highly politicized, is "Act of God." As opposed to the *peccatogenic* perception of disasters, however, it essentially relieves humans of having had any part in a disastrous event and thus lends itself to justifying the rejection of responsibility. It is important to keep in mind these diverse strands of terminological history, since, quite obviously, the perception of the causation of disasters also changes how societies react and adapt to them.

Early modern comparison: indigenous "superstition" vs. colonial "science"?

Whether Catholic or Protestant, all early modern European colonial powers who claimed territory in the Americas believed that extreme events such as storms, droughts, floods, fires, or thunderstorms with strong lightning (in particular if it hit important buildings such as church steeples) were portents, communications from God, signs that a community was being punished for its sins (→ Religious Beliefs, I/40). It was therefore common for priests to call for the improvement of the community and for processions to be held in the aftermath of such disasters (Alberola Roma 2015; Favier and Granet-Abisset 2009; García-Acosta 2017a, 2017b; Mauelshagen 2011; Mulcahy 2018). This did not preclude the close observation of nature (→ II/39) and the pursuit of an understanding of extreme natural phenomena. Religious interpretation and natural observation often co-existed and only during the 18th century did the balance start shifting toward natural "scientific" explanations with the spread of the enlightenment (→ I/8) throughout the Western world.

The Spanish were the first colonial power to get a taste of the awesome power of American "nature" in the form of hurricanes in the Caribbean, along the Gulf of Mexico, and the

Yucatán Peninsula. Several of the early chroniclers of the "discovery" of the New World mentioned them in their works and introduced them to their readers as a storm of unheard-of strength that blows from all directions. For this novel phenomenon they adopted the indigenous term "huracán," of which Fernández de Oviedo translates in his *Historia general y natural de las Indias* as "very excessive storm" (Arber, Eden, D Anghiera and Münster 1895, 81; las Casas 1875 [1575], 114–5; Fernández de Oviedo 1535, lib. VI, cap. III). To make the phenomenon graspable to their erudite European readership, the chroniclers, Thomas Lopez Medel in particular, described hurricanes in terms of Aristotelian meteorology (Lopez Medel 1990 [1570], 32; Rohland 2016, 76–7, 2018), and by including the peculiarity of changing wind directions. Fray Diego de Landa, the Bishop of the Archdiocese of Yucatán from 1572 to 1579 called the phenomenon a "huracán de quatro vientos," a "hurricane of four winds" (Landa 1966), and sometimes colonial documents also speak of a "terremoto de aire y agua" or an "earthquake of wind and water," which seems like a good description of what a cyclone feels like (García-Acosta, Pérez and Molina 2003). Simultaneously with those literal observations of nature, Fernández de Oviedo is noted as affirming that it was not coincidence that the hurricanes had waned since the start of the sacraments being celebrated in the churches of the island of Hispaniola, and furthermore, as the Christian faith was spreading through the island, the devil was losing its grip on the land. In due time, the Christian God would make these hurricanes cease (Fernández de Oviedo 1535, lib. VI, cap. III). This is one of many instances, in which, in the European (colonial) case, natural observation and religious explanation converged.

However, in Taíno mythology, "huracán" did not mean "excessive storm" as projected by Fernández de Oviedo. It was the name of a destructive demon who was, in fact, responsible for the creation of the Antilles. By breaking off part of the mainland coastline and then scattering this "debris" into the sea, he had created the Caribbean archipelago (Pérez 2001, 17). Stone engravings of Cuban origin depicting the deity huracán were described and analyzed by the Cuban ethnographer and historian Fernando Ortíz (1947). The symbol consists of a human-like head with two deep round holes for the eyes and an o-shaped open mouth. The figure has neither body nor legs, but two arms with five-fingered hands attached at either side of its head. The left arm is rounded backward so that its hand appears to reach behind the figure's head, while the right arm is bent forward with the hand resting in front of the head, thus creating an s-shape. Ortíz described the figure as performing a dynamic, counter clockwise rotation around its own axis (1947, 28–31). The counter clockwise rotation implied in the image indicates that the Caribbean Indians must have had knowledge of a feature peculiar to hurricanes which is not easy to observe from the ground and which American and European scientists only started theorizing in earnest about at the beginning of the 19th century (Farrar 1818, 95; Redfield 1832, 193). Clearly, the Taíno culture at the beginning of the 16th century was very different from the Spanish, and in many ways was not as technologically developed. However, the convergence of religious explanations for awe-inspiring natural phenomena with their observation and a sophisticated understanding for some of their features brings the two cultures on a very similar basis when it comes to understanding, "managing," and adapting to an environment. Rather, the Taíno clearly had a head start before the Europeans in the environmental knowledge of their homeland where they turned into hurricane forecasters for the European settlers (Rohland 2018). This is not just the case for the Caribbean, Hurricanes, and the Spaniards but, clearly, and maybe obviously, for all indigenous peoples of the Americas vis-à-vis the European colonists, as countless examples of failed early colonial settlements and European dependence on indigenous food crops show (e.g. Blanton 2003; Kupperman 1979, 2007; Rockman 2010).

While in the beginning, Europeans heavily depended on indigenous environmental knowledge for their survival and adaptation, this knowledge was swiftly included in and superseded by European knowledge infrastructures (Edwards 2010, 17) (→ Conquest and Colonization, I/7). With the extermination of indigenous populations at the hands and germs of Europeans, a large-scale, irrecoverable loss of cultural and environmental knowledge went hand in hand. In other words, the Christian *peccatogenic* perception of disasters supplanted the rich and variegated mythological landscape of the indigenous peoples of the Americas throughout the early modern period. By no means does this indicate, however, that the governance, or management, of disasters has turned out uniformly throughout the Americas and across time. A factor that appears to be universal across North, Central, South America, and the Caribbean, however, is that their systematically disadvantaged indigenous and black communities also, in many cases, became the environmentally most vulnerable parts of the respective society (→ Environmental Justice, II/8). That is, often indigenous, mestizo, and black populations were pushed to the least desirable and often riskiest parts of colonial settlements and became the victims of "natural disasters" to a higher proportion than European colonials or white creoles (→ Colonial Rule, I/5; Interethnic Relations, I/12). This is as much true for the past as it is for the present (Colten 2007; Lavell and López-Marrero 2014, 233; Oliver-Smith 1994; Padilla Lozoya 2016).

During the early modern period, disasters were largely managed locally with regard to the search and rescue of injured people as well as with collecting and appropriating funds to rebuild destroyed settlements. If a disaster surpassed the means of the local city or the provincial level, the colonial governor would petition for funds from the royal treasury. Depending on where those financial appropriations came from, this could take more time than a reaction in a disaster-situation required. Local self-help was hence indispensable. In the early modern disaster-prone (Circum-)Caribbean, this situation led to the development of an emergency provisioning network that piggy-backed on the contraband trade network, which, in turn, piggy-backed on the ancient indigenous trade routes, pointing back to the importance of indigenous knowledge and colonial socio-natural entanglement (Dawdy 2008, 107–10; Johnson 2011, 195; Rohland 2018).

Modern differences and similarities, transfers, and entanglements

In the largely Anglo-American-dominated United States, disaster management acquired a specific character during the 19th and early 20th century. Rather than differentiating between "man-made" and "natural" disasters as in Europe, the U.S. Congress' concept of disaster depended on the inability of victims to control or prevent loss and on their moral innocence. The basis for this focus on sudden deprivation and blameworthiness lay in the spiritual tradition of the U.S. founding fathers, such as Lockean philosophy, the British Common Law, and Puritanism. As a consequence of this focus on sudden loss and blameworthiness, Congress appropriated relief funds on a case-by-case basis for a wide variety of "disasters" ranging from material loss caused by riots, to losses from floods and fire during the 19th century (Dauber 2013, 14, Dauber 2003, 31–2, 35, 39–40). In 1881, the United States ratified the treaty of Geneva and Clara Barton founded the United States Red Cross. The "American Amendment" effected by Barton enabled the institution to grant relief from "great, overmastering calamities," such as storms, earthquakes, floods, etc., in addition to the effects of war (Dulles 1950, 16). The U.S. Red Cross depended entirely on private donations for its relief work and – when possible – stepped in before Congress got involved. This system of local self-help, Red Cross charitable donations, and relief work, together with case-by-case Congressional legislation, continued up to 1950 when it had become so cumbersome and inefficient that the U.S.'s first comprehensive disaster relief law, the Federal Disaster Assistance Act

(PL 81–875), was enacted (Bea 2007, 83). This Act moved the decision-making process to grant disaster relief from Congress to the President, who also directly administered the Disaster Relief Fund after he made a Disaster Declaration. Presidential Disaster Declarations could and can be made without the consultation of Congress.

From 1950 onwards, U.S. "natural" disaster relief developed in the context of Cold War politics (→ Geopolitics, II/34) and was closely linked to Civil Defense. Until the advent of Hurricane Betsy in 1965 and the consequent establishment of the National Flood Insurance Program (NFIP), disaster relief in the United States only worked after the fact, apart from building codes for earthquake- and fire-safe building. In 1979, the Federal Emergency Management Administration (FEMA) was created by President Carter. However, it was only after 1979 that disaster mitigation, that is, a focus on prevention and risk reduction, really started taking hold. In 1988, the Robert T. Stafford Disaster Relief and Emergency Assistance Act (known as the "Stafford Act" for short) was enacted, which is still in use today. It was the legislation that first properly enabled the mitigation of disasters by allowing post-disaster measures and federal finances to support mitigation projects (Sylves 2007, 133–35). This Act was updated after 9/11 and again after Hurricane Katrina in 2005, during which the institutional dismantlement, which had happened within FEMA under the Bush administration, became painfully apparent by the institution's failure to respond adequately to the disaster that followed Katrina (Gall, Boruff and Cutter 2007).

Similar to the United States, Canada's disaster management system also evolved from the Cold War context of civil defense. As in the U.S., Canadian first response in the aftermath of a disaster comes from the local level. Municipalities are in charge of operational decisions and deployment of personnel for search and rescue operations and recovery. In this, they are – like the U.S. – supported by the Canadian Red Cross and other humanitarian agencies. Only if the event surpasses local capacities, does the provincial or territorial level come into play, and only when these resources are exhausted, is the federal level called on. The same subsidiary approach is used in financing the cost of disasters. Only when costs exceed $1 per capita does the federal government step in with financial aid. A cost-bearing scheme has been in place since the 1970s, which has the federal government pay a percentage share of the actual costs of the disaster response and recovery activities of the province or local level. This cost-sharing principle has been so effective that since its inception, the Canadian state has appropriated some $1.8 billion for disaster relief, which, according to the *Encyclopedia of Disaster Relief*, is less than what the U.S. spent in the state of Mississippi after Hurricane Katrina (Hightower and Coutu 1996, 72; Rohletter 2011, 44). It is of course important to keep in mind population size and exposure to natural hazards when making such claims.

In Latin America and the Caribbean, most countries started establishing civil defense institutions from the 1950s onwards. As with the U.S., this was in part a response to the threats of the Cold War, but much more, and in opposition to the U.S. and Canada, it was a reaction to internal conflict, i.e. guerilla warfare (Lavell and López-Marrero 2014, 231). However, these national security organizations very soon also started functioning as institutions that administered "natural" disaster relief (→ Security, II/45). In a few Latin American countries, such as Mexico, this task is not in the hands of the army (→ Military, II/37) but rather in those of a "civil protection" federal agency.

The parallels to and influence of the United States during the 20th century development of Latin American disaster relief institutions are quite visible. Similar to the U.S., Latin American "civil defense" or "civil protection" organizations were at first only focused on granting disaster relief after the fact. Prevention and mitigation of disasters only came into the purview of individual states' organizations after the 1970s and were frequently related to big "events." In Mexico, for example, the Sistema Nacional de Protección Civil (National Civil Protection System) and the Centro Nacional de Prevención de Desastres (National Disaster Prevention Center) were created in 1986, after the devastating 1985 earthquakes, and are managed by the Secretaría de Gobernación (Secretariat of the Interior). Nevertheless, the effects and impacts of the recent earthquakes of 7th and 19th September 2017 on Mexican territory, have shown that social vulnerability and risk are still factors that are not being considered enough by the Mexican authorities.

Although great progress has been made in studies on disasters in Latin America, there is no concomitant advance in managing disaster risk reduction. This is largely due to the fact that governmental agencies, at a national and international level, do not recognize that the challenge for disaster risk reduction in the region is to understand and include the root causes and identifying the risk drivers related to territorial planning, environmental management, poverty, public investment and bad governance (Lavell 2017). This is one of the main reasons why the notion of "natural disasters" in the sense of "Acts of God," excluding the human socio-natural entanglement, is so pervasive in some scientific and political discourses in the region and beyond.

When it comes to disaster management, the Caribbean is a special case in the Americas with a very individual set of geographically and historically grown vulnerabilities. Apart from being, for example, more strongly exposed to hurricanes than the U.S. or Central American Gulf coast states, small island states are additionally faced with the problem of limited evacuation options, mobility, and resources for recovery. The Caribbean states' much later independence from their European colonial "mother lands" than the continental Latin American states has played a large role in the region's capacity to respond to and to manage disaster impacts. Until 1984, when the Pan-Caribbean Disasters Preparedness and Prevention Project (PCDPPP) was founded, disaster management was dependent entirely on international initiative and private donors. However, as the PCDPPP was sponsored mainly by U.S. and other international development agencies (→ Development, II/6), patterns of quasi-colonial dependence did not change greatly (Thompson 2010, 27). Only after the widespread destruction of Hurricane Hugo in 1989 did the Caribbean Community (CARICOM) start moving and founded the Caribbean Disaster and Emergency Response Agency (CDERA) with sixteen member states in 1991 (Kirton 2013, 6). Though institutional development was slow during the 1990s, CDERA was a step away from the dependence on development and international aid. In 2010, CDERA was renamed to Caribbean Disaster and Emergency Management Agency (CDEMA) in order to reflect a more encompassing approach, rather than merely responding to disasters after the fact. Though CDEMA is still largely funded by international aid, the institution has evolved since its foundation in 1991 gaining local and regional trust for handling the rising number of extreme events that have occurred in the Caribbean in the course of the last two decades.

With regard to disaster insurance, the Caribbean had its "last-straw moment" after the particularly active hurricane season of 2004 that had also left a mark on the U.S. Gulf coast states. In its aftermath, CARICOM heads of government approached the World Bank and requested improved access to catastrophe insurance. As a consequence, the Caribbean Catastrophe Risk Insurance Facility (CCRIF) was set up in 2007 (Bohle 2018; Ghesquiere, Mahul, Forni and Gartley 2006, 2). It is the world's first multi-country insurance risk pool and the first insurance instrument that operates with parametric policies. The latter release funds based on the assessment of the strength of the extreme event rather than on loss assessments and hence provide liquidity much more rapidly than traditional disaster insurance policies. With regard to Inter-American and global transfers, CCRIF has expanded its portfolio since 2014 to include Central American countries such as Nicaragua in 2016 and the multi-state risk pool model has since been adopted by other regions such as the African Union and the Pacific Islands Forum (The Economist 2017).

Conclusion

Clearly, the understanding of what "disasters" are, how to interpret them and react to them was and is culturally specific, but in the Americas was strongly influenced by colonial history (→ Colonial Rule, I/5). While the pre-Columbian mythological landscape and repositories of local environmental knowledge and science were likely as variegated as the many different peoples that inhabited both continents and the Caribbean archipelago, this multiplicity ended with the mass death of indigenous peoples (→ I/11) after European conquest (→ Conquest and Colonization, II/7). One effect of what Charles Mann called the "homogenocene" that started with the European "discovery" of the Americas (Mann 2011) (→ Colonial Exchange, I/6), was also that of spreading the Christian peccatogenic and providentialist interpretations of "natural" calamities across the continent (→ Religion and Missionizing, I/17) and raising specific legal structures of disaster relief in their wake. Indigenous environmental knowledge about extreme events such as hurricanes, earthquakes and floods, was relied on by early European colonists in all parts of North, South, Central America, and the Caribbean, and was subsequently incorporated in Europe's emerging scientific practice (→ Postcolonialism, I/38). In an almost circular motion, anthropogenic climate change (→ II/30) now has climate researchers, anthropologists, and social scientists from the Global North, and particularly from the Global South (García-Acosta 2017b), interested in recovering local environmental knowledge of indigenous peoples of the Americas (and other world regions) in order to help solve the unprecedented challenges facing humanity (Kronik and Verner 2010).

In Canada and the USA, modern disaster management institutions have evolved in the context of state-formation (→ Nation and State Building, I/16) of democratic, free market-based "first-world" states, which makes them structurally different from disaster management institutions in the Caribbean, Mexico, South, and Central America. Caribbean island states and the countries of South and Central America gained independence from European colonial centers much later (→ Independence Movements, I/10) and in the international political hierarchy only as "third-world" countries, where disaster management often came from the West in the form of development aid (→ Development, II/6). The economic dependence of those states on "first-world" states was thus perpetuated. This situation is in many (although perhaps subtler) ways ongoing, as global financial hubs that back disaster insurance programs and instruments such as catastrophe bonds are still concentrated and administered in the Global North.

With regard to Inter-American and global entanglements, it is also worth noticing that the structures of global climate politics, by dint of being centered in the United Nations through the UNFCCC, are closely tied to those of development politics (Mazower 2012). In other words, with the increase of natural extreme events that are already occurring due to the ongoing anthropogenic climate change (→ II/30), and that are affecting regions such as the Caribbean and Latin America disproportionally, global climate policy is gaining importance. The latter, however, is still piggy-backing on erstwhile colonial political structures, which makes for the paradoxical situation that the Global North – the main causal agent in global warming – is now telling countries of the Global South – mainly impacted by global warming and its new disasters – how to adapt to this new situation (Adamson, Hannaford and Rohland 2018, 201).

Works cited

Adamson, George, Matthew J. Hannaford, and Eleonora Rohland. 2018. "Re-Thinking the Present: The Role of a Historical Focus in Climate Change Adaptation Research." *Global Environmental Change* 48: 195–205.

Alberola Roma, Armando. 2015. "Tiempo, clima y enfermedad en la prensa española de la segunda mitad del siglo XVIII. Diarios meteorológicos y crónicas de desastres en el Memorial Literario." *El Argonauta Español* 12: 2–25.

Anderson, Mark D. 2011. *Disaster Writing: The Cultural Politics of Catastrophe in Latin America. New World Studies*. Charlottesville: University of Virginia Press.

Anonymus. 2008. *Anales de Cuauhtitlán. Noticias históricas de México y sus contornos*. ed. and trans. José Fernando Ramírez, Faustino Galicia Chimalpopoca, Gumersindo Mendoza, and Felipe Sánchez Solís, Mexico: I. Escalante. Orig. pub. 1885.

Arber, Edward, Richard Eden, Pietro Martire D Anghiera, and Sebastian Münster. 1895. *The First Three English Books on America [? 1511–1555]*. Westminster: A. Constable and co.

Bankoff, Greg. 2003. *Cultures of Disaster: Society and Natural Hazard in the Philippines*. London: Routledge Curzon.

Bastian, Dawn E. and Judy K. Mitchell. 2004. *Handbook of Native American Mythology. Vol. 2, Handbooks of World Mythology*. Santa Barbara, CA: ABC-CLIO.

Bea, Keith. 2007. "The Formative Years: 1950–1978." In *Emergency Management. The American Experience, 1900–2010*, ed. Claire B. Rubin, 83–113. Boca Raton, Florida: CRC Press.

Blanton, Dennis B. 2003. "The Weather is Fine: Wish You Were Here, Because I'm The Last One Alive. 'Learning' the Environment in the English New World Colonies." In *Colonization of Unfamiliar Landscapes. The Archaeology of Adaptation*, eds. Marcy Rockman, and James Steele., 190–200. New York: Routledge.

Bohle, Johannes. 2018. *Hurrikan-Riskscapes. Die Gouvernementalität von Risiko in der Karibik am Beispiel des Hurrikans 'Dean.'* Bielefeld: PhD Thesis, Bielefeld University.

Casas, Bartolomé de las, Feliciano Ramírez de Arellano Fuensanta Del Valle, and José León Sancho Rayón. 1875. *Historia de las Indias*. 5 vol. Madrid: Imprenta de Miguel Ginesta. Orig pub. 1575.

Caviedes, César. 2001. *El Niño in History. Storming through the Ages*. Gainesville, FL: University Press of Florida.

Colten, Craig E. 2007. "Environmental Justice in a Landscape of Tragedy." *Technology in Society* 29, no. 2: 173–179.

Dauber, Michele Lenore Landis. 2003. *Helping Ourselves. Disaster Relief and the Origins of the American Welfare State*. PhD Thesis. Evanston, IL: Northwestern University.

Dauber, Michele Lenore Landis. 2013. *The Sympathetic State. Disaster Relief and the Origins of the American Welfare State*. Chicago: University of Chicago Press.

Dawdy, Shannon Lee. 2008. *Building the Devil's Empire. French Colonial New Orleans*. Chicago: University of Chicago Press.

Dulles, Foster Rhea. 1950. *The American Red Cross: A History*. New York: Harper & Brothers.

Editorial Team of the Economist. 2017. "Hurricane Irma: The Caribbean's Pioneering Form of Disaster Insurance." *The Economist* online edition, September 2017. www.economist.com/news/americas/21729003-too-little-not-too-late-caribbeans-pioneering-form-disaster-insurance.

Edwards, Paul. 2010. *A Vast Machine. Computer Models, Climate Data, and the Politics of Global Warming*. Cambridge: MIT Press.

Farrar, John. 1818. "An Account of the Violent and Destructive Storm of 23rd September 1815." *Memoirs of the American Academy of Arts and Science* 4, no. 1: 93–97.

Favier, René and Anne-Marie Granet-Abisset. 2009. "Society and Natural Risks in France, 1500–2000. Changing Historical Perspectives." In *Natural Disasters, Cultural Responses. Case Studies Toward a Global Environmental History*, eds. Christof Mauch and Christian Pfister, 103–136. Lanahm: Rowman & Littlefield.

Fernández de Oviedo, Gonzalo Y Valdés. 1535. *Historia general y natural de las Indias. Vol. 19, Early Modern Spain*. London: King's College London.

Gall, Melanie, Bryan. J. Boruff, and Susan L. Cutter. 2007. "Assessing Flood Hazard Zones in the Absence of Digital Floodplain Maps: A Comparison of Alternative Approaches." *Natural Hazards Review* 8, no. 1: 1–21.

García-Acosta, Virginia. 2017a. "Divinidad y desastres. Interpretaciones, manifestaciones y respuestas." *Revista de Historia Moderna. Anales de la Universidad de Alicante* 35: 46–82.

———. 2017b. "Building on the Past. Disaster Risk Reduction Including Climate Change Adaptation in the Longue Durée." In *The Routledge Handbook of Disaster Risk Reduction Including Climate Change Adaptation*, eds. Ilan Kelman, Jessica Mercer and J. C. Gaillard, 203–213. New York: Routledge.

García-Acosta, Virginia, Juan Manuel Pérez, and América Molina. 2003. *Desastres agrícolas en México. Catálogo histórico*, Vol. 1 *Épocas prehispánica y colonial (958–1822)*. Mexico City: Fondo de Cultura Económica/CIESAS.

Ghesquiere, Francis, Oliver Mahul, Marc Forni, and Ross Gartley. 2006. "Caribbean Catastrophe Risk Insurance Facility: A Solution to The Short-Term Liquidity Needs of Small Island States in the Aftermath of Natural Disasters." *The World Bank*: http://siteresources.worldbank.org/PROJECTS/Resources/Catastrophicriskinsurancefacility.pdf

Groh, Dieter, Michael Kempe, and Franz Mauelshagen. 2003. "Einleitung. Naturkatastrophen - wahrgenommen, gedeutet, dargestellt." In *Naturkatastrophen. Beiträge zu ihrer Deutung, Wahrnehmung und Darstellung in Text und Bild von der Antike bis ins 20. Jahrhundert*, eds. Dieter Groh, Michael Kempe and Franz Mauelshagen, 11–33. Tübingen: Gunter Narr Verlag.

Grove, Richard and George Adamson. 2018. *El Niño in World History*. London: Palgrave McMillan.

Hightower, Henry C. and Michel Coutu. 1996. "Coordinating Emergency Management: A Canadian Example." In *Disaster Management in the U.S. and Canada. The Politics, Policymaking, Administration and Analysis of Emergency Management*, eds. Richard T. Sylves and William L. Waugh, 69–98. Springfield: Charles C. Thomas Publisher.

Hoad, T. F. 1993. *The Concise Oxford Dictionary of English Etymology*. Oxford: Oxford University Press.

International Federation of the Red Cross and Red Crescent Societies (IFRC). 2018. "What Is a Disaster?" www.ifrc.org/en/what-we-do/disaster-management/about-disasters/what-is-a-disaster/

Johnson, Sherry. 2011. *Climate and Catastrophe in Cuba and the Atlantic World in the Age of Revolution. Envisioning Cuba*. Chapel Hill: University of North Carolina Press.

Juneja, Monica and Franz Mauelshagen. 2007. "Disasters and Pre-industrial Societies: Historiographic Trends and Comparative Perspectives." *The Medieval History Journal* 10, no. 1/2: 1–31.

Keller, Edward A., Duane E. DeVecchio, and Robert H. Blodgett. 2015. *Natural Hazards. Earth's Processes as Hazards, Disasters, and Catastrophes*. 4th ed. Upper Saddle River, NJ: Pearson.

Kirton, Mark. 2013. "Caribbean Regional Disaster Response and Management Mechanisms: Prospects and Challenges." *The Brookings-LSE Project on Internal Displacement*. www.brookings.edu/research/caribbean-regional-disaster-response-and-management-mechanisms-prospects-and-challenges/

Konrad, Herman W. 1985. "Fallout of the Wars of the Chacs: The Impact of Hurricanes and Implications for Pre-Hispanic Quintana Roo Maya Processes." In *Status, Structure, and Stratification: Current Archaeological Reconstructions*, eds. Marc Thompson, Maria Teresa Garcia, and F. J. Kense, 321–330. Calgary: University of Calgary.

Kronik, Jakob, and Dorte Verner. 2010. *Indigenous Peoples and Climate Change in Latin America and the Caribbean*. Washington, D.C.: The World Bank.

Kupperman, Karen Ordahl. 1979. "Apathy and Death in Early Jamestown." *The Journal of American History* 66, no. 1: 24–40.

Kupperman, Karen Ordahl. 2007. *The Jamestown Project*. Cambridge: Belknap Press of Harvard University Press.

Landa, Fray Diego de. 1966. *Relación de las cosas de Yucatán*. 9ª. Ed.. México: Editorial Porrúa.

Lavell, Allan. 2017. "Preface." In *Reduction of Vulnerability to Disasters: From Knowledge to Action*, eds. Victor Marchezini, Ben Wisner, Luciana R. Londe, Silvia M. Saito, 9–14. São Carlos, Brazil: RiMa Editora.

Lavell, Allan and Alonso Brenes, eds. 2008. *ENOS. Variabilidad Climática y el Riesgo de Desastre en las Américas: Proceso, Patrones, Gestión*. San José de Costa Rica: LA RED/Oxfam/FLACSO/IAI. www.desenredando.org/public/libros/2008/enosvar/.

Lavell, Allan and Tania López-Marrero. 2014. "Disaster Risk Management in Latin America and the Caribbean. Four Decades of Evolution and Change, 1970–2010." In *Disaster Management. International Lessons in Risk Reduction, Response and Recovery*, eds. Alejandro López-Carresi, Maureen Fordham, Ben Wisner, Ilan Kelman and J. C. Gaillard, 229–247. London: Routledge.

Lopez Medel, Tomás. 1990. *De los Tres Elementos. Tratado Sobre la Naturaleza y el Hombre del Nuevo Mundo*. Ed. Berta Ares Quejia, Madrid: Quinto Centenario.

Ortíz, Fernando. 1947. *Cuban counterpoint: tobacco and sugar*. New York: Alfred A. Knopf.

Padilla Lozoya, Raymundo. 2016. "El surgimiento de una sociedad vulnerable y sus respuestas ante amenazas naturales: San José del Cabo, Baja California Sur, siglos xvi al xviii." In *Clima, desastres y convulsiones sociales en España e Hispanoamérica, siglos xvii-xx*, eds. Luis Alberto Arrioja Diaz and Armando Alberola Roma, 243–268. Michoacán, Alicante: El Colegio de Michoacán, Universidad de Alicante.

Malaizé, B., P. Bertran, P. Carbonel, D. Bonnissent, K. Charlier, D. Galop, D. Imbert, N. Serrand, Ch. Stouvenot, and C. Pujol. 2011. "Hurricanes and Climate in the Caribbean During the Past 3700 Years BP." *The Holocene* 21, no. 6: 911–924.

Mann, Charles C. 2011. *1493: How Europe's Discovery of the Americas Revolutionized Trade, Ecology and Life on Earth*. London: Granta.

Massard-Guilbaud, Geneviève. 2002. "Introduction: the Urban Catastrophe – Challenge to the social, economic, and cultural order of the city" In *Cities and Catastrophes: Coping With Emergency in European History*, ed. Geneviève Massard-Guilbaud, Harold L. Platt, and Dieter Schott, 9–42. Frankfurt am Main: Peter Lang.

Mauelshagen, Franz. 2011. *Wunerkammer auf Papier. Die Wickiana zwischen Reformation und Volksglaube*. Epfendorf: Bibliotheca Academica Verlag.

———. 2015. "Defining Catastrophe." In *Catastrophe and Catharsis. Perspectives on Disasters and Redemption in German Culture and Beyond*, eds. Katharina Gerstenberger and Tanja Nusser, 172–190. Rochester: Camden House.

Mazower, Mark. 2012. *Governing the World: The History of an Idea*. London: Penguin Books.

Mulcahy, Matthew. 2018. "Making Sense of Disasters in Early America – And Today." *The American Historian* 15: 37–42.

Oliver-Smith, Anthony. 1994. "Peru's Five Hundred Year Earthquake: Vulnerability in Historical Context." In *Disasters, Development and Environment*, ed. Ann Varley, 31–48. Chichester: John Wiley & Sons.

———. 1996. "Anthropological Research on Hazards and Disasters." *Annual Review of Anthropology* 25: 303–328.

———. 2002. "Theorizing Disaster. Nature, Power, and Culture." In *Catastrophe and Culture*, eds. Susanna M. Hoffmann and Anthony Oliver-Smith, 23–47. Santa, FE: School of American Research Press.

Pérez, Louis A. 2001. *Winds of Change. Hurricanes and the Transformation of Nineteenth-Century Cuba*. Chapel Hill: University of North Carolina Press.

Redfield, William Charles. 1832. "Hurricane of August 1831." *American Journal of Science and Arts* 21: 191–193.

Rockman, Marcy. 2010. "New World with a New Sky: Climatic Variability, Environmental Expectations, and the Historical Period Colonization of Eastern North Carolina." *Historical Archaeology* 44: 4–20.

Rohland, Eleonora. 2016. "Hurricanes on the Gulf Coast: Environmental Knowledge and Science in Louisiana, the Caribbean, and the U.S., 1722–1900." In *Works of Nature: Global Scientific Practice during the Age of Revolutions*, eds. Daniel Rood and Patrick Manning, 38–53. Pittsburgh: University of Pittsburgh Press.

———. 2018. *Changes in the Air. Hurricanes in New Orleans from 1718 to the Present. Environmental History: International Perspectives 15*. eds. Dolly Jorgensen Christof Mauch, David Moon and Helmut Trischler, Oxford and New York: Berghahn Books.

Rohletter, Wylene. 2011. "Canada." In *Encyclopedia of Disaster Relief*, ed. K. Bradley Penuel and Matthew Statler, 43–45. Los Angeles: Sage.

Rostorowski, María. 2002. *Pachacamac y el Señor de los Milagros*. Obras completas, vol. 2. Lima: Instituto de Estudios Peruanos.

Schenk, Gerrit Jasper. 2007. "Historical Disaster Research: State of Research, Concepts, Methods and Case Studies." *Historical Social Research* 32, no. 3: 9–31.

Smith, Shawn R., Justin Brolley, James J. O'Brien, and Carissa A. Tartaglione. 2007. "ENSO's Impact on Regional U.S. Hurricane Activity." *Journal of Climate* 20: 1404–1414.

Sylves, Richard. 2007. "Budgeting for Emergency Management." In *Emergency Management: Principles and Practice for Local Government*, eds. William L. Waugh and Kathleen J. Tierney, 299–318. 2nd ed.. Washington, DC: ICMA Press.

Thompson, Denise. 2010. "Building Effectiveness in Multi-State Disaster Management Systems: The Case of the Caribbean Disaster and Emergency Response Agency." PhD Thesis, Pennsylvania State University.

Watson, Peter. 2013. *The Great Divide: Nature and Human Nature in the Old World and the New*. New York: Harper Perennial.

34
GEOPOLITICS

Mirko Petersen and Dorothea Wehrmann

Geopolitics is the struggle over hegemony in places and spaces. More specifically, geopolitics relates to the control of territory as well as to the representation of spaces and places and their interpretation, for instance, as "last frontiers" or "military arenas" (→ Military, II/37). From a geopolitical perspective, the sovereignty over territory and the strategic relevance ascribed to places and spaces impacts political relationships. As a theoretical concept, geopolitics is examined in a cross-disciplinary field of area studies, political science, and political geography. In mass media (→ Cultural Industries, III/27), strategy and policy papers the term geopolitics is mostly used in a "classical" sense, meaning that it relates to the strategic aims of states (→ Nation State, II/38) ascribed to spaces and places (→ Political Communication, II/42). In this regard, the purpose of the concept has been discussed as being controversial because of its historical connection to colonialism (→ Conquest and Colonization, I/7) and imperialism and particularly due to its use in Nazi Germany. The approach of Critical Geopolitics, on the other hand, expands the understanding of geopolitics when considering political and cultural productions as well as the perception of geographical assumptions (such as the demarcation of national territories by borders). In critical geopolitical studies thus, a wider range of actors outside the military and political elites is taken into consideration as well as the distinct discourses to which they contribute (for the differences between Classical and Critical Geopolitics, see Ó Tuathail 1996, 21–74; for a short overview, see Dodds et al., 2013, 1–3).

The term geopolitics was first used by the Swedish political scientist Rudolf Kjellén (1864–1922), a student of the German geographer Friedrich Ratzel (1844–1904). His ideas formed what is known today as the perspective of Classical Geopolitics which evolved in the 19th and 20th centuries in Europe and the United States. In addition to the former authors, Classical Geopolitics was predominantly coined by the U.S. Navy Admiral Alfred Thayer Mahan (1840–1917), the British geographer Halford John Mackinder (1861–1947), and the German geographer Karl Haushofer (1869–1946) (Steinmetz 2012, 800). From the perspective of Classical Geopolitics, according to which the power of a state relates to its geographic location and control over territory (→ Land, II/15), the world regions are primarily classified in view of their geostrategic importance. In Mackinder's famous Heartland Theory ("The Geographical Pivot of History," first published in 1904) for example, Eastern Europe is considered a "Pivot Area," which, if controlled by a political entity, would facilitate the domination of other world areas. While Mackinder emphasized the significance of the Eurasian land mass, Mahan accentuated the control of the sea as the key vehicle for global hegemony (→ Atlantic, I/3). The regime of Adolf Hitler used the ideas of Kjellén and Haushofer as a justification for the aggressive German expansionism, arguing that it was the need of the Aryan race to persecute peoples of inferior races (→ I/39) in order to gain and defend their "Lebensraum" (living space).

After World War II "geopolitics" was regarded as a Nazi expression and seemed somehow outdated. The term disappeared from political and media discourses "although the ideas were still reflected in the thinking of the time" (Dodds et al., 2013, 4). As such, the European models of continental expansion were partly replaced by a "nonterritorial" strategy of the global hegemon, that is to say the United States. This strategy was rather marked by indirect control than by permanent occupation of territory (Steinmetz 2012, 803). In the 1970s, in his function as U.S. Secretary of State, Henry Kissinger (1923-) then repopularized the term geopolitics in political debates (Ó Tuathail 1996, 58). The term was later also adopted by the U.S. policy advisors Zbigniew Brzezinski (1928–2017) and Samuel P. Huntington (1927–2008). Brzezinki's book "The Grand Chessboard" from 1997, a sort of update of Mackinder's theories for the post-Cold War era, and especially Huntington's controversial work on the alleged "Clash of Civilizations" from 1996 encouraged many debates on 21st-century geopolitics.

New approaches: critical and radical geopolitics

The approach of Classical Geopolitics has been facing different academic and political contestations, especially since the late 1960s. In the context of the Vietnam War, a group of politically engaged geographers started to question "the imperial heritage of modern geography" (Ó Tuathail 1996, 57) and intended to transform their discipline. In this new academic movement called Radical Geography, issues like social justice, poverty (→ Social Inequality, II/20), underdevelopment (→ Development, II/6), environment (→ Nature, II/39), and gender (→ Gender Identities, I/28) have been brought to the center of attention (Mercille 2013, 129). While Radical Geography mainly developed in the Anglo-American realm, the Algerian War and later the Vietnam War triggered a new critical approach to geography in France. The main focus of this new French school of geopolitics was warfare and its connection with geopolitical knowledge. The school's most important representative was the geographer Yves Lacoste. His analysis of the Vietnam War not only received attention in France, but also in the United States. In 1976, Lacoste and his peers founded their own journal which they named *Hérodote* (Mamadouh 1998, 239–240).

In reaction to the political (re-)application of the term, in the early 1980s, the critical academic debates on global strategy and geopolitical practices expanded. Scholars associated with journals like *Political Geography*, *Antidote*, and the aforementioned *Hérodote* started to rethink the concept of geopolitics. These debates encouraged the formation of the approach of Critical Geopolitics. This school of thought amplified the already existing debates in the Anglo-American realm and France and became a domain of research in the disciplines of Political Geography and International Relations. In drawing on the Linguistic, Spatial, and Postcolonial turns, advocates of Critical Geopolitics are known for refusing to understand geography as a "natural, non-discursive phenomenon which is separate from ideology and outside politics" (Agnew and Ó Tuathail 1992, 192). Instead they emphasize that "[g]eography is about power" (Ó Tuathail 1996, 1) and consider this power as being enforced by political logics of territorial representation that determine the concept of order drawn upon. Predominantly coined by the geographers Gearóid Ó Tuathail (1962–), Simon Dalby (1958–), and John Agnew (1949–) Critical Geopolitics accordingly scrutinizes "geographical representations and practices" (Dalby and Ó Tuathail 1998, 2) and sheds light on the development and relations between geopolitical lines of argumentation and worldviews (Albert et al., 2003, 537). Critical Geopolitics scholars thereby try to contribute to a better understanding of how political power over territory is constructed, for instance, in terms of language (→ I/13) and cartography. In order to trace how a particular understanding of spaces and places evolves that determines specific perceptions of world order, Critical Geopolitics scholars differentiate between discourses shaped by political actors (practical geopolitics), strategic institutions (formal geopolitics), and mass media (popular geopolitics, Dodds 2014, 42; Ó Tuathail 2006, 8) (→ Media Flows, III/35). More explicitly, for example, Critical Geopolitics reflects critically on the use of the binary scheme of "Us" vs. "Them" (that is to say the representation of "self" and "other") as well as on geopolitical expressions such as "East," "West," and "Third World" that are used as instruments to construct a "simple model of the world, which can then be used to advise and inform foreign and security policy making" (Dodds 2014, 5) (→ Foundational Discourses). Similar to complexity-reducing cartographic maps, the production of imaginaries (Buitrago et al., 2016; Epple and Kramer 2016) of spaces and places is always based on selectivity (What is/is not depicted? What differences and similarities are considered/are not considered?) (→ Silencing) and as such imaginaries are understood as being influenced by unequal power relations, as something that has been constructed to enforce political and social order, as powerful instruments to shape one's view. Also, in this regard and with the growing significance and visibility of global environmental changes, Critical Geopolitics studies increasingly address the geopolitics linked to the representation of environmental concerns. Particularly this focus on the strategic use of geopolitical constructions (imaginaries) to legitimize policy decisions and actions distinguishes Critical Geopolitics from other constructivist approaches.

The concept of Critical Geopolitics, however, has also provoked criticism. Particularly in epistemological terms, for instance, criticism relates to the incompatibility of action-theoretical considerations and poststructuralist concepts of actors. More explicitly it is also argued that deconstructions of geopolitical interpretations lead to re-constructions, to new geopolitical narratives, which must be reflected and disclosed as such (Albert et al., 2003, 546–547; Dodds 2005, 3). Thus, similar to other critical studies, scholars related to Critical Geopolitics need to reflect that they are never detached observers, that is to say they can "know the world only through the conceptual schemas provided by our culture and languages" (Ó Tuathail 2006, 6). Critical Geopolitics studies are moreover criticized for focusing mostly on discourses either at the national or regional levels and for not considering both. Also, the categorization of actors into political elites and intellectuals of statecraft has been criticized as being rather essentialist (Reuber 2012, 169).

Another approach which contests the premises promoted by the concept of Classical Geopolitics is called Radical Geopolitics. It has its roots in the abovementioned Radical Geography which emerged in the late 1960s. Radical Geopolitics is a subfield of Radical Geography. It has a Marxist background and mainly focuses on political-economic factors in the study of places and spaces, be it in international relations or in politics. In Radical Geopolitics one can find influences by a broad range of scholars from different disciplines. Among its most important intellectual reference points are the works of the Marxist geographer David Harvey, especially his work on "The New Imperialism" (Harvey 2003). Advocates of Radical Geopolitics criticize the poststructuralist approach of Critical Geopolitics for highlighting discourses too much while neglecting "to identify the causes of political events and their crucial political-economic aspects" (Mercille 2013, 129). Radical

Geopolitics might constitute an important supplement to – or even an advancement of – the better-known Critical Geopolitics as long as it can circumvent the danger of presenting economic determinist interpretations of geography.

Geopolitics from the colonial conquest to the Cold War

Geopolitics in the Americas have a special history. The literary theorist Walter Mignolo points out that "[b]efore 1492, the Americas were not on anybody's map" and that "'America' … was an invention forged in the process of European colonial history and the consolidation and expansion of Western world views and institutions" (Mignolo 2005, 2) (→ America, I/2). After the Iberian colonization of the Americas (→ Conquest and Colonization, I/7), this space was conceptualized as an extension of Europe to another continent by European intellectuals. In this way, they constructed an overarching imaginary of the Occident (Mignolo 2000, 58–59). The name America (or América) is the female version of the seafarer Américo Vespucci's first name. The female name as well as the female portrayal of the continent (in contrast to the male conquerors) "suggests that the colonial project is built upon an implicit gender dimension" (Roth 2014, 140) (→ Gender Identities, I/28).

Ever since the invasion and invention of America, the definition of geopolitical entities in this part of the world was caught in a dialectics of outside interference and phases of internal integration and fragmentation. In the 18th and 19th century, North American settlers were able to form and expand the United States of America while the scattered independence movements (→ I/10) of the continent's southern part did not lead to the formation of a larger political power block. The formal independence from European colonizers and the foundation of nation-states (→ Nation and State Building, I/16) took place under the control of white settlers who wanted to prevent indigenous and black participation in "their" new political entities (Quijano and Wallerstein 1992, 551) (→ Ethnicity, I/25; Indigeneity, I/31).

The ongoing dependence of Latin America from Western Europe was to a large extent replaced by the U.S. domination of the whole hemisphere at the turn from the 19th to the 20th century, especially since the Spanish-U.S.-American-Cuban War of 1898 (Kaltmeier 2014, 175). Geopolitical interventions of the U.S. in the Americas served the purpose of obtaining and later maintaining its leadership in global affairs.

In the 19th and 20th centuries, U.S. foreign policy was marked by the so-called Monroe Doctrine from 1823, according to which the U.S. regarded any interference in the Americas by European nations as acts of aggression that would affect the entire sphere of the Americas and therefore require U.S. actions (→ Pan-Americanism, II/40). Later the 1904-Roosevelt-Corollary added to the justification of U.S. meddling (→ II/36) in Latin America. The subsequent territorial expansion of the U.S., as well as various political and military interventions in Central and South America, also followed geostrategic motives, such as obtaining economic benefits arising from agricultural resources in the so-called Central-American "Banana Republics" (in corporation with the infamous United Fruits Company) (→ Transnational Corporations, II/23; Global Commodity Chains, II/12). The same can be said about the formation of partnerships with regimes in Latin America and the Caribbean, among them extremely repressive military dictatorships (→ Authoritarianism, II/25), that served the purpose of containing alleged communist influences in the region during the Cold War era (→ Socialism, I/42).

Similar to the European and U.S.-American plans to dominate Latin America, the categories of Classical Geopolitics can also be observed in the thinking of Latin American political leaders. Sometimes the concepts of Ratzel, Haushofer, and Mackinder were directly adopted. The latter's category of the heartland, for instance, is used by Brazilian militaries, diplomats, politicians, and academics to describe their country and to develop strategies for it (Ostos and Del Pilar 2011). The use of Classical Geopolitical categories can be observed already in the 1930s and 1940s in the case of Argentine militaries (Child 1979, 95), but geopolitical theories flourished above all during the heyday of military dictatorships in the region (→ Military, II/37), in the 1960s and 1970s. The most prominent example was Chilean dictator Augusto Pinochet who was the author of different geopolitical writings. Pinochet was especially attracted to the idea of an "organic state" as described by Ratzel and Haushofer. He justified brutal repression against "subversives" by portraying it as a military rescue of the "sacred body" of the Chilean nation from terrible diseases (Sidaway et al., 2013, 170–171; see also Child 1979, 102–103).

In Latin America, geopolitics were and still are often interrelated with U.S. politics. The very name "Latin America" was established in the middle of the 19th century by political elites to form a loose bond of states against the expansionism of the United States toward the South (→ Interventionism). These elites tried to define Latin America as white (→ Whiteness, I/46), anti-imperial and democratic (→ Democracy, II/32) (Gobat 2013). While the understanding of what Latin America might be and which countries and peoples should be part of it has changed over time, it was especially the anti-imperial – or in more general terms anti-interventionist – tone that became a lasting element in the intents of defining Latin America, for example, in the context of the Cuban Revolution of 1959 (→ Revolution, II/44), the construction of the Bolivarian Republic by Hugo Chávez's government in Venezuela since 1998 and in many of the different projects of regional integration (→ II) (MERCOSUR, UNASUR, ALBA, CELAC) since the 1990s. Varying concepts of Latin America show, as Michel Gobat points out, "that geopolitical entities [...] are historical constructs forged in the crucible of political struggle" and that these "entities are anything but static" (2013, 1375).

Contemporary geopolitical developments and debates in the Americas

Already visible in the popular ideas summarized as Manifest Destiny in the 19th century, a defining characteristic of the U.S. geopolitical culture in the 21st century is still observed to be "the idea that the United States values are universal ones, that America is an exceptional country because it is the 'homeland of freedom'" (Ó Tuathail 2006, 27). In the recent past, especially the "War on Terror" on the global scene (→ Security, II/45), the negotiation of several trade agreements in the Americas (e.g. NAFTA, DR-CAFTA, the attempt of Free Trade Zone for the Americas (FTAA) and bilateral agreements with Chile, Peru, Panama, and Columbia) (→ Regional Integration, II/18) as well as the election of President Donald Trump, his "America First" campaign and the underestimation of climate change (→ II/30) in his polices has empowered the imaginary of the U.S. as a geopolitical agent driven by economic interests.

Similarly, however, also the geopolitical interests of its North American neighbor Canada have been closely entangled with its economic interests. In the context of the Americas, this has been especially visible since 1989, when the Canadian government started to promote the establishment of trade agreements with Central and South American countries. These agreements are often related to extensive mining activities carried out by Canadian enterprises, for instance in Mexico, Honduras, and Chile (Daudelin 2003) (→ Extractivism, II/9). Also in view of the rapidly changing Arctic, with the growing significance ascribed to climate change, Canada has often been criticized in newspaper reporting for prioritizing its economic interests in an "opening Arctic" over environmental concerns. On a sub-national level, in Alaska as well as in Canada's Northern provinces, geopolitical conflicts relating to the use of land and resources arose already in the 1970s between indigenous peoples and the respective federal state that resulted in land claim agreements (→ Land, II/15) and settlement acts. The more recent formulation of Arctic policies by the U.S. and Canada illustrate that interests of both countries in the Arctic region have grown, which are also inspired by the aims to defend sovereignty claims in the "Far North." Overall, these examples show that geopolitics is not only shaped by states but also influenced by the interests of non-state actors, such as representatives of industries and indigenous peoples (→ I/31).

Until today Latin America is of crucial strategic importance for the United States because of the richness in natural resources (Borón 2013, 99–112) and the network of military bases installed in the region (Borón 2013, 247–256). However, Latin America's relations to other important states on the global scene of the 21st century, like China and Russia, and the re-evaluation of ties to the United States and Europe have raised new questions about external dependencies and the region's role in the world.

The geographic position of the respective country, moreover, has been playing a key role in the strategic considerations made by political decision makers in Latin America. The main foci of Brazilian geopolitics were and still are the use and the protection of its large territory as well as its long Atlantic coast in terms of trade and security (→ II/45). The Argentine geopolitical thinking is mainly concerned with containing Brazils influence and its alliance with the United States as well as concerns over the South Atlantic (→ Atlantic, I/3). Different from these two most powerful South American states, Venezuela (among others) is more concerned with its position in Central America and the Caribbean.

Despite the impact of this strategic thinking, the struggles over places and spaces in the Americas are not limited to the plans of state actors and the fights over borders but also imply the involvement of broader parts of society for which life and well-being are at stake in geopolitical conflicts. The confrontations are not necessarily between different states; often they are rather about the way certain spaces are put to use. Similar to the North American Arctic, for Latin America this is especially important because of its vast reserves of oil, gas (→ Energy, II/7), water, important minerals and precious metals. The exploitation of these resources raises crucial societal questions related to territorial control, profits, development models (→ Development, II/6), environmental harms (→ Environmental Justice, II/8) and effects on local populations.

In the Americas, new forms of resistance as well as indigenous concepts of self-determination and autonomy started to question the standard understandings of space (→ Social Movements, I/41; Indigeneity, I/31). Moreover, alternative uses of spaces and places challenge "modern" geopolitical imagination which is closely tied to the nation-state (→ II/38) and its administrative, political, and economic categories (Preciado Coronado and Uc 2010, 85). An explicit example for this is the settlement agreements with indigenous peoples negotiated in Alaska and particularly in Nunavut which exemplify that the right given to indigenous peoples to control territory also empowered their say in policy making on the domestic but moreover on the regional level as the unique Permanent Participant-status given to indigenous organizations in the Arctic Council shows. In addition, especially since the popularization of the indigenous concept of *buen vivir* ("good living") in the early 21st century, classical notions of development (from the political right to the left) which often went hand in hand with the exploitation of nature, have been criticized, most intensely in Bolivia and Ecuador (Borón 2013, 133–160) (→ Nature, II/39). So far, these debates have not led to many concrete political changes on the national and regional levels. Latin American development strategies are still mainly footed on resource extractivism (→ II/9). The conflicts resulting from this strategy remain an integral part of Latin American geopolitics.

The importance of geopolitics as an analytical category

After the end of the Cold War, the optimism of an economic globalization which would lead to a conflict-free "flat world" without borders were widespread. Since at least the terroristic attacks of September 11, 2001 and the U.S.-led "War on Terror," this optimism has been subdued and geopolitical thinking has come back to the forefront of global politics and is now widely discussed in academia (Steinmetz 2012, 806–807; for a reflection on new forms of spatial separation, see Kaltmeier 2018, 93–109). The canonical authors of Classical Geopolitics like Halford Mackinder are again referred to frequently, not only by their critics, but also "by commentators who seek to apply geopolitical lessons for today's 'strategic dilemmas'" (Sidaway et al., 2013, 165). The persistence of determinist geopolitical analyses reminds us of the importance of critical research in this field. Geopolitics and the imaginaries of world order attached to it need to be conceptualized as permanently renewed and contested social constructions.

Although some of the lessons of 20th-century geopolitics are taught again nowadays, new interpretative frames had to be developed for new global developments of the 21st century. The "War on Terror" and its global consequences made clearer than ever that geopolitics is not exclusively shaped and produced by states. The global financial crises of 2007–2008 as well as recent cyberspace attacks (e.g. affecting sensitive infrastructure management programs or spying) are other examples which show that geopolitics is increasingly codetermined by non-state actors and that one also needs to take "virtual" places and spaces into consideration when examining the scope of geopolitics. Gerard Ó Tuathail highlights an "interesting paradox" with regard to "conventional conceptions of geopolitics" which "on the one hand, [...] address power struggles between states very explicitly yet, on the other hand, [...] usually contain little reflection on the social structures of power within states, how these shape geopolitical discourse itself" (2006, 9). It is therefore misleading to look at states as monolithic blocks within certain borders in geopolitical analysis. Instead, the combination of formal, practical, and popular geopolitics should be considered an important factor in the strategic positioning of states.

The sociologist George Steinmetz identified seven areas in which the study of geopolitics is valuable today: the identification of imperial strategies, the analysis of "states and politics as shapers of space and territory," the detection of spatial concepts in international relations, a dialogue with the ideas of neo-historicism developed in German geopolitics before 1933, the avoidance of economic reductionism in social science, offering alternatives to geopolitical imaginaries formed by governments, and providing corrective arguments to descriptions of globalization as a process of spatial unbounding (2012, 816–818). In addition to Steinmetz's suggestions, one might add a few aspects which have to be taken into account in research on geopolitics in general, and with regard to the Americas in particular. On a global level, multiple places and spaces are influenced by geopolitics simultaneously, which also corresponds to the observable change of power distribution in the international system (e.g. the changing world order: from a U.S.-dominated unipolar to a multipolar and perhaps future non-polar international order as predicted by Haass 2008). Against this backdrop and in line with the argumentation promoted by global governance scholars, analyses have to be broadened and have to take international and intergovernmental organizations and non-state actors into consideration, whether they are non-place or placed-based actors. With regard to the Americas, this can mean too look at the variety of continental and regional organizations and their spatial conceptions (as suggested by Preciado Coronado and Uc 2010, 76–77). Furthermore, as new forms of intra- and interstate warfare and actions of paramilitaries exemplify, it is particularly noticeable how non-state security actors have turned into informal actors that influence geostrategic relations in the Americas, which should not be overlooked (→ Security, II/45). Last but not least, with the growing significance ascribed to global environmental changes (→ Climate Change, II/30), scholars focusing on geopolitics should also consider the role of multinational enterprises (→ Transnational Corporations, II/23), and their practices of resource extractivism (→ II/9) in the Americas.

Works cited

Agnew, John A. and Gearóid Ó Tuathail. 1992. "Geopolitics and Discourse. Practical Geopolitical Reasoning in American Foreign Policy." *Political Geography* 11.204: 190–204.

Albert, Mathias, Paul Reuber and Günter Wolkersdorfer. 2003. "Kritische Geopolitik." In: *Theorien der Internationalen Beziehungen: Eine Einführung*, eds. Siegfried Schieder and Manuela Spindler, 527–555. Opladen: Barbara Budrich.

Borón, Atilio A. 2013. *América Latina En la Geopolítica del Imperialismo*. Buenos Aires: Ediciones Luxemburg.

Brzezinski, Zbigniew. 1997. *The Grand Chessboard: American Primacy and Its Geostrategic Imperatives*. New York: Basic Books.

Buitrago, Clara, Mirko Petersen, Paul Matthias Tyrell and Dorothea Wehrmann. 2016. "Introduction. Geopolitical Imaginaries in the Americas." *Forum for Inter-American Research* 9.1: 4–18.

Child, John. 1979. "Geopolitical Thinking in Latin America." *Latin American Research Review* 14.2: 89–111.

Dalby, Simon and Gearóid Ó Tuathail 1998. "Introduction: Rethinking Geopolitics: Towards a Critical Geopolitics." In: *Rethinking Geopolitics*, eds. Simon Dalby and Gearóid Ó Tuathail, 1–15. London and New York: Routledge.

Daudelin, Jean. 2003. "Foreign Policy at the Fringe Canada and Latin America." *International Journal* 58.4: 637–666.

Dodds, Klaus. 2005. *Global Geopolitics: A Critical Introduction*. Harlow: Pearson.

———. 2014. *Geopolitics: A Very Short Introduction*. Oxford: Oxford University Press.

Dodds, Klaus, Merje Kuus and Joanne Sharp. 2013. "Introduction. Geopolitics and Its Critics." In: *The Ashgate Research Companion to Critical Geopolitics*, eds. Klaus Dodds, Merje Kuus and Joanne Sharp, 1–14. Farnham: Ashgate.

Epple, Angelika and Kirsten Kramer 2016. "Globalization, Imagination, Social Space: The Making of Geopolitical Imaginaries." *Forum for Inter-American Research* 9.1: 4–18.

Gobat, Michel. 2013. "The Invention of Latin America: A Transnational History of Anti-Imperialism, Democracy, and Race." *American Historical Review* 118.5: 1345–1375.

Haass, Richard N. 2008. "The Age of Nonpolarity." *Foreign Affairs* 87.3: 44–56.

Harvey, David. 2003. *The New Imperialism*. Oxford: Oxford University Press.

Huntington, Samuel P. 1996. *The Clash of Civilizations and the Remaking of World Order*. New York, NY: Simon and Schuster.

Kaltmeier, Olaf. 2014. "Inter-American Perspectives for the Rethinking of Area Studies." *Forum for Inter-American Research* 7.3: 171–182.

———. 2018. *Refeudalización: Desigualdad Social, Económica Y Cultura Política en América Latina en el Temprano Siglo XXI*. Guadalajara: CALAS.

Mackinder, Halford John. 1904. "The Geographical Pivot of History." *The Geographical Journal* 23.4: 421–437.

Mamadouh, Virginie. 1998. "Geopolitics in the Nineties: One Flag, many Meanings." *GeoJournal* 46: 237–253.

Mercille, Julien. 2013. "Radical Geopolitics." In: *The Ashgate Research Companion to Critical Geopolitics*, eds. Klaus Dodds, Merje Kuus and Joanne Sharp, 129–146. Farnham: Ashgate.

Mignolo, Walter. 2000. *Local Histories, Global Designs: Coloniality, Subaltern Knowledges, and Border Thinking*. Princeton: PUP.

———. 2005. *The Idea of Latin America*. Malden: Blackwell.

Ó Tuathail, Gearóid. 1996. *Critical Geopolitics. The Politics of Writing Global Space*. Minnesota: University of Minnesota Press.

———. 2006. "Thinking Critically about Geopolitics." In: *The Geopolitics Reader*, eds. Gearóid Ó Tuathail, Simon Dalby and Paul Routledge, 1–14. Abingdon: Routledge.

Ostos, Cetina and María Del Pilar. 2011. "Aplicación de Modelos Geopolíticos en América Latina: Los Casos de Brasil y Colombia." *Revista de Estudios Latinoamericanos* 53.2: 147–167.

Preciado Coronado, Jaime and Pablo Uc. 2010. "La construcción de una Geopolítica crítica desde América Latina y el Caribe. Hacia una Agenda de investigación regional." *Geopolítica(s)* 1.1: 65–94.

Quijano, Anibal and Immanuel Wallerstein. 1992. "Americanity as a Concept, or the Americas in the Modern World System." *International Sociological Association* 134.1: 549–557.

Reuber, Paul. 2012. *Politische Geographie*. Stuttgart: UTB.

Roth, Julia. 2014. "Decolonizing American Studies: Toward a Politics of Intersectional Entanglements." *Forum for Inter-American Research* 7.3: 135–170.

Sidaway, James D., Virginie Mamadouh and Marcus Power 2013. "Reappraising Geopolitical Traditions." In: *The Ashgate Research Companion to Critical Geopolitics*, eds. Klaus Dodds, Merje Kuus and Joanne Sharp, 165–187. Farnham: Ashgate.

Steinmetz, George. 2012. "Geopolitics." In: *The Wiley Blackwell Encyclopedia of Globalization*, ed. George. Ritzer, 800–822. Chichester: Wiley-Blackwell.

35
HUMAN RIGHTS

Belén Olmos Giupponi

At the outset, it should be pointed out that the protection of human rights is a contested concept and a pervasive issue which has several strands in the Americas. It is also worth noting that "the Americas" consist of a heterogeneous group of thirty-five states with diverse historical, cultural, legal, and economic backgrounds (→ America, I/2). Necessarily, these characteristics translate into diverse approaches to human rights. There are thus a variety of dimensions to the protection of human rights in the continent.

First of all, traditional human rights theories stemming from the U.S.-American and French Human Rights Declarations find a contraposition in the de-colonization bibliography with Latin-American authors like Mignolo, Escobar, Gómez, Becker Lorca, and Barreto as some of the leading figures. Post-colonial theories bring about criticism regarding human rights as a long-held concept and a colonial legacy which overlooks inequalities at birth (→ Postcolonialism, I/38). From a related perspective, not only human beings are faced with inequalities, but also the current legal and political system is reproducing these inequalities (→ Social Inequality, II/20). Therefore, the human rights arena in the Americas is permeated by the struggle and confrontation against inequalities currently present in the Americas.

Second, from a legal standpoint, human rights are safeguarded within the Inter-American System of Human Rights (IAHRS) through the procedures that can be instituted before the Inter-American Commission of Human Rights (IACHR) and the Inter-American Court of Human Rights (IACtHR or the Court). Whereas the IACHR was created as an organ of the Organization of American States (OAS), the Court was established in 1979 by the American Convention of Human Rights (ACHR, also known as the "San Jose Pact"). Both Inter-American human rights bodies form part of an inter-governmental mechanism that monitors the compliance of states with international human rights law and has given rise to reports and case law on the protection of human rights throughout the continent.

Third, human rights issues have also been addressed within regional economic integration organizations (REIOs) aimed at establishing a common market although their initial scope was trade liberalization and the conformation of custom unions (→ Regional Integration, II/18). This is particularly true in the realm of Latin-American and Caribbean sub-regional REIOs; i.e. international organizations established through agreements signed between neighboring states generally with similar levels of economic development (→ II/6) and which share cultural and historical ties. These REIOs comprise the Caribbean Community (CARICOM), the

Central American Integration System (SICA), the Andean Community of Nations, and the Southern Common Market (MERCOSUR). Thus, they have developed institutional set-ups modeled upon EU law even if they are still inter-governmental processes.

Fourth, human rights have been at the heart of transnational law processes developed outside the formal governmental channels, particularly, in terms of the Peoples' tribunals and Truth Commissions (→ Civil Society, II/28), originally instituted to deal with gross human rights violations committed by authoritarian regimes (→ Authoritarianism, II/25) but which have also extended their action to cover other aspects such as the protection of environmental rights and access to water (→ Environmental Justice, II/8). These transnational mechanisms embody features of "peoples or citizens' tribunal" as commissions of inquiry that seek another form of accountability outside state-organized structures. To illustrate, the Latin American Water Tribunal offers expert knowledge to deal with alleged violations of environmental norms relating to water resources and to provide recommendations to resolve conflicts over access to water.

Notably, the interaction of these various strands has underpinned the evolution of human rights in the Americas. Protection is multifaceted and takes place not only through formal and institutional channels but also by virtue of bottom-up processes and is evidenced in the relationships between international human rights law and other sectors of international law, such as regional international economic law or international environmental law. Because of the growing significance of economic, cultural, and social rights in terms of inequality reduction, over the years there has been a shift from the initial focus on the safeguard of civil and political rights (→ Citizenship, II/27) to an emphasis on implementation of this set of rights in the Americas.

Against this backdrop, the entry's aim is to contribute a critical analysis of these different strands in the protection of human rights and to review other relevant aspects regarding the implementation of human rights norms in the Americas. Particularly, the main drivers behind the evolution of the defense of human rights in the Americas will be considered, identifying the key factors and features of the various systems set up to protect human rights and scrutinize pitfalls in this process. Human rights have been incorporated in different manners into these agendas and the various strands infuse a distinctive Inter-American approach to human rights. Thus, this contribution aims to set the scenario for the debate about new transnational dimensions in the implementation of human rights in the Americas with a focus on the interface between human rights and other realms, such as literature, economic integration, and environmental protection.

Processes and mechanisms of human rights protection

When it comes to the protection of human rights in the Americas, the concept is not free from controversy for several reasons. Human right is a contested notion, rather than an agreed upon term it definitely conjures up a process of struggle. In the Americas, there is a re-signification of human rights without proposing an alternative conceptualization but attributing the concept different meanings through re-signification of the elements involved in the notion.

Clearly, there is a tension (or a mismatch) between theoretical aspects (legal and ontological considerations) and reality. This is due to a marked inequality observed in the Americas, with a large percentage of citizens being extremely poor and, at the same time, there is accumulation of welfare in the hands of a small percentage of the population (→ Social Inequality, II/20).

It follows that the protection of human rights is not linear or straightforward. On an epistemological level, the notion of human rights is deemed as a Western concept and becomes criticized in the post-colonial context (→ Postcolonialism, I/38). Mignolo's contribution to the debate points out the need for the decolonization of human rights (2014). Historical inequalities are engrained in the social matrix, with elites still being predominant.

Indigenous peoples (traditionally marginalized) irrupted into the scene giving voice to the voiceless (→ Indigeneity, I/31). Concepts such as the Sumak Kawsay or Buen Vivir ("good living") rooted in the holistic comprehension of the world (*cosmovisión*) by Quechua peoples of the Andes brought about a new approach to human rights (in Quechua runa hayñi). Even if the international human rights texts, such as the Universal Declaration of Human Rights and the specific legal frameworks on the promotion of indigenous peoples are relied upon, trends toward the re-indigenization are more frequently proclaimed.

This is also reflected in the scholarship on human rights which has been traditionally dominated by a certain (male and white) perspective (→ Whiteness, I/46). From a "situated knowledge" standpoint these theoretical endeavors are also limited (Fox Keller and Longino 1996). Progressively, gender (→ Gender Identities, I/28) and ethnicity (→ I/25) dimensions are claiming a space for discussion in the protection of human rights in the Americas. Becker Lorca's (2015) contribution to the debate with the idea of "international mestizo law" represents a significant quantum leap in the manner in which human rights are perceived in the Americas. In turn, in her analysis of environmental justice González unveils the gender aspects often overlooked or invisibilized in traditional approaches to human rights.

Historically, human rights represented the legal battlefield during the authoritarian regimes and civil war period of the 1980s (→ Authoritarianism, II/25). Back then, civil and political rights were not safeguarded and human rights activists were persecuted and killed. Gross human rights violations occurred in that period, disappearances, and other atrocities were committed. Back then, the Inter-American Commission played a significant role in monitoring the situation of human rights in the continent. The restoration of democracy (→ II/32) and rule of law brought the need for truth, accountability and reconciliation. Truth commissions set up to deal with the aftermath situations paved the way for reconciliation. The heavy inheritance of the authoritarian past still casts a long shadow on the protection of human rights in the Americas.

Democracy and rule of law were praised as the two crucial elements which inaugurated a new era for the protection of human rights, focusing on social, cultural, and economic rights. New liberal policies and the push for the opening of markets following the Washington Consensus brought new challenges to the protection of human rights in the continent (Olmos Giupponi 2016) (→ Neoliberalism, II/16). A variety of human rights issues is emerging on various fronts. Migration and protection of migrants (→ Transnational Migration, I/44), equality in the access to essential rights (food, water, health), and the safeguard of environmental rights are contentious issues at the moment (→ Health, I/29; Environmental Justice, II/8). At present, human rights movements are entrenched with various identity processes, such as gender, women, street children, indigenous peoples, and the landless (Cleary 2007) (→ Social Movements, I/41). Other contemporary human rights issues include protection against police brutality, torture, and corruption.

Human rights have been a common subject in Latin-American literature. As Posner has argued, law is frequently a subject of literature which compels us to infer a deep affinity between these fields (Posner 2002, 11). Literature movements have echoed the protection of human rights through different genres: creative nonfiction, fiction, and poetry, exploring major issues in human rights protection through the lens of the humanities. Latin America's most acclaimed writers have been re-interpreted in terms of the protection of human rights (Agosín 2006).

Different theoretical considerations are in order. Literature aided the restoration of the rule of law after the end of authoritarian dictatorships in the continent. Memory, truth, and reparation are pervasive issues observed in the emerging literature after the end of the dictatorships (→ Memory Politics, I/34). This catharsis through literary means facilitated the normalization of the democratic life. The writer Ernesto Sábato led the Truth Commission in Argentina which investigated torture and forced disappearances. In releasing the final report "Nunca Más" (1984), Sábato described many cases of *desaparecidos*, human rights fighters which were subject to a witch hunt, de-humanized, and reified, reduced to abstractions in a living hell. In his book *Radical Evil on Trial* (1998), evoking Hannah Arendt's and Immanuel Kant's concept of radical evil, Carlos Nino further discussed the obligation of emerging democratic regimes to prosecute former dictators for crimes against humanity.

This particular strand of the Latin-American literature defined as *literatura testimonial* (testimonial literature) (→ Life Writing, III/11) developed not only in the Southern Cone after the 1980s but also in the rest of Latin-American countries that were subject to right-wing dictatorships (→ Trauma Literature, III/21). Space precludes an exhaustive analysis of the different writers but, for example, Gioconda's Belli book *Inhabited Woman* (Belli 1988) blends magical realism (→ III/12) with a political analysis of the conflict situation in Nicaragua. Main features and topics of this wave are articulated around violence suffered under dictatorships and repressive conditions; memory, distortion, and preservation of memory; memory politics (→ I/34) and justice; as well as citizenship (→ II/27); and reconciliation.

International law and human rights protection

The IAHRS remains at the core of the safeguard of human rights and its activity has been fostered by several tools and processes: a proactive approach to interpreting human rights norms (the so-called method of evolving interpretation and the *pro homine* principle); the increased judicial dialogue with the national courts and with the European Court of Human Rights (ECtHR); an enhanced cooperation between the IACHR and the IACtHR; and the affirmation of core international human rights law principles through the Court's advisory opinions.

The human rights system created under the OAS consisted originally of the Inter-American Commission, which in 1959 began promoting and protecting human rights as an autonomous organ of the OAS. The IACHR, as a committee of experts, has since developed a wide-ranging function in the promotion and protection of human rights under Article 106 of the OAS Charter overseeing compliance with the 1948 American Declaration of the Rights and Duties of Man.

The IACHR is the bedrock in the safeguard of human rights, as petitioners are precluded from lodging their grievances about the violation of human rights directly with the IACtHR. Additionally, the IACHR is an OAS organ tasked to monitor compliance of all OAS member states with international and regional human rights law, even if they are not parties to the ACHR. Accordingly, the IACHR has received several applications under the American Declaration in past years initially concerning the violation of civil and political rights and, more recently, also dealing with economic, social, and cultural rights. Since only a few cases progress to the next stage before the IACtHR, the Commission's reports are key to protecting human rights. In brief, the IACHR fulfills a prominent function in the protection afforded to petitioners, having laid the groundwork for a new era in the IAHRS.

The creation of the IACtHR by the 1969 ACHR represented a step forward in the defense of human rights within the institutional framework of the IAHRS, complementing the protection granted before the Commission. Although inspired by the ECtHR model, the functions of the IACtHR in the IAHRS possesses specific features. While the IACtHR was endowed since the beginning with jurisdiction in contentious cases and to hand down advisory opinions, its ECtHR was only given that function after the adoption of Protocol 16 in 2013. Regarding the relations with the Commission, the role of the IACHR is quite different from that played by the former Human Rights Commission in Europe. The IACHR, as the human rights body to which individuals have access, performs quasi-judicial functions over the admissibility of the claims and on the merits of the petitions. The procedure before the IACtHR can only be set in motion by the state Parties and the IACHR. As mentioned before, the IACHR is an OAS organ and, therefore, asserts its competence over all OAS member states, including those that are not parties to the ACHR.

In the IAHRS, the Court has developed a rich case law following its first ruling in the *Velásquez Rodríguez* case in 1988, a landmark case which set the court system in motion. The case arose when the university student, Angel Manfredo Velásquez Rodríguez, was seized and detained without an arrest warrant in Tegucigalpa, Honduras, and was subject to torture in two military locations. During the proceedings, the IACtHR ordered provisional measures to protect witnesses, as many were assassinated on January 5, 1988 and on January 14, 1988, and requested that the Government of Honduras adopt all measures necessary to prevent further infringements on the basic rights of witnesses who had been summoned to appear before the Court in all pending forced disappearance cases. This was the first of a long string of cases concerning *desaparecidos* during authoritarian dictatorships settled by the IACtHR.

Although the IACtHR focused initially on the investigation of mass human rights violations perpetrated during authoritarian regimes, it has broadened the scope of its activities over the years to handle complaints under the Protocol of San Salvador on Economic, Social, and Cultural Rights (OAS 1988/1999). Hence, the IACtHR's case law first reflected the transition to democracy of many Latin-American countries supporting the consolidation of democracy and the rule of law across the continent to then address the safeguard of economic, social, cultural and, more recently, environmental rights in the Americas. These include, among others, migrants' rights, environmental protection and indigenous peoples' rights.

In this vein, the IACtHR has evolved from being a relatively inactive court at the beginning to taking an active and innovative judicial approach to settling cases. Although the IACtHR issued its first Advisory Opinion in 1982, it was only in 1988, nearly ten years after its establishment in 1979, that the Court pronounced its first ruling in a contentious case. Since these early beginnings, the IACtHR has been progressively exercising its jurisdiction to settle contentious cases and has re-affirmed the significance of its role in the protection of human rights through advisory opinions. The Inter-American System has protected the victims' rights during post-conflict processes and has declared that amnesty laws enacted in several countries were null and void.

Notwithstanding the crucial progress achieved, the main caveat of the system is the lack of involvement of Canada and the United States. Although OAS members, both states do not participate in the IACtHR, creating a gap in the supranational legal protection. Equally important to note is the limited participation of Caribbean states as most of them have not recognized (or withdrawn) the contentious competence of the IACtHR.

Several landmark achievements have contributed to the escalation of activities in the IAHRS during the past decades. First, different methods of interpretation have paved the way for progress, giving judges greater scope to develop Inter-American human rights law in line with the ACHR. Hence, the IACtHR has pursued a progressive treaty interpretation of the ACHR set out in the Vienna Convention on the Law of Treaties (VCLT) and in light of the ACHR. To do so, the IACtHR relies on different hermeneutical methods, going beyond the constricting interpretation of the wording or the ACHR. Through a progressive interpretation, according to which the wording should be construed in light of present conditions, the IACtHR has established thresholds and tests to protect or balance different rights in conflict. Through this evolving interpretation of the ACHR, the IACtHR has expanded the scope of protection. As Lixinski points out, this approach "permeates much of the Court's activities, and it proposes some kind of hierarchy within international law in which international human rights law is at the top" (Lixinski 2010, 585). Another relevant interpretative tool is the *pro homine* principle put forward in article 29.1 and article 1.1 of the ACHR, whereby legal provisions must be interpreted in the most advantageous manner to protect the human being. However, this flexible interpretation of the human rights treaties also presents drawbacks, as the wording of the treaties cannot be overextended without the consent of the states as a necessary element in the evolution of the IAHRS. In Neuman's view, the reliance on a "consensus-building process" could improve the acceptance and effectiveness of the Inter-American human rights system (Neuman 2008, 108).

Second, evolution has been driven by an increasing judicial dialogue between the IACtHR and the ECtHR. Though the IACtHR has been mirroring its European peer, drawing on its jurisprudence to settle the cases, at the present stage there are cross references between the ECtHR and the IACtHR which translates into a more or less well-articulated judicial dialogue.

Third, one can observe another process of judicial dialogue between the IACtHR and national courts (particularly supreme or constitutional courts) which has been strengthened via the principle of *interpretacion conforme* (consistent interpretation) and *control de convencionalidad* (conventionality control) (IACtHR. Inter-American Court of Human Rights 2015). The first principle implies the obligation for national courts to interpret national legislation in conformity with the ACHR. Through the second mechanism (*control de convencionalidad*), domestic courts monitor the legality of state parties' actions in light of the obligations assumed under the ACHR. The "control of conventionality" was a development from the IACtHR's judgment in Almonacid Arellano et al. v. Chile (IACtHR. Inter-American Court of Human Rights 2006).

Core international human rights law principles have been affirmed in the reports of the Commission and in the decisions adopted in contentious cases and the advisory opinions of the Court. More precisely, the IACtHR has asserted the exercise of its advisory jurisdiction as a way to convey a clear message to all OAS member states, including those who are not parties to the ACHR. In the advisory opinions, the Court has identified and stressed *jus cogens* principles that are binding upon all states projecting a horizontal effect on relations between private parties. The IACtHR has issued, in particular, advisory opinions affirming principles of international human rights law, such as non-discrimination, equality before the law, and equal protection before the law and *non-refoulement*.

In the work of the Commission and the case law of the Court, three turning points have hailed this evolution: the protection of migrants' rights (→ Transnational Migration, I/44), the enforceability of economic, social, and cultural rights, and the consideration of environmental rights in relation to human rights (→ Environmental Justice, II/8; Nature, II/39). As for migrants' rights, the protection has taken on importance in the activities of the Inter-American specific bodies for the promotion and protection of human rights. Although petitions concerning migrants' rights have been submitted to the IAHRS since the 1980s, migration issues have only recently been included as one of its specialized fields. Thus, in 1996, the IACHR nominated a Special Rapporteur on Migrant Workers and Members of their families, taking into account their vulnerability and the need for special protection of their rights. This Special Rapporteur can arrange site visits to verify the working and living conditions of migrant workers, unaccompanied children and families of undocumented migrants (→ Family, I/26), addressing migration issues in general in the region. The Special Rapporteur has conducted various visits to monitor the situation of migrants with regular and irregular status at points of entry and detention places and has interviewed them. In the IAHRS' increasing specialization in migration issues, the IACtHR has contributed a significant case law concerning the protection of migrants' rights in the exercise of its advisory jurisdiction (Advisory Opinion 18/03 and Advisory Opinion 21/14) and in the contentious cases, establishing principles consistently reaffirmed in different proceedings.

In a recent line of jurisprudence flowing from the *Lagos del Campo case*, the Court has proclaimed the enforceability of economic, social, and cultural rights on the basis of the principle of human rights interdependence and indivisibility (IACtHR. Inter-American Court of Human Rights 2017, Case Lagos del Campo para. 141) using the principle to adjudicate socio-economic rights. In this case, the Court used interdependence to construe an Inter-American legal framework to reaffirm the states' obligation to enforce economic, social, and cultural rights. This doctrine has been confirmed in other rulings.

Environmental concerns and the safeguard of environmental rights have come under the scope of protection of the IAHRS in various rulings concerning indigenous property (→ Indigeneity, I/31). Specifically, the Advisory Opinion (OC-23/17 of February 7, 2018) on the Environment and Human Rights obliges the state to protect and guarantee the rights to life and personal integrity in relation to the environment (interpretation and scope of Articles 4(1) and 5(1) of the ACHR). The upshot of the Advisory Opinion is the recognition of a fundamental right (having both an individual and a collective dimensions) to a healthy environment articulated through the protection of human rights which could improve environmental protection.

Between human rights and regional international economic law in the Latin-American and Caribbean sub-regional integration, an evolution has occurred in terms of the protection of human rights (or, at least, specific human rights). In Latin America and the Caribbean, the development and progressive consolidation of provisions concerning human rights in REIOs has resulted in the creation of human rights system which raises the question of inter-systemic relationships in a similar fashion to what happened in Europe as these REIOs provisions co-exist with the IAHRS instituted by the ACHR.

The adoption of human rights norms in regional economic integration is a trend that emerged toward the end of the 1990s. During this period, the ideas of social dimension and social agenda became relevant in the Latin-American integration process. Scholars from the Latin American Economic System (SELA), NGOs, and unions (→ Labor Representation, II/14) criticized the regional free trade agreements because of their lack of commitment to address the social side effects of economic integration (Franco and Di Filippo 1999) (→ Regional Integration, II/18). Also, other scholars such as Grandi and Bizzozero stressed the need for a greater participation (→ II/41) of social actors (1997). Additionally, other commentators underlined the "democratic deficit" of these REIOs because of the marginal participation of third sector organizations. On the one hand, the demand for citizen participation in these REIOs increased, with a particular rise in requests on behalf of NGOs and unions, which depicts a "bottom-up process" (Tirado Mejía 1997, 52). On the other hand, sub-regional integration processes tried to address the regional governance's lack of social meaning and legitimacy by creating consultative bodies, such as MERCOSUR Consultative Economic and Social Forum for the participation of civil society (→ II/28), which describes more of a "top-down process."

From a theoretical standpoint, the dynamics of the inter-systemic relationships can be categorized into different types or models. Frank García (referring to NAFTA, MERCOSUR, and the unsuccessful Free Trade Area of the Americas FTAA) has proposed two models for the relationship between REIOs and regional human rights systems (RHRSs), the leverage model and the incorporation model (García 2003). The leverage model consists of "making effective participation in extrinsic human rights systems a legal or political condition" of membership (1–2). In contrast, the incorporation model is more similar to the patterns seen in Europe and is reflected "on the interpenetration of the two systems at many levels" (2). Drawing on García's analysis, a first model would be "coexistence and reference," according to which the two types of systems co-exist, and, sometimes, there is a reference to human rights instruments and the protection of human rights as a prerequisite for membership of the integration process, however, without any interaction between dispute settlement mechanisms. The second model would be "interrelationship and interaction" between systems; under this scheme, inter-systemic relationships between different judicial organs frequently occur leading to a judicial dialogue.

Intricacies of transnational human rights protection

In Latin America and the Caribbean, the articulation of more or less defined legal systems in the different REIOs is particularly relevant for the analysis due to their interaction with the IAHRS, as they lay down the groundwork for more complete inter-systemic relationships between the different dispute settlement bodies (courts of justice and arbitral tribunals). What follows, then, is a crucial question. Where do these sub-regional systems stand? At present, even if inter-systemic relationships similar to those established in Europe can be observed, the level of sophistication is significantly less. There are obvious constraints originating in essential features of the Latin-American and Caribbean integration. First, the integration in Latin America and the Caribbean does not exactly resemble the regional integration as happens in the EU, especially with regard to the development of Community law and the establishment of Community methods, mechanisms, and institutions. Although the creation of supranational organizations and Community law is envisaged in the founding treaties, in Latin America and the Caribbean the nature of the integration follows, in practice, an inter-governmental logic.

In the Caribbean, Central America, and the Andean States, integration processes bring together elements suitable for the development of supranational law and institutions, whereas MECOSUR still represents an inter-governmental model in practice. Particularly, in all of the different integration processes, the existence of a proper Community law is overshadowed by the implementation deficit, i.e. Community law norms go often unobserved. It should be clear, therefore, that the current legal systems do not possess all of the features of a true Community law, namely, current legal systems lack direct applicability and direct effect. Hence, these sub-regional integration agreements are still predominantly intergovernmental. Although binding rules emanate from them, individuals have no (or very restricted) access to specific mechanisms to expedite claims pertaining to the violation of human rights.

The key question lies in determining the features that characterize and define the integration schemes in the field of human rights and the scope and effects of each of the sub-regional integration processes in this area. In this vein, there are certain basic elements which constitute the foundation for the recognition and protection of human rights in the sub-regional integration that results in interactions with the IAHRS.

As a result, human rights norms have been passed, however, they are not complete human right systems in the sense of perfectly binding norms implemented through a compulsory dispute settlement mechanism. Simply put, they consist of provisions scattered in legal instruments, and the action of judicial institutions to resolve controversies may arise, if the application of Community standards results in the violation of fundamental rights. Therefore, development can be achieved through the establishment of a specific case law. The courts of these REIOs, as has happened with the Court of Justice of the European Union (hereinafter "CJEU"), have in certain cases undertaken protecting human rights. Obviously, the caseload cannot be compared to the caseload of the CJEU. The situation of MERCOSUR is atypical, because there is no court to resolve disputes arising within the integration process. Member States have opted to establish an inter-state arbitration procedure instead, which offers a limited opportunity for individuals to participate.

From a purely normative and institutional perspective, there are no complete systems of protection of human rights. To assert the development and consolidation of the protection of human rights in Latin-American and Caribbean integration processes, it is worth referring briefly to the legal instruments that have been adopted in the field of human rights in each of the integration processes: the CARICOM Charter of the Civil Society (1997); the SICA Treaties of Social Integration and Democratic Security (1995); the Andean Charter of Human Rights (2002); the MERCOSUR Social and Labor Declaration (1998); and the Protocol of Human Rights (2005). In most cases, based on the legal nature of these instruments, it cannot be concluded that they establish specific obligations for Member States or that they create the monitoring mechanisms; they are not legally binding, being either programs or purely recommendatory instruments. Yet, the significance of these instruments in the process leading to the development and establishment of human rights systems must not be underestimated. Therefore, human rights considerations are embedded in the economic integration, and there are different relations with the IAHRS through which one can proceed to the comparison between rights recognized in both regions.

In relation to the protection of human rights in the transnational arena, the Latin American Water Tribunal – LAWT (also known as TRAGUA for its acronym in Spanish) established in 1998 represent the most salient example of protection of human rights from a non-governmental perspective. The LAWT was originally created by the civil society (→ II/28) to address environmental degradation affecting water resources in Central America. For this reason, the Tribunal was previously known as "Central American Water Tribunal" and was subsequently renamed "Latin American Water Tribunal" (Olmos Giupponi 2018). Since its inception in 1998 the LAWT has emerged as a non-governmental body with a multidisciplinary composition and a mandate based on both formal and informal sources of law, which holds public hearings in order to address water-related complaints. The LAWT's mandate is twofold: to investigate whether or not an environmental dispute relating to water access has arisen and to provide an agreed solution applicable to the specific case (→ Environmental Justice, II/8).

The core principles that govern the proceedings are: systemic analysis, eco-centric ethical principles, indirect evidence, and inversion of the burden of the proof. If necessary, the LAWT can decide to organize an on-site visit to assess the severity of the situation described in the complaint. The "jurors" of the LAWT vary from case to case, as they are selected by an impartial Scientific and Technical Commission from a list of experts. The LAWT is distinctive because of its interdisciplinary composition; it is comprised not only of legal experts but a diverse range of professionals from different fields, such as history, literature, anthropology, geology, and hydrology. They come mainly from Latin-American countries, although some jurors are from other continents. The LAWT has dealt with more than sixty different cases.

On the completion of the proceedings, the jury issues a verdict containing recommendations for the settlement of the dispute. Although the LAWT's "verdicts" are not judgments *stricto sensu*, they contribute to raising and generating public pressure on states and increasing the "visibility" of environmental conflicts. The public hearings receive media attention and generate debate in society, helping to organize local communities to protect natural resources (→ Political Communication, II/42). Furthermore, the LAWT organizes other dissemination and training activities on sustainable water management in local communities and fosters the dialogue between the public authorities in charge of water governance and policy making, and the users.

In an overall appraisal of the LAWT's functions, it operates as a mediator in areas where the traditional model for inter-state dispute settlement only offers limited possibilities of redress to non-state actors (mainly individuals and groups). The LAWT provides petitioners with the opportunity to present their demands in a quasi-judicial forum.

Final discussion: what lies ahead for the protection of human rights in the Americas?

The protection of human rights in the Americas has oscillated between legal transplants and the search for the definition of a specific approach to human rights. The protection is fragmented, multidimensional, and heterogeneous. There is nothing permanent but the struggle.

Considering that the United States and Canada are not party to the American Convention, the effect of the IACtHR advisory opinions have on the OAS member states' legal orders is rather limited. The IACtHR's judgments should be enforced in national legal systems, however, advisory opinions do not carry any binding force. The IACtHR only exercises its contentious jurisdiction over the signatories to the ACHR, which are mostly Latin-American states. There is an increasing idealization of the Court, which is represented as a supranational court exercising its influence on all of the OAS member states. However, as previously discussed, the United States and Canada have not become parties to the ACHR, only a few Caribbean states have ratified it, and Venezuela denounced the treaty.

Turning to the evolution of sub-regional integration agreements in the field of human rights, they have followed different paths with various relations with the IAHRS. At the moment, the sub-regional integration agreements include specific provisions on social, economic, cultural, and environmental rights. These sub-regional integration processes have become more "human rights-friendly." Consequently, various human rights declarations and charters relating to the protection of fundamental human rights have been adopted. These instruments have often recognized human rights in similar terms to those set up in the Universal Declaration of Human Rights and the United Nations Covenants on Civil and

Political Rights and Economic and Social Rights. However, within Latin-American REIOs (→ Regional Integration, II/18), these provisions differ from those of traditional human rights agreements. This is the case because REIOs provisions do not establish monitoring bodies and tend to focus on the protection of specific rights, which are considered relevant for the integration process. In this context, labor rights and environmental protection have been included as human rights in the sub-regional integration processes. Only when such schemes evolve in terms of rules and case law in this area, will it be possible to establish fully-fledged inter-systemic relationships.

To better grasp the scope of the protection afforded within these REIOs, freedom of movement of citizens of the different Member States has been referred to as the core right for the establishment of a "regional citizenship" (→ Citizenship, II/27). However, in practice, freedom of movement is not fully operational, as it is understood by Member States to be comprised within the migration policy of each state (→ Transnational Migration, I/44). Cases before the Inter-American Commission and the IACtHR demonstrate this approach. It would be misleading to assert the existence of a citizenship in the EU sense, since it is just a mere statement of purpose. However, the IACtHR has issued the Advisory Opinion 21/14 on the Rights and Guarantees of Children in the context of migration and/or the need for international protection, following the joint request by MERCOSUR Member States (Argentina, Brazil, Paraguay, and Uruguay), which asked the IACtHR to determine the scope of state obligations regarding the rights of migrant children under the ACHR.

With regard to the relations between the IAHRS and the novel systems created in the framework of these REIOs in CARICOM, the Charter of Civil Society echoes some of the content and scope of the human rights instruments adopted in the IAHRS. The issue of human rights within MERCOSUR and SICA is linked to social rights and is considered within the framework of economic integration (freedom of movement). Only the Andean Community has developed a comprehensive and complete instrument on human rights, which goes beyond the content of the IACHR. The Charter for the promotion and protection of human rights in the Andean Community specifically mentions the IACHR in its preamble, but, at the same time, it makes a general reference to several other universal and regional human rights instruments.

With regard to transnational processes, the groundwork of the various Truth Commissions set up in the 1980s and 1990s to deal with the horrendous consequences of the dictatorships continues through other means (→ Memory Politics, I/34). In the field of environmental rights, LAWT provides the opportunity for claimants to present their cases and with recommendations for compliance with environmental legislation. The LAWT also facilitates voluntary compliance with water resources legislation, and indigenous norms and customs. In this way, the LAWT acts as a mediator recommending compliance with applicable environmental norms and identifying possible ways of solving the disputes. Additionally, the LAWT has proved to be an alternative forum to place water issues on the agenda, which contributes to mobilizing public opinion. The LAWT proceedings and verdicts raise awareness about water conflicts in Latin America and thus facilitate public pressure on states and private actors such as corporations. The LAWT increases transparency and environmental visibility in legal procedures (→ Environmental Justice, II/8), as evidenced in the cases involving approval of the construction of a new hydroelectric dam (→ Energy, II/7) or permission for the exploitation of mining concessions. Only through the intervention of the LAWT were the affected local communities able to raise their concerns. Finally, traditional water management and policy designed by governments adopts a top-down approach without considering the human rights dimension. In contrast, the LAWT offers a bottom-up approach that includes the demands of the different groups in society, such as the local population and indigenous people (→ Indigeneity, I/31). This approach represents an alternative to existing forums in which affected groups cannot access justice mechanisms and/or lack legal standing to do so. In sum, the remarkable activity of the LAWT opens the door to future opportunities to address controversial situations that may arise with regard to access to water where traditional justice mechanisms prove to be ineffective or inadequate.

Works cited

Agosín, Marjorie. eds. 2006. *Writing toward Hope: The Literature of Human Rights in Latin America*. New Haven, CT: Yale University Press.

Becker Lorca, Arnulf. 2015. *Mestizo International Law*. Cambridge: Cambridge University Press.

Belli, Gioconda. 1988. "*Inhabited Woman*." Barcelona: Seix Barral.

Cleary, Edward L. 2007. *Mobilizing for Human Rights in Latin America*. Bloomfield, CT: Kumarian.

Fox Keller, Evelyn and Longino, Helen E. 1996. *Feminism and Science*. Oxford: Oxford University Press.

Franco, Rolando and Di Filippo, Armando. 1999. *Las dimensiones sociales de la integración regional en América Latina*. Santiago de Chile: CEPAL.

García, Frank. 2003. "Integrating Trade and Human Rights in the Americas." *Research Paper* 26, *SSRN*. https://papers.ssrn.com/sol3/papers.cfm?abstract_id=470201.

Gonzalez, Carmen G. 2015. "Human Rights, Environmental Justice, and the North-South Divide." In *Research Handbook on Human Rights and the Environment*, eds. Anna Grear and Louis J. Kotzé, 449–4472. Cheltenham: Edward Elgar Publishing.

Grandi, Jorge and Bizzozero, Lincoln. 1997. "Hacia una sociedad civil del MERCOSUR. Viejos y nuevos actores en el tejido sub-regional." *Inter-American Development Bank*. http://10.iadb.org/intal/intalcdi/integracion_comercio/e_INTAL_IYC_03_1997_Grandi-Bizzozero.pdf

IACtHR. Inter-American Court of Human Rights. 1988. Velásquez Rodríguez v Honduras. Judgment on July 29, San José.

———. 2006. Almonacid Arellano et al. v. Chile. Judgment on September 26, San José.

———. 2015. Control de Convencionalidad, Cuadernillo de Jurisprudencia de la Corte Interamericana de Derechos Humanos 7. San José. http://corteidh.or.cr/tablas/r33825.pdf.

———. 2017. Lagos del Campo v Perú. Judgment on August 31, San José.

Lixinski, Lucas. 2010. "Treaty Interpretation by the Inter-American Court of Human Rights: Expansionism at the Service of the Unity of International Law." *European Journal of International Law* 21, no. 3: 585–604.

Mignolo, Walter D. 2014. "From 'Human Rights' to 'Life Rights'." In *The Meanings of Rights: The Philosophy and Social Theory of Human Rights*, Costas Douzinas and Conor Gearty, 161–180. Cambridge: Cambridge University Press..

———. 2009. "Who Speaks for the 'Human' in Human Rights?" *Hispanic Issues on Line* 5, no. 1: 7–24.

Neuman, Gerald. 2008. "Import, Export, and Regional Consent in the Inter-American Court of Human Rights." *European Journal of International Law* 19, no. 1: 101–123.

Nino, Carlos S. 1998. *Radical Evil on Trial*. New Haven: Yale University Press.

OAS. 1988/1999. Protocol of San Salvador on Economic, Social and Cultural Rights, signed November 17, 1988 and in force since November 16, 1999, San Salvador.

Olmos Giupponi, Belén. 2016. *Rethinking Free Trade, Economic Integration and Human Rights in the Americas*. Oxford: Hart Publishing.

———. 2018. "Assessing the Contribution of the Latin American Water Tribunal to Transnational Environmental law." In *People's Tribunals and International Law*, eds. Andrew Brynes and Gabrielle Simm, 230–256. Cambridge: Cambridge University Press.

Posner, Richard 2002. *Law and Literature*. Cambridge, MA and London: Harvard University Press.

Sábato, Ernesto. 1984. (re-edited 2016). "Foreword: 'Nunca Más'." https://librosycasas.cultura.gob.ar/wp-content/uploads/2015/11/LC_NuncaMas_Digital1.pdf

Tirado Mejía, Álvaro. 1997. "Integración y Democracia en América Latina y el Caribe." *BID-INTAL. Documento de Divulgación* 1. http://plataformademocratica.org/Publicacoes/7038_Cached.pdf.

United Nations. n.d. Universal Declaration of Human Rights in quechua. https://ohchr.org/EN/UDHR/Documents/UDHR_Translations/qul.pdf.

36

INTERVENTIONISM

Thomas Fischer

Before World War I, the political and diplomatic Inter-American relationships and connections could be characterized by the following five attributes. Firstly, as the 19th century progressed, a more asymmetric relationship between countries in the "North" and "South" developed. Time and again, the U.S.-American government proceeded with unilateral measures against formally sovereign nations of the "South" (→ Nation State, II/38). The U.S. confronted Latin-American and Caribbean nations that had consolidated as nation-states although they only shared a political-geographic border with Mexico. As a result, an adversarial relationship developed between the southern neighbors and the U.S. (with respect to settlers, entrepreneurs, and filibusters) that culminated in massive land losses and repeated military interventions in Central America. The relationship between Canada to the north, whose territorial consolidation was solidified through its westward expansion, and the U.S. was less conflictual. As seen in the relationship between the U.S. and its southern neighbors, asymmetric constellations also developed within South America between "stronger" and "weaker" nation-states. The consequences were massive land losses for the "weaker" ones, military interventionism with loss of life, and policies enacted that would undermine peaceful relations in the early centuries of nation-building (→ Nation and State Building, I/16).

Secondly, throughout the 19th century, U.S. foreign politics focused largely on the American double continent. These politics were justified by the Monroe Doctrine of 1823 as a guiding principle of foreign policy and the Manifest Destiny provided the moral drive.

Thirdly, even as Bolivarianism developed as an idea that was ever-present during the 1820s, the Latin-American elites failed to use this as a basis to develop an alliance. In the political reality, it did not present an alternative to the concepts driven by the U.S. The Drago Doctrine that was formulated in response to European violations of sovereignty, as well as the call for anti-interventionism articulated as part of Pan-Americanism were much more effective "weapons" to demand respect for the sovereignty of weaker states. To prevent the escalation of bilateral conflict between neighbors and end military conflict between neighbors (→ Military, II/37), the Latin-American side relied increasingly on the arbitration tribunals in the 19th century.

Fourthly, morally, ideationally and emotionally charged expansionism used in the U.S. to consolidate national space was not seen in South America. Land seizure (→ Land, II/15) and national campaigns were directed toward indigenous peoples (→ I/11) whereby a discursive contradiction between "civilization" and "barbarianism" was constructed. The consequences for the affected indigenous peoples were just as disastrous as in the U.S.

And fifthly, even the expansion of borders due to border wars followed no doctrine (→ Borderlands, II/26). Instead, these wars were justified merely with inconsistencies of colonial territorial demarcations before national independence.

Territorial expansion of the U.S. and Canada

Throughout the 19th century, the U.S. developed into a world power that dominated the American continent. The cornerstone was the massive territorial expansion on the American continent (Schoultz 1999, 14–38). However, this did not take place exclusively with military power. Large pieces of land were purchased from the Spanish, French, and English colonial powers. In 1803, the Thomas Jefferson administration (1801–1809) obtained Louisiana from Napoleon's France ("Louisiana Purchase") for $15 million. Even Spain, the other large colonial power in the region, was forced to relinquish large land parcels to the U.S. After West Florida declared its independence from Spain in 1810, President James Madison (1809–1817) laid claim to this area. At that time, Spain was occupied by French invasion troops rendering it incapable of acting. Napoleon forced Karl the VI and Ferdinand the VII to abdicate the Spanish crown and to declare his brother, Joseph Bonaparte, to be king. Until 1814, there was no legitimate Spanish power that could send additional troops or settlers to the "New World." When Ferdinand took the throne once again, negotiations between Secretary of State John Quincy Adams and Luis de Onis in 1819, cleared the path for cross-national agreements. Spain formally waived rights to East Florida, Sabine Free State, Oregon Country, and a small part of central Colorado.

However, the U.S. did not respect the border separating Mexico – which gained independence beginning in 1821 – from the U.S. as regulated by the Adams Onis Treaty. As a part of its empire-building, the U.S. militarily subjugated additional territories and assumed its national administrative apparatus and policymaking functions. After Texas declared independence with the help of propaganda by supporters of slavery (→ I/18), land speculators, and settlers in 1836, the U.S. annexed the widely "North Americanized" territory in 1845 and incorporated it as the 28th state in the union against the will of the Mexican president, Antonio López de Santa Anna (1833–1835; 1841–1842; 1843; 1844; 1846–1847; 1847; 1853–1855). New Mexico was occupied by the U.S. military in 1846 which resulted in a two-year war. In 1848, the Treaty of Guadeloupe-Hidalgo ended the Mexican-U.S.-American War but with Mexico also losing upper California. Mexico received over $15 million for relinquishing its territory. The U.S. took over the debt claims of U.S. American citizens to Mexico and 90 percent of Mexicans in regions ceded to the U.S. obtained U.S. citizenship as well. A few years later, the U.S. purchased the border area of La Mesilla in the current state of New Mexico and Arizona for $10 million in 1853 ("Gadsen Purchase").

As the U.S. expansion to the south began to flounder, the appropriation of land south of the new border with Mexico continued through entrepreneurs, warlords, and settlers who cooperated with local players (→ Land, II/15). As Robert E. May emphasized, their projects became part of the *popular culture* of the southern states. The leader enjoyed great respect there (May 2002). The most well-known filibuster was Nashville-born, William Walker who, together with soldiers, wanted to appropriate large pieces of land in Central America. His attempt to conquer Baja California and Sonora failed in 1853 after a confrontation with government troops. In 1856/57 he became one of the presidents of Nicaragua making use of the confusion of the civil war and simultaneously served as a promoter of slavery. While trying to establish himself along the Mosquito Coast and in British Honduras, a coalition formed that defeated his army and he was executed by a Honduran firing squad in 1860.

With the acquisition of Alaska to the north by Russia occurring in 1867, the same year in which the Dominion of Canada was confirmed, a sense of fear began to spread there. The fear that British Columbia would be next was used to territorially close ranks. Canada's concern was not unfounded since new states were being established and the population in the Northwest had increased. Considering this, U.S.-American politicians and citizens began demanding the appropriation of additional British-owned lands (Province of Canada, New Brunswick, Nova Scotia). In response, Canada acquired Rupert's Land and Northwestern Territory in 1870. British Columbia followed one year later as the sixth province. Canadian politicians pressed ahead with the consolidation of the Canadian Federation. Its own westward expansion sought to secure the required space under the protection of Canadian law and Canadian governance. In Canada, Manifest Destiny meant integration into the public sphere and the homogenization of former British territories westward (prairies) and northward (arctic). In 1871, the U.S. accepted the existence of the Dominion of Canada in the Treaty of Washington.

Against this backdrop, U.S.-American expansionism proceeded in the Caribbean (Schoultz 1999, 125–151). After the Spanish-American War of 1898, the so-called "splendid little war" (Secretary of State Hay), Puerto Rico was added to the U.S. The citizens thereby obtained U.S.-American citizenship. This separation of territory from Spain and the purchase of the Philippines and Guam were all regulated through the Treaty of Paris in 1898. The U.S. compensated Spain $20 million and for a long time, the three territories were governed through U.S. military governments (→ Military, II/37). Spain did not release its rights to Cuba's sovereignty, but also waived any claims. Only in 1902, did the U.S. pull its troops out. Through the Platt Amendment of 1901 (named after U.S. Senator Orville H. Platt) and a bilateral treaty in 1903/04, the right to intervene "for the preservation of Cuban independence, the maintenance of a government adequate for the protection of life, property, and individual liberty" and the right to oversee the public finances and foreign policy was written into the Cuban Constitution. The U.S. made use of this repeatedly. In addition, the "land lease" ensured access to the Guantanamo Bay "...for the time required for the purposes of coaling and naval stations."

In 1903, control over the Panama Canal (to be accomplished) also went to the U.S. as a gift in reciprocity to the Panamanian "fathers of independence" in gratitude for keeping the Columbian troops away from the isthmus and for immediately diplomatically recognizing the Republic that had separated from Columbia. The treaty was negotiated between the Panamanian envoy and Frenchman, Philippe Bunau-Varilla, and Secretary of State, John Hay. In doing so, Panama gave the U.S. exclusive rights to a 10-mile-wide zone including "all the rights, power and authority" for canal construction and operation. It included a compensation payment of $10 million originally set aside for Columbia. The U.S. gave itself the right to protect Panama's freedom ("independencia" in Spanish).

In 1914, the U.S. gained possession over the Corn Islands (Treaty with the U.S. protectorate of Nicaragua) that the Bryan-Chamorro Treaty leased to the U.S. for 99 years. Finally, in 1917, the U.S. acquired the Virgin Islands from Denmark. Ten years later, its inhabitants were granted U.S. citizenship.

Territorial expansion into South America

South America also experienced territorial shifts beginning with independence from Spain and then Portugal respectively. These can be characterized as national negotiation processes within the framework of so-called border conflicts. In the very bloody Guerra de la Triple

Alianza of 1864 to 1870, the allies, Argentina, Brazil, and Uruguay fought against Paraguay, the latter losing around half of its territory (Bethell 1996). Misiones and part of Chaco have belonged to Argentina since then and Brazil appropriated part of the federated state of present-day Mato Grosso do Sul.

Other conflicts between territories or with indigenous peoples (→ Nation State, I/11) resulted in shifting borders in the South and along the West Coast of South America. For example, characterized in the official historiography as *Campaña del/al Desierto*, the campaign of destruction against indigenous peoples viewed as "barbarians" resulted in the expansion of the Argentinian nation from 1878 to 1880 in the Pampas and in Patagonia (Shumway 1993, 168–187). The territories of Chubut, Neuquén, Rio Negro, and Santa Cruz were established in 1884. In the *Guerra del Pacífico* (or *Guerra del Guano y el Salitre*) of 1879–1883 against Bolivia and Peru, Chile won major territories in the North (Sater 2007). Chile incorporated the Peruvian province of Tarapacá as well as Tacna and Arica. With the loss of the coastal region around Antofagasta, Bolivia remained without access to the sea. It further consolidated its territory in the south as part of the war characterized by the invading government forces as "Pacificacíon" and by modern historiography as "Ocupación de la Araucanía" (Bengoa 1985, 205–326). Chile thereby reversed the sovereignty of the Mapuches that had been confirmed by Spain in the Treaty of Quilín ratified in 1641 and later by the Parliament of Tapihue.

Justification: concepts and doctrines

The territorial expansion of the U.S. was justified through the concept of Manifest Destiny (Johannsen et al. 1997). It was one of the most important driving forces for the appropriation of Spanish and Mexican territories. The term, "Manifest Destiny" was coined by the journalist, John L. O'Sullivan in 1845 in an essay published in the newspaper, *The United States Democratic Review* titled "Annexation." There, the New Yorker sketched out the idea of a central national destiny ("Providence") "to overspread and to possess the whole of the continent." This should cultivate "the great experience of liberty and federated self-government entrusted to us" (→ Foundational Discourses, III/8).

Driven by a strong sense of mission, this idea that captured the expansionistic mood in the U.S. appeared to justify the geographic expansion of the U.S. westward and southward mostly by white, European settlers by invoking the notion of a "higher law" (→ Whiteness, I/46). As Amy S. Greenberg demonstrated, *filibustering* was discursively constructed as a masculine activity (Greenberg 2006). O'Sullivan recommended that Texas be annexed which ended up happening in the war against Mexico (1846–1848) under President James K. Polk (1845–1849). At the end of these processes, the states of Arizona, California, Nevada, New Mexico, Texas, and Utah belonged to the U.S.

Many contemporaries invoked the Manifest Destiny whereby there was never a consensus regarding its identifying characteristics or implementation. Manifest Destiny equated the westward and southward expansion as destiny and extended the invitation to do so. Manifest Destiny became the mindset of many, but by far, not all people. No convincing political directives could be derived from it. "Democracy" and "Civilization" were values that distinguished the American nation and were achieved on settlement borders (→ Borderlands, II/26), but whose notable racist and religious foundations led to physical liquidation and the expulsion of indigenous peoples into reservations. Frederick Jackson Turner commemorated the related interaction between "wilderness" and "civilization" in a speech in 1893 before the Congress of the American Historical Association on the *Significance of the Frontier in American History* in honor of the World's Columbian Exposition in Chicago.

Canadian expansionism was in response to American expansionism. Thus, it has a defensive component. In contrast to U.S. American expansionism, it followed a political *nation-building* concept as opposed to a culturally loaded *Go West (and South)* idea (→ Nation and State Building, I/16). A direct military confrontation between the U.S. and Canada (regarding Great Britain) could thereby be avoided. Latin America, especially in Argentina, Brazil, and Chile, expansionism also followed a *nation-building* concept. As in the U.S. and Canada, it also involved brutal, violent processes used to bring under state control space and landscapes used by indigenous peoples. In a manuscript published in Chile in 1845 titled *Civilización i Barbarie. Vida de Facundo Quiroga. Aspecto Fisco, Costumbres y Ábitos de la Republica Argentina*, Argentinian writer and political scientist, Domingo Faustino Sarmiento (1845), president of his country from 1868 to 1874, cited the keywords used by white and mestizo elites in South America to draw attention to the problem: "civilization" versus "barbarianism"; development (→ II/6) versus underdevelopment; and order versus chaos. The deep-rooted loathing with respect to barbarianism primarily targeted indigenous peoples, the "salvajes," for which he saw no alternative other than to "exterminio [extermination]."

Although Manifest Destiny was imprinted in the consciousness of most Americans and was constitutive for personal identity, serving as a guiding principle, especially for settlers, entrepreneurs, and filibusters, concrete directives could not be derived at the political level. Instead, U.S. American foreign policy of the long 19th century referred to the Monroe Doctrine that President James Monroe (1817–1825) laid out in his annual address to the U.S. Congress. The speech made by the fifth president of the United States was a response to what was considered at the time to be the "Holy Alliance" of the conservative powers of Austria, Russia, and Prussia in 1814/15. Similar to Great Britain's Foreign Secretary, George Canning (1822–1827), Monroe viewed the European Alliance as a political security threat for America. Monroe explicitly mentioned four dimensions of the danger of Europe: colonization, political interference, intervention, and political-territorial control. As compensation for shielding Europe from the types of expansion seen in the "new world," he offered American restraint toward Europe (and the rest of the world) which was viewed as a commitment to continental isolation. In formulating parameters "to our peace and safety," Monroe included the Latin American Republics. If any of the European powers were to dare to intervene in the American double continent and thereby pursue recolonization projects, "such interposition" would not be viewed "with indifference." "It is equally impossible, therefore, that we should behold such interposition in any form with indifference."

Some Latin-American politicians viewed this proclamation as a guarantee for territorial integrity and political autonomy. However, since Monroe, the only time the U.S. stood up for the "southern brethren" was when this served the overarching goal of asserting its own interests and the maintenance of "our peace and safety." De facto, U.S. decision-makers conducted a cost-benefit analysis for every European intervention and there are many examples in the 19th century in which the U.S. did not hurry to the assistance of its "brethren in the South" even though they needed it. The U.S. was not present in 1833 when Great Britain occupied the Malvine Islands, in 1838, when France began the "Pastry War" with Mexico and simultaneously began occupation operations in the La Plata region, in 1861, when Spain took control over Santo Domingo in accordance with the wishes of the elite to repel Haiti, or in 1864, when France instated the Hapsburg, Archduke Maximilian, as emperor of Mexico.

There was no empirically verifiable principle of U.S. support for its "southern brethren" when it was required in order to avoid foreign intervention. Quite the contrary: Although President James K. Polk (1845–1849) translated Monroe's speech to mean that any intervention in America by Europe is prohibited, the newly formulated doctrine did not only primarily serve to protect against Europe's drive for expansion, but rather was also an instrument of North American power politics at the expense of the territorial integrity of the weakly consolidated "sister republics" in the South. In his speech presented to the U.S. Congress on December 2, 1845, the eleventh president of the U.S. attempted to dispel any doubts the British had regarding the annexation of Texas to the U.S. in the same year (Perkins 1993, 64–106).

From that point forward, U.S. presidents referred to the Monroe Doctrine for any sovereignty violations south of the Rio Grande River. The nearly ritualized invocation of the "doctrine" served to avoid explanations about the actual causes. Through repeated referencing and rhetorical confirmations, it became a sacrosanct principle. To force the acceptance of this mechanism both domestically and abroad, increasingly more real power had to exist than the U.S. actually possessed.

Latin-American governments had very little to counter such power. Nevertheless, there was no shortage of proclamations about alternatives. Simón Bolívar recognized the danger early on. He sought to avoid destructive conflicts between neighboring republics through a union of American states and simultaneously strengthen defenses against third parties. The South American *Liberatador* urged the American republics to help themselves and to build a coalition based on equality and balance. He supported the establishment of Hispano-America as an international actor, the strengthening of the region to repel any attempts of the Spaniards at recapturing it, and the solidification of the dominant republican principle. He considered the federation, as an organizational form, the best solution.

He hoped to lay the cornerstone to this structure before the Congress of Panama in 1826. All previous colonies of Spain and Portugal as well as the U.S., Great Britain, and the Netherlands were invited to the symbolic location between North and South America, where the Atlantic and Pacific oceans are closest (Granados García 2004, 44–48). Although Bolívar's wish for a grand American alliance was not met because only Mexico, the Central American Federation, Great Columbia, and Peru sent delegates, his analysis of the dangers of the sovereignty of the Latin-American Republics retained their validity. Therefore, publishers and politicians in the Americas continued to hold on to the notion of a Latin-American security alliance. The justification for such an alliance was not only the external threat presented to all post-colonial nations, but also the unifying cultural foundation of the new nations: the founding myths of the Latin-American Republics, the colonially imprinted *raza* (including the *mestizaje* process), Catholicism and exclusion of the "other" (→ Foundational Discourses, III/8). The components of community rooted in the notion of being "Latin American" were reinforced in Independence Day celebrations, memorial sites, speeches, manuscripts, newspapers and magazines, and supplemented national tales (Palacios 2009) (→ Memory Politics, II/34).

The Kingdom of Brazil differed from the rest of South and Central America whereby the postulate of independence that manifested itself with the departure of Portugal did not coincide with the rejection of the dominance of colonial masters, of slave trade (→ Slavery, I/18), and the principle of monarchy by the creole, Republican-leaning elite. In this country, the principle of monarchy was defended until the end of the 1880s and tied to the leitmotiv of civilization.

Interventionism in the early 20th century

In addition to territorial expansion, interventionism brought another form of control into use (Fischer 2012, 53–59). Instead of trusting primarily in negotiations, the Washington decision-makers developed an extensive repertoire of techniques and corresponding discursive justification strategies to assert their own interests in Latin America swiftly and without compromise. This instrument came to be used increasingly more frequently following the victory of the Spanish-American War, affecting Central America the most, although interventionist policies were common throughout South and Central America, well into the 1930s. Very often, the U.S. government refused to provide diplomatic recognition if irregularities occurred in the voting process, the U.S. blocked loans to nations, as well as interfered in their voting processes. In the latter case, the U.S., for example, even sent troops into countries south of the Rio Bravo although there was never an intention to occupy or to build colonies. U.S. Navy war ships and Marine infantry were deployed with increased frequency and whereby France, Great Britain, Germany, and Italy usually justified their constant pressure and military intervention by pointing to outstanding loan payments, the U.S. government justified sovereignty violations by pointing to the need to topple corrupt governments (to be defined on a case-by-case basis) and to eliminate mismanagement in the state budget and the lack of discipline in debt management, as well as to bring order to chaos, to set up democratically legitimate governments (→ Democracy, II/32), and to punish property violations and violence.

Military interventions occurred in Columbia (1903, cession from Panama), in Honduras (1903, 1907, 1919, 1924, 1925), in Cuba (1898–1903, 1906–1909, 1917–1922), in the Dominican Republic (1907, 1916–1925), in Nicaragua (1912–1925, 1926–1933), in Mexico (1914, 1915, 1916/17, 1918), in Haiti (1914, 1915, 1916/17), and in Panama (1925). For example, after the decision to build the Panama Canal, the U.S. focused its intervention in Nicaragua largely on preventing a second waterway from the Atlantic to the Pacific. Any Nicaraguan president who called the U.S. monopoly over the isthmus into question or who offered their land to other interested parties such as Germany or Japan, had to assume that he would be removed from office. For this reason, the enlightened despot, José Santos Zelaya was violently removed from office in 1909 with the support of the State Department (Schoonover 1991, 130–148; Langley 1983, 53–76). The rationale provided by the Howard Taft administration for his support for the coup was that it had to do with ending a dictatorship, protecting life and property of U.S. citizens, and defending neighboring countries from unrest. The *marines* stationed in that country from 1912 to 1925 were, however, not in a position to put these principles into action. The elections from 1912 and 1916 were accompanied by unrest and procedural irregularities and, as a result, no stable government emerged. Until the elections in 1928, the U.S. blocked all liberal presidents since the decision-makers in Washington mistrusted the liberal opposition due to their animosity toward the U.S., concurrence with the formation of a Central American union as supported by Costa Rica, and the adoption of underclass themes in their voting platforms. Nevertheless, using "neutral" U.S. citizens to administer external tariffs, the "National Bank," and the "Pacific Bank" were highly controversial among some local elites as they were excluded from these "national" resources. The single greatest success was in 1914 when the U.S. was able to secure from its Nicaraguan representative in Washington, from the conservative Emiliano Chamorro through the Bryan-Chamorro Treaty, the promise that no other power besides the U.S. would be permitted to undertake the construction of the canal (Schoultz 1999, 226–228).

As Paul W. Drake discovered, the more revolutionary, adversarial, or unstable Latin-American presidents were, the more determined the decision-makers in Washington were to remove them from office or to occupy whole stretches of land or countries. On the other hand, governments that were friendly and democratically elected could have great hopes of recognition and support from the U.S. (Drake 1991, 5). Interventions in Latin America usually had little to do with achieving the democratic participation (→ II/41) of its people. Indeed, it was preferable to have governments south of the Rio Bravo legitimized through elections. However, in contrast to white and somewhat less frequently mestizo governments, black, mulatto, and indigenous groups had little chance of obtaining support from the U.S. in their endeavors at democratic participation. With strong roots in the black and mulatto populations, the Cuban Liberal Party had firsthand experience with this. With undemocratic means and with the support of the U.S., they were kept out of power until the 1920s. This was felt particularly during the revolt against election fraud, the Guerra del Chambelona, during the administration of the conservative, President Menocal.

Justification: concepts and doctrines

Interventions in "black" and "mulatto" countries were justified in the U.S. using a paternalistic and racist discourse (→ Race, I/39). Modifying the idea of Manifest Destiny, the father-son metaphor, frequently depicted by publishers and illustrators, assumed that it was the pedagogical and moral duty of the superior, "civilized" (white U.S.-American) authority (→ Whiteness, I/46) to show the backward (Latin-American) countries the way, if necessary, by force. As Mary A. Renda demonstrated, paternalism was not only a justification that was not at all squeamish about the imposition of material and geopolitical interests (→ Geopolitics, II/34), but also the guiding notion behind white supremacy and preordained authority (Renda 2001, 89–130). White and mestizo elites in Latin America also adopted this concept to defend their privileges against most of the population.

At the international level, decision-makers in Washington justified interventions by referencing the Monroe Doctrine. President Theodore Roosevelt (1901–1909) reformulated it to mean that the U.S. would serve as the "international police" of last resort that would adjust conditions in Latin-American countries "if it became evident that their inability or unwillingness to do justice at home and abroad had violated rights of the United States or had invited foreign aggression to the detriment of the entire body of American nations" (Roosevelt 1904, n.p.). As a result of this discourse, diplomatic pressure and military interventions were used to install progressive regimes and to set development processes into motion in the southern part of the hemisphere. Roosevelt laid claim to the monopoly to decide if, when, and where interventions were to occur in the interest of progress. As justification, he also relied on the alleged supremacy of the U.S. "civilization." The American press understood the epochal meaning of Roosevelt's speech and thoroughly debated it (Veeser 2003, 320).

Woodrow Wilson (1913–1923) also created a new, paternalistic discourse. Interventions were to take place in the event of voter fraud or the overthrow of presidents. For Wilson, the Monroe Doctrine was not self-explanatory but rather a figure of argumentation that became part of his Pan American project (→ Pan-Americanism, II/40). He envisioned the construction of an international community of nations that all work collaboratively to secure borders and political independence. He partially followed the advocacy against the Monroe Doctrine published by Hiram Bingham in 1913. Bingham disliked how it had been reduced to an instrument used to justify aggressive interventions in Latin America that only served the interests of superpowers and their economic interests. He advocated for the construction of a cooperative Pan-Americanism (Bingham 1913, 109–112).

Latin-American publishers, statesmen, and intellectuals usually had very little to counteract American pressures. An additional difficulty was that American interventionism almost always found support among the local elites that relied on outside assistance to be able to exert power. Nationalists and elites displaced from power in Latin-American countries rejected interventionistic *monroísmo* as an unauthorized violation of sovereignty. Partly supported by anti-imperialist Americans, they attempted to construct a discursive wall of defense. The so-called Drago Doctrine played an important role here. On the occasion of the Venezuelan crisis of December 29, 1902, the Argentinian Foreign Minister Luis M. Drago (1902/1903) wrote the U.S. Secretary of State that stronger nations using gunboats to advance against weaker nations that were formally sovereign was a violation of international law. He referred to universal rights that supersede those of the U.S. and Latin-American human rights experts referred to this note whenever they criticized the gunboat politics of the European powers to assert their debt claims against private citizens (→ Human Rights, II/35).

A small success at the Hague Peace Conference in 1907 was achieved by Latin-American supporters of this view, whose invitation to the event was thanks to the support of Theodore Roosevelt. At this international conference, the codification of the Drago Doctrine that most of the "New World" delegates demanded did not obtain full approval. However, they were able to negotiate a convention that was in the spirit of the recommendation made at the conference of the American nations in Rio de Janeiro during the previous year and that was also supported by the U.S. delegation led by General Horace Porter. This initiated an arbitration tribunal for conflict resolution although they did not declare it to be obligatory and therefore did not condemn the use of force as a last resort. When compared to the gunboat politics usually practiced by imperialist powers in such cases, most viewed tribunal courts as the lesser evil in the face of delayed debt payments in other countries and complaints by international investors. This mechanism came to be used for international conflicts among Latin-American neighbors as well and led to the negotiation of numerous bilateral agreements.

Latin Americans also attempted to modify the Monroe Doctrine by invoking the sovereignty principle (Fischer 2012, 272–339). Its interventionistic components were sharply criticized in numerous articles, essays, and manuscripts. Whereas American caricatures depicted the actions of Uncle Sam south of Rio Bravo as a well-intended father figure, Latin-American artists presented him as a greedy, well-armed oppressor. These interrelated views of nation on the American continent could not have been more different: On the one side was the self-confident, successful U.S. American empire and on the other side, as contrast foil, were the predominantly weaker nations that were not able to effectively protect national sovereignty, the fundament of every nation-state (→ II/38).

The Mexican President Venustiano Carranza therefore rejected the interventionistic component of the Monroe Doctrine in the sharpest of tones in his speech before the delegates in1918. Another showground was the League of Nations that, according to Woodrow Wilson, was to increase respect for "great and small states alike." Latin American publicists and delegates used the arena of the League of Nations to push for what could be said. It was against the backdrop of the U.S. invasion of Nicaragua in 1926, that the anti-interventionist discourse regarding the Monroe Doctrine reached a climax. The League of Nations could not get around accepting the non-interventionist interpretation of the Monroe Doctrine. The Latin-American Republics also used this interpretation as a legitimation aid at the Pan American conferences (→ Pan-Americanism, II/40). However, the sought-after legalization of respect for national sovereignty was not achieved in the context of an Inter-American convention until 1933.

Works cited

Bengoa, José. 1985. *Historia del pueblo Mapuche: siglo XIX y XX*. Santiago: Ediciones Sur.

Bethell, Leslie. 1996. "The Paraguayan War (1864–1870)." *Institute of Latin American Studies Research Papers* 46.

Bingham, Hiram. 1913. *The Monroe Doctrine: An Obsolete Shibboleth*. New Haven, London, and Oxford: Oxford University Press.

Drake, Paul. 1991. "From Good Men to Good Neighbors, 1912–1932." In *Exporting Democracy. The United States and Latin America*, ed. Abraham F. Lowenthal, 3–40. Baltimore: John Hopkins University Press.

Fischer, Thomas. 2012. *Die Souveränität der Schwachen. Lateinamerika und der Völkerbund, 1920-1936.* Stuttgart: Steiner Verlag.

Granados García, Aimer. 2004. "Congresos e intelectuales en los inicios de un proyecto y de una conciencia continental latinoamericana, 1826–1860." In *Construcción de las identidades latinoamericanas*, ed. Aimer Granados García and Carlos Marichal, 39–69. Mexico City: El Colegio de México.

Greenberg, Amy S. 2006. *Manifest Manhood and the Antebellum American Empire.* Cambridge: Cambridge University Press.

Johannsen, Robert Walter, Sam W. Haynes, and Christopher Morris. 1997. *Manifest Destiny and Empire: American Antebellum Expansionism.* Arlington: Texas A&M University Press.

Langley, Lester D. 1983. *The Banana Wars: An Inner History of American Empire 1900–1934.* Lexington: University Press of Kentucky.

May, Robert E. 2002. *Manifest Destiny's Underworld: Filibustering in Antebellum America.* Chapel Hill: University of Northern Carolina Press.

Palacios, Guillermo. ed. 2009. *La nación y su historia: independencias, relato historiográfico y debates sobre la nación.* México City: América Latina, siglo XIX.

Perkins, Bradford. 1993. *The Creation of a Republican Empire, 1776–1865.* New York: Cambridge University Press.

Renda, Mery A. 2001. *Taking Haiti: Military Occupation and the Culture of U.S. Imperialism, 1915–1940.* Chapel Hill: The University of North Carolina Press.

Roosevelt, Theodore. "Roosevelt Corollary to the Monroe Doctrine." *Teaching American History.* https://teachingamericanhistory.org/library/document/roosevelt-corollary-to-monroe-doctrine/.Orig.pub.1904.

Sarmiento, Domingo Faustino. 1845. *Civilización i barbarie. Vida de Juan Facundo Quiroga. Aspecto físico, costumbres i ábitos de la República de Argentina.* Santiago: Imprenta del Progreso.

Sater, William F. 2007. Andean Tragedy: Fighting the War of the Pacific, 1879–1884. Lincoln and London: University of Nebraska Press.

Schoonover, Thomas. 1991. *The United States in Central America, 1860–1911. Episodes of Social Imperialism and Imperial Rivalry in the World System.* Durham and London: Duke University Press.

Schoultz, Lars. 1999. *Beneath the United States: A History of U.S. Policy Toward Latin America.* Cambridge, MA and London: Harvard University Press.

Shumway, Nicolas. 1993. *The Invention of Argentina.* Berkeley: University of California Press.

Veeser, Cyrus. 2003. "Inventing Dollar Diplomacy. The Gilded-Age Origins of the Roosevelt Corollary to the Monroe Doctrine." *Diplomatic History* 27, no. 3: 301–326.

37
MILITARY

David Pion-Berlin

Long ago, the United States marked out Latin America as its hegemonic sphere of influence. From its proclamation of the Monroe Doctrine in 1823 and Roosevelt Corollary in 1904, to its countless overt and covert interventions in Central America, the Caribbean, and South America (→ Interventionism, II/36), the United States established itself as the supreme power in the hemisphere (→ Geopolitics, II/34). From gunboat diplomacy of the early 20th century, to the Cold War in the second half of that century, Washington remained determined to advance its economic, political and security (→ II/45) interests in the region, and would resort to various forms of "hard power" to do so, and with great success. The U.S. dominance in the region is reflected in the titles of volumes such as *The Hovering Giant* (Blasier 1976), *Talons of the Eagle* (Smith 2007), and *Beneath the United States* (Schoultz 1998).

As the perennial superpower, the U.S. should be able to dictate to nations in the hemisphere what their defense and national security priorities should be. Its primary instrument would be the armed forces, which should, in theory, have considerable sway with the militaries and governments of its southern neighbors. Military to military ties are the avenues of influence, including foreign sales, assistance, training, and education (→ I/24). These links have been long-standing features of Inter-American relations, and they continue to this day.

Although the U.S. remains the greatest military power internationally, its influence in the region has declined. Washington faces strategic threats in other corners of the globe, diverting its attention away from Latin America. Other states meanwhile, have discovered the region as an attractive place for exports and investments. Episodically the U.S. has re-engaged, but has not been able to recapture the days of Cold War domination. Latin American states have devised ways of gaining advantages, even though they remain the weaker party. In the post-Cold War era, the degree of influence the U.S. still exerts and to what purpose is exemplified by the military educational programs that constitute a form of soft power projection. Important educational ties with its southern neighbors have been forged over decades, but their influence has been debated with both progressive and conservative critiques tending to inflate Washington's ability to shape Latin American military thinking and behavior through its educational institutions, either making dubious causal claims or focusing on good intentions rather than results. The U.S., however, is neither the hegemon of the past, nor is it inconsequential.

Is the U.S. an episodic hegemon?

The United States can be described historically as an episodic hegemon. Its influence ebbs and flows depending on regional and international conditions. This has less to do with its store of power, as measured by GNP, wealth, foreign investments, military capabilities, etc., where it maintains huge advantages with respect to Latin American nations, and more to do with its interest in and attention to the region, or lack thereof. Washington normally has plenty of power to wield; the question is whether it chooses to do so.

Unlike any of the other countries in the region, the U.S. has a global reach, global interests to protect, and thus a global perspective (→ Geopolitics, II/34). Its military bases and facilities number in the hundreds and are scattered worldwide, from which thousands of soldiers are deployed to support U.S. allies and confront its enemies (Vine 2017). Compared to U.S. security obligations in Europe, the Middle East, and East Asia, Latin America is often times treated as a side show. There are fewer military bases remaining in Latin America, and the U.S. troops that are deployed there are engaged in joint training exercises, or assisting in counter-drug operations, but not combat. Thus, in viewing Latin America through an international lens, Washington is prone to devote less attention to the region, unless or until events there reach crisis dimensions (→ Crisis, II/4), or somehow adversely affect U.S. interests in other places.

In the post-Cold War years, the United States has been unmatched militarily. The Soviet Union had collapsed and with that, so too did the East–West ideological rivalry which had previously given impetus to some U.S. interventions, though other more economically motivated interventions had also occurred. Cuba was hit hard economically by the Soviet fall, as it lost its customary subsidies from Moscow and faced growing scarcities. It turned inward to cope with its crisis, and could no longer exert the same political influence abroad it once had. Left-wing insurgents in Central America had disbanded, as the civil wars gripping El Salvador and Guatemala came to a close by the early 1990s. With no security rivals to worry about, U.S. dominance in the region was unquestioned (→ Security, II/45). And yet, it was precisely because threats from the south had subsided that Washington perceived there was less at stake there. Greater dangers were lurking in other corners of the globe and would rear their ugly heads by the end of the 20th century. Consequently, the U.S. would turn its attention to those challenges, and turn away from Latin America.

As a result of the 9/11 attacks, the U.S. ramped up its intelligence gathering capabilities, and set its military and other security forces loose in a hunt for the terrorist perpetrators and in a quest to deter future attacks. This of course meant that the U.S. focus would be largely centered on the Middle East, and parts of Asia and Africa as well. Latin America was a low priority. During the post-9/11 era, the George W. Bush administration "paid only lip service to Inter-American affairs," as Peter Smith wrote (2007, 398).

And it was U.S. neglect, adds Smith that gave Latin America "substantial room for maneuver" (2007, 399). The irony of the U.S. downgrading Latin America as a regional priority meant that states there could explore options that in decades past were thought to be off the table. A tide of left-wing governments swept to power, in Argentina, Chile, Brazil, Ecuador, Venezuela, and El Salvador with no resistance from Washington at all (→ Socialism, I/42). Economically, Latin America discovered good trade and investment deals with Washington's arch economic rival – China – thus lowering its dependence on the United States. If there is any proof that the Monroe Doctrine is dead and gone, it is China's uncontested penetration and exploitation of this hemisphere's markets.

Its store of power notwithstanding, it is doubtful that the U.S. can dramatically alter these developments, regaining the advantages it had in the 20th century. Trade and investment with China have forged new economic arrangements that cannot be easily undone by Washington. China, along with Russia, have been developing important defense economic relations with South American partners (→ Global Commodity Chains, II/12), bolstering Brazil's ground-based air defenses, exporting helicopters, jets, and tanks to Venezuela, while helping to modernize Nicaragua's military capabilities (Gouvea 2017). In the 1990s the U.S. accounted for 25 percent of the region's imports in defense products; in the first two decades of the 2000s, that is down to 10.2 percent (Gouvea 2017). Meanwhile, new South American political and security institutions seem to be here to stay. Hence, even if the U.S. suddenly turns its attention back to Latin America, it cannot resume where it had left off during the Cold War; it faces a new, more assertive and more autonomous set of southern neighbors.

By the same token, this does not mean that the U.S. has lost all of its influence; far from it. Cyclical downturns in Latin America's economic performance – not to mention China's – almost insure that there will be opportunities for the U.S. to regain some of its lost advantage, offering trade and investment deals that compete nicely with its rivals (Mares 2016). And security (→ II/45) concerns – especially the scourge of drug trafficking and organized crime and the violence they induce – will mean that countries there will not easily afford to turn down Washington's helping hand when it offers financial and technical assistance in combating narco-criminals.

The determination with which the U.S. chooses to engage Latin America, contest its choices, or ignore it has varied across time as has been said, but also by issue arenas. Arceneaux and Pion-Berlin (2005) distinguish between high and low politics in accounting for why U.S. influence, along with powerful international banks and financial institutions, would be greater on some issues, while national actors would exert more pull on other issues. High politics means high stakes, where governments believe their vital interests hang in the balance. Superpowers like the U.S. will be strongly inclined to intrude in the domestic affairs of Latin American states if doing so is perceived as necessary to protect or enhance its national security and economic well-being. Low politics is low stakes, where the superpower does not associate its own well-being with internal struggles of other states over questions of poverty reduction (→ Social Inequality, II/20), education (→ I/24), democratization (→ Democracy, II/32), or human rights (→ II/35), and is thus willing to let events take their course. Another way of visualizing this is in respect to the sovereign powers of states (→ Nation State, II/38). Sovereignty does not throw up the same set of defenses from issue to issue. It is a more formidable barrier in the realm of low politics than in the realm of high politics.

In short, outcomes are not predetermined. The U.S. may drive a tough bargain in certain circumstances and prevail, but in other circumstances lose out; in still other scenarios, it may not care enough to win, allowing the weaker states to get their way. David Mares sums up the choices nicely when he says, "In some cases, the U.S. is successful in getting what it wants, in other cases it does not care, and in still others it opposes what is happening and cannot stop it" (2016, 308).

A declining hegemon?

If this is the deal, it is certainly a less dominant situation for the U.S. than in decades past. There are a number of scholars who believe that the general long-term pattern, however uneven, has been one of declining U.S. power, but they do not agree on the cause. Is it simply U.S. inattentiveness? Probably not, though that is a serious causal contender. Scholars have also suggested the decline may be attributed to deeper, systemic shifts provoked by the great financial crisis of 2008 (→ Crisis, II/4), as the world moves from unipolarity to multipolarity (→ Geopolitics, II/34). The U.S. has lost its economic edge and even political standing to other states, and must now compete for opportunities. Others maintain it is Latin America's own counter-hegemonic thrusts, provoked by a certain anti-American sentiment (Long 2016).

Looking back over the last few decades, by and large what stands out is how the U.S. has struggled to gain control in the region, says Tom Long. In a recent book he asks how this could be, if power relations between the U.S. and Latin America are so asymmetric (Long 2015). He argues that economically and militarily weaker states have actually been able to modify relations with the U.S. to their advantage. They did so by "… affecting the U.S. policy agenda and the way in which the United States defined and pursued its interests in the region" (Long 2015, 217). Astute leaders were able to manipulate U.S. power for their own benefit. Creative agency can prevail over structural constraints arising out of power asymmetries.

For instance, Bogota, exerted considerable influence in the shaping of the 2000 U.S. assistance package known as Plan Colombia. Initially, lawmakers in Washington agreed to nothing more than counter-drug assistance to stem the flow of narcotics into the U.S. They were particularly reticent to direct any aid to the Colombian military, wary of entangling the U.S. in another Vietnam-styled quagmire. But the Colombian Government successfully conflated the fight against drug trafficking with the fight against the guerrillas, arguing the former could not be won without assisting the Colombian armed forces in its counter insurgency efforts (Long 2015, 174–216). Colombian leaders effectively lobbied the Department of Defense, the State Department and the U.S. Congress, eventually steering the aid in directions of their own choosing. Then, events on 9/11 would help Colombia even further as the struggle against insurgents (now labeled terrorists) became more urgent. This all occurred just as the FARC was gravitating toward the use of narco-trafficking to fund its operations, helping win the argument that guerrillas and drugs were two sides of the same coin. Rather than visualizing Plan Colombia as an intervention into a vulnerable state, it should be seen as an agreement that allowed Colombia to take advantage of U.S. resources.

In what remains a structurally asymmetric relation, weaker Latin American states still retain a strong element of agency. Those states will associate with the U.S. when it is in their interests to do so, but will also alter the terms of their alignment. For example, many Latin American states expressed solidarity with the U.S. fight against international terrorism, following the 9/11 attacks. The rhetorical pledge to fight terrorism alongside Washington was extremely useful in locking in greater amounts of U.S. military assistance, but at the same time often disguised an anemic commitment to follow through with actual policies. Most Latin American countries have not prioritized counter-terror operations, seriously doubting that Hezbollah, Al-Qaeda, ISIS, and other terror groups pose a grave threat to their region. But because Washington was not paying particular attention to the region in the years following 9/11, Latin America's verbal allegiance to the cause seemed to be enough.

Washington may at one point, have held itself up as the exemplar for Latin American states to follow – its military professionals, its counter-drug, counter-terror agencies and strategies, its development specialists (→ Development, II/6) – serving as guides for the less developed nations of the south. However, Latin American states are no longer attracted to the U.S. model; they are cautious, critical and discerning; they decide when or whether they will follow Washington's lead, and often choose not to. Latin America spoke in unison in its opposition to the U.S. effort to gain access to several military bases in Colombia after its 10-year lease of the Manta air force base in Ecuador had expired; refused to support various U.S. initiatives in the Organization of American States (OAS); and most recently took President Trump to task for his decision to build a wall at the U.S.-Mexican border (→ Borderlands, II/26), and his suggestion that he would not rule out military intervention to topple the Maduro Government in Venezuela.

The title of Brian Loveman's 2006 edited volume, *Addicted to Failure*, speaks to this change in the power dynamic. According to Loveman, U.S. policies to promote democracy (→ II/32), human rights (→ II/35), economic progress, peace and stability, have failed, and highlights the difference between U.S. foreign policy toward Latin America at the beginning of the 21st, compared to earlier decades, where the problem was not the undesirability of its programs, but the failure to see these programs through. Perhaps three or four decades earlier, a book written about U.S. imperialism would have not only criticized Washington's intentions, but lamented how Latin America had again fallen under the sway of its influence. However now, according to Loveman, the U.S. is no longer dominant, and instead, "… continues to pursue failed policies" (2006, 15). In one sense, the analysis is, perhaps unintentionally congratulatory, since it is conceding that the U.S. has expressed some worthy goals: democracy promotion, rule of law and competitive markets. Policies, were, the author argues, designed with these goals in mind. The difficulty, he suggests, is that the policies were misguided and self-destructive, undercutting the very goals the U.S. wished to pursue.

Rather than pushing back against Latin America's condemnations, U.S. administrations have tended toward either complacency or conciliation, tacitly admitting that the United States does not have the domineering presence it once enjoyed in the hemisphere, and that it must reconcile itself to a more co-equal relation with other countries in the region. President Obama set the tone early in his first term, when he attended the Fifth Summit of the Americas in Trinidad in April 2009 and said, "I pledge to you that we seek an equal partnership. There is no senior partner and junior partner in our relations; there is simply engagement based on mutual respect and common interests and shared values" (Randall 2013, 8). Washington's leaders had verbalized commitments like this many times in the past, even as they pursued coercive, unilateral interventions simultaneously. However, currently, as Stephen J. Randall noted, "the U.S. simply does not have the power or relevance it once had" (2013, 10).

Military educational ties: Evidence of U.S. hegemony or decline?

With these thoughts in mind, it is worthwhile to assess the impact of U.S.-Latin American military ties. The armed forces represent the ultimate power asset, and the U.S. remains globally unrivaled in this domain. If the U.S. is prepared to deploy that force, no Latin American state can stop them. Indeed, they did not, as U.S. troops stormed the beaches of the Dominican Republic in 1965, invaded Grenada in 1986, and overran Panama City in 1989.

The age of U.S. military interventionism (→ II/36) has passed, but what remains and is more critical are the long-standing relations the U.S. military has forged with its counterparts in Latin America. Based on sales, loans, grants, training, joint missions, and perhaps most importantly, education (→ I/24), Washington has tried and continues to try to build cooperative security relations through defense partnerships in the region, as a way of advancing its own security interests (U.S. Departments of Defense and State 2014) (→ Security,

II/45). If the Pentagon can develop relations with other militaries, it will have more reliable allies in the fight against terrorism and drug trafficking. Additionally, the Pentagon claims that it works to improve foreign military institutions so that they can play a more positive role in their own democratic societies, and that includes showing greater respect for human rights (→ II/35).

A critical component to this strategy is the International Military Education and Training (IMET) program that provide defense educational experiences for foreign troops. Founded in 1976, IMET is implemented through formal instruction in more than 4,000 courses delivered at some 150 military schools and installations. Approximately 6–7,000 international students from 135 nations participate annually (U.S. Departments of Defense and State 2014). IMET is funded and overseen by the Department of State, but is administered and implemented through the Department of Defense. It is a low budgeted program ($102 million in fiscal year 2013) but one advertised as being quite cost effective. Its purposes are to contribute to collective security, stability and peace by professionalizing foreign militaries willing to work with the U.S. (U.S. Departments of Defense and State 2014). Its intent is to build mutually beneficial military to military relations by providing critical training to participant nations. As foreign forces improve their understanding of U.S. military standards and values, their cooperation with U.S. forces is enhanced, thus helping the overall security effort in the region.

Its additional purpose is to "instill and maintain democratic values and protect internationally recognized human rights in their own government and military" (U.S. Departments of Defense and State 2014). These goals were given renewed emphasis with the creation of an expanded IMET (E-IMET) in the 1990s. E-IMET's five-fold focus was to engender a greater grasp and respect for democracy (→ II/32), civilian control, rule of law, military justice and human rights (→ II/35) (Cope 1995). The idea is that values can best be transmitted face to face; that soldiers from Latin America would be more likely to fully absorb and commit to a set of principles when directly exposed to those points of view within the classroom, mixing with U.S. soldiers and teachers. They would transmit their new-found knowledge and values back home to other soldiers, and especially to leaders within defense- related institutions, and government and society writ large.

The mere mention of human rights advocacy and U.S. military training in the same sentence is sure to raise eyebrows. The U.S. has earned real notoriety for its educational practices in the past. Its School of the Americas (S.O.A.), which received IMET funding, was infamous for having trained Latin American soldiers who then went on to commit atrocities in their home countries (Gill 2004). The School spawned an entire protest movement aimed at shutting the institution down (SOAW 2018) (→ Social Movements, I/41). Critics dubbed it the "School of Assassins," pointing to a number of infamous Latin American military leaders who had been S.O.A. graduates, and who had either overthrown legitimate democracies or were known for their inhumane policies (→ Authoritarianism, II/25). The S.O.A. was the subject of reports alleging the actual instruction in the use of torture – using human subjects – held at the School, when it was located in Panama (1946–84) during the height of the Cold War. But even later on, when the School moved to Ft. Benning, Georgia, it was revealed that while those practices may have been discontinued (if they were ever used) training manuals were still being circulated at S.O.A. that condoned if not encouraged similar behavior (U.S. National Security Archives 2017).

The S.O.A. has since (in 2001) been renamed the Western Hemisphere Institute for Security Cooperation (WHINSEC), and it too receives IMET funding. WHINSEC's mission is to "promote democratic values, respect for human rights, and knowledge and understanding of U.S. customs and traditions" (WHINSEC 2018). According to its own website, it has an Ethics Program and a Democracy and Human Rights Program. The latter seems restricted to a single course offered to new arrivals, which covers international human rights law, due process, and rule of law (WHINSEC 2017). Nonetheless, there is still cause for skepticism as to how seriously the Institute and its cadets take the human rights lessons, and just how much is actually transmitted back home.

Whether the U.S. military education has fostered repressive practices in Latin America, or conversely, has promoted greater respect for human rights and rule of law, in both cases its influence tends to be inflated. The leftist critique suffers from dubious claims of causality. It is true that some very notorious dictators and their subordinates took courses and earned degrees at S.O.A., as well as at other U.S.-based educational institutions, but those officers represented a small percent of the 58,000 who passed through the doors of S.O.A. Moreover, it should be asked, did those pedagogical experiences induce graduates to commit abuses, or were they already predisposed to do so? Leslie Gill's critical study of the S.O. A. states that in the case of Bolivia and Colombia,

> … earning the privilege to attend the School of the Americas depends on the number of arrests, eradicated coca fields, destroyed cocaine pits and in Colombia, dead bodies produced by soldiers … in their battles to halt drug traffic and suppress guerrilla insurgencies.
>
> *(Gill 2004, 239)*

This suggests pre-selection; that those admitted to S.O.A. were cherry-picked by commanders from both the senior host country and the U.S. because they had already fulfilled objectionable practices, which could have been reinforced at the School but certainly were not invented there.

The S.O.A., along with other IMET funded military institutions, represented just a small portion of the educational experiences of Latin American officers. Attributing too much influence to these schools is misguided, since those responsible for abuses have been subjected to many other pedagogical influences – especially their own country's military academies and training centers – which often did reinforce the same messages. This is not to absolve the S.O.A and other military schools of their responsibility, but rather to suggest the difficulty in establishing any clear, singular cause and effect between educational programs and the misguided behavior of the graduates.

Many of the worst human rights violators in Latin America seldom attended U.S. academies. Most notably the Argentines, who committed some of the worst abuses on the continent, had limited contact with the S.O.A. during the Cold War. Over the span of forty-eight years, from 1946–94, 660 Argentine officers attended the S.O.A., on average only fourteen annually – the smallest number among all South and Central American countries. And yet Argentina's military *Proceso* regime (1976–83) remains one of the most notorious abusers of human rights (→ Authoritarianism, II/25). Conversely, a country like Ecuador with a population one third the size of Argentina's and a substantially better human rights record, sent five times as many soldiers to the School during the same time period. Rather than attributing too much influence to the S.O.A., it is perhaps more constructive to analyze the particular historical circumstances of each country that helped predispose some soldiers toward committing such abuses.

Other analysts have regarded the military-military contacts more positively, expressing a confidence about their benefits that may be misplaced. Jerry Laurienti, in his 2007 book, *The U.S. Military and Human Rights Promotion: Lessons from Latin America*, argues that human rights promotion has been a vital component to U.S. military assistance programs. The key, according to him, is to "stay the course," in human rights by promoting long-term, consistent military to military contacts (Laurienti 2007, 132). He faults other scholars for focusing on absolutes; that if there were human rights violations, then the choices were to either cut aid to the offending nation or not. If a nation had a poor human rights record, then U.S. military assistance constituted, by definition, bad policy. This argument, Laurienti advises, left no allowance for the use of military assistance as a tool to impart well-intended human rights lessons. If, as he believes, Washington's goal was to improve human rights practices abroad, then of course more of its aid should be going precisely to those who were guilty of violating rights.

The difficulty with focusing too much on the content of a military assistance program is that it does not address the question of results: have these programs, in fact, been successful, or have they perpetuated undesirable behavior? If a country could be assured of ongoing assistance, year in and year out, without penalty for misconduct, this could be a disincentive for reforming bad practices. For instance, Laurienti points to Colombia as without exception, "the greatest success story for U.S. military human rights promotion" (Laurienti 2007, 90). And yet, a year after the publication of his book, revelations surfaced of widespread human rights abuses at the hands of the Colombian military. Human Rights Watch detailed the "false positive" scandal, where under intense pressure to produce results in its war against the FARC, Colombian commanders killed innocent civilians, dressed them in guerrilla fatigues and then claimed these as enemy combatant fatalities. About 3,000 of these cases were identified, between 2002–2008 (Human Rights Watch 2015).

In a similar vein, Carol Atkinson (2014) extols the virtues of U.S. military educational programs, as transmission belts for democratic knowledge and values, a form of soft power that oddly enough resides within the hardest form of power known to man, the armed forces. She analyzes the full range of U.S. military war and staff colleges, where ideas are transferred through international military networks. Soldiers interact with other soldiers, exchange ideas, form friendships, and forge professional and social networks. What emerges is a kind of epistemic community of like-minded professionals who can then spearhead reform in their home countries.

Can a soft power vehicle such as this really overcome institutional, bureaucratic inertia or outright resistance sure to manifest itself within defense ministries, governments, and armies unaccustomed to change? Atkinson seems to think so, based on statistical evidence accumulated from 169 countries, from 1972–2006. She found that countries that sent officers to study at U.S. military war and staff colleges were almost three times as likely to develop and consolidate democratic political institutions than countries that did not (Atkinson 2014, 135–136). The effect seemed to be strongest in autocratic countries where leaders had no intention of democratizing. Notwithstanding resistance to change from authoritarian leaders themselves, their regimes had poorer survival rates, succumbing to the influence of U.S. military educational programs. She finds similarly positive effects on democratic practices, noting that educational experiences reduce the propensity of regimes to deny basic freedoms to their citizens (→ Citizenship, II/27).

But how do the thoughts and actions of a collection of military students translate into wholesale regime change, let alone result in the fall of tyrants? What is the causal link between the education abroad experiences and the national, political changes she measures? It is a huge lift, to make the claim that somehow, foreign military students can not only bring valuable lessons back home, but can also transform long-standing, well-embedded practices (Omelicheva et al. 2017). Those students would either have to be numerous enough to achieve some kind of critical mass needed to push recalcitrant colleagues and superiors to enact major institutional reforms, or have risen to positions of prominence where they could single-handedly exert outsized influence over key power brokers. And all of this presumes that soft power strategies overcome the hard power realities that often dictate how militaries behave, especially within autocratic regimes (→ Authoritarianism, II/25).

In 2012, a report funded by the Defense Security Cooperation Agency (DSCA) and conducted by Thomas Bruneau and others at the Center for Civil-Military Relations, Naval Post Graduate School of Monterey, based on interviews of recent MA graduates, in-country security assistant officers, foreign service nationals and IMET policy makers from seventeen countries, along with data gathered from survey instruments and documents, explored the soft power strategies. By large proportions (95 percent) graduates said that the IMET experience increased their knowledge of U.S. democratic system and practices, and 84 percent said it had shifted their attitudes as well. Eighty-seven percent said they could apply what they had learned, and 90 percent claimed they could influence others after graduation (Bruneau et al. 2012, 34–38). The study concluded that IMET was a "very worthwhile investment to achieve U.S. goals" (Bruneau et al. 2012, 8).

At the same time, the study acknowledged that it was difficult to draw firm conclusions about IMET's actual impact on home countries. The authors recommended that a system be put in place to monitor just how or whether "recipient countries effectively utilize IMET graduates upon their completion of the program …" (Bruneau et al. 2012, 56). The report noted that since many IMET participants were mid-career officers, they were unlikely to be in positions of authority when they returned home (Bruneau et al. 2012, 34), and it would be years before they would advance sufficiently in their careers to sway others. Indeed, even as most *believed* they were having an impact on fellow officers, many of those interviewed expressed frustration at not being able to affect *institutions*, including their respective military organizations, joint staffs and defense ministries. To do so would require "buy in" from senior leadership that was not necessarily forthcoming. While the authors expressed great confidence that in time IMET graduates would make their presence felt, doubts can be raised about whether those entrenched in positions of institutional power would be open to enacting new human rights standards and practices, or to internalizing U.S. civil-military practices, just because a handful of officers return from the U.S. with glowing reports.

Conclusion

In sum, when General Bantz Craddock, former head of the U.S. European Command said "IMET remains our most powerful security cooperation tool and proves its long-term value every day" (Reveron 2007, 11), one must ask, how does he know this? Admittedly, there are well-intentioned individuals and programs within the Pentagon and its sprawling network of schools. But good intentions do not always translate into good results. The precise impact, beneficial or detrimental, of U.S. military educational programs on foreign countries' adherence to human rights (→ Citizenship, II/35), rule of law, and other democratic precepts is still unclear. In the interim, caution should be observed in attributing too much influence to this version of soft power, until more vigorous, systematic, and comparative studies have been done, which pin down the causal connections between pedagogical experiences and policy applications. For now, it should be said that U.S. military educational programs are neither hegemonic nor inconsequential.

During most of the Cold War, it may have been easier to assert that IMET and other U.S. educational programs were exerting harmful influences on Latin America. After all, Washington seemed firmly aligned, politically, financially, and militarily, with anti-communist right wing dictatorships notorious for their repression (→ Authoritarianism, II/25). Why would one not expect the Pentagon's schools to fall in line with the prevailing foreign policy of the time, and more specifically, with the preferences of the Secretary of Defense and President? Even if the best of intentions were present, (and that is a big "if") it is hard not to reach the conclusion that military to military contacts served primarily to support Washington's fierce commitment to defeating left-wing movements in the region, at whatever human cost. At the very least, as suggested earlier, schools like S.O.A. were probably reinforcing bad practices, even if they were not inventing them.

In the post-Cold War era, many question just what commitment the U.S. has to the region. The cause, if in fact it can be called one, seems to be to defeat a network of terrorists, organized criminals, drug traffickers, and the violence surrounding their activity. The U.S. Southern Command (Southcom) Commander, Admiral Kurt W. Tidd, in testimony before the Senate Armed Services Committee, in April 2017, defined "transnational threat networks" as the greatest risk to regional security and stability. These networks, says the Commander, engage in a host of illicit activities, and are "unconstrained by legal and geographical boundaries, unimpeded by morality, and fueled by enormous profits" (Tidd 2017, 5). While the threat to the U.S. looms ever present, most of these networks operate principally south of the border (→ III/3), wreaking havoc on public security (→ II/45), citizen security, and economic well-being.

But if these are the principle challenges, as perceived by U.S. commanders, the U.S. financial and manpower commitment to address them leaves something to be desired. Except for Colombia, no country in the region has received appreciable amounts of military assistance to address the threats. The U.S. footprint in the region is a light one. As Admiral Tidd admitted, the perception is that the "U.S. is disengaging from the region. Our partners plainly see that we are conducting fewer engagements; holding smaller and less frequent exercises; and that we have smaller U.S. military presence in regional embassies and fewer forces and platforms than before" (Tidd 2017, 11). Because it is not clear to Latin American states what is important to Washington, this translates into a lack of trust; that when push comes to shove, Latin American states cannot count on Washington's steady resolve to help counter the threats they face.

Unlike in the realm of economics (trade and investment), where the U.S. does face stiffer competition from other states and cannot simply assert its will, in the security realm, the U.S. has more room for maneuvering. China and Russia can sell arms, but neither competes with the U.S. when it comes to having such a large, well-established system of military to military contacts. U.S. military attaches, military groups (USMILGP), joint task forces, inter-agency partnerships (e.g. with U.S. AID) (→ Development, II/6), hemispheric army and defense ministerial conferences, and of course Southcom itself together comprise an impressive set of institutions and relations that can be used to advance worthy goals. Hence, the U.S. has the assets, and if it is not fully engaged, which it is not, it is because it has chosen not to be.

Admiral Tidd says that programs like Foreign Military Financing and Sales, as well as IMET are "foundational tools for building partner capacity, [and] sustaining trust" (Tidd 2017, 35). They are supposed to advance the cause of greater military professionalism, which entails adherence to civilian control, democratic rule of law, and respect for human rights (→ II/35). But are these tools being underutilized to achieve those purposes? Probably so. Southcom with its own Human Rights Initiative is now in its 20th year. It is structured to "bring together representatives of military, security forces, civilian government and civil society" to strengthen human rights commitments within the region's armed forces (Tidd 2017, 7) (→ Civil Society, II/28). Twenty years is more than enough time to yield results, and yet there is not much to show for it. Reports continue to emerge about human rights violations at the hands of the very security forces that have allegedly been schooled in human rights principles and practices. What is this an indication of? Is this poor or insufficient mentoring? Lessons not fully learned? A failure to prioritize human rights vis-à-vis other goals? Or insufficient commitment of time and resources? More well-designed research investigations are needed to unearth the principal causes of U.S. failure in this regard. But the bottom line is that the U.S. is not getting the results it purportedly desires. The human rights initiatives, like so many spearheaded by the military, reveals the limits of U.S. influence in Latin America in the modern era.

Works cited

Arceneaux, Craig and David Pion-Berlin. 2005. *Transforming Latin America: The International and Domestic Origins of Change.* Pittsburgh, PA: University of Pittsburgh Press.

Atkinson, Carol. 2014. *Military Soft Power: Public Diplomacy through Military Educational Exchanges.* Lanham, MD: Rowman and Littlefield.

Blasier, Cole. 1976. *The Hovering Gaint: U.S. Response to Revolution Change in Latin America.* Pittsburgh, PA: University of Pittsburgh Press.

Bruneau, Thomas, Kathleen Peggar, and Elisabeth Wright. 2012. "Impact of International Military Education (IMET) on Graduate Education." *Calhoun, Naval Post Graduate School.* June, 4. https://calhoun.nps.edu/handle/10945/7010.

Cope, John A. 1995. "International Military Education and Training: An Assessment." *McNair Papers* no. 44-45: 1–71.

Gill, Leslie. 2004. *The School of the Americas: Military Training and Political Violence in the Americas.* Durham, NC: Duke University Press.

Gouvea, Raúl. 2017. "US-Latin America's Security: Moving through an Inflection Point?" *Defense and Security Analysis* 33, no. 3: 223–241.

Human Rights Watch. 2015. "Colombia: Top Brass Linked to Extrajudicial Executions." On Their Watch: Evidence of Senior Army Officers' Responsibility for False Positive Killings in Colombia. Report, June 2015. www.hrw.org/news/2015/06/24/colombia-top-brass-linked-extrajudicial-executions.

Laurienti, Jerry. 2007. *The U.S. Military and Human Rights Promotion: Lessons from Latin America.* Westport, CT: Praeger Publishers.

———. 2016. "The United States and Latin America: The Overstated Decline of a Superpower." *The Latin Americanist* December 2016: 497–524.

Long, Tom. 2015. *Latin America Confronts the United States: Asymmetry and Influence.* New York: Cambridge University Press.

Loveman, Brian. 2006. *Addicted to Failure: U.S. Security Policy in Latin America and the Andean Region.* Lanham, MD: Rowman and Littlefield.

Mares, David R. 2016. "The United States' Impact on Latin America's Security Environment: The Complexities of Power Disparity." In *Handbook of Latin American Security.* eds. David R. Mares and Arie Kacowicz, 302–312. New York: Routledge Press.

Omelicheva, Mariya, Brittnee Carter, and Luke B. Campbell. 2017. "Military Aid and Human Rights: Assessing the Impact of U.S. Security Assistance Programs." *Political Science Quarterly* 132, no. 1: 119–143.

Randall, Stephen J. 2013. "Change or Continuity in US-Latin American Policy: The Obama Record." *Oasis* 18: 8.

Reveron, Derek S. 2007. "Shaping the Security Environment. The Newport Papers 29." *Online. Naval War College Newport Papers.* https://digital-commons.usnwc.edu/newport-papers/25.

Smith, Peter. 2007. *Talons of the Eagle: Latin America, the United States, and the World.* New York: Oxford University Press.

SOAW. 2018. Border. *School of the Americas Watch*. www.soaw.org/border/.

Schoultz, Lars. 1998. *Beneath the United States: A History of U.S. Policy toward Latin America*. Cambridge, MA: Harvard University Press.

Tidd, Admiral Kurt W. 2017. Before the 115th Congress Senate Armed Services Committee 6 April 2017. United States Southern Command, April 2017, Washington, DC.

U.S. Departments of Defense and State. 2014. Foreign Military Training: Fiscal Years 2014 and 2015 Joint Report to Congress, Volume.1. Washington, DC.

U.S. National Security Archives. 2017. "Fact Sheet Concerning Training Manuals Containing Materials Inconsistent with U.S." Policy https://nsarchive2.gwu.edu//nsa/archive/news/dodmans.htm. Accessed 30 October 2017.

Vine, David. 2017. *Base Nation: How U.S. Military Bases Abroad Harm America and the World*. New York: Metropolitan Books.

WHINSEC. 2018. Western Hemisphere Institute for Security Cooperation (WHINSEC). Mission. www.benning.army.mil/tenant/whinsec/Mission.html.

———. 2017. Western Hemisphere Institute for Security Cooperation (WHINSEC). Content. www.benning.army.mil/tenant/whinsec/HR.html.

38
NATION STATE

Olaf Kaltmeier and Mirko Petersen

Especially the American and the French Revolutions of the late 18th and early 19th century can be considered crucial for the development of the idea of the nation-state. Fundamental parts of this idea are an independent state ruled in the name of a community of equals (→ Citizenship, II/27), and a written constitution. Often, the implicit assertion of the linking of the two words – that is to say one nation lives on the territory of one state – does not correspond with reality. This regularly leads to political tensions and conflicts. Nonetheless, the nation-state ideals are today almost universally adopted to the different historic contexts that – in general terms – in the Americas are shaped by colonialism (→ Colonial Rule, I/5), slavery (→ I/18), migration (→ I/15), and dependence (→ Development, II/6). In the realm of the globalization-debate since the 1990s, the nation-state has often been labeled as outdated. Nevertheless, it still remains the fundamental unit of political agency in the Americas, with the exception of perhaps Haiti (often considered to be a paradigm of a "failed state") after the Duvalier-dictatorship (1957–1986) and the disaster (→ II/33) of the earthquake 2010.

According to German sociologist Max Weber, one can identify three different criteria which underlie the power of the nation-state. Firstly, it claims a territory within which local traits are subordinated to a central power. It usually disregards the plurality of cultures and ethnic groups on its territory and fosters the imagination of an ethnically homogenous space. Secondly, the nation-state claims control over the population living on its territory. To achieve control, an "imagined community" (Anderson 2006) must be created. This community is based on a "myth-symbol complex" (Smith 1986, 15) composed of factors like language (→ I/13), culture, religion (→ Religious Beliefs, I/40), norms, and collective memory (→ Memory Politics, I/34). Thirdly, the nation-state claims the monopoly on the execution of what Weber (1992, 157–159) calls "legitimate violence" over its territory and its population. In modern nation-states, this monopoly is justified by the principle of the sovereignty of the people. Pierre Bourdieu (1987) amplifies this Weberian perspective by highlighting that the state also claims the monopoly of defining the principles of the social division of society along various criteria.

Nevertheless, the new anthropology of the state has recently argued that the state is always an uncompleted project that constantly has to be imagined and put into practice through the conquest of its margins (Hansen and Stepputat 2001). In the field of symbolic power, the nation-state itself pursues different strategies to become visible and reinforce its potential for intervention through a "topography of power" (Ferguson 2006). Thus, the nation-state creates and compels others to believe in its power through semantics, narrations, symbols, and images (→ Foundational Discourses, III/8). Furthermore, to understand the process, everyday practices of state formation (Joseph and Nugent 1994), the agency of local actors and civil society, including those at the state's margins (Das and Poole 2004), have to be taken into account.

The ascent of nation-states over the past 200 years was a discontinuous process closely linked to the disintegration of various empires (Wimmer and Feinstein 2010, 765) (→ Nation and State Building, I/16). The first wave of nation-state creation unfolded in Latin America in the early 19th century after the collapse of a large portion of the Spanish empire. Different from North America, no larger political entity was created in Latin America (except for Brazil which was a Portuguese colony before). The new republics had been colonial administrative units before and a sort of belonging already existed in these territories by the time of independence (→ Independence Movements, I/10). This made the creation of larger geopolitical entities difficult. Short-lived projects of larger territorial units, like Simón Bolívar's Gran Colombia, disintegrated quickly.

Although the concept of a nation arose earlier in Latin America than in most parts of Europe, the development of an effective central state (and therefore the attainment of the monopoly on legitimate violence) after formal independence from Spain was difficult for many of the newly founded republics. The power gap was often filled by provincial landowning elites (→ Land, II/15). By the end of the 19th century, the Latin American nation-states were able to consolidate further. In much the same way, nation- and state-building was also a longer process in the northern part of the Americas. Until the Civil War of 1861 to 1865, the United States consisted of two different sociopolitical units: The Northern free-labor capitalist society and the Southern slave-based society (→ Slavery, I/18). The proto-national state of Canada, which gained formal independence from Britain only in 1982, was economically quite successful in the 19th century, but deeply divided between the English and French parts (Grunstein 2001, 9).

As the historian Michel Gobat notes, all geopolitical entities are "historical constructs forged in the crucible of political struggle," and they "are anything but static" (Gobat 2013, 1375). These political struggles do not have to coincide with the placement of borders (→ Borderlands, II/26), rather they are often about the way nation-states are imagined. All in all, the territorial units in the Americas have been stable (with some exceptions) since the end of the 19th century, but the battles for the meaning and the essence of the American nation-states have continued until the present. This is especially due to the lack of social cohesion which is caused by severe social and racial inequalities (→ Race, I/39; Social Inequalities, II/20). These two types of inequalities are closely entangled with each other in the form of "a socio-cultural hierarchy of European and non-European" (Quijano and Wallerstein 1992, 550). The lack of social cohesion has led to a variety of attempts at redefining nation-states in the Americas. Different phases of these attempts in the 20th and 21st centuries are described hereafter.

Welfare states

Despite the power of oligarchic elites in Latin America, social security programs were adopted in parts of the region in industrialized capitalist countries like the United States. Uruguay, Chile, and Argentina were pioneers of welfare state agency and developed welfare programs in the 1920s following a Bismarckian model (Barba Solano, Ordoñez-Barba and Valencia Lomelí 2009). The further development of the welfare state in the Americas then took place as a result of the world economic crisis of 1929 (→ Crisis, II/4), which caused the collapse of the global financial system, a dramatic decrease in world trade, and a sharp rise in unemployment and poverty.

In Latin America, the rapid decline in export opportunities and the increase in imports fueled an industrialization process based on the policy of inward-oriented import substitution. The so-called *desarrollismo* proposed not only the development (→ II/6) of national industries, but also the expansion of the industrial sector through the establishment of branches, especially in U.S. corporations. The modernization of agricultural structures was secondary. This led to the paradoxical situation that just at a time when the dependency of industrial products was about to be overcome, almost all Latin American countries had no national food sovereignty and had to import agricultural goods (Urquidi 2005, 189–197). Parallel to this process of industrialization, there was an acceleration in population growth and rapid urbanization (→ I/45).

In this constellation emerged the Fordist regulation (→ Fordism, II/10), which was characterized above all by industrial mass production and consumption as well as regulation by a social state, which largely pacified class conflicts (→ Class Struggle, II/3). Born of the necessity to manage scarce resources due to the crisis and to pacify social conflicts, the state took an increasingly proactive role – especially in the economic sphere (Halperín Donghi 1993, 208–232).

In the United States, the "New Deal," a series of programs including public work projects, financial reforms, and regulations enacted by President Franklin D. Roosevelt between 1933 and 1936, responded to the economic and social crisis. These programs included the Social Security Act which was the inception of the welfare state in the U.S. It established a retirement pension, unemployment insurance, and welfare benefits for handicapped and needy children. New Deal-like programs were also released in the U.S. colony of Puerto Rico. Two federal agencies, the Puerto Rico Emergency Relief Act (1933) and Puerto Rico Reconstruction Administration (1935) were installed to combat poverty, unemployment, disease, and hunger. But they were only partly successful in restructuring the political and economic systems and altering the traditional power relations in Puerto Rico.

The New Deal also had its repercussions in the South. This was intensified by the spread of Pan-Americanism (→ II/40) in the context of the "Good Neighbor policy." Inspired by Franklin D. Roosevelt, Brazilian dictator Getúlio Vargas followed a demand-driven economic policy with nationalist and protectionist traits. He established the so-called *Estado Novo*, a reorientation and self-description of the Brazilian nation-state based on nationalism, authoritarianism (→ II/25), and anti-communism, but also on populism (→ II/43) and welfare statehood. In addition, the industrialization of Brazil was strongly promoted. In the Argentina of the 1930s, the press and the principal political parties promoted a national reconstruction project similar to Roosevelt's and Juan Domingo Perón linked his reformist proposals to those of Roosevelt to win the 1946 election (Ruiz Jimenez 1998, 552).

The experiences of the socialist revolution in the Soviet Union (→ Revolution, II/44) and the general development of the labor movement (→ Labor Representation, II/14) also inspired different welfare state approaches in Latin America. In Chile, there was a period of social-reformist, populist regimes (the so-called *gobiernos nacionales y populares*) in the 1920s. The popular front government led by Pedro Aguirre Cerda (1938–1941) aimed at modernization of the capitalist model and a repression of the influence of the conservative agrarian bourgeoisie, especially with the founding of the state economic development agency *Corporación de Fomento*. From the 1920s to the 1950s, a kind of peripheral welfare state (the *Estado de compromiso*) emerged (Guillaudat and Mouterde 1998, 29) in Chile. Inspired by the communist experience in Europe, the Mexican government of Lázaro Cárdenas (1934–1940) introduced policies of redistribution, nationalized the oil industry, and carried out an agrarian reform. In Peru, Víctor Raúl Haya de la Torre propagated an independent national and anti-imperialist program of state formation.

However, not all states in Latin America were able to establish welfare state elements and governmental industrial promotion in this phase. Particularly in the non-industrialized states of Central America and the Caribbean, authoritarian regimes (→ Authoritarianism, II/25), largely supported or installed by the U.S., became "banana republics" under the influence of the United Fruit Company and the Standard Fruit Company (→ Transnational Corporations, II/23). This was the case in Honduras under the dictators Tiburcio Carías Andino (1933–1948) and Juan Manuel Gálvez (1949–1954), Guatemala under Carlos Castillo Armas (1954–1957), the Dominican Republic under Rafael Trujillo (1930–1961), and Nicaragua under the Somoza clan (1934–1979).

The expansion of the state in this period went hand in hand with new governmental practices. According to the sociologist Zygmunt Bauman, assimilation is a typically modern phenomenon that arises in the context of the modern "nationalization of the state" (Bauman 1995, 177). In this regard, the education systems are of crucial importance (→ Education, I/24). In Mexico, the *Secretaria de Educación Pública* was founded based on the revolutionary constitution of 1917 in 1921. In Chile, the constitution of 1925 decided to separate the state from the church, and a year later compulsory education was introduced. In Canada, compulsory education was introduced in 1920, which led to a sharpening of the ideological colonization of the First Nations (→ Indigeneity, I/31). The primary goal of the various educational institutions was to form homogenous national identities.

The control of the national territory was another goal declared by the administrations of the strengthened nation-states. The goal of the dictatorial *Estado Novo* in Brazil was to overcome the rule of regional political elites and to build a modern central state. An essential step was the founding of a new capital in the interior of the country. As early as 1922, the laying of the cornerstone for Brasília took place; the real expansion took place under President Getúlio Vargas (1930–1945 and 1951–1954). Architecturally, the city is committed to the ultra-modernism and the principles of the Charter of Athens. The city map is modeled after an airplane. The project consciously breaks with the traditional colonial architecture, leaves behind the alleged backwardness and catapults the Brazilian nation symbolically into modernity (Scott 1998). Similarly, modern urban planning projects have also occurred in Venezuela, where in 1961 the new city of Ciudad Guayana was created as a new industrial center, involving planners from MIT and Harvard University (→ Urbanization, II/45).

In many Latin American countries, the development of the lowlands of the Amazon region was an important and central point. In 1941/42, the U.S. sent the so-called *Misión Bohan* to Bolivia to explore the economic development prospects of the lowlands. As a result, the state economic development institution *Corporación Boliviana de Fomento* was founded to promote the agro-industry. Implementation of the colonization plans then took place only after the Bolivarian Revolution of 1952.

The first half of the 20th century also saw the rise of the nature-state (Hardenberg, Kelly, Leal and Wakild 2017) which was supposed to make nature legible and plannable. First national parks were established in the Southern Cone and in Mexico under the Cárdenas government. The parks were partly inspired by the U.S. model, but also contained European influences and new creations (→ Nature, II/39).

In many countries of the Americas, a new power bloc formed in the 1930s, consisting of an alliance of industrial bourgeoisie, middle classes, and sectors of the proletariat, with the objective of pursuing a project of national integration. In this period, the state established itself as a "hope-generating machine" for several social groups which were now addressing their demands (→ Political Communication, II/42). In Latin America, the crucial integration principle of this new phase was the modern concept of the people, "lo popular" (→ I/37). This idea of understanding the nation in terms of populism (→ II/43) – in contrast to the elite-centered visions of the traditional social stratification – found its highest expression in Argentine Peronism. Perón's most important goal was to transform the social imperative of the political system, abolishing the kleptocrat elitist state and installing a popular central state, which included the middle and under classes into the political process (→ Clientelism, II/29).

Nevertheless, the new state formations were not only inclusive. Efforts to build national identities through a strong state led to, often forceful, assimilation policies of the indigenous population. Examples of such policies include the idea of *Mestizaje* in Mexico, or the proposal of a substitution of the term "indio" by "campesino" by the Bolivian government which came to power after the revolution of 1952. Both examples highlight in a then-emerging trend in Inter-American indigenist policy (→ Indigeneity, II/31).

Revolution vs. reform vs. repression: the Cold War era

The "Short 20th Century" (Hobsbawm 1996) between the outbreak of the First World War and the collapse of the Soviet Union was marked by an epic struggle between capitalism (→ II/2) and communism (→ Socialism, I/42) on the global scale. After the end of the Second World War, this struggle was mainly represented by the confrontation between the Soviet Union and the United States. But the Cold War was much more than an issue of global geopolitics (→ II/34). It can also be considered a disciplinary strategy that defined the boundaries of national politics and identities (Campbell 1998, 153).

Even before the beginning of the Cold War, communism can be described as the enemy image per se of U.S.-American national ideology, which is founded on the idea of individual liberty and which is extremely anti-collectivist (Westad 2005, 8–38). The defense of this national idea reached a peak in the early years of the Cold War when a hysteric chase for "Un-American Activities" was launched by political hardliners who denounced all kinds of people as being communists. After a phase of relative relaxation, Cold War ideology was later used again massively by so-called neoconservatives to crack down on the New Left's counterculture (→ Subcultures, I/43) of the 1960s.

Latin America did not play a significant role in world politics in the early years of the Cold War. Nevertheless, the global block confrontation had a major ideological impact on the way North-South relations and – within this frame – the idea of the nation-state developed in the hemisphere. It was used as a counter-offensive against the political Left by the old elites, which had considered the welfare state a threat to their interests (for the U.S. case, see Campbell 1998, 140–141; for Latin America, see Bethell and Roxborough 1988, 179). The argument of the Cold War was not only used to exclude communist forces from political participation, but also to contain reformist nationalist tendencies which were considered an obstacle to the free flow of capital in the hemisphere (Grandin 2013, 36).

Most Latin American governments followed the U.S. line of conduct in the Cold War, both in foreign and domestic affairs, but this did not pay off for them in the form of investment programs. The United States focused on the reconstruction of Europe in order to contain communist influences there and paid less attention to Latin America where the Soviet Union did not maintain significant political relations. While Europe was reconstructed with a state-sponsored program, Latin America was left to private investments only (Grandin 2013, 32–33). In 1950, Latin America was the only region in the world without a U.S.-aid program (Bethell and Roxborough 1988, 186).

The economic situation in Latin America worsened and discontent rose. Poverty and inequality were not new phenomena in the region (→ Social Inequality, II/20), but in the early 1960s this situation was coupled with an outcry for immediate alleviation. It was especially the Cuban Revolution of 1959 (→ Revolution, II/44), as the historian Brands (2012, 40) highlights, which strengthened the belief in the possibility of rapid change in fields like property ownership and labor rights. The events in Cuba brought the Cold War closer to the hemispheric reality, especially since Fidel Castro announced his collaboration with the USSR (before he embraced a Marxist-Leninist state model, he appeared rather as a nationalist reformer). Cuba advocated revolution as the only possibility to rid themselves of oppressive governments supported by imperial powers. Revolution was supposed to lead to national liberation and real national independence. For this purpose, Ernesto Guevara developed a guerilla theory for government overthrows. This thinking was influential in Latin America for the rest of the Cold War era. While Guevara highlighted the importance of rural guerilla for national liberation, the 1970s saw a switch to urban guerilla warfare, for example in Uruguay and Argentina. On the economic level, Cuba failed to be an example of development for other Latin American nation-states. The regime's agricultural measures fell short and since the 1970s Cuba has economically been extremely dependent on the USSR (→ Socialism, I/42).

Besides military measures against Cuba and its influence in the hemisphere, the U.S. government under President John F. Kennedy announced the launching of the so-called "Alliance for Progress," a reform program for the region which was meant to be implemented by centrist governments with the aim of reducing communist influence (→ Development, II/6). The main guideline of the Alliance was provided by the Modernization Theory (→ Modernization, II/35). The most important intellectual behind this theory, Walt Whitman Rostow, was advisor to the U.-S. government. After the victory over fascism in World War II, its proponents were convinced that liberal democracy (→ II/32) in combination with market economy, that is to say the model of the United States, would pave the way to success for nation-states worldwide. The 19th century assumption that nation-states were in constant competition with each other for the best economic development was taken up again and transferred to the context of the Cold War (Breuer 2015).

A critical Latin American answer to the suppositions of Modernization Theory was the so-called Dependency Theory which was influential among scientists and policy makers in the 1960s and 1970s. *Dependentistas* emphasized the structural dependence of Latin American economies from the capitalist centers which makes modernization similar to that of the industrialized countries impossible.

Some of the hopes of the U.S. planners with regard to the Alliance for Progress were fulfilled. Several governments were able to expand light industry as well as commercial agriculture which caused economic growth. What the modernization programs did not tackle though were questions of redistribution of land and wealth (→ Social Inequality, II/20). The growth even strengthened the Latin American oligarchies since they were able to profit most. While some U.S. officials understood that land reform had to be a central part of the reforms, several U.S. politicians expressed their ideological concerns with what they considered socialist ideas and blocked these initiatives (Brands 2012, 59 and 63). When the presidency of Richard Nixon started in 1969, the Alliance for Progress and the Modernization Theory were already branded as a failure.

Beyond technical details of the reforms in the context of the Alliance for Progress, security policies (usually framed as measures for "stability") always enjoyed priority in relation to economic and social concerns. The Cold War foreign policy of the United States in Latin America disregarded the sovereignty of the nation-states in the region, from the coup d'état in Guatemala in 1954 to the interference in the Central American civil wars of the 1980s (→ Interventionism, II/36).

Yet it was not just the interference of the United States, but also the establishment of national security doctrines by the Latin American militaries which characterized the Cold War era. The anti-communism of the Latin American militaries had already spread in the 1920s and 1930s when Marxist and Leninist thought gained some popularity in several Latin American states (Harmer 2014, 138). This domestic anti-communism was fueled by the beginning of the Cold War and especially by the Cuban Revolution. Militaries came to believe that the fight against subversion was all-encompassing – political, economic, and military measures were taken to achieve internal security (Brands 2012, 74). Domestic politics were treated like a battlefield, within which competing imaginaries linked to Cuban-inspired national liberation movements (→ Freedom, I/27) had to be eliminated. These imaginaries were presented as threatening diseases against which the vulnerable body of the nation had to be protected. The military dictatorships of the 1970s went even further. They aimed at erasing their internal enemies completely and changing the mentality of the nation (→ Authoritarianism, II/25). This might be exemplified best by the Argentine military regime's practice of taking babies from "subversives" and giving them to supporters of the regime.

The neoliberal nation-state

The Latin American dictatorships of the 1970s, most notably the Chilean under Augusto Pinochet, also constituted the field of experiments for a new form of economic model: neoliberalism (→ II/16). This model spread in the Americas vis-à-vis multiple global crises (→ II/4). In 1973, the so-called Bretton Woods system, which was a guarantor of economic growth after the end of the World War II, broke up definitively. With the collapse of this system, money became a commodity. This gave capital new possibilities for action on booming, increasingly speculative financial markets, which led to extensive restructurings (→ Deindustrialization, II/5) and the end of Fordism (→ II/10). In 1982, a debt crisis broke out in Latin America. As a reaction, the major international institutions such as the IMF, the World Bank, and the creditor states of the Paris Club, decisively pushed the neoliberal turn in Latin America through structural adjustment programs.

The growing ideological significance of neoliberalism in the Americas was pushed by growing academic networks early on. In the 1950s and 1960s, Friedrich Hayek, who had moved to the University of Chicago in 1950, and Milton Friedman became the leading hubs of a trans-Atlantic network of think tanks and business-funded foundations (Stedman Jones 2012). Right from the beginning, Latin American economists, especially from the Catholic University of Chile, formed part of this network. In contrast to its European precursors, American neoliberalism took on a more radical and dogmatic character, especially regarding state-transformation (→ II/21).

The coup on September 11, 1973 against President Salvador Allende is of paramount importance for the establishment of neoliberalism in the region, as it not only ended the Chilean path to socialism (→ I/42) as a project of a peripheral welfare state, but it also made Chile a laboratory for neoliberal political recipes. Almost in their purest form, without having to take "market distortions" such as human rights (→ II/35), trade unions (→ Labor Representation, II/14) etc. into account, the neoliberal doctrines could be put into practice from 1975 onwards. As early as 1972, high-ranked militaries had contacted a group of neoliberal economists from the *Universidad Católica* and the Chilean newspaper *El Mercurio* which worked out an alternative government plan at the time of the coup, the so-called *El*

Ladrillo-manifest, which was financed by the CIA (Valdés 1995). However, the new model was by no means completely successful, even in terms of its own requirements. Immediately after the start of the "shock therapy," the country plunged into a deep recession, during which the gross domestic product decreased and inflation and unemployment rates rose rapidly. Only at the end of the 1970s did economic successes first become visible, and the talk about a "Chilean miracle" began.

After the experimentation phase in Chile, the neoliberal reforms were increasingly applied in the capitalist centers as well, especially in Great Britain under Margaret Thatcher and in the United States under Ronald Reagan in the early 1980s. The economic policies of U.S. President Reagan were based on monetarism, the deregulation of the financial sector, and tax reduction for the economic elites (→ Taxation, II/22) as a way of stimulating economic growth (following the so-called "trickle-down theory" the rest of society was also supposed to benefit from these measures). The welfare state was dismantled (→ State-Transformation, II/21) and the remaining public goods and enterprises were privatized to enhance the rule of the market forces (→ Privatization, II/17).

Neoliberal policies are characterized by the fact that the role of the state in the economic field is reduced. But it would be wrong to speak of a "weak state" per se. Instead, it is more appropriate to speak of a state-transformation toward a "national competitive state" (Hirsch 1995, 103). Unlike the (peripheral) welfare state, the state now aims at competing globally to create ever more favorable conditions for the exploitation of capital. This transformation cannot be reduced to the simple formula of "more market, less state," but rather a qualitatively different understanding of government. Michel Foucault's (2008) central thesis in relation to the neoliberal governmentality of the Chicago School is that the economic colonizes the social, so that the difference between the economy and the social ultimately disappears. The economic becomes the only valid rationality that claims validity for all areas of human action, including the social. In this sense, the neoliberal government is associated with specific forms of subjectivization, which are based on the idea of *homo economicus*.

Market radicalism and the economization of the social are central aspects of neoliberal policies, but they are also subject to historical change. In the so-called second generation of neoliberal structural adjustment programs at the end of the 1990s, structural reforms such as decentralization, reform of the legal system, and institution-building were – in accordance with the idea of "good governance" – considered central aspects of neoliberal state-transformation by the IMF and the World Bank.

The imagination of the nation's ethnos has varied in different projects of neoliberal state-transformation. In the initial phase, the neoliberal discourse was accompanied by a neoconservative discourse that drew on traditional values and conducted a crusade against Marxism. In the U.S., Ronald Reagan successfully brought ultra-conservatism, religious fundamentalism, and neoliberalism together discursively (a similar discourse brought the fascist Brazilian politician Jair Bolsonaro to power in the 2018 presidential elections) (Finn 2012). In Chile, the neoliberal military state carried out an ethnocidal policy that was committed to the ideal of a homogeneous, white Chilean nation of entrepreneurs (→ Whiteness, I/46). In the 2000s, neoliberal subjectivation has become more sophisticated. In Peru for example, the logics of marketing and corporate private management have been integrated into state practices, especially in city and nation-branding in order to reinvent national narratives and construct public subjectivities based on entrepreneurship (Cánepa 2017, 89). Thereby especially the Inca past is promoted as cultural heritage (→ Memory Politics, I/34), used as a tool to appeal to cosmopolitical tourists (→ Cosmopolitanism, III/5) and to construct a market-oriented national identity.

But the neoliberal state does not necessarily promote the nation's imagination as a homogeneous ethnoscape. Rather, with the indigenous protests of the 1990s, an increasing amalgamation of neoliberalism and multiculturalism can be observed, which is prominently reflected in the state formation. This is related to the spreading of multiculturalism as a discourse for state formation and the redefinition of the nation. In Canada, the Trudeau government (1968–1984) was quite successful in articulating multiculturalism (→ I/36) together with values considered to be Canadian in order to construct a specific form of Canadianness, that is also in contrast to the U.S. (Vieru 2013, 210–211) But also in the U.S., deeply shaped by the aftermaths of slavery (→ I/18), political culture changed with the multicultural politics of affirmative action and political correctness. In Latin America in the 1990s, there were several constitutional changes such as in Colombia (1991), Peru (1993), Bolivia (1994), Ecuador (1998), and Venezuela (1999) that recognized the specific cultural rights of indigenous peoples (→ Indigeneity, I/31). Furthermore, ILO Convention 169, which recognizes cultural rights and limited autonomy for indigenous peoples, was signed by nearly all Latin American governments, while Canada and the United States as well as other countries shaped by settler colonialism such as Australia, New Zealand, and South Africa have not.

These politics of recognition by the state have taken place against a background of neoliberal government policies, which have deepened socioeconomic disparities (→ Social Inequality, II/20). It is somewhat remarkable that indigenous demands for cultural recognition were partially fulfilled while claims for social justice and redistribution of wealth have been largely ignored (Bretón 2005; Kaltmeier 2017). The articulation of multiculturalism and neoliberal politics reflects the growing interest of international development corporations like the United States Agency for International Development (USAID), the Inter-American Development Bank, and the World Bank in indigenous peoples (→ Development, II/6). Part of this increased interest is without a doubt due to the increased mobilization capacities of indigenous movements, whom CIA reports in the 1990s labeled as more dangerous for liberal capitalist systems than even the last existing guerrilla movements.

The *Ley de Participación Popular* in Bolivia is a case in point, illustrating the articulation of neoliberal politics and the politics of recognition by the government of Gonzalo Sánchez de Lozada (1993–1997) in the context of the second generation of structural adjustment programs and its project of political decentralization (Postero 2006). In Ecuador, where the state demonstrated a great openness toward demands for ethnic recognition without taking into account demands of redistribution, the World Bank executed a pilot project for indigenous peoples (PRODEPINE) in cooperation with the state and the Confederación de Nacionalidades Indígenas del Ecuador (CONAIE), the biggest national indigenous organization. Promoting the concept of social capital, PRODEPINE (1998–2005) aimed to empower indigenous communities by integrating them into self-defined development projects.

Concurrently, new state-institutions have arisen in the Americas that put "*etno-desarrollo*" (ethno-development) at the center of their activities. After the strong critique of the Washington Consensus, and the neoliberal politics of the governments of its "first generation," new social and culturally sensitive programs were needed. Empowerment, social capital, political decentralization, and reforms of the educational and judicial systems were the new preferred areas of intervention. Together with national governments, these agencies established a regime of vision and division, which Charles Hale and Rosamel Millaman (2005) ironically refers to as "permitted Indian." Indigenous people who engaged in projects of ethnodevelopment were able to gain social recognition, while those who opposed and protested against them were marked as criminals or terrorists, especially after 9/11. In a similar way, neoliberal and penal practices in the U.S., especially against Afro-American and Hispanic people, have given rise to what some scholars call the transitions from welfare to workfare within a new carceral state regime (Wacquant 2009).

From "pink tide" and "change" to the right-wing backlash

After a series of protests against neoliberal policies, several center-left governments were elected in Latin America. This began with the election of Hugo Chávez in Venezuela in 1998. During the first phase of his government, Chávez was still isolated with his anti-neoliberal discourse, but after the elections in Brazil in 2002, in Argentina in 2003, in Uruguay in 2004, in Bolivia in 2005, in Ecuador in 2006, and in Nicaragua in 2006 a left turn (or so-called Pink Tide) was realized in large parts of the region.

The relations between the social movements (→ I/41) and the center-left governments was complex and at times paradoxical. Disillusioned by the traditional Left and trade unions (→ Labor Representation, II/14), many of the new social movements which came to birth in the 1990s had a clear anti-statist stance. Many followed the example of Zapatism in Southern Mexico, a movement which refused to aim for state power and instead called for a renovation of the Mexican nation (Thwaites Rey 2010, 28–29). In addition, the state still constituted a symbol of colonial (and neocolonial) exploitation for indigenous movements which gained importance in the 1990s and during the Argentine economic collapse of 2001 new forms of economic and political self-administration independent of the state emerged (→ Participation, II/41).

Although these social movements tried to establish new political paths, they helped – willingly or not – to bring politicians and parties to power through democratic elections. Some of these elected governments promised a redefinition of the role of the nation-state though. Hugo Chávez's "21st century socialism" highlighted the construction of "popular power" through the active participation of communities and workers (→ Socialism, I/42). However, the social property enterprises founded in Venezuela remain financially dependent upon the state and are therefore extremely vulnerable with regard to economic conjunctures (Larrabure 2018, 12). In Bolivia, the government of Evo Morales even called itself "a government of the social movements." Vice President Álvaro García Linera (2010, 87–88) defends this alleged contradictory expression by stressing that Bolivia on the one hand needs a strong influence of social movements to prevent the establishment of a new bureaucratic political class, and on the other hand requires a state which has sufficient power at its disposal for important decisions.

An important step toward the redefinition of the nation-state in Bolivia was the passing of a new constitution. Bolivia, as well as Ecuador, are now officially "plurinational states." This recognition of cultural diversity signifies a clear brake with the "one state-one nation" assumption (→ Multiculturalism, I/36). Nonetheless, the relations between indigenous communities and movements on the one side, and the Bolivian and Ecuadorian government on the other side remain difficult (Cordero Ponce 2012, 141–148). Often, the debates between the two sides revolve around the capitalist exploitation of nature (→ II/39).

A common denominator of the Pink Tide governments in Latin America was a strengthening of the nation-state vis-à-vis the market in order to stop the most devastating effects of neoliberalism. Latin America experienced an economic boom and this conjuncture was used by various governments to loosen the grip of international financial institutions and to realize improvements in fields like poverty, unemployment, inequality and women's rights (→ Gender Identities, I/28). The regained strength of the Latin American nation-states paid off during the global economic crises that started in 2008 (→ Crisis, II/4). The independence from financial institutions prevented bank failures or a renewed debt crisis in the region (Larrabure 2018, 2).

The changes in the region became especially clear in 2005 when an alliance of several Latin American governments repudiated the attempt of the U.S. administration of President George W. Bush to create a free-trade zone in the whole hemisphere. Instead of allying themselves with the U.S. government, the center-left governments increased regional cooperation (→ Regional Integration, II/18). Although different formats and organizations were created, most governments were not willing to sacrifice national sovereignty, which had recently been won back, for supranational forms of decision-making (Serbin 2010, 18).

The distancing of Latin America from the United States especially took place during the time of the Bush administration which encouraged the image of aggressive U.S. imperialism internationally. This changed to some degree when Barack Obama took over the U.S. presidency in 2009 although no major changes were made in the dealing with the countries south of the Rio Grande (except for the approximation with Cuba during the very last phase of the Obama administration).

The coming to power of the first black president who promised "change we can believe in" had a major impact on the self-image of the United States. There were high hopes that Obama would be able to lead the U.S. to a post-racial future (→ Race, I/39). The unity targeted by Obama never materialized. The U.S. today still witnesses a variety of intense social and racial conflicts, which have been fueled by the rhetoric of Obama's successor Donald Trump, especially with regard to migration from Central America to the United States.

While Obama's presidency did not bring an end to the almost globally condemned foreign policy of the Bush administration (marked by human right abuses linked to the so-called War on Terror), its records on the fields of economic policy and health care (→ Health, I/29) can at least be called a partial success. With a Keynesian style stimulus package, the Obama administration was able to milden the effects of the global economic crises in the United States. The health care reform, which aimed at insuring the most vulnerable parts of society for the case of illness, was a milestone in U.S. history since any similar attempt in history failed because of massive lobbying against it (such a reform has always been condemned as socialist and therefore "Anti-American" by its opponents).

As modest as some of the reforms might have been, a variety of the social and racial inequalities in the Americas have been tackled in the first one and half decades of the 21st century. The successes did not last as long as it was presumed though – on the contrary: The hemisphere is witnessing a major right-wing backlash in recent years. Keystones of this backlash are the elections of Mauricio Macri in Argentina in 2015, Donald Trump in the U.S. in 2016, Sebastián Piñera in Chile 2017 and Jair Bolsonaro in Brazil in 2018. The presidencies of Trump, Macri and Piñera also stand for a doubling of economic power (all named presidents are millionaires) in political power, which raises profound problems concerning democratic theory in the face of a worldwide dramatically increasing polarization of the social structure (Kaltmeier 2018). Many assumptions about the nation-state which were considered hegemonic before are now questioned again. The neoliberal nation-state is staging a comeback and racial exclusion has become socially acceptable again. Historical achievements of the past are no longer commonplace and have to be re-established.

Works cited

Anderson, Benedict. 2006. *Imagined Communities*. London: Verso. Orig. pub. 1983.
Bauman, Zygmunt. 1995. *Moderne und Ambivalenz. Das Ende der Eindeutigkeit*. Frankfurt am Main: Fischer.

Bethell, Leslie and Ian Roxborough. 1988. "Latin America between the Second World War and the Cold War: Some Reflections on the 1945–48 Conjuncture." *Journal of Latin American Studies* 20, no. 1: 167–189.

Bourdieu, Pierre. 1987. *Cosas dichas*. Barcelona: Ed. Gedisa.

Brands, Hall. 2012. *Latin America's Cold War*. Cambridge, MA and London: Harvard University Press. Orig. pub 2010.

Bretón, Víctor. 2005. *Capital Social Y Etnodesarrollo En Los Andes*. Quito: CAAP.

Breuer, Martin. 2015. "Development." *InterAmerican Wiki: Terms – Concepts – Critical Perspectives*. URL: www.uni-bielefeld.de/cias/wiki/d_Development.html.

Campbell, David. 1998. *Writing Security: United States Foreign Policy and the Politics of Identity*. Minneapolis: University of Minnesota Press. Orig. pub. 1992.

Cánepa, Gisela. 2017. "Cultural Management and Neoliberal Governmentality: The Participation of Perú in the Exhibition Inca: Kings of the Andes." In *Entangled Heritages: Postcolonial Perspectives on the Uses of the Past in Latin America*, eds. Olaf Kaltmeier and Mario Rufer, 87–108. London: Routledge.

Das, Veena and Deborah Poole. 2004. "State and Its Margins: Comparative Ethnographies." In *Anthropology in the Margins of the State*, eds. Veena Das and Deborah Poole, 3–34. Santa Fe and Oxford: School of American Research Press.

Halperín Donghi, Tulio. 1993. *The Contemporary History of Latin America*. Durham: Duke University Press.

Ferguson, James. 2006. *Global Shadows: Africa in the Neoliberal World Order*. Durham: Duke University Press.

Finn, Jim. 2012. *Sunday School with Franz Hinkelammert*. Buenos Aires: BAFICI, Buenos Aires Festival de Cine Independiente. https://vimeo.com/44431346.

Foucault, Michel. 2008. *The Birth of Biopolitics: Lectures at the Collège de France, 1978–1979*. New York: Palgrave Macmillan.

Gobat, Michel. 2013. "The Invention of Latin America: A Transnational History of Anti-Imperialism, Democracy, and Race." *American Historical Review* 118, no. 5: 1345–1375.

Grandin, Greg. 2013. "What Was Containment? Short and Long Answers from the Americas." In *The Cold War in the Third World*, ed. Robert J. McMahon, 27–47. Oxford: Oxford University Press.

Grunstein, Arturo. 2001. "Estado-Nación y Mercado. Reflexiones Comparativas Sobre Economía Y Política En Norteamérica Durante El Siglo XIX." Centro de Investigación y Docencia Económica, Documento de Trabajo, no. 75.

Guillaudat, Patrick and Pierre Mouterde. 1998. *Los Movimientos sociales en Chile: 1973–1993*. LOM: Santiago de Chile.

Hale, Charles and Rosamel Millaman. 2005. "Cultural Agency and Political Struggle in the Era of Indio Permitido." In *Cultural Agency in the Americas*, ed. Doris Sommer, 281–301. Durham: Duke University Press.

Hansen, Thomas Blom and Finn Stepputat, ed. 2001. *States of Imagination. Ethnographic Explorations of the Postcolonial State*. Durham: Duke University Press.

Hardenberg, Wilko Graf von, Matthew Kelly, Claudia Leal, and Emily Wakild, ed. 2017. *The Nature State: Rethinking the History of Conservation*. New York: Routledge.

Harmer, Tanya. 2014. "The Cold War in Latin America." In *The Routledge Handbook of the Cold War*, eds. Artemy M. Kalinovsky and Craig Daigle, 133–148. London: Routledge.

Hirsch, Joachim. 1995. *Der nationale Wettbewerbsstaat. Staat, Demokratie und Politik im globalen Kapitalismus*. Berlin: Edition ID-Archiv.

Hobsbawm, Eric J. 1996. *The Age of Extremes, A History of the World, 1994–1991*. New York: Vintage Books (Random House). Orig. pub. 1994.

Ruiz Jimenez, Laura. 1998. "Peronism and Anti-Imperialism in the Argentine Press: 'Braden or Perón' Was Also 'Perón' is Roosevelt." *Journal of Latin American Studies* 30, no. 3: 551–571.

Stedman Jones, Daniel. 2012. *Masters of the Universe: Hayek, Friedman, and the Birth of Neoliberal Politics*. Princeton: Princeton University Press.

Joseph, Gilbert M. and Daniel Nugent. 1994. "Popular Culture and State Formation in Revolutionary Mexico." In *Everyday Forms of State Formation. Revolution and the Negotiation of Rule in Modern Mexico*, eds. Gilbert M. Joseph and Daniel Nugent, 3–23. Durham: Duke University Press.

Kaltmeier, Olaf. 2017. "Politics of Indigeneity in the Andean Highlands. Indigenous Social Movements and the State in Ecuador, Bolivia, and Peru (1940–2014)." In *Indigeneity on the Move. Varying Manifestations of a Contested Concept*, eds. Nasir Uddin, Eva Gerharz, and Pradeep Chakkarath, 172–198. Oxford: Berghahn.

———. 2018. *Refeudalización. Desigualdad social, económica y cultura política en América Latina en el temprano siglo XXI*. Guadalajara and Bielefeld: Bielefeld UP, Universidad de Guadalajara.
Larrabure, Manuel. 2018. "Post-capitalist Development in Latin America's Left Turn: Beyond Peronism and the Magical State." *New Political Economy* 24, no. 5: 587–604.
García Linera, Álvaro. 2010. "La construcción del Estado." *Umbrales* 10: 63–89.
Cordero Ponce, Sofía. 2012. "Estados plurinacionales en Bolivia y Ecuador. Nuevas ciudanías, ¿más democracia?" *Nueva Sociedad* 240: 134–148.
Postero, Nancy Grey. 2006. *Now We are Citizens. Indigenous Politics in Post-Multicultural Bolivia*. Stanford: Stanford University Press.
Quijano, Anibal and Immanuel Wallerstein. 1992. "Americanity as a Concept, or the Americas in the Modern World System." *International Sociological Association* 134, no. 1: 549–557.
Thwaites Rey, Mabel. 2010. "Después de la globalización neoliberal: ¿qué Estado en América Latina?" *OSAL, Observatorio social de América Latina* 9, no. 27: 19–43.
Scott, James. 1998. *Seeing like a State*. New Haven: Yale University Press.
Serbin, Andrés. 2010. "Regionalismo y soberanía nacional en América Latina. Los nuevos desafíos." *Documentos CRIES* 15: 5–31.
Smith, Anthony D. 1986. *The Ethnic Origins of Nations*. MA: Wiley-Blackwell.
Barba Solano, Carlos, Gerardo Ordoñez-Barba, and Enrique Valencia Lomelí, ed. 2009. *Más allá de la pobreza: regímenes de bienestar en Europa, Asia y América*. Guadalajara: Universidad de Guadalajara, El Colegio de la Frontera Norte.
Urquidi, Víctor. 2005. *Otro siglo perdido. Las polítcas de desarrollo en América Latina (1930–2005)*. Mexico: Fondo de Cultura Económica.
Valdés, Juan Gabriel. 1995. *Pinochet's Economists: The Chicago School of Economics in Chile*. Cambridge: Cambridge University Press.
Vieru, Mihaela. 2013. "Whither Multiculturalism in Canada? The Turn that Challenges Postmodernity." In *Transnational Americas. Envisioning Inter-American Area Studies in Globalization Processes*, ed. Olaf Kaltmeier, 207–226. Trier, Germany and Tempe: Wissenschaftlicher Verlag Trier & Bilingual Press.
Wacquant, Loïc. 2009. *Punishing the Poor: The Neoliberal Government of Social Insecurity*. Durham: Duke University Press.
Weber, Max. 1992. "Politik als Beruf." In *Max Weber Gesamtausgabe, Abt. I, Schriften und Reden*, Vol. 17. eds. Wolfgang J. Mommsen und Wolfgang Schluchter, 157–254. Tübingen: Mohr-Siebeck. Orig. pub. 1919.
Westad, Odd Arne. 2005. *The Global Cold War. Third World Interventions and the Making of Our Times*. New York: Cambridge University Press.
Wimmer, Andreas and Yuval Feinstein. 2010. "The Rise of the Nation-State across the World, 1816 to 2001." *American Sociological Review* 75, no. 5: 764–790.

39
NATURE

Antoine Acker, Anne Tittor, and Olaf Kaltmeier

The invention of the Americas in the wake of the European conquests was based upon imaginaries and appropriations of nature (→ America, I/2). The idealization of the potential of soil and subsoil, the idea of frontier and physical proximity with the "wild," the perception of great distances and vast geographic spaces constituted social representations of nature in the colonial situation that persist until today (→ Foundational Discourses, III/8). The colonizers appropriated mineral resources on a large-scale and later on used part of the conquered territory, its soil, water, and its people to establish plantations for export products such as sugar, cotton, indigo, and later on bananas, coffee, and other products often introduced from other continents (→ Colonial Economies, I/4), which introduced complete environmental changes (→ Columbian Exchange, I/6). Colonialism (→ Colonial Rule, I/5) brought large-scale environmental transformations, making the interaction between humans and nature a central issue in the formation of modern American societies during the 19th and 20th centuries. The present entry addresses the concept of nature that derives from this history, and its impact on power relations, inequalities, and conflicts within and between different parts of the continent, as well as for the Americas in a global context. Rather than analyzing material change of the environment over time, the intersection between knowledge and politics is emphasized, from which new power constellations have emerged in the past five centuries, while also discussing existing and possible alternatives to the modern power regimes as ways to overcome the nature/culture divide.

Etymological considerations and history of the concept within the geopolitics of knowledge

Nature is derived from Latin "natura" which originally denotes "birth." In regard to its relationship to "birth," there are certain similarities to native American conceptions such as the Andean notion of "pachamama," mother Earth, who gives life (Medina 2001). Nevertheless, in occidental thought "nature" has come to mean also "essential, inner qualities." This is best expressed in the concept of natural laws, which conveys the epistemological separation of nature from society by creating a division between the instinctive and the rational, the innate and the acquired, the natural and the social, e.g. the "civilized man," according to the Western logic, is the one who has managed to overcome natural laws.

Anthropologists have argued that such a separation of nature from society cannot be conceived of as universal. It is rather a typically Western way of ordering the world, which has been globalized through processes of epistemological violence. The concept "nature" is linked with the Western vision of modernity that arguably exists to draw an artificial separation between what is human and what is not (Latour 1992) (→ Modernization, I/35). This conceptualization is put into question by a whole array of anthropological and ethnohistorical research in the Americas. In the Andean world, Joseph Bastien (1985) has highlighted that the local environment is often conceptualized in terms of the human body. Like the human body, the space underlies principles of metabolic flows and exchanges. For many indigenous peoples (→ I/11) across the Americas (from the Amazonian Xavantes to the Cree in Canada), humans evolve in the same web of exchanges and rituals as other actors, which can be animal or vegetal species, but also in some cases mountains, rivers, or even spirits and other beings which Europeans and white Americans would in turn categorize as "supernatural" (Descola 2005; Tanner 2007). Many afro-descendant syncretic rituals as they exist in black communities of Brazil, Colombia, Venezuela, Cuba, and other places, also promote a mystic connection to water, fire, air, and earth, which radically differs from the anthropocentric vision underpinning Christianism (Escobar 2008; Santos and Gonçalves 2011). The Americas are home to a multitude of such cosmogonies that do not articulate the universe along the nature/culture division (→ Religious Beliefs, I/40).

For the colonizers, the great divide between nature and culture served also as a backdrop for the explanation of the classification and the development (→ II/6) of human societies. Renaissance thinkers saw the "American savage" as a construct to conceptualize a state of nature. The special attribution of nature to the Americas was not limited to the 17th century. In the late 18th-century French naturalist Comte de Buffon developed a theory of degeneration in the Americas in which New World species were described as smaller and weaker than European ones, because of allegedly unfavorable climate conditions making healthy life impossible. U.S.-American and Latin American intellectuals, among them Thomas Jefferson, criticized these climate-based assumptions and their underlying racism (→ Race, I/39). In the midst of the 19th century, ideas of natural degeneration and inferiority – also inspired by racism and social Darwinism – justified internal colonization of indigenous peoples especially in the U.S. and in Patagonia (→ Conquest and Colonization, I/7). With the rising U.S. imperialism at the end of the 19th century, the U.S. established itself as a "civilizing power" against the "nature-driven" countries of Latin America and the Caribbean. By representing their Southern neighbors as emotional, primitive, wild, effeminate and/or childish, among other traits supposed to recall the innate and the natural, U.S. elites categorized them as incapable of mastering nature, which implicitly or explicitly amounted to a state of racial inferiority (Pike 1992).

Epistemological questions about "nature" and arguments for its domination and protection

From the 16th century on, counting, mapping, classifying, and representing have been basic operations in the creation of power-knowledge complexes about the (human and non-human) other. This has included in particular the production of knowledge about nature in the colonized areas and subordinated people and their surroundings all over the Americas into Western knowledge systems.

In doing so, Western-European epistemologies (knowledge systems) have been globalized, claiming to represent universal truth, while other knowledge systems have been minimized and delegitimized. A basic operation emerged in Western thought to separate human societies from the rest of the cosmos and gather in the concept of "Nature" everything that distinguished itself from allegedly "human" properties. This was a key element to legitimize the claim of (Western) men to dominate and exploit nature for one's own benefit.

In the early 1970s, the Deep Ecology movement emerged as an approach and new mode of activism that conceptualized nature differently and was influenced by the Hippie movement (→ Social Movements, I/41). Deep Ecology assumes that the "natural world" should be conserved for its inherent values, and not primarily in order to guarantee human development. Adhering to the *Gaia* hypothesis that the Earth was a naturally self-regulating organism, which should be protected from excessive human intervention, Deep Ecology was accused of actually contributing to the nature/culture separation. This is somewhat unfair, as Deep Ecology considers humans as an integrative part of *Gaia*, but still it is true that the movement related in many aspects to essentialist thinking. Moreover, criticisms to Deep Ecology have often served to dismiss the environmental movement as a whole, misinterpreting the latter as a project that is aimed at making nature sacred and impermeable to exchanges with humans. Yet, although the green movements have used the concept of nature to mobilize emotions in favor of environmental protection, what they actually did (consciously or unconsciously) was to promote a massive arrival of non-human actors into the (until then exclusively human) political and social spaces. This step, authors like Latour (2004) argue, took a decisive turn in making the concept of nature obsolete.

Social constructivists have pushed this tendency even further, arguing that "nature" does not exist apart from human perceptions and beliefs about it. According to this point of view, all concepts to describe nature and its qualities, such as wilderness, biodiversity, or habitat, are human inventions that carry cultural, political, and other meanings. Yet, this constructivist perspective from the social sciences caused a lot of contradiction among biologists, geographers, and environmental organizations. The latter accused constructivists of ignoring the scientific findings about the material causes and effects of "natural" disasters (→ II/33), biodiversity crisis and climate change (→ II/30), and thus, of indirectly contributing to legitimize the human colonization of the Earth: this "dangerous flirt with relativism" could end up being "as destructive to nature as bulldozers and chainsaws" (Crist and Hargrove 2004, xvi).

Yet, the concept of nature has not only been questioned from a constructivist standpoint, but also from a materialist one. Drawing on Karl Marx's work, Neil Smith argues that all nature is or has been transformed by capitalist forces (→ Capitalism, II/2), which now operate on a world scale (Smith 2008). Smith analyzes how capitalism and class power serve to make, unmake, and remake the natural and built environments throughout history. The argument is that even when in former times people struggled for their means of subsistence, they have appropriated, altered, and produced their various environments. He therefore argued that nothing is natural about nature, but that everything perceived as nature results from transformation induced by humans and capital.

Marxist ecology points to the fact that the labor process itself mediates and regulates the metabolic relation between humans and nature. Human production is based on the appropriation of nature (Foster 2015). Within the philosophy of social science, a broader debate is dedicated to the presumptions and (in-)compatibilities between a constructivist and a materialist understanding of nature (Evanoff 2005; Forsyth 2001). Drawing on science and technology studies, critical realism investigates the role of knowledge, which claims to have scientific solutions for pressing environmental problems and locates these within historical, political, and social relations. Even if it completely misreads the driving forces of environmental change, Western knowledge is often privileged at the expanse of local understandings of nature. Realist political ecology does not just seek to illustrate how knowledge about environmental issues and boundaries between nature and society are constructed. It also reconstructs proposals for environmental policy that are both biophysically accurate and socially more just, without claiming to convey the only true story (Forsyth 2001).

Latin American Political Ecology calls for the need to understand the epistemological foundations of the colonial regimes and the power-knowledge strategies that dominated peoples and appropriated their territories (→ Land, II/15) (Leff 2015, 35). Watts defines the goal of political ecology as to explain environmental conflict in terms of struggles over knowledge, power, and practice as well as over politics, justice, and governance (2003, 263ff) (→ Environmental Justice, II/8). Martinez-Alier conceptualizes political ecology as "the study of ecological distribution conflicts" (2002, 71), and Robbins sees the four key questions political ecology is concerned with as 1) degradation and marginalization 2) environmental conflict, 3) conservation and control, and 4) environmental identity and social movements (Robbins 2004, 14f). To frame demands in conflicts on ecological issues, different and competing meanings are attributed to nature. They span from nature as a commodity to be extracted to nature as territory, through nature as a sacred and cultural tourist destination. Meanings given to nature are hereby expressions of establishing or negotiating power, relating to intrinsic cultural, political, and physical aspects of particular territories. In this context, the importance of state agency (→ Nation State, II/38) has been recently discussed introducing the concept of the "nature state" (Hardenberg, Matthew Kelly and Wakild 2017).

Furthermore, there is an ongoing discussion of how sustainable societies have rooted in the ecological potentialities and cultural identities all over Latin America. "Traditional" or "indigenous" ecological knowledge and cultural imaginaries of sustainability are important points of departure (→ Indigeneity, I/31), where Latin American thinking offers new perspectives (Alimonda 2011; Leff 2015; Machado Aroaz 2014; Palacio 2006; Ulloa 2005). This is probably best expressed in the concept of Buen Vivir, (*sumaq kwasay* in Kichwa or *suma qamaña* in Aymara). Buen Vivir stems from Andean cosmovisions and conceptualizes the idea of a conviviality between different beings within an eco-system. This includes a debate on the importance of the commons (→ II, 31) as collectively owned and/or used spaces. Recently it was integrated in the constitutions of Ecuador (2008) and Bolivia (2009), with Ecuador being the first country in the world that constitutionally recognizes the rights of nature. From its Andean origins, the concept has been appropriated by other indigenous and ecological movements in the Americas, which have undertaken the task to translate it into their own cultural background.

Another approach to deal with nature and society is the field of environmental history, which especially in Latin America, is basically concerned with the three C's of colonialism (→ Colonial Rule, I/5), capitalism (→ II/2), and conservation and its impacts on the social production of environment (Carey 2009). This triad has been called into question as it fails to address other issues of environmental importance and because of its moral and political impetus. The tendency of some scholars to narrate the society-nature-relation in Latin America as a story of decay and fall from paradise due to colonialism and capitalism has also been criticized (Miller 2007). Furthermore, more "C's" have to be added such as catastrophe (→ Disaster, II/33) and climate (→ Climate Change, II/30), while the c of conflict is – especially in Latin America – an important cross-sectional issue.

Continued Columbian exchange, coloniality, and pristine myths

Since the invention of the Americas (→ America, I/2), local environments have been created through continuous acts of disruption, implantation, and development of incoming species, which in many occasions contributed to violent changes in the pre-existing ecosystems. The "Colombian exchange" (→ I/6) that started in 1492 brought large-scale environmental transformations, making the interaction between humans and nature a central issue in the formation of modern American societies (Crosby 1972). The proliferation of Eurasian species due to the colonial expansion is a crucial aspect of this process. In historical biology, 1492 is the recognized benchmark for the introduction of neobiota, (invasive) non-native species. But taking into account different conjunctures of coloniality, this "Columbian exchange" cannot be limited to the early colonial times. Therefore it is preferable to speak of "colonial exchange," meaning colonial not as a historical period but rather the ongoing field of force of coloniality, in the sense of a persisting order of social domination and territorial appropriation which is a legacy of historical colonialism (Quijano 1997) (→ Postcolonialism, I/38). Indeed, a renewed conjuncture of introducing new Eurasian species took place in the context of 19th-century settler colonialism in the U.S., where the dispersal vectors of colonization of non-native plant species correlated significantly with the settlement patterns of European settlers (Mosena, Steinlein and Beyschlag 2018) (→ Migration, I/15). This includes also the planned acclimatization of non-native species, especially in agricultural, forestry, and fish farming.

The history of rubber in the first half of 20th century, which involved the circulation of seeds and the more or less successful attempts to reproduce tree species between independent nations of South America, and European colonies of Asia and Africa, is also significant in that respect (Dean 1987). It shows that the Columbian exchange continued to exist in a global framework in which (formally) colonial and (supposedly) non-colonial contexts intertwined and superimposed each other. Still, it is remarkable that the transpacific biotic flows have not been as important as the transatlantic ones (→ Atlantic, I/3). Most Asian species have been introduced via the Eurasian dispersal vectors and the Atlantic. Other disciplines, such as Cultural Studies have sought inspiration in the "Columbian exchange" thesis. For example, Kunow (2011) analyzed to what extent the flow of germs has shaped the community-formation and governmental, often racialized, techniques in the U.S.-American metropolis.

Along with this production of new American ecosystems, geopolitical imaginations emerged (→ Geopolitics, II/34), be it implicitly or explicitly, that made some environments more appreciable to use than others. In colonial imaginaries, the double myth of untouched land to be conquered and the El Dorado to be exploited has been central (Sutter 2000). North America had been famously imagined as an open frontier (→ Borderlands, II/26), and a vast, grassy expanse teeming with game, with a low number of nomads who only left sporadic marks on the landscape. South America, too, or at least the Amazon rainforest, was thought of as an almost untouched Eden (→ Utopias, III/23). Nevertheless, newer archeological findings have evidenced the existence of sophisticated agrarian systems before the European invasions (Bezerra 2015; Cleary 2001; Miller 2007). Much literature has concentrated on questioning the pristine myth, both in environmental history and in political ecology. Conflictive debates and severe misunderstandings occurred about what it actually means to question the idea of wilderness (Crist and Hargrove 2004; Proctor 1998).

Transnational appropriations of resources

Since the colonial conquests, a central element of the societal relationships with nature in the Americas has been the extraction of mineral resources – especially gold, silver, tin, copper, coal, oil. The history of the entire continent has been shaped by the flows of extractivism (→ II/9). By the end of the 19th century, the asymmetric integration of Latin America into the world economy as a provider of raw materials was based on export enclaves with brutal social and labor conditions. In North America, the implementation of geological drilling in the 1860s enabled the United States to fuel its capitalist system with oil (→ Energy, II/7), on the road toward a strong economic growth. But this happened at the price of creating "sacrifice zones" in the petroleum producing areas, destroying entire landscapes and putting workers' lives at risk (Colten 2012; Jones 2014).

Several case studies in environmental history underline the destructive forces of capitalism (→ II/2), arguing that most deforestation and appropriation of indigenous lands (→ Land, II/15) was a product of a capitalist mode of production that started to bring massive transformation in the late 19th or 20th century. Although during the phase of import substitution (from the 1930s to the 1970s) other pillars of the economy were developed, at the end of the 20th century the role of the extraction of resources and the export of primary goods took on again an important relevance for societies all over the continent (→ Development, II/6). For example, neoliberal Chile under the Pinochet dictatorship (1973–1990) (→ Neoliberalism, II/16) fostered a selective integration into the world market based on primary products in sectors such as forestry, fishing, and fruits (Claude 1997).

However, this extractivist way of relating to nature is not exclusive to right-wing regimes. Even the left-leaning governments of the 2000s in countries such as Argentina, Brazil, Ecuador, Bolivia, and Venezuela expanded the extraction of resources during an era of favorable prices on the world market and used the commodity boom to finance expansive social policy. This new extractivism was based on the appropriation of nature in which Latin America continued to be dependent on the world market as an exporter of raw materials and little processed goods (Gudynas 2009).

Various protest groups, especially in connection with indigenous and local peasant movements (→ Social Movements, II/41), have mobilized against displacement, and the environmental as well as health consequences of this model (→ Health, I/29). Large-scale mining is often accused by such groups of being a Western way of exploiting the Earth, and that most benefits are transferred to other parts of the world. The intertwinement between extractivist practices and coloniality led Alimonda (2011) to elaborate on the concept of "naturaleza colonizada," ("colonized nature") as according to him, Latin America tends to be envisaged as a subaltern space that can be "exploited, devastated, reconfigured" according to global economic needs. He also makes an important point when he says that "nature" is not only "colonized" by industrial powers from the Global North, but also through the representations and actions of Latin American elites themselves.

Transnational dynamics of conservation

A wave of concern for the fate of nature having to struggle with the destructive effects of modernity grew strong in the second half of the 19th- as well as the start of the 20th-century Americas. This "early conservationism" resulted from mixed motivations, including the influence of European romanticism, a utilitarian preoccupation for forests, soils, and climate as the material basis of agricultural development, and a patriotic attachment to the wild as a source of "Americanness." It was particularly strong in the United States, where the writer Henry David Thoreau advocated the virtues of forest preservation as early as in 1860, while in 1892 the "Sierra Club" was founded as a pioneer organization for the protection of natural resources. Early conservationism helped create the world's first national park (Yellowstone in 1872) but also the nationwide measures against soil erosion and for reforestation, which accompanied Franklin D. Roosevelt's New Deal in the 1930s (Henderson and Woolner 2005). In the 8th Pan-American Conference held in Lima in 1938 (→ Pan-Americanism, II/40), the governments of the Americas agreed upon a common Pan-American Convention for protecting native flora, fauna, scenery, and objects of aesthetic, historic, or scientific values. The convention came into force in 1940 and was largely inspired by the U.S.-American conception of different stages of conservation (Scarzanella 2002). Later, other Pan-American agreements on preservation and conservation, like the Inter-American Convention for the Protection and Conservation of Sea Turtles, completed this convention.

For a long time, it was frequently (and wrongly) assumed that the United States was the only reference with regards to the history of conservationist thought in the Americas. However, since the 19th-century intellectuals, scientists, and later also governmental experts of Argentina, Brazil, Chile and Mexico have developed their own understandings and institutionalizations of protected areas (DeVries 2013; Pádua 2002; Wakild 2011, Kaltmeier 2020). In some cases, they took a critical distance to the U.S.-American model (Argentina), including in a revolutionary way, such as in Mexico under the government of Lázaro Cárdenas in the 1930s. Latin American conservation also sought inspiration in other intellectual traditions, such as Prussian forestry, based on the idea of sustainability (Chile).

Around the 1970s, traditional conservationism in many parts of the world gave place to more politicized, world-conscious, and socially critical initiatives converging toward a "new enlightenment" (→ Enlightenment, I/8), which saw the rise of modern environmentalism (Radkau 2011) (→ Social Movements, I/41). Mainstream politics attempted to appropriate this movement, as became visible through the multiplication of environmental agencies and acts all over the Americas and the world, and, at the global scale, with the UN conference on the human environment in Stockholm (1972). Here again, the United States have often been portrayed as the most fertile American country for the emergence of this "global environmental moment" (Eardley-Pryor 2014). Aldo Leopolds concept of "land ethic" (1949), Rachel Carson's *Silent Spring* bestseller against the devastating DDT pesticide (1962), massive popular events such as the Earth Day (1970) and early ecological legislation like the *National Environmental Policy Act* (1970) were indeed decisive milestones, through which segments of the U.S. society and politics gave a global impulse to environmentalism. In 1971, the foundation of *Greenpeace* in Vancouver also made Canada the world's cradle of modern ecological activism. Yet, similarly as for early conservationist thought, Southern contributions should not be underestimated. Brazilian environmentalists, for example, played a crucial role in the defense of biodiversity by turning the Amazon into a global deforestation symbol in the 1970s, after which they successfully lobbied to make Brazil's 1988 constitution a global pathfinder for environmental law (Acker 2017; Hochstetler and Keck 2007). In 1992, the Rio de Janeiro's Earth Summit created what can be considered a second "global environmental moment." Recently, smaller American countries also made their way to the foreground, such as Costa Rica, which has acquired the reputation of a green energy model for the 21st century (Evans 1999) (→ Energy, II/7).

From the 1980s onwards, powerful non-governmental organizations became global advocates for environmental questions (→ Civil Society, II/28). In social sciences, the role of environmental organizations has recently been a topic of controversial discussions. A few big international NGOs are controlling a rising amount of budgets for environmental conservation and are involved in projects that have displaced communities (→ Biopolitics, I/22). In the last decades, nearly 8.5 million people worldwide have had to leave their homes because the territory they lived in was transformed into national parks (Cernea and Schmidt-Soltau 2006, 1818). In many cases, NGOs have legitimized the transforming of spectacular landscapes into national parks or high-end touristic attractions, or have admitted that areas were destroyed for large-scale development, infrastructural, and extractivist projects (→ Development, II/6) as long as nature was protected elsewhere (Brockington and Igoe 2007, 5).

Against this background, Martinez-Alier (2002) describes three currents of environmentalism: the cult of wilderness, the gospel of eco-efficiency, and the mantra of environmental justice (→ II/8). The cult of wilderness defended the above presented idea of pristine nature, using the idea of the beauty of landscape and nature as basically a habitat for animals, which can be observed by conservationists. It was and still is promoted by the U.S. Sierra Club; the World Wildlife Fund (WWF), International Conservancy, Friends of the Earth and Greenpeace among others. A second current of environmentalism, which has a different take on nature, started to develop with a focus on efficiency, less pollution and is connected with the idea that if nature at one place is destroyed, this should be compensated for elsewhere. By backing this principle, environmental agencies throughout the Americas, and international lending organizations such as the World Bank or the Interamerican Development Bank, have enabled a market of environmental destruction to emerge. A third type of environmentalism follows the paradigm of environmental justice that refers to the right to live in a safe environment for all, and to reject the idea that especially the urban poor are forced to be exposed to many health risks due to toxic waste, industry, and traffic (→ Urbanization, I/45). At the same time, the rural poor in the Americas are threatened and displaced by dams, mines, oil, deforestation, and national parks. As they do not express their claims within the official discourse of environmentalism, the rural communities have had difficulties to make their voices heard (Palacio 2006, 150). Environmental justice (→ II/8) was therefore developed as a social movement's perspective on these issues.

The way state (→ Nation State, II/38) and society treat nature has changed over time (Hardenberg, Matthew Kelly and Wakild 2017). In Colombia, for example, a conservationist perception of nature only started to penetrate official language from 1980 onward, carrying with it new juridical and political ways of regulating questions of land and forest protection (Palacio 2006, 150). While in many other American countries a rhetoric of sustainability developed, however what took place in practice was often a neoliberal recommodification of nature (→ Neoliberalism, II/16).

The concept of nature has become a tool for several indigenous peoples worldwide to claim their rights and resist against an uncontrolled and full incorporation of their land and communities into the logic of capitalism (→ Indigeneity, I/31). Many native groups have appropriated Western concepts invented to separate the non-human from the human, such as "environment," "biodiversity," and "nature," which historically are absent from most indigenous societies in the Americas, and make little sense in the cosmogonies, which structure (or used to structure) their perception of the world. In that perspective, it is interesting to see how so many indigenous peoples throughout the Americas have (successfully) attempted since the 1970s to reframe themselves as guardians of the environment. This way, native people might enter a logic of self-government fostered by international organizations like the World Bank, which Astrid Ulloa (2005) termed as being an "ecological native" – the quasi-ontological articulation of nature and indigeneity in new forms of eco-governmentality.

The 2009 film *Avatar* by James Cameron is a case in point showing how this indigenous defense of livelihoods and nature against commodification and colonization has penetrated even the entertainment industry (→ Media Flows, III/35).

The imagination of nature is highly marketable. The tourist industry sells an image of tropical landscapes within the Caribbean as paradises for tourist consumption (Sheller 2003) (→ Consumerism, I/23). In this logic, local inhabitants tend to be perceived as "invaders" and "illegal occupants" of "virgin" nature who destroy biodiversity hotspots (Ojeda 2012, 364) (→ Biopolitics, I/22). In the past three decades, cosmetic firms, global organic food networks, advertising companies, the entertainment industry (→ Cultural Industries, III/27), and ecotourism have built on an exotic vision of the Americas as a "wild" and still largely "pristine" continent. Therefore, old colonial imaginaries are strengthened once again, and at the same time new forms of commercial appropriations of nature emerge.

The logic of Green Grabbing (Fairhead, Leach and Scoone 2012; Tittor 2016) – to sell nature so as to save it – is becoming increasingly present all over the Americas. Although intended to protect areas deemed pristine, the outcomes of these environmental initiatives are often modest at best. For example, the Yasuní ITT-initiative of Ecuador`s government in 2007 proposed to leave the oil resources in the National park untapped (→ Energy, II/7) in exchange for compensation from the international community. Nevertheless, in 2013 the initiative failed due to the lack of financial support and the extractivist-oriented economic policy of the Ecuadorian government. Additionally, debt-for-nature swaps are another instrument to protect nature and reduce CO_2 emissions that can have unintended consequences. In exchange for debt forgiveness, the debtor-government has to foster conservation or invest in climate-related expenditures. Critics have stated that this instrument leads to a further commodification of nature, and reduces countries of the Global South to a status of nature while production regimes in the Global North remain untouched.

Nature strikes back – "natural" disasters and climate change within the Anthropocene

Another narrative that was present in many other perceptions of nature was the idea of nature as a dangerous force that is able to bring catastrophic situations to humans (→ Disaster, II/33). There is a religious narrative that sees natural catastrophes like droughts, floods, hurricanes, and earthquakes as events through which God punishes "men," if humankind in general, or different groups of it, behave in an unholy way (→ Religious Beliefs, I/40). Although within the bible, humans have the right and duty to master non-human life for its own needs, evangelical churches all over the Americas have successfully pushed their interpretations of floods, hurricanes, and Tsunamis as having a biblical meaning.

A different strand of interpretation argues that most natural catastrophes are not natural at all, but that certain models of political dependency and colonial entanglements have made the consequences severe (→ Postcolonialism, I/38). As Davis shows, for example, great famines in the late 19th century the Brazilian Northeast might have been "materially" unleashed by climatic droughts, but they stood in tight relation with the production, exchange structure, and ideologies of global Victorian capitalism (Davis 2002). As a human counterweight to these perceived natural catastrophes, the modern history of the Americas abounds with mega-projects aiming to "win" against nature, such as the decision to reverse the flow of the Chicago river in the 1880s, the building of the Panama Canal (Baquero Melo 2015; Sutter 2000), or the giant farms of the Ford, Jari, and Volkswagen companies in the Amazon (Acker 2017; Grandin 2010) (→ Modernization, I/35). All of these examples, which show the aspiration of defeating natural laws, left concrete traces of the environmental effects, which Western, fantasized visions of nature could engender.

Humans have subjugated and transformed nature for millennia, but the intensity of resource extraction has accelerated a lot with colonialism (→ Colonial Economies, I/4) and capitalism (→ II/2). Although concerns with the damaging effects of anthropic activities on nature have much older roots, the idea that humanity as a whole can be a danger for the Earth's ecological balance has grown especially influential since the 1970s. The "Limits of Growth" report from 1972 was one of the first widely recognized signals that started the discussion about the effects of industrialization (Meadows, Meadows, Randers and Behrens 1972). The reduction of pollution of the environment in the industrial areas and the declaration of protected areas were the key political strategies that responded to this emerging awareness, but a real reduction of growth was not even intended.

The discussion about causes and impacts of climate change (→ II/30) essentially took form in the 1980s in continuity of these debates. "Sustainability" started to be a concept that was used for almost everything and made into a modern publicity slogan. Although often imagined under pressure of spectacular scenarios that predicted a catastrophic future for the Earth if pollution continued to grow, strategies to protect the environment, reduce carbon emissions and stop deforestation had limited effects. Later on, interdisciplinary teams (but mainly with a natural science focus) started to measure the planetary boundaries (Rockström 2009). But despite many expert reports, international conferences (Rio 1992, Kyoto 1997, Paris 2015, Bonn 2017 among many other), and an emerging global environmental governance as well as the recent intent to have a social-ecological turn within development policy (→ Development, II/6) and proclaim the sustainable development goals, the linear development of resource consumption remains far from being stopped. Up to today only severe economic crises (→ II/4) have had a significant impact in terms of reducing the ecological footprint (Krausmann et al. 2009).

Remarkably, the recent discussion about the Anthropocene seems to indicate an epistemological rupture: even within geology, human beings are now seen as a telluric force transforming nature in an irreversible way – a contradictory mixture of gardener and predators (critically: Görg 2016). Some works date the beginning of the Anthropocene back to the start of the Neolithic revolution 10,000 years ago, while others situate it during the industrial revolution in Western Europe 200 years ago, or even later, with a "great acceleration" that took place in the middle of the 20th century (Krausmann et al. 2009). From the perspective of the Columbian Exchange (→ I/6), Charles Mann has identified 1492 as the most important rupture and coined the concept of the homogenocene to analyze the merging of ecosystems from Eurasia, Africa, and the Americas that had been separated since the fragmentation of Pangaea (Mann 2011, 3–50). This brings a completely new time frame into the discussion about historical conjunctures – but is still an open, controversial discussion.

What all these debates have in common is that they imagine "humanity" as a collective actor equally causing the problems. Nevertheless, the danger of this approach is to ignore the differences between the Global North and the Global South, but also between different groups and classes within respective world regions (→ Social Inequality, II/20), especially in terms of consumption patterns (→ Consumerism, I/23) or even cosmological representations (Bonneuil and Fressoz 2016). Not all societies have a predatory approach to the non-human environment, neither have all humans the same carbon footprint. This is especially true in the Americas, where the United States and Canada have reached skyrocketing $C0_2$-emission rates, while in some rural areas of South America and the Caribbean people still have to struggle for basic resources. Promoters of the Anthropocene narrative often ignore asymmetric power relations and tend to frame problems in apocalyptic scenarios, but they offer a very technocratic and marked-based approach to handle them, if not even post-political managerial planning (critically: Lövbrand 2015).

Anthropocene research mostly builds on chronological milestones that follow the evolution of the European, North American and sometimes Soviet production models, such as the industrial revolution, the rise of the fossil fuel economy and the development of the nuclear sector (→ Energy, II/7). Historians still struggle to find a place for the Southern Hemisphere in this narrative, although recent works have started to discuss Latin America's ambiguous role (both as an extractive periphery and a rising contributor to global pollution) in the making of Anthropocenic change (Acker and Fischer 2018).

Discussion: Decolonizing nature?

Many of the examples mentioned above show how modern rationality should be subject to political and epistemological discussion. Indeed, it constructed an unsustainable world, whose ecological destruction is due to the exploitative appropriation of nature during the colonial regime (→ Colonial Rule, I/5), as well as prolonged and amplified through the present world economic order (Leff 2015) (→ Capitalism, II/2). This went hand in hand with the exclusion and oblivion of traditional practices, while Western knowledge attempted to extend its domination over the Americas. Yet, there are numerous struggles of urban and rural dwellers, indigenous and Afro-American communities, and advocate organizations aiming to defend local livelihoods against capitalist appropriation (→ Social Movements, I/41; Alter-Globalization, I/21). For example, conflicts against large-scale mining projects have become frequent in all parts of the continent. In their cultural dimension, these conflicts over territories and landscapes also represent antagonist representations of the world. They can be best understood as multidimensional conflicts over territories, ways of living, access to water and land, and the question of environmental governance.

In spite of the ethno- and anthropocentric origins of the concept, the category of nature in the Americas may not need to be abandoned altogether. Nature as a distinct category is deeply rooted in our contemporary models of imagining the world: as said before, even indigenous groups have embraced "nature" as an issue to fight for. Strategically, to revoke the concept of nature might not be the most rapid and efficient way toward stopping environmental degradation and social exploitation. Nevertheless, it is necessary to underline the colonial dimension which characterizes the history of the idea of nature (→ Postcolonialism, I/38), and to learn from intents to de-colonize it. Three dimensions appear crucial on this path: First, it seems important to foster new epistemologies beyond the nature-culture divide. In the Americas these new epistemologies can surge from a dialogue between Western and indigenous knowledge. These diverse forms of knowledge have to be conceptualized as social-cultural patterns to relate to environments. In this sense, it would be wise to stop amalgamating indigeneity (→ I/31) and nature. There is no inherent feature that makes indigenous people more "natural" than Western people. Instead, different knowledge systems and epistemologies need to be considered. Beyond the question of inter-cultural translation and dialogue, there is also the problem of cultural appropriation, especially in regard to indigenous environmental knowledge. As the debates on bio-piracy show, while denying the value of indigenous knowledge developed over many generations, Western powers now attempt to colonize life itself (Shiva 1997) (→ Biopolitics, I/22). The current use of patenting and genetic engineering is understood by Shiva as an attempt from the West to re-colonize the Global South.

Second, decolonizing nature should take into account the internal logics of environmental change as well as its materiality, and not only its representations. It would be misleading to relate all forms of a destructive use of nature to coloniality and capitalism. For example, while Andean indigenous-peasant communities have complex, sustainable reciprocity systems with their highland environments, they fail to relate to tropical environments in the lowlands. Also, archeologists suspect the collapse of anciently prospering civilizations of North and Central America, such as the Chaco Anasazi and the Maya, to be the result of an unsustainable way of extracting natural resources. Trying to take advantage of White colonization (→ Whiteness, I/46), Amerindians hunters of Canada and Quebec also actively participated in the animal massacres that made the transatlantic fur trade expand from the 17th to the 19th centuries (Ray 1998). It would be interesting to further research how certain dynamics of environmental exploitation have been shaped both by internal colonial logics, and by a homemade ignorance toward natural conditions in a specific place, interwoven with, but not necessarily deriving from Western ideas of progress and modernity (→ Modernization, I/35). A decolonial approach toward different understandings of nature has to handle the problem that these are almost always relational and shaped by multiple transnational relations and Inter-American entanglements.

Third, decolonizing the idea of nature means to undo the existing interrelation between society and a biotic environment based on exploitation, extractivism (→ II/9), and misuse. In many (not all) indigenous societies, these relations are thought in terms of reciprocity and substance orientation. This implies systems of care beyond the Western extremes of preservation of pristine wilderness and profit-maximizing extraction. To rethink and possibly reconceptionalize the category of Nature, the different imaginations of and modes of relation with the environment need to be considered. Proposals from Latin America (Leff 2015; Machado Aroaz 2014; Palacio 2006) or from a "world-ecology perspective" may contribute to overcoming the nature-society divide through conceptualizing the "web of life" (Moore 2015) and thus deepen the dialogue with (post-)colonial approaches to open new ways of conceiving the field of Nature/Environment/Society/Culture.

Works cited

Acker, Antoine. 2017. *Volkswagen in the Amazon: The Tragedy of Global Development in Modern Brazil.* Cambridge and New York: Cambridge University Press.

Acker, Antoine and Georg Fischer. 2018. "Historicizing Brazil's Great Acceleration." *Varia Historia* 34, 65: 307–314.

Alimonda, Héctor. 2011. "La colonialidad de la naturaleza. Una aproximación a la Ecología Política Latinoamericana." In *La Naturaleza colonizada. Ecología política y minería en América Latina,* ed. Héctor Alimonda, 21–60. Buenos Aires: CLACSO.

Baquero Melo, Jairo. 2015. "Entanglements, Nature and Inequalities in the Darien." *forum for interamerican research* 8, 3: 45–67. Available at: www.interamerica.de.

Bastien, Joseph W. 1985. *Mountain of the Condor: Metaphor and Ritual in an Andean Ayllu.* Long Grove, IL: Waveland Press.

Bezerra, Joana. 2015. *The Brazilian Amazon. Politics, Science and International Relations in the History of the Forest.* New York: Springer.

Bonneuil, Christophe and Jean-Baptiste Fressoz. 2016. *L'événement anthropocène: la Terre, l'histoire et nous.* Paris: Points.

Brockington, Dan and Jim Igoe. 2007. "Neoliberal Conservation: A Brief Introduction." *Conservation and Society* 5, 4: 432–449. www.conservationandsociety.org/text.asp?2007/5/4/432/49249.

Carey, Mark. 2009. "Latin American Environmental History: Current Trends, Interdisciplinary Insights, and Future Directions." *Environmental History* 14, 2: 221–252.

Carson, Rachel. 1962. *Silent Spring.* Boston, MA: Houghton Mifflin.

Cernea, Michael M. and Kai Schmidt-Soltau. 2006. "Poverty Risks and National Parks. Policy Issues in Conservation and Resettlement." *World Development* 34, 10: 1808–1830.

Claude, Marcel. 1997. *Una Vez Más la Miseria: es Chile un país sustentable?* Santiago: LOM Ediciones.

Cleary, David. 2001. "Towards an Environmental History of the Amazon: From Prehistory to the Nineteenth Century." *Latin American Research Review* 36, 2: 65–96.

Colten, Craig E. 2012. "An Incomplete Solution: Oil and Water in Louisiana." *Journal of American History* 99, 1: 91–99.

Crist, Eileen and Eugene C. Hargrove. 2004. "Against the Social Construction of Nature and Wilderness." *Environmental Ethics* 26, 1: 5–24.

Crosby, Alfred W. 1972. *The Columbian Exchange: Biological and Social Consequences of 1492*. Santa Barbara: Greenwood.

Davis, Mike. 2002. *Late Victorian Holocausts: El Niño Famines and the Making of the Third World*. London: Verso.

Dean, Warren. 1987. *Brazil and the Struggle for Rubber: A Study in Environmental History*. New York: Cambridge University Press.

Descola, Philippe. 2005. *Par-delà Nature et Culture*. Paris: Gallimard.

DeVries, Scott. 2013. *A History of Ecology and Environmentalism in Spanish-American Literature*. Lewisburg, PA: Bucknell University Press, 2013, Print.

Eardley-Pryor, Roger. 2014. *The Global Environmental Moment: Sovereignty and American Science on Spaceship Earth, 1945–1974*. Santa Barbara: PhD thesis at the University of California.

Escobar, Arturo. 2008. *Territories of Difference: Place, Movements, Life, Redes*. Durham, NC and London: Duke University Press.

Evanoff, Richard J. 2005. "Reconciling Realism and Constructivism in Environmental Ethics." *Environmental Values* 14, 1: 61–81.

Evans, Sterling. 1999. *The Green Republic. A Conservation History of Costa Rica*. Austin, TX: University of Texas Press.

Fairhead, James, Melissa Leach, and Ian Scoone. 2012. "Green Grabbing: A New Appropriation of Nature?" *Journal of Peasant Studies* 39: 237–261.

Forsyth, Tim. 2001. "Critical realism and Political Ecology." In *After Postmodernism: Critical realism?* eds. A. Stainer, and G. Lopez, 146–154. London: Athlone Press.

Foster, John Bellamy. 2015. "Marxism and Ecology: Common Fonts of a Great Transition." *Monthly Review* 67: 7.

Görg, Christoph. 2016. "Anthropozän." In *Wörterbuch Klimadebatte*, ed. Sybille Bauriedel, 29–35. Bielefeld: transcript.

Grandin, Greg. 2010. *Fordlandia: The Rise and Fall of Henry Ford's Forgotten Jungle City, Picador*. New York: Macmillan USA.

Gudynas, Eduardo. 2009. "Diez tesis sobre el nuevo extractivismo, en: Extractivismo, política y sociedad." In *Extractivismo, política y sociedad*, eds. Jürgen Schuldt, Alberto Acosta, Alberto Barandiarán, Anthony Bebbington, Mauricio Folchi, Alejandra Alayza, and Eduardo Gudynas, 187–225. Quito: Centro Andino de Accion Popular/Centro Latinoamericano de Ecología Política.

Hardenberg, Wilko Graf von, Claudia Leal Matthew Kelly, and Emily Wakild. 2017. *The Nature State: Rethinking the History of Conservation*. New York: Routledge.

Henderson, Henry L. and David B. Woolner. 2005. *FDR and the Environment*. New York: Palgrave MacMillan.

Hochstetler, Kathryn and Margaret E. Keck. 2007. *Greening Brazil, Environmental Activism in State and Society*. Durham, NC: Duke University Press Books.

Jones, Christopher F. 2014. *Routes of Power: Energy and Modern America*. Cambridge: Harvard University Press.

Kaltmeier. Olaf. 2020. *National Parks from North to South. An Entangled History of Conservation and Colonizationin Argentina*. Trier and Tempe: WVT/Bilingual Press.

Krausmann, Fridolin, Simone Gingrich, Nina Eisenmenger, Karl-Heinz Erb, Helmut Haberl, and Marina Fischer-Kowalski. 2009. "Growth in Global Materials Use, GDP and Population during the 20th Century." *Ecological Economics* 68, 10: 2696–2705.

Kunow, Rüdiger. 2011. "City of Germs: Biological Identities and Ethnic Cultures in the Metropolis." In *EthniCities: Metropolitan Cultures and Ethnic Identities in the Americas*, eds. Olaf Kaltmeier, Jens Gurr, and Martin Butler, 171–185. Trier: WVT.

Latour, Bruno. 1992. *Nous n'avons jamais été modernes. Essai d'anthropologie symétrique*. Paris: La Découverte.

Latour, Bruno. 2004. *Politics of nature: How to Bring the Sciences into Democracy*. Cambridge: Harvard University Press.

Leff, Enrique. 2015. "Political Ecology: A Latin American Perspective." *Desenvolv: Meio Ambiente* 35: 29–64.

Leopold, Aldo. 1949. *A Sand County Almanac*. New York: Oxford.

Lövbrand, Eva. 2015. "Who Speaks for the Future of Earth? How Critical Social Science Can Extend the Conversation on the Anthropocene." *Global Environmental Change* 32: 211–218.

Machado Aroaz, H. 2014. *Potosí, el Origen. Genealogía de la Minería Contemporánea*. Buenos Aires: Mardulce.

Mann, Charles C. 2011. *1493: Uncovering the New World Columbus created*. New York: Vintage.

Martinez-Alier, Joan. 2002. *The Environmentalism of the Poor: A Study of Ecological Conflicts and Valuation*. Cheltenham: Edward Elgar Publishing.

Meadows, Donella H., Dennis L Meadows, Jürgen Randers, and William Behrens. 1972. *The Limits of Growth*. A Report for the Club of Rome's Project on the Predicament of Mankind. CT: Universe. www.donellameadows.org/wp-content/.../Limits-to-Growth-digital-scan-version.pdf.

Medina, Javier. 1991. *Del alivio a la pobreza al desarrollo humano*. La Paz, Bolivia: HISBOL.

———. 2001. *Suma qamaña: la comprensión indígena de la buena vida*. La Paz, Bolivia: Federación de Asociaciones Municipales de Bolivia.

Miller, Shawn William. 2007. *An Environmental History of Latin America*. New York: Cambridge University Press.

Moore, Jason W. 2015. "Nature in the Limits to Capital (and vice versa)." *Radical Philosophy* 193: 9–19.

Mosena, Alexander, Tom Steinlein, and Wolfram Beyschlag. 2018. "Reconstructing the Historical Spread of Non-Native Plants in the North American West from Herbarium Specimens." *Flora* 242: 45–52.

Ojeda, Diana. 2012. "Green Pretexts: Ecotourism, Neoliberal Conservation and Land Grabbing in Tayrona National Natural Park, Colombia." *Journal of Peasant Studies* 39, 2: 357–375.

Pádua, José Augusto. 2002. *Um Sopro De Destruição: Pensamento político e crítica ambiental no Brasil escravista (1786–1888)*. Rio de Janeiro: Jorge Zahar Editora.

Palacio, Germán. 2006. "Breve guía de introducción a la Ecología Política: Orígenes, inspiradores, aportes y temas de actualidad." *Gestión y Ambiente* 9, 3: 143–156.

Pike, Fredrick B. 1992. *The United States and Latin America: Myths and Stereotypes of Civilization and Nature*. Austin, TX: University of Texas Press.

Proctor, James. 1998. "The Social Construction of Nature: Relativist Accusations, Pragmatist and Critical Realist Responses." *Annals of the Association of American Geographers* 88: 352–376.

Quijano, Aníbal. 1997. "Colonialidad del Poder, Cultura y Conocimiento en América Latina." *Dispositio* 24, 51: 137–148.

Radkau, Joachim. 2011. *Die Ära Der Ökologie. Eine Weltgeschichte*. München: Beck.

Ray, Arthur J. 1998. *Indians in the Fur Trade: Their Role as Trappers, Hunters, and Middlemen in the Lands Southwest of Hudson Bay, 1660-1870: with a New Introduction*. Toronto: University of Toronto Press.

Robbins, Paul. 2004. *Political Ecology: A Critical Introduction*. Hoboken, NJ: Blackwell Publishing Ltd.

Rockström, Johan. 2009. "A Safe Operating Space for Humanity." *Nature* 46, 1: 472–475.

Santos, Rosalira Oliveira dos and Antonio Giovanni Boaes Gonçalves. 2011. "A natureza e seus significados entre adeptos das religiões afro-brasileiras." *Revista Brasileira de História das Religiões* 3, 9. www.dhi.uem.br/gtreligiao/pdf8/ST12/002%20-%20Rosalira%20Oliveira%20dos%20Santos%20e%20Antonio%20Giovanni%20Boae.pdf.

Scarzanella, Eugenia. 2002. "las bellezas naturales y la nación: los parques nacionales en Argentina en la primera mitad del siglo xx." *Revista Europea De Estudios Latinoamericanos y Del Caribe/European Review of Latin American and Caribbean Studies* 73: 5–21.

Sheller, Mimi. 2003. *Consuming the Caribbean: From Arawaks to Zombies*. New York: Routledge.

Shiva, Vandana. 1997. *Biopiracy – the Plunder of Nature and Knowledge*. Boston, MA: South End Press.

Smith, Neil. 2008. *Uneven Development: Nature, Capital, and the Production of Space*. 3rd ed. Athens, GA: University of Georgia Press.

Sutter, Paul. 2000. "Arrancale los dientes al trópico": ambiente, enfermedad y el programa sanitario de Estados Unidos en Panamá, 1904–1914." *Papeles de Población* 8, 24: 61–93.

Tanner, Adrian. 2007. "The Nature of Quebec Cree Animist Practices and Beliefs." In *La nature des esprits dans les cosmologies autochtones*, eds. Denis Gagnon, Frédéric Laugrand, and Jarich G. Oosten, 133–150. Québec, Canada: Presses Universitaires de Laval.

Tittor, Anne. 2016. "Green Grabbing." InterAmerican Wiki: Terms – Concepts – Critical Perspectives. www.uni-bielefeld.de/cias/wiki/g_Green_Grabbing.html.
Ulloa, Astrid. 2005. *The Ecological Native Indigenous Peoples' Movements and Eco-Governmentality in Columbia*. London: Routledge.
Wakild, Emily. 2011. *Revolutionary Parks: Conservation, Social Justice, and Mexico's National Parks*. Tucson, AZ: University of Arizona Press.
Watts, Michael. 2003. "Political Ecology." In *A Companion to Economic Geography*, eds. Eric Sheppard and Trevor J. Barnes, 257–274. Oxford, UK: Blackwell Publishing Ltd.

40
PAN-AMERICANISM

Josef Raab

In the early 19th century, the desire to detach the "New World" from the "Old" and the resulting efforts to establish greater cooperation and unity among the young nations in the Western Hemisphere gained prominence in both South and North America. This sentiment was the root of Pan-Americanism, whose basis, according to Arthur P. Whitaker, is "the Western Hemisphere idea," the view that "the peoples of America are bound together in a special relationship which sets them apart from the rest of the world" (1954, 176). Among the idea's initial proponents were Simón Bolívar (who favored a union limited to Spanish America) and José de San Martín in Latin America as well as Henry Clay and Thomas Jefferson in the United States.

The term "Pan-Americanism" (sometimes written "Pan Americanism," without the hyphen) entered Inter-American discourse in the 1880s, and it continues to be a contested political notion to this day. While some interpretations have stressed the idea of Inter-American solidarity and unity, of a partnership of the nations of the Americas in pursuit of the greater good for them all (→ America, I/2), José Martí and others understood Pan-Americanism from its inception as a maneuver of United States hegemony. They suspected that under the guise of partnership and cooperation, the United States was really seeking exploitation and dominance. Despite this wide range of interpretations (diverging especially with regard to the United States as either a partner or an imperial force), Pan-Americanism has generally been understood as promoting diplomatic, political, economic, social, and cultural activities geared toward fostering closer ties among the states of the Americas by intensifying relations, supporting the establishment of Inter-American associations, and working toward a common defense (→ Military, II/37). The movement resulted in the founding of the International Union of American Republics in 1890 (renamed the Union of American Republics in 1910), and of the Organization of American States in 1948.

Early conceptions of Pan-Americanism

Originally, Simón Bolívar had envisaged a Spanish-American confederation, exclusive of Brazil and the United States. This partnership of Spanish-American republics was to serve as a defense against Spain and the Holy Alliance (forged in 1815) and as a counterbalance to the rising influence of the United States. Bolívar spoke out publicly for a Spanish-American union as early as September 1810, envisaging what he called "a nation of republics," in which the poor as well as the black population would also enjoy citizenship (→ II/27) – although Bolívar's writings on the topic are inconsistent (Blanchard 2000, 10, 11–12).

In North America, despite a general reluctance by the early U.S. republic to assist independence struggles elsewhere in the Americas (→ Independence Movements, I/10), Pan-American ideas were being formulated by President Thomas Jefferson, who wrote in 1813 that the unity of the American peoples extended to all their "modes of existence" (qtd. in Whitaker 1954, 2), and by Kentucky Senator Henry Clay, who "began in 1815 to agitate passionately for United States aid to and recognition of the nascent nations of the south" (Fagg 1982, 11). Jefferson held that

> America has a hemisphere to itself. It must have a separate system of interest which must not be subordinated to those of Europe. The insulated state in which nature has placed the American continent should so far avail it that no spark of war kindled in the other quarters of the globe should be wafted across the wide oceans which separate us from them.
>
> *(qtd. in Whitaker 1954, 29)*

His use of "us" to refer to Americans – whether they are living in the north or in the south of the American "hemisphere" – expresses a Pan-American consciousness and a distancing from Europe, which would later shape the Monroe Doctrine of 1823. According to John Edwin Fagg, Henry Clay's ideas,

> like those of other politicians and publicists who took up the cause, were [also] essentially Pan American: the western hemisphere had bonds of union in geographical propinquity, experience with European colonization and independence therefrom, a general devotion to republicanism, and a yearning for democratic institutions.
>
> *(1982, 11)*

According to the Monroe Doctrine (a term coined in the United States in 1850), the "New World" was to be completely separate from the "Old": The United States vowed to oppose any attempts by the Holy Alliance to reconquer any of Spain's former colonies in the Americas. Although the U.S.A. had not consulted with Latin-American governments before President James Monroe proclaimed these views in his 1823 State of the Union Address, the Doctrine was initially generally welcomed in Central and South America, where efforts were under way to establish a common defense. Gran Colombia (consisting of present-day Venezuela, Colombia, Panama, and Ecuador) "made pacts with Peru, Mexico, Chile, and Central America in 1822–1825 calling for united action for common security" (Fagg 1982, 14). While most historians in Europe and in the Americas stress Bolívar's central role in the efforts toward Spanish-American solidarity and consider those efforts the roots of Pan-Americanism, Soviet historian Marat Antyasov argued in 1982 that Pan-Americanism was from the start geared toward United States hegemony: "In reality, the idea of Pan-Americanism, that is, unification of the entire American continent under the aegis of the U.S.A., originated in the United States." He continues, "It was advanced by Alexander Hamilton, prominent U.S. statesman and public figure. Already at the beginning of the 19th century he predicted the establishment of 'one great American system' … [under] U.S. leadership" (1982, 34). Another Soviet historian, Sergo Mikoyan, went so far as to call Pan-Americanism "a derivative of the Monroe Doctrine" (1982, 151).

In his efforts to formalize Spanish-American solidarity, Simón Bolívar had invitations sent out in 1824 to most American governments to convene in Panama in 1826. While he did not invite the United States, Gran Colombia's acting president Francisco de Paula Santander later did. However, approval by the U.S. Congress to send two delegates to the Panama conference took until March 1826, stalled in part by U.S. politicians who feared challenges to the institution of slavery (→ I/18). One of the U.S. delegates died on the way to Panama, the other one arrived only once the congress was concluded, and discussions had been moved to Tacubaya, near Mexico City. The Panama Congress approved the "Treaty of Union, League, and Perpetual Confederation," which abolished the African slave trade in the newly established Spanish-American republics (see Blanchard, who writes that "the two issues were related: the abolition of slavery and related problems of citizenship were conceived around a larger Pan-American vision of a modern union of states" 2000, 9) (→ Citizenship, II/27). In the end, however, the treaty was ratified only by Gran Colombia, which would soon be at war with Peru (1828–1829), was becoming increasingly unstable, and ultimately dissolved in 1831. Lockey concludes that Bolívar "liberated half a continent, but failed to create a nation" (1967, 138). In these early years of Pan-Americanism, Brazil, the Caribbean, and Canada did not play any role.

The abolition of slavery (→ I/18) did not become a Pan-American mandate, as "Pan-Americanism ran headlong into national and regional political leaders whose primary concern was consolidating internal unity, often at the expense of national or international arrangements" (Blanchard 2000, 15). But while, according to Fagg, the Panama Congress of 1826 "seemed a fiasco," it did promote the Pan-American idea as a counter-movement to national interests. He writes,

> Bolívar came to be much revered a few years after his death in 1830, and his impulse to Pan Americanism, however interpreted, extolled. ... [But] [f]or more than half a century after Panama no one took an effective lead in bringing together the nations of the New World.

Fagg continues,

> The United States had a series of presidents whose interest in Latin America involved territorial expansion (Mexico, Cuba, and Central America) rather than hemispheric cooperation. Nationalism was developing among the ruling oligarchies of the republics in a way that impeded fraternity.
>
> *(1982, 17)*

Moreover, various wars between Latin-American nations ensued between 1836 and 1870, obliterating much of the earlier Pan-American spirit. The two biggest obstacles to Pan-Americanism that became apparent in the first half of the 19th century – national interests and (a suspicion of) U.S. imperialist tendencies – are still in place today.

In the years following the Panama Congress, Mexico tried to uphold the Pan-American sentiment in view of mounting conflicts with the United States over Texas, inviting other Spanish-American republics to a congress five times between 1831 and 1842. None of those congresses were held, however. The second Inter-American conference, the *Congreso de Lima*, eventually took place from December 1847 until March 1848, attended by the five Pacific nations of South America. Agreements on a common defense, non-interference in each other's affairs, and other matters were drafted, none of which were ratified in the end, however. Meanwhile the U.S.A. was waging war against Mexico (1846–1848), claiming almost half of Mexico's territory. Responding to the perception of the United States as an imperialist power, a third Pan-American congress was convened in Santiago in 1856. Peru, Chile, and Ecuador signed a Continental Treaty aimed largely at containing U.S. expansionism. Less than a decade later, in 1864 and 1865, a fourth Pan-American conference, also referred to as *Congreso de Lima*, followed, as France and Spain were launching attacks in Mexico, Santo Domingo, and Peru, while the United States was caught up in a civil war (1861–1865). The U.S.A. and Brazil did not participate in the congress, at which representatives of Spanish America drafted the Treaty of Union and Defensive Alliance, which, however, soon lost its relevance, as France and Spain withdrew once the U.S. Civil War was over. As Arthur P. Whitaker observes, during the two decades leading up to the second Lima congress, "the major trend … had been toward a division of the Hemisphere into the two Americas and the appropriation of the Hemisphere idea to the exclusive use of one of them – Latin America" (1954, 59).

Pan-Americanism and U.S. economic imperialism

In the 1870s, the Bolivarian dream of Hispanic Inter-American solidarity was revived and was extended into a Pan-Americanism that included the United States – most notably by Argentine writer, educator, diplomat, and President Domingo Faustino Sarmiento and U.S. Secretary of State James G. Blaine. Sarmiento, an *aficionado* of the United States, endorsed the Monroe Doctrine as long as it was "interpreted as a doctrine of equality and reciprocity among the nations of the Western Hemisphere, not a doctrine of the United States' hegemony or imperialism" (Whitaker 1954, 70). Blaine, for his part, sent out invitations for a hemispheric conference to be held in 1882, aimed at ensuring peace and reducing internal disputes. But when he was replaced as Secretary of State after the assassination of President Garfield, his successor called off plans for the conference. Nonetheless, Blaine managed to convince U.S. Americans of the business prospects that Latin America held, and his activities led to the expression "Pan-Americanism" coming into common parlance in the 1880s. Lockey traces its first usage in print to the New York *Evening Post* issue of March 5, 1888.

Once Blaine had regained the position of U.S. Secretary of State, a conference of Western Hemisphere states was to be held in Washington in October 1889. Canada, as part of the British Empire, was not invited, the Hawaiian kingdom received a late invitation and accepted too late, the Dominican Republic did not wish to participate because of a dispute with the United States. All other American nations accepted the invitation to the First International Conference of American States, which is also referred to as the First Pan-American Conference. Blaine formulated his two objectives thus: "First, to bring about peace and prevent future wars in North and South America; second, to cultivate such friendly, commercial relations with all American countries as would lead to a large increase in the export trade of the United States" (qtd. in Lockey 1967, 52–53; note the prominent position Blaine assigns to the United States). In his opening address to the conference, he proposed transportation routes that would connect "the political and commercial capitals of all America." He also declared "that hearty cooperation, based on hearty confidence, will save all American States from the burdens and evils which have long and cruelly afflicted the older nations of the world" and "that friendship and not force, the spirit of just law and not the violence of the mob, should be the recognized rule of administration between American nations and in American nations" (qtd. in Lockey 1967, 74–75). On April 14, 1890 (which has been celebrated as Pan American Day since 1931), the International Union of American Republics was created along with the Commercial Bureau of the American Republics, which was to have its seat in Washington, and which was to be headed by the U.S. Secretary of State. In Laura Lomas's view, what the United States understood as Pan-Americanism in the last two decades of the 19th century was very dissimilar from Simón Bolívar's aspirations in the first two decades of that century. She writes:

> No longer representing a Bolivarian coalition of American republics that would commit to mutually guaranteeing one another's independence and sovereignty against the threat of imperial invasion, Pan-Americanism was from its inception in English usage always freighted with the expansionist and duplicitous economic designs of the United States.
>
> *(2008, 219)*

The Cuban exile poet and independence fighter José Martí, who reported on the Washington conference for various Latin-American newspapers, saw United States imperialism as the main obstacle to Pan-American union. In his article for the December 19–20, 1889 issue of the Buenos Aires newspaper *La Nación*, he warns against "the domination [of Spanish America] by a nation reared in the hope of ruling the continent" (qtd. in Foner 1975, 367). Lomas points out that

> [i]n Martí's own usage, the adjective 'Pan-American' carries connotations of deceit and fabrication … Sarcastic references to 'los panamericanos' – by which he meant the U.S. and Latin-American delegates to the 1889 conference who toured the major industries in the United States – reveal Martí's animosity toward this term and the concept.
>
> *(2008, 218–19)*

There was a general suspicion in Spanish America that – in view of the monopolies and trusts that were starting to dominate the United States – Pan-Americanism might be primarily aimed at ensuring U.S. industrial domination in the Western Hemisphere and at securing markets for U.S. goods. According to Mexican historian Alonso Aguilar, "Latin Americans, for their part, proposed that the conference adopt … basic principle[s of] American international law" because

> [t]he flow of foreign capital into the continent was growing rapidly; foreign investors frequently sought to obtain privileges of all kinds and in cases of conflict appealed to their home governments for support, in violation of the principles of national sovereignty.
>
> *(1968, 39, 40)*

Martí was inspired by the Washington congress and by the growing preponderance of the United States to write his best-known essay, "Nuestra América," which was published in the New York *Revista Ilustrada* on January 1, 1891 and which is generally considered to encapsulate his interpretation of Pan-Americanism. In the essay he argues that Latin-American nations need to stop imitating foreign cultural and political models, that the United States needs to see the other American nations as partners rather than subordinates, and that all nations in the Americas need to work together toward common goals. Like Bolívar's Pan-Americanism, that of José Martí "was predicated on a discourse of shared historical legacies, cultural imaginaries, and language, or Hispanismo" (Allatson 2007, 188). According to John Edwin Fagg, "[a]t least since 1889 Pan-Americanism has shown the two entities [the United States and Latin America] as adversaries despite the rhetoric of unity" (1982, 3). What Alonso Aguilar calls "the front of generous 'big-sister' concern" of U.S. President William McKinley would soon become "the 'Big Stick' policy made notorious in America by the picturesque and headstrong Theodore Roosevelt [U.S. President from 1901 to 1909]" (1968, 43).

Further Conferences of American States were held in Mexico City in 1901, in Rio de Janeiro in 1906, and in Buenos Aires in 1910. Fagg states that "[b]y then it was becoming traditional that Brazil and the United States were natural allies in facing the Spanish-speaking states" (1982, 30). Theodore Roosevelt's "Corollary to the Monroe

Doctrine" envisaged the United States as an international overseer in the Western Hemisphere. In his annual message to Congress delivered on December 6, 1904, he declared his respect for the self-management of nations in the Western Hemisphere but added that

> [c]hronic wrong-doing, or an impotence which results in a general loosening of the ties of civilized society, may in America, as elsewhere, ultimately require intervention by some civilized nation, and in the Western Hemisphere the adherence of the United States to the Monroe Doctrine may force the United States, however reluctantly, in flagrant cases of such wrongdoing or impotence, to the exercise of an international police power.
>
> *(Roosevelt 1904, 101)*

The U.S.A. originally promoted Pan-Americanism for economic and commercial reasons – often on the verge of economic imperialism (as with the opening of the Panama Canal in 1914 and with the onset of "dollar diplomacy," i.e., the use of U.S. force to further U.S. business interests abroad). With Roosevelt's Big Stick Policy, military interventionism (e.g., in Nicaragua 1909–1910, 1912–1925, and 1926–1933) was added to the U.S. interpretation of Pan-Americanism. At the same time, with the onset of the modernist movement in Latin-American literature (→ Modernism, III/14), there was a growing self-confidence in Latin America and a courage to stand up against U.S. interventions.

> The Nicaraguan poet Rubén Darío called for 'Pan Hispanism,' which deliberately excluded the United States. In his poem 'Salute of the Optimist' ('Salutación del optimista'), Darío calls for the 'fertile Hispanic blood' to awaken and to 'sing new hymns' of glory.
>
> *(Weeks 2015, 64)*

In 1908 dignitaries from across the Western Hemisphere gathered in Washington, D.C. to lay the cornerstone for a building to house the Pan American Union (the permanent secretariat or "commercial bureau" of the Union of American Republics founded in 1890), which today serves as the headquarters for the Organization of American States. While the Pan American Union's stated goal was to collect information on the histories and cultures of the nations of the Americas, its major problem was that this information was organized to highlight U.S. accomplishments and possibly to facilitate U.S. interventionism (→ II/36) (Park 2014, 1–3).

Accordingly, as Aguilar writes, "interventions and abuses perpetrated by the United States multiplied between 1906 and 1916 under the widest range of pretexts" (1968, 53). He adds that what the United States "really wanted … was not the solidarity but the subordination of the hemisphere" (1968, 55–56). According to Arthur P. Whitaker, in the first two decades of the 20th century, the United States assumed a so-called "'civilizing mission,' which connoted unilateral action, both political and economic, supported by missionary zeal and, if necessary, by armed force as well," as Pan-Americanism was fused with the idea of Manifest Destiny (1954, 115). Ricardo D. Salvatore (2006) has spoken in this context of "imperial mechanics," pointing out the central concern of the United States with transportation routes connecting the Americas in the "machine age."

Yet in a speech held on December 7, 1915, U.S. President Woodrow Wilson denied any imperial aspirations, maintaining

> that the states of America are not hostile rivals but cooperating friends, and that their growing sense of community of interest, alike in matters political and in matters economic, is likely to give them a new significance as factors in international affairs and in the political history of the world.
>
> *(qtd. in Lockey 1967, 9)*

Further on, he notes, "This is Pan-Americanism. It has none of the spirit of empire in it. It is the embodiment, the effectual embodiment, of the spirit of law and independence and liberty and mutual service" (qtd. in Lockey 1967, 9). Indeed, Wilson did manage to establish cooperation among Latin-American nations who had been rivals until then. But ultimately his Pan-American aspirations were not credible, since while he spoke of "the principles of absolute political equality among the states," the United States was militarily involved in Northern Mexico and was "invading and occupying multiple countries in Central America and the Caribbean" (Weeks 2015, 86).

Subsiding Pan-Americanism

In academia, establishing a shared history and culture of the Americas, Herbert Eugene Bolton proclaimed in his 1932 presidential address to the American Historical Association that the First World War (during Wilson's presidency) was the period of greatest Pan-American solidarity because

> [t]he essential unity of the Western Hemisphere was revealed by the Great War. Every nation had to answer the question of participation or neutrality. ... It is a significant thing that all America, from the north pole to the south pole, was either on the same side of the great struggle or remained neutral. There was emphatic Western Hemisphere solidarity.
>
> *(1939, 49)*

This view has been contested especially by Latin-American historians like the Irish-Mexican writer and philosopher Edmundo O'Gorman, who called Bolton's vision of Pan-American solidarity and cultural unity "a beautiful and false illusion" (1964, 111).

By the time of the Fifth Pan-American Conference, which was held in Santiago in 1923, Yankeephobia was strong in Spanish America, and, according to Fagg, "Washington was now isolationist and had no intention of relinquishing its monopoly of the Monroe Doctrine" (1982, 39). Tensions continued to flare at the Sixth Pan-American Conference in Havana in 1928, and the division of the Americas became even more apparent as Spain was trying to intensify its relations to Latin-American nations at the expense of Pan-Americanism. Whitaker notes that at that conference "Pan-Americanism was at ebb tide" (1954, 130). Aguilar adds that in the 1920s "the most characteristic feature ... was the massive flow of foreign capital, especially from the United States, into the main Latin-American countries whose economies thereby became more dependent and underdeveloped" (1968, 61). Against this background, labor organizers – primarily from the United States and Mexico – established the Pan-American Federation of Labor in 1918 (Harvey 1928), which was dissolved in 1934 (→ Labor Representation, II/14).

Nicaraguan guerrilla leader and political thinker Augusto César Sandino proclaimed in 1929 to "*the Representatives of the Governments of the Twenty-one Latin American States*" the need for Latin-American solidarity against U.S. economic imperialism (Sandino 1929, 61, italics in the original) when he wrote,

> Deeply convinced as we are that North American capitalism has reached the final stage of its development, transforming itself into imperialism, and that it no longer heeds theories of law and justice, passing over without regard the immutable principle of independence for the component parts of the LATIN AMERICAN NATIONALITY, we consider an alliance of the Latin-American States to safeguard that independence from the ambitions of United States imperialism, or from any other power that tries to subordinate us to its interests, to be indispensable and unpostponable.
>
> *(1929, 61)*

He called for "the fusion of the twenty-one States of Our America into a single, unitary Latin American nation" (1929, 62). Yet again, U.S. dominance was an obstacle to Pan-Americanism and promoted instead Pan-Hispanic-Americanism.

Sandino's resistance to U.S. interventionism is credited with having helped to bring about a change in the United States from the Big Stick Policy of Theodore Roosevelt to the Good Neighbor Policy of Franklin Delano Roosevelt, who declared that

> [a]mong the nations of the Western Hemisphere the policy of the good neighbor has happily prevailed. … [In the Americas there has never existed] a greater spirit of mutual understanding, of common helpfulness, and of devotion to the ideals of self-government than exists today in the twenty-one American republics and their neighbor the Dominion of Canada.
>
> *(qtd. in Lockey 1967, 9)*

On April 12, 1933, speaking in front of a special session of the Governing Board of the Pan American Union in Washington D.C. in celebration of Pan American Day, Roosevelt vowed, in his famous "Good Neighbor" speech, to respect Latin-American nations in the spirit of Pan-Americanism, saying that "the essential qualities of a true Pan-Americanism must be the same as those which constitute a good neighbor, namely, mutual understanding, and, through such understanding, a sympathetic appreciation of the other's point of view" (qtd. in McPherson 2016, 121).

The Good Neighbor Policy also needs to be seen in the context of increasing scholarly engagement in the United States with Mexico, Central, and South America, as "the study of Latin America became an academic specialization" (Berger 2000, 46). Aguilar comments that the Good Neighbor Policy was "a step forward as far as the aggressive behavior of the United States was concerned, behavior which had culminated in armed interventions in Mexico, Central America, and the Caribbean" (1968, 69) (→ Interventionism, II/36). He concludes, however, that the Good Neighbor Policy did not "affect the very basis of United States–Latin-American relations. The countries south of the Rio Grande remained subjugated to the great power in the north and very soon the illusion vanished that things would change radically" (1968, 69). At the Seventh Pan-American Conference, held in Montevideo in 1933, the U.S. A. finally agreed to the principle of nonintervention; nonetheless, "the United States continued to interfere in Latin-American affairs in one way or another" (Aguilar 1968, 71).

Against this political and historic background Diego Rivera was asked to create a mural for the Golden Gate Exposition in San Francisco in 1940–1941 (→ Muralism, III/37). The resulting work, entitled "Pan American Unity," envisions a utopian version of San Francisco and presents multiple scenarios from which to view it (Park 2014, 227) (→ Utopia, III/23). While other murals by Rivera at that time had created a stronger contrast between – especially – Mexico and the United States, the attitude foregrounded here is complementation rather than rivalry. The various panels depict activities and accomplishments in indigenous, Anglo- and Hispanic America (→ Indigeneity, I/31). These are presented side by side, not in competition with each other but complementing one another in the pictorial creation of San Francisco and other places as combining features and faces associated with a variety of American locations. Rivera stresses the Americas' history of democracy (→ II/32) and has the different nations and peoples of the Americas unite in their opposition to European dictatorships (→ Authoritarianism, II/25). As Stephen M. Park notes,

> [r]ather than mapping the hemisphere, Rivera chooses to locate its rich array of cultures in a single city. His aim is to include the disparate parts of the Americas without simplifying their cultures into knowable categories. … Rivera presents us with multiple views of both the city and the hemisphere that resist an easy synthesis.
>
> *(2014, 228–229)*

The spiritual South and the machine-driven North are depicted as complementary and as interrelated in the vein of Pan-Americanism. Artists, workers, intellectuals, and athletes of different parts of the Americas – red, brown, black, and white – work together in the mural.

After the death of Franklin Delano Roosevelt, the U.S. government's interpretation of Pan-Americanism changed quickly toward efforts geared at U.S. hegemony – now in military (→ II/37) terms. In the Inter-American Reciprocal Assistance Treaty passed at the Eighth Pan-American Conference in Rio de Janeiro in 1947 the United States required Latin-American states to support any military action it might take. Alarmed by the rise of fascism in Europe and by the growing strength of the Soviet Union, the United States strove for a "hemispheric defense" treaty to formalize the Act of Chapultepec, which had been adopted at the Inter-American Conference on the Problems of War and Peace in Mexico City in 1945. In effect, rather than Pan-American partnership on an equal footing for a common goal, the treaty subjected Latin-American foreign policies to outside approval (by the United States). As Alonso Aguilar sees it,

> [t]he Inter-American Treaty of Reciprocal Assistance was not only the first military treaty signed in America in peacetime; it was also an instrument intended to undermine Latin-American sovereignty, to submit the most important national decisions to the vote of other countries, and to try to hold back the course of history by alleging that the advance of Socialist countries and of liberation movements was the worst threat to the world that had arisen out of the war.

He adds, "The United States attitude clearly revealed the inability of its governing classes to comprehend that the desire of the people for progress and change could not be sacrificed to privilege and vested interests" (1968, 83–84).

Donna J. Guy reminds us that despite the general emphasis on "commerce, diplomacy, and military intervention" in discussions of Pan-Americanism, the movement also involved other aspects: For the period leading up to the 1950s, she stresses the importance of groups like the Pan-American Sanitary Commission and the Pan-American Scientific Congress as well as the Pan-American Child Congresses, all of which were "important component[s] of Inter-American cooperation … linked to the child rights movement and, through it, efforts to promote the welfare state in the Americas" (2000, 34).

Another aspect not often mentioned in the context of Pan Americanism is sports. The first Pan-American Games were to be held in Buenos Aires in 1942, but plans did not come to fruition until 1951 (Torres 2011). Since then, Pan-American Games have taken place every four years, always the year before the summer Olympic Games.

Increasing U.S. military and economic interventionism

The Ninth Pan-American Conference held in Bogotá in 1948 approved the Charter of the Organization of American States, which privileges U.S. interests. The economic agreement reached at the conference was likewise not geared toward promoting economic development (→ II/6) in Latin America but assigned to Latin-American economies primarily the function of supplying natural resources and raw materials, thus increasing their dependence on United States capital. Another resolution proposed by the United States demanded Latin American support for combating "the activities of international Communism" (qtd. in Aguilar 1968, 91) (→ Socialism, I/42). The pattern of exchanging U.S. financial aid and private investment for Latin-American political support continued throughout the 1950s. U.S. efforts to halt the spread of Communism came to a climax with the Cuban Revolution, whose representatives denounced those efforts as imperialist. For example, at an August 1960 meeting in San José, Costa Rica, Cuban Foreign Minister Raúl Roa told the assembled representatives that the

> cunning weapon wielded by United States propaganda against the Cuban Revolution ... has been ... to brand it indiscriminately as 'influenced by Communists,' as acting as a 'Soviet satellite' or 'the spearhead of international Communism.' This is the scratched record we have been listening to in crescendo for seventeen months...

His ultimate charge is as follows:

> [i]n the name of the revolutionary government of Cuba, I accuse the government of the United States of making this false charge in order to first safeguard and then recuperate the privileges of exploiting corporations who carry more weight with the State Department than the legitimate interests of the people of the United States.
>
> *(qtd. in Aguilar 1968, 112)*

In the 1960s, when John F. Kennedy forged the "Alliance for Progress" as a Pan-American initiative (→ Development, II/6; Modernization, I/35), the goals ostensibly shifted toward combating social inequalities (→ II/20). According to the U.S. State Department, the program was

> [t]o make the benefits of economic progress available to all citizens of all economic and social groups through a more equitable distribution of national income, raising more rapidly the income and standard of living of the needier sectors of the population.
>
> *("Objective" 1961)*

However, at the same time, the U.S. attacks on Cuba at Playa Girón and at the Bay of Pigs revealed the interventionism (→ II/36) of the U.S. – carried out in violation of the Organization of American States (OAS) Charter. Carolyn M. Shaw has appropriately spoken of "the ebb and flow of U.S. dominance" (2004, ch. 5). That Kennedy used the Alliance for Progress "as an instrument of the cold war instead of economic development, as Operation *Pan-America* [launched by Brazilian President Juscelino Kubitschek de Oliveira in 1958] had proposed, led," according to W. Michael Weis, "to the effective end of pan-Americanism and a functioning inter-American system" (2001, 344). Interventions by the United States would continue throughout the 20th century, and socialist Latin-American governments would stand up against U.S. hegemony into the 21st century (→ Socialism, I/42).

But all too often situations arose in which, as Alonso Aguilar puts it, Latin-American states "allowed the caprice of a powerful country to take precedence over principle and to undermine the right of self-determination," resulting in "the subjugation of Latin-American policy to United States demands" and a routine of "domination and plunder" (1968, 122, 131, 155). Such frictions demonstrate that the idea of a Pan-American solidarity keeps being tested but also continues to be reasserted – with changing alliances that sometimes include the United States as a genuine partner and that are at other times dominated by or directed against them. For example, at the Tricontinental Conference of Asia, Africa, and Latin America held in Havana in January 1966, it was resolved that "[g]overnments emerging from liberation movements will not be obliged to respect the agreements … of the OAS and especially those which invalidate the principles of nonintervention, free determination, and sovereign equality of nations" (qtd. in Aguilar 1968, 147).

The United States desire to combat and prevent the spread of communism in Latin America led to numerous covert and overt interventions by U.S. military and secret service (→ Interventionism, II/36; Military, II/37). A CIA coup d'état overthrew elected Guatemalan President Jacobo Árbenz in 1954, a coup to overthrow left-leaning Brazilian President João Goulart was supported by the U.S. in 1964, and in 1965 U.S. soldiers deployed to the Dominican Republic prevented the transition of power to a left-wing government. Support by the United States for the installation of right-wing dictatorships in Chile in 1973 and in Argentina in 1976 were just two of the most salient cases in the alleged U.S. fight against the spread of communism that would lead to U.S.-backed authoritarian regimes in numerous countries of South America in the 1970s (→ Authoritarianism, II/25). The U.S. could count on Latin Americans being divided between supporting and fearing socialist revolutions (→ Revolution, II/44). While some welcomed U.S. financial, military, and secret service assistance, the majority rejected this new form of U.S. interventionism – an old hegemonic practice with a new justification. The various campaigns illustrated the U.S. paranoia about the threat of communism in its backyard as well as an attitude toward the rest of the Western Hemisphere that was not in the spirit of Pan-Americanism but rather in the tradition of feminizing and infantilizing Latin Americans as weak and therefore unable to resist potential communist manipulators. Another major assault on the idea of Pan-Americanism in the late 20th century occurred with the financial and military support offered by the United States to the Contras in Nicaragua throughout the 1980s. Some have argued that all these interventions were motivated by the U.S. desire to prevent the success of the Cuban Revolution of 1959 (McPherson 2016, 148). Since the end of the Cold War, the main reason given by the U.S.A. for intervening in Latin-American countries has shifted from combating communism to efforts in the "war on drugs."

Toward the end of the 20th century, looking past U.S. support for Latin-American right-wing dictatorships and beyond high-level negotiations on Inter-American security (→ II/45), Pan-Americanism was invoked, among others, in the creation of the Inter-American Indian Institute, in the work of the Inter-American Human Rights Commission (→ Human Rights, II/35), and in environmental causes throughout the Americas (→ Environmental Justice, II/8) (Sheinin 2000, 3). In the 21st century, writes Carolyn M. Shaw, the OAS has given up its focus on anticommunism as "a guiding principle to assure regional security. Member states have placed new emphasis on the principle of representative democracy, even at the expense of nonintervention and state sovereignty" (2004, 186), as exemplified by the Democratic Charter adopted in 2001. Still, many Latin-American nations remain wary of U.S. hegemony and the threat of U.S. interventions. That is why since the late 20th century, there have been numerous re-interpretations of Pan-Americanism as a united

Latin American front against the United States – returning to Simón Bolívar's original interpretation of the concept. From the creation of MERCOSUR in 1991 via the assumption of the presidency of Venezuela by Hugo Chávez in 1999 to the founding of ALBA in 2004 and the establishment of UNASUR (the Union of South American Nations, which expressly excludes the United States) in 2014, there has been a sort of emancipation of Latin-American nations resisting U.S. dominance (→ Regional Integration, II/18). As Gregory B. Weeks comments, UNASUR opposes U.S. hegemony as well as "international capitalism and … dependency. The entire flavor of the founding document is utopian, a new era dawning that would renew the age-old desire for regional unity and harmony" (Weeks 2015, 215). CELAC, the Community of Latin American and Caribbean States, founded in 2010 and comprising thirty-three nations, has as its mandate "to provide a counterweight to U.S. Cold War policies and to help Latin-American countries coordinate responses to key collective challenges they faced" (Weeks 2015, 218). More often than not, these "challenges" are tied to the United States.

Nonetheless, the notion of Pan-Americanism remains influential in various scenarios of the 20th and 21st century: for example, it was invoked by the Chicano Movement (→ Latinidad, I/33; Social Movements, I/41), it was instrumentalized in the frequent references to Bolívar and Martí by Venezuelan President Hugo Chávez in his call for resistance to U.S. hegemony, it is seen at work in the alliances of indigenous groups throughout the Americas (→ Indigeneity, I/31), and it was rekindled in December 2014. Facilitated by Pope Francis and the Vatican, U.S. President Barack Obama, and Cuban President Raúl Castro held a phone conversation of almost an hour, vowing to exchange prisoners and to improve relations between their countries. As Obama said in a televised address at the White House on December 17, 2014,

> Today, the United States of America is changing its relationship with the people of Cuba and the most significant changes in our policy in more than 50 years. We will end an outdated approach that for decades has failed to advance our interests. And instead … create more opportunities for the American and Cuban people and begin a new chapter among the nations of the Americas. … Todos somos Americanos.
>
> *("Transcript" 2014, no pag.)*

This "new chapter" in which "[t]odos somos Americanos" ["we are all Americans"] was in fact one closely tied to the 200-year-old idea of Pan-Americanism that had for so long suffered from U.S. hegemony. In April 2015, Barack Obama and Raúl Castro met face to face at the Seventh Summit of the Americas in Panama City, they shook hands and talked extensively. Yet on his way to the summit, Venezuelan President Nicolás Maduro, for his part, laid a wreath to commemorate the 1989 U.S. invasion of Panama and rallied a cheering crowd: "Never again a U.S. invasion in Latin America!" (qtd. in McPherson 2016, 1). A year later Obama became the first U.S. president to visit Cuba since 1928. But in 2017 his successor announced that he would cancel many of the less strict regulations put in place by the Obama administration. In addition, signaling the opposite of Pan-Americanism, he pushed ahead with plans for a border wall between the United States and Mexico (→ Borderlands, II/26; Security, II/45). In 2019, finally, a U.S. invasion of Venezuela is a distinct possibility, as the Venezuelan government is becoming increasingly repressive and is alienating its neighboring American nations. While the idea of Pan-Americanism remains alive, the reality of Pan-American solidarity and a partnership of equals is not at all well today.

Lawrence E. Harrison has spoken of "a cultural divide in the Hemisphere" (1997, 5) between the United States and Canada on the one hand and Latin America on the other, between "the Anglo-Protestant and Ibero-Catholic traditions" (1997, 18). He has asked (rather paternalistically) whether the political traditions and cultural values of "traditional" Latin America are not so radically different from the "progressive" U.S. and Canada that Pan-Americanism must necessarily remain a dream (1997, 5). Much has also been made of the argument of Latin American "dependency" (Harrison 1997, 20–21). Cooperation has sometimes coincided with competition, even with a "history of hostility" between the United States and Latin America (McPherson 2006, 9–28).

The notion of Pan-Americanism has been invested with very different meanings at different times, in different places, and in different political/social/academic circles in the Americas. In his 1925 essay on "The Meaning of Pan-Americanism" Joseph Byrne Lockey stated that concerning the position of the United States in Pan-Americanism there is "much confusion of thought," since uses of the term vary from "group[ing] the American republics under the hegemony of the United States" to asserting "the political or the legal equality of the independent states of America" (1967, 2, 4). Likewise, David Sheinin calls the notion of Pan-Americanism "elusive," situating it between "a vision for friendly inter-American exchange" and Latin-American associations of Pan-Americanism "with a U.S. agenda for political, strategic, cultural, ideological, and economic influence in the hemisphere" (2000, 1). The major obstacle to a genuine Pan-American partnership remains the exceptionalism of the United States, and to a lesser degree of Canada and Brazil.

A concept that has recently partly come to replace Pan-Americanism is that of "Americanity" (Quijano and Wallerstein 1992), which also recognizes the unequal power division between Latin America and North America. In expanding "Americanity" to "Trans-Americanity" as a term designed to capture the situation in the 21st century, José David Saldívar notes that

> [t]he key historical and structural difference between Latin America and the United States in the nineteenth century and today, in the twenty-first century, … is that Latin America and the United States of America (through globalization) are now part of what Quijano and Wallerstein … presciently called a *single world order*, for the Americanization of the Américas is coming into 'full bloom'.
>
> *(2012, xiv–xv, emphasis in the original)*

The steady rise of the Latino population of the United States (→ Latinidad, II/33) may be adding another facet to the future of Pan-Americanism.

Works cited

Aguilar, Alonso. 1968. *Pan-Americanism from Monroe to the Present: A View from the Other Side*. 1965. New York: Monthly Review Press.

Allatson, Paul. 2007. *Key Terms in Latino/a Cultural and Literary Studies*. Malden, MA: Blackwell Publishing.

Antyasov, Marat. 1982. "Pan-Americanism: Its Origin and Evolution." In *Pan-Americanism: Its Essence and Evolution*, eds. P.N. Fedoseev and I.R. Grigulevich, 33–42. Moscow: USSR Academy of Sciences.

Berger, Mark T. 2000. "A Greater America? Pan-Americanism and the Professional Study of Latin America, 1890–1990." In *Beyond the Ideal: Pan-Americanism in Inter-American Affairs*, ed. David Sheinin, 45–56. Westport, CT and London: Praeger.

Blanchard, Peter. 2000. "Pan-Americanism and Slavery in the Era of Latin American Independence." In *Beyond the Ideal: Pan-Americanism in Inter-American Affairs*, ed. David Sheinin, 9–18. Westport, CT and London: Praeger.

Bolton, Herbert Eugene. 1939. *Wider Horizons of American History*. Repr. 1967. Notre Dame: University of Notre Dame Press.

Fagg, John Edwin. 1982. *Pan Americanism*. Malabar, FL: Robert E. Krieger Publishing Company.

Foner, Philip S. ed. 1975. *José Martí: Inside the Monster*. New York: Monthly Review Press.

Guy, Donna J. 2000. *White Slavery and Mothers Alive and Dead: The Troubled Meeting of Sex, Gender, Public Health, and Progress in Latin America*. Lincoln, NE and London: University of Nebraska Press.

Harrison, Lawrence E. 1997. *The Pan-American Dream: Do Latin America's Cultural Values Discourage True Partnership with the United States and Canada?* Boulder, CO: Westview Press.

Harvey, Rowland H. 1928. "Pan-Americanism through Organized Labor." *Social Service Review* 2, 3: 414–434.

Lockey, Joseph Byrne. 1967. *Essays in Pan-Americanism*. Port Washington, NY: Kennikat Press. Orig. pub. 1939.

Lomas, Laura. 2008. *Translating Empire: José Martí, Migrant Latino Subjects, and American Modernities*. Durham, NC and London: Duke University Press.

McPherson, Alan. 2006. "*Antiyanquismo*: Nascent Scholarship, Ancient Sentiments." In *Anti-Americanism in Latin America and the Caribbean*, ed. Alan McPherson, 1–34. New York and Oxford: Berghahn Books.

———. 2016. *A Short History of U.S. Interventions in Latin America and the Caribbean*. Malden, MA: Wiley Blackwell.

Mikoyan, Sergo. 1982. "America at the 'Moment of Truth' or the Collapse of Some Concepts." In *Pan-Americanism: Its Essence and Evolution*, eds. P.N. Fedoseev and I.R. Grigulevich, 33–42. Moscow: USSR Academy of Sciences.

O'Gorman, Edmundo. 1964. "Do the Americas Have a Common History?" In *Do the Americas Have a Common History?: A Critique of the Bolton Theory*, ed. Lewis Hanke, 103–111. New York: Alfred A. Knopf.

Park, Stephen M. 2014. *The Pan American Imagination: Contested Visions of the Hemisphere in Twentieth-Century Literature*. Charlottesville, VA and London: University of Virginia Press.

Quijano, Aníbal, and Immanuel Wallerstein. 1992. "Americanity as a Concept, or the Americas in the Modern World-System." *International Journal of Social Sciences* 134: 549–557.

Roosevelt, Theodore. 1904. "The Roosevelt Corollary to the Monroe Doctrine." In *Latin America and the United States: A Documentary History*, 2000, eds. Robert H. Holden and Eric Zolov, 100–102. New York and Oxford: Oxford University Press.

Saldívar, José David. 2012. *Trans-Americanity: Subaltern Modernities, Global Coloniality, and the Cultures of Greater Mexico*. Durham, NC and London: Duke University Press.

Salvatore, Ricardo D. 2006. "Imperial Mechanics: South America's Hemispheric Integration in the Machine Age." *American Quarterly* 58, 3: 662–691.

Sandino, Augusto C. 1929. "Plan for the Realization of Bolívar's Ultimate Dream, March 20, 1929." In *Sandino Without Frontiers: Selected Writings of Augusto César Sandino on Internationalism, Pan-Americanism, and Social Questions*, 1988, eds. Karl Bermann et al., 61–74. Hampton, VA: Compita Publishing.

Shaw, Carolyn M. 2004. *Cooperation, Conflict, and Consensus in the Organization of American States*. New York: Palgrave Macmillan.

Sheinin, David. 2000. "Rethinking Pan Americanism: An Introduction." In *Beyond the Ideal: Pan-Americanism in Inter-American Affairs*, ed. David Sheinin, 1–8. Westport, CT and London: Praeger.

Torres, Cesar R. 2011. "The Limits of Pan-Americanism: The Case of the Failed 1942 Pan-American Games." *The International Journal of the History of Sport* 28, 17: 2547–2574.

"Transcript: Obama's Remarks on U.S.-Cuba Relations." 2014. *The Washington Post*. Dec. 17, 2014. www.washingtonpost.com/politics/transcript-obamas-remarks-on-us-cuba-relations/2014/12/17/08366538-8612-11e4-9534-f79a23c40e6c_story.html?noredirect=on&utm_term=.111606631776.

Weeks, Gregory B. 2015. *U.S. and Latin American Relations*. 2nd ed. Malden, MA: Wiley Blackwell.

Weis, W. Michael. 2001. "The Twilight of Pan-Americanism: The Alliance for Progress, Neo-Colonialism, and Non-Alignment in Brazil, 1961–1964." *The International History Review* 23, 2: 322–344.

Whitaker, Arthur P. 1954. *The Western Hemisphere Idea: Its Rise and Decline*. Ithaca, NY: Cornell University Press.

41
PARTICIPATION

Wagner de Melo Romão

The term participation refers to the involvement of a community or society in political life in many different ways. A great deal of what has been conceptually developed in relation to the term refers to the opposite of the idea of representation. Thus, participation is an activity associated with direct action in political life, in which the individual acts on their own – without the mediation of representatives or intermediaries – to influence decision-making in the political system or in private political organizations (Pasquino 2010). Beyond the difference in relation to mediated practices of political action, the term participation encompasses a great variety of actions in terms of form, impact on the political system, and interaction with other individuals.

A distinction should be drawn as to whether these actions are individual or collective: the former are characterized by a continuum, starting with exposing oneself to political overtures or voting in elections and consultations such as plebiscites and referendums (→ Democracy, II/32), to the occupation of public positions (Milbrath 1965). Collective forms of expression and the pursuit of political influence through unions (→ Labor Representation, II/14), political parties, social movements (→ I/41), civil society (→ II/28) organizations and many other forms of collective action should be considered as well. Currently, different forms of online interaction on social media (→ III/41) and the internet have also expanded the many possible ways of exercising influence or political pressure (→ Digital Culture, III/28).

More specifically – and within the scope of the so-called democratic innovations (Fung and Wright 2003; Smith 2009; Gurza Lavalle and Isunza Vera 2010) – the concept of participation has also expanded to include a more personal interaction between citizens (→ Citizenship, II/27) and the State (→ Nation State, II/38). The terms "citizen participation," "social participation," or "institutional participation" (Isunza Vera 2006; Romão 2015) all describe political action that generally develops in forums with a degree of formality and, to a great extent, that exists with the mediation or direct action of the state. These forums allow the interaction between socio-political agents in civil society through the discussion, reflection and, possibly, the deliberation on themes they hold in common. Generally, the interaction between these agents and those that represent governments and other state bodies also occurs in these forums.

Authors such as Arditi (2005) and Zaremberg (2012) posit that the role of these mechanisms is similar to that of the alternative circuits to Parliament in decision-making, originated within the context of the state of social well-being in Western Europe and analyzed by authors such as Schmitter (1974) and Offe (1985) in the literature on neo-corporativism. They in fact can take on the form of complex deliberative structures which, in some cases, can be compared to the Legislative or Executive branches, such as the universal system of Brazilian health care, or Ecuador's Transparency and Social Control Branch of the new constitution. However, in more general terms, this rarely occurs, and the spaces for citizen participation tend to have reduced deliberative power when compared to traditional state powers, though they might constitute important focal points for socio-political mobilization.

It is not feasible, considering the limits of this entry, to cover the wide variety of forms and meanings of participation. Therefore, some of the forums in which the abovementioned civil society and governments interact will be highlighted. These forums can usually be observed more frequently in local governments, but they can also develop in higher levels of government, including at the national level. The creation of alternative mechanisms of political representation is closely connected to the interaction between state and civil society.

These forums of participation can occur within and with the backing of national governments themselves, via specific legislation or the decision of the national Executive (*top-down*) , or through the voluntary initiative of civil society, or local governments (*bottom-up*). However, as McNulty (2014) observes when analyzing the case of Guatemala, this difference should always be tempered by the knowledge that the emergence of such forums and processes are almost always reciprocal. For example, the municipal health councils in Brazil emerged from the local experiences of citizen participation in informal follow-up and demand councils concerning health policies. Afterwards, with the creation of a national health system, the federal government induced local governments to create their councils since, without them, they would not have access to budget resources.

In a general sense, participation processes involve the allocation of the public budget for the execution of works and services. This can involve, on the one hand, social actors who are based in the areas where they live or, on the other hand, actors who are more directly connected to public policy sectors, such as health (→ I/29), education (→ I/24), social assistance, culture, etc.

In the first case, one of the main models of inspiration is the Orçamento Participativo – OP (Participatory Budget), created in Porto Alegre, as well as in around a dozen other Brazilian cities at the beginning of the 1990s, all governed by the Partido dos Trabalhadores (Worker's Party). The OP's proposal was to divide the city into regions, promote the meeting of residents to identify the problems that take place in their neighborhoods, and find ways to solve these problems. Usually, a list of measures is drafted that should be considered by the municipal governments with some degree of compromise. In subsequent years, the OP has spread to practically all the countries of the Americas, accounting for thousands of events. It is estimated that around three thousand events based on the Brazilian experience occur today worldwide (Sintomer, Herzberg and Röcke 2014). In the second case, the creation of councils was established by agents of public authorities and representatives of civil society, or only social agents. These are permanent forums of decision-making, formulation, monitoring and evaluation of policies, diffusion of information, and conferences that marshal organized sectors of civil society (→ II/28) that, by their turn, influence public policies, which Rhodes (2008) calls *policy networks*.

The participatory democracy agenda

In most American countries, with the exception of for example United States, Canada, and Cuba, the dissemination of these participatory mechanisms took place with the onset of re-democratization from the beginning of the 1980s onwards (→ Democracy, II/32). The transition from authoritarian regimes (→ Authoritarianism, II/25) to democratic ones in Latin America (O'Donnell, Schmitter, and Whitehead 1986) (→ State Transformation, II/21) incorporated the need to go beyond democratic representation *strictu sensu.* Invariably, the fall of dictatorial regimes occurred amid strong popular manifestation, relevant effervescence in civil society (→ II/28), and the creation of new forms of participation in which the demand for free general elections and the legalization of left-wing political parties came hand in hand with the expectation that mechanisms for direct citizen participation on public issues be included, especially in the sphere of local governments. A huge variety of community associations and social movements (→ I/41) had an important role in the elaboration of new constitutions that would include mechanisms of participatory democracy in countries such as Brazil (1988), Colombia (1991), Peru (1993), Argentina (1994), and Paraguay (1992). A second wave was marked by a new Latin-American constitutionalism (Nolte and Schilling-Vacaflor 2012) that combined constitutions produced in junctures of national "re-founding," with the appearance of political parties and movements positioned to the left of power after the neoliberal period of the 1990s (→ Neoliberalism, II/16). This occurred in Venezuela (1999), Ecuador (2008), and Bolivia (2009).

In these two waves, in which new constitutions were drafted, there was an increase in the number of nations that included provisions in their legal landmarks for popular deliberation (referendums, plebiscites, mandate repeals) as forms of decision-making based on universal suffrage, as was already the common case in other American countries such as the United States, Canada, and Uruguay. However, this has not necessarily guaranteed that people will have a central role in the most important political decisions in Latin-American countries, especially in the case of mandate repeals (Lissidini 2011). These tend to be a solution for impasses among political elites, as in the mandate repeal concerning Chávez's term in Venezuela in 2004, and in Bolivia in 2008 (Eberhardt 2017; Kornblith 2014). Or, diversely, mandate repeals may turn out to be destabilizing factors for established governments, where consulting the population in the middle of a term is the result of the weak institutionalization of the party system and the laxity of rules in proposing a repeal, as was the case in Peru, where over 5,000 repeal polls in municipalities occurred between 1997 and 2013, with a total of about 1,737 repeals (Welp 2016).

In countries such as Mexico and Chile, the process for new constitutions did not take place. In Mexico, the Federal Constitution was not affected by the moment of relative flexibilization of the political system, in which there was a change in the leadership of the national state after more than seventy years of absolute control of the Institutional Revolutionary Party (PRI), which occurred with the victory of the National Action Party (PAN) in 2000, which continued working within the nation's central government for twelve years. Likewise, in Chile, though there were some specific reforms, the transition to democracy did not bring with it a new constitutional process. The country has maintained the same constitution since Pinochet's dictatorship. These are cases of very slow transitions in which one can see more continuity than rupture with the previous political order, with special emphasis on the fact that they did not bring about the re-structuring of constitutional order.

Aside from the efforts that participation be included in the new constitutions of the first and second waves, many of the countries in the American continent developed supplementary legislation related to the decentralization of public policies and citizen participation. "Laws of citizen participation" appeared in 1994 in Bolivia, Colombia, and Peru – taken up once more in the latter in 2003 – including the legal obligation that municipalities carry out participatory budget processes in their budget decisions. In 2002, Panama established its own citizen participation mechanisms for the control of transparency in public administration. In 2006, Venezuela regulated its *Consejos Comunales*, laid down in the 1999 constitution and, thus, introduced a new phase of political mobilization in the country. Uruguay approved a decentralization and citizen participation law in 2010. In the current decade, new citizen participation laws have been introduced in Chile and Ecuador in 2011; Bolivia in 2013, and Colombia in 2015 – this last occurring amid negotiations for a peace treaty with the guerilla of the Revolutionary Armed Forces of Colombia (FARC). Furthermore, between 2000 and 2010, mechanisms of participation were created in specific sectors of public policy in most of these countries, as can be seen in the cases of Brazil and Argentina, for example. Councils and other institutional participatory forums have been provided for as elements of inspection, social control and, in some areas, of deliberation on the future of political policies.

It is important to consider that these "waves" of participatory legislation are related to a regional and international agenda encouraging citizen participation in public administration with the aim of guaranteeing the rights of political citizenship (→ II/27), in which organizations such as the United Nations, the Organization of the American States, the Organization of the Ibero-American States, the European Committee, among many others, as well as international agencies, all participate (→ Development, II/6). Beyond that, a great deal of importance is given to the development of specific sectors of public policy, or more broadly, to the internal political-institutional conjunctures of each country.

Popular outcry for greater participation and control over public agents – almost always amid scandals pertaining to corruption or the ill-use of public funds – may trigger the emergence of specific events or new participatory legislation. This occurred, for instance, with the political crisis in Argentina at the beginning of the 2000s (→ Crisis, II/4), which brought with it the creation of several events of institutional participation, such as the Buenos Aires OP, starting in 2002 (Welp and Schneider 2011); the manifestations in Brazil, in June 2013, which led to the drafting of a proposal for a National System for Social Participation by the Dilma Rousseff government – subsequently rejected by the conservative Parliament (Romão 2015); or, still, mobilizations such as the "Water War" and the "Gas War" at the peak of neoliberalism in Bolivia, and the indigenous insurrections between 2000 and 2003 (→ Indigeneity, I/31), which gave rise to the critical juncture (Pierson 2004) that preceded the rise of Evo Morales to power in 2005 and the call for the Constitutional Assembly that transformed the nation's political system (Webber 2011).

National experiences: political context, decentralization, and public policies

Diverse experiences can be found in American nations – especially in Latin America – as a result of the renovation in their democracies emerging from mechanisms of participatory democracy, centered on institutional participation. Although there is a predominance of forms of participation related to local governments or local public organs, some countries have integrated two or three levels of government in federative nations and national forums in unitary states.

The resurgence of citizen participation after the 1980s brought about a great deal of expectation in the academic community and civil society as to possible benefits for the expansion of democracy (Fung and Wright 2003; Santos 2005). The confidence in growing democratic political systems directly connected to popular demand intensified as left-wing political parties and social movements won elections and reached the leadership of national governments in Venezuela (1998), Brazil and Argentina (2003), Uruguay (2005), Chile, Bolivia and Nicaragua (2006), Ecuador (2007), Paraguay (2009) and later, Peru (2012), El Salvador and Costa Rica (2014), and Mexico (2018). As was mentioned above, in the 2000s even countries that continued under the command of right-wing or center governments in the political sphere developed laws that contemplated the popular demand for more direct participation.

The effectiveness of citizen participation in many American countries has been debated as well as its connection with the broader institutional-political context of each political system. One example, Mexico, has a solid legislation regarding local and regional participation with the creation of the National System of Democratic Planning in 1982. In subsequent periods, the School Councils of Social Participation – a result of the change in educational laws – and the Advisory Councils on Sustainable Development were created. With President Fox's PAN government, the Municipal Councils of Rural Sustainable Development were created, under the new law for Sustainable Rural Development (→ Development, II/6). However, works such as those by Zaremberg et al. (2017) posit that only the School Councils – which were mandatory for the allocation of government funds to schools – in fact mobilized the Mexican population, with 19 percent of citizens stating that they participate or have participated in these councils. Most of the institutional participation in Mexico remains symbolic and fictional, especially in the context of the neoliberal and conservative governments of recent decades.

Other examples include countries such as Brazil, where the requirement that councils, with the participation of civil society, be created for the allocation of federal funds to municipalities stimulated their development in several political sectors. The municipal – as well as the state and national – councils have expanded in the more than 5,500 municipalities in the country. The legal landmark for this process was the Federal Constitution of 1988, which brought with it the strengthening of municipalities and the decentralization of public policies. The most solid example is the creation of the Sistema Único de Saúde (Central Health System) – a public, universal health care system in which responsibilities are divided among federative entities, and with mandatory forums of citizen participation, such as councils and conferences. Throughout the 1990s and 2000s, participation and social control forums were created in several public policy sectors, e.g. health (→ I/29), education (→ I/24), children and adolescent rights, the rights of the elderly, social assistance, environment, historical, and cultural heritage (→ Memory Politics, I/34), inspired by this model.

With Lula da Silva's victory in the 2002 elections, there was the assumption that the Worker's Party would adopt participatory practices at the federal level. The main model disseminated was that of national conferences of public policies and the incentive for the creation of dozens of national councils, as well as the opening of municipal councils for public policies. Though the model was well known, especially in the more traditional policy sectors such as health, social assistance, and human rights (→ II/35), the national conferences spread from 2003 on, totaling over eighty conferential processes at the local, state, and national level, in several government action sectors. Deliberations aim at influencing ministerial action concerning the implementation of policies. Romão et al. (2017) identified at least three types of conference: the more institutionalized kind, with greater capacity to influence public policies; the kind characterized as being an agenda dispute, in which a struggle between divergent ideas on policies prevails; and finally, mobilization conferences which aim at activating networks in civil society and the government to strengthen – and even create – new sectors of governmental action.

Regarding the Mexican case, Zaremberg et al. (2017) point out that the mechanisms of citizen participation present very little effectiveness. Mediating actions between the population and the state are still carried out almost exclusively by the political parties (PRI, PAN, and PRD). Similarly, in Brazil, the logic of political-party coalitions, in a highly competitive system, has an effect on the mechanisms of participation, both in the polarity between the government and opposition – with effects on the creation or erosion of mechanisms – and the eventual chances for the forums of civil society participation to exercise pressure and wear out governments (Gurza Lavalle, de Melo Romão and Zaremberg 2014).

Thus, to understand the political meaning of institutional participation, its connections with political-party disputes must be established. This is even more intense in countries that have been carrying out profound reforms in their political institutions by distancing themselves from liberal democracies, such as Venezuela, Bolivia, and Ecuador.

Hugo Chávez's rise as president of the Republic of Venezuela in 1998 and the elaboration of a new constitution created a new political regime and a new party system. There was a shift from a low-intensity democratic system to a growing political polarization in society and its contact with the state, which saw political participation (in the form of direct consultation in plebiscites, referendums and mandate repeals) as its main channel. However, the most important wager of the Chávez regime can be seen in the proposal of Communal Councils of a territorial nature and in the connections with public policy sectors, which led to thousands of community councils throughout the country (McCarthy 2012).

This was effectively a search for an alternative in re-structuring networks that would lead to a new form of participatory power – certainly articulated by a strong, superior central element which, ultimately, was anchored in the presidential Cabinet itself. The Communal Councils relied on the flow of resources derived from the oil bonanza of the 2000s (→ Extractivism, II/9) – which coincided with Chávez' most ebullient period in power.

In the Councils, public funds are formulated, decided on, and administered territorially, in part by public servants designated for social mobilization, and in part by individuals belonging to the local population. According to the legislation created in 2006, each Council occurs in urban areas with between 150 to 440 families, and in rural areas with up to twenty families. Because these organizations act directly with the identification of urban problems in communities and the raising of public funds to solve these problems, the Communal Councils became the hegemonic form of community participation in Venezuela during the Chávez years. With the highly polarized political context in the country that deepened after Chávez's death in 2013 and the rise of Nicolas Maduro, the Councils became spaces restricted to activists and those who favor the regime. Therefore, the difficulties in institutionally strengthening participation in Venezuela derive from extreme political polarization.

Something similar occurred in Bolivia, though with the distinction of attempting to include native populations in the country's political and administrative system. The Law of Popular Participation (Law no. 1551/1994) gave rise to decentralization by transferring new responsibilities to municipalities, mainly in the areas of education and health. The law guaranteed the distribution of 20 percent of national revenue to the 314 Bolivian municipalities that were counted at the time. Right after Evo Morales' election, and since the 2009 constitution, Bolivia's political process has focused on respecting and encouraging the forms of "community democracy" of the nations and peoples of indigenous rural origin (→ Indigeneity, I/31), creating a new political system characterized by a pluralism of nationalities and based on the *Ley Marco de Autonomías y Descentralización "Andrés Ibáñez,"* ratified in 2010.

The main point concerning citizen participation in Bolivia has been to overcome the discrimination and political exclusion of native populations within their original territories. A new institutional model was proposed, which, at the same time, articulated political and budgetary decentralization and the construction of a state whose judicial design incorporated the diversity of the nations who lived in an area, allowing for communities to "equitably express themselves and live according to their forms of organization, thought and understanding of the world" (Freitas 2014).

Still, one must be aware of the many difficulties that arise in the actual establishment of new autonomies. Aside from the difficulty of building something new – a political autonomy that will never be absolute – there are also important aspects related to a model of economic development (→ II/6) that tends to be incompatible with the way indigenous peoples (→ I/11) live. Although the 1998 constitution in Ecuador already included a series of mechanisms for citizen participation, the rise to power of Rafael Correa and the PAIS Alliance – after a highly troubled historical period, marked by the intense participation of social movements, especially indigenous – brought about a new political movement in the country. The *Revolución Ciudadana* and the new constitution of 2008 triggered a renewed legal and institutional framework of participation, transparency, and accountability, with the creation of a specific power, called The Transparency and Social Control Branch and the National Council of Citizen Participation, made up of members from civil society with executive attributions for the nomination of public service sectors in the national government.

Though to a lesser extent, the tensions stemming from the process of decentralization encouraging participation also took place in Uruguay. Since the Frente Amplia (Broad Front) party rose to power in 2005, Uruguay has gradually altered its centralist tradition. Though it is true that departmental governments have in fact taken on new tasks since the end of the dictatorship in 1985, this had not really materialized as a law until the 1996 constitutional reform which reinforced decentralization. Nevertheless, very little had truly moved forward before the 2009 Law for Political Decentralization and Citizen Participation (complemented in 2014). This law granted the creation of municipalities and elected authorities in areas with more than 2,000 inhabitants, also allowing towns to implement institutional innovations for participation, thought there are no binding rules. The only forum of citizen participation that the municipalities must implement is an annual public hearing in which the accounts of the previous administration are presented (Freigedo 2017). There is also the possibility of Local Popular Initiative: 15 percent of those registered to vote can present initiatives, including the creation of a new town.

However, these changes still have drawbacks that need to be pointed out. First, there is no level of fiscal autonomy for municipalities in Uruguay – these remain dependent on the Departmental Government and the National Executive Power. Aside from that, the law does not establish an amount or percentage of a set budget for municipalities and, thus, everything depends on the political relations between mayors and the departmental and national leaders. This situation is extremely disruptive for the establishment of permanent mechanisms of citizen participation. After all, without a budget there is no power and, with no power, there are very few practical stimulants for participation.

If in countries such as Uruguay one can say that the principal undertaking for citizen participation lies in the strengthening of local structures of governance, in Peru the process started at the beginning of the 2000s. With the experiences of Villa El Salvador and Ilo, which had initiatives of community participation on governmental decisions in the 1980s and 1990s, the nation began to develop national laws on the subject in the 2000s.

The Constitution of Peru (1993) and the Law of Citizen Participation (1994) broadened the mechanisms for direct participation with mandate repeals, referendums, accountability, and the removal of authorities which had begun during the authoritarian Fujimori period. At the beginning of the 2000s, during Alejandro Toledo's government, Peru introduced new legislation concerning administrative decentralization, the organic laws of regional governments and the organic law of municipalities, through which Regional and Local Coordination Councils were created and the Law of Participatory Budgets began, determining the municipalities' obligation to establish participatory processes in budget debates. The members involved in the Regional and Local Coordination Councils are the mayors of the provinces (or districts, in the case of local councils) of a specific region and representatives of civil society organizations, with a 60 percent to 40 percent proportion, respectively. These councils decide on the agreed regional (or local) development plan and the annual participatory budget.

The decision-making process for the participatory budget begins with debates between civil society and local government representatives in the municipalities, then moves on for approval of regional councils – which are a type of local Legislative – and only then are sent to the Ministry of Economy and Finance which evaluates its technical and financial feasibility. In other words, there are significant filters in this process after the civil society participation phase. According to McNulty (2012), those who participate in the process acknowledge the difficulties in its implementation – especially because decisions are made only on investments (and not on the whole budget, most of which is already committed to the payment of existing public service and government structures). Besides that, the completion of projects itself is compromised: on the one hand, by the uncertainties imbedded in any budget process; on the other hand, by decisions made at higher levels in government that do not consider what has been decided by civil society at local government levels. The Peruvian model prompted similar experiences in the Dominican Republic and Ecuador.

Citizen participation in Colombia is linked to the country's process of pacification after the agreement between the Revolutionary Armed Forces of Columbia (FARC) and the Colombian State. The pathway to peace is directly connected to the approval of the current Law of Citizen Participation of July 2015, which reforms the previous one of 1994. The new law was the result of an agreement between the Ministry of the Interior and the civil society organization *Foro Nacional por Colombia*, consisting of a participatory process that began in 2011 and evaluated the previous law, elaborating new proposals. According to Velásquez and González (2015), there was an institutional oversupply (over fifty laws creating forums for citizen participation were issued in the last two decades) which produced a fragmentation of social agency and the control of spaces by specific actors. On the other hand, fragmentation led to circumstances in which the same leader belonged to different forums of institutional participation, leading to a concentration of political resources and, gradually, a distancing from his or her base. Hence, the same dilemmas of political representation can be seen in forums of institutional participation. In Nicaragua, Guatemala, and El Salvador (Vargas and Petri 2009) citizen participation was also a part of a negotiation and concentration process which ended civil wars.

In Argentina there also seems to be a prevalence of a progressive institutionalization and diversification of participatory mechanisms, especially in municipalities (Rofman and Foglia 2015), related to gradual advances of the municipal agenda. Some municipalities, especially large and midsized, have developed administrative and political capacities, as well as promoting initiatives for the participation of civil society. The participation of civil society in governmental organs began with social welfare policies at the end of the 1990s in local councils that promoted and protected the rights of children and adolescents, aiming at articulating citizenship and governmental actions directed to the advancement of rights (→ Human Rights, II/35). After the period of street manifestations during the 2001–2002 crisis, local governments incorporated mechanisms such as participatory budgeting, ventures that created employment and income managed by governmental actors and civil society, events in territorial development, and mechanisms of participatory administration in some sectors of public policies, such as safety, childhood protection, and education.

Although its development has been slow in these countries from the beginning of the 2000s, more recently there has been significant expansion concerning participatory budget events, especially in the large metropolises of the United States and Canada. Different from Latin America, the participatory budget events in these countries have been limited to districts or specific issues with scarce resources. On the other hand, especially in the United States, participatory budget events have intensified among populations that have little electoral representation, such as immigrants (→ Transnational Migration, I/44), adolescents and minority groups, granting them political expression. Chicago, New York, Toronto, San Francisco, and St. Louis are some of the cities that have adopted this system. In all, there have been around 250 events in the countries mentioned, taking into consideration the extreme diversity of the political communities (schools, universities, districts, communities in housing complexes) where they are held (Goldfrank and Landes 2018).

Closing remarks

Citizen participation is still underway in practically all countries due to permanent processes of political-institutional decentralization and recentralization, and because these experiences are still relatively recent and constantly being improved. There are numerous contentious aspects regarding the growth of institutional participation related to political disputes within the context of each nation, administrative and institutional difficulties, and the lack of political leadership that commits to expanding democracy (→ II/32) via participation, all of which can bring about setbacks or limitations in growth.

It is imperative to recognize that recurrent street manifestations in American countries in the last years indicate that institutional forms of participation were not able to help the political system overcome the ever-present "crisis of representation," characterized by a high level of mistrust in political institutions and in politicians. The participation of citizens in combination with state agencies should not be the only form of attempting to atone for the inadequacies of democracies in the continent.

Nevertheless, it is unquestionable that the way to improve democracies demands the diversification of citizen participation. In this sense, it is the task of researchers on the Americas to investigate how these events develop, what are the factors for their success or failure, what is their relationship with the political scenario and what is their capacity to survive the traditional authoritarian policies (→ Authoritarianism, II/25) that still permeate the relations between the state and society on the continent.

Works cited

Arditi, Benjamín. 2005. "Introducción: la idea de un 'segundo circuito' de la política." In *Democracia post-liberal? El espacio político de las asociaciones*, ed. Benjamín Arditi, n.p. Barcelona: Anthropos Editorial.

Eberhardt, María Laura. 2017. "La revocatoria presidencial en América Latina. Ventajas y limitaciones. Los casos de Venezuela, Bolivia y Ecuador." *Colombia Internacional* 92: 105–133.

Freigedo, Martín. 2017. "Political Rights and Intermediation: Municipal Decentralization and Democratic Innovation in Uruguay." In *Intermediation and Representation in Latin America: Actors and Roles beyond Election*, eds. Gisela Zaremberg, Valeria Guarneros-Meza, and Adrián Gurza Lavalle, 77–94. London: Palgrave Macmillan.

Freitas, Caroline C. M. 2014. "O processo de regulamentação das autonomias indígena originário camponesas na Bolívia: tensões entre pluralismo, descentralização política e soberania." *Pensamiento Propio* 40 (Julio-Deciembre): 125–155.

Fung, Archon and Eric Olin Wright. 2003. *Deepening Democracy: Institutional Innovations in Empowered Participatory Governance*. London and New York: Verso Books.

Goldfrank, Benjamin and Katherine Landes. 2018. "Participatory Budgeting in Canada and the United States." In *Hope for Democracy: 30 Years of Participatory Budgeting Worldwide*, ed. Nelson Dias, 161–176. Portugal: Epopeia Records.

Gurza Lavalle, Adrián and Ernesto Isunza Vera. 2010. "Precisiones conceptuales para el debate contemporáneo sobre la innovación democrática: participación, controles sociales y representación." In *La innovación democrática en América Latina: tramas y nudos de la representación, la participación y el control social*, eds. Vera Ernesto Isunza and Adrián Gurza Lavalle, 19–80. México: CIESAS, Publicaciones de La Casa Chata.

Gurza Lavalle, Adrián, Wagner de Melo Romão, and Gisela Zaremberg. 2014. "Partidos políticos e innovación democrática: más allá de purezas y perversiones." *Revista Mexicana de Ciencias Políticas y Sociales* 220 (Enero-Abril): 21–54.

Isunza Vera, Ernesto. 2006. "Para analizar los procesos de democratización: interfaces socioestatales, proyectos políticos y rendición de cuentas." In *Democratización, rendición de cuentas y sociedad civil: participación ciudadana y control social*, eds. Ernesto Isunza Vera and Alberto Olvera, 265–291. México: CIESAS, Universidad Veracruzana, Miguel Ângel Porrúa Editorial.

Kornblith, Miriam. 2014. "Revocatoria del mandato presidencial en Venezuela: definición y puesta en práctica." In *Democracias en movimiento: mecanismos de democracia directa y participativa en América Latina*, eds. Alicia Lissidini, Yanina Welp, and Daniel Zovatto, n.p. México: Universidad Nacional Autónoma de México.

Lissidini, Alicia. 2011. *Democracia directa en Latinoamérica: entre la delegación y la participación*. Buenos Aires: CLACSO.

McCarthy, Michael. 2012. "Las posibilidades y los límites de la participación politizada: Consejos Comunales, coproducción y poder popular en la Venezuela de Chávez." In *Nuevas instituciones de democracia participativa en América Latina: la voz y sus consecuencias*, eds. Maxwell Cameron, Eric Hershberg, and Kenneth E. Sharpe, 167–198. México: Flacso México.

McNulty, Stephanie. 2012. "An Unlikely Success: Peru's Top-Down Participatory Budgeting Experience." *Journal of Public Deliberation* 8, no. 2: 1–19.

———. 2014. "Mandating Participation: Evaluating Guatemala's Top-Down Participatory Governance System." *Pensamiento Propio* 40 (Julio-Deciembre): 95–124.

Milbrath, Lester. 1965. *Political Participation: How and Why Do People get Involved in Politics?* Chicago: Rand McNally.

Nolte, Detlef and Almut Schilling-Vacaflor. 2012. *New Constitutionalism in Latin America: Promises and Practices*. Oxon and New York: Ashgate.

O'Donnell, Guillermo, Philippe C. Schmitter, and Laurence Whitehead. 1986. *Transitions from Authoritarian Rule: Comparative Perspectives*. Baltimore: John Hopkins University Press.

Offe, Claus. 1985. "The Atributtion of Public Interest of Public Status to Interest Groups." In *Desorganized Capitalism, Contemporary Transformations of Work and Politics*, ed. John Keane, 259–299. Cambridge: Polity Press.

Pasquino, Gianfranco. 2010. *Curso de ciência política*. 2nd ed. Lisboa: Princípia.

Pierson, Paul. 2004. *Politics in Time: History, Institutions, and Social Analysis*. Princeton: Princeton University Press.

Rhodes, R. A. W. 2008. "Policy Network Analysis." In *The Oxford Handbook of Public Policy*, eds. Michael Moran, Martin Rein and Robert E. Goodin, 428–447. Oxford: Oxford University Press.

Rofman, Adriana and Carolina Foglia. 2015. "La participación ciudadana local en la historia argentina reciente (de los '90 a la actualidad): asistencia, movilización, institucionalización." In *Revista Estado y Políticas Públicas* 5: 41–61.

Romão, Wagner. 2015. "Reflexões sobre as dificuldades da implementação da participação institucional no Brasil." In *Idéias - Revista do Instituto de Filosofia e Ciências Humanas da Unicamp* 6, no. 2: 35–58.

Romão, Wagner, Adrián Gurza Lavalle, and Gisela Zaremberg. 2017. "Political Intermediation and Public Policy in Brazil: Councils and Conferences in the Policy Spheres of Health and Women's Rights." In *Intermediation and Representation in Latin America: Actors and Roles beyond Election*, eds. Gisela Zaremberg, Valeria Guarneros-Meza, and Adrián Gurza Lavalle, 31–51. London: Palgrave Macmillan.

Santos, Boaventura de Sousa. 2005. *Democratizing Democracy: Beyond the Liberal Democratic Canon*. London: Verso Books.

Schmitter, Philippe. 1974. "Still the Century of Corporatism?" *The Review of Politics* 36, no. 1, (January): 85–131.

Sintomer, Yves, Carsten Herzberg, and Anja Röcke. 2014. "Transnational Models of Citizen Participation: The Case of Participatory Budgeting." In *Hope for Democracy: 25 Years of Participatory Budgeting Worldwide*, ed. Nelson Dias, 28–46. São Brás de Alportel and Portugal: In Loco Association.

Smith, Grahan. 2009. *Democratic Innovations: Designing Institutions for Citizen Participation*. Cambridge: Cambridge University Press.

Vargas, Jean-Paul and Dennis Petri. 2009. "Participación ciudadana y cohesión social en América Central." In *La lucha contra la exclusión social en América Latina: una mirada desde Europa*, ed. Fernando Carrillo Flórez, 197–217. La Paz: BID, Eurosocial, Comisión Europea, Plural editores.

Velásquez, Fabio C. and Esperanza González. 2015. "La reforma de la Ley de Participación en Colombia: Una experiencia de gobernanza democrática." *Desacatos* 49 (Septiembre-Diciembre): 48–63.

Webber, Jeffery. 2011. *Red October: Left-Indigenous Struggles in Modern Bolivia*. Chicago: Haymarket Books.

Welp, Yanina. 2016. "Recall Referendums in Peruvian Municipalities: A Political Weapon for Bad Losers or an Instrument of Accountability?" *Democratization* 7, no. 23: 1162–1179.

Welp, Yanina and Cecilia Schneider. 2011. "Orígenes y contradicciones de la participación ciudadana institucional. Análisis de las experiencias de Buenos Aires, Montevideo, Barcelona y Zúrich." *Revista Mexicana de Ciencias Políticas y Sociales* 56, no. 211: 47–68.

Zaremberg, Gisela. 2012. "Fuerza, proyecto, palabra y pueblo: circuitos de representación en consejos de desarrollo municipal en América Latina." In *Redes y jerarquías. Participación, representación y gobernanza local en América Latina*, ed. Gisela Zaremberg, 35–70. Mexico City: FLACSO-IDRC.

Zaremberg, Gisela, Ernesto Isunza Vera, and Adrián Gurza Lavalle. 2017. "The Gattopardo Era: Innovation and Representation in Mexico in Post-Neoliberal Times." In *Latin America Since the Left Turn*, eds. Tulia G. Falleti and Emilio Parrado, 264–282. Philadelphia: University of Pennsylvania Press.

42
POLITICAL COMMUNICATION

Carlos Del Valle Rojas

Broadly speaking, political communication is any communication that is political in nature and in purpose. The study of political communication is, on the one hand, a type of applied research that focuses on understanding the effects of media, in order to optimize political results (electoral campaigns, public policy, etc.), the basic principle being that there is no politics without communication. On the other hand, one can argue that *politics* is an intrinsic condition of *communication* and, therefore, political communication should be understood through a lens of established power relations and control. In this case, the principle would be: There is no communication without politics.

The different circumstances surrounding the origins of political communication do not allow for a clear distinction between communication and propaganda. In fact, the concept of political communication emerged within the framework of World War I propaganda and developed in the context of electoral campaigns. For this reason, the work of the Committee on Public Information (CPI) in the U.S. is considered a milestone and an effective example of war propaganda on a large scale. Journalist George Creel directed this committee, and Edward Bernays, one of the inventors of Public Relations, was a member (1923, 1928, respectively).

It follows that political communication originates from two particular contexts: one related to war and characterized by the use of communication strategies to persuade the United States' population to support participation in World War I; the other related to electoral politics, with the aim of getting public support for electoral candidates. Notwithstanding the foregoing, some of the more common techniques, like the poster, can be seen being used even before World War I.

Harold Laswell is considered to have founded the concept of political communication with his book, *Propaganda Technique in the World War* (1927), and he is thought to be responsible for formally introducing this term (1969). The concept is also considered a precursor to political psychology. Other authors argue that the origin of political communication is the book *Political Behavior*, edited by Eulau, Eldersveld, and Janowitz and published in 1956.

Regardless of the different but related understandings, political communication is the most common way to refer to the integration of communication and politics, and specifically to a form of communication that is: 1) political in nature and 2) political in purpose. The first implies that politics is an intrinsic condition of communication, which means it is impossible to consider communication in isolation from politics. The second suggests that communication can be *used* in politics, from which communication as a political strategy is understood.

Inter-American discussion and critical reflections

From a general perspective, there are two identifiable approaches within the field of communication, and both of these can also be seen in the study of political communication. Through the first approach, communication is viewed from a functional and instrumental perspective, derived from two traditions: 1) Mass Communication Research, primarily developed in the United States (→ Cultural Industries, III/27) (Lazarsfeld, Berelson and Gaudet 1944; Katz and Lazarsfeld 1955); and 2) development (→ II/6) and modernization (→ I/35) theories from a diffusionist perspective (Schramm 1949; Lerner 1958; Rogers 1962), a widespread tradition in Latin America (particularly in Colombia, Brazil, and Mexico), though also in the United States.

Within this first approach, various models exist, ranging from political psychology to propaganda, as well as Rogers's 1962 model of diffusion of innovations (and its subsequent updates and revisions), and social marketing models, in which communication constitutes a technique within a strategy.

From this perspective, the contributions made by propaganda studies, which would have an early presence in the United States, would prove essential. Such was the case of the CPI, or the "Creel Committee" (1917), led by George Creel (1920), and included Edward Bernays (1923, 1928). The committee's work is considered one of the most effective examples of war propaganda on a global scale. This period corresponds with the creation of close to two thousand posters between 1914 and 1920, in the context of World War I. The methods used in the production of these posters in the United States at the beginning of the 20th century is the same we see now in Latin American electoral campaigns. The principles behind these methods include simplification, hyperbole, association, appeal to emotion, and transmission (for example, recurrent nationalist mythology). Take the case of Michelle Bachelet's 2014 campaign in Chile, with slogans like "Yo Quiero Chile" (I love Chile) and "Chile de Todos" (A Chile for Everyone), or Mauricio Macri's 2015 campaign in Argentina with slogans like "Estoy con vos" (I'm with you) and "Unir a todos los argentinos" (May all Argentines unite). In all of these, the role of communication is key, particularly the role of social media (→ III/41). For example, Macri took first place in Argentina and third in the world, when he got 600,000 mentions on Twitter and gained three million Facebook followers. In fact, he earned the nickname, "President of Facebook," as he reached millions of Argentines through Facebook – 350,238 registered volunteers; 92 percent of Argentina's active Facebook population reached; and 3.4 million video views. In the United States, Donald Trump, for his part, with his 2016 slogan, "Make America Great Again," managed to continue the effective use of social media that Barack Obama had pioneered in 2008. In effect, despite his opposition to traditional media, especially the press (→ Journalism, III/32), Trump used Facebook and Twitter extensively, was the first candidate optimized by the Google News algorithm and tweeted more than any other candidate; there was one day when he was the person most talked about on the planet. The history of propaganda shows that Roosevelt was the president of radio (→ III/40), Kennedy of television (→ III/43), Obama of the internet (→ Digital Culture, III/28), and Trump of social media.

In contrast, through the second approach, communication is viewed through a combined social, critical, economic, and political lens, beginning with critical theories such as the neo-

Marxist tradition and its subsequent revisions like the Frankfurt School (Adorno 1954), and continuing with the political economy of information, communication, and culture, the development of which occurred across the Americas: Smythe (1981), who was born in Canada and studied in the United States; Schiller (1969) in the United States; Mosco (1996) in Canada; and Sierra (1999), who was Spanish but had a long career in Latin America and was later recognized as President of the International Centre of Advanced Communication Studies for Latin America, CIESPAL; among others. These traditions would intermingle significantly over the course of more than two decades, indicating fruitful Inter-American relations, and would later produce new branches of thought like communication for development and communication for social change, among others. With all of these, the political constitutes a critical component of communication.

From this perspective, not only is the role of traditional media (radio and television), internet, and social media important, but so is the role of "alternative," "citizen," "community," or "participatory" media (→ Media Participation, III/36), which began to play a dominant role in Latin America in the 1980s (Antonio Pasquali, in Venezuela; Rosa María Alfaro, in Peru; Armand Mattelart, in Chile; Luis Ramiro Beltrán, in Bolivia; Néstor García Canclini, in Mexico; Mario Kaplún, in Uruguay y Jesús Martín Barbero, in Colombia). Important milestones include the MacBride report (1980), which identified the problem of the high concentration of mass media and the lack of horizontal communications (→ Cultural Industries, III/27), as well as the failure of the New World Information and Communication Order (NOMIC). These both highlighted the need for new media, like community radio, local television, and extensive use of info-centers and Telecenters. In the 1990s, projects playing a central role included the Communication Initiative, with Inter-American cooperation; the World Association for Christian Communication, based in Canada; and the Communication for Social Change Consortium, an initiative sponsored by the Rockefeller Foundation in the late 1990s in the United States with a robust presence in Latin America that had launched the work of Wilbur Schramm and Paul Lazersfeld in the United States in the 1940s.

Etymological considerations

Evidently, communication is as old as politics. Considered separately, the term "politics" is understood as the art of governing (from the Latin "politicus" and the Greek "politikós," which essentially means "of the citizens" or "of the State") (→ Citizenship, II/27; Nation State, II/38), or more recently as an activity related to the community.

The current and widespread use of the concept includes diverse epistemic and theoretical traditions, whose expressions are not always properly differentiated; for this reason, many believe that the term refers to the same idea, even when it is being applied to completely different situations. Accordingly, it is important to identify the different disciplinary areas that are in dialogue with political communication, such as: linguistics (political language) (→ Language, I/13), communication (rhetorical construction, use of media, influence on public opinion, advertising, and electoral campaign design), politics (government, communications, policy proposals), and sociology (social and political movements). Additionally, consideration should be given to the political economy of communications, a comprehensive approach that analyzes production conditions; power relations and the concentration of property, as they relate to the presence of media (→ Media Flows, III/35); and the political psychology of communication, which investigates psychological strategies of communication for a political purpose.

Political Communication should therefore be understood as an interdisciplinary science, as it involves an interaction among different disciplines of knowledge, which themselves address many diverse social, political, economic, and cultural factors. These factors include: actors (journalists, politicians, consultants, political parties, the media, governments), their roles, the production of discourse, and relations in democratic contexts (→ Democracy, II/32). In summary, three types of actors can be seen: political organizations, the media, and citizens (as audience), all interrelated because of the intentional nature of political communication (McNair 2011).

Considering the above, political communication is all communication of a political nature and for a political purpose. It appears in various psychological and discursive strategies and techniques, for political purposes, and can be used by different actors in different contexts, as previously mentioned.

Final discussion

Political communication is based on two different approaches and traditions, with different purposes and natures. Both make for an interesting geopolitical relationship between North and South America (→ Geopolitics, II/34).

In the first case, the approach of Mass Communication Research (often called "classical" to differentiate it from later research), emphasizes the uses of communication to achieve political objectives. Beginning with Rogers's work, it developed over time in Latin America, as seen in the transformations that took place in the agricultural sector (notably, the incorporation of technology). There remains a constant tension between the theories and their application in Latin American contexts. In the second case, neo-Marxist studies, and critical theory in general, came to have a strong presence in North America, especially in the United States and Canada, but in Latin America, too, of course, where these studies (despite tensions and disagreements) formed part of dependency theory.

The two traditions resulted in a productive tension between an empirical epistemology, represented by Paul Lazarsfeld, and a critical epistemology, represented by Theodor Adorno. Indeed, one can see this tension concretely manifested in the Princeton Radio Research Project. This project, carried out between 1937 and 1939, was led by Paul Lazarsfeld, who invited Theodor Adorno to participate. Their encounter proved key to the trajectories of communications research, namely, the empirical approach (Lazarsfeld) and the critical approach (Adorno). In this sense, political communication had geopolitical tensions, as well, especially in Latin America, where one or the other model was adopted; the region then had two potential means by which to communicate politics and policy to establish a bridge between government and citizenry (→ Nation State, II/38; Civil Society, II/28). The distinction remains to this day in communications schools and departments, though there is a tendency to integrate aspects of both the empirical and critical approaches.

This integration is evidenced in the works of various international associations focused on political communication, whether at the Latin American level, such as the Asociación Latinoamericana de Investigadores en Campañas Electorales (Latin American Association of Electoral Campaign Researchers) – ALICE; the Ibero-American level, such as the Asociación de Comunicación Política (The Association of Political Communication) – ACOP; or at the North American level, such as the American Association of Political Consultants – AAPC. With all of these, approaches can be found that integrate both the empirical (characteristic of electoral campaigns), and the critical (characteristic of the sociocultural impact of electoral processes).

Works cited

Adorno, Theodor. 1954. "How to look at television." *The Quarterly of Film, Radio and Television* 8, no. 3: 213–235.

American Association of Political Consultants-AAPC. https://theaapc.org.

Asociación de Comunicación Política-ACOP. http://compolitica.com/acop/sobre-acop/.

Asociación Latinoamericana de Investigadores en Campañas Electorales-ALICE. www.alice-comunicacionpolitica.com/asociacion/.

Bernays, Edward. 1923. *Crystallizing Public Opinion*. New York: Liveright Publishing Corporation.

———. 1928. *Propaganda*. New York: Horace Liveright.

Creel, George. 1920. *How We Advertised America: The First Telling of the Amazing Story of the Committee on Public Information that Carried the Gospel of Americanism to Every Corner of the Globe*. New York: Harper & Brothers Publishers.

Eulau, Heinz, Samuel Eldersveld y Morris Janowitz. 1956. *Political Behavior. A Reader in Theory and Research*. Chicago, IL: Free Press.

Katz, Elihu and Paul F. Lazarsfeld. 1955. *Personal Influence: The Part Placed by People in the Flow of Mass Communication*. Glencoe, IL: The Free Press.

Laswell, Harold and Arora Satish. 1969. *Political Communication: The Public Language of Political Elites in India and the United States*. New York: Holt, Rinehart & Winston.

Lazarsfeld, Paul F., Bernard Berelson, and Hazel Gaudet. 1944. *The People's Choice: How the Voters Makes up his Mind in a Presidential Campaign*. New York: Duell, Sloan and Pearce.

Lerner, Daniel. 1958. *The Passing of Traditional Society: Modernizing the Middle East*. Glencoe, IL: The Free Press.

MacBride report. 1980. *International Commission for the Study of Communication Problems. Many Voices, One World*. London: UNESCO/Lanham, MD: Rowman & Littlefield.

McNair, Brian. 2011. *An Introduction to Political Communication*. New York and London: Routledge.

Mosco, Vincent. 1996. *The Political Economy of Communication: Rethinking and Renewal*. London: Sage.

Rogers, Everett. 1962. *Diffusion of Innovations*. New York: The Free Press of Glencoe.

Schiller, Herbert. 1969. *Mass Communications and American Empire*. New York: Augustus M. Kelley.

Schramm, Wilbur. 1949. *Mass Communications*. Urbana, IL: University of Illinois Press.

Sierra, Francisco. 1999. "Comunicación educativa y economía política. Apuntes sobre políticas culturales e innovación tecnológica." *Ámbitos. Revista Andaluza de Comunicación* 2: 39–48.

Smythe, Dallas Walker. 1981. *Dependency Road: Communications, Capitalism, Consciousness and Canada*. Norwood, NJ: Ablex Publishing.

43

POPULISM

Mirko Petersen

Populism is a frequently used term in political and scientific debates. For a long time, the term was rather marginal and mainly used with regard to Latin America. Nowadays it is also ubiquitous in the analysis of the recent political changes in Europe and the United States of America, that is to say the rise of right-wing nationalists, above all Donald Trump in the U.S. The term can even be found in economic analyses of the International Monetary Fund (2016, XV, 267, 2018, 85) and prominent articles on foreign policy (e.g., Zakaria 2016).

Calling someone a populist is often meant to denounce his or her idea as irrational, or mere rhetoric, and evokes the image of a charismatic leader who seduces the masses. Often populism is presented as dangerous, primitive, or manipulative (→ Political Communication, II/42), which leads to a serious obstacle when attempting to use it as an analytical category.

A very general definition of populism was given by the Argentine sociologist Torcuato S. Di Tella, who defined it as "[a] political movement that emphasizes the interests, cultural traits, and spontaneous feelings of the common people, as opposed to those of a privileged elite" (Di Tella 1995, 985). Although from a more structural perspective, English political theorist Margaret Canovan gives a similar definition, but she refers to populism as an "appeal" instead of a movement (Canovan 1999, 3). Both Di Tella and Canovan emphasize that populists prefer direct addresses to the population over debates within political institutions. Due to the fact that mobilization plays an important role in populism, it is often described as a movement, however it is also often referred to as a type of regime, an ideology (e.g., Albertazzi and Donnell 2008), discourse strategy (e.g., Imbusch 2012), or a political style (e.g., Knight 1998). In all definitions of the term, the role of a leadership figure is considered an important aspect.

However Argentine theorist Ernesto Laclau introduced a new and influential approach by which populism was not understood as a movement, regime, or style (on the influence of Laclau's ideas in Latin America and Europe, see Damin and Petersen 2016). For him, the commonalities of different populist movements could not be defined by the governments or leadership figures that propelled these ideas. Rather, his theorization of populism is that of a political logic (Laclau 2005, 117) and can be read as a critique of the other definitions and used as an instrument for analysis.

Populism in the Americas

Historically, the term populism first appeared in Russia during the 1870s to refer to the *narodniki*, a group of political activists that tried to establish a social system based on popular institutions and traditions (Di Tella 1995, 985). In the Americas, the term was first applied to a protest movement in rural areas of the United States in the late 19th century (e.g., Priester 2007, 78–91) (→ Social Movements, I/41). This so-called agrarian populism was a protest against the transition from competitive to organized capitalism (→ II/2). The involved farmers articulated their interests against the political domination by urban centers. This early form of American populism has been interpreted "as a revolt of small and medium-sized entrepreneurs against Big Business and the one-sidedness of a capitalist economic system, which might have failed as a revolt, but which enjoyed success as a persistent demand for reforms" (Imbusch 2012) (→ Class Struggle, II/3).

This demand for reform took many different shapes. It was present in Roosevelt's New Deal policy after the world economic crisis (→ II/4) at the beginning of the 1930s, as well as in the rises of certain famous political figures in the second half of the 20th century. George C. Wallace, Ralph Nader, Henry Ross Perot, and Jesse Ventura all presented discourses which can be described as combinations of very different ideological elements (for example, some argue for state intervention, others strictly against it).

Until the success of Donald Trump in the U.S. the term populism was mainly applied to Latin America rather than North America (Di Tella 1995, 986). In Latin America, the notion of populism has generally been linked to the construction of a strong centralist state (→ Nation and State Building, I/16) in opposition to the landowning oligarchy. In some cases, for example, the government of Hipólito Yrigoyen in Argentina, it was possible to absorb the increasing demands of the subaltern classes for social and political integration by introducing moderate reforms (Laclau 2005, 192–193). These possibilities of absorption came to an end with the global economic crises after 1929, when the profits of exports fell and the economic situation declined. Since that point in time, it has been possible to observe three different "waves" of populism (Imbusch 2012) in Latin America.

The first of these waves is often referred to as classical populism. It started with the questioning of the oligarchic and liberal economic model after the economic crisis of 1929–30, and ended with the beginning of the neoliberal epoch in 1980 (→ Neoliberalism, II/16). Sociologist Carlos M. Vilas offers a list of the characteristics of classical populism: a strong political mobilization, the integration of the popular classes into a multiclass political project (→ Class Stuggle, II/3), industrialization, an interventionist state (→ Nation State, II/38), non-alignment in foreign policy, nationalism, and the existence of a leadership figure (Vilas 2004, 136). The most prominent representatives of this first wave included President Getúlio Vargas, in power in Brazil from 1930–45 and 1951–54, President Lázaro Cárdenas of Mexico, from 1934–40, and President Juan Domingo Perón of Argentina, between 1946–55, and from 1973 until his death in 1974. Contemporaries often associated these regimes with fascism, due to their corporatist economic attempts and their political iconography. Though fascism was a source of inspiration for these leaders, their actual politics cannot be adequately described by the term.

The second populist wave was marked by the comeback of democracy in various Latin American countries after the epoch of military dictatorships (→ Authoritarianism, II/25). Whether this wave during the late 1980s and 1990s, periodically called the neopopulist wave, can really be thought of in these terms, is contested. Unlike the regimes that were part of the first wave, its socioeconomic orientation was extremely market-oriented. Often, Carlos Salinas de Gortari, Mexican president from 1988–94, Carlos Saúl Menem, Argentine president from 1989–99, and Alberto Fujimori, Peruvian president between 1990 and 2000, are listed as representatives of this second wave. For Vilas, only the political style of these regimes can be considered populist, but not the politics they stood for. He agrees with political scientist Denise Dresser (1991), when he states that this style of government "was a remake of populist practices which tried to improve the governability of the neoliberal reform process" (Vilas 2004, 137). For Vilas, Latin American populism is clearly defined by its classical historical examples and their interventionist, progressive politics.

The third populist wave was closer to the tradition of classical populism. It occurred at the turn of the millennium, after strong popular resistance against the neoliberal model. For the description of these governments, similar attributes, such as the ones suggested by Vilas to describe classical populism are used (e.g., Follari 2010, 103–104). In comparison to past populist experiences, the focus on Latin American regional integration (→ II/18) became a more important part of the political agenda of these governments. It was especially important in the regimes of Hugo Chávez, and later Nicolás Maduro, in Venezuela, Evo Morales in Bolivia, and Rafael Correa in Ecuador. Occasionally, Néstor Kirchner, and Cristina Fernandez de Kirchner in Argentina are also associated with this third wave. Analysts tend to denounce these politicians as demagogic, nationalist, and populist, and contrast them with a pragmatic, realist, and modern Left, represented by Lula Da Silva and Dilma Rousseff in Brazil, the Frente Amplio in Uruguay, and the governments of the Concertación in Chile (Ramírez Gallegos 2006).

Meanwhile, the third populist wave linked to the Latin American center-left governments has come to an end or at least entered a severe crisis. New right-wing governments such as the ones of Mauricio Macri in Argentina, Sebastián Piñera in Chile, and Jair Bolsonaro in Brazil came to power. The latter is frequently called a right-wing populist while Macri and Piñera are usually not associated with populism.

In addition, the term populism can also be found in the language of Inter-American relations. The United States is frequently concerned with Latin American governments that are said to follow a populist agenda. Why populism is seen negatively becomes clearer when looking at an analysis of the changes in Latin America since the turn of the millennium, written by Hal Brands for the Strategic Studies Institute of the United States. Brands draws a negative image of populist regimes, especially the governments of Chávez, Morales, and Correa. In his view,

> [t]hey promote prolific social spending, centralize power in the presidency, and lash out at Washington. This program is … strategically problematic for the United States. Populist policies ultimately lead to authoritarianism, polarization, and economic collapse, and certain populist leaders have openly challenged U.S. influence and interests in Latin America.
>
> *(Brands 2009, V).*

This example shows how debates over populism are entangled with the geopolitical role of the United States in Latin America (→ Geopolitics, II/34). Since many regimes which have been labeled populist can be described as critical of its role in the region, the negative image associated with the terms "populism" or "populist" is used by the United States to delegitimize these governments.

Populism as a political logic

As described above, there have been several attempts to classify movements, governments, or politicians in the Americas as populist. For the U.S.-American case, social movements

(→ I/41) and certain persons are usually considered populist, while in Latin America, this notion is most often used to characterize governments. However, one must question critically if it is possible to logically put all of these actors in one analytical category. Ernesto Laclau states that

> [a]ll the attempts at finding what is idiosyncratic in populism in elements such as a peasant or small-ownership constituency, or resistance to economic modernization … are … essentially flawed: they will always be overwhelmed by an avalanche of exceptions.
>
> *(Laclau 2005, 117)*

Therefore, Laclau refused to understand populism as type of movement or regime, but rather as a political logic.

Political crises are the starting points for the emergence of this logic. It "can either be a result of a fracture in the power bloc" or of problems "of the system to neutralize the dominated sectors" (Laclau 1977, 175). In order to replace the power bloc and establish a new hegemony, heterogeneous social demands have to be brought together, so as to define what "the people" is supposed to mean in a specific context. "The people" is a part of society that claims to be the only legitimate representative of society as a whole.

Populist alliances are formed when the different actors share a negative perspective or experience, usually, according to Laclau, "their opposition to a common enemy" (Laclau 1996, 40–41). Every variety of populism forms itself through its antagonistic opposition to the dominant discourse. This can also be discovered during the neoliberal 1990s in Latin America which Vilas does not consider populist. As just one example from this second populist wave, a new fiscal policy was presented as an opposition to the hyperinflation during the mandate of the regimes that were in power before.

To bring heterogeneous social demands together, empty signifiers are used, for example ambiguous terms such as "order" or "justice" receive a specific meaning based on their context (Laclau 1996, 36–46). For Laclau, the use of these empty signifiers was considered a necessity in order to unify demands. An example of this was the 2008 presidential campaign of Barack Obama in the United States. After eight years of a Republican government led by George W. Bush, a large variety of social groups found themselves in a dissatisfying situation. The tactic of Obama's campaign was not to make detailed references to reforms for each of these groups. Instead, the campaign chose a phrase that was supposed to express the desires of all of the groups in a very vague way. In the slogan "Change we can believe in," Obama's campaign found a formula to represent the heterogeneous demands.

Often, the heterogeneous parts of a group are brought together by a leadership figure. In some sense, leaders have a similar task to empty signifiers, or even become empty signifiers themselves. One example of this was in the case of Juan Perón during his exile from Argentina, between 1955 and 1973. Perón himself was the only common thread that made the leftist Peronist guerrillas and the rightist Peronist trade-union bureaucracy cooperate (→ Labor Representation, II/14), to a certain extent, in the political struggle of the time (Laclau 2005, 214–221).

As mentioned previously, heterogeneous demands must be brought together, however the very success of this goal also bears dangers. Laclau points out that alliances formed within the populist logic, the constructed "people," can be very fragile, for example, if the empty signifiers change their temporal fixation in the eyes of some parts of the alliance (Laclau 1996, 44–45), or if the common enemy is defeated or disappears (Laclau 1996, 30).

With this understanding of populism, it is not possible to label certain political actors as populist and others not. Rather, it is about looking at the extent to which logic is present in different political lineups. This is not to say that populism is politics as such. Populism is only one political logic among many others, and cannot, for instance, explain phenomena such as secession, where a part of society does not claim to represent society as a whole, but instead wants to separate itself from it (Aboy Carlés 2010, 25) (→ Independence Movements, I/10).

Populism can occur in many different political entities, and for the Americas, it is not possible to distinguish between a populist south and a non-populist north or vice versa. The conceptualization of populism as a political logic is a possibility to pay tribute to a variety of regional differences which should be considered. Used in the way proposed here, populism is not an umbrella word for the characterization of regimes, persons, or movements, but rather an analytical tool for investigating power relations and the practices behind them.

Works cited

Aboy Carlés, Gerardo. 2010. "Populismo, Regeneracionismo Y Democracia." *Postdata* 15, no. 1: 11–30.

Albertazzi, Daniele and Duncan Mc Donnell. 2008. "Introduction: The Sceptre and the Spectre." In *Twenty-First Century Populism – The Spectre of Western European Democracy*, ed. Daniele Albertazzi and Duncan Mc Donnell, 1–11. New York: Palgrave Mac Millan.

Brands, Hal. 2009. *Dealing with Political Ferment in Latin Aamerica: The Populist Revival, the Emergence of the Center, and Implications for U.S. Policy*. Carlisle, PA: Strategic Studies Institute, U.S. Army War College.

Canovan, Margorat. 1999. "Trust the People! Populism and the Two Faces of Democracy." *Political Studies* 47: 2–16.

Damin, Nicolás Javier and Mirko Petersen. 2016. "Populismo Entre Argentina y Europa. Sobre La Transnacionalización De Un Concepto." *Iberoamericana* 16, no. 63: 15–32.

Di Tella, Torcuato. 1995. "Populism." In *The Encyclopedia of Democracy. Volume III*, ed. Seymour Martin Lipset, 985–989. Washington, DC: Congressional Quarterly INC.

Dresser, Denise. 1991. *Neopopulist Solutions to Neoliberal Problems: Mexico's National Solidarity Program*. Center for U.S.-Mexican Studies, San Diego: University of California Press.

Follari, Roberto. 2010. *La Alternativa Neopopulista: El Reto Latinoamericano Al Republicanismo Neoliberal*. Rosario, Santa Fe, Argentina: Homo Sapiens Ediciones.

Imbusch, Peter. 2012. "Populism." In *Online Dictionary Social and Political Key Terms of the Americas: Politics, Inequalities, and North-South Relations*, Version 1.0. http://wiki.elearning.uni-bielefeld.de/wiki farm/fields/ges_cias/field.php/Main/Unterkapitel164.

International Monetary Fund. 2016. *World Economic Outlook October 2016: Subdued Demands. Symptoms and Remedies*. Washington: International Monetary Fund Publication Services.

International Monetary Fund. 2018. *World Economic Outlook October 2018: Challenges to Steady Growth*. Washington: International Monetary Fund Publication Services.

Knight, Alan. 1998. "Populism and Neo-populism in Latin America, especially Mexico." *Journal of Latin American Studies* 30, no. 2: 223–248.

Laclau, Ernesto. 1977. *Politics and Ideology in Marxist Theory: Capitalism – Fascism – Populism*. London: NLB.

———. 1996. *Emancipation(s)*. London and New York: Verso.

———. 2005. *On Populist Reason*. London: Verso.

Priester, Karin. 2007. *Populismus: Historische und Aktuelle Erscheinungsformen*. Frankfurt am Main: Campus.

Ramírez Gallegos, Franklin. 2006. "Mucho Más Que Dos Izquierdas." *Nueva Sociedad* 205: 30–44.

Vilas, Carlos M. 2004. "Populismos Reciclados O Neoliberalismo a Secas? El Mito Del 'Neopopulismo' Latinoamericano." *Revista de Sociologia e Politica* 22: 135–151.

Zakaria, Fareed. 2016. "Populism on the March: Why the West is in Trouble." *Foreign Affairs* 95, no. 6: 9–15.

44
REVOLUTION

María Josefina Saldaña-Portillo

In its current political iteration, indicating a complete regime change in favor of a new order, the term revolution derives its meaning from the late 19th century liberal overturnings of the aristocratic administrative units: United States Revolution (1776); French Revolution (1789); Haitian Revolution (1801). These modern revolutions collectively initiated the end of monarchical empires premised upon the absolute power of a single sovereign, instituting instead nation-states (→ II/38) that redistributed the sovereign power of the state to the people through some form of liberal representative government (→Democracy, II/32). "Revolution" comes from the old French word *revolvere* – to turn back, to return – suggesting that this overthrow of an exploitative and outmoded aristocratic order was no more than a return to an original authority that belonged to a sovereign people. Thus, revolution returns a people to itself, returns to the people their natural sovereignty, even if it is the act of revolution itself that constitutes the people retrospectively as a national ethnos, as scholars of nationalism argue (→ Foundational Discourses, III/8).

In a Marxist context, the concept of revolution has a distinctly class character (→ Class Struggle, II/3), with the proletariat leading a revolutionary overthrow of capitalist hegemonic forces (→ Capitalism, II/2) in the interest of installing a communist mode of production, where not only do workers direct the economy by displacing managerial and capitalist classes, but they also provide for a return of the political system to the people, though the means of such direct representation has taken various diluted forms of representative governance in actually practicing revolutionary governments (→ Socialism, I/42). The two most famous communist revolutions, in terms of geographical extension and temporal duration, are the Russian Bolshevik Revolution (1917) and the Maoist Chinese Revolution (1949). While diametrically opposed in terms of their political methods and economic paradigms, liberal, and Marxist revolutions do share the presumption of returning political power – usurped by improper forces – to the people, to its proper owners, and in this sense, both are premised on overcoming an initial alienation of a sovereignty that resides naturally in the people themselves.

For the purposes of this Handbook to "rethink the Americas," however, it is appropriate to remind readers that the first socialist revolution began not in Europe or Asia, but in Latin America, with Mexico's 1910 uprising against the oligarchical dictatorship of Porfirio Díaz. Mexico had already promulgated its 1917 Constitution by the time of the first Russian Revolution in March of the same year. The Constitution established universal, free, secular education

(Article 3) (→ Education, I/24); the end of debt peonage and other forms of indenture (Article 5) (→ Unfree Labor, I/19); agrarian reform for the redistribution of lands in communal holdings (Article 27) (→ Commons, II/31); the nationalization of all natural resources including oil, minerals, waters, and hydrocarbons (→ Energy, II/7) (Article 27); worker's rights to unionize (→ Labor Representation, II/24), to strike, for an eight-hour work day, for equal pay between women and men (→ Gender and Work, II/11), as well as for three-months paid maternity leave (Article 123). As the first national constitution to instantiate the economic rights of citizens, the Mexican Constitution served as a model for the Russian Constitution of 1918, later ratified as the *Declaration of Rights of the Working and Exploited People*.

On the one hand, it is possible that the Mexican Revolution's role in the global history of communist, socialist, and anarchist revolutions is underestimated, when not entirely overlooked, because of the unorthodox brand of socialism the country practiced, premised as it was on the principle of a "mixed economy," combining large government-led public development projects (→ Development, II/6) that required the nationalization of key industries with private capitalist development in the vast majority of industrial sectors. In agriculture, Mexican revolutionary leaders negotiated constantly between the demands from millions of dispossessed small-scale farmers for communal lands (→ Land, II/15), primarily in southern Mexico, and the powerful interests of large-scale agroindustry on private farms and ranches in northern Mexico. Indeed, when the Mexican revolution is commemorated by historians of Marxist revolutions, as in Florencia Mallon's *Peasant and Nation: The Making of Postcolonial Mexico and Peru* (Mallon 1995) or Eric Wolf's *Peasant Wars of the 20th Century* (Wolf 1969), it is usually analyzed as a peasant revolution. Thus, the lack of a proletarian leadership at times associated with the Mexican Revolution may have also contributed to its minimization as a model, though the centrality of the peasantry in the Mexican Revolution presaged the centrality of peasant consciousness to Marxist revolutions worldwide, with peasant leadership of revolutionary movements not only emerging across the American continent but also in Eastern and Southern Asia.

On the other hand, the broad alliance of Mexican anarchists, communists, liberals, workers, indigenous peasants (→ Indigeneity, I/31), students, and intellectuals who together constituted the revolutionary forces anticipated popular front strategies in Europe and the United States by two decades. This prompts the question, also asked by Jean Franco, if forgetting the priority of the Mexican Revolution, in the global history of leftist revolution, is not an effect of Eurocentric exclusion, discrimination, and failure of recognition in the global metropolises? Mexico, as part of the Latin American Third World, can only be "the place of the instinctual" – its revolutionary intellectual production always marked as mere experience – "subordinate to the rational knowledge produced by the metropolis" and thus always "irrelevant to [metropolitan] theory" rather than the bearer of such theoretical knowledge for the world (Franco 1988, 504). Latin American revolutionary movements of the 20th century were uniformly attributed to the Soviet Union's interference in the United States sphere of influence, but it was most often the Mexican Revolution that provided the model for economic restructuring in the wake of revolutionary transformation.

Meanwhile, a half-century later, the remarkable 1959 Cuban Revolution turned its guerrilla method into a revolutionary theory taken up by anti-colonial movements throughout the global south. A band of eighty-two men launched a yacht from Mexican shores on November 25, 1956, landing in Cuba a week later. Within a few days, more than half the troop was felled in an attack by dictator Batista's Air Force. Nevertheless, a mere three years later, this tiny band of rebels had successfully overthrown one of

Latin America's most brutal dictators, President Fulgencio Batista. Aboard the *Granma* as part of this original revolutionary troop was Ernesto "Che" Guevara, who would give this revolutionary movement much of its international character, as he himself was an official envoy of the Cuban Revolution, sent to participate on Cuba's behalf in theory and praxis of revolution in African and South American combat. The guerrilla's rapid success led Che Guevara to elaborate the theory of *foquismo* in his *Guerra de guerrillas*, first published in Havana in 1960. Guevara famously concluded in this manual of guerrilla warfare that it was unnecessary to wait for the conditions of revolution to arise, because instead, "*el foco insurreccional puede crearlas* [the insurrectional cell can create them]" (Guevara 1960, 4 [translation by author]). Guevara describes the guerrilla combatant who is a member of this foco "as a person conscious of a role in the vanguard of the people," as a person needing "a moral conduct that shows him to be a true priest of the reform to which he aspires" and finally, "[t]o [whom] the stoicism imposed by the difficult conditions of warfare should be added an austerity born of rigid self-control that will prevent a single excess a single slip" (Guevara 1998, 39).

Foquismo was taken up by revolutionary vanguards across Latin America (Argentina, Bolivia, Brazil, Colombia, Mexico, Uruguay) and the African continent (Algeria, Angola, Mozambique, Tanzania). Both rural and urban foco groups appeared in South America following the Cuban revolution, including the *Movimiento de Izquierda Revolutionaria* (MIR) in Bolivia; the *Ejército de Liberación Nacional* (ELN) in Colombia; the *Montoneros in Argentina*; the *Tupamaros* in Uruguay; the *Guerrilha do Araguala* and the *Comando de Libertação Nacional* in Brazil. According to Jorge Castañeda, roughly one third to half of the guerrilla members pertaining to these groups who were tortured, killed, or imprisoned were intellectual elites from the middle and upper classes of Latin America (Castañeda 1993, 75).This vanguardist model of an ascetic guerrilla cell who miraculously appear among the peasantry as "a sort of guiding angel who has fallen into the zone, helping the poor always" has been roundly critiqued for its elitist condescension, racist undertones, and its masculinist hierarchy by such scholars as Ileana Rodríguez (1996, 2001), John Beverley (2004), and Saldaña-Portillo (2003). Moreover, as a method of revolutionary transformation, this "early" *foquismo* failed spectacularly in South America and ushered in ever more brutal tactics by military juntas there (→ Military, II/37; Authoritarianism, II/25). A later wave of *foquismo* unfolded in Central America during the 1970s and 1980s and was considerably more successful. This was principally because revolutionaries in Nicaragua, El Salvador, and Guatemala combined armed insurrection by small cells in cities with long-term peasant organizing by cells embedded in rural areas, and most importantly, with a much broader popular front strategy that mobilized urban and rural civil society (→ II/28) into a massive social movement (→ I/41).

In Cuba, the self-declared Marxist-Leninist foco did succeed in establishing socialist relations of production in agriculture and industry on the island nation (→ Socialism, I/42), and to provide exceptional universal healthcare (→ Health, I/29) and education (→ I/24) – including higher education – for the entire population. And while racism still exists in Cuba (→ Race, I/39), the revolutionary changes wrought by Cuba's Communist Party vastly improved conditions of inequality among whites, mestizos, and blacks on the island (→ Social Inequality, II/20). Moreover, Cuba was the only client-state of the Soviet Union to survive the fall of the Berlin Wall. In short, Cuba, like Mexico, established permanent social reform through their respective revolutionary processes, and it is unlikely that the population of either country would opt for returning to their shared disenfranchised and exploitative pre-revolutionary pasts.

Of popular fronts and *foquismo*

Movements for revolutionary change across the Americas have most often entailed the use of both popular front and *foquista* strategies, as made evident in Central America, and again in the case of the Zapatista uprising in Mexico in the 1990s. Democratically elected regimes that ushered in socialist policies also relied on popular front strategies for achieving government office (→ Democracy, II/32), as in the case of Jacobo Árbenz Guzmán's Guatemala in 1944 or Salvador Allende's Chile in 1970. The politics of the popular front *and* of *foquismo* found fertile ground in Latin America because of the economic infrastructure imposed upon its countries by centuries of Spanish colonialism and U.S. neo-colonialism (→ Postcolonialism, II/38). The structurally reduced size of bourgeois and working classes in Latin American countries made it essential for revolutionary movements to build popular front coalitions that brought together these small class sectors with students, intellectuals, peasant groups, political parties of all ideological stripes, but also with the lumpen proletariat, the itinerate proletariat, and with those employed in the informal sector (→ Informality, II/13); or alternately, to form an armed vanguard foco, in the hope of pushing a politically repressed population to the politics of a popular front (Beverley 2004). Brutal military dictatorships (→ Authoritarianism, II/25) and right-wing populist governments (→ Populism, II/43) made the combination of popular front and *foquista* approaches essential, as these revolutionary approaches provided the necessary protection for each other.

The rampant, irrepressible expression of revolutionary desire in the second half of the 20th century, through both popular front and/or *foquista* movements, across virtually every country in Latin America (and across the Global South), made it painfully evident that revolutionary change would *not* come first to the fully developed countries of the First World, with their fully articulated proletariat classes (→ Modernization, I/35). To the contrary, revolutionary movements in the Global South made it clear that the working classes in the First World were the beneficiaries of an international division of labor that boosted their buying power in the center by hyper-exploiting the working classes and informal sectors in the periphery. Revolutionary praxis in Latin America, from 1910 until the close of the century, was not just raw experience, or even just a theory of action, but provided theoretical advances in the analysis of global capitalism (→ II/2), particularly of its reliance on neocolonial modes of labor exploitation in the Third World to guarantee the continued growth of the rate of profit for the First.

The division of the world system, following Immanuel Wallerstein, into First, Second, and Third world may seem dated, and indeed imprecise. Nevertheless, for the historical period under discussion – the post-war anti-colonial and revolutionary period – such terms were not only operative terms of economic analysis, but also political rally cries, especially for eliciting solidarity across what is referred to today as the Global South. Thus, this entry continues to use these terms, with a recognition of their limitations for diagnosing the present, because of their historical importance in Marxist revolutionary theory and praxis.

American revolutionary movements generated a body of knowledge about enclave economies, about unequal terms of trade, about the racialized international division of labor, and about the history of colonialism and neo-colonialism in the engineering of "underdevelopment" in the Third World (→ Development, II/6). This knowledge found its scholarly articulation in the Dependency and the Unequal Development schools of economic theory, coming out of Latin America and Africa respectively. Though a rigid geographic divide between the two schools could be drawn, this was an effervescent period in development studies, with much collaboration and exchange between the proponents of each approach (See exchange between Andre Gunder Frank (1966); Ernesto Laclau (1971); Samir Amin (1977); Cardoso and Faletto (1979); Rodolfo Stavenhagen (1981)).

Just as armed revolutionary movements shared tactics and strategies, guerrillas and arms, across the Global South, leftist economists and sociologists who were critical of modernization (→ I/35) and diffusionist theories of development shared data and analyses globally to permanently dislodge these theories of economic progress that papered over the foundational role that colonialism had played in the primitive accumulation of capital (→ Capitalism, II/2; Colonial Economies, I/4). Rather than attribute the differences between First and Third World modernization and economic development to the cultural attitudes, dependency theorists identified the structures of permanent extraction enjoyed by corporations in the richer countries (→ Transnational Corporations, II/23), structures that were repeatedly defended with First World military might (→ Military, II/37) when revolutionary movements challenged or dislodged them.

Revolutionary actions, economic analyses, and political theories have always been transnational affairs, beginning with the lead up to the Mexican Revolution. Mexican-American communities and labor unions along the United States side of the U.S.-Mexican border provided safe harbor for revolutionaries of all stripes (→ Borderlands II/26), playing a pivotal role as the staging ground for various factions involved in the effort. In 1904, for example, a group of Mexican anarchists, including the brothers Ricardo and Enrique Flores Magón, sought political exile in Laredo, Texas, where they established one of the first anarchist parties in the United States, the *Partido Liberal Mexicano* (PLM). Though a liberal party in name, its principles were anarcho-syndicalist. Moving on to San Antonio, and eventually St. Louis, Missouri, the Flores Magón brothers and other anarchists set up the publication of their paper, *Regeneración*, which at its peak had 20,000 subscribers in Mexico and the U.S. combined. During their years in exile, the Flores Magón brothers and other anarchists met repeatedly with the American anarchist Emma Goldman and the Spanish anarchist Florencio Bozora.

The PLM was active along the border for the duration of the revolution because of the constant financial support and political harbor provided by U.S. citizens. From these bases of operation, the PLM organized forty-four small, democratic guerrilla cells inside Mexico for overthrowing the Díaz regime, with clandestine practices of horizontality and secrecy that would later be adopted by urban guerrilla across Latin America. This might even be called the original *foquismo* movement, focusing on urban populations with large proletariats rather than rural peasant classes, and on sabotage and general strikes, rather than armed insurrection.

In 1906, a PLM group made up of nine Mexicans and seven U.S. citizens helped organize a strike by miners at a mine in Sonora, located close to the Arizona border. The cell held educational events and fund raisers, helping to identify and coach leaders among the miners. Owned by the U.S. Cananea Mining Company, a subsidiary of the Anaconda Mining Company, the mine was a perfect example of the consequences of Díaz' economic policy of selling the rights to the country's resources to the highest foreign bidder (→ Extractivism, II/9). As John Hart describes it,

> The miners and mill workers of Cananea were part of an enclave economy, a highly capitalized enterprise devoted to the extraction of raw materials, controlled by foreigners...like enclave economies worldwide, [it] increased social inequality among the indigenous population and between it and the foreigners, increased spatial inequality, increased landowning inequality.
>
> *(Hart 1990, 185)*

The June 1, 1906 strike was a key episode leading up to the revolutionary war against Díaz for several reasons. The striking workers demanded a national minimum wage, a six-day work week, safety standards, compensation for work-related disability, and the abolition of child labor (→ Labor Representation, II/14) – all demands that were championed by northern revolutionary forces and met in the 1917 Constitution. The company executives, however, rejected the demands out of hand, firing into a crowd of protestors, killing three. Workers immediately staged an armed takeover of the mine, lynching two of the managers. Roughly 300 vigilantes from Arizona immediately invaded Mexico, organized under the command of the Arizona Rangers and with the approval of John Henry Kibby, the governor of the Arizona territory whose appointment had been endorsed by Anaconda mine executives. The Rangers coordinated with the Mexican Army to put down the strike, resulting in an estimated thirty to one-hundred deaths of workers and their family members (Hart 1990). This incident underscored the degree to which foreign companies controlled the economy (→ Transnational Corporations, II/23), and were free to abuse workers and their families with impunity. Moreover, it demonstrated the degree to which Díaz's regime was propped up by U.S. government, making it clear that U.S. armed forces could still invade Mexican territory at will (→ Interventionism, II/36). The indignity of this U.S. invasion fueled the Mexican revolution, which was an international affair from start to finish, with U.S. citizens and governmental forces involved on both sides of the conflict.

Revolutionaries from many Latin American countries cut their teeth by participating in the Mexican Revolution as well, but the two men who had the most lasting impact on the revolutionary imagination in the Americas were Agustin Faribundo Martí from El Salvador and Augusto César Sandino from Nicaragua. Each travelled to Mexico in exile, persecuted for their political activities. The "Che Guevaras" of their age, Martí and Sandino would become the most notable international revolutionaries of the early 20th century. Martí landed in Mexico in the early 1920s. Initially deported to Guatemala for running afoul of the oligarchic regime of the Melendez-Quiñonez family, he quickly left for Mexico with the specific aim of studying the agrarian roots of the revolution and the agrarian reform legislated by the 1917 Constitution. He joined Mexico's Communist Party, and later went on to found the communist parties of Guatemala, of Central America, and eventually, upon his return from exile, of El Salvador. Martí met Sandino while in Mexico, and this meeting would prove vital in both their lives. Sandino fled to Mexico after the failed attempt to murder the scion of a powerful oligarchical family in Niquinomo in 1920. Sandino worked for two different U.S. oil companies while in Mexico, but like Martí he spent most of his time with communists and anarchists, who helped shape his anti-imperialist analysis. After five years in Mexico, Sandino set sail in 1926 for Nicaragua to form the *Ejercito Defensor de la Soberanía Nacional de Nicaragua* [Defending Army of Nicaraguan National Sovereignty]. U.S. Marines had invaded Nicaragua multiple times in the early 20th century, and having raised sufficient funds for his Army, Sandino returned with a plan of ousting the Marines and instituting free and fair elections to challenge the oligarchic interests in the country. Sandino's war of liberation went on for nine years until his assassination in 1933. And though he was assassinated during the negotiations for free elections that never materialized, his Army forced the Marines to leave Nicaragua in defeat in 1932.

In 1928, Martí travelled to Nicaragua to join Sandino's Army, reaching the rank of Colonel before returning to El Salvador in 1930 to found the Communist Party. Martí was instrumental in initiating a popular insurrection against the Salvadoran oligarchy in the first days of 1932, following corrupt national elections that propped up the U.S.-backed dictatorship. The Communist Party led a popular front of students, communist intellectuals, laborers, and indigenous peasants against the Salvadoran National Guard, but it was brutally defeated just weeks after it started by the infamous 1932 massacre of 30,000 revolutionaries. Martí was captured and executed in prison, along with other revolutionary leaders.

Despite the assassinations of Martí and Sandino, their anti-imperialist and nationalist visions, forged in the crucible of the Mexican revolution, would live on as inspiration for generations. In the 1970s, Nicaraguan and Salvadoran guerrillas named their armed movements after these heroes: The *Frente Sandinista de Liberación Nacional* (FSLN) and the *Frenti Faribundo Martí de Liberación Nacional* (FMLN). These guerrilla movements also adopted Sandino and Martí's anti-imperialist platforms for revolutionary change, taking up arms to topple puppet regimes backed by the U.S. military and CIA; to establish full and effective suffrage for all citizens (→ Democracy, II/32); to expropriate monopolistic foreign interests in the economy and the nationalization of key industries; and most centrally, to redistribute lands to dispossessed peasantries (→ Land, II/15).

When the Sandinista revolutionary war successfully overthrew the Somoza dictatorship in 1979, they came to power as the dominant force in a broad popular front coalition that had participated in the overthrow of the Somoza dictatorship. Though the Sandinista government was most often compared to the communist government in Cuba, their economic and political program more closely resembled the Mexican model of a mixed economy. Precisely because they did not follow the Cuban model of a political economy of exclusively state-run industries, the Sandinistas were faced with the politically difficult task of balancing the interests of the working and agricultural masses who had supported the Sandinistas for more than a decade of guerrilla and clandestine operations, at great personal costs, with the interests of the vastly more powerful and entrenched private sector that had initially formed a coalition with the FSLN to oust Somoza but did not share their revolutionary vision of redistribution of national wealth (→ Social Inequality, II/20). Under these difficult circumstances and while fighting a notorious U.S.-backed counter-insurgency, the FSLN nevertheless achieved significant advances in the universalization of healthcare (→ Health, I/29), and education (→ I/24); in the democratization of higher education; in the redistribution of political power; in the expropriation of oligarchical agricultural interests; in the massive redistribution of land to the peasantry; and in the institutionalization of electoral democracy.

The FMLN in El Salvador and the *Unidad Revolucionaria Nacional Guatemalteca* (URNG) in Guatemala did not achieve revolutionary victories, but the civil wars they led did bring about a stalemate. Despite the extraordinary amount of military aid that was given by the U.S. to the right-wing National Guards and paramilitary groups in Guatemala and El Salvador, the URNG and the FMLN – in coordination with popular fronts – forced the oligarchic elites of their countries to the negotiating table. The peace accords reached between these revolutionary groups and the political elites of Guatemala and El Salvador, held under the auspices of the United Nations in the 1990s, disbanded the brutal National Guards and police forces in both countries, and led to their re-constitution as civilian branches of government. The FMLN and the URNG became political parties. While the URNG has not had significant electoral gains in Guatemala, in 2009 the FMLN-candidate Mauricio Funes won the presidency of El Salvador, and in 2014, his Vice-President, Salvador Sánchez Cerén, succeeded him. The revolutionary struggles spearheaded by FSLN, FMLN, and URNG deserve the credit for ending decades of brutal dictatorships in Central America, and for transitioning these countries into electoral democracies (→ II/32), even if neoliberal constraints have made significant socialist reforms impossible under FSLN and FMLN civilian governments (→ Neoliberalism, II/16).

The subject of revolution and development

American revolutionary movements of the 20th century have been soundly critiqued for their homophobia, sexism, and racism by scholars such as Ileana Rodríguez (1996), Jean Franco (1988), María Milagros López (2001), Alberto Moreiras (2001), José Rabasa (2010), and Saldaña-Portillo (2003) among others (→ Gender Identities, I/28; Race, I/39). An understanding of the confluence of the American revolutionary imagination and the Western model of capitalist development helps explain how revolutionary movements and their leaders misidentified the interests of large swaths of the constituencies they sought to liberate from imperialism and emancipate from capitalist exploitation. A Eurocentric discourse of development (→ II/6) captured the imagination of almost all 20th-century revolutionary movements. Post WW-II development projects proposed by the World Bank (WB), the International Monetary Fund (IMF), and U.S. AID not only endorsed export-led growth and free trade, they also reiterated the social and economic demands that have animated revolutionary movements in Latin America since their first articulation in the 1917 Mexican constitution: work, land (→ II/15), housing, education (→ I/24), healthcare (→ Health, I/29). Liberal development theories, projects, and promises were clearly part of a First World strategy, spearheaded by the United States and Britain, for the containment of communism (→ Modernization, I/35), and this explains why liberal proponents of development theories have parroted revolutionary goals in Latin America since President John F. Kennedy's Alliance for Progress.

But what explains the inverse relationship? Why did American revolutionaries adhere to Western models of development in their revolutionary platforms and praxis? Revolution and development could explain this phenomenon as both are animated by a particular theory of subjectivity. Not only do these two discursive terms depend upon each other dialectically for their mutual constitution as historical alternatives, but *both* revolutionary and development discourses also depend upon colonial legacies of race (→ I/39) and gender (→ Gender Identities, I/28) in their theoretical elaborations of subjectivity, agency, consciousness, and change. Even as revolutionary movements in the Americas situated themselves against the capitalist models of national development prescribed by U.S., Britain, and international agencies, they nevertheless proposed a liberal model of development for revolutionary subjects and for the transformation of consciousness. Similarly, even as Cold War development paradigms defined themselves in contradistinction to revolutionary movements, they nevertheless articulated the requirement for revolutionary agency and change in the development models they engineered for Latin American nations.

A normative theory of human transformation and agency, then, is at the heart of the confluence between revolutionary and development discourses. Why might this be so? As narratives of liberation and return to natural popular sovereignty, both of these discourses share an origin in imperial reason, in those Enlightenment (→ I/8) doctrines of progress, evolution, and change that were historically articulated with the practice of European colonialism (→ Colonial Rule, I/5) and colonial capitalism (→ Colonial Economies, I/4). Thus, even as post-World War II discourses of development and revolution were specifically articulated *against* colonial and neocolonial relations of power (→ Postcolonialism, I/38), both shared a theory of human perfectibility that was itself a legacy of the various raced and gendered subject-formations animating colonialism. It is precisely the prevalence of this meliorist model of subjectivity and theory of agency in revolutionary movements that contributed to the failure of decolonization and liberation struggles in Latin American and the U.S. (i.e., the Black Panthers, the Brown Berets, the American Indian Movement) in the late 20th century. The formation of revolutionary consciousness in these movements was predicated on the transcendence of a pre-modern "ethnos." The attainment of a universal condition of revolutionary agency was repeatedly figured as the leaving behind of one's own particularity, as leaving behind the feminized "ethnos" of indigenous, peasant, or religious identity (→ Indigeneity, I/31; Religious Beliefs, 40). Revolutionary movements of the 20th century are not simply understood as movements against colonial and neocolonial capitalism (→ II/2). They must also be understood as *within* a racialized and gendered Marxist developmentalism (→ Development, II/6; Modernization, I/35).

While liberal development theories were proposed by the United States, Britain, and Europe in response to massive post-war decolonization movements, there were continuities between colonial categories of subjectivity and developmental categories of national citizenship (→ II/27). Ethnos, religion, and race were metaphorized as cultural attitudes to be overcome by development, while gender is allegorized within the domain of active (European) nationalism and passive reactive (Third World) nationalisms (→ Gender Identities, II/28). Development theory normalized hierarchical and exploitative relations of exchange in a global capitalist system, by simply attributing wealth to differing levels of productivity. To achieve these normative levels of productivity, liberal development theory proscribed an epochal change in the subject. It required the subject to become an agent of transformation in their own right, one who was highly ethical, mobile, progressive, risk-taking, and masculinist, regardless of whether the agent/object of a particular development strategy was a man or a woman, an adult or a child.

In stark contrast to proponents of liberal development, some 20th century revolutionaries wanted to overthrow the hierarchical and exploitative relations of capitalist production in favor of workers and peasants. However, the majority of revolutionary movements wanted simply to introduce a socialist model of production in key economic sectors, and to redistribute wealth, land, and work equitably (→ Social Inequality, II/20). Nevertheless, in their efforts to achieve these goals, almost all revolutionary leaders promoted models of revolutionary consciousness and change that deeply resembled the liberal development model. Remember Guevara's guardian angel who falls from the sky fully formed to help the oppressed? He is stoic, potent, and austere, capable of making ethical choices for his less-evolved constituents in this revolutionary errand, constituents who he must lead and discipline with religious fervor. American revolutionary leaders adhered to a model of revolutionary-transformation-as-epochal-conversion, requiring – much like liberal development models – the epistemic death of a prior ethnic, religious, raced, or sexed subject. Adherence to other modes of consciousness – to, for example, indigenous religious cosmologies – marked one as the subject of a pre-revolutionary and pre-modern consciousness to be superseded by revolutionary transformation. Revolutionary leaders had to be transformative agents in their own lives and the lives of others. In doing so, these revolutionary heroes represented indigenous peoples (→ I/11) and peasant subalterns as the horizon of their messianic, revolutionary errands, as the agent/objects of their own revolutionary developmentalism. Revolutionary vanguards had to act as the catalysts for the transformation of subaltern consciousness, a transformation that inevitably entailed the transcendence of all ethnic, racial, religious, sexual, and gendered particularity (→ Intersectionality, I/32).

This revolutionary model of change did not go unchallenged. Indigenous participants in these revolutionary struggles, like Rigoberta Menchú, who was a member of the Guatemalan URNG, critiqued this revolutionary subject who oddly required her to transcend everything that marked her specificity as an Indian woman (→ Indigeneity, I/31). She launched her critique from her specific gendered, classed, and ethnic position (→ Ethnicity, I/25; Gender Identities, I/28). In *Me llamo Rigoberta Menchú y así me nacío la conciencia*, the process of coming to consciousness is not represented by her as epochal or revelatory (Burgos 1988). Rather, her revolutionary understanding of exploitation accrues precisely through her experience with the mundane – with the territory of women, of indigenous peoples and of peasants. Where other revolutionaries represented this mundane consciousness as a pre-modern ethnic formation that had to be superseded in order for nationalist change to occur, Menchú offered a "non-modern" positionality for indigenous revolutionaries, a positionality that allows the K'iche' Indians to negotiate a limited participation in modernization – liberal or revolutionary – that encroaches on indigenous people from all sides (→ Indigenous Literatures, III/10). In claiming her authority over her own experience, Menchú demanded, on behalf of Mayan Indians, authority over any revolutionary model of development to come (→ Life Writing, III/11).

Similarly, the Zapatistas began their insurrection in southern Mexico by demanding full participation in revolutionary Mexico as well. The Zapatista insurrection demanded the re-constitution of the Mexican revolution so that the state and economy would once again benefit the disenfranchised, including the perennially excluded indigenous population. The Zapatistas re-conceptualized the meaning and practice of revolutionary citizenship for the entire nation through their critique of the PRI's model of neoliberal development, but also through the critique of their model of revolutionary agency: the fully capable *mestizo* subject. The Zapatista demand for indigenous rights exposed the inherent developmentalism in the term *mestizaje* (→ Hybridity, I/30), as it is predicated on the erasure of the indigenous subject in favor of the tropologically more advanced revolutionary *mestizo* subject. In addition, the Zapatistas threaten the triumph of neoliberalism (→ II/16) and globalization represented by NAFTA by demanding control over economic resources for indigenous people (→ Regional Integration, II/18). They do so, however, not in order to exclude themselves from a national development process. Rather, the Zapatistas claimed the role of the state for themselves through their autonomy movement, in order to dictate the terms of a development project in which they are already fully implicated. Indigenous actors across the continent are demonstrating how indigenous movements are re-writing revolutionary projects to include indigenous people as authorities over their own experience.

Indeed, the indigenous/peasant cultural and political production exceeds the terms of the revolution/development dialectic. Rejecting developmentalist notions that interpret their indigenous and peasant subject positions as pre-modern, indigenous subjects like Menchú and the Zapatists offer a model of revolutionary consciousness predicated on the global politics of local "everyday life." These subaltern insurgents challenged a model of revolutionary subjectivity and a theory of agency not from a position of indigenous purity, but from an indigenous and peasant subject position simultaneously produced by modernity and in reaction to its developmentalism. As such, the deployment of the categories of universalism and particularism must be reconsidered, so central in Western political thought, as well as the future of revolution in America.

Works cited

Amin, Samir. 1977. *Imperialism and Unequal Development.* New York City: Monthly Review Press.

Beverley, John. 2004. *Testimonio: On the Politics of Truth.* Minneapolis: University of Minnesota Press.

Burgos, Elizabeth. 1988. *Me llamo Rigoberta Menchú y así me nacío la conciencia.* Mexico City: Siglo Veintiuno, S.A. de C.V.

Cardoso, Fernando Henrique and Enzo Faletto. 1979. *Dependency and Development in Latin America.* Berkeley: University of California Press.

Castañeda, Jorge G. 1993. *Utopia Unarmed: The Latin American Left After the Cold War.* New York: Vintage Books.

Franco, Jean. 1988. "Beyond Ethnocentrism: Gender, Power, and the Third-World Intelligentsia." In *Marxism and the Interpretation of Culture*, eds. Cary Nelson and Lawrence Grossberg, 503–515. Chicago: University of Illinois Press.

Frank, Andre Gunder. 1966. "The Development of Underdevelopment." In *Monthly Review* no. 4: 17–31.

Guevara, Ernesto Che. 1960. *La Guerra de Guerrillas.* Cuba: Ediciones "Lucha."

Guevara, Ernesto Che. 1998. *Guerrilla Warfare.* Lincoln: University of Nebraska Press.

Hart, John. 1990. "Revolutionary Syndicalism in Mexico." In *Revolutionary Syndicalism: An International Perspective*, eds. Marcel van der Linden and Thorpe Wayne, online. Libcom online library. https://libcom.org/library/revolutionary-syndicalism-mexico-john-m-hart.

Laclau, Ernesto. 1971. *Feudalism and Capitalism in Latin America.* Great Britain: New Left Review.

López, María Milagros. 2001. "Solidarity as Event, Communism as Personal Practice, and Disencounters in the Politics of Desire." In *The Latin American Subaltern Studies Reader*, ed. Ileana Rodríguez, 64–81. Durham: Duke University Press.

Mallon, Florencia. 1995. *Peasant and Nation: The Making of Postcolonial Mexico and Peru*. Berkeley: University of California Press.

Moreiras, Alberto. 2001. *The Exhaustion of Difference: The Politics of Latin American Cultural Studies*. Durham: Duke University Press.

Rabasa, José. 2010. *Without History: Subaltern Studies, the Zapatista Insurgency, and the Specter of History*. Pittsburgh: University of Pittsburgh Press.

Rodríguez, Ileana. 1996. *Women, Guerrillas and Love: Understanding War in Central America*. Minneapolis: University of Minnesota Press.

———. 2001. *The Latin American Subaltern Studies Reader*. Durham: Duke University Press.

Saldaña-Portillo, María Josefina. 2003. *The Revolutionary Imagination in the Americas and the Age of Development*. Durham: Duke University Press.

Stavenhagen, Rodolfo. 1981. "Changing Functions of the Community in Underdeveloped Countries." In *Underdevelopment and Development: The Third World Today*, ed. Henry Bernstein, 83–95. New York: Penguin Books.

Wallerstein, Immanuel. 2004. *World Systems Analysis: An Introduction*. Durham: Duke University Press.

Wolf, Eric. 1969. *Peasant Wars of the Twentieth Century*. Norman: Oklahoma University Press.

45
SECURITY

Lucía Dammert

The challenges to security in the Americas are many. An increase in the use of violence and the regularization of organized crime are only some of the many facets to the problem in the region. In the past decades three changes in regard to crime stand out: (i) exportation of crimes; (ii) greater organization and complexity in criminal phenomena specially link to drug trafficking and (iii) difficulty for governmental institutions to address the problem. This situation has come hand in hand with substantial changes in the way in which public security is understood in the Americas – moving from a centralized vision focusing mainly on the role of criminal justice institutions in crime prevention toward a new, multidimensional approach that recognizes the importance of integral proposals for intervention.

Latin America remains one of the most violent regions in the world – by some measures the most violent one. During the past decade alone, 1.4 million people in Latin American and the Caribbean have lost their lives as a result of violent crime. The perception that State authorities (→ Nation State, II/38) are unable to protect the citizens' most fundamental rights (→ Human Rights, II/35) is visibly damaging the support for democratic institutions in the region and becoming a breeding ground for authoritarian attitudes (→ Authoritarianism, II/25). The way in which the crime issue is approached has shifted away from the domestic security perspective developed during the civil wars in Central America and dictatorships in South America, whose principal objective was the consolidation of an internal control system that prohibited social and political movements (→ Social Movements, I/41). Thus, an internal enemy was consolidated and characterized as one who went against a political system with ample police and military (→ II/37) functions that ultimately led to the obvious violation of human rights (→ II/35).

The "crime crisis" experienced in the United States (U.S.) demonstrated the many factors associated with this problem as well as the need to consolidate public policies at every level in order to address these different factors. This led to the development of a new way to conceptualize security in the Americas, forming a new integral perspective that recognized the importance of prevention and also generated profound changes in policing strategies.

Hence, conceptual frameworks and public policies on security issues are deeply interconnected and influenced by the U.S. The vital role of the U.S. in defining the national security strategies, developed during the 1970s and the 1980s, by the dictatorships has been extensively studied (Long 2015; Schoultz 2016) (→ Authoritarianism, II/25). After the democratization process, the situation has not changed significantly (→ State Transformation, II/21). Quite the contrary, the process of transmission, diffusion, and hybridization of knowledge remain of special relevance (Tulchin 2017). The rising presence of transnational criminal acts, such as human and drug trafficking, has established a clear south-north channel that strengthens the common challenges that should be faced in the inter-American region.

This entry highlights the production of knowledge related to public security in the Inter-American context. Although mostly linked to northern conceptual development, there are clear differences on how the same topic (or policy) is understood. This is still a novel process since prior to the 1960s there was little debate on public security issues in Latin America, but this practice is key to the way public security is being analyzed in multiple different contexts.

Keeping this in mind, two different and sometimes complementary practices can be described. The first analyzes the importance of transmission and dissemination of concepts and policies, using three examples: war on drugs, zero tolerance, and community policing. At different levels of development and implementation, each shows the relevance of the Inter-American relationship as well as the difficulties that come with the transference of "solutions" without consideration of elements of national context. In each country there is a general process of adaptation that certainly changes the focus and its original meaning. Secondly, in some cases the north (specially the U.S.) does not only play the role of concept producer, but also intertwines within a process of conceptual interdependence and even hybridization (De Beaugrande and Dressler 1981). There are multiple cases to explore but perhaps the most interesting and recent one is the *maras*-terrorism link developed after 9/11 and the alleged participation of Central American youth gangs (*maras*) in transnational drug-related crimes that have affected multiple cities north and south of the Rio Grande. This new perspective has redefined how the problem of the *maras* has been approached in both the U.S. and in Latin America, and thus requiring that key questions be redrawn and that analytical process of production of knowledge on public security issues for Inter-American studies be continually developed.

Transfer of knowledge on public security

The concepts and practices of public security in Latin America are directly influenced by the North American experience, more specifically by the U.S. This influence has multiple elements and sources ranging from the training of Latin American police officers in the U.S., the active involvement of the Drug Enforcement Agency (DEA) in multiple countries, and the participation of several institutions and experts that disseminate concepts about "good practices," "evidence-based initiatives," or "promising lessons" (Swanson 2013). However, most of the concepts and practices developed in the U.S. responded to a problem of urban crime and violence in the 1980s and 1990s where the country underwent its most intense crime-related security crisis (→ Urbanization, II/45). Since then, there has been a significant improvement in violence indicators and crime is no longer a key issue for many U.S. cities. However, the literature shows mixed evidence regarding the explanations and factors that can be considered key in such a contraction in crime and violence (Blaustein 2015). Many of the tactics that were developed at a local level in the U.S. during this period were imported during the next decades to Latin American countries. For instance, cities such as Lima, Mexico City, Buenos Aires, Santiago, and Quito requested the services of the former mayor of New York, Rudolph Giuliani or his former police commissioner William Bratton (Gerber 2001). Along with the experts, the media played a key role in the "conceptual journey" of the initiatives that were subsequently implemented in Latin America (→ Media Flows, III/35), often without any adaptation (Blaustein 2015).

The terrain in Latin America for importing concepts on public security is fertile. The increase in crime, since the early 1990s throughout the region was linked not only to high levels of violence but also to corruption and inefficiency of police and justice institutions (Bailey and Dammert 2006). In the last two decades, there has been a clear influence and transfer in the Inter-American region where three concepts played a particularly relevant role: war on drugs, zero tolerance, and community policing.

War on drugs

The Americas face serious drug problems related to a complex process of production, distribution, and consumption that involves multiples countries (Rosen 2015). For many years, the main concept developed in the U.S. and implemented throughout the Americas was the "war on drugs" that included a wide variety of initiatives mainly focusing on drug-producing countries to enhance efficiency in intercepting and destroying drug trafficking networks (Youngers and Rosin 2005). In the 1980s, "tough on crime" laws were passed at the National and State legislatures in the U.S. that resulted in an increased prison population since most laws were directed towards drug consumers that resulted in incarceration for long periods of time. Public opinion was fundamental in this policy, as general perception linked urban crime to drugs (Fukumi 2008).

Drugs were the "enemy" and the main policy to confront it was the police. In fact, the experience developed and implemented in the U.S. was included in the training of police officers throughout the Americas using interdiction and urban strategies to control drug-related crimes. The same pillars to fight organized crime were first assembled in Colombia via Plan Colombia and then later in Mexico via Plan Mérida. In many cases, the difficulties encountered in police institutions led to the inclusion of the armed forces (→ Military, II/37) in these strategies based on the idea that "new threats" included crime in its various dimensions (Rocha and Zorovich 2015).

Undoubtedly, the "war on drugs" as a concept has significantly influenced the policies of virtually every country in the region. Most practices reflect the perspective developed in the U.S. but has also been strengthened by multiple bilateral and multilateral bodies. In other words, it is possible to visualize a strategic process that has culminated in an Inter-American vision on drugs and that focuses on the proposals that were first developed in the U.S.

The outcomes have not been entirely positive. In fact, a report by the United Nations recognizes that in 2016 there has been a rise in the land dedicated to the production of coca in Colombia and that drug trafficking has become a key factor in the amount of violence in the region. Since the law-and-order approach driven by the U.S. has not had the expected results, alternative perspectives have emerged from Latin American political actors (Long 2015; Rosen 2015). For instance, in the late 2000s, several former Presidents of the region joined in the proposal for the legalization of marijuana, as well as the need to define public policies that recognize the public health (→ I/29) component to the "war on drugs" (Global Commission on Drug Policy 2016). The proposal highlights the importance of the U.S. recognizing this aspect of the drug problem, given that high demand levels fuel conflicts especially in Mexico and the Central American region (Bruneau, Dammert and Elizabeth 2012; Gledhill 2015).

Despite the efforts made by diverse political actors in countries such as Colombia, Uruguay, Argentina, and Mexico, the results have not been successful from the global point of view. However, it is important to recognize that Canada, who shares a less punitive view of drug-related problems than the U.S. government, recognized the need to move forward with a different perspective with illegal drug use. The war on drugs continues to prevail in the hemisphere and undoubtedly impacts Inter-American security and all its related institutions.

Zero tolerance

The experience gained in New York City in the early 1980s has become one of the most analyzed practices in the world regarding the best way to effectively deal with crime (Blaustein 2015). Although there are multiple interpretations of the factors that led to the reduction of violence and crime in the city, there is no doubt that the changes made in the police institutions served to increase its effectiveness (Ungar and Arias 2012) (→ Urbanization, I/45). But in addition to policy strategy, the New York experience focused on the conceptualization that most crimes are developed in places where small crime was not previously effectively confronted, named the "Broken Windows Theory" (Wilson and George 1982). This analytical perspective goes hand in hand with the recognition that those who commit criminal acts based their actions on rational analysis of the context. Thus, increasing punishments is a central element of the strategy considered successful in major North American cities. Also, situational crime prevention focused on developing initiatives to limit public spaces that were in precarious situations to prevent small crimes such as vandalism or public drinking to create a sense of order and lawfulness (Parks 2008).

The concept of zero tolerance was coined to express the "hard hand" that the government should adopt in any act that transgresses laws. U.S. literature has been extensive in affirming, or at least, installing doubts about the effectiveness of this perspective, but the criticisms did not come as quickly in the rest of the hemisphere (Jefferson 2015). An element from the analysis of the North American experience is the increasing level of public investment that involved all processes of professionalization, modernization, and articulation of diverse institutional actors. In Latin America, "zero tolerance" was fully assumed as an effective way of fighting crime, especially in political electoral discourse. Therefore, the dissemination of concepts brings with it the increase of "punitive populism" (→ Populism, II/ 43) that proposes initiatives focused on a punitive discourse that often does not recognize the context-wide differences (Ungar and Arias 2012).

The process of conceptual transfer has had multiple stages, most of which are built on an initial pillar of the New York experience being recognized as successful. For instance, at the beginning of 2015, former New York Mayor Giuliani stated in El Salvador's media that "gangs must be destroyed and that this process can be efficiently carried out by implementing a program such as the one effectively developed in NY: Compstat" (Mallonee 2015, n. p.).Of course, this statement leaves aside the police situation in El Salvador that institutionally lacks the capacity to systematize criminal information, not to mention its high levels of institutional corruption.

However, the conceptual transfer emphasizes the "arrival" of proposals rather than on their feasibility. The gap between the proposition of certain ideas and their implementation is not a coincidence but responds to the exponential growth of the private security industry, who frequently "offer" concepts such as those previously described. According to Cálix, the responses that the region has come up with yield "to the temptation of an unrestricted supply of more police agents, tougher punishments and more prisons" (2007, 41), which are the measures considered to be more successful in curbing crime. However, harsher policies and punishments do not necessarily achieve the expected results, namely, increased public order and security, but may, on the contrary, imply more radical consequences such as an excessive growth of the prison population, the criminalization of vulnerable groups, or socio-spatial stigmatization (→ Social Inequality, II/20). The more conservative positions – not necessarily in the political sense of the term – seek to promote a series of measures to control insecurity by enhancing police work and the prison system, preventing lawbreakers from committing new crimes by disabling them in jail. Despite some advances, the situation in the region is quite critical. In addition to the negative externalities of the use of incarceration measures, the cohabitation of first-timers with more experienced inmates allows for the exchange of experiences, practices, and networks that "professionalize" the criminal experience.

Finally, the aptitudes learned in the implementation of the "zero tolerance" policies in Latin America have not been a topic in the debates found in the U.S. literature. In fact, criminological debates focus on theoretical proposals mainly developed in the north, with little interaction with the experiences of the south. Consequently, it is not possible to speak of an Inter-American criminological analysis, but rather of multiple displaced processes whose consequences in the southern hemisphere are still unknown.

Community policing

Police institutions in Latin America face multiple challenges that lead to high levels of citizen mistrust (Corbacho, Philipp and Ruiz-Vega 2015). Citizens, in most countries, express their suspicion at institutions that are considered corrupt, slow and inefficient not only in the fight against everyday crime but also against organized crime. The return to democracy (→ II/32) has not generated effective programs of modernization (→ I/35) and police reform, but instead has left traditionally ineffective institutions to tackle citizen´s insecurities. Latin America began to generate processes of police reform to address these issues only at the beginning of the 1990s (Cruz 2011). The majority of reform efforts have not been successfully accomplished due to multiple factors, such as the political inability to sustain reform, barriers within institutions, as well as the lack of a comprehensive view of police work (Bailey and Dammert 2006; Ungar and Arias 2012).

In most cases, the U.S. experience served as a "model" to follow because of the changes that were made in the police in the early 1980s. As mentioned before, the increase in violence and crime in the U.S., in addition to the recognition of the need to change the way the police developed their work, especially with the most vulnerable populations, generated important institutional changes. Accordingly, various concepts and practices were installed in the vocabulary of Latin American security that were (and still are) key to police development in the region. Among them, the community police perspective plays a major role (Frühling 2012). The search for greater involvement with the community, more decentralized police decisions and focus on crime prevention at the local level are some of the pillars of this concept. The U.S. experience involves small local police institutions and even some at the State level where this model of police work was developed. It has had a wide range of effects that varies from the way police is distributed in the territory to the type of patrol and uniform used. Therefore, based on local information, an array of initiatives was developed that have had a positive impact on the community as well as the perception of police work.

Community policing was a concept that traveled quickly to the rest of the hemisphere. There were multiple cases where the proposal was adapted and programs that sought the same results were implemented (Frühling 2012). However structural problems of police institutions in Latin America such as low salaries, limited training, secretive logistics, and little concern for the relationship with citizens were not taken into consideration. The search for "good practices" to be implemented led many countries to develop this type of initiative with very different scales and results (Ungar and Arias 2012). In some cases, the adaptation of the concept was rather superficial, resulting in the generation of a special police group that carries out foot patrol and seeks to establish contact with the citizenry, while maintaining the same repressive practices throughout the rest of the institution. Therefore, although in the early 2017 most countries in Latin America and the Caribbean had community policing programs, its characteristics varied significantly from the original idea. The process of diffusion of the concept has had several sponsors, possibly one of the most important is the Inter-American Development Bank (IDB) that from the 1990s strengthened lines of technical cooperation and loans in several countries that, for the most part, included the creation of community policing programs (→ Development, II/6). The Organization of American States (OAS), through the Meeting of Public Security Ministers of the Americas (MISPA) has also highlighted the importance of this type of initiative as well, despite the fact that in most cases results have not been evaluated or shows mixed outcomes.

Thus, the conceptual journey does not develop autonomously but is driven by various organizations that contribute to its consolidation. There is an open question regarding the consequences of misinterpretation of the concept and its development in the south, where despite the various initiatives developed, levels of citizen mistrust remain at the highest compared to any other governmental institution.

Finally, the impact that these experiences have had on the way policing is being implemented is sporadic. Meanwhile, the U.S. police have developed an increasing emphasis on intelligence-based police work, where the need to confront local but also transnational threats especially linked to terrorism, have developed sophisticated systems that allow to model (or even predict) criminal incidents.

Entanglement of Inter-American security: Maras and terrorism

Security in the U.S. was redefined after the 9/11 attacks. The vulnerabilities of the security system were considered high priorities to tackle and to do that multiple institutional changes that allow progress in identifying potential people or groups linked to possible terrorist actions were developed. While the so-called "war on terror" has various components of global action, the impact on the Americas has been especially unavoidable when linking various new threats to the security landscape (Rodgers and Adam 2015; Tulchin 2017; Vanden 2014). These new threats range from organized crime to transnational migration (→I/44), natural disasters (→ II/33), and epidemics that can develop and weaken governments and even states.

For the U.S., the threats associated to the new security strategy are linked to any actor who could support radical groups in other parts of the world and carry out attacks of various kinds. It is in this context that migration became not only a humanitarian, economic, and social problem, but especially a security one, increasing the already massive deportation policy (Williams and Disney 2015). Moreover, organized crime started to be considered a matter of national security that involved human and drug trafficking but also opened the possibility for other types of criminal activities. Unlike the cases previously analyzed, there is a clearer process of interaction at the Inter-American context regarding the new threats to security and the importance of terrorism. Despite limited evidence of a possible radicalization process in Latin America, the perception that it could become a host for terrorist activities is not irrelevant (Johnson 2012). In this new era, an emphasis on the security problems with the relationship between the Venezuelan and Iranian Governments, for example, was clear at the conceptual and policy framework (Johnson 2012). By the same token, in the South American border region between Argentina, Brazil, and Paraguay (Triple Frontier), there is a long history of organized crime activities (→ Borderlands, II/26). But after 9/11, some security experts "suspected jihadist were taking safe harbor there" (Folch 2012, 12). Similarly, there are many changes in the security agenda of the U.S. with Mexico, not only as a gateway to illegal migration but also as a possible illegal arms market and even the connection between drug trafficking and terrorism.

The possible relationship between the *maras* and international terrorism is arguably an excellent example of the metamorphosis of knowledge in the Inter-American security context. Thus, the Central American youth gangs have had an especially important presence in the countries of the so-called northern triangle (El Salvador, Honduras, and Guatemala) for more than three decades (→ Family, I/26). However, recently, their identity transformed from being considered a local crime actor to a possible Inter-American terrorist threat.

The evolution of the *maras* has its roots in U.S. street gangs (Bruneau, Dammert and Elizabeth 2012). In fact, many studies of the *maras*'s first actions emphasize the relationship with mass deportation processes of Central American migrants who were part of U.S. gangs (→ Subcultures, I/43). The vicious circle was consolidated and nourished the increasing violent process of gang development throughout the Americas. Considered a problem of public security, the *maras* in Central America have been confronted by hard-hitting policies that include long prison sentences and consolidation of violent practices. At the beginning of the 1990s, the concern was no longer localized and became a regional issue that was not being dealt with efficiently and the practices that were imported without local adaptation became fertile ground for the increase use of violence and extortion (Bruneau, Dammert and Elizabeth 2012).

In 2012, for the first time in U.S. history, the Mara Salvatrucha was officially designated a transnational criminal organization. That definition allowed police and other security institutions to target the group and to either deport or incarcerate some of its members linked to organized crime in U.S. cities. A few years later, in 2015, the Supreme Court of El Salvador ruled that both *maras* (Salvatrucha and MS18) will be deemed a terrorist group due to the systematic use of violence and increasing punishment for any of their actions. Finally, in April of 2017 the Attorney General of the U.S. stated that the Mara Salvatrucha could be designated a terrorist organization by the Federal Government due to increasing levels of violence.

It should be noted that the literature on the subject is still limited and that many of the analyses of the *maras* and their involvement in regional criminal organizations are mostly based on police information whose quality is not always high (Bruneau, Dammert and Elizabeth 2012; Cruz 2011). In fact, many of the statements that propose the consolidation of an organized and coordinated strategy at a regional level have not been corroborated by studies carried out in each country (Bruneau, Dammert, and Elizabeth 2012; Dudley 2011). However, in the context of the debate about the new threats and strategies to combat terrorism, *maras* were considered potential collaborators in the international threat terrorism represents (Johnson 2012). In various documents from the U.S. government, statements can be found that open questions about the possible closeness of both processes, describing the *maras* as an organized and available army to introduce practically anything in the U.S.

The process is still developing. Available information shows that the *maras* have a presence in the streets but also in prisons in many countries; they execute violent acts that seem to be linked to drug trafficking, but their possible connection to international terrorism is not as obvious. Beyond the characteristics that these groups would adopt in the future, the interpretative process that they have undergone in the last decade is of special importance and recognizes the complexities of the Inter-American security scenario as well as the constant interaction and hybridization processes that occur in this topic.

Final words

The importance of the U.S. voice in the America's security agenda should be researched from an integrative perspective. In fact, an international cooperation agenda that focuses on tackling structural factors that generate and reproduce criminal violence, rather than simply on the control of crime, would be a welcome addition in the theoretical and policy debates. As a part of the agenda there is a clear need to reframe the discussion. This means resisting appeals to fight crime through iron-fist methods, that is, through the twisted repressive populism that almost always fails to reduce crime rates but never fails to undermine basic civil rights (→ Human Rights, II/35). However, social prevention must be calibrated with the strong sense of urgency that the situation demands and the recognition that state coercion, within the boundaries of the rule of law, is unavoidable in the fight against crime.

Another area for future development relates to the need for robust indicators. Better public safety indicators would allow for more informed diagnoses and policy decisions. In most of the countries, information on crime behavior and trends are weak or non-existent and for this reason policies are routinely crafted based on intuition rather than knowledge. Transferring the expertise of developed countries in this regard is a potentially rewarding pursuit.

The Americas must confront an important, yet under analyzed, agenda on security issues. There is a clear need for more in-depth and comparative analyses that would open multiple opportunities to identify the dynamics of entanglement in the Americas. The topics vary from multiple disciplinary approaches and theoretical perspectives, however there is a simultaneous process of knowledge production that needs to be identified and analyzed in an integrative perspective. Security issues are at the core of most political, social, and economic processes in the Americas and there are multiple open questions that need to be faced with a new perspective that would recognize the importance of the mutual construction of meaning and concepts.

Works cited

Bailey, John and Lucía Dammert. 2006. *Public Security and Police Reform in the Americas*. Pittsburgh: University of Pittsburgh Press.

Blaustein, Jarret. 2015. "Exporting Criminological Innovation Abroad: Discursive Representation, 'Evidence-Based Crime Prevention' and the Post-Neoliberal Development Agenda in Latin America." *Theoretical Criminology* 20, no. 2: 165–184.

Bruneau, Thomas, Lucía Dammert and Skinner Elizabeth. 2012. *Maras: Gang Violence and Security in Central America*. Austin, TX: University of Texas Press.

Cálix, Álvaro. 2007. "La falacia de más policías, más penas y más cárceles: el problema de la inseguridad y el castigo desde una visión alternativa." *Nueva Sociedad* 208: 40–55.

Corbacho, Ana, Julia Philipp and Mauricio Ruiz-Vega. 2015. "Crime and Erosion of Trust: Evidence for Latin America." *World Development* 70: 400–415.

Cruz, José Miguel. 2011. "Criminal Violence and Democratization in Central America: The Survival of the Violent State." *Latin American Politics and Society* 53, no. 4: 1–33.

De Beaugrande, Robert and Wolfgang Dressler. 1981. *Introduction to Text Linguistics*. London: Longman.

Dudley, Steven. 2011. "Central America Besieged: Cartels and Maras Country Threat Analysis." *Small Wars and Insurgencies* 22, no. 5: 890–913.

Folch, Christine. 2012. "Trouble on the Triple Frontier. The Lawless Border Where Argentina, Brazil, and Paraguay Meet." *Foreign Affairs, Snapshot*. Washington, DC. www.foreignaffairs.com/articles/argentina/2012-09-06/trouble-triple-frontier.

Frühling, Hugo. 2012. "A Realistic Look at Latin American Community Policing Programmes." *Policing and Society: An International Journal of Research and Policy* 22, no. 1: 76–88.

Fukumi, Sayaka. 2008. *Cocaine Trafficking in Latin America: EU and US Policy Responses*. Aldershot and Hants: Ashgate.

Gerber, Jurg and Eric Jensen. 2001. *Drug War, American Style: The Internationalization of Failed Policy and Its Alternatives*. New York: Garland Publisher.

Gledhill, John. 2015. *The New War on the Poor: The Production of Insecurity in Latin America*. London: Zed Books.

Global Commission on Drug Policy. 2016. "Advancing Drug Policy Reform: A New Approach to Decriminalization." Washington, DC. www.globalcommissionondrugs.org/wp-content/uploads/2016/11/GCDP-Report-2016-ENGLISH.pdf.

Jefferson, B. J. 2015. "Zero Tolerance for Zero Tolerance?: Analyzing How Zero Tolerance Discourse Mediates Police Accountability Activism." *City, Culture and Society* 6, no. 1: 9–17.

Johnson, Stephen. 2012. "Iran´s Influence in the Americas." *A Report of the Center for Strategic Security Studies Americas Program*. Washington, DC. https://csis-prod.s3.amazonaws.com/s3fs-public/legacy_files/files/publication/120223_Johnson_IranInfluence_ExecSumm_Web.pdf.

Long, Tom. 2015. *Latin America Confronts the United States: Asymmetry and Influence*. Cambridge: Cambridge University Press.

Mallonee, Laura C. 2015. "Rudy Giuliani Will Advise El Salvador on Security, Justice Reform." *LAND, Latin America News Dispatch*, online edition, January 12. https://latindispatch.com/2015/01/12/rudy-giuliani-will-advise-el-salvador-on-security-justice-reform/.

Parks, R. B. 2008. "Broken Windows and Broken Windows Policing." *Criminology and Public Policy* 7, no. 2: 159–161.

Rocha, Marcelo and Silvia Zorovich. 2015. "Trends in Drug Trafficking and Organized Crime in Brazil." In *New Approaches to Drug Policies*, eds. Jonathan Rosen and Brienen Marten, 35, 57. Basingstoke: M. W. Palgrave Macmillan.

Rodgers, Dennis and Baird Adam. 2015. "Understanding Gangs in Contemporary Latin America." In *The Handbook of Gangs*, eds. Scott H. Decker and David C. Pyrooz, 478–502. Hoboken, NJ: John Wiley and Sons, Inc.

Rosen, Jonathan. 2015. "The War on Drugs in Colombia: A History of Failure." In *New Approaches to Drug Policies*, eds. Jonathan Rosen and Brienen Marten, 58–72. Basingstoke: Palgrave Macmillan.

Schoultz, Lars. 2016. *National security and United States Policy toward Latin America*. Princeton: Princeton University Press.

Swanson, Kate. 2013. "Zero Tolerance in Latin America: Punitive Paradox in Urban Policy Mobilities." *Urban Geography* 34, no. 7: 972–988.

Tulchin, Joseph. 2017. "Regional Security in Latin America after US Hegemony." In *Power Dynamics and Regional Security in Latin America*, eds. Marcial Suarez, Rafael Duarte, and Brigitte Weiffen, 27–51. Basingstoke: Palgrave Macmillan.

Ungar, Mark and Desmond Arias. 2012. "Reassessing Community-Oriented Policing in Latin America." *Policing and Society* 22, no. 1: 1–13.

Vanden, Harry. 2014. "Maras, Contragoverned Spaces, and Sovereignty." In *US National Security Concerns in Latin America and the Caribbean*, eds. Prevost, Gary, Harry Vanden, Carlos Campos and Luis Fernando Ayerbe, 81–92. Basingstoke: Palgrave Macmillan.

Youngers, Coletta and Eileen Rosin. 2005. *Drugs and Democracy in Latin America: The Impact of U.S. Policy*. Boulder, CO: L. Rienner.

Williams, Ginger and Jennifer Disney. 2015. "Militarism and Its Discontents: Neoliberalism, Repression, and Resistance in Twenty-First-Century." *US-Latin American Relations. Social Justice* 41, no. 3: 1–28.

Wilson, James and Kelling George. 1982. "Broken Windows: The Police and Neighborhood Safety." *The Atlantic, retrieved* 2017-05-26.

INDEX

For Product Safety Concerns and Information please contact our EU
representative GPSR@taylorandfrancis.com
Taylor & Francis Verlag GmbH, Kaufingerstraße 24, 80331 München, Germany

www.ingramcontent.com/pod-product-compliance
Lightning Source LLC
LaVergne TN
LVHW080117011026
849160LV00013B/1118
9781032400822